Concrete for Breakfast

More Tales from the Shale

Jeff Scott

Methanol Press

First published in Great Britain by

Methanol Press
2 Tidy Street
Brighton
East Sussex BN1 4EL

For a complete catalogue of current and forthcoming publications please write to the address above, or visit our website at www.methanolpress.com

ISBN 978-0-9553103-6-2

A catalogue for this book is available from the British Library

(Hardly suffering) Editor: Michael Payne
Word Wrangler: Graham Russel
Technical Advisor: Billy Jenkins
Proof Readers: Caroline Tidmarsh and Vy Shepherd
Book and Cover Design: Vicky Holtham
Cover Photograph: Jeff Scott

Printed in the UK by Cpod, Trowbridge, Wiltshire

Contents

Introduction

The book you have in your hand continues my examination of the question 'what is speedway?' that I embarked on when I travelled to every track in the country in 2005 and 2006. This odyssey resulted in the publication of a couple of books *Showered in Shale* and *Shifting Shale*. So this is really more of the same but also something different. *Concrete for Breakfast* is also not a club history nor the (auto) biography of a rider but a snapshot and my personal journey round every stadium that staged the sport in Britain - this time during 2007. Again, it was a pleasure to be able to have a reason to visit every track in the country, often more than once albeit slightly tempered by a summer of wet weather. Though I could only write about what I encountered, I have again tried to capture some of the characters that make up some parts of the speedway world as well as vaguely attempt to delve beneath the surface of what I've seen. All of life was there at speedway in our nation and many people went out of their way to be kind, tell me their thoughts on speedway or comment on my books.

Anyway, when writing this book I have tried to adhere to the lessons I was given previously by my editor, mentor, advisor and writing coach Michael Payne as well as encouragement from the late Michael Donaghy who suggested I write about what I know or love.

Sadly, anyone familiar with my blog or my books will know that I'm not adverse to some pointless navel-gazing and pretentiousness or facetiousness. Nonetheless, I hope that you can forgive these faults and mostly enjoy the chance to travel to the tracks again in my company as much as I relished the visits.

Lastly, without the riders prepared to risk their lives on high-powered bikes without brakes on various different tracks - for our entertainment and to make their living - there would be no sport to watch in this country. In our everyday lives, we often take our own mortality for granted and, equally, we make light of speedway injuries as part and parcel of the sport. The 2007 season was a particularly poor one for serious injuries in the UK. From the 2007 season, injuries to Gary Stead, David McAllan, Stuart Robson and Mark Loram spring immediately to mind. Numerous other riders allegedly 'recovered' from their battle scars. Clothed in their racing gear, unlike their loved ones, we often forget that every rider is someone's brother, son, partner, husband or father. Hopefully we can all remember this every time a critical comment nearly passes our lips without need of further injury to remind us of the real situation.

There you have it. I hope that you enjoy your journey.

Brighton

1 June 2008

For George Grant, who kindly took me to Smallmead
every Monday night in the mid 1970s

and

In loving memory of
Gladys Trotter
1923-2008

**"So much is chance,
So much ability, desire, and feverish care."**
Michael Donaghy

Chapter 1. Newport: New Year Classic 2007 rain-off

7th January 2007

"The greatest show on dirt" Sky strap line

Inevitably as soon as Tim Stone, the promoter of the Newport New Year Classic, spoke in congratulatory fashion to the *Speedway Star* about the fact that this winter speedway event could and had run in all weathers, he was bound to irk the speedway weather gods. In other years, whether the wintry conditions ranged from just plain cold and cloudy to snow throughout the Newport area, or even when there was sleet, rain, overnight frost and snow, the show must and did go on. This morning, with the rain coming down heavily four hours before the tapes are due to fly, the track looks decidedly soggy. In fact, it looks hugely wet to my untrained eyes as puddles near the inner white curb of the track - that on a golf course would be called 'lateral water hazards' and would definitely merit a dropped ball - lie visibly on all the bends and on both straights. Elsewhere the track surface itself looks generally sodden but not waterlogged. But then this isn't golf and I'm not a track curator, so everyone is quick to inform me at every opportunity: "the track isn't a problem; it's the weather". This is the party line peddled by all and sundry, so much so that I'm happy to be a believer and would repeat it to anyone, were I to be asked. Not that I am ever consulted, since I am asking the questions - though a quick glance at the expression on Tim Stone's face suggested that it might be politic if I kept these to a minimum with him and, indeed, generally keep out of his way. Not that he has much time to talk as his mobile trills constantly and when it's not bleeping like a demented space invader machine on the fritz, he charges about the place in a frenzy of vital proprietorial activity. Given the weeks of preparation already put into maintaining the track, continuous rain is the last thing he needs.

The centre green also looks waterlogged but then the riders don't race on that so they're unlikely to use it unless they pull up with an engine failure or end up on the podium spraying the Tesco own-brand Cava round with gay abandon. Perhaps, this isn't a surprise given the stadium was originally built on reclaimed marshland. Already at work on the heavy infield and (bravely) attending to the electrics in the downpour are Peter Brookes and David Dean. As far as their hooded anoraks go, they both sensibly favour the attire worn this season by the more fashionable deep-sea trawlermen, in contrast to Tim who prefers the florescent yellow jacket beloved by so many motorway maintenance people everywhere, albeit without anything as jaunty as a baseball cap or hood.

Before I left a rain-swept Cardiff to travel to the Queensway Meadows Industrial Estate, I conducted an extensive search of the Internet in an attempt to get conflicting accounts of the weather in the vain hope that the heavy rain forecast on one of the sites wouldn't materialise. Some forecast showers and others a downpour. The night before, my favoured forecaster of choice, 'Metcheck', had promised a deluge of 4.8 millimetres between the *New Year Classic* speedway witching hours of noon to 3 p.m. but now had suddenly veered towards a more optimistic light sprinkling for the NP19 area. However, that said, other forecasters spoke in more generalised terms of passing bands of rain throughout the day. Nonetheless my hope sprang eternal at the thought of possibly selling a few more copies of my books by the turnstiles while the crowd surged through en route to bagsy their key spot on the grandstand.

Down by the turnstiles this hope looks decidedly ill founded, especially as there was a giant puddle-cum-flood to navigate directly upon entry. Any arriving fans would have to splosh through it to access the path to the grandstand or to reach any of the bends (or for that matter the downstairs toilets inside the bowels of the stand where the bar used to be located; once there, they would also be confronted by a further water hazard of a slightly flooded corridor).

The optimism and dedication that it takes to run your own stadium and found your own speedway club - in an area subject to a severe economic buffeting over the years since the closure of the traditional local industries of coal and steel - require stubbornness, bloody mindedness, resilience, tenacity and a cast of mind always prepared to look on the bright side. Tim has all those qualities, though the bright-side aspect is subject to occasional strain. Indeed, to have achieved all he has with Newport speedway, he must really be possessed of an optimism allied to an indomitable view of life to have ensured the continued existence of Newport speedway at the Premier and Conference League levels. Understandably enough, his approach to one of his major revenue-earning speedway meetings of the year was one of determination in the face of difficult odds (and weather conditions). In fact, there was some brightness just before 10 at the stadium - sadly though, not in the speedway office where Tim was, but in the far distance to the West in the general direction of Bristol. At the behest of Tim's disembodied voice from within ("what way is the flag blowing?") I stand on tiptoe and peer over the barbed wire topped perimeter fence of the stadium towards the flagpole of the car dealership building - sited nearby on this light industrial estate - to establish the wind direction. I report back that the direction was favourable since it blew roughly from the east and theoretically should shortly bring the fair sky towards us. Instead, preferring the evidence of his own eyes ("not that I disbelieve you"), Tim comes out to inspect the brightness and the billowing flag for himself before he retreats back to the inner sanctum of the dry Speedway Office but notes once more, as he passes, "it's not the track it's the weather." Some people have prepared for the eventuality of rain, notably trackshop entrepreneur John Jones. He is predictably "freaking professional" enough to have strategically pitched his stall (with its sensible waterproof covering for the roof and sides of the stall) on the slightly higher ground in the corner by the steel gates and adjacent to the catering facilities, just to the side of the giant puddle by the turnstiles. Like the puddle, no one would miss his stall. With his delightful lady wife busied elsewhere, my greeting of "alright?" is greeted by an automatic response of "fine" belied by his tone of voice, the weather conditions and the scowled look on his face as he sploshes grimfacedly towards the bowels of the grandstand.

Earlier I'd spoken to the always-cheerful Dave in the new "upper bar" area that has been installed on the top level of the grandstand since my previous visit last summer. He didn't hold out much hope that the racing would proceed but like so many of the other loyal volunteers that the club relies on throughout the season to ensure it runs successfully, he'd still turned out and busied himself helping with whatever was to hand or was required. The relocated bar occupies a good-sized section of the grandstand and overlooks the track magnificently and also provides a restricted view through the windows of the away side of the pits to the left. I welcome the shelter inside and quickly gather that some last-minute outfitting is still in progress as another man is crouched but busy in the far corner, though in press accounts the bar has been "fully operational" since October. It's a splendid addition to the ongoing gradual development of the Hayley Stadium facilities and in this week's *Speedway Star* Tim proudly expected that some riders would have the odd libation (or ten) there after the meeting, when he felt that the irresistible lure of the new facilities would inevitably cause them to "take liquid refreshments" on site.

For now, the only liquid easily available falls from the sky. Constantly occupied throughout my time there, the dedicated track staff in the form of the always-welcoming Peter and David are busy painstakingly sweeping and tidying the covered areas of the pits of sawdust (on the home side) and of sizeable puddles on the more exposed away section. Peter reckons the forecast is "rain, rain and more rain", and my thought that I might be a bit of a 'Jonah' is met with, "but, at least, he had a whale to shelter in and you seem to have forgotten yours!" Listening to the collective chatter, the general opinion comes down on the side that "Tim should have called it off yesterday 'cause of the forecast, but didn't!" Equally, early cancellation would also probably have brought complaints from someone. It's clear that in the unlikely event the racing can proceed smoothly, then the crowd levels will suffer from the uncertainty and the ugliness of the actual or forecast weather. The arrival of the SCB Official Craig Ackroyd - who has travelled down from Preston - in the next few minutes will remove this decision from Tim's reluctant hands, particularly as the rain remains heavy and the track continues to look sodden. Though, again, I'm reassured: "The base is dry and firm below the surface so the riders'll be able to race - we'll put on a show - the track holds up well and with a bit of sawdust, it'll be no problem!" I had hoped to check this confident opinion with the experienced Newport track curator, Andy Dean, but he's absent and his son tells me, "He don't work here no more 'cause he had a falling out with Tim over some things". Though I don't learn what these were, I do learn from David, when talking about the objections that the S.W.A.R.M. ladies expressed regarding the comments I attributed to them about the club in my book *Showered in Shale*, "there's always problems when you mix women and

Lateral water hazard on the home straight.

Peter Brookes and David Dean sweep the pits.

Tim towers over Bomber and his big brolly (actual size)

sport." Unable to comment, I imagine that this afternoon the mixture of shale, water and sawdust would be the problem that will most occupy the male half of the species gathered here.

Not that there will be any need to spread out the sawdust since, by the time I wander round to the circle of umbrellas by the catering outlet, it's clear that the referee has immediately abandoned the meeting. It will now be run, weather permitting ("we'll postpone it on the Saturday next time if it's this bad again") at the same time in the same place in a week's time. The diminutive Chris 'Bomber' Harris chooses that moment to arrive with what, in his hands, appears like a giant umbrella only to be greeted by Tim saying in his singsong Welsh accent, "Sorry Bomber, it's off! We thought the rain would hold up but it's carried on so we's had no choice." In his own rich regional accent (Cornish), Bomber remains nonchalant and unbothered, "Yeh, I've already looked at it - I just wonder why I'm not still in bed." After some chatter among the officials and Tim ("Thank you, ladies, for all coming in today!" he calls to the retreating helpers before his mobile trills "ah, Lubos, sadly it is off!") I wander back along the edge of the grandstand with Bomber and his friend. Our talk moves jokingly from the track conditions to take in his selection for the 2007 GP series. His assured "we'd have been alright, we could have raced" is wittily interrupted by an older man I assume to be a mentor, "it'll get us used to it for the GPs." If we ignore this sly reference to the television induced habit of the GP series organisers to continue to run these meetings with apparently scant regard for rider safety, irrespective of actual weather conditions or track quality - Bomber laughingly retorts, "I'll just knock a few people off!"

Back under cover on the home side of the pits David Howe, with his mum in tow, has arrived to immediately and gleefully stake his chosen place in the pits with, in the absence of his bike, a small pile of possessions - namely his bike stand, an empty fuel can and a dirt deflector. I'd heard how polite, conscientious, thoughtful and thorough David Howe was when interviewed by the excellent Tim Hamblin, the ace speedway reporter of the *Wolverhampton Express & Star*. Tim is a shrewd judge of people, so I'm not at all surprised when this judgement on his character is borne out when David warmly congratulates Bomber on his selection for the GPs. However, he then appears, despite the weather conditions, genuinely shocked and amazed at the news that the meeting has been cancelled. His incredulity is touching and he seeks confirmation from the chain-smoking older man sat next to him with a clipboard of official paperwork ("don't ask me - he hasn't told me yet and I'm the farking one signing everyone in!").

"You're farking kidding! That means I'll have to wash the bloody bike again as it's on the back of the car! Seriously, I was ready to race - I was just getting the driest bit of the pits, I was ready to go - I've been training hard."

"Doin' what?" asks Bomber.

"Heavy bag boxing, you know, with the big bag on the rope - it nearly killed me. It's the hardest training I've ever done! Me hand swelled up and everything.

Look it's stopped now; perhaps he'll run it. There's not much grip out there though."

"Just you and me, David!" grins Bomber.

"It always was anyway [smirks]. I can't believe that I'll have to clean the bike again! I haven't even unloaded it but it's been on the back of the car held on with a couple of bungee straps and board - retro style just like the old speedway riders used to."

The talk then moves onto Bomber's trip to Denmark for something I don't quite catch to do with his engines before they rather illuminatingly get down to casual gossiping about when a certain rider whose name I've redacted rode at Redcar, "you only get away with three or four moves like that a season and he tried them all at once. Gary and Freddie have been around, so they just thought, you can have that if you want it that much!"

Entertaining though this banter is, the lure of a long drive home in the rain proves too much for me to resist. It's not until I reach the Severn Crossing that the rain temporarily stops and the skies brighten but then - like the notorious hugely dangerous currents of the river below - the weather around here obeys the laws of its own microenvironment. Just like Hayley Stadium runs to its own uniquely engaging rules and rhythms - those managed, dictated and generated by the proud, energetic Welshman Tim Stone. Except, of course, on those days when the weather gods occasionally intervene to rain on his parade.[1]

7th January 2007 New Year Classic - postponed rain

[1 SCB ruling (SR 7.5.2) is instructive with regard to the limited number of close season meetings. *"In respect of Out of Season Meetings (outdoor or indoor), the SCB will grant a maximum of 1 permit per month (November to February, inclusive)"*. This explains why during the close season there is only Brighton in December, Newport in January and Telford in February. There is some jealousy among promoters about these meetings since it's pretty well known these one-offs can make good money and other promoters can't break into these possible lucrative winter speciality markets through any previous stakeholder claims. Arguably, this jealousy made sure during the close season that Tim would lose his geographically influenced regular cartel of meetings either side of the British Grand Prix at Cardiff, when he regularly ran Newport v Glasgow on the Friday night and the Welsh Open on the Sunday afternoon. These meetings usually attracted his best crowds of his season by far. But the BSPA vetoed his previous rights to the Friday meeting when they unexpectedly allocated the 2007 Premier League Pairs Final to Somerset on that Friday night. Effectively, this deprived cash-strapped Tim from one of his significant "keeping his head above water" meetings and so hit his business hard.]

Chapter 2. Telford: Ice, Y-fronts and the law of three

11th February

The always interested Kelvin Tatum

The indoor version of ice speedway held in Telford brings some much-needed spiked-wheeled glamour (though, in reality, they're actually self-tapping screws inserted into the tyres) to the close season calendar and, given that 2007 is the 22nd staging of the event, nowadays it's become an institution within the sport. My trip to see the racing is a double first since it's my first-ever trip to Telford, let alone to watch the event that is the slight mouthful known as the 'Telford International Indoor Speedway on Ice'. For some reason, I'd always associated it with mail order catalogues and imagined that Telford was a new town built during the heyday of these developments in the 1960s and 1970s but, until I had to figure out how to get there, I had no real idea where it was in the country. I suspected it was in the North but it turned out to be the largest town in Shropshire. The council website claims that it is one of the fastest-growing towns in the country (140,000 people) and named after the famous Scots civil engineer, Thomas Telford. Like many political inventions (and similar to how what outsiders call 'Stoke' is really an area made up of five distinct towns), the place we know as 'Telford' was created from the fusion of other more exotic sounding independent but smaller towns - namely Dawley, Donnington, Hadley, Ironbridge, Madeley, Oakengates, Shifnal (home of Wolverhampton team manager, Peter Adams) and Wellington. Weirdly the town incorporates half of a UNESCO World Heritage site known as Ironbridge Gorge. My level of ignorance about this country shocks me sometimes.

Though the journey from the M6 onto the M54 and into the town centre is easy enough, like all places you've never been to before, actually locating the ice hockey rink where the racing on ice will happen is altogether another matter. Still, all roads seem to lead towards Telford Plaza and, after defeating the vagaries of the one-way systems I encounter, I soon find myself pulling into the riders' and officials' section (having persuaded an officious man of my legitimacy to enter) of the extensive car park they have adjacent to the rink. The place is already crowded with riders' vans and, though the shutters have yet to be officially open to admit them, many have already started to unload their equipment or work on their machines. Though this isn't really a pits area - it is usually where the Zamboni ice-smoothing machine is handily parked when it's not resurfacing the rink - the hive of activity could lead you to imagine it was. Apart from the car park location, the most immediately noticeable difference to normal is the frightening number of spikes required on each tyre in order to be able to race on ice effectively. Obviously, I knew they were needed but the sheer number is impressive. Edward Kennett's mechanic Chris Geer suggested that I run my finger along one to establish how sharp it really is. In fact they're far from razor sharp but then they're needed for grip and to slice past your opposition not cut them to ribbons. Even though every bike has each wheel encased in the protective sheath of a metal mudguard (something you don't see on a traditional speedway bike), you'd soon get colander looking skin should you enjoy the misfortune of being run over. You can't buy these tyres ready-made and each one has to be constructed by hand in bespoke fashion. In this case by Chris Geer, who has pierced the rubber casing of the body wall of the tyre from inside with an individual screw on each knobble of the tread. Viewed side on, each tyre is a forest of spikes and looks extremely punky. There are five spikes per section - three on the central part of the tread and another on either rim so that the rider of the bike can lean his machine almost horizontal with the ice in the corners, should they so desire! The riders are given their special tyres on arrival, so that all the tyres are the same. Any rider found to be using a different tyre would be thrown out of the meeting. It takes Graham Drury seven hours to prepare each tyre!

Just like outside, the mood inside the ice rink is cheerful and light hearted. Because of the layout of the ice rink, the Collectors Fayre is spread over two floors. Upstairs, almost immediately after the fans have shown their tickets and passed through the turnstiles-cum-entrance way, they're confronted by the doorway to a manager's office, a lift for disabled access to the downstairs ground level of the ice rink itself as well as the full glory of the memorabilia stand manned by Nick and Johnny Barber plus Martin Dadswell. A prime feature of the display is a sea of bright red and yellow garments (anoraks, scarves, shirts and the like) and speedway paraphernalia - all prepared for the start of the season when Birmingham Speedway will once again take to the shale at Perry Barr (albeit a different stadium than before although this was the stadium they originally raced at from the Second World War until 1969). Today will be the first chance that the mad-for-it Brummies fans will have to lay their hands on some Brummies branded gear and wear their allegiance - signalled through the colours themselves and a giant red B - with pride and distinction. This is a shrewd move, given the pent-up demand for all things Birmingham speedway and how close Telford is to the second city, but also it's an example of commercial good sense since the Brummies promoter Graham Drury is one half of the promotional team that has run the Ice Speedway for the last 22 years. The magnitude of the re-opening is further emphasised by the presence today of serial speedway club owner and "Kidderminster based businessman Tony Mole" (as Nigel Pearson invariably describes him in the *Speedway Star*). Indeed, close by there is a small table set up for fans to pre-purchase Birmingham Speedway season tickets, actually from Tony Mole himself causing some fans to joke later, "He wants to make sure none of the money goes missing!"

Straight on from the entranceway glass doors there's a nylon-tiled passage that leads to the ice-rink seating area that runs the length of one side of the auditorium, while to the right of the memorabilia laden tables are the stairs that lead down to the basement and the ground level of the ice rink itself. The rink, encased by a protective wall partly constructed from toughened Perspex, allows clear sight lines for the spectators while at the same time protecting them from injury from flying rogue pucks - and at its base has the solid blocks-cum-fence that you find at ice rinks everywhere. Though the Perspex wall encases the whole of the rink (but still allows easy access at the far end) fans will only be able to stand and watch the meeting clustered round the third/fourth bend area and along the length of the back straight. Also downstairs in the basement is another Collectors Fayre housed at the bottom of the stairs in an overheated room that also houses some toilets and vending machines and affords a restricted view of the rink that will immediately be blocked when fans arrive to stand and watch the action on the ice. I'm not quite sure what any of the stallholders located here have done to offend, but there's a sense that they have been cast into the stygian gloom of a rubber-floored dungeon that smells faintly of melted ice, stale sweat and reeks strongly of industrial strength disinfectant (probably used to mask the musk of sweaty feet as this is usually where the hired skates are removed). The majority of the stalls are found here though I imagine fans will have already been sated by the goodies on display for sale upstairs, should any of them even have the desire or inclination to linger any longer than is necessary in this slightly unprepossessing environment. The rubber flooring to protect against the damage caused by skaters' spikes is pretty well everywhere in the basement. Later, ignoring the contrast that upstairs there is mainly new stock on display and downstairs superseded stock from seasons past, a glistening Dave Rattenberry will morosely say, "I bet you're glad you didn't pay to come and have a stall here!"

On my first reconnaissance trip to inspect the rink, I bump into the avuncular force of nature that is ice speedway co-promoter Ian Thomas. He's on his way to change into the cream-coloured "Savile Row suit" and dark collared shirt he carries on coat hangers

Edward Kennet and Chris Geer

A spiked ice speedway wheel

along with the slip-on white dress shoes that will complete his showman's attire. Old theatrical habits die-hard for someone schooled for many decades in (what Ian invariably calls) "showbusiness" who has forgotten more than some people will ever know about the entertainment industry, let alone about the speedway promotional game.[1]

Only a minute of conversation with Ian will quickly reveal that while he performs, the primary function of 'The Ian Thomas Organisation' is to manage and gain bookings for other performers. There is a wealth of choice offered to any potential customer including; close-up magic, caricaturists, comedians, tributes, speciality acts, look-alikes, named groups, party bands, discos, 50s-60s-70s bands and, of course, the most recent addition to the stable Mr Woo. I believe Ian is a close-up magician, something I initially thought was magic for the short-sighted, but is a definition more to do with the dexterity, wonder and skill the performer possesses (qualities that would, elsewhere, qualify you as a pickpocket). Like his speedway persona, Ian has strong, plainspoken opinions on what should or shouldn't be done and who is "quality" and who isn't. So for him, illusionist Derren Brown and Poole co-promoter Matt Ford are both quickly dismissed as hoaxers or charlatans rather than the genuine article (albeit Ian is much more vituperative about Matt). The site nowadays has honed and refined its mission statement (what sort of sad world is it that someone like Ian Thomas is forced by commerce to have such a thing?). "Fronted not surprisingly by Ian Thomas, we offer a personal service, quality and importantly, value for money. We provide entertainment for virtually any type of event. We will always give you an honest opinion on whether any particular act is suitable for the function you are organizing. You will find our prices competitive. We only offer top class performers. After many years in the business and a first class reputation to maintain, it is important that you are satisfied with the acts we supply. Please feel free to contact us to discuss your proposed function."

Unlike many other contemporary speedway promoters, Ian has the gift of the gab, a keen eye for a storyline and a natural flair for creating news or controversy (usually through his plain speaking). He's definitely someone who always puts his heart into his work and also metaphorically puts a capital P into Promotion and then double underlines and highlights it in yellow for additional emphasis. The well-oiled machine that is the Telford International Indoor Speedway on Ice promotional partnership of Thomas/Drury (or Drury/Thomas,

[1] Almost as I walked in back home after Telford, I logged onto Ian's website (www.it-org.co.uk) to find out more about 'The Ian Thomas Organisation' - tagline "a whole world of entertainment". Given the site had only just gone live, it wasn't quite the sleekly refined version that you'll find nowadays, nonetheless it still had the music hall feel or, at least, the completely different era of theatrical entertainment atmosphere it still retains. Listening to Ian's wealth of "showbusiness stories" (and for Ian, you sense the word is always split into its constituent parts of show and business), you quickly gather that, despite his comparative youth, he's part of a long-standing theatrical tradition of hard-working, jobbing performers who travel from venue to venue - whether it's a club, a works function, corporate event or a birthday party. Our quick fix, always-on-the-run-culture has no real time for the dying tradition and ethos of the somewhat slower acts and performances that require participation as a group or being together as part of a community rather than the more modern atomised, individualised consumption in your own home approach that increasingly dominates. In some ways, Ian is unintentionally (rather than self-consciously) following a similar trajectory in his showbusiness life as he is in his speedway one since he manages and, in a sense, performs in both spheres with each, ultimately, part of a rich tradition but slowly stumbling to extinction in competition with other media for the limited free time of its patrons. Even more spookily, in authenticity terms you could argue that speedway is only authentically appreciated when seen live at the track rather than enjoyed in the modern way as a viewer at home (since, unlike football, community live screening in pubs and bars is non-existent) served up with an ersatz version - albeit an enhanced simulacra - of the experience.]

I'm not quite sure which order they should appear in) has been burnished and perfected over many years to the point of second nature. Nonetheless, both men have a fastidious attention to detail and take nothing for granted. Getting dressed up is all part of the day and an essential component of the overall effect. "I always try to wear a satin collar at every speedway meeting. I bought my cream Savile Row suit from the Middleditch's [salvage] business. It was £120 but should have been £1,000 on Savile Row. I shop at the same place as Terry Russell - when I saw him I said 'I buy my suit at the same place as you!' 'What Savile Row?' 'Nah - the Middleditch's!' He didn't say nowt to that." Ian then manages to surprise me on two counts - firstly with news that he's embraced the world wide web thingy and gained his own URL but secondly, and with a show of proprietorial pride, Ian invites me "to have a look round the changing rooms - come on I'll show you while I get changed!" Inside the changing room he quickly strips down to his large sized Y-fronts and socks (dear reader, I won't give you a description but you'll have to conjure your own image of a man of a certain age undressing and then sprucing himself up) while carrying on talking throughout. As ever, Ian has a wealth of engagingly told or witty stories and his recent cruise holiday with his wife was no exception. "They say things happen in three's. On Boxing Day, we went to a Christmas Party in India and, when I arrived, a farking dog bit me! On the 29th of December, I was shat on by a monkey at Singapore (it's a lovely zoo) - there was a Singapore television crew filming who creased up when they saw it but kindly helped clean me up. Then I bumped into a man on Orchard Road who said ' I know you and I've just bought your book'. He'd bought the book second-hand on Amazon for £2.50 signed (To Wendy) and everything!" If Ian was unlucky during his travels abroad, then recently he'd been much luckier on the UK road system when involved in a car crash. "I was slowing down and was crashed into from behind. I got four broken ribs - they were wonderful at Chesterfield Hospital where they gave me an MRI scan that showed an 'abnormality on my kidneys'. Thank fark I'm in BUPA! I was delighted when they said it wasn't cancer." By now Ian has transformed himself from a figure in giant Y-fronts into his smart, impresario persona with showtime threads to match and project that image. He waves expansively at the 16 specially produced tabards for the later ice speedway meetings that hang in numerical order on individual hooks in the cavernous and deserted changing room, while they await the arrival of the riding talent. "After so many years, this thing runs itself!" says Ian confidently as he escorts me out of the changing room and points me to the Press Centre housed up some stairs at the far end of the ice rink.

To enter the room that serves as the Press Centre, you have to go up some stairs and pass through a couple of fire doors to find yourself inside the media inner sanctum. I've got to say I'm impressed at the professionalism of the organisers that such a facility even exists as it certainly doesn't at the Brighton Bonanza or any of the Super7 events. The press room has a cash bar - probably sensible when you consider the reputation that journalists have for the amber nectar - a large, highly polished boardroom-style table that dominates the centre of the room as well as a huge number of chairs that surround the table and line the walls. There are also some comfy chairs but these have no takers. If, as they say, possession is nine-tenths of the law then it's likely the other sports journalists who have already congregated in the room would give the average German family a good run for their money on holiday when it comes to securing the ideally placed pool loungers. The only window in the room that overlooks the ice rink has already been completely blocked with strategically placed chairs laid out in the manner of church pews. The equipment of local sports journalism is laid out on each seat along with anoraks, battered canvas bags and the like ostentatiously signalling that these seats are taken. As a first-time visitor myself and bucking the speedway trend to friendliness, no one says hello or attempts to introduce themselves but prefer to chat among themselves or stand around territorially. I clutch my sky blue "World Indoor Ice - Official Pass Admit One" (with the word "Press" - chosen from a range of alternatives that include Rider, Mechanic, Official, TV, Radio and Guest - circled in biro) to silently indicate I belong here but to no avail. The men of a certain age prefer their own rarefied company to that of strangers and clearly many have decided to base themselves here for the duration of the event. They will get a good view as they watch through the glass, so what they lose in atmosphere they will (hopefully) gain in accuracy for their reports for Radio North North West of Stevenage or whatever regional outfit they write for. I look around for Richard Bott - the legendary speedway journalist and the indefatigable writer of a continuous stream of exciting press releases in the month prior to the event - but can't find him.

Instead, I retreat to the gloom of the downstairs Collectors Fayre where Dave Rat introduces me to Kevin Little - who's here to press the fresh and drum up interest for his forthcoming testimonial at Redcar in the early weeks of the season - as well as Julie Reading and Stephanie Babb. These two ladies are an essential part of the hidden administrative, planning and support network

As worn by Terry Russell

Dave Rat and John Rich savour the basement atmosphere

committee that any rider will need to have if they wish to have a successfully organised and run testimonial arranged (by willing volunteers). I quickly gather that they have been at the nerve centre of operations for countless rider testimonial events. They are characteristically modest about their skills and contributions, though the reality is "we're promoters for the day - we do the whole day and whatever it involves. We help organise the sponsors, riders, presentations, race format - everything that you can think of that would have to be organised for an ordinary speedway meeting plus all the bits and bobs you also get at testimonials! It's often a bit more complicated than a league meeting 'cause everyone comes from all over - everyone wants to help but the problem is usually getting hold of people and the hardest thing is putting the sponsorship together. At the moment we're working on both Kevin Little's and Jesper B Jensen's testimonials. You'd be amazed at all the things you have to think of and get right on the day. For Jesper's we have Mark Sawbridge putting the programme together and Willow Print doing the programmes - they're both fantastic to work with. For Kevin, Mike Hunter is doing the programme and George English is printing. Everyone pulls together and most people just can't do enough." They're "both Wolves fans" but by background Stephanie is a nurse ("if they get injured and I'm at the meeting, there's lots of little bits of advice you can give to the riders before they go to hospital to ensure they get properly diagnosed and treated") and Julie works for Yorkshire Bank, so "does the banking for all the riders" she's involved with. I gather they've helped organise the testimonials for Peter Karlsson, Robbie Kessler, Richard Juul and Michael Max plus they intend to organise Nicki Pedersen's in 2008. Later in the season, events will ensure that they will also throw themselves with gusto into helping organise the Garry Stead Grand Prix.

I bump into referee Chris Durno who informs me, "you can tell it's the start of the season 'cause there's already a dispute over tyres. One of the riders wants to use solid blocked ones and all the other riders say he should change his tyres 'cause he'll have too much of an advantage otherwise! All the riders are on a guarantee with something extra for a win so it's important to them all. With the soft tyres they all have, they'll give much more than solid blocks - I'll just find out what Graham Drury says to resolve it." He continues, "I was here really early but, as it's the first meeting of the season, I'm really nervous! I've just been given the list [of his forthcoming fixtures] and I have the first two *Sky* meetings of the season. Even better, I've been given Birmingham's first-ever meeting - I can't tell you what a huge honour it is, I'm really thrilled!"

Upstairs at the glass doors of the reception, there's a huge crush of fans waiting to burst into the ice rink and survey the mound of carefully selected merchandise on the Barber stall before heading to other areas of the building. There they'll be greeted by a slim line Johnny Barber who has "dropped two trouser sizes already walking a mile and a half a day. I don't have scales and it's all how you feel - and I'm really feeling the benefit!" Also passing is Mildenhall team manager Laurence Rogers who has just completed his first draft of the Michael Lee story, "it's already written but just waiting to be checked - Michael's just back from France where he looked after [Len Silver's] chalet all winter." There is bound to be a lot of interest in such a book, both given Michael's achievements on the track and his notoriety off it. Laurence intends to print the book via successful businessman and speedway collector extraordinaire Allen Trump's LCD Publishing company. Laurence has been offered unbelievably competitive rates but knows that as a result other work might take priority over the printing of his book (and still isn't). Another man in attendance is Eastbourne centre-green photographer Mike Hinves who tells me that the arrival of Bob Brimson has led to some interesting appointments and changes off the track. Coming from a music industry background, Bob is well aware of the power of promotion and the need to harness the Internet. Consequently, he has appointed David Taylor to re-design and revamp the Eagles website into an all-singing and all-dancing multimedia web portal that it is intended will feature all the usual information of match reports, fixtures and the like along with videos of rider interviews and recent meetings, regular photo updates, an online trackshop, a blog from their Writer in Residence and various other bells and whistles. According to Mike, Bob's lack of speedway experience in general and promotional experience specifically, has meant that he has tended to listen to those who have immediately volunteered to help him or who claim to be tried and tested experts. This new-found power went to the heads of some people and they started to throw their weight around. Mike feels that the website was a case in point because while Bob had heard extraordinary stories about the huge volumes of visitors ("millions"), he's unaware that allegedly many of these often only logged on to check the live score updates. This, thereby, skewed the visitor totals and exaggerated the pent-up interest Eastbourne speedway fans actually held for accessing their information via the World Wide Web. As a regular at Eagles fixtures home and away, Mike often used to text through the scores but will no longer be doing so since, rather significantly, live updates will not be a feature on the new-look Eastbourne website. For Mike, this goes down in the brave-decision school and reflects a misplaced (and untested) confidence that the re-vamped digital age content of the website will still drive visitor numbers in the same manner as a proven need for basic information. There has been some initial tension and teething problems after David Taylor's appointment ("I'm track photographer now") to various job functions in the Brimson-led organisation. Mike had been informed that his photographic services were no longer required though this was subsequently rescinded, "they then had to eat humble pie when they discovered that I owned the domain name for the website."

One of the shrewdest aspects of the staging of this event every year in Telford by Ian Thomas and Graham Drury is the low cost of the changes they have to make to the venue in contrast to the other indoor meeting of the close season held in Brighton. At that event, the organisers put on a show at a multi-use venue that requires them to invest considerable time, money and effort to create an indoor shale track for the racing, whereas in Telford pretty well everything is already in place at the rink. Indeed the stadium infrastructure is already in place - though during the preceding weeks the rink owners build up the thickness of the ice to ensure that the spiked wheels don't penetrate the freezing pipes beneath the surface - since there's a solid fence with plastic safety shield and the configuration of the seats in the balcony requires no alteration at all. I imagine that they can command a better deal on rental costs since the number of alternative uses to which you can put an ice rink is severely limited - even despite the fact that Telford Ice rink is a Regional Centre of Excellence for Ice Hockey - compared to a multi-purpose auditorium. One problem that has to be overcome is how exactly do you mark an inside white line on an ice surface that is also that colour? Ingeniously, the solution is to get an aerosol can of spray paint (blue) and use this to mark dotted blue lines on the surface. One of the few other significant investments is a large rectangular green felt mat to serve as the centre green, the starting gate tape mechanism and sixteen black buckets that are turned upside down to indicate the track shape on the ice. The drawback of this practical bucket-led solution is that riders with greater experience of racing on ice at Telford can alter the shape and topology of the track as they ride by accidentally on purpose kicking the buckets aside as they pass. Even after only a couple of races it quickly becomes apparent that many riders favour this tactic and, should you be an alien beamed down from outer space to the Telford Ice Rink, you'd be forgiven for thinking that the number of times you literally kick the bucket somehow contributes to the skill of your performance in the event. Another issue is the danger the ice surface presents to the start (and red flag) marshal who has to slide across the rink during the races to retrieve bits of fallen equipment (mud guards and the like) as well as repeated try to rearrange the buckets back into some semblance of an oval shape. It's a thankless and endlessly repeated task that enthrals the crowd since he only ever seems to scramble back to the safety of the rubber matting from the marauding spiked wheels by the merest fraction of an inch.

A thorn between two roses

The afternoon entertainment is provided by an England versus Rest of the World team meeting and within minutes of the bikes starting to race on the tight ice circuit, the air inside the auditorium is filled with the rich aroma of exhaust fumes. Though the riders are slightly tentative for the first few laps of competitive action, their innate skill on their machines allied to the grip provided by the spiked wheels soon has their collective level of confidence improve appreciably. The confined nature of the space means that passing manoeuvres are at a premium but careful timing or strategic kicks to the buckets that line the final bend creates opportunities for the cannier riders to sneak past their rivals. It's fortunate that the fans are protected from the racing by transparent Perspex sheets because every rider appears to delight in trying to create a huge spray of ice with their back wheel as they broadside-cum-powerslide into the corners. Some races shoot by as though the slippery ice surface is of no concern to the contestants, whereas others proceed at a tentative pace that appears to increase the chances of possible disaster through a loss of traction rather than reduce them. If any team really adapts to the conditions, it is the England one; and with three 5-1s in the first four races, they establish a lead that they are never going to relinquish. By heat 11, confidence levels are such that Aidan Collins waves to the crowd during the race and Edward Kennett does wheelies on his celebratory lap. Aggression on the rink doesn't necessarily gain the required results either, as Stephan Katt finds in heat 12 when he annihilates the opposition in the first bend only to discover that the dynamics of a four-lap race on ice is different to that on shale, since all three other riders easily sneak past him hugging the inside white (blue aerosol) line. Other than the slippery surface, there are hidden dangers - well they are hardly hidden - in the form of the upturned buckets that attempt to mark the so-called boundaries of the track. Rider after rider boots them aside or brushes them with their spikes in order to gain fractional advantage by cutting the corners to reduce the total distance they have to cover. It's a tactic that works well until Wayne Broadhurst gets a bucket impaled on his front wheel spikes as he exits the second bend, then massively struggles for control down the backstraight before smashing into the fence on the fourth bend. After wiping away the slush, he tentatively heads back to the pits and England comfortably run out victorious at 53-25.

During the break between the International meeting and the Pairs competition also staged during a big value afternoon of entertainment, David Howe promises over the often inaudible tannoy system yet greater excitement for the waverers in the audience who haven't yet purchased their tickets for the evening racing, "it does get a bit more aggressive in the evening - so I'm looking out for that!" In the six-lap Final of the Pairs competition, Craig Branney is so determined to excel that he smashes into more-or-less exactly the same spot on the fourth bend at even greater speed than Broadhurst (since he has a bucketless front wheel) and the thunder clap cum crunching sound of the smash reverberates inside the auditorium. As the cause of the stoppage, Branney is excluded and the race is awarded. Because of the 4-3-2-0 point scoring format, no matter where his partner David Howe was adjudged to have finished would have made no difference to the destination of the trophy (won by the pairing of Edward Kennett and Tony Atkin). However, I could have sworn Howe led at the time of the crash yet was surprisingly announced as third by Dave Hoggart, an error made as he rushed to get on with the subsequent presentation. After the Pairs trophy presentation, the National Anthem crackles loudly over the loudspeaker system though many of the crowd appear keener to leave the Ice Rink for the fleshpots of downtown Telford than linger and bathe in patriotic contemplation. Those who do stay are treated to the sight of the riders going mental racing the quad bikes and monkey bikes during the interval. It's clear to see that riders love just riding bikes - any bike they can lay their hands on. Edward Kennett, who has become something of an indoor specialist, appears to do about 60 laps.

I retreat to the inner sanctum of the Press Room and take a seat by the massive boardroom table. Having bagged seats in a prime position by the windows, despite the fact that the racing has stopped, many of the reporters seem reluctant to move that far away and, instead, stand around forlornly in the manner of train spotters temporarily without trains to spot. Before the catering arrives, Ian Thomas tries to tempt assorted members of the media to try the cakes he's brought with him but claims to be unable to manage to eat all on his own. The one-man sports commentary empire (stretching to speedway via darts and football) that is so ably and knowledgeably fronted by Nigel Pearson, also requires him to file copy on a weekly basis for the *Speedway Star* on Wolverhampton, Workington and, from this season, Birmingham. Ian Thomas is in no doubt about what the content of the Workington copy should comprise next week if judged by his conversation with Nigel, "The headlines write themselves! Branney head butts the fence and afterwards says he didn't feel it! Oh, and Tony Jackson on his first night as team manager takes the Rest of the World side to their largest ever defeat!" Once the food arrives, everyone attacks it with gusto and there are plenty of conversations to randomly overhear. An excited Graham Drury catches up with his co-promoter, "Tell you what - there was some fantastic racing this afternoon! People who say it's just a bit of fun, don't know what the fark they're talking about if you looked at the racing." Many people want to congratulate Graham on his appointment to promote at Birmingham and the idea that racing will once again take place in the Second City clearly causes widespread interest in the pressroom. Particularly if judged by the number of times Graham is asked about some aspect of the stadium ("superb!"), team ("we think we're going to do well but I'm making no forecasts"), track ("there's some contamination - I don't know what it is"), opening night plans ("it's going to be really special") or season ticket sales ("fantastic response and on sale here"). "I tell you what, Perry Barr is a rough place! When I got lost, I realised we weren't far from where [Handsworth] they had the riots that time!" Though in demand, Graham still has time for a few words with me and marks my card about who to look out for during the evening, "The German kiddie - don't know his name - has won a couple of times [in a similar overseas event] and is a real indoor expert!"

Back at the upstairs Collectors Fayre, Tony Mole sits resplendent in his shockingly bright Birmingham Brummies team coloured anorak (on sale at a bargain £39.99) waiting for season ticket purchasers. There's a reasonably steady stream of people venturing over to his table but, this being speedway, they're keener to find out some gossip, inform him of their connections with the club, or just out to express delight at the impending return of the club rather than part with hard cash. Nearby to where Tony Mole is talking up a storm, Johnny Barber brushes off ill-informed suggestions ("I've heard the area to watch from at Birmingham is very small") and also waxes lyrical, "the bar is just fantastic - it just goes on for days - over 1,000 people can watch from behind glass I reckon!" Steve and Sarah Miles (speedway fanatics and Peterborough fans) banter with the trackshop staff. The cause of some amusement is Steve becoming the Panthers 'Fan of the Year' (I can't tell whether this is true or Johnny taking the mickey), "I hear you had a ruff ride to win and Thomas the Dog was highly commended - may be nearly losing to a dog is paws for thought?" As I'm hovering behind the stall, when two fans in bright red Stoke anoraks linger over the copies of *Showered in Shale*, I can't help myself but strike up a conversation. "What team do you support?" [said just as the colouring and name on their clothing sinks in], "Stoke!" I leave them to contemplate a purchase after I add, "I've always seen good racing there!" Seconds later a gleeful Martin Dadswell informs me, "Well, you frightened them off; they practically ran away as soon as your back was turned!"

There's no doubt that this occasion provides huge value for money as the evening events comprises even more races (22) than the afternoon one (20) and that's without counting the quad bike racing during the interval. With pride and individual glory at stake, the racing is noticeably much more competitive and, since all the riders have by now acclimatised to the conditions, there is more passing let alone the fact that the corners are much more combative. Arguably one of the most entertaining aspects of the evening is a virtuoso performance from Phil Morris who appears to covet an award for gamesmanship and high calibre moaning. Heat 11 sees him mime his disgust at referee Chris Durno for having the cheek to stop the race when he led at the first

VIP area door sign

time of asking. Though he also won the re-run he obviously still felt sufficiently hard done by and actually had reason to be aggrieved when Wayne Broadhurst knocked him off on the third bend of the first lap of heat 16. Phil is quickly on his feet to have a word with Wayne and then to ostentatiously shake his head at Chris Durno for having the cheek to call all four riders back for the re-run. I'm sure trying to get fellow riders excluded isn't good etiquette and breaks the unofficial speedway riders' code that pits them against officialdom rather than each other. However, Phil still has plenty more to say on the subject and bravely butts into Wayne's conversation with his wife Andrea (who is also his mechanic and knows her way round bikes since she won the 1996 British Ladies Autograss National Championship too) to share some further bon mots. All this gamesmanship is for nought as Wayne wins the re-run comfortably. The contrast of racing indoors on ice rather than shale is emphasised in heat 18 when Morris cuts up the inside of Christian Hefenbrock on the second bend through the proverbial gap that isn't there and aggressively moves him over. In fact, it really isn't there at all since, in order to gain the advantage required to pass his rival, Phil has taken it upon himself to create his own racing line - skirting the rubber matting of the centre green - inside the notional boundary of the obliterated inside (blue) line. Having failed to be excluded for his sneaky manoeuvre, Morris ploughs onwards while Hefenbrock tries to catch him, only to then lose control and crash with a resounding thump into the fence in almost the same spot one lap later. Unperturbed, Phil Morris then cuts up aggressively inside Jack Hargreaves at the end of the third lap to ride to victory in the race and possibly in the Championship itself, unless Wayne Broadhurst can win his final race (heat 20) and force a run off. This race is hardly likely to be a gimme with Les Collins also needing a win to force a race-off with Phil Morris for the championship. Broadhurst leads but then, in his haste to occupy the outside line hits the fence exiting the fourth bend and is then excluded by Chris Durno when he skitters off his machine on the next bend causing the race to be stopped. However, you clutch any straw in such a situation and the fact that Wayne has one of those pesky black buckets he'd been kicking aside all meeting stuck under his front wheel when he crashed gives him some justifiable grounds for complaint. Appeals to natural justice by both Graham Drury and Ian Thomas see him re-instated by the referee; thereby giving Phil Morris the hump and notional cause for complaint throughout the rest of the season to anyone who shows interest or will listen. The re-run has barely started before John Branney causes mayhem on the third and fourth bends of the first lap when he cuts the corner to get the lead from Wayne Broadhurst who then promptly falls from his machine and only lightning reflexes from Les Collins prevents him from being badly spiked. Presenter David Hoggart appeals to the crowd in the balcony to stand up if they wish to see "all four back". Popular sentiment rests with Wayne, so he finds himself reinstated yet again and wins the race to force a race-off for first place with Phil Morris after Stephan Katt and Les Collins have settled the ownership of third place via their own run off. Almost from the off the result is never in doubt and Wayne 'King of Telford' Broadhurst wins the crown for the fourth time in his career (and retires with a record that sees him also achieve two seconds and a third in ten years on the ice). He celebrates enthusiastically and sends the crowd home happy after another day of speedway entertainment on ice.

11th February

England v Rest of the World 53-25

International Best Pairs, Winners: Tony Atkin & Edward Kennett

19th British Open Championship, Winner: Wayne Broadhurst

Chapter 3. High Beech: Electricians in short supply at 79th anniversary celebrations

18th February

SKYBALLS ON WEATHER

Kelvin *"We've had all sorts of weather this afternoon - rain, hail, little bit of snow - but the important thing is that we're on"*

The Kings Oak Hotel located in Epping Forest is the venue for the celebration to mark the 79th anniversary of the start of speedway in Britain at High Beech. Sadly nowadays the track is no more, but only a short distance away from the hotel you can quickly find yourself walking on a true slice of speedway history and what clearly was once part of the racetrack itself. In typical speedway fashion, the event isn't supported by any modern-day promoters or publicised by the speedway authorities at all. Sadly, history is often only ever mentioned in the context of making a real or imagined plea to some notional part of the tradition of the sport in this country in order to try to drum up some interest or flog a few more tickets. Apart from that, we live in a perpetual present where we pretend there are no lessons to be learnt from past experience or conclusions to be drawn from previous experiments with the rules, regulations, league structure etc. Each year the new and often more complicated tablets come down from the BSPA mountain to tidings of great joy (and occasional reluctance) from the promoters and with the acquiescence of the trade press. The typical speedway supporter remains loyal but drawn from an ageing demographic that probably spells disaster for the longevity of the sport in the medium to long term. On the Internet forums, everyone has a proposal - invariably a highly speculative and totally uncosted one - about what needs to be urgently done to restore speedway to its former glory and prominence in the national consciousness and/or media.

If the halcyon days have long gone, then to all intents and purposes the majority of the people who come along to displays their memorabilia, catch up with friends or look at what is on show really don't care about the travails of the present-day incarnation of speedway. Often they are some of the few living links we still collectively have with the salad days of the sport when it was wonderfully vibrant and truly a national pastime. Despite what feels like a Siberian wind, on the tarmac of the car park outside the Kings Oak a variety of stalls have been erected that feature the real meat and potatoes of the day for many of the older generation of riders and fans in attendance - the bikes and body colours that saw active service on the cinder tracks of yore. Inside the hotel, the bar that overlooks the swimming pool houses the Collectors Fayre part of the event and is also packed with a variety of stalls selling or displaying memorabilia drawn from different generations. Fayre organiser Andy Griggs, along with John Rich and Bill Gimbet who've made the journey down from the Midlands to man the Dave Rattenberry stall, represent the modern-day trackshops. Also in attendance are Tony McDonald and Susie Muir, publishers of retro speedway magazine *Backtrack* and a rich variety of books including the autobiography of Simmo (Malcolm Simmons) who will attend later to sign copies for any interested fans. Tony is a savvy publisher with a keen sense of commercial acumen, so his mere presence fills me with optimism that it could be a big day for book sales until he tells, "I doubt it's going to be anything special." There's a slice of history with a stall of race jackets run by Alan Morgan, and a stall of speedway DVDs plus there's a line of three sparkling, shiny and proudly cared-for speedway bikes that attracts admiring glances and loving touches all day. Later I overhear some gentlemen, "he's done a really good job at polishing it up - look at the points cover - we'll have to work harder on our polishing!" there are also a range of framed (£35) and unframed (£22) action photos taken by Stockport fan Steve Ridgeway on sale and, if paintings are your thing rather than photos, then Jim Blanchard has a stall full of these artefacts for you to display in pride of place at your home. Representing the Speedway Museum and raising further funds for its construction from donations or purchases of a limited but snazzy range of branded memorabilia are George and Linda Barclay who have thrown themselves into the fundraising with a dedication, gusto, belief and charm that really should get wider recognition than it has. They've travelled countless miles to an endless number of meetings to put the best foot forward for the Speedway Museum and represent these plans, the sport and themselves with great knowledge, capability and grace. Despite some sceptical opinion, they clearly really believe in the project and (modestly) delight in the success of their fundraising efforts. "We've raised £72,000 at the last count - seventy percent of that from the public - they said it couldn't be done but we've proved them wrong! April 28th is the tentative opening date - the VRSA started it and we've finished it." Apart from the displays to be erected in the physical museum itself (inside Paradise Park, located near Harlow), there are still some important administrative details to be resolved including its charitable status but also a bid for supporting funds from outside agencies, "we're fighting with the Lottery - maybe they'll just be giving all their money to the Olympics?"

The official opening hours of the Fayre is from 11a.m. to 4 p.m. but, given the natural constituency of such events being predominantly men of a certain age, they're likely to be up early and keenly excited enough to arrive well in advance. By 10 a.m. there are already quite a few visitors and I'm warned, "it'll be busiest between 11 and 12.30 before it subsides - many of them will probably need a nap by 2 p.m." My stall is in pride of place (albeit also in the slipstream of the Siberian wind blowing down the corridor from the entrance) and is the first to be seen as the fans enter. There's a steady flow of people and, given everyone likes to linger over the merchandise or catch up with old friends, the room is soon full and almost gridlocked. Many people look at my books quizzically as though they're not quite sure what place books on contemporary British speedway have at such an event. Many people stop for a few words as they pass. The start marshal with the most distinctively patterned trousers in speedway, Ian Glover, has strong links with speedway in Kent having gone to his first meeting at Canterbury in 1968 when he was nine years old and speedway was "a new phenomenon in the area". The track was only three miles down the road from his home and, like his father, he's always been interested in bikes (and ridden road bikes), while later he became the supporters club secretary for Canterbury. He now works at Sittingbourne but has also sought out his regular fix of speedway action at all the tracks in the surrounding counties, namely Lakeside and Eastbourne.

By late morning the aisles of the room are so crowdedly impassable there must genuinely be a fire risk, particularly given the high average age of the attendees. Inevitably there is a good smattering of men who used to ride and one of those is Eric Hockaday who (if I understood correctly) rode for a long list of clubs including Eastbourne, Coventry, Rayleigh, Exeter, Stoke, Cradley and Sheffield. He tells me "I won one major meeting" (the Sussex Championship) and that he's proud to have ridden for Charlie Dugard, "I know his son Bobby who runs it there now." To his mind, "the supporters on the Northern tracks are better - more generous - an engine was only £110 in those days and in the bar one of them gave me an open cheque saying 'there you are' no questions asked."

Though I'm sure that the majority of the men in the room could change an engine, replace the electrics or build a speedway bike from scratch, the problems that Fayre presenter Craig Saul has with his microphone appear to be beyond the abilities of everyone at the Kings Hotel. Craig has to resort to accosting everyone who passes with the questions, "do you know anything about electronics?" The new-fangled electronic technology is a stumbling block for all who try to rectify it and it looks likely that we're not going to be treated to interviews with assorted ex-riders like Malcolm Simmons, Bert Harkins and the like. That is until Pete Sampson from Paradise Park arrives at 1 p.m. and soon has the sound restored. Craig immediately says, "this man requires no introduction - it's Mister Bert Harkins!" Ironically the sound equipment has been fixed so that we can listen to someone speak in what - to Southern English ears - sounds like an impenetrable Scots accent. Bert is soon replaced by Malcolm who is yet again on the road to promote his book. He cuts a dapper figure, signs many copies and draws a crowd to listen - Craig closes the peroration with, "well, Malcolm, you'll always be Super Simmo to us!"

Whenever memorabilia is on sale or where the riders and equipment of yesteryear gather, Allen Trump is never far away. In his attempt to bring speedway back to the Exeter area he's had wide-ranging experience of the variety of people and bodies you have to work with or placate in order to finally get planning permission for a speedway track. Everyone has put their tuppenceworth in and, often, their approval has expensive strings attached with regard to the prospective site chosen at Haldon Hill. For example, the Highways Agency has worries about increased traffic volumes caused by the speedway and insists that the road will require the construction of a mini-roundabout. This blithely ignores the fact that the land is shared with "Haldon racecourse who've been there 200 years without them worrying about the horse boxes or needing a roundabout!" Resident

Well cared for shiny bikes

Backtrack stall vaguely mobbed

The legendary Malcolm Simmons

objections to the granting of planning permission in the general area isn't solely directed at the speedway plans since the national house builder Bellway Homes have had their housing development "reduced from 180 to 116 homes 'cause of residents objections on parking. Once you get involved with planning permission, all these different people get involved - English Nature, the Fireman's charity, the Highways Agency, the council - and it's always heads you lose, tails you lose! City-centre politics is unbelievable and that's before you try to sort the outside environmental concerns. For example with the Fireman's charity objection, the planning application cost £8,000 plus it was £800 per noise test - both for mine and the council's, which I pay for! I've had no change out of £25,000 and then there's the expectation and pressure of 1,500 Exeter speedway fans. If the modern planning regime applied to speedway in 1928, it would never have happened! Can you imagine a track in Epping Forest?" Having had first-hand experience of the difficulties in securing approvals, Allen sympathises with the ongoing protracted search for a suitable location for Wimbledon speedway conducted abortively by the PLC. Equally he thinks there are two sides to every story when it comes to the eventual acrimonious demise of the recent Conference League version of speedway at Plough Lane, "I spoke to the GRA and it wasn't quite as I understood it to be reading the reports. They tried to run on a shoestring and you can't do that with a stadium like Plough Lane. They were polite about Ian Perkin but you could read between the lines."

Fresh from his successful series of interviews on finally functioning equipment, Craig Saul stops by and is warned by *Backtrack* supremo Tony McDonald. "You've got to be careful what you say around Jeff - the worry isn't that you'll be misquoted but that you'll be accurately quoted!"

If speedway isn't hugely popular with the residents and some of the elected representatives in Devon, then the same applies in Workington. "The council don't want speedway. If someone makes Tony Mole an offer for his outstanding lease, he'll accept it, as he's a businessman. Speedway is too difficult for the council to be bothered with - unlike football and rugby. They say the new stadium is gonna cost £20 million, whereas both the soccer club and the rugby club would take £1 million each and put the stadiums they have right. But that would be too sensible!" Outside the front door of the hotel Stuart Towner and his wife-to-be Sue Jackson-Scott have a pasting table stood next to their van laden with a variety of publications including the always interesting and highly regarded independent speedway magazine, *the Voice*. To raise money for charity, they also have a speedway bike rigged up and attached to a light and a stop watch so interested punters can test their reaction times in a simulation that they have to imagine approximates the rise of the tapes for the start of a speedway race. Fortunately, not only do all contestants not have the complication of another three riders all hurtling competitively for a narrow section of shale in the first corner but many can also be grateful they don't have to depend on their reaction times and skills on a speedway machine to try to make a living. Once you've come under orders, the only way to get a flyer from the start is to anticipate the rise of the imaginary tapes and do the speedway equivalent of hitting and hoping, namely just release the clutch almost immediately in the hope random chance will dictate that the tapes have risen a fraction of a second beforehand. Fans complain whenever riders are excluded for a tape-touching offence when attempting to predict their rise and they also complain when referees vary the release times by holding them inordinately or just letting them go. Perhaps the lesson of the day should be that you clearly can't ever win if you're a rider, a referee or a would-be promoter seeking planning permission.

18th February - the tradition goes on …

Chapter 4. Swindon: Behind the scenes with the Abbey Stadium track team or Fencing and an important tip on how to handle equipment

8th March

SKYBALLS WITH ADDED ROSCO, PART I

Jonathan *"You could talk to Rosco all night - he likes to talk"*

I have had a long-standing invitation from Graham Cooke to come along and help the Swindon Robins track team with their winter work on the Blunsdon track. When he said "fencing" I imagined that I might have to buy an épée or foil specially to look the part, or even, perhaps given this is speedway, help with some stolen goods but apparently he meant the air variety. Graham is the author of the most unique speedway Blog in the country - the *Blunsdon Blog* - which covers the trials and tribulations of the (mostly volunteer) track team as they fight with the elements, the track and the invisible evil enemy of the vexatious staff that have responsibility for the greyhound track. Well, more the battle with the sand that forms the greyhound track surface, particularly when the rain makes it run and leech onto the hallowed shale surface. Not that I want to get too technical here as this has all been covered with humour in a wonderfully informative way by Graham on a week-by-week basis throughout the long winter months of the close season. It has become a hugely popular site and Graham informs me that traffic is an incredible average of 5,500 visitors per week to their home page (just the sort of visitor numbers I'm incredibly but quietly envious of)! I'm keen to meet in person some of the many, vividly described characters that I've learnt about on the site and get to appreciate first hand the dedication, hard work and artisan levels of skill that goes into the maintenance, upkeep and creation of the Blunsdon track. It's something that as speedway fans we almost take for granted. How can you have speedway without a track? Though we all know that staff regularly at work on the track doesn't necessarily mean that it will have been prepared to the exacting standards that the Swindon track curator Gerald Richter demands in Wiltshire (and at Lakeside where he also works). I think that some fans still believe that the promoter just throws open the turnstiles on a race night, the tractor twirls round the track a few times and some lines are painted at the start gate and once the riders have got changed and warmed their bikes up then you're just about ready to go.

Graham has warned me that they make an early start. I arrive along the foggy road that is the A420 from Oxford and then travel via the A419 (North) to Cirencester into the almost deserted but extremely well coned car park of the Abbey Stadium just before 8 a.m. A quick walk inside the equally deserted stadium grounds through the partially open gate reveals a totally locked up grandstand and an apparently desolate stadium. After a sit in my car listening to the *Today* programme on BBC Radio 4 and another brief foray inside the grounds, I meet a bloke who cheerfully directs me down the road to the smaller sky blue painted gate that provides access to the pits. Apparently everyone will be there already. I quickly find that everyone has indeed already assembled for an early-morning hot drink and banter inside a cosy but slightly decrepit hut by the pits. It's a room of sufficient size to easily seat seven people (with space for more to stand) that also boasts a table, sink, work benches - with an impressive display of mugs and a rich array of variously sized sandwich boxes piled up for later by the track team - and a kettle. There are four framed speedway action photographs on the wall directly in front of the entry door and on the adjacent wall the famous *Blunsdon Blog* calendar. This can be downloaded from the website and each month features a photograph (luckily clothed) of a member of the close-knit track team. Like the speedway season, the calendar doesn't run the full year and so only covers the vitally important months February to October. Though, that said some bloke in Cumbernauld hasn't quite grasped this since he bombards Graham with emails saying that every time he downloads it, the months of November and December are missing!

I'm soon introduced to everyone in the hut and a friendly, unassuming group they are too. They remain completely unaffected by their newfound notoriety on the Internet and Ernie makes the point to rib Graham about how news on the site about future work has got him in trouble with his wife (Rita) since he chose to spend his additional free time at the track rather than helping round the house or at the shops. Like many people involved in many unsung tasks of the speedway world, they work without payment for a love of their club and the chance to be involved behind the scenes. Ernie Poole explains to me that the blokes who helped paint the changing rooms are mad keen Robins fans convinced that the 2007 season will see Elite League Championship success "and they know if we lift the trophy that they'll be able to say that they played their own part in that too!"

All the regulars are here inside the hut with a mug of tea or coffee already in hand. There's the highly regarded track curator Gerald Richter who's presently incapacitated by his recent hernia operation - something that the rest of the crew correctly predict will definitely irritate him since he's a relentless man of action - and so ruefully tells me that he'll "be standing in the sun watching" today in an accent that I could mistake for South African (when in fact he's from Rhodesia/Zimbabwe). There's the exceptionally hard working character Rod 'Punch' Ford whose age is variously put somewhere between 67 and 69. Whatever the exact number he has the confident demeanour and physique of a man younger than his years who's unafraid of hard work. As if his work at the track wasn't already enough he has also three giant allotments to tend to though he has yet to get to work on them "as it's too wet up there". John Nobbs is in his 13th season on the track staff at the club and is of the opinion "you know, I can't see us losing at home this season - not once". The others are also pretty confident but reserve the right to look out for possible unexpected pitfalls through injury and mechanical failure. John tells me "on race day I'm on the tractor with Gerald blading the track between races", while away from Blunsdon, like many round this neck of the woods, he's a Swindon Town Football Club fan (as well as a machine operator for a recycling and quarrying company). Graham, the *Blunsdon Blog* founder and webmaster far better describes everyone in the track team with more insight and acuity than I ever could and so it is when it comes to describing himself in one of the early Blogs:

"The fact is that I am not used to manual work, having spent 25 years teaching at a Wiltshire Comprehensive school, the last few years of which were spent behind a desk as part of its management team. I now spend my time working as a ceramic artist, designing commercial web sites, resourcing and purchasing IT equipment for individuals and teaching basic IT skills to those unfamiliar with computers. None of these are physically demanding and I admit - I have become soft in middle age." Graham's work as a ceramic artist has its peaks and troughs, so after notionally or actually exhausting himself at Blunsdon the next day he will find himself "making 200 fingerbowls for an East Anglian restaurant chain." He patently relishes the variety that his early retirement permits him.

Completing our small team today is the friendly Ernie Poole who has followed the Robins since 1974 when he was 17. He met his wife at the track and, apart from a couple of years when the kids were younger, has followed the club obsessively. "With me wife, son and daughter we never missed a meeting for two years in 2000 and 2001. I can really honestly say I've enjoyed myself here and met a lot of true friends through speedway. I love coming here and I tried for years to get on the ground staff here". Demand for these voluntary positions is huge, not only for the closeness to the club but also for the insight that involvement behind the scenes confers. It's definitely a case of dead man's shoes at Blunsdon. Away from his work here - and he is a tireless, metronomic worker - Ernie is a HGV lorry driver, "if ever I've got any tension or anger I just save it all up for here and put all that energy into some shovelling or hard graft. It's wonderful in lots of ways here."

When the talk of the tearoom isn't the Robins prospects for the coming season we also get to adventitiously learn about the reinvigorated atmosphere and enthusiasm that has swept the organisation and outlook of the Lakeside Hammers where Gerald also works. He praises the passion for speedway and the strategic approach to the business taken by the newly formed partnership of owner Stuart Douglas and promoter Jon Cook, who he speaks exceptionally highly of for his energy, insight, pragmatism and commitment. Together they've been like a whirlwind in every department of the club and the future outlook looks extremely rosy. Gerald also pointedly acknowledges the huge contribution made to the club by Ronnie Russell "you couldn't ask to meet anyone who knew so much about speedway and cared for the club so much - we'll all miss him terribly. If there could be any criticism of Ronnie, and it sounds a silly thing to say, he was too nice sometimes. He had six different riders wanting six different track conditions and you can't promise them that they'll all be happy. The change in management is going to be good for

Let the (patriotic) party begin

Here's one I made earlier

the riders who've been there for ages too - Leigh Lanham rides the same line every race, it's like he's on rails, you could shut your eyes and still overtake him. In the past riders would be able to come in and say 'it's too wet' but now Jon Cook won't sympathise; he'll say 'fark off out there and ride the track!' Some riders are about to have the best years of their careers with him in charge. Hopefully this year we won't suffer with injuries either. Last year we lost four riders in ten days - people said sign some more but where the fark are you supposed to find them, Ronnie looked but it's easy to say, not do - if that happens to Swindon they'll finish bottom of the farking league too!" One thing is for sure, in Gerald's considered opinion, there's a new outlook and rekindled enthusiasm at Lakeside that will really take the club places during this and future seasons. "We want to beat everyone this season and with Jon around I think we can" even more interestingly given Gerald works at both tracks, "you know, I think the one he really wants to win is Swindon!"

When it comes to predictions of how other teams will fare in 2007 these come thick and fast. The consensus is that either Ipswich or Belle Vue will snatch the wooden spoon, though they're keen to tell me that they think Eastbourne won't fare so well nor, perhaps, will Oxford. Incredulity is expressed that on the forums there is a groundswell of opinion that has Coventry as likely champions. I preach the gospel of a settled squad but this only gets a "yeh, but who's going to really improve their averages?" My answer is almost any rider but particularly their American not-so-secret-weapon, Billy Janniro, though this gets the more elliptical response "maybe but it all depends which Billy turns up".[1]

We all troop outside where it's a remarkably sunny morning and Gerald notes "the forecast was for rain today but I don't farking see any clouds". As a close reader of the Blog, I had already noted over the winter that Blunsdon was allegedly twinned with Siberia - though today it was temporarily twinned with Barbados - and so I dressed accordingly in strong boots, waterproof trousers (with long johns underneath) and numerous layers to protect against any wind chill. I'd also brought my trusty gloves worn with distinction these last couple of years at the Brighton Bonanza, plus I'd invested in some knee pads - not quite *à la* Martin Dugard but fit for purpose as they rarely say about the Home Office nowadays. I'd cunningly bought these knee protectors because I'd gathered from the latest Blog entry that today's task was most likely to be the back breaking nightmare that is fixing the kickboards to the air fence on bends one and two of the Blunsdon track. Once you get out and walk on the surface you appreciate how huge this circuit really is. I also gather how proud Gerald is of

[1 This was a prescient remark since Billy scored an incredible 100 bonus points as an ever-present rider for Coventry during the 2007 season. Arguably Janniro was one of the first riders to really appreciate (and act upon) the significance of the fact that bonus points do not count towards your CMA (Calculated Meeting Average). So, for example, on many occasions a rider can be paid the same whether they finish ahead or behind their team mate. This means that not only is there no incentive to win *but* also a rider can sensibly maximise their future chance of employment by knocking off the throttle during the run in to the line and thereby artificially reduce their average. In all meetings during 2007, Billy averaged 6.75, yet his starting CMA is 5.17 for 2008. Contrary to some opinion, he's less of a silly Billy than a clever Trevor. In his *Speedway Star* preview for the 2008 Elite League season, respected and plain-speaking Wolverhampton team manager, Peter Adams, was forthright on this BSPA decision. "Taking away the bonus points from a riders' averages was a huge mistake. I don't know why it was done, but the sooner we revert back to like it was, the better it will be when it comes to points limits. I know of riders in the Elite League who purposely finish races behind their partner to try and keep themselves in work!"]

what has been achieved here, "this year we've used the motorway blade all winter - we started in October and we've been doing a bit every week and packing it down properly. I'm really, really pleased with it this season [waves arms expansively], put a top dressing on and you won't even see a different colour. Last year Reading borrowed the blade and farking returned it with the gears broken. They paid for it but it took months to get repaired so I couldn't do all that I wanted. This year we could and it shows!"

By now we've arrived at the far end of the track from the pits - bends one and two - and I find myself in a small but perfectly formed gang that comprises Graham, Ernie, John and myself. Ernie professes great optimism, unaware that I could potentially be a handicap to smooth progress through my innate cackhandedness, "this is great if we all work as a team, there's more of us today, we'll really be able to build up a pace and get it done quickly". The "it" in question sounds simple enough - attach the kickboards to the air fence. In practical terms this means unfurling shale-covered thick black rubber sheets from the pile in the nearby wheelbarrow to then place them at the base of the air fence, which is itself studded with metal ringed holes through the length of each inflatable panel. These ringed eyelet holes, with the addition of another one drilled one inch away, will be used to attach the rubber kick boards to the air fence by the cunning use of cable ties. Though these are fiddly to attach, since they require a pair of matching holes to be drilled in the kick board to then attach it via the cable tie to the actual base of the air fence[2]. This requires a lot of bending down or the kind of work on your haunches you'd have to pay good money to experience at a gym. It also requires patience, strength and dexterity along with aptitude to ignore the cold wet gloop that is the shale surface on this part of the track after the previous few days of torrential rain. 22 panels form the Airtek (motto "working for British Speedway") air fence for this particular bend, all clipped snugly together in position and slowly starting to inflate. Well, it is now that Graham has staggered round with the incredibly heavy military look generator that is the air pump itself, then filled it with petrol and fired up the noisy motor. The panels were modified for this season with the addition of a bright yellow inflatable base cushion that will adapt them sufficiently to overcome a previous design flaw. This will make each section stand almost as tall and proud on race day, just like Len Silver at the head of his rider parade. This is a doubly positive move since the riders will hit the air bags rather than slide underneath them. While, from the curatorial staff perspective, the rubber kick board can then be attached almost seamlessly and so work much more effectively as a barrier to the shale deposits that rapidly accrue with each bike that broadsides past during the races.

I suggest that I would be best suited to the grunt work that requires little skill and no patience so, with Graham, I get assigned the task of unfurling and dragging the kickboards into position by each panel. Ernie soon points out, in jovial fashion, that I somewhat lack common sense since rather than drag each of them greater and greater distances to place in position, I could transport them close by on the wheelbarrow I'm robotically unloading them from. Doh! Ernie is already crouched at work with John in the slop that is the damp shale surface and alternates between using drill and tying the cable ties. Earlier I'd overheard them comment that Charlie Gjedde had borrowed a brand new battery-powered drill but hadn't treated this equipment in a respectful fashion and had eventually returned it in a somewhat battered condition. There was a collective tut and raised eyebrow that I gathered indicated that this was probably typical of the thoughtlessness of the breed. After a while we get into a rhythm with our individual tasks. Once I've laid out the kick boards, I drill the additional holes in the air fence, Ernie drills them in the altogether trickier and thicker surface of the kickboards, John inserts the cable ties and Graham tightens them. I definitely have the easiest task. For a break, I go back over their work and clip off the excess ends of the cable ties - this is the speedway equivalent of pruning the roses!

When we're hard at work a cry goes up and I mistakenly think I hear them say something about Norman Cook but, instead, it turns out to be a shriek that heralds the arrival of Swindon team manager Alun 'Rosco' Rossiter. He chats animatedly to Punch for a while and I pop over and introduce myself. Rosco belies his slightly mardy reputation to be friendly and welcoming though he's clearly pigeonholed me as a vague representative of the Eastbourne Eagles rather than an independent minded writer. He jokes, "Have you come to sabotage our fence?" When I point to the entry to the first bend and say, "Yeh, just there is where Nicki is

[2 the BSPA refer to them as "Inflatable Fences" in their regulations after one particular manufacturer - with strong historic Swindon connections - felt they had claim to the term "Air Fence".]

Practical drainage in action

Graham Cooke explains the Great Sand Scandal, part 27

gonna put your riders in the fence," he laughs and points to the second bend "Nah, it'll be over there", before he goes on to make a point to stress how much he respects and admires ("I haven't got a problem with him at all") the Eagles Danish destroyer. The rest of the curatorial team banter with him (and then among themselves about him) after he's returned to the comfort of the speedway office to notoriously make the first in a lengthy series of continuous mobile phone calls. "Whenever Terry Russell's around he always says look what we've done!" Ernie relates a hilarious story about the stress levels everyone felt before *Sky* televised the World Cup at Swindon that has the punch line "I said to Rosco - stick a farking brush up me arse and I'll sweep the farking pits for you too!" Everyone is a joker at Blunsdon it seems, so it's no surprise when bearded Robins senior start marshal Stan Potter joins the track team for a bit of further banter that Ernie stops to bat off politely, as he fiddles with a tin of mini-cigars that he resists before carrying on with more painstaking work.

Another unexpected nuisance that has hampered the steady-state approach to the work round the stadium over the winter has been the arrival of giant moles in the form of a phalanx of archaeologists who proceeded to dig trenches pretty well everywhere. Four were dug on the centre green, another took up the entire length of the pits yard and car park and these were joined by another set of two located elsewhere in the stadium car park. Scotching rumours from rival clubs that this site is so old that the last trophy won by the club was buried at the stadium, it transpires that apparently Blunsdon is the site of an ancient burial ground - well a Roman or pre-Roman burial site - of possibly considerable interest to said archaeologists. The council were spurred into action by the imminent closure and redevelopment of the stadium to hire Cotswold Archaeology to conduct a survey on their behalf. Their interest in the local heritage that is possibly buried hereabouts has also been spurred by other very visible developments in the nearby area, which includes the extensive workings of what will ultimately become the Blunsdon bypass and also the giant Motorola building that has been erected. The company logo dominates the horizon sightline, though the building itself looks much more like a remand centre than anything that approaches delightful office space. Still it's handy for the speedway! Initially Graham thought that the sudden appearance of the trenches on the centre green were part of an elaborate joke concocted by Punch but the sight of some archaeologists dressed in clichéd fashion on a dig soon persuaded him of the earnestness of their intent. Sadly, the site had been desecrated long ago - when the stadium was originally constructed in 1948 - so all they found for their troubles was the random detritus that the bulldozers and levelling work originally created (and buried). The track staff had taken some quiet satisfaction when one day in torrential rain they watched as a "lank haired youth dressed in trainers, jeans and T-shirt but no coat - your typical archaeology student" continued to dig with great persistence while his trench rapidly filled with water. He eventually abandoned the task and when asked 'did you find anything?' replied "Nah, only trench foot". Unfortunately, though the trenches have been filled, the centre green still bears the scars of the excavation and remains slightly hazardous to walk across. Graham confides, "it's still a mess and we're unlikely to do anything with the training track this season."

A subject much closer to Graham's heart is the vexed problem of the sand that leaches from the greyhound track onto the track surface. He was politely asked by Rosco to tone down his Blog comments on the competence of the greyhound track maintenance people but clearly struggles to remain diplomatic about their attitude and approach. To be fair, they do seem to wilfully ignore the work that has been put in by the speedway track staff on the drainage and the gullies ("we dug a channel to run rainwater off the greyhound track and down to the centre green where it can do what it likes to that surface"). Any loss of sand is resolved by piling the stuff ever higher to combat this shrinkage. Clearly sand and shale don't mix at all! In fact, "their sand runs off over the track - it's washed off every week - the water runs through but the sand is deposited throughout the shale. This stops the shale binding. This is a real problem in the corners as the riders hit the corner at full revs, kick into the corner and, as they are hitting an area of weakness in the surface, they're literally bouncing when the shale comes away in cakes. So the bike goes down, grips, bounces and lands again and, last season, the track couldn't cope with the speeds. Leigh flew into the fence last year 'cause of it and broke all the spokes in his wheel!"

Back in the tea room, Gerald is ensconced on his chair with a copy of this week's *Speedway Star* ("there's a photo of Rosco in it this week - so it's half price!") in his hand, close by to the container of cakes that the friendly, helpful and hard-working Shirley - the club tea lady and general behind-the-scenes powerhouse - has brought along to tempt the hungry and thirsty track workers. Lured in by the tea and cakes, Rosco affects some introductions "this is the legendary Shirls - well that's what they call her on the Internet!" As you'd expect the news that there is in the *Star* attracts comment, "what is it with this Daniel King thing? Peterborough say one thing and Ipswich another - they both can't be right!" News that the Reading programme was voted the best of 2006 is greeted with some incredulity but some resignation though still some pride since Swindon tied joint second with Somerset. There's an element of an apples with onions comparison here in final points scores awarded by the anonymous *Speedway Star* reviewer. The excellent looking Reading version is judged to be worth a mark of 980 points (with 20 points lost for the "Quality/Racecard") while the Swindon version scores 945 points (with 25 points lost for "page paragraphing" and 15 points for both "Visitors" and "Design"). Something that immediately sprang to my mind is that not only was the Bulldogs programme 20% more expensive - so cost an additional £10 or five Swindon issues extra during the season - but a meeting I attended used an 'old' programme with a less impressive insert, though this is a common customer unfriendly 'Spanish custom' practised throughout the sport. Still, the mystery reviewer has to make decisions/distinctions based on the actual issue of the programme placed in front of him. Though, perhaps, in another year price and/or value for money could replace or be added to some of the more wilfully obscure and recondite categories?

With the break over again all too soon, while we walk back to the track Graham explains the pride and fastidiousness with which Gerald prepares the track and areas of the stadium for which he is responsible. "It has to look good as well as be good! He takes huge pride in his work and it'll be doing his head in that he can't work as normal today 'cause of his operation. Punch and I try to work to his standards. By the way, Punch loves to drive the JCB, once he's in there you can't get him out though you've got to be a little wary of him in the JCB - the power steering doesn't work, the brakes judder and it often violently veers to one side". I make a mental note to keep a close eye on Punch when he's in the vehicle, as I don't fancy getting run over. Later when Punch works with the energy and strength of a much younger man shovelling gravel at the first-bend curb, Ernie asks "How many other farking 69 year olds could you imagine doing that? He's unbelievable! He doesn't know when to stop sometimes though. I worked with him one time, we shovelled all day and I just about kept up with him. My hands came up in huge blisters whereas his were without a mark. He said 'you gripped that too tightly, hold the shovel like you would if you were, you know, w**king' It's advice I've never forgot!"

Another vehicle that makes it onto the track for an outing is Gerald's silver BMW. Though still recuperating he just has to help, so he drives round and round the circuit - hugging the white line - in an effort to further tyre pack down the surface and thereby still usefully contribute. Never judge a book by its cover and in my brief conversations with Gerald, I quickly learn that to pigeonhole him as a track curator would be to seriously underestimate his background, intelligence, skills and experiences. Before I leave he outlines a brief history of his speedway life that includes track curation, 12 years as a referee, the resurrection of a derelict track

Punch goes for another spin in his tractor

Shirls multi-tasks

in South Africa (Walkersville), never mind that he also ran his own insurance and financial brokerage company. No wonder Stuart and Jon at Lakeside have ensured that he continues to have some involvement with the marketing, branding and promotion of the Thurrock based club. He's also not frightened of hard work or a full week. Just as well really since during the season each Monday and Tuesday finds him at Lakeside, while Wednesday and Thursday are taken up with work at Blunsdon, Friday night it's back to Lakeside again, before he returns to Swindon (where he lives) on Saturday. It's not uncommon for him to be at Blunsdon over the weekend as well. Many people underestimate what the significant level of work is that's required to create the ideal racing surface.

Our work on the kickboards is drawn to a premature end - with the additional help of Roy who saw the first-ever meeting at Blunsdon in 1949 when his father took him and, impressively, has been a loyal Robins fan ever since - when we start to run out of cable ties, so under Ernie's expert guidance we have to improvise and only attach alternate holes. Gerald notes sardonically, "It'll be another temporary job that'll last the whole season". Nonetheless we've attached the kickboards to 14 sections of air fence and, for the statistically minded, each section has an average of 13 cable ties that have to be laboriously attached by hand. When you consider the sheer size and surface area of the air fence found on both bends at Blunsdon, this is a mammoth task! Though we could have finished the job on the first and second bends should more cable ties have been available. The remainder of this particular job will be completed on Saturday and there won't be a shortage of alternative tasks for any of those minded to come along and volunteer to help. Talk turns to who exactly will be the first rider to test the cushioning effect of this safety feature at Blunsdon. Gerald's in no doubts, "The first in will be farking Bager or Gjedde!"

Back in the tea room the cast of helpers has increased further but Shirls flutters efficiently about to ensure that everyone has some refreshment and is well looked after. Sadly I have to desert the crew so don't get the chance to join Graham - or Punch as he works like a man possessed - in an archaeological dig of his own (with shovel gripped in the sensitive manner approved by Punch) on the first and second bends where further work is required to "top dress" the drains with shingle and stones. I haven't helped that much really though everyone kindly claims that I have. However, I do have a much greater appreciation of the sheer difficulty and complexity involved in speedway track preparation. Never mind how much time and fastidiousness even so-called simple jobs require. I also know how lucky the Swindon management and riders are to have such a hard-working crew of volunteers to ensure that these and so many other thankless tasks are completed with good cheer and considerable élan! I would almost say that I couldn't wait to get back there next week to help these lovely people some more …

8th March - Swindon: the track work continues …

Chapter 5. Swindon v Reading:
Blunsdon twinned with Siberia

15th March

Chris Gay   *"I know things haven't gone your way so far, but I don't have the discretion to award it!"*

Rosco   *"I don't believe you can't award it. Well, you referees need to get it together - when one ref does it on one lap and another does it on the third"*

The thick fog that I'd driven through in Berkshire and other parts of Wiltshire still lingered in the area that surrounds Blunsdon Stadium when I parked once more in the gravel covered pits just after 8 a.m. By that time the construction workers were already hard at it on this section of the relief road that will ensure "there will be no roundabouts from here to Cirencester". The demolition workers have also already set to work on the factory type building that for a couple of hours continued to overlook the second bend of the circuit before a giant digger arm rapidly smashed the whole structure to the ground. It's quite an addictive spectacle to watch - as the brickwork crumbles and falls almost in slow motion after it has been 'tapped' by the giant arm of the demolition vehicle - though Graham Cooke gives me some pause for thought when I learn the workers who were on its roof last week "were removing all the asbestos".

Inside the lair that is the track staff hut, Gerald Richter and Punch have already arrived and are deep in discussion about the disrespect that they suffer at the hands of the greyhound track staff. It's bad enough that the sand causes real problems with the track itself but the lower level crimes irk them much more, particularly the unauthorised use of equipment. Whether they break into the staff hut or use the machinery without permission ("we think Rosco gives permission for use of equipment that's not the property of the stadium"), they then compound their lack of grace and courtesy by consuming tea or diesel without its replacement and by moving the heavy plant equipment and then abandoning it wherever they fancy. Today Punch and Gerald have arrived to discover the lorry has been used ("they must have got the keys from someone") and then left without fuel. While the container they need to regularly access some of the many tools they require for track preparation work in advance of the first Swindon Speedway meeting of the season has been blocked or, as Punch so elegantly puts it, "Which farking muppet put the trailer in front of the container?"

The huge amount of work put in over the winter has already shown to be completely worthwhile at the recent 'press and practice' day for the club albeit with a lot of effort by the volunteer track staff that mostly has gone unrecognised and unappreciated. For example, Graham "ached all over in my back, shoulders and legs at 8 p.m. on Monday" after work on the track has seen him successively at Blunsdon for four out of the previous five days. The track curator is matter of fact about what has to be done today to prepare the track for the Don Rogers M4 Trophy start-of-season challenge meeting between the Robins and local rivals Reading. "We'll pack down the track with the vibrating roller - after we've worked at the first bend [where sand mixed in the shale has caused the track to come up in slabs during the practice day] - sweep the white line; inflate and wash the air fences and kick boards as well as put up the green catch netting". Fortunately or otherwise, every track curator simultaneously has people who take his work for granted, think they could do it better or have a right to tell him what to do. Consequently, Gerald has many people to advise him on his work, whether they're the fans, the riders or the club management. He treats everyone the same, so ignores their advice and gets on with what he has to do. The fans are often the most misguided in their opinions, "people say you've done this or you've done that but if they were on the inside they'd know how much you've really done." Before he circles the track many times in the large yellow bowser lorry used to water the surface, Gerald remembers to "put on

Punch in action, part 1

Do not feed the animals

Air compression made easy

the showers - Rosco was upset there wasn't any hot water after practice; so was I as I wanted to shower before going to Arena", where he also prepares the track. I stand with Punch on the track by the pits gate. The shale surface has the kind of quality and consistency that you'd be delighted to find in the soil in your own garden (or three allotments in Punch's case). Punch draws his foot through the loose shale of the surface and remarks, "the track is lovely, almost in perfect condition - made all the better 'cause we had some dew last night but Gerald is obsessed with water and watering it even though the forecast says it'll rain at 4 p.m. It's a nightmare to know what's best. If you water it and it rains you're farked and if you hold off for the rain but it doesn't, it's then too late even if you do water it - there's not enough time to pack it down; we're packing it down all day normally - so everyone complains about the dust." Punch has seen it all before and has worked at the track "since my eldest daughter was 8, she's 44 now so let's see … that's 36 years - I've seen promoters come and go!" He then proceeds to list them in chronological order as the giant yellow bowser slowly passes us and sprays brackish coloured water onto the track surface. Though now 67, Punch will work with relentless determination and capable efficiency in a breezy manner that a man 30 years his junior would definitely consider 'hard work'. "I've always worked hard and long days don't bother me at all; the easiest job I've ever had is the plumbing I do now and I love comin' here so it don't seem like work though we do work hard just to make sure everything is just right!"

Punch scampers off to join Gerald, Roy arrives, Mick Richards heads off to jet wash the air fence adverts ("it's soap that does it, then I rinse them off afterwards") - something that he does before and after the meeting - and I help Graham load his car with the generators that will be needed to inflate the first and second bend air fences. Both generators are hugely heavy to lift from the car, transport across the blue tarpaulin covered sandy surface of the dog track and place into position. After Graham has pulled the cord to start them both and ensured that they're properly attached, we set to our first task of the day - the attachment of the fine gauzed green netting above the air fence "partly to keep the shale off the dog track but also partly to try to keep it on the track!" The netting has pre-sewn holes close to its corded edge and my job is to ensure that they're firmly attached into position on metal hooks and consistently pulled taut. We work well as a team and make steady progress round all the bends of the track. We leave a small section on the third bend as this section is badly worn and should already have been replaced. Gerald instructs us to remove it completely (" in case it flaps around and distracts the riders"), when I ask Graham who has responsibility for the provision of the netting, he replies, "Whoever is in charge is supposed to provide it; certainly not the volunteers who work for free and bring their own tools". This is a sore point because in October Punch had had his own toolbox stolen by thieves: "His toolbox took him 40 years to amass - some of his specialist wrenches cost £30 each 30 years ago - and are irreplaceable, literally 'cause they haven't been, and 'cause you can no longer get many of these tools".[1]

Mid way through our work on the netting, we're joined by Bob Crowther ("no relation") who is the modest and affable designer of the revolutionary 'double' start gate mechanism that has been installed at Swindon, Coventry, Reading, Cardiff (for the Grand Prix) and also, this season, Birmingham. "I watched ours go up and down and said to Terry Russell I could do better. He said 'go ahead and show me' so I sketched out some plans. The initial delay was finding where to source all the materials from, though I've done that now. There's £1500 worth of bits in each one. I build them at home - I s'pose if you add up the hours it takes to make them the rate of pay ain't so great. They have them here. Funnily enough it's the ugliest one really - and at Coventry and Redin and I've just put one in at Birmingham. Double tapes! We use stainless steel pipes rather than scaffolding poles like they used to and I've replaced the metal bracket with a plastic one, which is the secret really. The problem with the old one was there was nowhere for the velocity to go but the plastic one solves that and goes up and down much quicker. So quick it catches some riders out. When I built one for the GPs, I was gonna test it here on the Thursday before but it was rained off so we just had to use it without a proper test at the GP. I didn't tell Terry in case he worried, but it turned out alright!"

The most important work of the day is the track repairs (and general tender loving care) that Punch and Gerald affect on the first and second bends. Punch works with fastidious and skilful pride to transfer shale from the digger and evenly distribute it across the surface with a graceful, rhythmic sweep of his shovel. It's hypnotic to watch. Graham explains that during practice they had discovered "half an inch down there's an inch thick layer of sand that has to be dug out, replaced with fresh shale and the area is then soaked in the hope it will bind. We'll get the heavy roller on it when it arrives at noon, though we don't use the vibrating mechanism as it makes the shale come up in slabs. It'll be replaced four foot out - we don't want to do all the bend in case we ruin it. We'll do the rest later in the season." While there's still some work to be done, everything is pretty well in hand before "we do the last few jobs: check the fence, pin the air fence to the safety fence and dig up the start gate ten yards forward [with an implement known as 'the Ripper'] as last year the Robins riders liked a lot of grip at the start!"

A good friend of mine works as cabin crew for British Airways and she talks of the few snatched minutes "before the enemy arrives" and though the opposite is the case when it comes to the great esteem the track staff hold the riders in, they still lock them out during the early afternoon on race day. "It goes mad when they start to arrive so we lock the pits gate until Punch says they can get in around 4 p.m. or when we feel we're pretty well ready to allow them in!" Everyone goes their separate ways and gets on with their own tasks independently. Gerald goes to Sainsbury's for petrol, Punch storms hither and thither (but shows me the area where sponsors' advertising boards from previous seasons go to die) and Graham goes off for some diesel. However, he returns almost straightaway covered in 'eau de diesel' after the decayed pipe there gave way, something he playfully highlights with a resigned exclamation of "the day just gets better and better!" There's nothing for it but a tea break and hot drinks await us brewed by the friendly and industrious Shirley. We have a new large and quite fluffy pink towel brought in by Stan Potter to join the towels and tea-towels that already line one of the workbenches-cum-cupboards, "My Sandra's auntie passed away". It's an addition to our creature comforts Punch greets in his own way, "You're giving us farking dead people's stuff now!" After the tea break, Shirley heads for the riders' dressing rooms where she cleans and disinfects the showers, toilets and both changing rooms - one of which has a great sign that reads "all body jewellery to be removed before racing". These tasks aren't officially part of her responsibilities, "My job is to sweep the pits but no one does the changing rooms and toilets so I does 'em too!" Not that anyone is that observant: "last year we were half way through the season when I pointed out the water wasn't running through the urinals." Start marshal Stan is so conscientious he has arrived to prepare for his work well over eight hours before the tapes are due to rise. He's a fountain of information and I learn that of the Robins riders, "all have GMs, there's no Jawas or whatever they call them nowadays. At practice Leigh Adams was down the road before the rest had started but it helps if you've got eight engines to choose from. For racing it's got to be the Premier League!" He then chats much more revealingly with other members of the track team but sweetly instructs me to "turn your ears away".

Though I'm here to look and learn as well as just generally research the work of the Blunsdon track staff, I'm also a spare pair of hands. Often the emphasis is upon the word 'spare' since it's easier to automatically just get on and do, rather than slowly

[1 as luck would have it Rosco later brings Punch a box that contains a Du Pont toolbox set that the invoice inside says costs £439. This price causes some incredulity among the track staff when they compare this to the actual tools provided inside it. Punch remains grateful but philosophical, "it doesn't replace what I've lost and they are pretty awful but Rosco didn't have to replace the stolen ones so overall I'm happy that he has decided to do so."]

Punch in action, part 2

Mick Richards clean the air furniture signage

Where advertising signs go to die

explain to me what has to be done and then watch it done slowly or half as well. Instead I chat to Roy who came to the second-ever meeting at Blunsdon 58 years ago when he was six and "they still had a cinder surface". Talk of Blunsdon - "I only live a quarter of a mile away as the crow flies" - has Roy come over wistful: "I'll be sad to see it close as it's been part of my life for 58 years, man and boy. It's only gonna move 200 yards away - over there towards the car park. They say it's no good any more - why not just tidy up the grandstand? Sure that's not too great but the stadium and track itself is generally fine. I just don't understand it unless there's something I don't know. I can still name the team from all those years ago: Ray Lambourne, Bob Jones, Ginger Nicholls, Bill Downton (notorious for never being seen without his helmet on his head - in person and in photos - though the pits at that time were more visible to the paying customer), Alf Webster, George Craig, um and then there's one I forget. [later remembered as "Ivor Atkinson - he only rode in a couple of meetings"] We break off our conversation since Rosco pulls up in his lorry to interrupt his work on the wiring of the stadium speaker system to ask me very politely if I can pass on a message, "Can you ask Graham to get the diesel jet wash and clean the kick boards?" It sounds an innocuous enough request but when I pass it on verbatim to Gerald as he passes with Punch a few moments later he takes umbrage, and expresses some doubts about his cognitive capacity and parentage, "Tell him he can fark off! I'll farking tell him what I think, if he wants to do the farking track I'll go home". With no one able to dissuade him otherwise, Gerald storms over to the start line to gesticulate by the driver's cab of the lorry Rosco drives. I quickly gather that Rosco is a bit of a hero for the track staff and he knows that without his help it would be best to assume the professionalism of the staff will ensure that all is tickety boo by the time the riders or public enter the stadium. Punch remains phlegmatic, "Alun has always been like it, he just piles on the jobs if you let him!"

Anyway, since the next task that the track staff planned to accomplish was to prepare the environs of the track for the meeting ahead anyway, Punch and Graham set to jet washing the inner bricks that form the white line, the green netting and also clean the kickboards. They work well as a team. Punch methodically cleans everything in sight in an experienced and scrupulous manner. This means that he cannily rather quickly douses each kickboard before he then painstakingly removes the layer of shale that has accumulated on its surface. "It loosens it so I can blast it off quickly, if you did otherwise you'd flood the track 'cause it would take longer". Graham is happy to drive the lorry slowly, while Punch works away contentedly, "It's a toy so Punch loves to use it and I just love driving the tractor".[2]

With this task soon out of the way, the only sensible response is to retire back to the hut to regroup and for a refreshing cup of something hot. I commit the *faux pas* of accidentally sitting down on the chair by the table. "Hold on, that's

[2 Clearly the track staff subconsciously desire to specialise in certain exciting items of the track equipment. Later Gerald tells me, "Graham is only happy when drilling and Punch is only happy when on the tractor!" I suspect use of the power washer would run the tractor close in Punch's world. I'd love a go with the jet wash - since it looks such fun - but know better than to presume to ask to blast the shale away from the kickboards (pristine or otherwise) never mind dare to suggest to clean the white line so it gleams so much that you'd think it had just been painted.]

my chair!" says Punch with calm authority. Suitably refreshed and though it is still over eight hours until the tapes rise only routine tasks remain to be done. Everyone does his own race day tasks. I help Graham block the last few holes in the metal fence that surrounds the track and ensure the kick boards are correctly in place with no edges on show in the riders' direction of travel. The roller does its work and all is well with the world. Our lunch break soon comes round and afterwards Gerald is in a contented and expansive mood, "The track is ready now, in fact everything is ready - we just need to put some water on and take the grader round; they could race at 4 p.m. if they wanted". He takes a mobile call and from the conversation I gather the caller grills him about his progress with the track. I imagine that it's Terry Russell but it's not, "my daughter is a fanatic - she never misses a meeting here, she just can't get enough!" The black clouds away in the distance concern some of the track staff but not Gerald who can't wait to splosh some more water everywhere.

Not that I was a great deal of help anyway this week but there are now many hours to kill. I drive off to sample the delights of a local housing estate nearby to the Sainsbury's superstore, which I temporarily lose. When I return it's still ages until the pit gates are locked and then ceremoniously unlocked a short while later to allow the riders admittance. The track staff get on with some 'busy work' that occupies them while I kick my heels and read the 16-page supplement that has been included with today's edition of the *Swindon Advertiser*. If only all speedway clubs could boast this level of pre-season coverage. It's a tribute to the importance of the club within the town, the success of the Press and Practice day, the keenness of the local reporter Dave Eaton and the publicity skills of Robins Press Officer Robert Bamford. Oh, and of course the potential of the talented team assembled by Rosco along with sponsor turned co-promoter Gary Patchett and Terry Russell that has made them bookies' favourites to land the Elite League crown in 2007. The front page describes the situation succinctly as it features a photo of Lee Richardson and Leigh Adams with the headline "THEY MEAN BUSINESS! But can Richardson and Adams help end Robins' 40-year drought?" It's a good question and the speedway cliché that you need luck and a season free from injuries springs immediately to mind. Tactical cunning and exemplary performances will also help, particularly away from the home advantage the riders enjoy at the incredibly fast Blunsdon circuit.

It's an entertaining read. Gary Patchett admits, "I'm pretty much hanging on Terry's shirt tails, because I'm new to this but I could not have anyone better to learn from. Terry's had his knockers in the past, with people questioning his commitment to one club, with his interests at Eastbourne and Arena Essex. But that isn't an issue. Terry told me two years ago that Swindon was his favourite." Terry Russell is equally enthusiastic and sings from a similar hymnbook. "Swindon is a good business and I've been pleased to be involved and, as I think I stated before, I didn't wish to be a multi-club owner. I did it because the Elite League wasn't stable. It's stabilised a hell of a lot now, we had a really healthy year and promoters came along to take my positions in those clubs. That's allowed me to wear the colours and support the team. I enjoyed Eastbourne, but I'm happy to move on and support the team."

Rosco candidly admits how he's grown in his managerial position at the club and looks to the future with pride and great optimism. If there's been a cloud on the horizon it was technology driven, "I have to say for a couple of seasons the internet (fans' forum) were a big evil in my life." With the advice and support of his boss Terry Russell, Rosco has changed his outlook and put the real or perceived criticisms into context and now takes a 'not in front of the children' perspective. "At the end of the day, you are reacting to criticism from people who often don't know what the whole story is. There is always 10 per cent they don't know - and 10 per cent they should not know." We also learn that boss Terry has a straightforward approach to management that you don't often read about in business textbooks, "Terry has been fantastic. He'd be the first one to b*ll*ck me, make no bones about it. But he does keep me on level pegging. He doesn't give me too many compliments, so if he does, I take it as a massive one! His argument is he doesn't look at what I do right because he expects me to do it. He looks at what I do wrong. He's instilled into me that things have to be professionally done. If you do a job, you do it right." When it comes to the prospects for the Robins for the season ahead, Rosco manages to sound optimistic but is sensible enough to introduce a note of *faux* caution. "We're all excited, but I don't want to get over-excited." It's a case of once bitten, twice shy, "last year we had a good side and great expectations, but really they didn't deliver what they should have," says Rosco apparently forgetting that, as team manager, he's ultimately responsible for motivation and performances on the track! Alun is definitely keen to dampen expectations and appears to emphasise that Swindon will definitely qualify for the play-offs but not win them, "There is not talk of winning the league here.

Shirls spring cleans

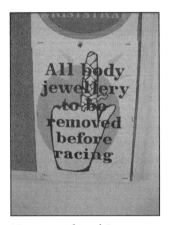

Necessary safety advice

The talk will be of going for the top two places." However, like the Spice Girls he's got what he really, really wants, "The team we have this year is probably the most exciting we have put together. I'm not frightened about it - but we really are going for it, that's for sure, hence the team we have." There are always worries and Alun provides quite a list of these but, strangely, forgets to mention lack of team spirit as a potentially inhibiting factor. "Injuries could happen. Something else could go wrong. Somebody might not hit form, or might have a nightmare of a season." When quizzed on who might snatch the Elite League crown, Rosco draws on his many years' experience as a rider and, recently, as a manager to pronounce, "I see Peterborough as a threat and Wolverhampton too, while at home, not many people are going to beat the Lakeside Hammers.[3] Peterborough are the ones we've got to watch. They really stick out for me."

If Rosco prefers optimism tempered with caution then Andrew Moore is also quite happy to look to the future positively but unblinkingly confront the traumas of his past at Eastbourne. "I was put in the team at number 2 and struggled badly, lost a lot of money, got into debt and decided enough was enough. Riding at two with Nicki Pedersen is soul-destroying even though he is your partner … I was destroyed in almost every way. I was a victim of the way many Elite League teams are put together, losing confidence and interest and blowing my brains out financially." However, now he's decided not to turn his back on the sport and with a reserve slot at the Robins guaranteed along with a "good package", Andy feels rejuvenated and looks forward to "some good meetings, scoring plenty of points and being part of a championship-winning team." Lee Richardson is another rider who has done some "soul-searching" after finding himself on a "downward spiral" and in "about the darkest place a professional sportsman can be." This turns out to have been a dark teatime of the soul brought about by poor performances, low morale, injuries and "horrendous mechanical problems" rather than a description of a visit to the pub Rosco runs. Things got so bad, Lee discussed them with her indoors, "I sat down and chatted to my wife and said I don't want to do this any more." A note for teacher wasn't forthcoming for the diminutive Lee and, after mature reflection, he has come to appreciate the privileged life led by a speedway rider plying his trade in leagues throughout Europe and decided to manfully persevere. Without the distraction of the GPs, Lee expects to repay the loyalty shown to him by the Swindon management and fans, "I owe Swindon and I want to help them win the league title because they are favourites." Another ambition is to eventually replace Leigh Adams as captain and leader of the club to further emphasise his dedication to the Robins cause, "I never had any doubts about staying here, never talked to any other clubs and never contemplating going anywhere else."

They say talk is cheap, and ultimately everyone will be judged by his results where it matters most - on the track itself. Despite the cold breeze of a damp March night, Blunsdon is packed with fans keen to witness the team start to gel

[3 they lost 4 times]

together and start to burnish their collective spirit in a challenge meeting with local rivals, the Reading Meridian Lifts Bulldogs. By the time of the rider parade, there has already been quite a bit of celebrity spotting in the form of 1969 League Cup match-winning moustachioed hero and meeting sponsor Don Rogers ("he's always here!"). He's paraded past the adoring crowd on the track before all the riders are introduced to him prior to competing for the attractively named 'Don Rogers Sports M4 Trophy'. While mingling amongst us is the new blonde-haired *Sky* presenter lady who's here tonight to practise her skills with some random interviews with members of the crowd. More cynical and sexist members of this particular section of the Wiltshire speedway congregation claim that sleeping with a speedway rider is a contractual rite of passage for *Sky* lady presenters. They banter among themselves about the prospective identity of the first speedway rider or team manager (?) she'll sleep with, unaware that she's happily married to a rugby player! The press are out in full force and I meet the friendly Chris Seaward who "covers all meetings as a match reporter".

I imagine he works closely with best-selling prolific speedway author and Robins press officer, Robert Bamford who's stood under the home straight grandstand overlooking the activity by the start line with Robins (and Leeds) fan Steve Thorn. Before Rob disappears to continue his extensive range of match-day duties in the press box elsewhere in the stadium around about the time of heat 7, I'm lucky to be able to listen and learn from their conversation. Rarely off message for even the briefest moment, Rob talks up the prospects for the meeting, team and season. "We have a long, hard seven months ahead - but we know what we have to do! We have a great team, promotion, fans and stadium - it's just getting better and better. It's 147 days ago since the last action at Blunsdon and, here we are with an expectant crowd and the atmosphere pumping!" Robert seems nonplussed that I should want to spend my time learning the work of the track staff and doubts the education benefit of helping out, "are there any skilled jobs for the track staff?"

Though they hold the Swindon Robins team assembled for the 2007 season in high esteem, as the riders leave the pits to line up for the first race Rob and Steve are much more excited by their first opportunity to check out the start girls as they line up with their coloured umbrellas in tight-fitting costumes. As you'd expect from someone who has thoroughly researched speedway for his annually produced *Yearbook* (and other publications) Rob is extremely knowledgeable about every speedway rider in the country, let alone the Swindon ones. This fastidious attention to detail also extends to the start girls and I half expect to hear a factually based statistical run down on each young lady but, instead and somewhat surprisingly given the precise attention to facts in his written work, Rob's descriptions are founded on emotions and couched in impressionistic language. "Steve has a crush on the start girl in yellow Emma Dixon (I haven't) 'cause she's stunning!" The chance to ogle the staff is all too brief and the season starts, predictably enough, with a comfortable win for a fast-gating Leigh Adams in a drawn heat that sees Greg Hancock finish second for the John Postlethwaite owned Bulldogs managed by Jim Lynch. The heat is drawn because Zdenek Simota relegates Tomasz Chrzanowski to last place, thereby prompting Rob to observe, "that was fast - the track is so smooth - that's Simota's best ever ride here!" Another early season opportunity to study the form of the start girls has Steve and Rob lapse into silence while they intently study the girls stately progress as they parade up and down close to their respective start gates wearing weather inappropriate and remarkably thin/skimpy clothing. Expert on all things Swindon, Rob observes excitedly, "red and yellow retained! I'm not sure about blue, green is definitely new!" The second race sees the riders strung out like a line of washing after Mark Lemon and Danny Bird display the opposite of telepathic understanding since both display a favour for the comforts of the white line and so get completely in each others' way. This allows Mads Korneliussen to escape to victory and this processional race is drawn. The third race follows the same pattern with a win for a Swindon rider (this time Seba Ulamek) with the minor placing occupied by the visitors. Steve notes, "Charlie got squeezed out on the first corner, didn't he?" Thereby prompting a resigned, long-suffering sigh from Robert, "it's Charlie's notorious gating!" Before the start of heat 4, he's optimistic, "I expect to see the deadlock broken here!" This is well founded since not only does Bird get excluded under the two-minute warning (and is replaced by Lemon) but Korneliussen also moves at the start without penalty from the referee. The resulting 5-1 effectively ends the meeting as a contest. From this point in the meeting, the Bulldogs fall away badly and only record one heat advantage all night. Heat 6 sees the start line girls finally acknowledge the elements when they don red, blue, green and yellow track suit tops, while Leigh Adams combines with Tomasz Chrzanowski for the second maximum heat advantage of the night. Robert leaves for the warmth of the referee's box, after gleefully noting "it's exhibition stuff from the Robins" before he double underlines the fact that the "Robins are in the ascendancy".

Punch in action, part 3 (with Graham getting a rare go on the tractor)

There's little in the way of drama or close racing, though the blue helmet colour turns out to be popular in heat 8 when Chrzanowski and Korneliussen both wear one to the start line before Tomasz changes his to the correct colour. This must have discombobulated them because Simota then passes the pair on the third bend, thereby providing the rare example of a passing manoeuvre on a night when apparently these weren't allowed anywhere other than the first corner. By heat 9, the riders appear to struggle with the arrival of mid-track bumps on the racing surface on the first bend. Unrelenting drizzle starts immediately after the Lee Richardson interview in which he reveals the crowd are "fantastic" at Blunsdon and that "obviously, people know we are the strongest side on paper this season!" If the Speedway Riders Benevolent Fund received a one-pound donation every time a rider or a promoter said, "speedway is won on the track not on paper", then injured or retired riders would no longer have to worry about their financial futures. The drizzle gets gradually heavier but the need to practise and to get some 'competitive' track time overrides any hint of concern about the possible danger of a greasy surface. Indeed, Mads Korneliussen enjoys himself so much in these worsening conditions that he provides the only authentically exciting pass of the night on the third lap of heat 12. That said, Charlie Gjedde uses considerable aggression to vanquish Danny Bird in the penultimate race. Based on this display, it would be hard to assess the championship credentials of the Robins since the ease of their victory appears to be based on home track familiarity along with a brittle performance from their notional local rivals from Smallmead.

15th March Swindon v Reading (Challenge - Don Rogers Sports M4 Trophy) 55-37

Chapter 6. Reading v Swindon: Dustbowl derby
8th April

The first leg of the double header Easter Sunday meeting between Reading and Swindon is enticing enough to attract a good-sized crowd to Smallmead. The number of spectators through the turnstiles has been swelled by a good contingent of Swindon fans who gather on the third bend, which allows the keener ones to press themselves against the perimeter fence to try and catch a glimpse of what's happening in the pits. Originally the meeting was advertised to start at noon but during the week before was put back by half an hour "for the crowd". Many Swindon fans see conspiracy everywhere and claim it was to allow extra leeway for Matej Zagar, who flew in this morning. In the programme, Jim Lynch is full of optimism and hopes for "a win under our belts this afternoon [to] ensure that people sit up and take notice that it's not just the Robins and the Bees that are the teams to worry about this season."

The jet-set life of the modern speedway rider is such that they're at a different track almost every day and so encounter a huge variety of track surfaces. At Smallmead today, they will get to face a range of these conditions all in the space of a couple of hours since the perils of staging a meeting during the day is compounded when it's beautifully hot and sunny. The track staff have soaked the track - which looks to have a good layer of dirt on it, particularly towards the safety fence - in the full knowledge that it will dry out quickly. Out in the first heat is Leigh Adams who Greg Hancock in his programme notes describes as "such a fair competitor". I assume this is a tacit reference to Nicki Pedersen and is always easy to say about someone who fails to transfer their league form to the individual stage and so never ultimately really challenges you in the Grand Prix series for the crown. Leigh wins this latest race according to the Queensberry rules and when he drives aggressively into the third bend for the first time - wet gloopy lumps of the shale are thrown over the crowd stood closest to the greyhound track wall. It sticks to everything it touches including the kevlars of Simota and Hancock who spend the race trailed off behind the fast-gating Aussie. The end of the heat is the signal for the first of many track grades to commence.

The absence of Mark Lemon at reserve has brought together an interesting partnership for Reading since they've paired guest Jason Bunyan with Danny Bird. They have some previous together since, during the Spring Bank Holiday of 2005 Bunyan, aggressively crashed into Bird in a manner that prematurely scuppered his season and some felt was deliberate. Such is the nature of the guest system and the frequent movement of riders from team to team that bygones are mostly bygones. They get little chance to find out how they will ride together as a partnership since Bird soon falls and thereby incurs the wrath of Mads Korneliussen ("Mads hasn't scored less than eight for us all season") who lays down his bike with alacrity but leaps to his feet equally smartly to gesture his annoyance at the fallen bottle blond. The referee today is Ronnie Allan and he allows extra time before the re-run for Mads to fix the silencer he damaged. It gives me the chance to chat to Darcia Gingell who works as part of the track staff team at Blunsdon and who joins the contingent of travelling Robins fans whenever she can. Big things are forecast for the Robins by the bookies and pundits this season ("everyone's desperate for it") and this has been reflected in the early-

Greg, Leigh and Travis discuss the track

A hint of dust

season crowds: "We had a big one on Thursday night [for Poole] that was bigger than when we had the World Cup. They've been great ever since they first talked about the stadium closure, though they say the crowds haven't been great here."

This is the theme actually taken up in the programme by Joel Hufford of *BBC Radio Berkshire* who is blunt in his assessment, "only a couple of weeks into the season and already concern has arisen over the size of the crowds the Reading Bulldogs are attracting." He goes on to make a fallacious apples with oranges comparison with the attendances at the football club and grants only limited validity to the commonly held and deeply sensible explanations that these low numbers are to do with the "weather, the price of admission and the move to racing on a Wednesday or Friday." Ignoring how the seemingly always-absent Bulldogs supremo John Postlethwaite has ridden roughshod over tradition in the name of innovative marketing, Joel prefers to claim the cause is the exciting heterogeneity of alternative sources of entertainment available to the modern consumer ("movies on demand, the internet, video games etc tempting people to stay at home"). "If speedway is to flourish", he sounds a clarion call for "much more aggressive and innovative" marketing. Ignoring that it was always thus, just more so nowadays, Joel then undermines his case with his suggested solution with the hardly revolutionary but tried and tested proposal of a few school visits to help, "ensure a new generation of fans will be around in the coming decades". Sadly fans today and not fans tomorrow are needed to fulfil the BSI business plan. This desire for increased marketing expertise is hugely ironic when you consider that around the time of the creation of BSI Reading in early 2006 it was put about in the media that Postlethwaite had a proven track record in this particular area and, consequently it was implied, would really shake things up around here. We all looked forward to him sprinkling some of the bountiful quantities of marketing magic dust that lined his pockets onto Reading speedway, but sadly we're still waiting for what he has done to bear positive fruit. To be fair to him he has tried and did invest in the team and the management as well as aggressively marketing the club on television and regional radio (BBC Radio Berkshire, for example!). He also experimented with free entry for kids (abandoned in 2007) and changed the name of the club *without* effective market research to supposedly appeal to a wider demographic/more affluent audience. Indeed it must be galling for BSI Reading to have assembled a strong team to take the club into the Elite League only to encounter a sustained campaign of apathy (once the initial enthusiasm died away), if judged by average crowd numbers. With hindsight and common sense, some initial thorough analysis prior to the purchase, name change etc. might have highlighted this failure to excite as a possibility! Like many baubles, Reading Speedway has only been a temporary attraction to John Postlethwaite and he's again notable by his absence, leading some wags to christen him the Lord Lucan of Smallmead.

If the crowd numbers are missing at the typical fixture held at Smallmead so, disappointingly, are the start girls! Maybe they're on holiday or, perhaps like the lack of a Sporting Director (Sam Ermolenko) or an Account Manager (Torben Olsen) this year, they have been let go as part of a rumoured cost-cutting exercise? Something that is also let go today is the score when the Bulldogs suffer four consecutive lost heats. Talk on the Swindon section of the terraces before the third heat is that Sebastian Ulamek and Matej Zagar has "a bit of a history" together and that Charlie Gjedde's variable performance this season is down to his "engines - when he borrowed Moore's he got 14, they say he's putting all his money into his house in Denmark." The bad blood that supposedly exists doesn't get any further expiation since Ulamek wins from the gate and Gjedde has a "sensational ride" when he uses his knowledge of Smallmead and general cunning to gain sufficient speed to pass both Zagar and Kolodziej on the fourth bend of the penultimate lap. At least Smallmead is a track where some passing is more likely to be witnessed, unlike Blunsdon where Darcia notes, "at the end of the day if you get on the line you can't really get passed".

Another point of interest in this race is provided by Zagar's red helmet or, to be more exact, the black stripes that are incorporated in its design on the side of the helmet. Only two days previously the same referee (Ronnie Allan) had showboated in the pits and made a song and dance about Nicki Pedersen's green helmet (insisting that he wear a helmet colour) though its surface was less obscured by a design feature than appears this afternoon on Zagar's. If the same referee can be so inconsistent from one day to the next in the application of the rulebook when it comes to helmet colours, you have to wonder how he will manage to apply the increasingly complicated rules and regulations of the sport. This kind of inconsistency gives referees in general an unfairly won but nonetheless bad reputation. It also confirms that Ronnie sometimes prefers to be 'the big I am' rather than consistently judicious. Luckily for the fans and both sides, the need for interpretation was minimal and so controversy was absent from this meeting.

What wasn't absent was the frequent sight of a puzzled Jim Lynch who fated himself when he sympathised with Belle Vue and Oxford, "It's been tough for all the tracks up and down the country trying to get track conditions right". Or, a gaggle of Bulldogs riders (first Hancock, Zagar and McGowan, later Hancock and Kolodziej) deep in puzzled conversation stood on the third bend of the track. Everyone who conducted an inspection repeatedly kicked the surface, as if this might help, and every man and his dog had their say as though the track surface were solely to blame for their astonishingly poor start to the meeting. It seemed a bit rich to obliquely blame the track surface when so many riders in the Reading team appear uninterestedly lacklustre. It would be easier to concentrate on those riders that perform well - they are both out in the fourth heat: Travis McGowan (who falls when in a good position) and Jason Bunyan (who departs from the team script to ride with verve and determination). If the start had been put back to better suit Zagar's schedule he looked decidedly uninterested in his first ride, after which I confidently expected him to gain the measure of whatever troubled him to then buck up, kick on and perform in his usual highly capable manner. After another lengthy track grade he did return to the track for heat 5, but finished stone last without even causing Leigh Adams to have to accelerate aggressively under him on the third bend, as he consistently did with any rider who briefly had the temerity to challenge his pre-eminence. The score is now an embarrassing 9-21 and the Bulldogs play-off credentials look somewhat suspect, if judged by this performance.

If there's an apology for a performance on the track, then off it, Tadley-based announcer Paul Hunsdon fulsomely acknowledges the loudspeaker difficulties the club experienced at the Good Friday meeting with Oxford, "we apologise for the speaker failure and for those of you that experienced sound problems, particularly on bend 3 and bend 2, so apologies for that!" Part of me is happy to acknowledge that the new corporate Bulldogs feel the need to offer regret but the other part hates the infantilisation of modern safety and customer announcements that pervade so many contemporary experiences nowadays. I much prefer the old style way of doing things where speaker (and lighting) problems went with the territory at Smallmead and, therefore, were never really acknowledged enough to merit an apology. Before you know it, Paul will be asking us to 'ensure that you take all your belongings with you when you leave the stadium!'

The 'weaker' Robins pairing of Lee Richardson and Andrew Moore tempts the energetic Jim Lynch to use the black-and-white tactical option as early as heat 6 to great effect when he gives this to the experienced Greg Hancock. It's hardly an innovative choice but supremely effective in reducing the overall deficit to a much more acceptable 17-22. In this race Richardson relived his early Smallmead years by falling and being excluded. Darcia, like the rest of the Robins fans, isn't that bothered by Lee hitting the

JP watches incognito

deck, "you don't mind if he's trying!" After the race, a small cameo between the returning victorious Bulldogs riders and Jim Lynch gives an insight into his current level of authority with them. In the manner of an impatient geography teacher dealing with stragglers on a day out trying to broaden the educational outlook of his bored charges, just as Greg Hancock and Sam Simota return to the pits gate Jim ostentatiously waves an instruction with his programme board that they continue round again for a (rare) victory lap. Greg pointedly ignores him and just carries on straight back to the pits but Sam, still at an earlier stage in his career, obliges.

In Heat 7, Reading manage their second drawn heat of the meeting after a win by Travis McGowan but, with Danny Bird trailed off at the back looking completely out of sorts and never straying from the white line, the heat is drawn. The unseasonal warmth of the sunshine has completely dried the shale surface of the track and the dust clouds are starting to mount ("the dustbowls coming - it's getting dustier and dustier," chokes Darcia). A trio of riders return to the track as Paul the announcer tries to drum up interest among the Reading faithful for the return trip to Blunsdon in the evening ("they've been getting some excellent crowds down there"), though at this point many bookies would already pay out on the Swindon win without the formality of a contest. Jason Bunyan gives another display to the rest of the team of how to aggressively ride a circuit that he won't have placed a wheel upon for over 18 months. Paul Hunsdon the announcer attempts to create some excitement before heat 9 with some welcome talk of horses, "sponsored by our good friends at Equestrian Vehicle Services - so give them a call if you're interested in equestrian!" A glance in the programme shows that the amount of heat sponsorships has improved at the club from the poor level of last season since 2007 sees only four of the fifteen slots unsold - though suspicions remain that some adverts may have been included gratis. Matej Zagar finally stirs from his inexplicable torpor to win a race, though I'm still much more taken with his ostensibly red helmet with the large black motif on its sides (even though the rest of the field only see the back of it) after the first bend when he cuts across them all from gate 4.

An unexpectedly early interval for more work on the track allows Paul Hunsdon to feel pride at the second prize in the Reading prize draw (free entry for the next meeting), and to poke fun with an old joke to distract from the pitiful nature of the home performance with mention of the even more execrable local rivals, Oxford. "I heard in the prize draw at Oxford, first prize was free entry to the next meeting and second prize was two free entries" 'Boom! Boom!' as Basil Brush would say. Track conditions deteriorate further despite the additional attention and TLC lavished on it to the extent that it's hard to watch through the dust cloud that thickly billows over the first corner every time a rider circuits the track. The cloud is so thick, it's like the London fog in old black-and-white films, albeit that at Smallmead you have the added bonus of choking shale dust. Paul employs some understatement in his latest public service announcement, "we must apologise for it getting a little bit dusty - you can see we've been watering and apologies for those of you on the bend getting a little bit filled in!"

Like the earlier races, the Robins riders continue to approach each race with vim and gusto. Seb Ulamek wins from the start in 12 and in the next Leigh Adams brooks no argument in the first lap when he cuts hard under McGowan on his favoured third bend. Even Lee Richardson appears comparatively indomitable as he holds Greg Hancock back in last place, though he looks from side to side so often (in a kind of deranged Green Cross Code way for a hyper-aware speedway rider) for the challenge that never comes from the American, that I worry that self-induced dizziness might soon cause him to fall.

When we learn over the tannoy just before heat 14 that "Danny has unfortunately withdrawn from the meeting due to illness," a loud cheer bursts from the large contingent of Swindon fans on the third bend as they realise a three-rider race in heat 14 eliminates the slim mathematical possibility of a Bulldogs win. The race itself is a cameo in miniature of the difference between the attitudes of the two teams since Mad Korneliussen really aggressively harries Janusz Kolodziej - the leader from the gate - for two laps before he manages to pass him as they hit the bend for the third lap. Charlie Gjedde follows in his wake for the third 1-5 of the meeting. It's a dispiriting spectacle for the Reading fans and many of them walk out of the stadium at that point without waiting for the nominated heat that will also result in another maximum heat win for the visitors. Any wavering fans won't feel like rushing back after a performance as appallingly lacklustre as this and, if by any fluke some new fans have actually ventured along to Smallmead for their first ever meeting (doubtless attracted by the family-friendly and benign Bulldog brand name), they'll probably think twice before they return if they anticipate a dust-obscured spectacle (albeit one provided with the possibility of some free pneumoconiosis). Fortunately, we'd already learnt that there would be no post-meeting press conference in the bar afterwards, otherwise you'd have to suspect that severe embarrassment and the absence of a plausible explanation for this display has led to its cancellation. On principle rather than with deep conviction, announcer Paul Hunsdon looks ahead to the return fixture at Blunsdon, "let's hope the Bulldogs can re-find their form and push the Robins all the way!"

8th April Reading v Swindon (Elite League A) 39-54

Chapter 7. Swindon v Wolverhampton.
The search for tyre heaven continues

7th June

Though I only called at late notice, Wayne Russell (son of Terry) was kind enough to let me launch my new book of photographs - *Shale Britannia* - at Blunsdon. "We're only too pleased to have you - you're welcome anytime," he tells me inside the speedway office located just within the entrance gates of the stadium. Wayne toes the party line and so plays down the Robins chances of Elite League success, "it's too early to say anything!" Instead we revert to that hardy perennial of British conversation - the weather. It's still warm and apparently, "the forecast is to be fine". Swindon has reputedly attracted big crowds to Blunsdon all season, though the visit of Wolverhampton is unlikely to prove as popular as the "top of the table clash" with Coventry last week.

When I arrived, Nick Barber and his sister Bev had already unloaded their navy blue transit van and were on the way back to the trackshop they run as one of the outposts of their empire at Blunsdon. The actual location of the shop appears to be a moveable feast dependent on the weather and the time of year. Today it is a line of tables set out under the lee of the roof of the main grandstand with a view towards the first bend/start gate, while handily placed for the snack bar. I excitedly show them my book of photographs and they spend some time leafing through it. It's quickly clear that the speedway community is so tightly close knit that many people are instantly and obviously well known to each other by name or, at least, by sight. Bev kindly thinks, "It's great. They're really interesting shots - very unusual - people will have a quick look, find bits but go back to it again and again!" Her brother Nick worries that the market might not be flooded with photographic books like this for a very good reason, "How many have you done then? Hopefully no more than 500!" News that the print number figure is higher and that I hope to sell the book to people outside speedway has him pull an expression that simultaneously expresses a concern for my sanity and indicates he's recalled the taste of something unpleasant. Lucy Aubrey - the Robins loyalist who runs the trackshop ("she's worked here for years") along with her boyfriend Lee - is surprised to spot herself in the background of one photograph, "when the trackshop was inside there" she says pointing a few yards further down the concourse.

All night the book attracts gasps of recognition, confident assertions of which track is pictured or disappointment from some browsers that they're not pictured inside. Swindon Press Officer, consummate speedway statistician and prolific speedway author, Rob Bamford, (his latest co-authored book on the history of Oxford Speedway presently finds the presently clubless Cheetahs fans with more time on their hands to read it) notes dryly, "It's a behind-the-scenes-look at speedway that I don't imagine every promoter in the country is exactly going to be overjoyed with - particularly as, sometimes, it doesn't portray their business in the most glamorous light! You've even got some pictures of some toilets." Still they do say the camera never lies and that everyone has to go to the toilet.

I've hardly set up my stall before the amiable and hard-working volunteer member of the track curatorial staff here, Graham '*Blunsdon Blog*' Cooke, drops by to become the first person to buy a copy of the book. We chat about recent meetings, my blog on the televised encounter with Coventry here ("I had tears of laughter in my eyes when I read it - I've pinned a copy up in our hut for the others") and the present state of the Blunsdon track. Even more significantly for the Robins prospects of championship success this season, the camaraderie and team spirit that exists among the dedicated track staff applies to some members of the speedway team too, "Leigh Adams gave Andrew Moore a real masterclass in the pits and on the track - identifying faults, passing on tips and ideas on how to put it right. Gating isn't his strongest suit so hopefully this will help him improve that. We rigged up a temporary start line on the back straight and Leigh has given him a lot to think about. We've all really taken to Andrew for his all-out and honest effort." Though not all the team share universal love for each other, at least if the article about the "altercation" between Seb Ulamek and Charlie Gjedde in tonight's edition of the *Swindon Advertiser* is to be believed. The riding order of the team has been changed so they no longer have to exchange handbags or ride regularly together. 'Rosco' dismisses idle talk about the incident as, "heat of the moment stuff".

Tonight's SCB Official Christina Turnbull wanders over on the way to the referee's box high up in the main grandstand. The always polite and well-informed Graham appears to know her well but, afterwards, says, "Who was that?" Given the strength of her Scots accent (still retained despite her missionary work in the South), Nick slightly unnecessarily tells us "She's Glaswegian". He then ponders the alleged internecine antipathy that exists between the Scottish speedway clubs, "There's only one club to support in Scotland - Glasgow - people always talk about the rivalry but I reckon it's the Edinburgh lot who highlight this the most." Stupidly I say, "you could always support Berwick as your Scottish team rather than choose between them," before Nick immediately reminds me, "Well you could - if it wasn't in England!"

Having tried vaguely to help at the track with the Blunsdon curatorial team a few times earlier this year, I confidently thought that I was now on nodding terms with Alun 'Rosco' Rossiter. Though he'd conspicuously ignored me half an hour earlier as he scuttled by, this time when the red-anoraked Alun came down the steep grandstand steps that lead from the toilets with club co-owner Gary Patchett (I only know this because he has his name emblazoned on his white shirt), I accost him by my table display and proudly say, "It's my new book!" With a mystified look on his face, he says "Oh? Right!" in a nonplussed, slightly suspicious manner before he very politely lingers for a moment. Even though (as usual) his mind was no doubt buzzing with tactics, stratagems and cunning plans to best the opposition during the night ahead. I imagine promoters everywhere have to regularly cope with totally bonkers people who feel they can stop the (great) man in question to share with them the full vacuity of their opinions at great length with added copious boring detail. Alun looked briefly at the book as though distractedly inspecting some badly completed child's homework poisoned by radiation. Luckily Rosco's eye is caught by the giveaway postcard held in his hand which features the cover image (piles of tyres) I've used for my forthcoming *Shifting Shale* book, thereby instantly giving us something more to talk about since I ask, "Where do all the used tyres go?" Alun double checks I'm not some weirdo environmentalist before he answers warily, "We dispose of them properly!" When I ask, "Where?" he seeks to retain his authority by drawing himself up to his full height and also couple it with an air of mystery, "Dunno!" He's already started to walk away when I wonder aloud, "Is it tyre heaven?" without reply.

One of the pleasures of selling my books at speedway meetings is the sheer variety of people that I meet. I chatted to keen motor sports enthusiast Graham Ramsey who'd only started coming along to speedway recently after noticing the sport on *Sky* and liked what he saw. He liked how "competitive" it was, the "ability to see everything" and the "courtesy - the very first time I went someone showed me how to score". Apart from Swindon, he's been to Poole ("more structure, much more to it") and Reading ("despite being dilapidated still friendly - it has quirky charm"). Many people wander past without stopping to even look at the books never mind agonise over a purchase. Rob Bamford has returned and kindly points out, "There is the legend that is 'The Don' [Don Rogers] with daughter Lucy and grandson Josh!" With a few minutes still to go before the tapes actually rise for the first time, Rob doesn't hold out high hopes of a closely fought meeting against Wolverhampton, "this is as close as they'll be all night". Another visitor to the stand is Malcolm - the man who'd won a copy of my book *When Eagles Dared* for correctly and rather cleverly answering every question posed in the *Blunsdon Blog* Christmas quiz. He modestly plays down what must be his encyclopaedic knowledge of all things speedway ("everyone could have read things up or looked on Google").

Freshly qualified as the wild card for the Cardiff Grand Prix by way of the British Final (and apparently on a mission to repeatedly say when interviewed on the telly, "a year ago I couldn't have imagined this" - a statement widely seen on the terraces as an oblique reference to his admiration-inducing signing-on fee and guaranteed match payments), David Howe comprehensively burst

Christina Turnbull

Picture book briefly captures Rosco's interest

Charlie Gjedde always shops with his calculator while Robert Bamford looks on approvingly

through the tapes to a loud ironic cheer from the always keenly competitive Blunsdon faithful. Though *Schadenfreude* quickly turned to disbelief when it was announced: "All four back as there's a fault in the box". The incredulity increased further still in the re-run when Leigh Adams found himself relegated to fourth place for two laps before he just about managed to struggle past (pollen victim) David Howe. After they'd both gated well, up front there was a duel between Peter 'PK' Karlsson and Charlie Gjedde before the Wolves man secured a comfortable win. Any thought of stern resistance from Wolves soon ended with a 5-1 for the Robins reserves in the next race. It was such an easy win that it caused Lucy to remark, "Their reserves can't be that good as Andrew Moore looks like a world beater - not that I'm criticising him or his efforts but he has one good one and one bad meeting usually". The dose of 5-1 medicine is repeated for the visiting patient in the fourth heat, though this race is effectively ended as a contest when Lee Richardson wins the battle of wits with Freddie Lindgren by aggressively riding him towards the fence on the apex of the first bend. Sensibly, Lindgren shuts off and Richardson departs to win with an impressive show of speed that's not really reflected in the final race time.

Between races I take the chance to catch up with the Barber family. Bev wasn't impressed by the lack of interest and attentiveness shown by Jonathan Green when *Sky* recently televised the meeting at a rain-soaked Birmingham, "When he's not on air he spent most of the time texting and not watching the meeting - he had no interest at all. It's just a job to him!" I soon gather her brother Nick isn't a big fan of the newly opened Speedway Museum (which I must confess I'm looking forward to visiting). He professes to be scandalised by the cost of entry to the Wildlife Park, "£12 to get in for an adult - you won't get much change out of £50 if you take a family" and the fact that when you get inside many of the historic programmes on display are "only photocopies". As a keen collector of speedway memorabilia he's recently noticed a sudden flood on eBay of rare historic programmes and wonders at the reasons for this recent availability. "I stopped bidding for a Walthamstow 1934 one - they only rode one season pre-war, they were known as the Wolves then - when it reached £210. It went for £250 in the end - the seller lived in Broxbourne."

The chance of any kind of further token resistance from Wolverhampton looked unlikely with the rider replacement in operation for Billy Hamill ("Virus? Fark off! He just doesn't want to ride speedway here - he should be on a seven day ban really, but they won't") and becomes impossible with the withdrawal from the meeting of David Howe before heat 5 starts. At the trackshop Lucy is amazed at this news, "He's withdrawn due to hay fever! Is he a speedway rider or what?" When I say it's a shame because he's gating so well at the moment, she retorts, "Yeah brilliantly; shame it's through the tapes". Weirdly, the revised combination of Karlsson-Lawson secures a surprise heat advantage for Wolves. Though the race itself is notable for a dramatic fall for Mads Korneliussen - who is thrown like a rag doll on the fourth bend when his bike comes to an unexpected halt. Nick receives a text from his brother at Ipswich to say that Simon Stead has crashed badly ("his bike hit the stock car fence") at Foxhall

Heath, "they're all trying to keep up - the young riders - that's the trouble". On the subject of young riders, Lewis Bridger stops long enough at my stall for me to show him the two photos of a much younger looking him that appear in my book.

The Blunsdon crowd cheer loudly when Lee Richardson overtakes Freddie Lindgren on the last lap to win the next race. Nick notes, "He's the new hero round here this year - he's been invincible the last month or so, now he hasn't got the crap of the GP to distract him. He'll never need to work again - nice for him but trouble for British speedway because anyone from this country who shows any talent, everyone praises them - before they've done anything - and they soon lose ambition." Someone who shows ambition tonight but doesn't enjoy much luck is Mads Korneliussen who repeats his dramatic fall again in heat 9 - this time on the last bend of the last lap when placed third, albeit he's slightly less rag dollish in his departure from his equipment this time round. He remains prostrate on the track for a considerable time and over the tannoy we're told in the manner of the solemn tone usually reserved for redundancies or bereavements, "our thoughts are with Mads - he appears to be talking to his team mates who are with him". Rumours that you have to nearly get injured to manage a chat with your Swindon team mates can be dismissed as an exaggeration put about by jealous fans of other teams. Things could have been much worse but for the superb reflexes of the closely following Matthew Wethers, whom referee Christina Turnbull singles out afterwards for deserved praise for "his quick thinking". The time is then passed with an interview with Steve 'Johno' Johnston who doesn't mention the £8,000 he's reputedly owed. He does, however, revisit the thoughtless manner in which the news of the immediate closure of Oxford Speedway was communicated to him (a lady from the office rang his mobile to advise of his redundancy) before he adds, "I need to get back out on the track". Shortly afterwards we learn, Mads is, "battered and bruised - nothing broken according to the track doctor but he has officially withdrawn from the meeting."

Also withdrawn, albeit totally unofficially, from the meeting are the Wolverhampton team who between them only win three race advantages all night - one of these in heat 11 when PK rides in a black-and-white helmet colour. I'm impressed by the often subtle attention to detail shown by the promotion at Swindon - this is illustrated before the tapes rise for this particular race when the start-line girl on gate 2 parades about with black-and-white umbrella rather than a green one. Magnus Karlsson shines in heat 10 when he rides to a hard-earned nil points after he drifts wide on the penultimate lap and thereby allows the 'never-say-die' battling Andrew Moore to hurtle past.

The Robins take full advantage of having Tomasz Chrzanowski at reserve all night and he scores a paid five-ride maximum. I enjoyed his pass of Lindgren (on the fourth bend of the first lap in heat 12) whom he made appear slow to the point of stationary before he shot off into the distance to win by around 40 yards. The penultimate race of the night featured Freddie Lindgren as a tactical substitute in a black-and-white helmet colour off a 15-metre handicap and, consequently, he indulged in battle royal for third place with his team mate Magnus Karlsson. Arguably this was one of the most entertaining tussles and illustrates that - contrary to visual evidence on the night - the Wolves riders really do actually race for each point when the fancy takes them. Afterwards I overhear Rob Bamford say to a friend, "Not very good tonight was it, John? The track wasn't that great and the opposition were worse!"

7th June Swindon v Wolverhampton (Elite League B) 57-36

Chapter 8. Rye House v Glasgow:
Night of flying haggis and fire starters
9th June

Eric Boocock *"We'll go back to what we thought of in the first place before we changed our minds and got it wrong again!"*

Having worked in Harlow, it's always an embarrassment not to be able to find a short cut through the town and thereby avoid the toll bridge (50p) by the sewage works that leads to the speedway stadium in Hoddesdon. This time I even managed to lose myself enough to go past the rather posh Harlow greyhound stadium, the football club and golf club before realising I'd gone the long way round. I then eventually found myself as practically the first to arrive in the hot, dusty car park outside. Inside Andy Griggs was already setting out his stall for the evening and when, a short while later, he was joined by Doug Boxall - for all the world it looked as though they were restaging the photograph of this trackshop that appears in my book, *Shale Britannia*. Not long afterwards, Edward Kennett would arrive and ask, "Am I in it?" Though I've taken many photos of this rising star of the shale - mostly at the Bonanza - sadly to operator error, the shakes and poor light had dramatically hampered the end result. Andy delights in the situation and tells Edward a number of times during the evening, "I'm in it and you're not!"

As ever at Hoddesdon, the behind-the-scenes activity is frenetic on race night and with the trackshop right by the speedway office I get to see firsthand how hard Hazel Silver and her staff work to ensure everything runs smoothly. Len buzzes enigmatically about before the gates open but he's soon away down to the pits to conduct the speedway end of the race night performance.

Before he heads off, Hazel looks at Len and says, "we have a collection for Garry…" "Stead" adds Len as though part of a speedway mind reading double act before he continues, "Tai will help with that". The horrendous news that Garry will be confined to a wheelchair as a result of his crash at Somerset has shocked the sport generally in a week when news has circulated that two European riders were killed when riding in Continental Europe league meetings. Everyone knows the dangers of speedway and the innate perils of competing on bikes without brakes - but the level of carnage there has already been this season has provoked many people to wonder about the actual cause, along with some wild talk of the need for (unspecified) safety improvements.

When the jovial Rye House and Peterborough speedway track announcer Craig Saul arrives, he lets me know that the Rockets unofficial speedway forum have thought up an innovative way to raise funds for the also badly injured 30-year-old Sunderland-born Rye House 'veteran' rider, Stuart Robson. Namely, they have rather innovatively sponsored Craig for every time he can work the words "fire starter" and "flying haggis" into his comments during the night. On the surface, these don't sound the most propitious words to casually drop into any speedway conversation until you remember that Craig, as a part of his race night spiel, has a pet name for every speedway rider who ventures through the Hoddesdon pits gate. Luckily tonight's visitors the Glasgow Tigers feature Shane 'fire starter' Parker and David 'flying haggis' McAllan. "Even Len is in on it and promises to get in a few mentions during the rider parade" smirks Craig before he heads off to the referee's box with his trademark banana and comprehensive notes (plus my book) in hand. Craig is being unduly modest since although the Glasgow nicknames are the invention of others, he has deserved reputation for ingenuity and creativity when it comes to the invention of rider nicknames, which then subsequently become the moniker that stays with the rider throughout their careers. You only have to think of "Flyin'" Ryan Sullivan, Jan "The Hammer" Andersen, "Speedway's Most Wanted" or "The Total Package" (Hans Andersen) and "The

Thunder Down Under" (Jason Crump). Though I have to say that this always calls to mind farting or Rod Stewart's ex-wife Rachel Hunter who allegedly described her orgasms as something along these lines in respect of the tremors it caused in her pants.

Craig is deservedly known as one of the country's foremost announcers and, if truth be told, there was need for some aural entertainment on a night when not so many of the Glasgow riders put up anything like a real fight against a Rockets team supremely confident on their own track. As usual at Hoddesdon, Len Silver leads out the track staff and riders in mock military marching on parade fashion to the sound of 'Those Magnificent Men in their Flying Machines' before he treats us to some of his trademark, slightly idiosyncratic introductions in true Master of Ceremonies fashion. Naturally, we're introduced to each rider in turn, "Robert - I can't pronounce it - SEA-ACK. Is that it? You know who I mean." All this happens before Len reprises his thoughts on the recent performances by the club, particularly the cup meeting at Birmingham during the week, where Rye House ended the night with only three fit riders (out of the six they started with) and hopeful appeals to the referee to call a halt the meeting fell on deaf ears. The defeat still rankles with Len days later, "On Wednesday - when we raced at Birmingham - we raced on a track that was a disgrace!"

The racing is soon underway and the Rockets open with a 5-1 that effectively ends the meeting as a contest before it has hardly even really started. Were I a Tigers fan - and there weren't many in evidence on this particular leg of their mini-Southern tour - I'd be irked by the lack of fight shown by the experienced George Stancl. The race is won by "they call him the English German, Robbie Kessler" - now in Hertfordshire as a replacement for Ray Morton (having started his season at Stoke before going via Workington to now end up at Hoddesdon) - who forms an exciting and dominant partnership with "Mr Big Stuff" himself, the diminutive Chris Neath.

Confirming the evidence of our own eyes, Craig mentions, "the tractor is on the track already." It's the first of many track grades on a warm night when the heat of the atmosphere makes control of the dust difficult, even on a track normally not known for the thickness of the shale that covers its surface. It gives me the time to catch up with Reading Racers uber-fan Arnie Gibbons who is nearly half way through composing his exciting sounding manuscript on the 'History of Reading Speedway 1968 Onwards'. As a long-time fan of the Racers I'd be interested in his book anyway, but from how Arnie describes his thorough but eclectic approach to research (so that he can properly place each year in its own local social and historical context) it sounds like it will fascinate many fans, even those who feel they want to learn nothing about the club. I wish it had already been written so that I could read it now. Arnie hovers by my table and when I occasionally sell a copy of my book he repeatedly makes my favourite (well-worn) joke to every customer: "It would be rarer to have an unsigned copy!" Perhaps my sales would have been helped if I'd chosen a different night to attend since Andy Griggs finally had stock of the Rye House history book (that I'd seen elsewhere) on sale at Hoddesdon. The pent-up demand is such and this, allied with the enthusiasm for all things Rockets among the fans in this neck of the woods, means that he's sold all 30 copies he had before the tapes had even risen. Blimey is all I can enviously say.

With frequent breaks in the proceedings, we're kept well entertained by Craig but also treated to some virtuoso riding of the dusty but regularly graded Hoddesdon track by the home riders. They repeatedly and ruthlessly exploit their home knowledge of the circuit on those rare occasions when they haven't already established their dominance by the first corner. Heat 3 sees the return of "the 'Tommy Gun' Tommy Allen - back three days after that knee ligament injury," though he can only finish third behind second-placed Shane Parker. As ever, if any Tigers rider is to shine, it will invariably be Shane but, though he is the highest points scorer for the visitors on the night, even he looks slightly out of sorts. To my mind, the most impressive Glasgow rider of the night is - rather surprisingly given he couldn't catch a cold last season - Lee Dicken. That said, Robert Ksiezak and Trent Leverington also ride with verve and some determination that ultimately isn't quite reflected in their final points totals.

The next race features "The Boxmeister Steve Boxall" but the race ends before it has started. "Heat 4 didn't quite get off the ground as Adam Roynon was guilty of tape touching or, rather, tape demolition." Luke Bowen then replaces him in the re-run of the race. He's a rider who apparently is involved in his own unique 'elbowing' fund-raising scheme, if judged by the aggression he shows towards the 'flying haggis' as they enter the first bend in the re-re-run. It's an approach that relegates McAllan to last place but allows 'Sea-ack' to escape for second. The series of harsh manoeuvres is continued next time out by Tommy Allen who

Raffle tickets on sale

Another 5-1 beckons

Prime view of the fourth bend

super-aggressively rides George Stancl wide for a really close inspection of the links of the first corner safety fence that thereby maroons him out there in an impressive flurry of dust. This manoeuvre knocks out any remaining nascent desire Stancl might have had for this particular contest and, with ostentatious glances down at his engine, he pootles slowly round to the fourth bend before he retires without even completing a lap. Arnie notes matter of factly, "that's one thing the Elite League does - it gives you a lot more 'rigour' on the first bend! - to put it politely".

The Neath-Kessler partnership fires in another 5-1 to take the score to 25-11 after six heats. Craig is delighted: "They've already shown what they can do in heat 1 - their message is quite simple, 'if you want more of that, you can have more of that'!" The Tigers then throw their dice and send out Shane Parker in black-and-white but the race is stopped after Luke Bowen hammers into the first-bend safety fence and comprehensively demolishes it. He appears less than happy with Trent Leverington but, in fact, gets a reprieve from the SCB Official that greatly surprises me. It's a decision that Craig diplomatically describes as "a very tight entry to that first bend - the referee has ordered a re-run with all four back." We're then treated to another extensive trade grade session and a painstaking repair of the fence that I'm sure is completely and totally unconnected with Luke Bowen having to get himself and his equipment back together for the re-run of the heat. Craig kindly promotes my photo book with a description that includes the phrase, "shows the sport in a light it's rarely seen in". I chat with a bloke by my display table who has come along as a tribute to his recently deceased Rye House supporting father. It has been an emotional experience for him - memories of his dad and going to speedway with his late father have come flooding back, "when the first race started I was nearly in tears - my dad loved speedway!" Though Luke Bowen takes to the track in the re-run, it is Steve Boxall who aggressively steams past Trent Leverington on the second bend before he closely tracks Shane Parker for the next couple of laps who provides the real excitement. The experienced Aussie has to use all his guile and accumulated years of track craft to remain in front but, after another blocking manoeuvre on the penultimate corner, has no answer to a magnificent blast round the outside for victory perpetrated by the determined Rocket. Because of the use of the tactical ride option, it is still the first Tigers heat win of the night.

Back at my table, Arnie is worried that crowds at Reading remain poor though he's of the opinion that the Bulldogs promotion haven't helped themselves with the monumental stupidity of sometimes running Smallmead fixtures either side of a weekend, often resulting in a choice for fans of watching the racing on a Friday and/or on a Monday. "Even ignoring the impact of *Sky*, people simply choose to go to whatever meeting looks the best one and ignore the other. For Reading versus Lakeside I counted the crowd - I've often counted Conference League crowds, that's not difficult to do - and there were only 752 there." I query the exactitude of this figure but, even if you allow a significant margin for error, these aren't the type of attendance figures that will keep the club bank manager happy or puff up entrepreneurial Mr Postlethwaite's fragile ego.

Speedway justifiably enjoys a reputation as a genuine family sport and, whenever I visit Hoddesdon, I'm particularly struck by the truth of that statement. The terrace outside the bar (close by to my table and the trackshop) is thronged every time I'm here with younger families absorbed in the racing or their own conversations, while their kids run around happily nearby. There is also always a real mix of generations throughout the stadium and a high proportion of children regularly enjoy themselves by playing in the sand of the dog track that circles the speedway track here, completely oblivious to the hidden threat of what my dad would call "dog's muck". Unlike many other stadiums in the country, children can easily access it and, since it's uncovered, the sand also gets doused in healthy quantities of flying shale (though I believe that this isn't so good for the delicate feet of the dogs). Tonight we're all getting showered in a thin film of dust and the Tigers riders feel more shale than most as, on the whole, they trail their Rockets counterparts. However, they do enjoy a mini revival that starts in heat 10 when the talismanic Shane Parker rides skilfully to pass Robbie Kessler and then pressures Chris Neath without quite managing to get past him. This is the signal for successive 4-2s for the visitors teed up by wins for Lee Dicken and Shane. Naturally, Craig takes the opportunity to mention incendiary activities as often as possible. Normal service is soon resumed when, in heat 13, Stancl finishes third and the 'flying haggis' finishes last behind the fast-gating Neath-Boxall partnership, "the Tigers were picking up a bit of steam but the Rockets soon squashed that!" Craig notes triumphantly.

Glasgow gate well in the next heat but the race has to be re-run after Tommy Allen smashes into the perpetually collapsing first-bend fence. I felt he was fortunate not to be excluded - something that Craig's neutral and diplomatic announcement obliquely confirmed, "with Tommy Allen running out of room, we can tell you it will be re-run with all four riders". There is another delay for fence repairs, though after it has been restored to its former glory, we're treated to a fascinating duel that has Luke Bowen repeatedly try to find a route past Trent Leverington for third place. Luke uses the entire track to probe and harry but never quite passes his opponent until he makes one final desperate burst for the finish line only to lose out by a tyre-tread width. With the Rockets already 20 points ahead this level of effort isn't required (but nonetheless impresses) and has the unfortunate consequence that he crashes and careens into the (first-bend!) safety fence during the so-called warm down. Craig notes *sotto voce*, "Luke Bowen giving 120% - better make it 130%, you know what you get every time he takes to the track!" The meeting closes with a four-lap exhibition of confident team riding from the Neath-Boxall combination, who both end up with paid 14 points on the night. "A t'riffic race to sign off tonight's Premier League racing - entertaining for all the right reasons: pride, passion and determination!"

The news of the Garry Stead collection is excellent and Len Silver sounds genuinely delighted at the generosity of his fans, "I can tell you it's a record collection for us - £2600 - a wonderful, wonderful gesture, thank you!" Afterwards I learn from Craig that the sponsored use of the words 'fire starter' and 'flying haggis' has also raised £420 from the members of the Rye House unofficial forum for the injured Stuart Robson. Since we all watch a sport with a strong statistical emphasis, it's really no surprise that Craig can immediately tell me that he used "32 fire starters and 10 flying haggises - which was good when you think neither of them rode well tonight!"

9th June Rye House v Glasgow (Premier League) 57-35

Chapter 9. Sittingbourne v Buxton: Embodiment of the ethos

10th June

Nigel	*"Who says speedway races are all about who makes the start first!"*
Sam	*"I don't think there's any kind of advantage in speedway unless you make the start"*
Jonathan	*"Once again Greg Hancock proving that starts are so important!"*
Sam	*"It's all about getting out of the start."*
Kelvin	*"It's clearly important to make the starts in speedway, if you can hit that fresh air it's easier!"*
Nigel	*"Who says first from the gate always wins? That is NOT TRUE!"*
Hans Anderson	*"Speedway is easy when you make the start"*
Sam	*"It's all about making the starts"*
Sam	*"It's one of those tracks where you have to make good starts!"*

It's already a warm day when I arrive at Sittingbourne though it's still only mid-morning. One of the first people to greet me is Chelsea Lee-Amies who tells me rather proudly that she "got here at half eight with my dad to help with the track". Her father Stuart (aka 'Rat') is one of many people who rush purposefully about to ensure that all the last-minute tasks that need to get completed actually do get completed before the tapes rise on this afternoon's Conference League clash between the Sittingbourne Crusaders and the Buxton Hitmen. Arguably these two clubs most embody the ethos that originally led to the creation of the Conference League itself - namely a desire to ensure young riders can get the match action they require to hone and develop their riding skills as part of an apprenticeship, where winning remains an option but isn't the obligatory be all and end all of the equation! Whenever you visit them, both clubs have a very homely atmosphere along with a make-do-and-mend attitude that places the greatest emphasis on safe enjoyment for the riders as much as cut throat success or instant results. Though, if this Conference League fixture were to be symbolically transplanted to the world of Spanish football, today would represent the clash between Barcelona versus Real Madrid in the imaginations of the participants and fans in attendance in this part of Kent.

In fact, Sittingbourne don't win that often at home (let alone away) so any club that visits invariably expects the chance of a comfortable win or, if they adopt similar team-building policies like Buxton, this represents the best chance the visiting club will have of a closely fought, competitive meeting on the road and, possibly, an away win all season. Consequently, pretty much all of the opponents arrive in the pits charged up and keen to compete in this flat part of the county of Kent. The whole place is built on the willingness of volunteers to commit their time and energy to the club. This morning is no exception as some scamper around or, in the case of Graham Arnold (dressed in his trademark green boiler suit that makes him look like a pilot or paramedic), politely issue requests to others in a laconic fashion. He calmly gets on with filling the adapted transit van that serves as the bowser from a well apparently located underneath the rider changing rooms.

Like so many clubs in the country, Sittingbourne Speedway welcomes children and they take full advantage of their licence to roam. Those close by to the clubhouse and my table are either distracted by the games they're playing among themselves, pretending to be speedway riders on their push bikes and executing a series of skids and wheelies or else they're crowded round my book display. They're ignoring my new photo book completely since Chelsea is showing her curious gaggle of friends my first book *Showered in Shale,* "Look I'm in it [leafs excitedly through the pages], I have a copy at home and it's signed and everything!"

I've set my table up by the slope that would allow disabled people to just about squeeze into the portacabin that serves as the tea bar and refreshment room here. This cabin overlooks the finish line that, at Sittingbourne, is staggered some yards ahead of the starting gate. Some people stop to buy a book and others just want to chat. One man gives me a potted history-cum-lecture on the traditions and brilliance of the now defunct and often lamented Cradley Heath speedway club as well as an unasked for geography lesson on the technical definition of the whereabouts of the Black Country. I know that rivalries throughout the Midlands are complicated, deep-seated and often bitter but I had, rather stupidly, always considered West Bromwich if not Wolverhampton as part of this unique country-within-a-country location. In fact, I'm told in no uncertain terms that neither are within the boundaries of the two square miles that constitutes the Black Country with Tipton somewhere on the periphery of its ideological border in an area apparently historically famous for "chain and nail making and foundries". The conversation soon moves on to the bile and hatred that allegedly characterises the typical Wolverhampton speedway club supporter brought on by the enviable success of its local rival Cradley. Strangely, as a counterpoint, I've often been told that many people have an abiding memory of unfriendliness and implied menace at Cradley in marked variance to the popular view of the iniquity of its demise. "As a club we produced more world champions - Bruce Penhall, Eric Gundersen, Jan O Pedersen, Billy Hamill and Greg Hancock - and won more trophies than any other club. Cradley were always in the Inter-League KO Cup every year, oh, and I forgot that Schwartz and Penhall won the World Best Pairs!" It's a managerial truism that lions are always led by donkeys but in the case of Cradley, the perils of planning permission (according to this man) are compounded by the alleged ideology of geographic purity of the chief campaigner in charge of the quest for its resurrection. "Bob King or Andrews or someint, I'm not quite sure - whatever he's called - he's holding it back 'cause he wants it to definitely be in Dudley Wood and that ain't gonna happen whereas it might elsewhere, if only he'd listen!" I mentally thank my lucky stars that I don't have any part to play in this campaign since I've too quickly got inadvertently embroiled in passionate debate some might see as located upon bald men fighting over a comb territory.

Luckily Lakeside's Adrian Kearney strolls by and I can instead talk about the impact of the changes that there has been at the club in Thurrock since Stuart Douglas took over from Ronnie Russell and the experienced Jon Cook also joined the club. "It's refreshing to have someone who will listen and try new things. With Ronnie - love him to bits - he was old school so he just used to open the gates and expect people to turn up. Whereas now we're trying all sorts and trying to get people to notice how things have changed."

Sat on the chairs behind me are some members of the Moss family - Buxton co-promoter Jayne, her mother-in-law, Janet, whose husband set up the club and Jayne's baby son Kieran who is now nine months old. He's already a veteran of many speedway meetings and is clearly a happy, smiley baby who is content to thoroughly gum his plastic key ring. Also scampering about the vicinity is her elder son Josh who has shot up and is a bottle of pop in energy terms as well as highly knowledgeable about speedway (along with being club mascot and a hugely enthusiastic fan of the club). As ever Josh wears his Buxton Hitmen tabard proudly. Baby Kieran chooses to break the minute's silence that is observed during the rider parade to pipe up with a few cute gurgles. Jayne notes that she always enjoys her visits to Sittingbourne and that both clubs continue to exist on a financial shoestring held together by devotion and dedication. She's mystified by the spate of severe accidents that have afflicted the sport this season, "there've been so many crashes this year everywhere - lots of different tracks and riders so you can't say it's for any one reason!"

Bowser/Transit Van

Practice available

Chelsea and friends study Showered in Shale

Typical pits scene

Before the meeting can get underway there is a further delay for what announcer Steve Ribbons mysteriously calls a "paperwork problem". This requires the first of his relatively frequent pits interventions by the SCB Official for this fixture, Chris Gay. Because of the intensive watering of the track, when the racing gets underway there are no eddies of shale dust thrown up by riders as they pass our position during the first race but instead there is a slight splattering of gloopy shale. Jayne remarks that she believes that one of the conditions of being able to stage speedway at Sittingbourne is "not having any dust - I recall one farmer is zealous about it - though it's hard to keep the dust down at any track, never mind on a hot day like today". Kieran's grandmother Janet agrees that dust and speedway go together like gin and tonic, "you get dust everywhere!"

During the delay we learnt from Steve Ribbons over the tannoy that Ken Burnett has won the raffle and my attendance is mentioned, though mysteriously for reasons I can't explain I'm described as a "bon viveur" which - for some reason - reminds me of the advert for Listerine that features Clifford the Dragon, notorious for his bad breath. Once the racing has started at 12.25 p.m., Sittingbourne immediately concede a 5-1 to the James-Roberts partnership in a race won very impressively in some style by Jack Roberts. The swift arrival of the next heat has Buxton reserve Lewis Dallaway endure a frustrating start to his afternoon. First he fails to get his bike to start - despite some vigorous pushing by his mechanic in the reverse direction around the fourth bend - and is excluded under the two-minute time allowance for his troubles. Then he's pushed out again in an optimistic attempt to join the re-run off a handicap of 15 metres but still finds himself excluded once more when his bike again fails to start. Sittingbourne's Luke Goody also endures an engine failure in this race but is already so close to the line that he is able to gain a point for third place.

Heat 3 has the Crusaders claw back some of their deficit with a heat advantage and features a win for Mark Baseby that is described as "fast or what?" by Steve Ribbons whose announcements are so brief I begin to wonder if he charges by the word. Another heat advantage in the next race restores the scores to parity at 12 each when Sittingbourne's Danny Warwick wins comfortably. I've been in a long conversation with a well-spoken man ("I would buy one of your books but haven't brought any money") and Danny's win inevitably brings up the topic of his distinctive white man with dreadlocks hairstyle. Admittedly I playfully gild the lily with my claim that Danny is, in reality, as bald as a coot - it's a claim that's soon rejected but incredulity still seizes the man at the fashion news that this unique tonsorial arrangement might involve artificial help in the form of hair extensions: "You don't mean they clip on, do you?" The next week he makes a point of coming over to tell me, "I asked Danny about his hair afterwards and he said they're real!" (before he also tells me, "I might buy one of your books later in the season but haven't got any money today"). It's the kind of remark that brings to mind Mandy Rice-Davies's famous answer during the Profumo scandal, "well he would [say that], wouldn't he?"

The lead briefly see-saws until Heat 8 when, given his imperious form up until this point, I am expecting Jack Roberts to win convincingly. It is a good theory but sadly, though he shoots away from the tapes, Jack then hammers spectacularly into the safety fence at the apex of the first bend. In fact, he bounces off the fence and performs an acrobatic manoeuvre with his bike that sees him somehow somersault over it before he swiftly leaps to his feet to try to clear the track of his equipment. Chris Gay stops the race in the interests of safety and Roberts is excluded, despite his much-appreciated efforts to clear the track before the arrival of the remaining three riders on their next lap. With a drawn re-run, the next race provides a real test of referee Chris Gay's observational abilities and knowledge of the rulebook since it requires him to be almost able to simultaneously watch incidents on two different sections of the track at once. Though Mark Baseby leads comfortably, the real action of the race is an intense two-lap battle between Jonathan Bethell and Andre Cross that eventually leads the Buxton rider to come to grief and fall but not be excluded for his troubles. This is because race leader Mark Baseby receives this honour since he has fallen unchallenged seconds beforehand on a different section of the track. To my mind, referee Chris Gay makes the right decision though a split second either way would have altered his final judgement. After the meeting, Chris takes the time to puff thoughtfully on a thin cigar and carefully outline the exact detail of his thinking to keenly knowledgeable speedway fan Arnie Gibbons who'd questioned this by helpfully outlining every possible scenario and ramification of the sequence of events that led to the stoppage of the race. Intuitively the decision made felt right to me at the time, though it is only listening to Arnie's encyclopaedic outline of the permutations that I realise how complex the rules are and how much had to be instantaneously weighed up by the referee on this occasion.

The referee also has cause to visit the pits a couple more times during the afternoon. Speedway is a dangerous adrenalin-based sport where feelings often run high and things are said or done in the heat of the moment that more sober reflection might have avoided. As younger people are also involved so there can be an element of the nightclub confrontation about exchanges of opinion ("what are you looking at?"). One such incident reportedly has Aaron Baseby brush Jack Roberts that results in an exchange of mutual staring followed with a threatening offer from Jack. A shake of the hands soon calms the situation. Later, Sittingbourne team manager Chris Hunt draws the referee's attention to a confrontation between Scott James and a member of pits staff - a situation again resolved by Chris Gay with a word in the shell-like of those involved and with both team managers.

By the start of heat 12, Buxton have again edged into the lead after Jack Roberts resumes his normal service to defeat the Crusaders most impressive rider of the afternoon, Danny Warwick. However, the possibility of a Sittingbourne fight back arguably flounders on the last bend of the third lap when Andre Cross falls unexpectedly and loses position when placed second. The home fans groan and a man on the centre green - that I take to be Sittingbourne team manager Chris Hunt - throws his arms into the air in a disgruntled and exasperated fashion. Salt is comprehensively rubbed into this wound when Buxton secure a 5-1 in the race that takes the score to 33-39 with only three heats to go.

Not that all hope has been extinguished and the flame starts to flicker once more with a third win on the day for Danny Warwick and a heat advantage. From the commentary box, after the race Steve Ribbons is keen to ask some rhetorical questions over the tannoy, "You must ask yourself - does that give us a sporting chance?" In the absence of any crowd response, Steve waits a minute or so before he replies to his own question (is this one of the first signs of madness?), "the answer is yes!" It's a hope of a fight back that turns out to be misplaced when plumes of exhaust smoke belch from Luke Goody's bike prior to the start of the race, only for him to then be excluded for touching the tapes. He's replaced by Aaron Baseby, though surprisingly because he rears at the gate it's his more experienced brother Mark who finds himself placed fourth when a stunning burst of speed has him overtake the whole field ahead of him before he's barely reached the middle of the back straight. The Buxton riders pack in behind him for a drawn heat and thereby leave Sittingbourne requiring a last heat 5-1 to draw the meeting. Sadly this possibility ends when Mark Baseby quickly falls, though we're still treated to the spectacle of a forceful pass by Jack Roberts on Danny Warwick (on the last bend of the penultimate lap) to definitively secure the race points, although the overall result was already a foregone conclusion. Buxton mascot and vocal cheerleader all afternoon, Josh Moss is amazed and delightedly pipes up, "Buxton won away - for once!"

One Minute Silence

Ian Glover waves the chequered flag

Buxton mascot Joshua Moss

Afterwards I catch up briefly with referee Chris Gay when we're joined by a man with wet hair who interrupts to quietly say, "I just wanted to tell you that these are the best showers in the league - they're warm, clean and powerful and also to say that you're the best referee in the country - honestly! - the lads in the changing room were talking about you and the way you handled things today. It was lovely that you came down and consulted in the pits with us. It makes all the difference - thank you!" I'm still not exactly sure who this polite and sincere gentleman is. Later the invariably modest Chris says, "you must think I plan these" since it's the second time I've had a post-meeting chat with Chris that has been interrupted by riders who wish to congratulate him (the last time was at Plymouth) on his diplomacy and skills as an SCB Official. "Young riders don't want to lose face in front of each other and as referee I can give all an opportunity to move on without losing face".

Before he leaves for his van this rider turns to me and says, "Yours is the best speedway book ever - honestly! My mum has read every single page and, even though you gave me a right going over, I still think it's the best. As a matter of interest, how many has it sold?" Jonathan Bethell (for it is he) looks disappointed when he hears the actual figure and consoles me, "Well it should have sold more!" I'm not sure that I can imagine any other sport where the referee is so sincerely thanked by one of the participants - it's the kind of thing that makes you proud to follow speedway and reflects so creditably on the young men (and volunteers) that go to make Buxton and Conference League speedway so special!

June 10th Sittingbourne v Buxton (Conference League) 42-48

Chapter 10. Wolverhampton v Reading:
Attack of the table smasher
11th June

When I arrive early at Monmore Green Stadium, the Dave Rattenberry trackshop stall is already erected and almost completely stocked, despite the fact that there are nearly four hours before the tapes rise. As usual, Dave is there along with John Rich - who I immediately apologise to since he's regrettably been cropped out of one of the photos in my new book *Shale Britannia* that he might otherwise have appeared in. They have a young helper with them today in the form of Kayleigh Jones who tells me about her attraction to all things speedway, "well, Freddie Lindgren mainly - that's the only reason I'm here". John protests, "you're bloody Wolves". She's only been coming along since June 2006 but already has an impressive number of photos that feature Freddie and herself that she proudly shows me. Kayleigh loves the "buzz of the bikes, the speed and the dangerousness" but, most of all, Freddie! Later she admits, "I'm trying to get up the gear to ride myself". Apart from lingering round the pits to engage Freddie in conversation or have another photo taken with him, she says she "helps Rat" though, to the untrained eye, the opposite appears to be the case. Rat and John appear to treat her with the affection and care of a surrogate daughter, "helps the fat man, aye" says Rat. Dave has already studied my photo book at Mildenhall, "it's a good book - it's unusual" whereas it's new to John and he's still leafing through it, "it's a bit dull isn't it? Bill isn't in there either". At that point a man called Tony - whom I recognise from a similar performance last season - interrupts us. His role on race nights at Monmore Green seems to be to berate Dave every time I come here for some previously promised item of merchandise that he expects to be in stock and already awaiting his arrival. "Have you got my mugs?" he demands only to learn from Rat, "Tony - I can promise you - you will get your mugs off me!"

A tall blond-haired man stands by my book display to study the merchandise and I soon learn he's Paul Harvey who's "spannering for Magnus Karlsson not Peter Karlsson". He has his "own business - a removal business - so I'm fortunate 'cause I can have the time off to do this". He lives in Hull and it sounds as though enough speedway riders to form a team live in the nearby vicinity to him. "Opposite my house lives Emil Kramer, the Pickering family are next door and down the road is Emiliano Sanchez. Further down the road is Joel Parsons - round the back of him to the east of where I live is Lee Dicken and the Nortons - Danny and Kyle - live in that area too and, of course, Magnus lives at my house when he's here too! It's a right little collection of us all in one area - we all beg, borrow and steal off each other." Paul got into speedway "when I was small" - a significant admission given that he's now around two metres tall - "I was 11, I think, when I first went, I'm 44 no 45 now and it was the Rayleigh Rockets".

Kayleigh with her idol Freddie Lindgren

Avuncular welcome always assured at any Rattenberry trackshop

Paul Harvey (Danny Warwick eat your heart out)

Like many people in the speedway community, he feels that the issue of safety needs to be urgently addressed. "There's got to be some safety done somewhere, it should be compulsory to have air fences. Why do they still have to attach wooden fence boards to metal fence posts? It beats me! Sod's Law is a rider never goes between them but hits the post. We come to see racing not accidents. There's been so many bad accidents this year - Stuart Robson and Garry Stead, he lives over the back from me. It's come as a real shock, normally he just walks down my garden path and shouts 'get the kettle on!' It's hit me really hard that he won't walk again - he has a baby daughter too - a strange name I can't remember - four months old. He has a son from a previous partner, Lewis, who's five. He's devastated, he says, 'life's over for me' but I say, 'life's just starting again for you'. They know what they do - they know - but forget the risks. Once they're injured they're all too easily forgotten it seems though! There's Carlos Villar - the first time I saw him I thought 'that's a matter of time' - there's the Polish kiddie Cegielski, his girlfriend used to spanner for him and Lawrence Hare, of course. I can't think of any more off-hand but there's plenty of them whose lives have been changed by speedway- yeh, there's still some mentions but mostly they're just forgotten about!"[1]

After a few moments lost in his own thoughts he abruptly changes the subject, "You should chat to some of the riders for your books - they have so many stories. That Emiliano Sanchez has some hilarious ones about when he first came to this country. He came over in a car with just a bike and one telephone number of someone he didn't know - an Aussie, I forget his name. He could hardly speak English and they stopped him at customs when he arrived and searched everything. The sniffer dog ate his sandwiches too! You should hear him tell them, he's got some great stories but, then, so does everyone. My first job in speedway was on the away side of the pits at Hull. Ian Thomas used to say 'stand there with a hose for an hour and wait until it's up to your knees'. When the away riders used to arrive they didn't know what to think. He used to try all sorts to gain an advantage."

My giant poster advertising my photo book has attracted quite a crowd of onlookers keen to identify the exact whereabouts of each photograph. Dave Rattenberry points to one picture and says, "I know most of these but I dunno where that one is - is it Sittingbourne?" My hilarity quickly gives the game away that, in fact, it's his own trackshop on the Isle of Wight, "Jesus, I never knew it was mine!" Rat then attempts to say it was before his time there but soon learns otherwise, "oh no - it was when I was there!" My delight is short lived when I incorrectly claim that another featured photo that mystifies Rat is Buxton, luckily I soon correct myself (it's actually Sittingbourne). One lady who effortlessly identifies each image correctly is Wendy Jedrzejakski - "it's said Jed-RA-Jedski although everyone says Jedi on a jet ski". She's so good I'm

[1 Ironically the *Speedway Star* a fortnight later (June 23 2007) included a hard-hitting and provocative article from Lawrence Hare that is required reading for all interested in considering safety standards within speedway. There was also news of a sponsored two-day, 165-mile bike ride for Krzysztof Cegielski organised by Poole Pirates fans Robert Hawkins and Rob Green. Steve Johnston joined the same bike ride to raise funds for Garry Stead.]

tempted to ask her to move along but instead try to fox her with more recondite pictures from the book. She studies the cover of the book and says loudly, "I could have been on there - I've still got my 'Miss Long Eaton' sash, well 'Miss Fina Invader' it says really". For a track where the fans are so passionate and knowledgeable, I've rarely done well with my book sales trips at Monmore Green and tonight is no exception.

Away in the pits there's some drama when SCB Official Margaret Vardy rules that tonight's visitors Reading can't replace the absent Sam Simota with their number 8 rider Phil Morris (as they intended) because he has a higher average than Simota. Instead the Bulldogs have been forced to bring in Ben Barker to ride at reserve. This isn't good news for their prospects of a vaguely competitive performance, particularly given that Matej Zagar is already missing from the team and for whom they'll have to use rider replacement. I think about leaving my display to buy a programme but Bill assures me, "don't worry they won't run out, it's only Redin!" Over the tannoy we learn that "Wolves legend Don Goodman is in the crowd tonight". He was a well-travelled footballer and one that I know well, since he played for Sunderland. He's very strongly associated with the area, partly because of his million-pound transfer to Wolves and his fighting performances for his various clubs. A glance at his career statistics shows that he scored more goals for West Brom and Sunderland than Wolves but then he played more games for the Baggies. Later I see a man with impressive dreadlocks who escorts and carefully supervises his son in the gents loos in the plush Monmore Green grandstand - I assume it's Don but don't ask in case I'm mistaken, particularly since it's not quite the place or the time to ask.

Tonight is an important night for Chris van Straaten since he has organised a collection at this meeting for the 'Promise Dreams' children's charity[2] that is close to his heart. The Wolverhampton based charity "raise funds to make dreams come true for terminally and seriously ill children, no matter what their dream might be". Later I see a smiling CVS stagger past with three collection buckets towards his speedway office. He answers, "they're heavy too!" when I ask, "have you got enough buckets, Chris?" Later we learn over the tannoy system "well done, you've raised over £700!"

Also in the crowd tonight is *Radio Five Live's* sports reporter, Phil Mackie. He's come along to the Monmore Green stadium to try to soak up the atmosphere of a 'typical speedway meeting' as well as grab some vox pop interviews with riders, staff and fans for a very brief item on the Simon Mayo programme that will look at summer sports you might like to consider visiting. When I listen to the programme they exaggerate and say the crowd was 1,900 people, though with the presence of building works on the main grandstand terraces, to my untutored eyes it didn't seem quite as crowded as normal. The meeting itself was a long way from exciting as the Bulldogs get up and go - with the exception of Greg Hancock - had apparently gone absent without leave, thereby effectively undermining the meeting from a closeness or entertainment point of view from the outset. Plus, there is the unique not-found-elsewhere factor on race night at Wolverhampton - the almost continuous aural accompaniment throughout of the thoughts and comments of presenter Ian 'Porky' Jones who appears to perform under the impression that we've all come along to hear/see him rather than watch the speedway. I'm sure you could get used to him over time but, I'd like to think, that someone kindly tipped Phil Mackie the wink that such is the presentational quirk of his extreme self-love, it isn't at all 'typical' or the norm within speedway generally.

Kindly and observant security man, Ian Price, rushes up to me to interrupt my enjoyment of the meeting, "your table has been broken - I was just coming up towards it and I watched him jump on it". Though not expensive, it's pretty important to have something to display books on when I travel to speedway tracks to sell them. Luckily, after I have confirmed the wrecked and splintered nature of my table, Ian is able to take me elsewhere in the stadium to chat with the young man who has been so poorly behaved and so thoughtlessly treated my property. I found when I was younger that adults who reacted calmly when I'd transgressed got their message across much more effectively. Ian stands silently by when I speak with the youngster in question. He is with his granddad, though this overweight and slightly resentful man appears to have abdicated any supervisory responsibilities in favour of just wheezing in his chair for the night. The young man (with green iced lolly in hand) is tearful and decides the best approach is to have his granddad repeat a totally false and barely believable story, flatly contradicted by the reality of events seen by Ian.

[2 To contact Promise Dreams call 01902 378595 or email info@promisedreams.co.uk]

ICA Crook aka Mushy Pea

The Monmore pits

Tai and Lewis queue for ice creams

The story is that he'd been "chased by bullies and when trying to get away the table had been accidentally broken". It would be something that would elicit sympathy if true but, though totally unconvinced, I decide to suggest that if he was bullied anywhere in future then he should always try to confide in a nearby adult, whether or not he actually knew them. There is a scarcely audible but mumbled "sorry" and I think I honestly expect his granddad to waddle over from his seat and come to inspect the full horror of the damage himself or, as I believe most people would in this situation, offer some form of restitution. Instead he steadfastly takes the view, "he was being chased by bullies and he's said sorry - what more do you want?" Better brought up children or grandchildren would be fortunate to enjoy the company of supervising adults with greater levels of social responsibility and some understanding of the concept of leadership by example. Unfortunately, this young man appears to have been rewarded with refreshments for lying and treated insouciantly for deliberately damaging the property of others. It's a sad reflection on the values of his adult carer at the speedway and doesn't bode well for his future development. I definitely blame the parents and the grandparents, though clearly lack of intelligence plays its part.

When I return to my table, John Rich is already in the process of finding strips of wood to temporarily bind and fix it back together for the night ("I remembered I had a Phillips screwdriver in the car"). Security man Ian also then gets involved and, after a few minutes of practical skills and impressive craftsmanship, they have restored the table to something approaching its former glory so that I can again continue to use it tonight. "It's better than it was now!" says John before he adds, "and you missed the chance to take a photograph". John and Ian brush off my protestations of gratitude, while Graham (who also helps Rat on race night at Wolverhampton) remains amazed that no offer of help or compensation was made to rectify the damage. Interestingly when the meeting finishes, granddad lollops by while studiously ignoring me, though I do pointedly call out "goodbye" and "remember what I said about bullies" to his grandson Pinocchio.

With the result of the meeting already beyond all doubt, the Wolves team manager, Peter Adams, chooses to reward David Howe for his four-ride paid maximum with a deserved place in the nominated heat 15 alongside Freddie Lindgren. The Reading partnership of Hancock-McGowan then choose that race to finally show some concerted determination and the race effectively ends as a contest when they gate and ride Lindgren hard to the fence, thereby causing him to stutter to retirement. David Howe chases manfully but McGowan eventually blunts his challenge on the second bend of the last lap with a blocking manoeuvre that leads Howe to shut off. The difficulties of satisfying your fans, even when you win easily, is typified by the presumption and reaction of the man next to me, "[Howe is] bloody hopeless in heat 15 - it's the sort of farking decision that'll cost us the bonus point and, possibly, a farking place in the play offs!"

11th June - Wolverhampton v Reading (Elite League A) 54-39

Chapter 11. Lakeside v Eastbourne: "Speedway has lost its mojo"

15th June

After any clash with Poole, for many Eagles fans the clash of Lakeside against Eastbourne is the most eagerly awaited fixture on the speedway calendar in this part of the South-East of England. It has been given added spice in 2007 because of the departure of Jon Cook from East Sussex to Thurrock. I'd certainly made sure I could go to the first encounter following what many Eastbourne people believe to be Jon Cook's defection and, in fact, I so comprehensively beat the traffic through the Dartford Tunnel that I arrive at the stadium nearly five hours before the tapes are scheduled to rise. The whole place is deserted apart from intense activity on the track and Davey Watt unpacking his bike in the pits. Even the speedway office is empty and the phone continually rings unanswered. However, the unattended grounds give me the chance to investigate the visible signs of the revolution that has happened here at the speedway club since the ebullient Ronnie Russell departed and the entrepreneurial Stuart Douglas took over. The subsequent shock appointment of Jon Cook as his experienced co-promoter has been widely seen as a shrewd move in speedway circles for the possible future development of the club and an opportunity to end their status as perpetual wooden spoonists in top-flight British speedway.

The talk in the press and on the Internet has been about the whole new spirit and culture that the co-promoters have tried to instil throughout the club. There was also the heavily publicised and widely praised experiment to allow free entry into the club on the night *Sky* televised a fixture here for the first time this season. It was an experiment that indicated that there were around 6000 people in the vicinity who were quite prepared to come along to a free speedway meeting. Whether or not they would continue to do so if they had to pay to get in was another question but, at least, they'd had a taste and sampled, what was by all accounts, a vibrant atmosphere reminiscent of the heyday of speedway's popularity. The most visible change effected within the stadium under the new regime runs the length of the back straight where the fans are now able to stand in an enclosure that allows them to be much closer to the track and the action. Though the raceway at Thurrock can be viewed from any point on its oval, this sensibly addresses the historic complaint that fans were always somewhat distant and removed from the action. The track staff who are here work attentively distributing the metal crash barriers and carefully placing them in their correct positions for later.

One of the first people to arrive in a glistening black pick-up truck is Jon Cook and I'm suddenly all overcome with the idea that I'm Alexei Sayle so I greet him with "hello Jon - got a new motor?" Jon treats this poor attempt at levity with the contempt it deserves. According to reports in the *Speedway Star*, during the racing this truck is parked just by the pit lane and the Lakeside riders congregate to stand as a team on its open back to watch the racing from a more ideally elevated viewing position. An impressively tanned Jon has hopped out of this fashionably sleek shiny black vehicle to set about adjusting the crash barriers that line the grass verge closest to the pits before he moves on to adjust the configuration of the crash barriers that line the back straight. He works with speed and some determination but finds the time to chat. "The day-release boys help out with doing all

Home side of the pits at Lakeside

Cover girl Sheila

Alf soaks up the sunshine

this - they're great! They put the stuff out but don't stay - though they could - which says it all about the current appeal of speedway with precisely the type of group of people we need to be attracting to the sport. It'd be free for them but they have other better things to do. Speedway has lost its mojo!" I ask Jon about his work at Lakeside and from his description, it's clear that he's excited by the opportunity to work with Stuart Douglas and has been relishing being a key part in driving through many of the behavioural and attitudinal changes at the club, "though there's still so much more to do!" They say 'don't look back' and that is a mantra that Jon has adhered to when it comes to Eastbourne. "I haven't really had the time to do anything but concentrate on here to be honest. You hear things but I've got a job to do here and that's what I'm concentrating on - to make it a success. That's how I've always done it. I can't say I've looked at the website or tried to keep up but obviously I hear this and that, but I can't really comment nor would I think to. When it comes down to it, speedway is a simple business - riders ride and promoters promote. One risks their life and the other risks their money. Like lots of people I noticed the fixture but I want to win every meeting and this meeting is just like any other in that respect. You can't work somewhere for so many years and not still feel something but my job is at Lakeside now. I have seen that there are 17 guests on the list for 'The Men in Black' tonight - I can't imagine who they all are or what they're doing here and I can't remember ever going anywhere with a number like that. It's a bit ridiculous but that's their business, I'd imagine we'll only be taking around three people to theirs when we go but, as I say, it's not my business. Bob [Brimson] is new to the sport and he's going to want to do things his way. We've kept in touch and I've helped behind the scenes because I want Eastbourne to do well and the team they have is pretty much the team I selected so I'm gonna want them to be successful. Equally, it's for him to run and, being new to the sport, he's got to learn for himself! Lots of people will give or offer advice, push themselves forward as experts and he's got to decide who knows something and can really help and who doesn't. I worry that some of those with the loudest voices don't know as much as they think they do! Anyway I have to get on and my interest now is building this club up much further to what it can really be and I'm going to carry on working hard to make sure that happens."

By the time I get back to the arcade that houses the café and the various shops at Lakeside, Alf Weedon has pulled up in his car to start his race-night routine of unbolting the shutters, unloading the new stock and readying the shop in preparation for the arrival of the fans. Ever since his knee operation the other year, he's struggled with his mobility and now has to use crutches to ease his progress around the place. All this, combined with his age (87 this year), has had a knock-on effect on his outlook on life that now has a default setting of slightly to majorly frustrated. He's even had to cut back on his beloved photographic duties, though that's probably sensible since, if looked at from a safety perspective, he'd definitely no longer be able to evade any rogue stray speedway bike he encountered heading towards him at speed on the centre green. After some consideration, he kindly allows me to set up my table in pride of place next to his shop. It's an ideal spot from which to watch the racing and, since the turnstiles have now opened, a great location to watch the world as it wanders by en route to the various parts of the stadium they favour to watch from. I proudly hand a copy of my new book of photographs to Alf with some trepidation because of the lifetime he's spent making speedway photography his career. A minute or so later, I notice that he no longer has the book. I question its whereabouts, "I've already sold it," he tells me with some satisfaction. "It's the sales talk innit! You just don't chat to them, you say [caresses cover and flicks the pages] 'it's a beautiful book, lovely paper, unusual photos!' Easy."

Over the tannoy Nicki Pedersen is interviewed about the prospects for the meeting ahead, "the home riders have an advantage here but we're here and focused - all the riders have been injured and some still are - we do our best!" Whether this best will be good enough remains to be seen. Though the Eagles welcome back David Norris from injury, they are still without Dean Barker - who stands with his girlfriend and various friends on the slope just in front of me throughout the meeting. Trevor Harding is in at reserve along with Ryan Fisher as a guest in place of Lewis Bridger at number two, hardly a like-for-like swap. When Greg Brimson rushes by on a mission to get a bottle of Diet Coke for his brother Bob, he asks my opinion on our choice of guest, "Trevor [Geer] tells me Ryan normally rides really well here - but then Trevor's a nice man!" After he's held third place for two and half laps Ryan succumbs to the pressure from behind from Henning Bager and this last place doesn't bode well for the Eagles prospects. Afterwards I learn that Bob Brimson dressed Ryan down in the pits for accepting a guest booking and arriving with a dirty bike and kevlars. Depending on your point of view, and with appearances counting for so much in all walks of life nowadays, it definitely shows a busy schedule or a lack of preparation and respect!

One person who leaves before the Elite League meeting starts is Derek Barclay, Conference League fan par excellence who still mourns the passing of Wimbledon at Plough Lane and nowadays gets his regular fix through his involvement with Sittingbourne. He's come along to watch the Academy League meeting that at Lakeside starts before the contest that features the experienced riders and tonight features the Hammers versus the Eastbourne Eaglets. This decision to put on the junior riders first at 6.45 p.m. and 'develop the young talent' as the speedway parlance usually has it, bucks the nationwide trend to put such things on as an afterthought. Whether or not this actually attracts the fans to arrive early is open to question. But, people like Derek - solely committed to the starter levels of speedway who are prepared to pay Elite League prices (later it transpires he has a press pass "I'm not that mad that I'd pay to get in and then leave") to watch this racing and then depart - remain in a definite minority. He's very happy with what he's seen and, as he leaves, notes "most of them are Sittingbourne really". He has to pick his way through the last of the arrivals - reportedly a crowd of 1,900 - who're still coming through the turnstiles as he heads in the opposite direction for the car park.

Heat 2 features an advantage for the visitors, mostly due to the determination of Trevor Harding who withstands the close attentions of Paul Hurry for a couple of laps. It's not long until the home side establish a lead although it remains nip and tuck until heat 8. The races come along with noticeable rapidity though there's enough time to listen to the commentary box banter ("there's a lot of Geminis follow speedway, Bob") or admire the new glossy, large-format programme they now sell at Lakeside. It's an artefact of some lustre with a pleasing but appropriate mix of columns, features, rider photos, information and adverts. It follows on from the full-colour programme the Reading Bulldogs introduced to the Elite League but, I'd suggest, is a much more sophisticated product (without really breaking new ground) and represents better value. Though it too has been priced at the rather steep new price point of £2.50, what you get means that you don't quite resent this premium rate so much as you do at Smallmead. Even more interestingly, though huge attention has been paid to the contentious switch of Jon Cook and Adam Shields from Eastbourne to Lakeside even the 2005 award-winning Eagles programme printers, it appears even Fineprint ("Proud Printers of the Hammers Programme"), have defected. Though they still produce the Eastbourne programme, they now clearly do their best and most exciting work for Lakeside.

Quite a few things stand out - notably the varied catalogue of Lakeside branded merchandise for sale at the trackshop or online and the fact that Stuart Douglas signs off his column as "Stan" as well as refers to his residence as the "House of Stan". Stan sings the praises of the items for sale at the trackshop too; he highlights "a fabulous memento in the miniature riders, every one of them hand-painted. They make a great gift, and although they are not dirt cheap [£28] (remember, every one is unique), they are very, very limited, so if you fancy one, get in there sharpish. It took me a long time to find them - all the other models seem to

First bend

Track shop and bar

be bikes only - and KK came up with these. I have one of him in his Leszno gear - looks brilliant!" In recent years, the injuries the riders have suffered have sometimes made the score lines here look as though models actually rode on behalf of the club. Eventually, Stan moves on to some relatively low-key discussion of the visit of Eastbourne, which he contextualises as "one of the BIG ones". He then extends a "very special welcome to Bob Brimson who has come in with vitality and energy [he sounds like a shampoo] and who, I know, wants to see the sport move forward in much the same way as we do".

In his column, Jon Cook straightaway mentions the significance of the clash with the Eagles, "tonight's will be a very strange experience for me having headed north to the Hammers this winter but it is a match the whole team know is going to be one of the toughest of the season". Jon imbues the clash with greater significance and subtly writes off the Elite League play-off chances of both teams who'll "look to set down a marker for our KO Cup clashes later in the year, a competition that is both clubs' most realistic chance of a trophy this year". Living as he does on the south coast, all roads lead north for Jon so travel to the real geographic "North" gets another mention when he discusses the narrow defeat that was the trip to Belle Vue. He then also dedicates almost as much space to correcting a "misapprehension" initiated by a report in the *Speedway Star* about the abolition of the "free refreshments" as part of a general clearance of the Lakeside pits during racing as he does to the visit of Eastbourne. This eradication of the "Piccadilly Circus situation" in the Lakeside pits is another part of the increased professionalism the new promotion have brought to so many aspects of their business. Nonetheless, despite press reports, it's a change that has been handled with some sensitivity, so Jon thanks and apologises to "the ladies that did such a sterling job in providing refreshments for the pits [who] were not a problem and were not bothering our boys at inappropriate times".

The widely expected tension of the clash isn't evident on the track but heat 8 represents a real turning point in the contest with the battle between Ryan Fisher and Henning Bager for second place. On the fourth bend of the second lap, a self-induced error has Ryan nearly hit the fence before on the next bend, Henning takes his rival out to the fence in order to pass him before he then accidentally rears to allow the American back through. However, a determined drive to the line sees Bager once again snatch second by a hair's breadth on the finish line to give the Hammers a 5-1 and extend their lead to unassailable levels. Bager becomes a bit of a one-man thorn in the Eagles side when in heat 10 he delays and blocks the Watt-Norris combination sufficiently to allow Adam Shields to escape for an easy victory. The following race features a weird incident that finds Ryan Fisher lapped and thereby eliminated from the race. However, a sudden competitive urge (or, possibly, ignorance of the rules) causes him to abandon the centre green and bizarrely rejoin the race to compete with Joonas Kylmakorpi under the bizarre delusion that this is somehow possible or permissible. If it were possible to be excluded twice Ryan would have managed this feat but instead escapes with a "public warning" from referee Chris Gay because the announcer informs us, "he pulled off the track and pulled back onto the track". There is also much muttering from the crowd - "Ryan Fisher shouldn't have been racing Joonas there as he'd been lapped", is the consensus (albeit without the qualifying adjectives I've deliberately omitted).

Heat 12 has "KK" ride Davey Watt hard to the fence on the fourth bend of the second lap on the way to his race win. It's not something that the Aussie appreciated if judged by his post-race on-track gestures and it's a discussion that he continues once the riders have returned to the pits. The massed ranks of the Eastbourne 'Men in Black' immediately scatter towards the mouth of the pits entrance (if this were the school playground a shout of "bundle!" would have gone up) as riders, staff and mechanics from both teams protectively assert their territorial rights and try to separate the angry and aggrieved parties. Harsh words are the least of the exchanges - even Floppy and Jon Cook suspend their friendship for an alleged frank mutual transfer of opinions - and it's clear if viewed from the terraces that the simmering rivalry has briefly flared into a full-scale display of handbags. Dean Barker looks on nonchalantly and notes pithily, "looks like it's all going on down there!"

During a gap in proceedings Deano keeps his promise ("I might have to have a look at that later") to come over to study my photo book, which he does in the company of the *Speedway Star's* Dave Fairbrother and Glenn, Deano's ex-mechanic, who away from the track is really a bookmaker. Deano already knows my cover girl, Sheila Le-Sage who has been tirelessly committed to the supporters club here for years, "that's Scary and she is Scary. Heart of gold but I gotta say I've seen better!" Deano flicks through the stadium shots ("what an advert for speedway! It ain't Chelsea is it?") to quickly find the images of start line girls ("that's more like it - why don't you do a bird book?") and then also spots a fan he recognises ("you've even got the grumpiest bloke in speedway!"). Glenn is pleased to find a picture of himself ("I was on the phone to a bookmaker") and quick as a flash Deano says to me, "do ya want that signed?" Deano is keen to help me, "I gotta think of someint inspiring for you to do - but I don't know what it is yet! I know why don't you do a book of photos of the tracks?" When he learns it's already been done by the prolific speedway author Robert Bamford and John Jones in their best-selling *Homes of Speedway*, he shrugs and laughs, "I'm full of good ideas!"

The tension from the pits continues onto the track in the next race when a black-and-white helmeted Nicki Pedersen finds himself in a biter bit situation (at the start of the second lap) when a very determined Adam Shields enables the Dane to conduct his own close inspection of the first-bend air fence. It's a manoeuvre that enables both Lakeside riders to escape and relegates Nicki to third, though he soon sets off in swift pursuit. Sadly it's a pursuit that ends in failure when Joonas dramatically falls under pressure from the Dane on the first bend of the last lap. I think Nicki fails to touch Joonas and is the victim of a theatrical 'professional' fall, but afterwards referee Chris Gay assures me that "Nicki definitely touched him; Joonas stayed on before he fell but there was definitely contact". Eastbourne trackshop manager Martin Dadswell was another witness of this incident and reported "He wasn't anywhere near him - Nicki came back to the pits laughing as it was so ridiculous!" Something that isn't a laughing matter is the re-run that sees the Hammers gain an easy 5-1 against Trevor Harding and thereby confirms a victory on the night that is greeted loudly and triumphantly by the home fans. Even though the result is a foregone conclusion, the last heat of the night is still a very competitive affair in the contest for the minor placing after Nicki Pedersen has shot off into the distance. Davey Watt endures another aggressive on-track manoeuvre, this time from Joonas Kylmakorpi who 'cuts off the nose' of the Aussie rider on the exit of the second turn of the first lap. This relegates him to the rear and effectively ends his participation in a drawn heat that finally sees the Hammers win the meeting 54-36.

I gather from the departing Eagles fans that they thought Eastbourne could have mounted more of a challenge. Interviewed over the tannoy, Jon Cook is thoughtful and magnanimous in victory, "the score doesn't do justice to the visitors but we're in this to win matches. I certainly wasn't looking forward to it! At a personal level, my life was at Eastbourne and you just can't erase that overnight". He discusses the fine detail of the win ("it was Adam's best meeting, by far, at home this season") and looks optimistically to the future. Away from the Lakeside stadium microphone, Brian Owen interviews Bob Brimson for tomorrow's edition of the Brighton-based local newspaper, the *Argus*. Bob is in forthright mood, "our riders were extremely unhappy with some of their riders and the general attitude of their promotion. They are a bunch of Big-Time Charlies. I can't wait for them to come down to our place." In reply Jon Cook refuses to be drawn into a stinging reply but instead settles for subtlety, "I think the

Dave, Dean and Glenn

Big-Time Charlies comment was disrespectful to our club but I will let Bob Brimson concentrate on his spin and we will concentrate on winning speedway meetings." He then added, "fair play to the Eagles. They won more races than we did and the result didn't do justice to their performance. They are a better side than some of their fans give them credit for."

15th June Lakeside v Eastbourne (Elite League A) 54-36

Chapter 12. Sittingbourne v Scunthorpe: Gordon for Cardiff

17th June

Jonathan	*"Why is no-one using the 15 metre tactical? Why would they vote it in, if they're not going to use it?"*
Jonathan	*"It's not very good for the sport or the fans - we used to have close meetings, but now we're not having them!"*
Nigel	*"Under 2007 regulations - that option isn't open to them, so they have to go with traditional arrangements"*
Nigel	*"The aggregate bonus point - a SUPERB rule that came in twenty years ago"*
Nigel	*"Under the old system, I think it must be pointed out, this would be the night when Coventry won the league but it means nothing now!"*

Jonathan Green serenades Terry Russell

As ever it is a beautiful sunny day when I arrive at Sittingbourne speedway club. Also as usual I've driven my car across the rutted tracks that lead to the temporary car park in a field and the small knot of chairs that form what counts as the entrance gates of the club. The route across the adjacent fields appears to change slightly every time I come here.

The place is already a hive of activity in the pits, on the track and in the general environs of the club grounds. On the way to the loos I bump into Scunthorpe Scorpions team manager, the endlessly hale and hearty "Kenneth Smith" (as the programme calls him), who's so smartly dressed in jacket, collared shirt and tie that he could easily have just come from conducting some local Sunday School services. He's always affable and chatty whenever I meet him and looks fit and healthy. I mention this only because the *Speedway Star* reported that he's recently 'battled' with cancer. Last time I saw him I studiously didn't mention it - I understand the last thing you need if you have cancer is prurient albeit well-meaning curiosity about the exact details and the present state of play - but this time I do. Kenny makes very light of the situation and appears genuinely embarrassed that public record of the news has somehow made him unnecessarily the centre of attention when his preference would have been to keep it quiet. Almost predictably given his attitude to people and life, he couches his comments in the language of good fortune, opportunity and respect for the skills of all the medical practitioners he met as well as concern for the worry and stress that it's caused his family and friends. He has a strong life force about him and an easy confidence, allied to a self-deprecating sense of humour that can only come naturally rather than be affected. "When the news came out in the *Star*, I didn't know until the phone rang and I was asked if I was selling my Long Track bikes. I'm not but when I asked 'why?' they said, 'well you won't be needing them any more!'" After some more chatter, Kenny bustles off to get on with something he loves and relishes - his speedway duties.

Riders on parade

Smartly dressed Rob Godfrey helps out

After I've set up my table festooned with my new photography book *Shale Britannia* in my traditional place by the disabled access ramp that leads up to the tearoom, I'm ideally placed to consider the bustle of on-track activity that is still taking place just a few minutes before the scheduled start time. It's a position that commands an excellent view of the track itself and the flat marshlands beyond studded with electricity pylons and distant cranes as well as enlivened by the odd passing boat. Sittingbourne announcer and their *Speedway Star* round-up reporter, Derek Barclay, soon bounds by on his way to the commentary position. I eschew the chance to question him about his provocative and erroneous comments about myself on the private members Dons Forum run by Ian Perkin - the man at the helm during the latest, rather sudden, demise of (the Conference League incarnation of) Wimbledon speedway club. I decide silence is the best response to his fallacious claims that he 'knows' I have a "pig hatred" of Wimbledon and so choose to chat idly and, hopefully, sell him a book. Scunthorpe's success over the past two years has made many people resentful of all they've achieved on and off the track. I believe Derek admires the drive and ambition shown by Rob Godfrey and Norman Beeney but, nonetheless, he's in typically waspish mood, "there was a fight last night at Rye - nothing to do with them [Scunthorpe] of course, though they get into fights everywhere! Should I mention the 'Third World track' comment these made about here in your book [*Showered in Shale*]?" I advise Derek against being needlessly albeit playfully antagonistic before he adds, "to be fair to them, they did say that after they'd just had some problems here."

The arrival of Scunthorpe in this part of Kent is greeted with some enthusiasm by the Sittingbourne speedway club - not because they expect to win against such a strong side ("this team would do well in the Premier League") but more that they're notoriously well supported by Conference League standards. They often travel with a good-sized contingent of die-hard Scorpions fans. Whether or not the rumoured coach-load ever arrived I don't know, but judging by the overall crowd numbers I'd say not. A knot of fans of the Lincolnshire club had congregated just in front of my position on the grass banked hillock that overlooks the finish line sandwiched between the portacabin-cum-clubhouse that houses the Crusaders tearoom and the main home-straight grandstand. Further to the left is the thick-walled gun position that houses the commentary-cum-referee's box and the start line, which here is of the staggered variety and placed almost on the fourth corner well behind the finish line. Consequently all races here involve four and one-sixteenth laps. Just before the racing starts, I abandon my pasting table of books and stand behind the gaggle of Scorpions fans. I finally get to meet *Speedway Star* deputy editor, Andrew Skeels - a keen Scunny (football and speedway) fan and recent proud first-time father - who wonders, "will the crowd make three figures?" I then make a complete mess of my programme before the racing has even commenced when Derek Barclay initially mis-announces the Sittingbourne team order. Though he corrects himself moments later, Pavlov's dog like (without the salivation, obviously) I'd already made these erroneous amendments. "That's Derek for you", says keen Scunthorpe fan and Press Officer (and occasional cover there for the Clerk of the Course) Richard Hollingsworth, before he denies the claim that violence marred last night's encounter with Rye House, "it was handbags at the pit gate that's been blown out of all proportion!" Extremely unusually the Scorpions actually lost a meeting - you'd expect this to be the case for most speedway clubs in any league away from home but the strength and dominance of the Lincolnshire club is such that, even away from Normanby Road, such an occurrence still counts as significant news! In fact it is their first defeat of the season, though the 52-41 score made little overall difference as they still progressed to the next round of the Knockout Cup by the comprehensive aggregate score of 100-83.

If bookies were ever to offer odds on the result of a Conference League fixture, then they would have stopped taking bets on this fixture a long time ago. Should Asian betting syndicates ever branch out their activities to include speedway, then they'd probably amuse themselves with the permutations of how many heats out of the fifteen that won't finish as 1-5 results in favour of the visitors. On the expected basis that there will be many such heats in this clash of Conference League team-building philosophies - a match up of David versus Goliath that could be characterised as a difference in time scales since one team is invariably 'riding for improvement' whereas the other is always 'riding for success' - then the initial 2-4 represents a comparative triumph for this afternoon's underdog team.

The Sittingbourne riders are determined to put up some concerted resistance as typified by Aaron Baseby who charges under Scott Richardson on the fourth bend of the third lap of heat 2, thereby painfully trapping his rival's foot in his back wheel. After he's calmly untangled his foot he powers off again to resume his second-place position. The Scunthorpe team is unusually blessed with a couple of riders with the Christian name Scott ('knock, knock' 'who's there?' 'Scott' 'Scott who?' 'Scott nothing to do with you!") and the Baseby family appears to have definitely taken against them. On the first bend of the third heat Mark Baseby collides with the latest Scott to venture upon the track - in this case of the Anderson variety - who in turn continues across the track to wipe out Andre Cross before any of these riders has even managed to reach the apex of the first turn. By dint of his fast gating Richie Dennis somehow avoids the carnage. Looking at the initial scene of devastation, I'm stood by the witty Lynn Hunt who's here with her husband David to watch her son Daniel compete in the second half of the meeting - this features round 2 of the Sittingbourne speedway 'Club Championship'. She tirelessly organised the Shaun Tacey testimonial at Mildenhall last season and pointedly notes that a substantial discrepancy existed between the number of members of the public she herself counted at the meeting (over a thousand) and the formal number as evidenced by the gate receipts actually handed over. This is a crime literally and metaphorically and deprives one of speedway's gentlemen of his just deserts from his testimonial day. We watch as the steward nearest to us - wearing a mysterious 'Crusaders Walking Bus' yellow fluorescent tabard - runs to help the stricken riders closely followed by the medical team. "It's that bend - it's notorious!" remarks Lynn matter of factly. Later the mystery of the tabards is solved when I'm told the 'Walking Bus' scheme is "a local campaign for kids to walk to school and not get driven".

We're also kept entertained by Derek Barclay on his microphone duties who chatters on to fill the time before the re-run "with all four back" called by referee Christina Turnbull. Derek takes it upon himself to spread the milk of human kindness when he loudly and gleefully proclaims, "just to confirm last night's result: Rye House 52, Scunthorpe 41!" The politer Scunny fans close by me say, "Alright! Alright!" while others append more colourful modifiers to their descriptions of him. Lest we doubt his ability to bring the arcane or the obscure to life, Derek highlights the contribution of the *East Kent Gazette* - owners of a handsome advertising sign displayed at the stadium that simply says '*East Kent Gazette*' - "we get excellent coverage every week - it comes out on a Wednesday - they must be doing well since it's the first time I've ever known them to be sold out when I went to the village". We don't learn what else Derek attempted to buy in down-town Sittingbourne, but we do then get treated to some news about the 'Club Championship', "safe to say we hold the most eccentric second half in speedway!" This stream of consciousness from Derek (that he'd have to pay good money to indulge in with a psychoanalyst) is cut short by the riders shuffling about at the start for the re-run of the race. They then hammer off into the distance only to be stopped by the referee putting on the red lights - at a point when Mark Baseby has already reached the third bend in the lead ahead of Richie Dennis. It's a decision greeted with incredulity by Gail Godfrey, the wife of Scunthorpe co-promoter Rob, "What!" she exclaims only to be told by the lady next to her Julie Harrowven (Kenny Smith's partner), "It's Christina Turnbull - she does things like that to keep the meeting closer!" The next re-re-run takes markedly less time to organise and we're treated to Mark Baseby and Richie Dennis aggressively exchanging the

Scunthorpe fans offer words of encouragement

The Hunt family

lead with each other for the first two laps before Mark pulls away to win comfortably. A drawn heat represents a mini-triumph for the Crusaders and Derek delightedly praises the winning youngster with lawyerly precision, "certainly the most exciting rider in the league [lengthy pause] on this track!"

The bowser at Sittingbourne takes the form of a converted transit van with water tanks inside that manically circles the track (driven by Rat usually) spraying its payload liberally on the surface. Consequently, some stray wet shale from the gloopy track surface has sprayed my programme to add to the mess caused by the earlier Derek Barclay inspired team line-ups confusion. Sittingbourne is a track with many varied Arena/Lakeside connections - for example, Graham Arnold is Clerk of the Course in Thurrock - and so it's no surprise to see fans in Arena replica tops or Adrian Kearney stroll by. We briefly chat about some of the controversial incidents from the much-anticipated clash between Lakeside and Eastbourne two days earlier, particularly the Nicki Pedersen exclusion. "I felt sorry for Nicki - Joonas left a huge gap and fair enough Nicki did catch his front wheel, more of a touch really, but Joonas went down dramatically." When I wondered if the quoted attendance figures were borne out by what I saw, Adrian reassures me that they were packed in like penguins under the roof of the home-straight grandstand.

Mark Baseby doesn't get to show his speed round the circuit when he lifts at the start of heat 5 and then watches Josh Auty live up to his reputation with a win by a country mile in the fastest time of the day. Later in heat 11, more used to conditions and with even more appropriate bike set up, Josh wins in an even faster time. A third successive 5-1 for the visitors has Dean Felton admonish himself profusely when he fails to catch the Cockle-Richardson partnership. Dean's profile in the programme lists his "inspiration" as "winning" and his "best speedway moment" as "any time I win a race", but with the Scorpions in town a couple of second places is as good as it gets this afternoon. Heat 7 starts with the drama of an exclusion for Jon Stevens and ends with an awarded race when Scott Anderson falls for the second time on the third bend. This decision gifts Sittingbourne number 5, Gordon Meakins, his only points of the afternoon. The chances of the Crusaders minimising the differential in the scoreline aren't helped by mechanical difficulties and in the next race an engine failure for Joe Reynolds before he reaches the start line has him excluded under the two-minute time allowance. Keen to make no more errors in my programme and with my brain not starting like Joe's bike, I absent-mindedly but stupidly turn to Lynn and say, "do I put an EF in my programme for that?" This is a cue for great hilarity, "no it's an 'x' - how long have you been going to speedway, Blondie?" News that it's 32 years doesn't help regain my long-lost authority.

Sittingbourne send out Mark Baseby in a black-and-white helmet colour in heat 9 and this race is stopped almost as soon as it starts, ostensibly for a fall by Scott Richardson on the second bend that has Julie Harrowven exclaim, "She didn't need to do that!" (imagining he was just about to be excluded). The dulcet tones of Derek Barclay soon come over the crackly tannoy to explain the rationale behind the referee's decision: "The red light was put on before the rider fell 'cause the ref wants to warn the rider in green [Cockle] for moving at the start". It's a reprieve for Mark Baseby as he was third when the race was stopped and in the re-run this improves to a second place that ties the heat score at four each. Derek relates the result as though this represents some sublimated form of triumph for the Crusaders and gets so carried away he's back on the tannoy moments later to say, "the winning time, I forgot to give you".

Dean Felton nearly fulfils his stated speedway aspirations when he leads heat 10 for a couple of laps before Richie Dennis finds a way past him. The tapes fly up and the riders roar away at the start of heat 11 only for the red light to be immediately illuminated. Derek informs us, it has been halted "for movement at the start". This is news that Julie greets with disbelief, "she's getting like Barbara Horley!" This race features Gordon Meakins who flatters to deceive according to Lynn Hunt, "Gordon only races for two and half laps then he coasts. He bought Joe Screen's last season stuff but I reckon he's frightened to use it - most kids would kill to have it but can't afford to!" The race ends with the sixth 5-1 of the meeting for the visitors and starts a sequence of five consecutive maximum heat wins. They're helped in this achievement by a collision between Aaron Baseby and Andre Cross worthy of the Keystone Cops that has Andre excluded (and throw his goggles to the shale in exasperation) and the race awarded. A lady called Helen has won a copy of my book in the raffle and asks me to sign it - I manage to continue with my errors when I sign my own signature correctly but sadly misspell 'congratatulations'.

Dean Felton wins an exclusion for an elegant fall on the third bend of the first lap of heat 13 and Gordon evades crashing into him by the cunning tactic of lagging behind the field, "Gordon managed to stop because he wasn't hard up behind!" Only a tear in the space-time continuum will probably see him ride to a maximum in any meeting but the prospect of a re-run with only three riders - Auty, Cockle and Meakins - doesn't thrill Lynn, "gonna be a close race then!" She playfully continues, "It ensures Gordon will get another point!" I playfully suggest that I'll start my own variation on the 'Back the Brits' campaign, namely "Gordon for Cardiff GP reserve!" The expected 5-1 duly arrives and has Derek Barclay try to salvage some local pride by clutching at more verbal straws over the tannoy, "Josh's time was a slow one there". With the score poised at 22-58 I say to Lynn, "it's closer than I thought". A fair comment to my mind in view of the widely predicted massacre of 15-75 but another cause for hilarity with Lynn who takes great delight in my Murray Walker-esque malapropisms. The spirit that is the Sittingbourne approach to speedway is typified by the choice of Aaron Baseby to ride in heat 15. With the result of the meeting long since decided rather than try to massage the overall final score line, the club prefer to give Aaron Baseby more big race experience against the Scorpions Josh Auty-Joe Haines combination. It's something Derek Barclay announces in trademark fashion, "yes it's Aaron - unusual to put a reserve in heat 15" he says, ignoring that the visitor's Joe Haines is also a reserve.

Lynn savours the Conference League clash but is really here to watch her son Daniel (21) race and when he comes back in his race gear she asks, "are you a Knight or a Lancer?" She sums up the life of a speedway mum briskly, "he always thinks with his head in the first race but then he grew up with grass track and speedway with his dad. At 11, he kept hassling all the time - just what I didn't want - and at 16 Mervyn Cox at the Eastbourne junior track said 'he's got talent'. He's worked so hard to pay for it all - he's bought Shaun's [Tacey] bike and he's just bought an Adam Allott bike. Each week he does something that cost £200-£300 to put right but that's speedway for you. Shaun keeps saying to him 'sell the bikes 'cause you got a decent job' - he's just done the flooring at the Festival Hall and he earns more than Shaun did last season. He's had one ride for Arena in the Academy League - they ran out of time and lacked first aid cover - and then heard nothing until he found out they use Mark and Aaron Baseby. It's now got to the stage where he now realises it's a hobby whereas before it was his dream!"

On the subject of dreams, the Scunthorpe riders have come out on their bikes for a victory parade to celebrate their convincing triumph. One of those on a machine is Kenny Smith who cuts an incongruously dashing figure in collared shirt, jacket flapping along with his ponytail. He pootles past grinning broadly and smirkingly catches the eye of his partner Julie Harrowven stood on the grass hillock in the knot of Scunny supporters, "that was to wind me up 'cause I told him I don't want to push him in a wheelchair!" The backstory, as they've started to say in fashionable media circles nowadays, is slightly complicated since it mixes Kenny's desire to show he has beaten his illness and pay tribute to a deceased young rider and his family. "He often says to me 'I just want to ride four laps'. He wants to ride in the David Nix memorial meeting - 'cause he was there that night - but when he

Jacketed Kenny Smith on victory parade

had his glands out it weakened a plated shoulder. He'll make light of it and I know how good he is on a bike but if he needed to correct things, he'd be too weak to do it since the operation and that's what I worry about!"

Sadly I have to leave before the second half starts. One can't help but ponder on the fact that if Sittingbourne could secure more sponsorship - from fans and local companies alike (as well as the sports' authorities I'd suggest) - they could have the real recognition and reward that their efforts so rightly deserve. Particularly when you consider the amount of talent they have found and developed for the 'better off' teams over the years. I had hoped to see a few races but when I left the bowser transit was circling the track. Lynn fills me in on the remainder of the afternoon later, "Daniel only scored three had two crashes as the track was balder than Uncle Fester and they just watered the blue groove (interesting), his last race was good with riders flying everywhere due to track conditions, luckily nobody was hurt and the most damage sustained was the bum he ripped in his race suit, I think he still has all the skin he started with on his posterior thanks to the sacrifice of the seat of his pants!"

As I leave towards the car park I come across Adrian Kearney who marvels at how the Sittingbourne club manages to survive, "it's a real struggle to keep going here. The hours Graham does - though he doesn't like to talk about it - is unbelievable and so many others dedicate themselves. This is a hard man's sport! Today's meeting showed the difference in levels in this league, never mind to the others. They could have done better but their heads dropped but they shouldn't see it as a disgrace." Afterwards, the *Speedway Star* notes that the 24-68 score is believed to establish a new record score for a home defeat. In the car park, I bump into Kenny Smith lurking by his car, charming as ever, I gather he's really determined to take to the track, "I was team manager at King's Lynn the night David [Nix] got killed. I want to do four laps at the testimonial - I've got metal all over my body and a plated shoulder from the last one, but I want to ride!"

17th June Sittingbourne v Scunthorpe (Conference League) 24-68

Chapter 13. Sheffield v Birmingham: "The track's good, mate – I think we're gonna get a track record tonight!"

21st June

It's Midsummer's Day when I arrive at Owlerton Stadium in Sheffield, though with the thick dark clouds overhead it looks nothing like it. Neil Machin is ensconced in the speedway office with the ladies who work there with him and all of them are smoking like crazy. I suggest that they get a sign that says, 'Thank You for Smoking' and I quickly gather that they view the impending smoking ban as another example of the creeping tentacles of the 'Nanny State'. The office has a new glass door of the kind people have fitted to their patio extensions, except this one is frosted and has a speedway rider emblazoned on it. Not that many people are coming through the door at this time of the afternoon with over five hours to go before the scheduled start time. However, they are ringing up constantly to check on the weather and the likelihood of the meeting going ahead. Part of the job of a promoter on race day is to take on the role of glorified but unpaid weatherman. Some promoters are allegedly not always completely honest when it comes to relaying track and weather conditions to the curious punters. Neil is from a much more straightforward school that tells it bluntly as it is. Albeit tinged with optimism as well as a tried and tested repertoire of stock phrases that he's honed over the years. These practised statements tell you everything and nothing, plus they can be interpreted both ways.

I can only hear one side of the conversation as I stand sipping my black tea at the office counter cum half partition wall that separates the enquiring hordes from the inner sanctum of the office proper.

"When God waters our track he does it evenly!"

"I can't comment on the weather where you are - but here we haven't had a drop!"

"We have a few dark clouds but the forecast is showers and our track will soak it up."

"The track's good, mate - I think we're gonna get a track record tonight!"

The suggestion by Neil (said in a slightly hushed voice as though imparting confidential information) that the track record might get broken is a psychological masterstroke and powerfully suggestive to any waverers who call. It's notoriously fast at Owlerton anyway (the front of the free programme proudly announces "Welcome to the Fastest Track in Britain"), so the prospect of lightning-fast racing and broken track records should be enough to tempt anyone out. Neil suggests this often and confidently, but between calls he tells, "half the time the people who ring up have more or less decided not to come anyway, though what the weather's doing at their place is irrelevant to what's going on here - it can rain sometimes quarter of a mile away and yet we get nothing. Or vice versa. So if it's raining in Rotherham, I don't farking care! It did rain heavily here last week when we had the 'Top Gun' meeting. In fact last Thursday was the second wettest day in the last 140 years - we got three and half inches of rain". I have so much time that I decide to head off into town and leave Neil to tell all callers about the possible fall of the track record - jointly held by Simon Stead (8th August 2004) and Chris Holder (12th October 2006) of 59.5 seconds - and to allow all the members of the office to continue their marathon Olympic standard smoke in. Neil asks if I find myself a brolly to buy him a large

Optimistic fans muster

Impressive machinery trundles past

black-and-white umbrella if I see one on sale, "we have all the other colours for the start girls but we're missing that one for the tactical rides." Given the size and the speed of the track at Sheffield, many teams struggle to assert themselves over the dominance of the home riders and, invariably, they soon find themselves having to explore their tactical ride options in order to try to keep the score line close. So I'm sure the absence of said brolly is apparent to any keen-eyed observer around heat six or seven most weeks.

When I stay in Sheffield I always stay at the nearby Garrison Hotel. They have special room rates for speedway fans if you ask them, it's warmly welcoming in a typically slightly distant South Yorkshire way and the rooms are comfortable with good facilities (tea and coffee making stuff plus a good quality telly with a reasonable range of satellite channels). Breakfast is served until late and it's really close to a large Morrisons supermarket and a drive-in McDonald's so some ends of the culinary spectrum are handily catered for. It is also pretty handy for the Sheffield Supertram and, obviously, the speedway (and greyhounds). However, one thing it doesn't have - like many other parts of the city it will transpire over the next week or so - are drains able to cope with the monsoon-like deluge that blasts in for 15 minutes or so. You genuinely have to go to more tropical climes to experience the level of rainfall that hits the hotel and this part of South Yorkshire. The walkways are soon temporarily flooded along with the car park and the rain cascades off every surface. Hopefully, the legendary drains and absorbent shale of the track will cope easily but I worry that this book sales trip might suddenly prove fruitless. Unbeknownst to me at this point, less than a quarter of a mile away the back straight has flooded.

Though the velocity of the rain lessens considerably, I decide against a trip into town in the drizzle so the speedway club will have to remain without a black-and-white coloured brolly suitable for tactical rides. Given their notoriety round the Owlerton circuit, it will be a rare occasion indeed that you ever see a Sheffield rider don this helmet colour. When I return, Neil remains as I left him - in the speedway office with his ear glued to the constantly ringing phone with a cigarette burning in the ashtray. With most callers, he acknowledges the sharp bout of "heavy rain" but still maintains a relentlessly optimistic outlook regarding a possible alteration in the track record. We have a brief conversation that ranges widely over many issues within speedway - from performance-enhancing drugs ("cannabis isn't going to help your performance but cocaine is") to problems in the 2007 Elite League ("some people have a cost base that doesn't match their revenues and that's a problem for them in that league") and even referees. Despite his recent £300 fine (from referee Graham Flint for foul and abusive behaviour at Edinburgh), Neil maintains he's still "always happy to have honest discussions with referees".

Because of the dark clouds and the forecast threat of further rain, I decide to pitch my stall next to Mick Gregory's trackshop based under the spacious roofed grandstand of the home straight. His merchandise is already neatly set out over a number of tables and various items of Tigers and Wulfsport branded clothing are now on temporary hangers on the glass windows of the grandstand building itself. My just published photography book *Shale Britannia* is closely studied by Mick and the friendly Sheffield co-promoter (and one half of the race-night presentation team), Dave Hoggart (who's in his first season actually holding the management reins of a speedway club). They intently study the whole book but the photo of a smiling Mick Gregory stood by his stall catches their eyes. "Somebody must have £100 to catch me smiling like that!" claims Mick. It's a claim Dave only too readily confirms, "he must have been counting the money!" Discussions then turn to the start line girls pictured in my book, "you ain't got any of our start tarts in there have you? They're as tough as nails and have had more pricks than a second-hand dartboard." They are interrupted by a man who's determined to quiz Dave and get to the bottom of the "real reasons why the ELRC has moved from here to King's Lynn so suddenly - I don't believe it's the 'technical reasons' it says it is on the BSPA site. What is it really?" Dave plays a straight bat and refuses to answer any of the questions, discuss the relative merits of air fences (the alleged reason for the change is that King's Lynn now have one - rumoured to be the one previously used during the defunct Elite League incarnation of Oxford - and Sheffield very obviously from where I'm stood, very much doesn't) or go into specifics but eventually offers the thought, "It's bollocks!" Dave appears much more worried by the impact of the behaviour of rival promotions on the club, "We can take anything but a rise in our costs due to the incompetence of others!" The answer is more prosaic as a glance at clause 9.2.1 (a) in the SCB Rulebook shows that an approved inflatable fence is mandatory for all Elite League meetings. So, the ELRC is clearly an 'Elite' meeting, notwithstanding concerns expressed by the SRA that riding without one would set a dangerous precedent.

The turnstiles open on time and some of the keener members of speedway's watching fraternity make their way to their favoured spots on the terracing opposite the start line or adjacent to the pits. The other half of the speedway race-night presentation team, Shaun Leigh, wanders past my table a short while later. He remains confident that the meeting will go ahead, "It's a bit wet on the second bend" he notes with some understatement given the very visible, large puddle there a short while earlier, "but after a couple of races it'll be okay". With nothing to do and potentially nothing to see, many people are in philosophical mode. "I went to speedway lots in the 60s and 70s" says one man before he proudly adds, "and now I'm a returnee these last couple of years. I just love the speed and excitement. I've no interest in motorbikes but speedway is different but, like all things, politics spoils it." It's a theme echoed by the next man who lingers for a chat by my table, "I've been coming 60 years and seen lots of changes - all for the worse! Each year they change the rules and they [the promoters] wait until the new rules come out and try to bend them without thinking. Their job is to promote the sport not drive people away. I've been chatting to Paul Cooper [the Sheffield reserve] and he says it'll be on once they scrape the surface 'cause it's okay beneath!" Whenever there's a hold up or delay at any speedway meeting it's important that something is seen to be happening, even if it really accomplishes nothing. This is particularly true when fans wait with varying degrees of patience for the drizzle to stop or subside. At Sheffield they use giant-sized equipment appropriate to the proud industrial heritage of the area to create the effect of concerted effort. So on the track itself, we witness a giant red super-grader - that looks like it should be involved creating new roads or railways - which slowly and inexorably circles the track. Notionally it's attempting to remove the sodden shale but, instead, appears to be slowly scoring problematically deep grooves into the already completely soaked surface.

Sadly all hope of any racing taking place disappears in the continuous drizzle that sets in strongly once the turnstiles opened. The meeting is formally abandoned at 8 p.m. and, given the appalling conditions the first leg of this fixture was held in at Perry Barr for the benefit of the *Sky* cameras, there is some truth in the opinion I hear as departing fans pass by my table towards the car park, "it always has to rain for Birmingham meetings!" For any promoter, it's a tricky situation to judge correctly - you're damned if you do and damned if you don't - especially when the sky is overcast and rain is forecast. If they keep the turnstiles shut, the fans get disgruntled in the car park and if they open them and subsequently postpone the fixture, the fans get disgruntled in the stadium on the terraces or in the bar. It also creates an additional problem for the promotion in that anyone who has paid to get in, then owns an admission ticket that is valid for readmission at the next three meetings, so takings from those meetings will be reduced by the number of notionally 'free' admittances. Mick Gregory takes an old-fashioned and slightly morose but pragmatic view, "next time it rains or looks like rain, no one will come 'cause of what happened tonight!" Nonetheless, there is general incredulity among some members of the track staff at the news that Graham Trollope (pronounced tree-lope-pee) had watered the track that morning despite the forecast of rain, "I think he just loves riding in that machine [the bowser] - he must have an

Track TLC continues

orgasm each time!"

With the track record resolutely unbroken and all the fixed costs (and many of the variable ones) of staging a meeting incurred, Neil Machin isn't a happy smoker in the speedway office, "Fark! Fark! Fark!" he says angrily to no one in particular even though his recently retired ex co-promoter Malcolm Wright is just taking his leave from the room, "I will see you in two weeks - enjoy the wonderful world of speedway!" Unluckily for the promotion, and for me, having travelled 250 miles, this is the only Midsummer's Day speedway meeting in the country that is lost to the weather. Sod's Law dictates that the moment the abandonment is announced the sky will immediately brighten - and so it proves tonight as I pack away my things. Without seeing a wheel turned even in practice, I retire back to the comfort of the Garrison Hotel, vaguely content in the knowledge that I have sold nine books. A total that is many more than I sell at some tracks that have actually managed to stage a meeting!

21st June Sheffield v Birmingham (Premier League) - postponed rain

Chapter 14. Edinburgh v Redcar: Mood darkens under blackening Armadale skies

22nd June

The drive to Edinburgh allows me the chance to call in at the Wooley Edge services on the M1, where Area Manager Rob Grant (no relation to the speedway rider, I imagine) warmly welcomes visitors with a sign on the wall. The gents toilet here was nominated for the 'Loo of the Year Awards' in 2003 but things must have dramatically declined since then. Next door in the ladies facility standards have apparently been maintained if judged by the fact that their loo also has award plaques from 2003 to 2007 prominently displayed on the wall outside is anything to go by. All roads lead to Edinburgh or, at least, that's the way it seems on the congested roads north. The weather remains fair until around about the Berwick on Tweed area, when the A1 suddenly becomes enveloped in a misty fog (along with some drizzly rain) that comes straight from film casting central. It doesn't bode well for the prospects of the meeting between the Edinburgh Monarchs and the Redcar Bears going ahead tonight. Once I've negotiated the jammed M8, I find myself outside the resolutely locked gates of Armadale Stadium under fine skies except for some really high cloud. Through the gates I can see that there now appears to be a large vacant area that was once occupied by the alternative entrance turnstiles that I think the sponsors used to use. Later I learn that the club have decided that only having one entrance ensures everyone who should pay pays and everyone who's a sponsor or guest of the club still gets in for free, but without confusion.

I only have to wait a short while before the gates are unlocked and, along with some other people who've gathered at the bars of the gates, I'm allowed through its portals. Before long I get to chat with the friendly but slightly taciturn Edinburgh co-promoter,

4077 M.A.S.H. Meets Armadale

Panoramic view of both sponsors lounges

John Campbell. The club had suffered their first low attendance of the season last week for the meeting against Newport. No real travelling support was expected but "due to heavy rain in the east" crowd numbers fell below normal/standard levels and, consequently, so did revenues through the turnstiles. It's a shortfall that meant the club failed to break even on the night and is something, John notes matter of factly, "we're not gonna get back!" The weather is a topic of conversation on everyone's lips and many take the chance to call the speedway office to find out the present situation or to confirm their prejudices. "People ring up and I always say we have two chances - It's on or it's off. I think they just want confirmation of their own decision not to come half the time". At that moment we're interrupted by the arrival of SCB Official Jim McGregor, who's wearing his official SCB jacket and carries an important-looking briefcase. John fills him in on the broad-brush detail of the Monarch's defeat the previous night in Redcar, "anyone who goes there when Josh Auty rides for them [at reserve] will lose as he's pretty good!" Once Jim and John have exchanged further information and pleasantries, John returns to the theme of the weather and its deleterious impact on attendances, "[last night] people kept saying to Chris van Straaten he was 'lucky' that the rain held off and the meeting ran but he knew that he'd lost three or four hundred 'cause of the poor weather in the local area!"

Many fans think they know best how to promote any club or the sport and (according to John) this is an outlook that afflicts many newcomers to speedway, particularly on the promotional side of the fence, "New promoters come in and think if they spend a thousand pounds on some advertising and run a board around town that the crowds will flood in - of course, they don't! Getting ten new speedway fans to come along is always the hardest thing to do." John is very proud of the support and effort on behalf of the Monarchs by his volunteers at the club and when a man in overalls nods as he passes, John sings his praises, "that's our raker - he's a Glasgow fan - comes a long way to get here. He volunteered for the dirtiest job, I'm very grateful for his help and I'm not going to say no. So many clubs have unsung people behind the scenes who make it tick - often the fans don't see or notice them, but they're vital to making many clubs work week in and week out." He's also been very impressed with Lee Complin, "I don't know if you know him. He just rode for us at Newport and tried really hard. He was keen to ride in heat 15 too. It was a hot day and he'd already had six - so most guests wouldn't be fussed - but when Ronnie [Correy] asked him which gate he wanted he said, 'it doesn't matter 'cause I'm going to win anyway'. Of course, we sorted out some tactics - Ronnie would clamp Morris down on the inside and he'd escape round the outside. And that's how it worked out. Jim McGregor said 'he's the best I've seen anyone ride Newport in ten years'. We did invite him to ride for us again but I had to ring back and tell him that we couldn't honour the booking 'cause Matthew [Wethers] had recovered from injury. It was disappointing for him 'cause he's so keen but, you'll never guess what, he said, 'thank you for Sunday!' How many would think to say that? We'll definitely book him again if we can."

Rider wages is another topic dear to John's heart, specifically the strict control of them. "So many get spoilt with the crazy money! It's always best to send them to Buxton as they pay nothing and then he'll always be grateful to come here." Nonetheless, natural parsimoniousness aside, the level of wages paid out in the Elite League really shocks him, "Even Theo was on £XXX a point when he was at Wolverhampton. He's the sort of rider who gets nothing or might get a maximum [incredulous pause] imagine paying £YYYY to Theo!" Since we're stood close by the safety fence we can see the bowser slowly make its way round the circuit, "there's always a point when you have to water the track to get the meeting on even if you think it's going to rain. People hate the dust more than they do a track that's too wet. At Berwick, people come dressed up to go out in Berwick afterwards - for whatever they have there - and with the curfew they know it won't be too late before they get into town. Getting covered in dust means they won't come back!" John bustles off to ensure everything is as it should be at the entrance gates before they officially open to admit the public. As he heads away, some members of the track staff wander by and one man stops to laughingly say, "put down how handsome the track staff are here!" walks a pace or two and turns to add, "oh, and how hard working."

Stood by my table of books, I don't sell that many but people often stop to share their opinions. One of these is local author Gary Lough, who penned the really enjoyable *10th yer Baws*! - his blunt account of the recent (ish) championship winning season for the Monarchs. Gary predicts a close scoreline of 46-44, though afterwards I realise I'm not exactly sure if he meant the Monarchs or the Bears would triumph. Earlier his father had passed and sympathised about the piles of stock that any author inevitably gets landed after the publication of their book. While I wait for sales that never quite come, once a few people have sauntered off to their favoured viewing positions the sky darkens appreciably, roughly 40 minutes before the tapes are due to rise. A man stops to inform me, "We lost 51-40 without that twat [Henrik] Moller - he's invented an injury after he got 13 paid 15 in Denmark, just 'cause he wants to ride in Italy in the Under 21". It sounds a fair enough ambition to me, though having to resort to deception isn't so helpful. After he's got that off his chest and various other complaints about the composition of the present Monarchs team this man then acknowledges, "it's hard to attract decent riders up here!" Another man who introduces himself is that doyen of the Scots speedway scene, Dick Barrie, who looks forward to the 40th anniversary celebration meeting at Berwick. An event where the "field will be drawn from nine nations". He likes my photography book, "I can tell what is going on in most places as I've been involved - but many people who buy wouldn't have any idea at all".

The meeting gets underway promptly at the allotted time and before that happens we learn from the announcer, "there's no parade tonight due to the forecast of heavy rain." He then runs through the team and mentions the apparently controversial absence of Henrik Moller who "picked up a midweek injury in Denmark". The meeting opens with three drawn heats, all of which are with some interest. In the opening heat Gary 'Havvy' Havelock emphasises his superiority at this level when he scythes under Theo Pijper on the second bend before he smoothly continues to win effortlessly. Matthew Wethers leads the second heat twice - the first time out the race is stopped when Jack Roberts takes his duties to delay the chasing pack too seriously - he appeared to get stuck in each and every corner - and is excluded for his troubles after a three-rider pile up on the apex of the third and fourth bends. Wethers then gates again to win comfortably but it's also noticeable that Josh Auty appears to stutter on his bike in most corners as though an invisible ghostly impediment kept delaying his progress by repeatedly getting in his way. The third heat has James Grieves withstand initial pressure from Ronnie Correy (before he falls away) to win easily in a race notable for a pearler of a fall by Chris Kerr.

The contours of the track appears to cause some of the visiting riders problems and the fourth heat sees Matt Tresarrieu rear massively at the gate and then nearly go massively out of control on the fourth bend but just about manage to hang on. The Monarchs record a 5-1 in this race to establish an early 4-point lead. To my mind the ambient temperatures have started to cool. Nonetheless, Monarchs co-promoter John Campbell is apparently oblivious to the cold in his white short-sleeved collared shirt and appears to be absolutely everywhere in the stadium at once. One minute he's by the pits entrance on bend 4, during heat 2 he's on the centre green and by heat 5 he's on the perimeter of the first bend apparently watching the crowd and not the racing. You don't have to listen hard in the crowd to hear the grumbles of discontent about the application and ability of Ronnie Correy and, with the arrival of heat 5, these complaints progress from a gentle susurration to gale force. Ronnie outgates Havvy but,

Fans mingle on first bend

since he appears completely content to occupy mid track position into the bend, Havvy is able to easily and imperiously blast round the outside for a comfortable victory.

We soon learn from the meeting announcer, Scott Wilson, about "Ian J Brown and company - the accountant sponsors of heat 6". Referee Jim McGregor must still be drinking in this exciting news (or having a 'senior moment') because he seems totally oblivious to a third-bend third-lap fall for Josh Auty, who luckily manages to clear the track by a whisker after some struggle to retrieve his bike. Scott has an obsession with the use of the trope "separated from" to describe the race positions in every race and, from this point onwards, it is usually the Monarchs riders who find themselves separated from the Bears. Indeed, from this stage of the meeting onwards, the home riders only manage to win one more race and fail to record any heat advantages. The Bears start to claw back the overall deficit when "Armadale specialist and former home boy James Grieves" gates from the inside and proceeds to aggressively drive wide under Matthew Wethers who, sensibly, slows slightly to avoid catastrophe.

In the absence of excitement on the track for the Monarchs fans, meeting presenter Scott Wilson tries to stir up the thrill level with talk of the innovative fund raising scheme they have at every meeting here at Armadale - "the Monarchs Golden Double". For a £1 stake, you can win an "accumulator prize" if you correctly guess the correct result (in helmet colour sequence) of heats 2, 8 and 13. Statistically, this is a difficult thing to achieve, though if you don't fancy the chances of winning this you can also bet on the meeting result (maximum bet £10 with odds displayed on "betting boards"). In one of the chosen races, although it's still only his second away meeting of the season, Josh Auty shows the speedway intelligence that has justifiably garnered him many plaudits in his brief career so far, when he rides an exceptional opening lap. Mostly he evades some determinedly belligerent-cum-hard-riding from Derek Sneddon before Josh, somehow, bravely squeezes past on the second bend of the second lap to escape to a well-deserved victory. Scott marvels and looks for explanations at the same time, "he does know what it's like here after the Under 15 Championship, so he knows his way round!" A few heats later Scott amuses us with his pronunciation of Redcar's exotically named Arlo Bugeja ("AR-LOW BIG-E-GAYJAH"), who rides to an unwanted negative maximum - zero - on his first ever visit to Armadale stadium.

A brief interview with Havvy enlivens things between races. We quickly learn (at length) that injuries have blighted the Redcar season so far ("one after each other we've all been injured"). We also gather that he thinks highly of the work of Armadale (and Monmore Green) track curator, the plain spoken Alan 'Doc' Bridgett, "if more tracks round the country were like this we'd have more exciting speedway!" A run of four drawn heats ends with heat 12, though it's a race more notable for a fourth-bend crash for Matthew Wethers that elicits a scream at the moment of impact from a sympathetic but worried fan in the crowd. My view - down the sight line provided by the safety fence itself - enabled me to watch Matthew's head and neck get violently thrown by the velocity of his impact into and over the top of the fence, almost as though his neck was spring loaded. "Good news, Matty is fully conscious and has indicated his injuries to the medical staff. We're just getting the backboard as a precaution!" Rumour soon sweeps the terrace that he's ruptured his knee ligaments badly, though quite how people can claim to know this stood on the terraces I just don't know. Theo Pijper is interviewed to pass the time and he notes with some understatement, "the track is inconsistent on the outside and, if you hit it wrong, it can launch you!"

After I retreat from the pits, I watch the remainder of the meeting on the second bend favoured by long-time Monarchs fan Dougie Copland. He's not overly impressed with the team this season and has a particular animus towards Ronnie Correy, whom he suspects doesn't really give his all for his latest club. "When there's a young, wild rider he just hangs back and looks down at his machine. Not to vary your tactics four laps out of four is poor. If you visit here, you just know what they [the Edinburgh riders] are going to do before they do it! Henrik is one of those guys with so much talent but doesn't show it. He is very capable of beating most of the top European riders abroad but at the same time be pretty hopeless on British soil. Equipment and preparation play a vital part in any rider's make up. Apart from Matthew Wethers, though, no one got in amongst them. I suppose we've been spoilt when you think of the riders we've had over the years. Ronnie Correy was once a great international speedway rider in the 1980s and 1990s but has now reached the end of his career and should know it's time to pack it in. Peter Carr and Kenny McKinna, two Monarchs legends, knew when to stop - still at the top! Sure Ronnie looks like he should be going fast, almost spectacular sometimes - he's got all the right mannerisms and gestures - but watch, he never gains on the rider ahead of him!" Later in heat 15, Dougie points out to me, "Ronnie can make this look really good here - he's going way out high but he's going nowhere!" It's definitely a dispiriting end to the contest for the home support as Redcar run away with the last three heats 5-13 to win the meeting (and the bonus point) at a canter 40-50. The Monarchs fans under the low roof of the grandstand on the back straight show their disapproval, "look at them booing Pijper and giving him the finger!" Another disgruntled man stops by my display table as he leaves and says sarcastically, "you should have taken a photo of them pretending to be heat leaders!"

22nd June Edinburgh v Redcar (Premier League) 40-50

Chapter 15. Berwick: "Get a photo of Rob 'cause your mum used to fancy him"

23rd June

SKYBALLS ON TRACKS

Jonathan	*"Track conditions are good - this rain has actually helped!"*
Floppy	*"Rain - a natural way of watering it"*
Jonathan	*"We'll have more talk about the track in a moment"*
Kelvin	*"If it stops raining it will only get better, if it continues it will get greasy"*
Jonathan	*"The track's still a bit greasy - we've had a lot of wet rain!"*
Sarra Elgan	*"Jason, the tracks looking patchy".*
Jase	*"It is very patchy - good way to describe it!"*
Kelvin [sympathises with God]	*"It's a bit of a track creator's nightmare!"*
Kelvin	*"There's really a strong wind here tonight Sam, how's that gonna affect track conditions?"*
Sam	*"I think it's gonna play a big part."*
Kelvin	*"Track conditions change as the seasons change"*
Jonathan [at Isle of Wight]	*"It's a very big track"*
Kelvin	*"Yes - it's a very physical track, quite wavy"*
Jonathan	*"Is the track improving?"*
Kelvin	*"No, it's staying very similar"*
Jonathan	*"Why have they created the adverse camber?"*
Jonathan	*"What does a rider like?"* [in a track]
Kelvin	*"The rider likes what he's given every week"*

They say the line between success and failure is a fine distinction that is easily crossed. If that's the case then the Berwick Bandits appear to have simultaneously killed an albatross and run over a black cat as it's only a couple of seasons ago that they nearly won the Premier League. Since then a rip in the space-time continuum or, more likely, a slight tightening of the purse strings, has seen a chasm open up of massive proportions that such aspirations of championship success seems like a distant dream to loyal Bandits fans. They've had to suffer watching their team stumble from one defeat to another at Shielfield in recent weeks (against Somerset, King's Lynn and Glasgow) and, if they travelled, they got to see the team monstered on the road away from the Borders. With title dreams already definitively at an end, the chance to celebrate the history and longevity of the club at its 40th anniversary meeting is a welcome distraction and promises to be a night of great nostalgia.

The individual meeting to be staged in celebration is really incidental in comparison to a gathering of many riders who have thrilled the fans over the past four decades (albeit not continuously) in the Bandits black and yellow colours. The advance publicity suggested that "100 former Black & Gold Bandits were expected to make the trip", some from great distance, and these invitees included notable riders such as Doug Wyer, Maury Robinson, Jim McMillan, Bruce Cribb, Graham Jones, Richard Knight and Alan Mogridge as well as ex-promoters Kenny Taylor and Davie Fairbairn. Nostalgic recollection is hard wired into any speedway fan, so the chance to socialise and chat with the heroes of your youth or middle age should prove irresistible. Perpetually cheerful Berwick promoter, Peter Waite, confidently expects a "great night" and notes, "for once everyone can forget about all the problems we are having on the track and celebrate 40 years of speedway at Berwick". Sadly for all concerned, the weather gods have decreed otherwise. When I arrive at the compact rather old-fashionedly beautiful stadium that houses the speedway club as the tenant of Berwick Rangers Football Club (known as the Duckets due to sheltered stand on the back straight), the wet drizzly weather appears to have set in for the day and only a supreme optimist would expect the clouds to lift. Luckily that person is on hand in the form of the diminutive and usually perma-tanned Peter Waite, who this afternoon is smartly dressed in the brightly coloured 40th Anniversary commemorative club anorak (£45 from the track and available in bigger sizes too). Ever one to look on the bright side, the anniversary meeting has coincided with some shock speedway film news that has caught the attention of the national press. "We got a whole half page in the Scottish Sun and 10 minutes on the radio, which should attract a big crowd if the rain holds off!" In the press, Peter speaks film lingo and so stresses the "boost the club and the district will get once this movie hits the big silver screens globally". Perhaps notable international film stars like Jude Law or George Clooney can be persuaded to put themselves on the map further by associating themselves with Berwick.

After quizzing a number of people about the exact details of the film, I gather it will be called "3456" - a brave or brilliant choice of film title depending on your point of view. It will tell the life story of ex-Bandits rider Lex Milloy who retired from the sport after three seasons when a crash saw him break his thigh. He then went on to have a successful career as a movie stunt man and has now finally brought to fruition his dream to make a "full length motion picture". Filming is due to start shortly ("on location") at the club and take place from mid-July and during August when it is hoped to recreate speedway footage to represent the glory days of the 60s and 70s as well as the present day. The notable nearby public house 'The Grove' will also feature and a number of people involved in this film production have come along to the meeting for reconnaissance. Like the rest of us, they mostly take shelter from the elements under the home straight grandstand. I meet the pleasant enough but distracted feature "writer and director" Rod Woodruff who projects such an aura of luvvieness that he might as well travel with a chair with the word 'Director' in large capital letters on the back and one of those megaphones so he can shout "action!" He operates on the assumption that I'll already know all about it, consequently he's vague with me on the exact detail. He waves his arms expansively and suggests I speak with his colleagues-cum-minions while he gets on and suggests I also later via email.

With more time to explain and less ego altogether is freelance researcher Candida Boyes who knows next to nothing about speedway but, nonetheless, still has the important task of researching, finding and sourcing the various props for the film. From her I learn that there is "massive action content, but also humour and a love story woven into the script" that is "fictional" but "loosely based around the life of Lex Malloy." Verisimilitude is extremely important in any movie to avoid the anoraks subsequently highlighting your continuity errors. Candida is particularly keen to find "clothes" (leathers), "paper memorabilia" (programmes) and various other crucial items like bikes, tools, helmets and the like from the 1960s and 1970s but they are somewhat thin on the ground this afternoon. I suggest that she asks Berwick club photographer Graham Platten in the trackshop for his help (though I doubt he stocks such items on a regular basis) and promise to put her in touch with Nick Barber who runs some popular speedway collector memorabilia fairs in addition to his trackshop empire. When I call into the trackshop later, I soon see that Candida would have been disappointed in her search for props. Inside, Graham morosely tells me, "This might be the last week we're in this 'cause they're going to convert it into two junior [football] changing rooms". Also with the crew is the "line producer", a lady called Shirlpa Sharma whose ethnicity visibly signals the 'speedway meets Bollywood' aspect of the film production written about in the *Speedway Star*. In fact, the film will be masterminded by "experienced Bollywood producer Manu Kumaran" whose film company Medient Film has offices in London and Mumbai. Shirlpa instantly fits into the speedway world since she smokes in louche fashion with impressive zeal all evening. Indeed, she draws so heavily on her cigarettes that she

*Peter Waite models 40th
anniversary designer anorak*

*Danny Warwick and Kevin Doolan enjoy
the liquid sunsine*

Peter Waite 'gardens' in his tractor

makes notable speedway smokers Jason Lyons, Kauko Nieminen and Bob Brimson look like novice part-timers on their first smokes behind the bike sheds. Less than two weeks later, Candida writes to inform me that sadly the "film has been postponed indefinitely due to legal complications". Berwick speedway had temporarily brushed shoulders and crossed paths with the international film world but, before fame and award ceremonies could even beckon, the Bollywood dream had faded.

By the speedway office in the grandstand, Peter Waite surveys the scene below him. The stadium is basically deserted apart from helpers and guests huddled under the cover of the grandstand. Before us all, the lush and verdant centre green is also deserted but visibly sodden by the liquid sunshine. A nearby phone rings and Davina from the programme stall patiently answers the enquiry about tonight's meeting, "Yes, it's drizzling but the track is in good condition." Before he bustles away towards the glamour of the film people and the pits area, Peter reveals, "If we get them in [the fans], we'll race it!" Unlike some other promoters Peter doesn't really want to create false hopes that he then dashes by opening the entrance turnstiles but, since a good-sized number of cars have already parked on the grass outside, he's shortly going to have to make a decision. By his favoured spot on the fourth bend, Berwick club presenter Dick Barrie surveys the scene. His comparatively youthful look belies the fact that 2007 is his 58th successive season involved in speedway "as a happy spectator or otherwise interested party". Perhaps his youthful vigour has been aided by his recent 10K charity 'run' through Edinburgh to raise money for some of the disadvantaged children of Central Scotland? He first took up the microphone at Berwick speedway in 1972 and has enjoyed his latter-day renaissance back here at the club, after the persuasive Peter Waite suggested he return, once again, to these duties. Like many people, he's anxious that the meeting goes ahead since it will be difficult to ever reassemble this unique cast of characters for any restaging, never mind that many fans, like me, have travelled from far afield to specifically attend this meeting. This particularly applies to the handlebar heroes of yesteryear as much as the field of riders assembled to race for us tonight. Dick expects a competitive meeting should the rain abate, "it's not like a team meeting when they know if they don't like it they can come back another week. This is a real one-off! They're racing for good money and every race is a heat 15, so they'll really go for it. I'm really lucky because it's so exciting watching them from here - I really never tire of it especially Michal Makovsky - he's wonderful round here! People know it's going to be good racing, well it would be if it hadn't rained so much. Bad promoters would just open up the gates now but Peter's honesty is such he refuses!"[1] Dick leaves me as he has things to do as well as people to see or ex-riders to gladhand.

[1 In April 2008, Peter Waite would explain his responsibilities in an interview in the *Speedway Star* with Peter Oakes. "Most tracks have a load of people doing everything, I'm doing every single thing here. Sink or swim, it's down to me. I do the track, I do everything, I do all the programme advertising, all the marketing, all the team managing away from home, you name it, I do it. I speak to the riders, I do all the administration, all the financial side, all the money side, everything. I do the corporate stuff, I go out and get the sponsors, I do the whole thing, I don't think there will be another promoter in the country that does it all; it's not because it is greed or anything like that, basically the money is not there to pay people. I go to the High Street to give out leaflets, I go to the supermarkets, the schools, I'm putting posters up. Twenty-four seven is not the word."]

The rain sets in heavier around 5.20 p.m. While many would tear their hair out at the possible impending disaster of postponement (let alone the lost income), Peter smiles warmly as he passes and calls out above the loud music that plays over the stadium tannoy, "It's fun Jeffrey - we've got an hour [to avoid an abandonment] - we can always have a disco!" A break in the rain has Dick announce, "Message for those outside: you might be thinking 'oh no' but after discussions with the riders and referee, and since it's stopped raining, we will be opening the gates." As the fans file through the turnstiles, they're greeted by the sight of Peter ensconced in his tractor dramatically digging up huge slushy piles of shale right by the starting gate. It looks to be extremely radical curatorial work but, at least, signals that every effort is being made by the club management to prepare a track as suitable as possible for this anniversary meeting (or, possibly, plant some vegetables). Not all the fans are pleased with what they witness, "it's just sludge out there - they'll be filled in before the first corner. It won't go ahead and, if it does, we'll be paying Premier League money for processional, Conference League performance". I'm not sure I agree but the renewed onset of the drizzle doesn't bode well for the possibility of racing.

Referee Jim McGregor sees the funny side

It was only a matter of time before the organisers bowed to the inevitable and Dick Barrie conveys the bad but predictable news. "The referee [Jim McGregor] promised Peter Waite and his staff that he'd wait and consider the situation before making a decision. Sadly there can be no racing tonight for the safety of the riders. The ref has examined the track and, though the riders were prepared to ride, he has over-ruled them! We'll be back in a fortnight against Newcastle and your ticket is valid for the restaging of this meeting or the next three meetings here at Shielfield. There are hordes of past Bandits in our reception area - lots of very handsome men there and Rob Grant - and we're here for the duration until the last Bandit wanders home so come along and join in the fun, take part in our history!" Afterwards, Dick apologises to me for the weather ("we've been washed away") as though I'd assumed that this somehow forms part of his responsibilities. He also admitted he was frustrated with the postponement but remained determined to live for the moment and "enjoy the old guys!"

Lacey, Muriel, Davina and Bob savour the moment

If this were a marketing campaign, I think you'd have to describe the rush of people to the far end of the grandstand adjacent to the pits as a 'Grey Surge' to befit the predominant hair colour. This impromptu gathering of Bandits fans, ex-riders and staff quickly creates a loud hubbub with an ongoing buzz of greetings and nostalgic saunters down Memory Lane. One who's completely captivated and totally energised by the situation - in true child in a sweet shop fashion - is Penicuik taxi driver and long-time obsessive Berwick speedway fan, Jim Brykajlo. Ostensibly, he's also here with his son Steven and cousin Dougie Copland, but the reality is that tonight his role is that of cameraman par excellence - one half of a double act with Mike Hunter as they seek to film and record interviews with every rider here who ever had any connection with Berwick. Instantly they all seem to recognise each and every rider, while Jim appears shocked that I often have no idea who these "instantly recognisable"

Jim Brykajlo and Mike Hunter should be hired by Sky

Vandals graffiti board

people are, let alone that I can't recall the exact fine detail of their individual speedway careers. He pursues them all - giddy with excitement and runs about like an extremely friendly one-man paparazzo - to capture every last word, gesture and flicker on film for posterity. Steven has his own camera and is honorarily the film runner to whom Jim loudly dishes out a continuous stream of instructions, observations and orders, "Steven get a photo of Rob [Hollingworth] 'cause your mum used to fancy him!" Before he pauses for breath and observes, "he still has his really good looks!" Between interviews, Jim scans the area for the next ex-Bandits rider to rush over to and invite for a brief exclusive. No less excited but masking it much better with a display of nonchalance on the sidelines is Dougie, "I've been coming since I was four, Berwick's 40th is actually 2008 but it's a fantastic night to have all these riders together again all in one place. Look at Jim [at that moment masked behind a bulky camera but completely in the moment silently counting Mike down into his interview with hand gestures from behind his lens] and Mike too - he's in his element interviewing past riders. They both are. We all are. It's a shame about the racing but no one wants this to end!"

23rd June Berwick 40th Anniversary meeting - postponed rain

Chapter 16. King's Lynn v Mildenhall: "If I leave now, I can still see *Emmerdale* at seven"

27th June

Nigel   *"By the start line - perhaps making a psychological point to the referee"*

Mick Bates [to Peter Oakes] *"I don't need to look at a replay, I've made my decision"*

The clouds and the heavy rain I drive through in the last 10 miles before I arrive in King's Lynn fails to fill me with any great hope that the local derby meeting with Mildenhall will go ahead as planned. The car park at the Norfolk Arena is littered with large puddles and there's already a reasonable sized queue of riders' vans parked outside the locked pits entrance gates waiting news of an abandonment or permission to enter. The track itself looks thoroughly soaked and heavy to my untutored eyes but I quickly gather from club co-promoter Jonathan Chapman that while stress levels within the Chapman family are high, he still feels the meeting will go ahead as planned. That would definitely be the preferred option for the promotion, as a postponement late in the day, with only a few hours to go before the scheduled start time, translates into the worst financial news possible since you've maximised your costs (it's much cheaper to postpone early in the day) but then gain no revenues through the turnstiles. Going ahead would also avoid later season fixture congestion, something that is already a real problem across all three leagues because of the seriously inclement weather that the British summer of 2007 has already provided. Any decision to proceed with the meeting by the promoters will be taken in the context of the full knowledge that rain in the area and the forecast threat of more rain later will have a deleterious impact on the size of the crowd (and reduce it below what could reasonably be expected for this fixture in fine conditions).

A short while later an impressive number of riders from both teams have gathered by the safety fence and the entrance to the track itself to consider the gloopy conditions but apparently ignore the brightly lit message on the electronic scoreboard that intermittently flashes up 'King's Lynn Stars versus Mildenhall Pussycats'. Buster and son, Jonathan, are also there along with SCB Official Mick Posselwhite. Everyone looks suitably serious, as if collectively they were doctors about to deliver news of a terminal illness to an anxious relative, and jokes are at a minimum. Partly in jest but mostly seriously, always-charming Mildenhall number two Shaun Tacey loudly remarks, "if I leave now I can still see *Emmerdale* at seven!" Buster appears to have his own personal dark cloud in close attendance and, having gained the assent of the referee, outlines his intentions to the riders, "I will take off the crap and rough it up as quick as I can to make it raceable and we will take it from there." I take this to mean that "we will take it from there" with regards to further rain rather than the idea that there will be any further debate as to whether the meeting goes ahead or not! On both sides, the faces and body language of some riders, particularly the more experienced ones, indicate that they have either just eaten something distasteful or are far from in agreement with this plan. Whatever the logic or benefit of proceeding with the meeting, Jonathan Chapman cajoles the downcast crowd of riders with some further instructions, "we want everyone in kevlars straight away so we can get it on quick - no faffing about!" He then rushes off purposefully towards the stairs that lead to the referee's box (which also houses Jonathan's office too) perched high above the home-straight grandstand that overlooks the start line. He tells me, "the ref's fine with it and we can get it on, but you have to think of the crowd!"

The trackshop is a hive of activity and inside Johnny Barber is as keen as the promotion that the meeting goes ahead, particularly as the Barber trackshop empire has suffered because of the recent poor weather "six rain-offs in eight weeks". The Barber family run the trackshops at both Mildenhall and King's Lynn so many of the fans will use or be attired in articles sourced, produced and provided by them. I ask Johnny:"How come the yellow-and-black Mildenhall Tigers 2007 anoraks look almost identical to the

Threatening clouds hover

Disconsolate track walk ends

Track readied for action

Berwick Bandits 40th anniversary version I'd just seen the previous weekend?" He playfully denies they look alike or have any similarity or connection when it comes to their manufacture or provenance, "Not in the slightest - I don't know what you mean - shut your face!" Even Forrest Gump would strongly suspect the hidden hand of the Barbers is behind the supply of these exceptionally stylish and collectable garments.

The fashion symmetry isn't the only connection the King's Lynn trackshop has with Berwick, as Johnny's regular helper Mike Moseley is a columnist for their programme as well as the wordsmith for the 'Life of Riley' feature (and quizmaster) in the Lynn one. He's also a Wimbledon speedway fan exiled to this part of the country and recently (albeit briefly) got the chance to see ex-Dons rider Grant McDonald return to speedway to fill the jinxed Lynn reserve berth. Well, at least until a crash in only his second meeting ended his comeback. In an attempt to rival my own love of convoluted and lengthy sentences, in the programme Jonathan Chapman announces the arrival of Simon Lambert at reserve and discusses the injury Grant sustained. "It was a great shame though to lose Grant in only his second meeting here at home, just in that one race he was showing all the ingredients of why we had brought him to this club, lots of determination and skill, surely it would only have been a matter of time before he started winning races, unfortunately he suffered a broken wrist, which was pinned on Sunday and bad ligament damage to his ankle, he is now back at home but it is unlikely we will see him again this season, he has vowed though to be back next year if we want him and 100% race fit. The bad news is the medics had to cut his kevlars off and now he is left without a race suit so next week we will be holding a collection so we can replace them for him." According to Johnny, Grant is prone to misfortune, "every career he has goes wrong - he retired from speedway to become a window cleaner and fell off the ladder, he then became a taxi driver and crashed the taxi and, in his speedway comeback, he fell almost as soon as he'd started!"

They say you can never mistake a Scotsman for a sunbeam and with visual entertainment at a premium, apart from Buster, on his tractor, industriously and expertly scraping the slop from the track surface on his tractor, all that's left is for Glasgow-born club "Presenter" Mike Bennett to step into the breach to try to entertain. Luckily he has a lot to say about one of his favourite topics - himself. The advent of post-modernism in literature, the visual arts, music and theatre has seen self-reference and parody become the *lingua franca* of any contemporary artist worth their salt. Unbelievably Mike Bennett has brought the techniques of this school of artistic practice to speedway, albeit without the knowingness or the humour, light touch and sense of parody. "If you're after my job, you're welcome to it!" The shaft of light between the dark clouds is just like the wit - there's just about a glimmer of it - "it's 15 to 20 minutes before we start and, hey, we've got some sunshine". In fact Sod's Law dictates that as soon as the track has been readied into something approaching superficially raceable, the sun bursts through so strongly in true late evening summer fashion that the start of the meeting is further delayed because it causes interference with rider visibility. Mike Bennett isn't happy, "we were going to do some racing but, wouldn't you know it, the sun is in the way! Just to state the bleedin' obvious - they're working on the track at the moment as you can see." Jonathan Chapman gives the crowd a brief but well deserved break from the stream of consciousness Guantanamo-style aural entertainment offered by the presenter to explain the situation to the fans. "I'm sorry about the delay but we're just getting the whole thing sorted for the referee. We were a few minutes away from calling the whole thing off but we'd spent all the money anyway so we thought 'why not?' after we saw a few rays of sunshine. Thank you for your patience but we'll be getting going as soon as we can!"

When the meeting finally starts, getting going would be too strong a way to describe the riders' initial approach and attitude to the slippery track conditions. As you'd expect, home number one Tomas Topinka uses his local track knowledge to win the race but without his usual grace since he slows into each bend and negotiates the distance to the apex of the corner in almost upright position before then accelerating towards the next corner to repeat this manoeuvre. When you consider that he's not broadsiding in traditional fashion, his winning time of 66.2 seconds is impressive and testament to his track craft. Safe in the thought that he has a video of Emmerdale to watch at home later and exhibiting the exciting leg trailing style that appears to benefit him in these conditions, Shaun Tacey finishes second and Chris Mills squeezes past Tom P Madsen for third on the last bend. This enables the Stars to take a lead that isn't really threatened from then onwards.

There's then a considerable delay before heat 2 while Buster again attends to the track. To my untutored eye though, he appears to be on some kind of peculiar sabotage mission since as he circles in the tractor, the grading implement he pulls behind him gouges deeper and deeper grooves into the surface. After a few circuits, he appears to have created something that more approximates a mid-track trench than the burr you often hear them talk about on the telly. Somehow Buster manages to smooth this back over again and then spends considerable time madly pirouetting in his tractor on the last bend. In the stands, the chatter ignores the thinly disguised groove Buster has carved in the surface and instead is much more concerned with the effect his work will have on the apparently well-known bobble on the apex of the third and fourth bend. "I don't think that they're gonna get rid of that bump there, it's always a problem corner!" Garrulous as ever, with a hint of self-deprecation that the usual ego-fest wouldn't suggest, Mike Bennett informs us, "they're still getting that bottom corner sorted - if I went on *Mastermind*, my specialist subject would be stating the bleeding obvious - they're still working on the track!" If he keeps up this level of insight, there's an outside possibility that future television work might beckon for Mike as a ready made understudy-cum-stand-in for *Sky*'s Jonathan Green should he ever fall ill or have a prior engagement.

Fortunately the tedium of the presenter racking his mind for something distractingly vacuous to entertain the crowd with is interrupted by a *mea culpa* issued by Buster Chapman fresh from his exertions on the track surface. "Some of the riders ain't happy. Obviously, it's my fault, we put too much dirt on it!" With that admission, we're back on with the action, though collectively the riders warily trundle round to the line and James Brundle completes a shaky looking practice lap. Mark Thompson then immediately treats us to a virtuoso display of bike throwing at the start gate. If there were marks for artistic merit, he'd definitely reap the rewards for this throw-cum-fall before he'd even reached the first bend. Despite the drama and attractiveness of this departure from his machine, referee Posselwhite is not persuaded that this fall was caused by anything other than rider error (rather than the expected 'first-bend bunching' decision the rider so clearly expected). His team manager, Laurence Rogers, is surprised too if judged by the theatrical manner of speedway-meets-Southern-European-style-football protest that sees him ostentatiously fling his arms in the air in a beseeching manner - initially as part of the appeal for leniency - and subsequently then conspicuously flutter them in chagrin. King's Lynn gains another heat advantage and, though the race itself isn't exactly a classic, Mike Bennett can't help but again promote the oh-so-startling fact that his company relentlessly produce DVDs of every King's Lynn meeting. By his standards it's an almost subliminal mention since we learn that he's "looking forward to playing that back on the DVD". The Tigers then almost silence Mike when they hit back with a 5-1 to level the match when the pairing of Kyle "LAY-GOW" (as announcer Edwin Overland likes to call him) and Jason King combine with such confidence that you half expect that the track will totally suit the visitors for the rest of the night. It's an expectation that's punctured by a win for Paul Lee in the next race that has Mike drool, "isn't he fantastic to watch in full flight?" before he advises the home fans on the correct etiquette and manner in which to display their excitement, "I'm sure that you'll all be cheering him round the stadium."

Loyal Lynn fans gather

Under orders

It's unusual for King's Lynn not to find themselves ahead by Heat 4 of most meetings at the Norfolk Arena. While the track gets yet more attention, I wander back to the trackshop where Johnny Barber worries like a die-hard local, "some meetings have to be called off - if I was Jonathan Chapman I'd call for a track inspection even though his dad has prepared it! If someone gets injured, they won't be happy especially if it costs Lynn the league." A steward by the tall first-bend open-air grandstand is equally anxious, "this is the worst I've ever seen it here for years, it's like the old days! Mildenhall are used to riding this type of rough track as they did it all last season." The further tender loving care Buster has lavished onto the surface appears to have paid handsome dividends since the riders suddenly race with something much more closely approximating to traditional racing. That is until Tom P Madsen smashes into the fence at the apex of the last bend on the second lap and, keen to minimise yet further delays to the action, the referee Mick Posselwhite awards the result as a 5-1 to the Stars. Once again on the centre green, Laurence Rogers flails his arms around in the style of a manic traffic policeman with great theatrical effect, but with little result on the ref's decision. It's the first of four successive home heat advantages that gives the Stars what appears to be an unassailable lead. The heat wins aren't won without a struggle, particularly in Heat 6 when the experienced Paul Fry challenges Tomas Topinka for the lead throughout the race. Mike Bennett approves, "once again Paul Fry putting on a good show, we like Fryer!" Mike then reverts to his presentational house style of seeing his role to act as a glorified cheerleader content to merely confirm the evidence of our own eyes - in this case about the track surface, "its definitely getting better!" I'm not sure he's paid to highlight deficiencies in the quality of the conditions but, the fact he often does is what makes him unique and, to my mind, always essential listening!

Someone who makes light of the conditions in his first two races is Paul Lee. He's particularly impressive as he wins Heat 7 and Johnny remarks, "they can turn the bike now and then Paul Lee goes round and burns them all and they think 'bloody w*****!'" The rhythm of the meeting improves and the races come thick and fast, invariably punctuated by Mike Bennett who has the irksome trait of starting his erstwhile wrap-up of each race before it's even finished, often just at the moment the leading rider enters the last bend. Johnny misses some of the track action because of dawdling shoppers, "I cannot understand why during a meeting like today - which is two and a half hours old - why do they still come into the trackshop when the race is on? I can only assume they got in for free or have no interest in speedway!" With the scores after eight heats 30-18 and the Stars poised for another comfortable home, it slowly becomes clear that the Tigers haven't read the script but, instead, are keen to fight back. Paul Fry starts the resistance with a tactical ride win and by the time Heat 13 arrives the Tigers have won three out of four races. Mike Bennett praises them, "what can you say about Mildenhall? They're flying - attacking it!" The suggestion that the Lynn riders have taken their collective hand off the throttle, assuming victory, while not quite firing on all cylinders and racing on the track that's there in front of them, isn't a fair comment about the performance of Daniel Nermark.

The twelfth heat finds him relegated to the rear after he finds himself the meat in the sandwich on the first bend. Some riders might react by looking down at their engine or ostentatiously struggling with the variable surface of the track, but not the determined Nermark, who chases resolutely for the remainder of the race and nearly beats Tomas Suchanek on the line with a sneaky inside cut back on the last corner. I question Johnny as to whatever happened to Mike inelegantly calling Daniel the "Nerminator"? "Mike only recently learnt that Daniel Nermark hates being called 'The Nerminator' but only after he'd said it every week for a year and a half!"

Normal service appears to resume in the 13th with a comfortable triumph for Tomas Topinka who wins by such a distance he can indulge in some minor wheelies even before he takes the chequered flag. The next race sees Trevor Harding have a ding-dong mini-race within a race with Jason King for second place. A daring overtake on the third bend of the third lap appears to settle the positions in his favour until an unforced error on the apex of the last corner allows King to sneak past. This 5-1 takes the scoreline to 45-42 and raises the possibility that a maximum heat advantage in the last heat decider could see the Tigers grab a shock win that would establish local bragging rights for quite some time to come. Even though Paul Lee falls in this race, Topinka wins in the fastest time of the night to ensure a drawn heat and that Fortress Norfolk Arena remains unbreached by the opposition yet again. The crowd slowly drift away after a stop-start rather protracted meeting in difficult conditions but nonetheless, the riders still served up drama, some good races and a nail-biting finish. Something that couldn't have been predicted five hours beforehand with a sodden track, grumbling riders, and dark clouds overhead. With the car park still emptying and the rider's equipment not yet packed away in their vans, the post mortems have already begun. A key member of staff who helps so many things run smoothly at the stadium, Nathan Hoolands, notes, "there were a couple of hundred terrace team managers not really understanding the basic mechanics of track preparation." Buster hasn't enjoyed what he's witnessed but I remain unclear as to what or who exactly, "things that have gone on tonight I'm really not happy about. It leaves a bad taste and that's unusual for me!" His wife Cheryl sums the situation up phlegmatically, "we just about broke even 'cause we got a good crowd, despite the rain. I'm pleased considering it was 300 or 400 down on what we would expect. If you rain off so close [to meeting start time], you have all the costs and have to restage. We've had so many off this season - they have everywhere - it's not funny! We usually either run or we don't so everyone knows where they stand. I think the track caught our riders out to start with as they've come to expect it'll be excellent!"

27th June King's Lynn v Mildenhall (Premier League) 48-45

Chapter 17. Somerset: Vortex of traffic chaos

29th June

Jonathan *"Great for the fans watching in their lounges"*

The decision to stage the 2007 Premier League Pairs Championship at Somerset's Oak Tree Arena enabled the new era at the club under the co-promotion of Mike Golding (also the long-time experienced co-promoter at Poole) to showcase the highly regarded track and the many recent changes made to the stadium infrastructure. The grassy car park outside remains the same but sign of development is visible even as you stroll up to the turnstiles. These have been relocated and enhanced, while nearby there are now some impressively tall wooden gates. Once you're through these, the full scale of the development ambitions that the landlord harbours for the club become immediately apparent. The entranceway past the gate area has been spruced up with sauna effect type wood that I don't recall from previous visits and now divides off the grass banking immediately to your right as you look towards the first bend. Close to that there's a partially completed large building that will soon serve as the clubhouse and bar area (also to house skittles and a bowling alley) though, since it remains out of bounds, tonight the temporary bar is located under a tent-cum-marquee on the second bend. It's also clear that the grass banking of the final bend and, I think, some if not all of the back straight has been further built up to improve the view the spectators get. It was already an area that provided a good outlook down onto the track (and the passing traffic of the nearby M5 motorway) but now, with the increased elevation, the view is even more panoramic while it provides room for greater numbers of spectators than previously.

Predictably enough, the decision to award this prestigious meeting to Somerset raised some eyebrows with complaints about its distance from Cardiff, perceived home track bias that would benefit the Rebels pairing of Zetterstrom and Kramer, possible motorway delays during the Friday night rush hour and unsubstantiated grumbles that Matt Ford's position on the Management Committee had somehow influenced the choice of this venue for this leg of the *Super7even* series. The only person with legitimate grounds for complaint would be Tim Stone, the promoter at Newport, the nearest rival track to here, who now found that he would be unable to run his traditional Grand Prix curtain raiser fixture (versus Glasgow). Like the promoters at many clubs, Tim enjoys a hand to mouth existence, though he remains blessed with loyal volunteer staff and an indomitable cohort of Wasps fans. Only a few meetings staged at his track each year contribute really significant revenues to his business, namely the New Year Classic, the Welsh Open (traditionally staged on the Sunday after the GP) and the pre-Cardiff meeting he'd now suddenly lost. Given that Tim is one of a small number of promoters who own their stadium, the income provided by the large crowd happy to venture 10 miles down the road from Cardiff to watch an entertaining Premier League meeting would be impossible to replace. Whatever his feelings, Tim kept his own counsel in public and stressed the quality and attractiveness of the field of riders who'd compete at the Welsh Open.

Like all major events, the field originally assembled for the Pairs has undergone some last-minute changes to the line up. Consequently, we'd see Emiliano Sanchez replace Jason Lyons and Tommy Allen replace Steve Boxall. This would reduce the chance of success in the competition for both Birmingham and Rye House. However, when I arrived at the stadium on a warm, sunny afternoon many hours before the scheduled start time, there was all the usual frenetic activity associated with last-minute preparations on and off the track. Though that said, track curator Ez Curtis and his team approached their tasks in the calm manner of people who do this every week of the season, whereas time pressure, along with the desire to create the best impression possible at such a showpiece event, had slightly ruffled the calm equanimity of the invariably placid Mike Golding. This manifested itself in his quickened step and perfunctory, by his standards, greeting. The changes in the stadium has seen the trackshop relocate and the portacabin is now placed on the fourth bend and, for this meeting, has been extended with the addition of a large gazebo-cum-awning style blue tent. Mike's partner Anita is absorbed in concentratedly ensuring the stock is laid out attractively helped by her daughter Katie and their good friend Andy Griggs, the Rye House and Peterborough trackshop franchisee. Later I also see Dave Rattenberry, the wealthy owner of the lucrative Midlands trackshop empire, also help out dressed in his trademark apron. The merchandise on display not only mixes the best of the stock usually found at both Poole and Somerset but also has an international flavour since it's also been supplemented with the branded gear of a variety of riders who'll race in the Grand Prix tomorrow. Though, that said, it's notable that some of the newer riders in that competition like Chris Harris appear to have missed a trick by failing to supply such materials in bulk.

Anita and Mike expect tonight to be a bumper night of earnings at the trackshop. In the weeks and days before the event they have been besieged by phone calls and emails from people like me who're keen to come along and display their wares in the full knowledge that an enthusiastic crowd of many thousands will be on the look out to spend. Sensibly enough, they have decided to refuse all requests from other potential stallholders who might dilute their share of this significant one night only increased spend. Anita did explain this decision to me in her sweet way and left me in no doubt that I'd be welcome on any other night to sell my books at Somerset. In fact, I'd come to the track direct from the printers with my new book *Shifting Shale* and just as with my book *Showered in Shale*, the Somerset track was the first place it ever went on sale. Mike and Anita did kindly give me permission to hand out my leaflets to fans as they entered the stadium. I'm delighted to be in the sunny south-west of England, particularly since my northern road trip would have tried the patience of anyone. After a rain-off at Berwick, I drove from there to Glasgow - when I set off for the meeting a light drizzle was reported by Alan Dick, as likely to be still on, despite the forecast - though by the time I'd arrived the torrential rain I'd encountered en route had wreaked its toll at Ashfield too. Cutting my losses, I drove to Manchester for my Writer in Residence duties for Eastbourne speedway at their meeting at Belle Vue only to find this meeting abandoned on the morning of the fixture. Financially speaking, clubs prefer to call off meetings early and often emphasise it's to stop the riders and fans having a wasted journey. This was the first Belle Vue versus Eastbourne fixture to bite the dust, well sodden shale actually, since 2001. Ironically for a city reputed to be a tad on the wet side, Manchester was to miss the full impact of the wet, stormy weather that caused severe floods in the Yorkshire cities of Sheffield and Kingston-upon-Hull.

Luckily compared to many other fans journeying to the Pairs, I had only been slowed by grunky traffic when I travelled cross-country to Somerset speedway from my printers in the Glastonbury area. Though the gates opened at the pre-advertised time, the volume of fans that trundled through them wasn't at the level anticipated because the Oak Tree Arena suddenly found itself locked in a bizarre vortex of traffic jams. If there were to be any road accidents that afternoon, it appeared they were only allowed to happen within a few miles radius of the track. In fact, a couple of hours before tapes up, the main road through the area - the M5 - was jammed because of nearby accidents in both directions as well as hampered by additional complications caused by crashes in the perennially gridlocked Portishead area (some miles away near Bristol). As a result, the stadium became accessible only to drivers with the ingenuity to leave the motorway early and make a massive circular detour round the often picturesque minor local roads. This would have been the case if they had been able to avoid the further jams then caused by the volume of diverted traffic or, yet another accident on the road outside the stadium within mere yards of the car park. The back-straight grass banking provided a great view of the gridlock on the motorway (apparently exacerbated by an overturned caravan in the queues) and, as the occasional car eventually filtered through into the car park an hour later, the chatter was of stationary queues and pandemonium. With five accidents to choose from, the air ambulance was in huge demand and the meeting would have been delayed further than it finally was, if the club hadn't refused the emergency services request for the assistance of their (statutory) paramedic. So, with weather conditions perfect (unusual in a rainy summer) and with an exciting meeting in prospect, numerous fans in coaches and cars were stuck almost within touching distance. Anyone living locally tempted by the prospect or attractiveness of the event sensibly wouldn't even venture out of their houses.

It was a situation that did nothing for the mood of the promotion and even less for the outlook of the trickle of fans who came through the gates after hours stuck in their vehicles, ironically often having set off early in order to drink up the atmosphere. Many also missed the organised pre-meeting photo and autograph session with the casually dressed riders (and the *Sexy7even* start girls in their figure-hugging race suits) that has come to exemplify these events since reinvigorated by the advent of the *Super7even* series umbrella concept. The brains behind this rebranding and many of the little touches that have increased the presentational professionalism of these blue riband events of British Speedway is Jonathan Chapman. With trademarked gelled

Persuasive raffle ticket sellers: Judith and Sheila

Mobbed rider autograph session

Crowded rider parade

hair, he rushes purposefully about the place - from car park to stadium to pits - in the hours before the scheduled start, albeit with the odd break to snatch a few brief moments to enjoy the trappings of success in the form of a brief rest in his deluxe car in the company of his striking girlfriend. Mostly though, he chats to riders, organisers and fans. If not, he peers worriedly into the distance as if convinced that by sheer effort of will he can magnetically draw the expected crowds of fans into the car park. He retained a phlegmatic outlook, "I've booked the weather but forgot about the traffic! I've never seen anything like it! The motorway is blocked in both directions and If there's any accident it's nearby here. We've delayed the start by 15 minutes already and we don't want to cheat the public who've bought advance tickets but we'll have to start shortly 'cause of the curfew they have here."

In the interests of market research, the Somerset speedway promotion tried to encourage visitors to their meetings to fill out a blue information card and place it in the box provided inside the trackshop or marquee. "One lucky winner" of the monthly draw will be given a £25 M&S voucher for revealing any use of selected "facilities within a ten mile radius of the Oak Tree Arena during your visit". These ranged from use of a garage/pub/café or restaurant as well as a guest house/hotel/caravan/camp site with an additional query about a "local town visit". There was no mention of the in-car and in-coach sightseeing and dining that the jams caused many attendees to compulsorily experience prior to this Premier League Pairs meeting. Once people have finally fought their way through the traffic, paid at the turnstiles (or for advance ticket purchasers for the whole series of *Super7even* events, gained VIP fast-track access supervised first-hand by Mike Golding and Jonathan Chapman) and bought their programme, they're immediately confronted with a phalanx of people keen to part them from their money (for good causes) or hand them information. Many people have a desperate need to use the toilets so can't stop to chat or vaguely linger, while some others haven't enjoyed the unexpected delay to their journeys. For those who can linger to savour the atmosphere of this part of the stadium, there's a number of options. They can place a donation for the Speedway Riders Benevolent Fund in the buckets held by Rob Peasley and his dad Cliff or buy raffle tickets from Somerset fans Sheila Shabin and the 'Mighty Atom' Judith Rourke. If anyone attracts a queue, it's these ladies who appear to already know almost everyone, and even if they don't, they still have a smile and kind word for everyone else as they pass through. They meet and greet whenever they break off from loudly roaring out "Raffle tickets!" Later I buy a Garry Stead wristband from ladies collecting on his behalf. With 45 minutes still to go before the original start time, rumour has it that 20 coach loads of fans are still missing in action and I overhear someone say, "when we met Jonathan Chapman this afternoon he was six foot two but with all the stress and strain of it all, he's back down to his normal speedway rider height!" Not only are the fans stuck, but some of the riders are too and, at one point, Craig Watson, Ricky Ashworth, Tommy Allen and Ulrich Ostergaard don't enjoy the ideal preparation for the meeting. Also delayed is half of the presentational team, so Craig Saul - the half who has arrived - tells me, "its not just the riders but Mike Bennett who's held up in traffic". Craig is a charming man and such a skilled practitioner of the speedway presentation arts that he - on a weekly basis during the season - invariably manages to perform with wit, enthusiasm and knowledge. He also has a particular linguistic gift for off-the-cuff bon mots and, unlike some others, doesn't feel the need to display needless condescension or flourish his ego. Craig is a curious man but wears his insider information with complete discretion, though he looks forward to the forthcoming Michael Lee autobiography produced by Laurence Rogers that is widely rumoured to be close to publication. "Sizzle sells" he notes. Minutes later, we all breathe a sigh of relief when Mike Bennett bounds into the stadium having apparently come straight from his job as a croupier at Butlins, if judged by his bright scarlet red jacket and black trousers.

After a brief delay to wait for stragglers, the rider introductions and parade goes ahead, bathed in sunshine, though technical gremlins beset Craig Saul's microphone and the presentational team becomes much more of the Mike Bennett Show than was originally intended. Particularly so since he clasps the working roving microphone with a tenacity that suggests it may be the Olympic flame or that tonight has become some form of ad-hoc audition for the Cardiff presentational gig. His initial pronunciations indicate that Kevin Coombes probably has a job for life if Mike is his only serious rival for the position. We're soon introduced to (local favourite) "Mag-Nuss Zita-Strumm" who sounds like he might be distantly related to Swansea's finest, Catherine Zeta Jones. Later Mike excels himself when he gleefully asks, "any Elite League fans here this evening? That was REAL racing - we see it every week and just love it! Better than what's shown every Monday night or what you see!" Despite the delayed start, many fans sadly don't get to see the initial races and coaches are still arriving in the crowded car park after heat 6. By which time they've missed the shock first heat that sees "Zita-Strumm" win the first race but leave his partner Emil Kramer straggling at the rear having apparently forgotten that the likely victors in a Pairs meeting require a modicum of teamwork. Consequently, Shane Parker and Craig Watson pack the other scoring positions in the race that, under the 4-3-2 points system in operation at this event, sees them thereby gain a 5-4 heat advantage. Similar success in subsequent heats will be required if the Glasgow Tigers are to fulfil their ambition to win the Pairs title for the third year in succession. The third heat sees another fancied partnership - the Compton/Ashworth pair from Sheffield - start as poorly as they continue throughout the night. Arguably the star attraction at this event, the experienced ex-World Champion Gary Havelock, scuppers Redcar chances with a tapes infringement in his first race.

The crowd in the stadium are warmly appreciative of the action played out before them in the sunshine. There's also a smattering of riders here in the crowd to watch proceedings. These include Ryan Sullivan - who no longer rides in the UK since he prefers the less manic schedule of Russian club speedway (and the inflated pay) - along with Tai Woffinden who's stood with a gaggle of girls as he queues at the burger van on the first corner. The secret to success in any Pairs meeting, obviously enough, is to ride as a team and the points system is weighted as such. The key is to avoid the disastrous nil points of any last place finish (though this is sort of just about okay if the other rider wins). Many of the highly fancied teams drop out after the group stages including King's Lynn and Somerset, thereby confirming what a good choice the Oak Tree Arena had been as a venue since the so-called home bias hasn't proved to be relevant in the final analysis. The semi-final would also feature the unfancied teams of Newcastle and Workington, who you'd have secured good odds on beforehand, should bookies offer odds on such speedway meetings. The sense of grievance about the actual selection of the teams involved in this *Super7even* meeting felt by Edinburgh Monarchs fans I spoke to before the meeting wouldn't have been assuaged either by the good form shown by Newcastle or the semi-final qualification of the Glasgow pair. "We should have been in this before Newcastle, Glasgow and Birmingham! Many of them didn't even bother to bring any supporters when we've brought two coachloads".

If the racing entertained prior to the semi-finals, then the last four races of the night are worth the admission money alone - and would be seen by every fan no matter how long they've been delayed by the traffic problems. The quality (along with the team riding) is exciting and even the often anodyne third-place race-off manages to thrill. The most consistent partnership of the night is the Glasgow twosome of Shane Parker and Craig Watson who exemplify this all-for-one-and-one-for-all ethos right up until the final race of the night since, up until then, they are never separated. The rider of the night is Chris Holder who is only headed once (in the semi-final); with his partner Jason Bunyan, they become the surprise winners of the competition. Not that this is handed to them on a plate by the Tigers pair who, at one stage in the final race, look highly likely to repeat the medicine of their earlier group stage encounter that saw Holder win and Bunyan finish last to give Glasgow a narrow 5-4 heat win. However, with Holder

The close racing gets a warm reception

Race action and a nearly completed clubhouse

Showered in shale

and Parker racing in their own personal duel up front until Jason Bunyan sneaks past Craig Watson on the last lap, more of the same appears to dictate that the Tigers will emerge victorious through the clever but often undervalued tactic of sensible team riding throughout the event. Ultimately, the Islanders combination of the fastest rider of the Premier League (Holder) and his partnership with their most resurgent one (Bunyan) prove to be the most potent. It's traditionally awkward for fans based on the Isle of Wight to journey to watch their team ride away from home, as ferry sailings back to the Island are infrequent during the later hours of darkness. However, club captain Jason Bunyan is only too keen to dedicate the victory to this small, loyal but hardy contingent of their followers, "this was a fantastic night for the Isle of Wight. The club really deserves it, as do the supporters who travel to watch us away from the Island. They have earned some reward and it was nice to put a trophy in the cabinet for them."

29th June Premier League Pairs Championship, Winners: Isle of Wight

Chapter 18. Cardiff: Bomber excels in luxurious surroundings

30th June

The weather on the morning of the Cardiff Grand Prix dawns drizzly and overcast, so it's a delight to know that the meeting will definitely go ahead because of the modern retractable roof on the Millennium Stadium. This year I'm at the Speedway Collectors Fayre run by the Barber family that is housed in the clubhouse bar of Cardiff Rugby Club adjacent to the state-of-the-art stadium that towers over it. While the Millennium is a temple of worship to the various sports it hosts, the Rugby Club stadium is also impressive in itself. Despite the comparative luxuriousness of our surroundings, collectively there aren't many happy faces among the stallholders as we unload our cars and vans to trudge in through drizzle with our boxes of stock up the external stairs to the clubhouse. I'm lucky since I don't have the range of stock that others have, though equally they will enjoy greater sales as a result. Even without any fans keen to purchase speedway memorabilia, the area already looks crowded. Stallholders include the Barbers, Martin Dadswell, the "Polish people" [Pawel Ruszkiewicz], Re-run Videos (now really Re-run DVDs), various programme sellers, *Backtrack* who have the stall next to me as well as the legendary freaking professional stallholder from Manchester, John Jones along with his lady wife. Afterwards I'm told that John was left in tears at the end of the fayre when the breakdown of his stall marked the end of an era for him before he retired to overseas climes and probably delight the people of Portugal fortunate enough to encounter him.

My stall overlooks the parked cars and the rugby pitch but I don't get the chance to enjoy the view since I have my best-ever sales day, helped along in no small part by the interest shown in the arrival of my new book *Shifting Shale*. Sadly, this day is to prove that one swallow does indeed make a summer when it comes to my book sales for the rest of the speedway season, although on the bright side I didn't have a box of them stolen this year. The 40 copies of my new book sold pales in comparison to the huge sales enjoyed by Tony McDonald who launches his Kenny Carter biography at the Fayre. Along with his partner Susie Muir and their son, he occasionally struggles to keep up with the demand and boxes empty with great rapidity. The atmosphere in the hall mixes frivolity, high spirits and, as ever among speedway fans, an element of earnest anarokishness when searching for hidden speedway treasures among the stalls. For most of the day the place is rammed with people - despite the fact that there is an entrance fee of £1 - and the sheer volume of bodies means that the room temperature is rarely below sauna-like. The other

Lower tier

Roof closed

Fayre I was kindly invited to display my wares at by Andy Griggs last year also runs and attracts keen interest. Talk slowly filters through that though my space in the corridor en route to the toilets remains unused, plus some form of confusion over the booking, means that Andy and Dave Rattenberry have to set up their displays in the less than ideal location of the bar area after they find the main display room already occupied by Wulfsport. I sympathise with their disappointment at their exclusion from this key sales area since last year I also experienced that possession is nine-tenths of the law when I was relegated to the corridor.

Over at the rugby club, many people stop by for a chat at my stall and the hall buzzes with conversation about the meeting ahead along with speedway gossip in general. I try to catch a few words with Johnny Barber who says, "not now when I'm holding my Hans Andersen mints - mints? Yes he does!" Anyone who is anyone to do with the sport of speedway in this country will try to make their pilgrimage to Cardiff today (if they can afford to), so it's no surprise to see the great and the good wander past during the day. There are the traditional dramas, of course, including the temporary loss of his hearing aid by Workington promoter Ian "I've lost me farking ear thing" Thomas. Conversations are many and varied, ranging from a few words with friends to encounters that highlight the rich tapestry of people who make up one of the joys of following speedway. Paul 'Grizzly' Adams tells me passionately about the difficulty the contours and topology of the rugby pitches that Plymouth constructed their track upon in the lee of the A38(M) caused, particularly the vexatious "water table" that he kindly promises me a thorough tour of on my next trip to Devon. I also meet an obsessive baseball and speedway fan (as well as the Belle Vue and Birmingham club physio!), Steve Williams, who has been on his own *Showered in Shale* type odyssey to every baseball stadium in North America. He's written up some chapters on his journey but, like many before him, has found his enthusiasm taxed by a lack of time and the responsibilities of everyday life. It's a theme explored many times in Literature. Most notably by Laurence Sterne in his brilliant (and my second favourite book of all time) *The Life and Opinions of Tristram Shandy, Gentleman* (1759). In this novel, Tristram's dad tries to write an encyclopaedia that explains how to rear a child properly but gets so bogged down in the minutiae of the project that Tristram has almost grown to maturity before his father has completed the section on the care and development of the six-month-old baby.

At one point I even volunteer to share my table with hard-working speedway/sports commentator Nigel Pearson who arrives for a couple of hours to try to sell the Birmingham Speedway history book that he's invested his money in. Standing around with your books can be a thankless and soul-destroying task at the best of times but, at least, he's brought company in the form of a distracted and bored ex-speedway rider whose name I don't catch and whom I don't recognise. This turns out to be Neil Evitts who rode for a variety of clubs including Birmingham, Stoke, Halifax, Bradford and Wolves. He rode in a World Final, was England captain at one point and was also British

Champion. No wonder standing round with a table of books didn't ring his bell! Nigel tells me, "we gave the printing to some bloke in this country but it turned out he was just the intermediary for some printers in Eastern Europe - Rumania, Bulgaria or somewhere like that - so it took a bit longer than we thought." Nonetheless the enthusiasm for all things Brummie is such that the book pretty well broke even upon publication and will receive prominent attention on the BSPA website that Nigel controls in his capacity as BSPA Press Officer. The book itself is a glossy papered publication packed with black-and-white photos. Boredom soon seizes the ex-rider and Nigel cuts short his foray into speedway bookselling to go off and network or prepare for his commentary ahead on *Sky Sports*. He's an easy and interesting man to talk with a plainspoken approach to life and work.

I take the chance to show him the article - photocopied from an old edition of the excellent football magazine *When Saturday Comes* - that Wolverhampton speedway club historian Mark Sawbridge had earlier gleefully passed on to me. Clearly written by someone with experience of speedway it's entitled "DULL SPORTS: No.3 Speedway" and features a drawing ("Eat Dirt Bjorn!") by a cartoonist who no longer draws in the magazine. It goes on to read:

"THE RULES: Four grown men on teenagers' motorbikes ride four times round a cinders track. First to the first corner always stays in front and thereafter the drama level is equivalent to that of watching four nuns on mopeds lapping a roundabout, i.e. it only gets exciting if two collide or one falls off. Variants may take place on ice or elongated, but Rule One always applies. Occasionally it takes place indoors, where it has all the excitement of competitive hoovering.

THE PARTICIPANTS: Any Scandinavian male with one leg shorter than the other.

THE SETTING: A decrepit track on the bleak side of town, perhaps near a sewage farm, [he's been to Reading & Rye House then] sometimes self-consciously and misleadingly named 'The {insert name of town} Stadium'. Somerton Park 20 years ago, when Newport Wasps' fans blinded by flying gravel on a Friday night could sometimes be found still wandering the terraces, *King Lear* style, when the County kicked off the next afternoon.

THE FANS: The sort of poor-but-honest families who voted Tory to stop immigration, then found themselves flattened by the Poll Tax. Barely articulate, but they can calculate Torbjorn Smorgasbord's average to five decimal places. Baby gets an air horn and clipboard as christening presents."

Sadly this photocopied article gets cut off just as the author warms up to denunciate how riders can appear for many different clubs throughout Europe AND for many different clubs in the same league as a guest (SOCCER IN A SPEEDWAY CONTEXT: "Anders Limpar is contracted simultaneously to..."). It's a situation that baffles even the most open-minded of those fans keen to make the transition from others sports to our own, even though, obviously, in recent decades the tendency has been for speedway to lose fans to other codes of sporting entertainment. If a visitor from outer space from, say, Mars arrived on the planet for only one evening and happened to pick Cardiff to experience the human race, then they'd leave with a very misleading impression of the popularity and status of speedway in contemporary modern Britain. For this one day only, the city is thronged with speedway fans from all the speedway nations to create the one-off, one evening only in the year, high-water mark of a speedway audience. In a definite break with the tradition of the F.I.M. declaring suspiciously even/rounded attendance figures, this year the crowd is announced as being 41,247. This figure still represents a continued five-year decline from the still unbeaten record of 42,000 set in 2002, despite relentless year-round print and broadcast media promotion. Questions remain about how far these 'official' final figures have historically been inflated by the widespread circulation of complimentary tickets by the organisers. However, looked at on the telly or viewed via the optic of reports in the *Speedway Star*, the Cardiff GP is represented as a festival of speed without parallel anywhere in the known universe and little attention is ever given to the vast swathes of empty seating throughout the stadium that (every year) remain resolutely unfilled. It's not a problem that besets many sports that stage events at the magnificent Millennium Stadium but would be immediately obvious to our first-time alien visitors. Something that wouldn't be quite so clear to them - since they wouldn't have seen speedway raced on outdoor tracks with a distinctly higher standard of preparation and quality - would be the traditional processional awfulness of the racing often provoked by man-made indoor tracks at stadiums such as this. The event is staged with great spectacle and so enthusiastically celebrated as if it's a real festival by the general speedway public that this effectively disguises the lack of shale and the concomitant unpredictable ruttiness of the track surface. This invariably ruins the quality of the vast majority of races staged and, consequently, eliminates the advantage the most

View from the heavens

gifted performers of the age would usually have over their less-skilled rivals.

From a xenophobic and nationalist perspective, this turns out to be excellent news for British speedway since the never-say-die attitude and grass-track background of the eventual winner Chris Harris enables him to ignore or cope with the irregularity of the surface that defeats or catches off-guard some of his more illustrious contemporaries. For some years, the business plan of the organisers has extended the range and locations of the venues used to stage rounds of the Grand Prix series. It has focused much more on the environment and spectacle that 'guest' stadiums provide rather than the actual quality of the track. The new Wembley pitch would be an example from another sport of this approach that sees concentration on the wrapping not the present itself. The organisers can regularly provide processional racing on an execrable surface in the full knowledge that, come hell or high water, the fans will still turn out in droves (well somewhere around 40,000 people). Given the rumoured staging costs of around £300,000, the event is a clearly huge revenue-generating machine for the organisers. If we take a conservative view of the average ticket price (at say £35), paying customers (say 39,000) and programme sales (say 30,000 at £8 each), then my calculator already shows a figure of over £1.6 million and this might be an underestimate of gate receipts which themselves may only form a fraction of earnings since these will also be boosted by the sale of television rights. This is before we even factor in monies gained through sponsorship or advertising. The total figures involved would bring a complacent smile to the steeliest and most modest of successful businessmen, let alone the features of speedway visionary John Postlethwaite. Build it and they will come has proved totally correct and, with a win for Harris swelling national breasts with pride, future prospects look bright that this cash cow will continue to lay its golden eggs.

Once the prime seats have gone, one cost-saving suggestion for fans could be to buy the cheapest available ticket each year and then sit wherever they liked in the stadium since there are acres of free seats to choose from. I soon moved from my position on the third bend to a much better location to sit with a contingent of Weymouth fans and officials. Obviously, in what feels like the rafters of the auditorium, you can rarely hear the announcements because of the combination of the sound system deficiencies (though I wish I hadn't heard Chas & Dave during the interval) and the incessant parp of the air horns that continually echo throughout the stadium. I like the typically speedway atmosphere that these air horns create and, if you watch the giant screens, you can still mark your programme without the muffled (to inaudible) dulcet tones of Kevin Coombes to explain things.

Once the meeting gets underway, the track surface appears relatively smooth - well it does from the great height I look at it from - but the 'best riders in the world' appear to struggle with it to the extent that you'd be forgiven for thinking it's a rutted field. Smoothly stylish riders who 99 times out of 100 ride with effortless grace are immediately struggling. Riders like Nicki Pedersen, Jason Crump, Greg Hancock and Leigh Adams - hardly nearly men when it comes to

World Championship success or being thereabouts - genuinely look to have difficulty with the random lumps and bumps that regularly throw their finely tuned balance off kilter. The person who adapts best to this adversity is the eventual winner C. Harris, whose nickname 'Bomber' has been banished from the *Sky Sports* airwaves by something that isn't usually associated with their speedway commentary team - political correctness! No major or minor speedway meeting is ever complete without some form of mechanical failure or malfunction. Luckily for Jason Crump, after he's comprehensively trashed the tapes at the start of Heat 3 the referee, Krister Gardell, rules that it's 'all four back' because of an apparent "tapes malfunction". A sign of the shock result that is in store on the night is signalled at the outset of the re-run race when the imperious 'Bomber' Harris beats both the 2007 GP leader (Nicki Pedersen) and the current 2006 World Champion (Jason Crump) from the tapes! To my mind, the referee loses control of the meeting "early doors" [as Kelvin Tatum would say] and never regains authority but prefers to indulge the riders with a series of poorly officiated starts and some questionable decisions. Heat 4 is a case in point when the tapes rise so quickly that the riders have hardly stilled their wheels, let alone come under orders, before they are let go to race.

Though overtaking is at a premium after the first corner, there is enough occasional action on the track to legitimately stir the crowd, though the incessant blare of the air horns continues throughout the night without need for an excuse or justification. Another Brit, David Howe, is able to warm national pride and gain his best result of the night in Heat 7 with a second place (behind the season-long disappointing Pedersen, B.) that he then celebrates in the manner of a recently confirmed world champion. David is always likely to struggle and qualified for the event through this season's made-for-TV qualification procedure via the televised British Final, something that fails to inject any passion into that night or into the imagination of the speedway fans generally at Cardiff since we all know he is merely fodder for the qualification process on the night. Any GP round attracts aggressive riding manoeuvres but the track is to prove a great equaliser in this respect - since riders could hit an unexpected divot or bump at any moment to lose position. Before the interminable "rabbit, rabbit, rabbit" of Chas & Dave during the interval break, Leigh Adams serves up an overtake of Nicki Pedersen on the back straight of Heat 11 to win the race and leaves Nicki so comprehensively behind that it looks as though he was stood stock still. The last race before the interval 'entertainment' sees Scott Nicholls move from second into the lead by aggressively powering under Rune Holta, though sadly for him Jason Crump follows in his slipstream. After probing for a way past for a couple of laps, the Australian times his run to the line to perfection and powers round the final bend to win by a short head at the flag.

With all the skill and correct preparation in the world, you still need a slice of good fortune and this arrives for Chris Harris in Heat 13. To gain the lead, he cuts across a lifting Andreas Jonsson who then proceeds to clatter into the back wheel of the Cornishman, only to then be excluded for his troubles. It is a double slice of good fortune since such racing incidents often spiral into something more serious than a brief encounter with the air fence. The re-run gives Leigh Adams another chance - this time to fly away with alacrity - from which he then takes full advantage. Three heats later, Scott Nicholls falls theatrically at the back of the first-bend bunch like a dying swan to amazingly somehow convince the referee to stop the race and declare a re-run with all four back rather than the more widely anticipated exclusion of Sophie Blake's beau. On the subject of glamorous women in speedway, another re-run gives the start line girls a chance to strut their funky stuff and twirl their brollies in a manner Bruce Forsyth used to suggest salaciously to Anthea Redfern to show off her clothing to the best effect. Where I'm sat in the Wildcats enclave, a disconcertingly camera-less Julie Martin isn't impressed with their nimble foot and umbrella work, "I've never known people take holding a brolly so seriously!" Weymouth away team manager, Jem Dicken, doesn't beg to differ but instead continues to avidly train his binoculars on the start line girls in a manner that might lead you to think he's been tasked to score them on artistic merit, style and performance before every single race. The re-run of the race has some excitement on the final bend when Scott bursts powerfully under Nicki to force him towards the fence. It's a manoeuvre that would defeat less gifted or brave riders but not Nicki, who opens his throttle and wheelies to the line to win by a short tread.

If the 2007 GP series is almost Nicki's from the outset of the first meeting then, Cardiff brings the best out of Bomber to the extent that he is even occasionally gating rather than having to rely on his signature fight back from behind. Probably already definite to qualify for the semi-finals with 9 points from four rides, a point or two for him in Heat 19 would most likely ensure a more favourable choice of gate position in the elimination races. In the flow of the moment and temporarily forgetful of his trademark ponderousness at the tapes, he flies from the gate in the lead only then to be called back when the referee stops the race. A real sign of his intent and the mark of a potential winner, Harris repeats the medicine to again lead from the tapes and win ahead of Tomasz Gollob. A Brit, in the form of Scott Nicholls, wins the final qualification race of the night (how often do you see successive victories for British riders in the GPs?) to ensure that the patriots in the crowd really had something to shout about. Even those of a more taciturn disposition can't help but get caught up in the atmosphere of hope crossed with jingoism that echoed and surged throughout the Millennium Stadium during those moments.

The atmosphere builds further, since Scott and Chris found themselves in separate semi-final heats and the prospect of a double chance that a home-based rider might finally triumph on the night in Cardiff still remains a tangible prospect. Sadly, the collective nationalistic rollercoaster took a dip almost as sharp as Hans Andersen's who, after a poor gate, found himself initially jostled in the first bend by his arch-rival Nicholls before he executed a swallow-dive of a fall. He does this at the rear of the pack and in a manner that has him careen dramatically into the air fence at the apex of the bend. A blind man on a galloping horse officiating at his first speedway meeting ever would have ruled - nine times out of ten - that this was all the fault of the Dane. True to a night of gifted fence sitting where he's failed to take any decisions at all, referee Krister Gardell then bottles it again to order a re-run with all four back. A three-way match race with Crump off gate one and Hancock off two potentially getting the chance to stymie each other would have suited Scott's purposes and whatever form of natural justice applies in the world of speedway. Instead, his reflexes and gate 3 defeats him, though he's temporarily second at one point, Scott eventually trails in fourth. Even in this race, the referee manages to miss an infringement by Hans when he crosses the inside white line with both wheels on the second bend of the last lap. Jules leaps to her feet in disgust, loudly aggrieved at this further example of his incompetence as an official but, since we're miles up in the gods of the stadium with the riders displayed distantly below us like particularly clever performing ants, her protests go unheeded.

If there's a lump or bump on the track (well actually there are many) Nicki Pedersen is bound to find it and, since his smooth but aggressive riding style is much more finely calibrated than, say, Bomber's, the second semi-final isn't the time to discover them. The Eastbourne fan in me is convinced that Nicki has been shoved just prior to finding the specially placed burr on the track that sees him fly with true jet-propelled speed into the air fence. Champions are never wrong and, definitely, never at fault but even this referee couldn't fail to exclude him. That said, Nicki amused his doubters with a cameo leap to his feet and some virtuoso head shaking en route to the pits while on the further look out for someone to remonstrate with or blame (other than himself). This was a fortunate outcome for Bomber who'd suddenly reverts to type and not only forgets his gating gloves but also apparently finds himself on a lead bike (if judged by his shockingly ponderous exit from the tapes). But for the stoppage, this would have eliminated him and killed the patriotic fervour immediately. As it is, the re-run finds him comfortably third (out of three) until the last bend of the penultimate when Jaroslaw Hampel obliges by getting shockingly out of shape (or Bomber used the Sylar-esque powers he's kept hidden until that vital point) to thereby enable the Cornishman to secure second place.

If you were attending the 2007 GP with smell and hearing as your only senses, then the food would repulse you and you'd be driven mad by the air horns and musical interludes. However, in the final you'd not need to be told that Chris Harris is in pursuit of a rival or been in any doubt about the exact moment when - with the true devil-may-care gambler's proverbial last roll of the dice for **** or bust - Bomber cleverly cuts back onto the inside of Greg Hancock on the last bend to, thereby, win with flair and flamboyance by what technically is known as 'not much'. Joy is unalloyed and barmy throughout the stadium - jingoism and national pride swell collectively into noisy pandemonium. Personally, for me it doesn't eclipse the joy of Martin Dugard's wild card triumph now many years before, but it is still something to behold and witness first hand! Outside the Poles trudged off into the torrential rain that blitz the streets of Cardiff and deeply soak the initial throng of British speedway fans contentedly lurching away into the darkness.

30th June Cardiff Grand Prix 2007, Winner: Chris Harris

Chapter 19. Newport: Breathtaking skill lights up the Welsh Open

1st July

SKYBALLS ON CELEBRATIONS

Jonathan	*"I just wondered - have you ever done a wheelie like that?"*
Kelvin	*"No, I haven't"*
Nigel	*"Watch for Ulamek's celebration when he wins - he loves it here - maybe he's not going to bother 'cause of that damaged hand and ruins my theory"*
Tony Millard	*"The wheelie of celebration, the Reading fans are going to enjoy that!"*

Nigel [implies the Swindon team are going slightly over the top after early season win at Coventry]

"The way they're celebrating, you'd have thought they'd won the title".

Jonathan *"Yes, hugs all round"*

The staging of the Welsh Open Championship is to all intents and purposes the Welsh National Championship but for the small matter of official F.I.M. recognition. It's the event that Tim Stone (billed in the programme as "Promoter/Mt Organiser " and also as "Training Officer") has staged at Hayley Stadium since the Grand Prix moved to Cardiff. He used also to stage a Premier League meeting on the Friday night prior to the GP as well when Newport would usually take on Glasgow. Speedway fans only in the area for the weekend would often be tempted to include one or both meetings in their itineraries but the advent of the Super 7 series put paid to that tradition. Tim is one of the few promoters within British Speedway to own his own stadium and, given the size of his regular crowds, he continually needs to find ways to attract people to use the facility for other purposes other than just speedway in order to balance the books. Despite the fact that he runs the club on a shoestring, Tim studiously doesn't complain about this loss of much-needed revenue (most likely five figures). Instead, he prefers to proselytise about the virtues of the principality and to see this event as an additional service or adjunct to that provided by the Welsh Tourist Office. He needs no second invitation to concentrate on the positives of the quality field of riders he's attracted to compete in the event. With defending champion Chris Holder on display, one of the most in-form and exciting young riders in the country will, hopefully, attract the casual punter who might not otherwise get to regularly see the talented Aussie ride. "We've always regarded this weekend as an important part of the Grand Prix weekend, and hopefully many people will pay us a visit on their way back from Cardiff. I've said it before [every year in fact] but I feel it's a very open field, and once again I've put together a line-up which I feel will provide the best afternoon's racing possible."

It's a field of tried and tested competitors who Tim knows (from his previous stagings of the New Year Classic here) will not only entertain but will also get on with the meeting irrespective of track and weather conditions should they deign to become an issue. Indeed, it's a line up that echoes what any sensible superstitious bride ensures she does at her wedding by wearing something old, something new, something borrowed, something blue. On display we have clubless "three times British Champion" Andy Smith allegedly in his "final season of domestic racing", Eric Andersson "putting himself in the shop window this afternoon" plus another rider no one will have seen ride in this country before, Marek Mroz, who hails from the hot bed of speedway talent that is

Poland and "has been brought to the attention of British promoters under the MSJ Speedway Promotions banner."

As there's still a few hours to go before the turnstiles are open the gates are locked, but inside the stadium is a bustle of activity with a variety of last-minute preparations going on in various locations - the pits, on the track, the catering caravan, stallholders industriously setting up their stalls and the bar (now apparently fully functioning). It offers a great view of proceedings since its relocation to the top of the grandstand away from the cool, darkened recesses of the interior it previously occupied. Already in pride of place strategically positioned where everyone will have to walk past him after they enter the stadium, is John Jones - a man always happy to give me a studied glower - who engrosses himself professionally laying out the final few items of merchandise with his delightful lady wife. Having been round the memorabilia circuit for some time, Mister Jones has *the* essential piece of equipment that any forward thinking stallholder will need - something to protect all of the gear he has on sale from the likely rain. The forecast is for showers - either heavy or intermittent depending on whether the person you speak to is an optimist or a pessimist - though, in my opinion, the thick black clouds overhead promise a deluge sooner rather than later. Everywhere you look everyone is busily absorbed. As Tim passes I ask if I can pitch my table under the lee of the stand on the home straight if it rains. He doesn't break his purposeful stride to reply other than to say, "my head is all over the place, I'll talk to you later!" When we spoke on the phone the week before, he kindly agreed to allow me to display my books here and said that the fee he'll charge me for doing so depends on how many I sell and I'm to see him at the end to sort that out.

While we all collectively wait for the rain to arrive or pass by the Queensway Industrial Estate, I pitch my table. It's good to catch a few words with some of the willing volunteers I've met on previous visits to the stadium as they bustle past or stop briefly to look at my new books. I've hardly been there five minutes before I'm told (rather proudly), "we're fourth from bottom this year!" This news comes from some of the friendly people who give many hours voluntary service to Newport Speedway and I soon learn that average attendances week in and week out haven't, like the rest of speedway, bucked the national trend of decline, "the crowds average around 400, I reckon, I dunno how he survives!" It's good to catch up again with characters like Hywel Lloyd ("photographer"), Peter Brookes ("Race Day Maintenance"), Gavin Morrison ("Incident Recorder") and David Dean, who isn't listed in the programme but has taken over track curatorial duties from his now retired father Andy. Like some others on the staff he's spent time in the past week helping out with the huge logistical task that is the annual installation of a temporary man-made indoor circuit inside the Millennium Stadium and, immediately afterwards, dismantling it all again. In the "Tim Stone Writes" section of the programme we learn, "most of the Newport track and medical staff were working at last night's GP and the practice on Friday. As we get ready for our meeting today, it's amazing to note that all the track dirt at Cardiff has been transported away, the air and retaining fences have been dismantled and packed up, the cleaners have been in and the stadium is without any trace of speedway. It is all quite amazing." David is of the view that Tim should have assembled an even better field for today's meeting than he already has, "if he'd paid £200 or whatever appearance money Bomber asked for - he's a GP rider now and it's his living - since he always goes well here and would bring people in. It would have been amazing! Today would now be the first meeting he'd done since he won! Tim says he's gonna pop in for a few heats and ride the New Year Classic - when he's testing his engines - but that's no good for today."

Over by the turnstiles, Jayne Morris and Janet have the High Octane Club S.W.A.R.M. table strategically positioned to entice customers willing to buy a raffle ticket or pen to raise "funds for your Newport Wasps and then it passes it to the riders in the form of tyres". This fundraising initiative has been in existence since 1999 and further emphasises the community-minded attitude of many Newport speedway fans. Their support goes some way to defraying the essential costs faced by all riders and is gratefully received on a regular basis. I purchase a black pen with yellow embossed lettering proclaiming my support for all things Newport. I believe, but forget to ask her to confirm, that away from her fundraising Jayne is so involved at the club that she has also sometimes stepped into the breach to turn her hand to team management duties for the Conference team here, the Mavericks. If so, I can't immediately recall any other club using a female speedway team manager, other than Jayne Moss and Vanessa Purchase. Also nearly ready for the off is Dave on the programme stall who has sensibly placed himself in an area with vague shelter to the right of the entrance turnstiles where despite a good number of cars already in the car park, a long expectant queue is conspicuous by its absence. Most likely, many have still to recover from a night of exuberant celebrations in honour of Bomber's triumph.

When the gates do open on time, the heavens open pretty well at the same moment, thereby dampening any lingering initial optimism about sweltering conditions. It's a heavy downpour that almost immediately leaves the track looking more suited for use in a pottery class than a speedway meeting. I cover my books up which isn't exactly going to help sales before I retreat with them and set my table up adjacent to the first set of steps in the grandstand. I make sure I don't obscure anyone's view as well as block any of the access ways. It's not a great day for sales (three in total) but then tracks all round the country find that for a month after the Grand Prix so much money has been hoovered out of the speedway public that attendances remain static at best, while trackshops report a noticeable lack of impulse purchases compared to the norm. The rain has turned to drizzle but appears to have had a dramatic effect on those fans coming an hour or so early to bagsy their favourite spots within the stadium. So few people have passed my position let alone stopped that I wander over to the entrance to have a look for myself at the volume of arrivals. In fact there's a coach full of fans outside, supposedly from Glasgow, but to Tim's apparent chagrin they're all staying put on the vehicle until they're completely satisfied that the meeting will go ahead. Given the summer so far, this is a sensible precaution, especially when they're so far from home but, with the sky definitely brightening and the drizzle slowed to almost imperceptible, I think it's safe to say that Tim and the riders have a 'show must go on' attitude that will ensure the racing definitely happens, barring a sudden monsoon.

An OAP couple who have paid to enter and walked about two yards inside the stadium, look up and decide to debate re-entry terms and conditions with Ros Curtis ("Office Administration") who's lurking purposefully there. News that their tickets would be valid for the "next four meetings" doesn't thrill them and they retort, "but we live in Sussex!" After some further chit-chat, they go to buy a programme to check what it says in there about rain offs. What they'll find there appears to have been drafted by the same people who compose the regulations in that special language employed in the SCB rulebook (notoriously a document that includes phrases that can have multiple interpretations) since it mixes clarity and obtuseness in equal proportions. Judge for yourself, "in the event of a meeting being abandoned before the holding of the eighth race in the programme the promoter honours that days admission ticket to any meeting of the same demeanour, excluding test matches, international events or cup finals or special meetings." Leaving aside that test matches appear to have dropped from the speedway calendar almost completely nowadays (let alone be staged in Wales), this qualification specifies no time period and a meeting of the "same demeanour" appears to rule out re-entry at Newport league meetings. Luckily the meeting does go ahead so this is all academic (but instructive). My stall has the advantage that whatever the weather it's dry in the drizzle and shaded in the sunshine. Stopping by to chat is attractive ex 'Miss Fina Invader', Wendy Jedrzejakski. She draws my photo book to the attention of Mrs Mark Lemon ("I must get one for Mark, he'd love it") who, like so many throughout the season, doesn't have enough money with her but promises to buy it later or online (at www.methanolpress.com). I also get a number of fans stop to share their views on everything from the GP, to the weather and someone who unsolicited tells me they didn't thrill to the sight of Buzz Burrows in full flow gliding past teenagers at Plough Lane, "I've been going since 1960 and the worst thing I ever saw was that pissy little track at Wimbledon." I retort that many other fans would vehemently disagree and were consistently thrilled, almost to the point of orgasm, by superlative racing action served up on a narrow track during the brief Wimbledon Conference League era. The French language has the wonderful and untranslatable word *jouissance* that suffices better than plaisir to describe this life-affirming experience. Indeed, the famous psychoanalyst, Jacques Lacan, invented the more appropriate and descriptive concept of *surplus-jouissance* unaware that it would so well describe the thrill of the CL Plough Lane experience.

Because of a printer's error with the race card, the programme is a bit of a collector's item in itself since it already has an insert, though the meeting hasn't yet been rained off or re-staged. The original version of the programme would have halted the meeting at race 16 without the necessity of the final four heats, a possible race off and the final itself. As a result we're treated to the thoughts of Jason 'Jase' Harrold ("Club Announcer") twice, though this is no sacrifice as it's well worth a read. To fully appreciate his observations you need to be both a speedway fan and an avid watcher of soap operas on every television channel. My mum would qualify on the soaps side of the equation but I reckon the only speedway person I know who could really fulfil the criteria would be Shaun Tacey, who sadly hasn't been included in the field so couldn't verify the veracity of these suggestions. Jase is also a local radio broadcaster for *Red Dragon Radio* (and modestly had a full-page picture advert of himself and co-host in the Cardiff GP programme) so I reckon he must have to watch the soaps for his work or else has a huge interest and significant free

Sawdust top layer is applied to the track

Coming to the tapes

time. Provoked by a letter to the *Speedway Star*, Jase has overlooked his "dream about bedding Anne Robinson" to entertainingly ponder long and hard to come up with what he calls the "definitive list of speedway lookie-likeies"

> Steve Bishop = Richard Arnold (TV presenter)
> Kelvin Tatum = Paul Whitehouse (TV funnyman)
> Mark Loram = Rob Minter (EastEnders)
> Jason Crump = Chris Martin (Coldplay lead singer)
> Tomasz Chrzanowski = Jim Carver (The Bill)
> Adam Skornicki = Stuart Cable (rock and roller)
> Grzegorz Walaszek = Greg (Coronation Street)
> Morten Risager = Ole Gunnar Solksjaer (Footballer)
> Piotr Protasiewicz = Brian Johnson (the dad in My Parents are Aliens)
> Ritchie Hawkins = Danny (from Grease is the Word)
> Ryan Fisher = Mark Arden (from The Full Monty)
> Ben Barker = Barney Rubble (cartoon character from Flintstones)
> James Brundle = Jonas Armstrong (played Robin Hood)
> James Brundle = Dr Fox (DJ and TV judge)
> Bryn Williams = Phil Spector

The unpredictable joy of a typical summer is illustrated by the fact that, after the heavy rain subsides and with less than an hour to go before the rider parade, the sun then starts to beat down with sufficient ferocity that you really wonder if sun cream would suddenly be more useful than a brolly. With the dramatic change in weather conditions, the mood lightens and suddenly the stadium has gone from empty to noticeably crowded with fans. Luckily I'm in the shade of the grandstand and business is so slow that I can read the paper without fear of interruption. All that's to be seen on the track is a battered red tractor pulling a brightly coloured yellow hopper, filled with sawdust for distribution onto the track surface manually by David Dean. They circuit a few times to deposit an absorbent layer of sawdust in hopper-width strips on the track surface. Incident Recorder Gavin Morrison potentially fates himself for the meeting ahead when he comments about the lack of accidents at Hayley Stadium this season, "there's been less to write down [for the SCB] this year - Phil Morris has been doing the Winter Schools as he's just down the road and I reckon Tim has listened to him. So the track is smoother the way he likes it!" In fact, there was to be a fair share of incidents to entertain and worry the fans but, what is to be deemed an "incident" in SCB form-filling insurance terms (and what isn't recorded as such) is the type of mystery only known to the charmed circle of those qualified as speedway officials.

Josef 'Pepe' Franc immediately decides to attempt to win a prize for the most bizarre pirouette of the afternoon in the first race (on the first bend) when he somehow manages to enter the bend in one direction and exit it in the direction he'd just come from. It's a manoeuvre that fires Jason Harrold's admiration more than Anne Robinson or the race itself, "that's the first time I've seen a bike go in reverse!" Much more significantly, Andre Compton speeds away to an untroubled win, while behind Ryan Fisher drove under the high-fancied Chris

Holder with such aggression that it isn't a surprise that the young Australian finishes third. Not exactly an auspicious start and, given his recent exemplary form, not something that would have been widely predicted beforehand. It certainly shows that the riders aren't just going through the motions and the chance to win some silverware and prize money is all the motivation that is required to instil a strongly competitive spirit. To further add to variables (though it remains bright), after a few heats we're treated to some cliché Welsh weather in the form of another quick burst of rain.

Anything the BSI can do at the Millennium, Tim Stone can equal or better. Well that is the light-hearted attitude taken by Jase over the tannoy, "there's a tapes malfunction there - if it's good enough for the Millennium Stadium, it's good enough for us I can tell you! I know what the problem is - it's Chris Durno! Whenever he's spectating he ends up officiating. So if you see him, point him out to security and we'll have him ejected from the stadium!" The next outing for the young in-form Australian lets Jase remind us, "Chris Holder - the holder of the Welsh Open title!" As would have been expected beforehand if there'd been a show of hands in the crowd, Holder wins by the proverbial country mile from Ricky Ashworth, who himself had won by an inordinate but similar distance in Heat 2 from Mroz on his debut race in this country. Former Welsh Open champion Andre Compton looks a likely early contender to be a finalist when winning Heat 7, but only after a re-run due to a rider tangle that appeared to be instigated by Mroz under the mistaken impression he could play dodgems on the second bend during the initial running of the heat. This must have exhausted his luck since he withdraws from the meeting after his next ride with a knee damaged when he falls heavily after David Howe dives under him with some venom. This is a different David from the one who kindly interrupted his gardening at the start line before Heat 9 to stop and sign autographs for a couple of cheeky young fans. In between times, Josef 'Pepe' Franc has developed a psychological block of some sort about the first-bend corner, though this time he manages to wait until the second lap to give another virtuoso display of weird riding skill. This takes the form of two 360 degree revolutions on the bike before he then resumes in the traditional direction of travel with a peculiarly slow motion roll from his machine that would have him sacked as a stuntman on any self-respecting action feature film. Jase rather formally called this a "failure to negotiate the first turn", while referee Dave Dowling must be a keen reader of Halliwell's and the SCB rule book since he excludes him for his troubles as the primary cause of the stoppage. Since it is a fall with great artistic merit, it would have been no surprise if Pepe were to perform a first-bend triple salchow on his next outing. In fact, more prosaically he trails in last and withdraws from the meeting, thereby joining "knee ligament" victim Compton in the car park much earlier than expected.

By now the sun is back and the first sign of problems with dust unbelievably rears into the equation of the meeting (some claim the track is made of dust not shale). If the first bend is Pepe's nemesis then the third bend is Ricky Ashworth's equivalent hurdle. In Heat 10 chasing late entrant to the field, Krzysztof Stojanowski, he smashes into the fence (of the wooden not air variety as this is the Premier League) with great velocity on the last lap. This race is also notable for Ryan 'Green Fingers' Fisher incurring the wrath of the start marshal for excessive pre-race gardening that leads some to believe he is digging for buried treasure. It is an effort that must have exhausted him since he retires before the race ends. Though he takes no action for Fisher delaying the start, the referee endures a busy afternoon with seven re-run races and a host of incidents to adjudicate on along with a couple of awarded races. The most notable heat of the afternoon is another re-run affair, after the initial attempt to complete it is derailed by a horrendous smash for Marek Mroz who loses control on the first lap and appears to want to re-enter the pits head first through the pits gate. The St John Ambulance staff crowd round and, judged by the impact and awkwardness of the fall, it wouldn't have been a surprise if a trip to the hospital were the bare minimum for the Pole. However, with an echo of the thrillingly exciting Poles of my childhood who always comprehensively demolished the Smallmead safety fence before they leapt to their feet with a broad smile and a few words of broken English, Mroz rises from the shale waving enthusiastically. Afterwards Tim notes, "Marek impressed us all with his attitude, and the fans really took to him. He had a prang with Andre in his second ride and then almost took the safety fence out later on, only to get up and wave to the crowd!"

This drama is as nothing compared to what we witness from Chris Holder in the re-run, who gives new meaning to the concepts of bravery, riding skill and nerve, for which, it's genuinely a struggle to find enough superlatives. In a nutshell, not only does he explore every possible racing line to get round four laps of the track (in every race) but, when he comfortably leads his second

Adam Shields with fans

lap, his approach to the vexatious third corner causes him to lose control, get totally out of shape at high speed and career inexorably towards the wooden boards of the safety fence for the seemingly inevitable crash. Somehow with automatic reflex and intense breathtaking skill on and almost off the bike - you wouldn't call it composure since his limbs flail in concert with the bucking movement of his machine - he showcases a manoeuvre that appears to cause him to traverse the boards just about still on his bike before he lands back into the saddle in an upright position on the exit of the fourth bend. This detour causes him to temporarily lose position by a couple of places but his full-throttle resumption sees him fearlessly and determinedly flash past his rivals round the outside to win the race easily. I would rarely ever buy a DVD of a meeting I'd been to (except a Mike Bennett one) but this manoeuvre was so breathtaking it would enjoy endless replays and, in my opinion, makes the famous Rickardsson air fence wall-of-death impression look pedestrian (albeit this was at the so-called 'higher' level of a GP). It is so stunning and an almost cartoon-like manoeuvre - built on a verve and an adaptability you'd have to tick in the box marked natural grace and skill, rather than luck. I feel like wiping my eyes in disbelief and, in years to come, the number of people who'll claim to have been part of the crowd inside Hayley stadium to see this will probably multiply one hundred fold. It was worth a season's admission money in itself and was, in my opinion, the instinctive ride of genius. Jase observed with some understatement, "that's how to entertain the crowd!" Referee Margaret Vardy's partner Steve later remarks to me, "I can't remember when I last saw motorcycling like that - it was unbelievable!"

The next race is staged in a way that could make you think it had been styled in the manner of what is traditionally the last Banger car race of the night - the Demolition Derby. Ronnie Correy leads until the second bend of the second lap before he suddenly crashes over onto his left shoulder. Jase tells us authoritatively, "seized an engine, threw a chain, not quite sure ..." In the re-run Lubos Tomicek produces a slow motion fall in the same spot that must have distracted Ryan Fisher who, before the red light comes on, smashes into the fence on the very next bend. The race is awarded to the sole survivor of the heat Leigh Lanham. "Andre Compton sadly withdraws with knee ligament trouble and I don't think we'll be seeing any more of Josef 'Pepe' Franc either." In the next race, having had a few rather extended himself races to dust down and fix his equipment, Ricky Ashworth then crashes again in almost the same place on the third bend to provoke Jase to contemplate whether, in true Grand National fashion, it should be renamed "Ashworth Corner". Fortunately, the other riders stop promptly without too much difficulty, despite the fact the centre green flag marshal has a senior moment at the very moment of the fall since he prefers to gawp rather than raise the flag in his hand. Apart from the crashes, re-runs and dare-devil racing, another notable feature of every race is the increased dust levels that quickly head much more towards choking than light. "I apologise once again for the dust but with all the black clouds around if you put water down, Sod's Law says you get a shower and ruin it. If you don't, and we didn't, you get dust!"

What we also get is a thrilling set of closing qualifying races and a great finale. Before then the riders continue to drop like flies - both Ronnie Correy and Eric Andersson didn't ride their final heats and were marked in the programme as non-starters. I'm more of the school of thought that says if you lead on points after all the heats have been completed then you win, though this has become a rarity nowadays. Consequently, we have one more race - the Final - to determine the champion, though thankfully the four finalists are so clear-cut as not to require the eventuality of a run off between riders tied on the same points tally. The points totals has Lanham, Shields and Howe all tied on 12 points with Holder next on a comparatively meagre 10. David Howe looks the likeliest winner until Holder again shows his talent to zoom thrillingly past through a non-existent gap only to then nearly obliterate his advantage by flirting dangerously with the safety fence. There's something almost Polish about him and, given his youth (19), something engagingly unpredictable in his full-throttle gifted, harum scarum style of racing. He's a worthy (defending) champion who served up the race of the season, if not the decade. Anyone who'd come along to Newport would travel further to see Chris Holder line up again next year. A delighted Tim Stone laconically commented to the *Speedway Star* afterwards, "I think Chris Holder fancied an excursion to Newport with the lines he was taking to win the Final."

1st July Welsh Open Championship, Winner: Chris Holder

Tim Stone R.I.P.

Tim Stone was sadly prematurely snatched from his family, his friends, and all the speedway community, aged 55 on April 26th 2008.

What you saw is what you got with Tim. Without his dedication and vision, Newport Speedway wouldn't have survived. Like he had helped so many youngsters, Tim quietly and without fuss always helped me too (in a slightly schoolmasterly way leavened with a sharp wit). Unlike many other promoters of his generation - and though he didn't know me from Adam - he spent a couple of hours on the phone to go through in thorough and painstaking detail the nuances of my draft chapter on Newport in *Showered in Shale* prior to its publication ("do you have to say 'meagre crowd'? Can't we say small or not mention it all?").

In my brief experience, Tim was an idiosyncratic, modest, strong-minded and plainly spoken man who marched to his own tune and adhered to his own strong sense of values. In my view, he typifies why speedway remains community based and, despite attempts by commercial and vested interests, resolutely isn't corporate. He remembered his (working class) roots and was passionate about South Wales too*. He will be sadly missed.

* See *Showered in Shale*, Chapter 23 'The House that Tim Built'

Chapter 20. Mildenhall v King's Lynn: Banter flares in the fens

7th July

Jonathan	*"Fast field in Heat 13 - that's something to look forward to."*
Kelvin [without a hint of emotion in his voice]	*"Yeh that should be a special race."*
Jonathan	*"All the heats are important but this one could be very important!"*
Kelvin	*"Drama before it even starts!"*
Jonathan	*"Where did that come from?"*
Kelvin	*"It came from the top drawer"*
Jonathan	*"We'll big you up as we always do!"*
Kelvin	*"I think the coin toss could prove pivotal"*

The poor summer weather forced the postponement of the derby fixture between Mildenhall and King's Lynn at the end of May but was soon rearranged for a rare Saturday night meeting at West Row. Like many clubs, the Tigers haven't had the best of luck with the weather gods but also have had to cancel a couple of fixtures because of work at the stadium. In fact, it will be the first meeting there since June 10th when they won 49-44 against Stoke. Since then the track has been re-laid, stock-car debris removed and 150 tons of new shale put down. Some of this has been subsequently lost without a wheel turned in anger because of flooding caused by monsoon-like rainfall. A big crowd is expected though they'll have to make do with an insert inside the already printed programme unused from May. A glance at the team sheets reveals that each club has a number of riders who've also ridden for their local derby rivals. The ex-Stars in the Tigers line up are Shaun Tacey, Tom P Madsen and Tomas Suchanek, while the Stars track ex-Tigers Paul Lee and James Brundle. This should add extra spice to a meeting that's often keenly contested by the riders and passionately felt by the fans in local bragging rights terms. Six weeks is a long time in speedway as well as politics and this is best illustrated by the swap of one Mark (Thompson) for another (Baseby) in the Tigers line up. In his notes for the superseded programme, team manager Laurence Rogers praises "Thommo" for "getting amongst the points with a tremendous paid 9 return" against Glasgow. By the time of the actual fixture, Laurence has "thought long and hard" about axing Thommo and reluctantly done so in true mercy-killing fashion, "he cannot be knocked for his commitment and effort but it was just not going right for him and his confidence was clearly at a low point". His replacement previously rode for Mildenhall in the Academy League in 2006, but Mark Baseby has mainly served his speedway apprenticeship at Sittingbourne. Also missing tonight is Kyle Legault because he's made it through the semi-final of the GP qualification tournament and so, Laurence notes, finds himself only "ten rides away from being a GP rider in 2008!"

The club have kindly given me permission to sell my books and I've arranged to stay the night on Queensway in downtown Mildenhall. After I've checked in at the local Queens Arms hostelry recommended by club Press Officer Simon Barton ("never stayed there myself so I don't know what it's like") and noted the sign on my door - "take away food (Indian and Chinese) will not be eaten in the rooms" - I soon found my table set up in the alcove between the burger outlet and 'The Fenman' bar, next to the trackshop run by Johnny Barber. From this vantage point in the grandstand, you get an excellent view of the whole track particularly the run from the starting tapes towards the first and second bends. The King's Lynn trackshop is also part of the Barber Empire, so I pay great attention to the pre-meeting forecasts I hear. Johnny diplomatically plumps for a 45-45 all draw, his brother Nick expects a 48-42 win for King's Lynn and Mike Moseley (here tonight with his convalescing wife and a man of many hats (helper at the Lynn trackshop, exiled Wimbledon fan and Berwick programme contributor to name but a few) opts for a similar score, albeit in favour of the Tigers. The always-friendly Shaun Tacey has come over for a chat with the Barbers only to be told by Nick, "you're getting fat and going grey!" Shaun smiles, "I can't afford to cut me hair! I could do with a good meeting 'cause I ain't been doing so good to be honest this season." The track is bathed in sunshine and looks in perfect racing condition from this distance, though close up the reality might be somewhat different. Shaun wanders off to get on with his preparations but, as he leaves, reminds us that he's not adverse to the odd abandonment of a meeting if it means he can continue to be an avid watcher of his favourite soaps on telly, "it's sunny so you know there's no *Emmerdale* on!"

No trip to Mildenhall is ever complete without the obsessive-compulsive attentions of Michael, a teenage Tigers fan who haunts Johnny Barber at the trackshop throughout each and every meeting of the season. He's already hovered a couple of times by my table as I set up my stall of books in between constantly fingering, inspecting and generally checking the speedway merchandise laid out on the many tables of the trackshop. He's keen to know my planned whereabouts for the evening and when EXACTLY I'll be leaving, "are you here 'til the end of the meeting?" he asks every five minutes or so. Michael refuses to be reassured on this point nor about his other frequently asked questions, "will you sign them?" and, the one that really concerns him, the fact that my books are stocked by the shop as well as myself, "will you both sell them?" Johnny affects to pretend intolerance under the constant fire of this frequent questioning and claims to find that Michael gets under his feet. However, actions speak louder than words, so Michael often sneaks round to cuddle up to Johnny only to be admonished, "Michael don't you wipe your snot on my clothes! How many times have I told you?" They must come from a theatrical family because, oblivious to the strong smell of burning sausages wafting over from the food stall nearby, Nick Barber is soon screwing his face up in mock disgust at the contents of my Tupperware container of food (a delicious combination of brown rice, seafood salad, broccoli, spinach and cauliflower), "what's that? You ain't gunna sell none if they get to see that!" As if he's the missing half of a shale-based comedy double act, once he's established the contents of my meal Johnny chimes in, "it's like being at a Gordon Ramsay speedway track!" Nick doesn't hold out much hope for my prospects of a book sales triumph tonight, "if you sell 10 I'll be surprised - let me rephrase that, I'll be pleased for you."

As the first fans already filter into the stadium and, apparently mandatorily, immediately set out their blankets or garden chairs on the grassy hillock of the back straight, I rush to the pits to thank Laurence Rogers for his hospitality. I don't find Laurence but I do find Peter Thorogood who's immortalised for posterity pictured sat topless in a large shed in my book *Showered in Shale*. It's a memorable photo described by Mildenhall Webmaster David Crane as "a scary topless shot of Thorogood." Peter is a taciturn man who's been round the metaphorical speedway houses many times, "I've been involved for so long, there's photos of me knockin' about everywhere. I've been going ever since West Ham in 1946. I used to go straight from school to join the queue at half four in order to get our seats a couple of rows back from the fence by putting out our West Ham scarves. I was promoter at Rayleigh when I marked out the track for Allied promotions for Reg Fearman. When it shut I couldn't go elsewhere! But, gradually I got involved again." Peter is clearly a huge lover of the thrill of the speed and lure of the shale. I listen to him enthuse about the performance of Chris Holder in the Welsh Open and, in particular, one daredevil breathtaking manoeuvre, "he rode right up the fence higher than Rickardsson - how he didn't fall I don't know - his foot left the footrest and touched the back wheel. I was stood with Neil Street and he knows his father and has known him since he was a baby. He says his balance is exceptional - no matter how out of control or out of shape he gets, he rarely falls off. He's got the talent to go all the way, if he doesn't have an accident of course!" Peter isn't listed in the Tigers programme as a club official but I know that he also travels round to a few other selected tracks, like the Isle of Wight, to help advise on matters of the shale. Or he would but for mechanical problems with his motor, "me BMW engine blew up on Thursday. The red light came on but it was lashing down and I didn't want to stop on the M11 so I carried on to Stansted where I turn off (I live in Southend) 'cause you hear all those stories about the foreign lorries not seeing people on the hard shoulder and running them down not knowing they have and not stopping!"

Track staff gather

Spares van

Back at the trackshop, Kevin Long has arrived and is already deep in conversation with Johnny. Kevin is the always-dapper Mildenhall (and Ipswich) "announcer/presenter" renowned for his sharp tongue, quick wit, proclivities and effortless use of the double entendre. Today he sports a pink tie, a smart white jacket and dark trousers. Later his identity is questioned on the British Speedway forum, "is he the chap in the Showaddywaddy suit who announces the teams?" It's not a suit but someone offers the observation, "got a slaphead like honey too." Kevin is also a man who relishes the chance to exploit (real or perceived) local rivalries and all night will take studious delight to playfully insult and generally bate the more thin-skinned of the King's Lynn faithful in attendance at West Row. In my view, he aims to get a reaction to his lively repartee but offers his more caustic comments in a playful tongue-in-cheek style that can, sometimes, get misinterpreted or cause offence. No stereotype remains unexplored or cutting phrase unuttered, though this is smoothly combined with encyclopaedic knowledge of the sport and its riders. Some loathe his approach but there's no doubt it usually adds to, rather than detracts from, the overall entertainment on offer and it definitely builds the passion on the terraces amongst both sets of fans. Speedway isn't a working class motorbike version of the Royal Garden party and doesn't require or exhibit manners appropriate to such an event. While speedway is first and foremost a family sport, we do need to break away from identikit presenters blathering about the results in favour of some with spunk and brio to add much-needed colour. I'm sure he does overstep the mark on occasion and afterwards the forums would bemoan this and chastise him for his objectionable comments along with accusations about his comparative lack of respect. He promises to announce that I'm here to the crowd at regular intervals, "don't worry you'll get equal billing as I don't want any squabbling in the merchandise area!"

Despite his best efforts at promotion, sales remain slow but I am treated to some customer feedback about my photo book, *Shale Britannia*. "When I first got it and saw all those empty stadiums and car parks, I thought 'well!' But once I read the two pages at the front where you explained it, I thought I'll look again. And now I can see it's brilliant - it's a fictional meeting done so well. We can all get photos of the riders on the track but you've really caught something." Another man echoes this later, "I've been going 40 years and your book really captures what speedway is all about - you get the atmosphere and everything!" The lovely Wendy with the unique surname - Jedrzejakski (pronounced "JED-RA-JEDSKI") - is also at the meeting. From her I learn the word "otoresu" which she tells me is "Japanese for speedway" Blimey! I also gather she's well connected in the speedway world, "I rang Garry [Stead] but couldn't speak to him as he was in the gym building up his upper body!"

Some people really love a moan and speedway fans are no different but proximity to the trackshop seems mistakenly to lead them to the belief that I must have some involvement or power in decision-making at the club. "Where do you get the programmes? I can't believe how much it costs to get in here! We've already spent £20 that's £4 more than Lynn. It's our first time here in 10 years and we won't be coming again to get ripped off!" If I could have found him, I'd have asked Kevin Long to cap off his enjoyable start to the evening by saying a few words and summoning up some of his key insights into the consequences of the types of close family relationships he claims is allegedly commonly practised in Norfolk. The man grumbles off in search of a programme that, when he finds it, will confirm his feeling that he's being gouged since in reality all you really get for your money is an insert. Over the tannoy, Kevin breezily informs us, "if you've just joined us - the programme is as per programme!" Bathed in sunshine, the stadium looks pretty full. There's a good selection of garden furniture throughout with the back straight grassy hillock particularly well served with a varied selection and in front of me there's very little room left in either direction within the grandstand that houses the trackshop. There's also a full accompaniment of storm flies and other insects stimulated by the warmth to venture from wherever they live in the fields, ditches and hedgerows of the nearby flat fenland horizon. An older man repeatedly tries to swat them away without success, "you always get a good selection of insect life here!" People close to him try to asphyxiate the insects by ostentatiously smoking but are loudly sent from the grandstand. It's the first speedway meeting at West Row since the smoking ban came into effect in England and clearly there will be some teething problems with its implementation and the exact demarcation of where you can and can't smoke. It's rather like the disputes between local and Icelandic fisherman off the coast of Scotland fighting over what cod has been caught within British territorial waters and what hasn't. Understandably, many smokers are habitual people and consequently struggle to shake off learned behaviours, such as the long-held 'right' to fill the air with toxic and carcinogenic fumes when and where they choose irrespective of the wishes of others. Now that the stormtroopers of the health and safety lobby have intruded on this pleasure, they're somewhat tetchy and irritable at these recently altered circumstances. On this occasion, they grumble and depart but are soon back smoking in that spot again, drawing deep on the evil weed and gulping lungfuls of smoke. The lady smoker (and like swearing, smoking is rarely ladylike) takes particular umbrage and mistakenly simultaneously sees herself as a 'victim' of political correctness and a kind of speedway/smoking prisoner of conscience prepared to suffer and fight the forces of oppression. Well, she screams her objections when told to go "outside" [the grandstand], "this is farking outside, I'll farking show you!" I think her objection is based on an architectural misperception since our grandstand has a roof and is 'enclosed', therefore, counts as an enclosed space under the new legislation.

Entertaining though incendiary smokers are while fighting for a spot from which to exercise their right to slowly kill themselves or others, the action on the track completely absorbs. Things start poorly for King's Lynn when the fast-gating Tomas Topinka has an engine failure on the last lap to loud ironic cheers from the home fans, thereby gifting Mildenhall a 5-1. The race also features a very loud interruption from an overflying plane that leads me to think we may be about to be dive bombed, but doesn't even merit a glance away from the action on the track by the locals well used to noisy interruptions from activities on the nearby air base. If a 5-1 is a bad start, then a 5-0 in the next race "in memory of Shirley Gill" is even worse. With the Stars James Brundle excluded after the finish by referee Dave Watters for starting the race without a dirt deflector fitted and guest reserve Simon Lambert stymied with mechanical gremlins that caused him to retire, the result provokes yet more unfettered delight from the Mildenhall faithful. They certainly appear to relish the misfortune of their local rivals and gleefully celebrate a stonking 10-1 advantage. Kevin plays up the drama by savouring the heat details and the accurate pronunciation of riders' names, in particular, that of the Czech heat winner, "Thomas SUE-CAR-NECK" whose winning time sets a new track record of 50.22, thereby narrowly pipping the record held by Paul Lee (50.25) since 2004. Said in the correct manner, the Czech's name sounds totally alien to me but Johnny remarks, "it is the correct way to say it so Mister SUE-CAR-NECK says but he'll always be a SOO-SHAH-NECK to me!"

With King's Lynn hopes of an away win already looking dicey, the likelihood of an aggregate point appears less possible with another wildly celebrated heat advantage that takes the score to 14-3 after three races. Michael pops by to wistfully touch various items of memorabilia and to buzz around to check that the exact mathematical position of the merchandise on the trackshop tables remains as he'd previously left it on his last visit five minutes ago. He stops to linger and look at my books again and, with a vague nod towards Johnny Barber, knowledgably reveals, "You're both selling them!" The Stars then fight back with what tonight almost counts as a mini-revival but in reality is usually only a heat advantage, albeit won forcefully by Trevor Harding when he passes Paul Fry on the last corner. Fryer came into the team after Mildenhall sacked their number one 'Super' Mario Jirout - after an apparently lacklustre display at Glasgow ("as a consequence of what happened in the meeting at Ashfield

Levity reigns at track shop

Advertising opportunity

[appeared not to give a monkeys and pootling round faraway at the rear of each race he 'competed' in] we have had to dispense with the services of Mario"). It's obligatory to refer to Paul Fry as "evergreen" or to say, to quote Bryn Williams' description of any speedway rider aged over 35, "like good wine and cheese, he just gets better with age". Laurence Rogers breaks the cliché mould with some hyperbole of his own with a description that styles him as a "real battler", someone who "always gives his all" and as "one of the sport's 'Peter Pans'". In fact he doesn't enjoy the best of nights and this second place is as good as it gets for him all evening. He with the interesting surname when translated from Dutch, Theo Pijper, also isn't in stellar form in his role as guest replacement for Kyle Legault. He races to an untroubled last place in Heat 5 in a drawn race sponsored by "Out soon: British speedway track directory: routes and maps to every track £3.50. See Laurence for details." Tom P narrowly avoids an exclusion in the next heat ("would you like to be a match day mascot - only £10?") under the two-minute time allowance by riding dangerously fast on a short cut across-cum-around the centre green, thereby suddenly drawing my attention to the noticeable lack of the Mildenhall Grid Girls here tonight. In the first corner, Shaun Tacey shoves James Brundle with such ferocity that I wonder if he's accidentally taped over an unseen episode of *Emmerdale*. Brundle soon has to take up the chase since his partner Trevor Harding appears to be unable to slide his bike with any degree of competence. It's a determined chase that nearly, but not quite, pays dividends on the line. The scores are now at an unfeasibly large 24-11 but, ever the optimist, stood by the trackshop Nick Barber sagely observes, "Lynn only need a couple of 5-1s and they're right back in it." In fact, the King's Lynn team management shrewdly opt to give Daniel Nermark the black-and-white helmet colour and he then combines with Paul Lee for an important 8-1. Michael pops by to ask, "when are you packing up?" and tells Johnny, "you're both selling the books!" On the centre green, presenter Kevin Long congratulates the Lynn team management on their actions, "the tactical ride is there to be played and was played there with great affection [?] in Heat 7!"

Johnny reassures me with news that in his confident opinion *Shifting Shale* will "be a slow burn". The chance of any further sales is then unexpectedly cut short when a lady with her jumper tied round her waist gets it snagged on the corner of my display table, thereby dragging it to an angle sufficient to spill most of the books on the floor. Most clumsy people would apologise, but she says angrily, "you want to get some hazard tape on that!" I make a mental note to add this to my list of essential publishing requirements for erstwhile travelling authors. Shaun Tacey enjoys the effective night he aimed for and combines with Tomas Suchanek to reassert the Tigers dominance with a 5-1 in Heat 8 that stretches the lead for the home team back to a handsome 10 points. There's an exchange of drawn heats before Topinka and Mills treat us to some formation overtaking action on the first corner of Heat 11. Topinka distracts Fry with an outside pass while Mills sneaks cannily up the inside to join his team mate. Mark Baseby hasn't quite read the script and nearly sneaks second place on the line from Mills who appears to have his mind on his intended celebrations.

These seem somewhat OTT, given the Stars still trail by 6 points but, if nothing else, indicate his determination and commitment. Kevin is keen to quiz the crowd and build the meeting up to an exciting finale in the minds of the spectators, "can King's Lynn come back with four races to go?" he asks rhetorically. Chris Mills has had years of interview training with Mike Bennett so serves up some bland 'sick as a parrot' responses to some probing questions when Kevin interviews him after the race. Excitingly we learn from Millsy, "we've gotta take each race as it comes and see if we can sneak it!" Kevin basks literally and metaphorically in the glow of the moment and dons an imaginary apron to talk in culinary metaphors, "sunshine speedway we're cooking up for the fans." If Millsy showed tenacity then Suchanek displays something in spades that, when spotted, causes Nermark to back off dramatically after a competitive first corner. Pijper overcomes his meeting-long torpor to rouse himself sufficiently to gain second place in a race sponsored by "Coming soon. The Michael Lee story *I Did It My Way* £16.99 - see Laurence to order one." This is the type of book to excite many speedway fans, though some still disparage Michael for 'not fulfilling his talent', which I understand to be a coded objection to some of his recreational activities that, in the past, got him in trouble with the law. With the order of the evening now apparently to exchange alternate 5-1s, Trevor Harding stalks Paul Fry for four laps. He often attempts to pass but finds his route blocked by his more experienced rival until he cuts inside during the dash to the finish line. It's too close to call and Kevin milks the tension with his announcement of another 5-1, "Second [pause] shush - Trevor Harding!"

With the match score at 43-37, Mildenhall hold the aggregate advantage by three points and their 4-2 in the penultimate ensures they will gain those three points no matter what the Stars do in the final race. The delight amongst the Tigers fans verges on the unalloyed. "SOO-CAR-NEK" then caps off his match-winning performance from the reserve berth by scything through the field from third to first on the first corner. It's a manoeuvre that many fans take as their cue for yet more loud exuberance. Kevin Long joins the riders on their victory parade and takes the opportunity to banter with some of the King's Lynn fans who remain watching from the terraces. One particularly voluble couple take defeat badly enough to offer hand gestures and vitriol to Kevin who retorts over the tannoy, "it's nice to see you waving at the riders - you've got five fingers on one hand; I expect you've got webbed feet where you come from." Quite a witty, off-the-cuff put down, in the face of abusive hecklers that plays with some conventional stereotypes. Kevin also said as an aside to other Mildenhall staff and riders with him on the truck that was also audible over the tannoy, in the manner of Leslie Nielsen going to the lavatory with a microphone in *Naked Gun*, "inbreds". Subsequently, this was reported on the British Speedway forum as, "you really are an inbred!" I don't hear his comments [though Kevin recounts them later], but afterwards on the British Speedway Forum some upset King's Lynn fans vent their feelings and repeat his alleged comments at length, though in true speedway internet fashion some of the posters weren't even at the meeting or, if they were, also didn't hear the comments! This deflects attention from what an enthralling meeting we all witnessed and conveniently obscures any embarrassment felt by King's Lynn fans at the loss. An angry poster from Norfolk with the moniker 'Shooting Star' burns up on re-entry and notes, "if I were the Mildenhall promotion I would feel totally and utterly embarrassed to have Kevin Long on my staff" and, like a few others, demands an apology otherwise he's never going to darken the doors (well turnstiles) of West Row ever again. Keeping the pound in your pocket is the only language apparently really understood by the Mildenhall promotion (or that they can be impotently threatened with), while repeated appeals for "a statement" from club Press Officer Simon Barton falls on deaf ears. Though given he was standing with Kevin at the time of his remark and his aside, he still could be called as a witness to the show trial that will undoubtedly take place soon when they convene the great speedway courts of justice. Someone else apparently misunderstands both racism and the Race Relations Act, whilst simultaneously losing all perspective (as is traditional for some on the forums) to claim this was "a bordering racist remark." And to think I thought insulting the Welsh was the last bastion of this improper use of language until Kevin expanded the genre? It's probably best not to be provoked, but caustic repartee is all part of the élan and appeal of Kevin's own unique presentational approach. It should be taken in the spirit of fun intended and remains infinitely preferable to the inane/witty banter of some of his erstwhile presenter rivals who, in the words of Charlie Brooker when discussing *Katie & Peter Unleashed*, "remain scarily upbeat, like a barman cheerfully ignoring a death in his pub."

Fans gather at pits fence

Important notice

Unaware of this furore unfolding, I'm later joined by Kevin - after he's conducted a series of post-meeting rider interviews replete with penetrating questions in a packed 'The Fenman' bar - who picks up my photo book *Shale Britannia*, "it's a Mildenhall and Ipswich fans kind of book - no complicated sentences or difficult words! Have you sold out and is my cheque in the post?" I tell him it is, "well, that's not a phrase you hear much in Mildenhall."[1]

7th July Mildenhall v King's Lynn (Premier League) 52-40

[1 When writing up the events of this meeting, I asked Kevin for his view on the post-meeting furore now the dust had settled and the carrot harvest was in. He replied:

"What surprised me about the whole incident was the way that it 'snowballed' thanks to the erstwhile intervention of some forum members with obvious ulterior motives. What we had witnessed had been a terrific Premier League encounter between Mildenhall and King's Lynn. Obviously emotions run high in local derbies, but for the most part the King's Lynn supporters were very sporting indeed as we made our way round the track on the victory parade - but for this one couple. Just as we pulled out of the second bend going down the backstraight, they stood right up against the fence and launched into a tirade of abuse (all the strongest expletives F's, C's, and W's) and using a combination of accompanying hand gestures.

What I actually said directly to them was that "it was nice to see them waving at the riders with their webbed hands". Chinese forum whispers has since seen this comment bearing no resemblance to what was actually said. But that never stopped anyone on any message board from having their say did it?

As we passed by this couple and the 'communication' between parties had been exchanged, I literally said just "inbreds" under my breath, whilst turning away and chatting to the Mildenhall riders and management on the parade truck. In no way, whatsoever, did I say that all King's Lynn fans were "inbreds" or any other comments like that. In fact, during the course of the meeting itself, I was congratulating the Lynn riders after successful heats and for providing some great entertainment. Can the same be said of when Mildenhall or any other team for that matter are the away team at other tracks, like King's Lynn (for example)? Having attended a number of meetings at Saddlebow Road during the course of 2007, I know for sure, having witnessed it, that the comments I made pale into insignificance when compared to some of those from the King's Lynn camp.

It is also fascinating when supporters comment on the situation, having not even heard anything for themselves, simply going by what they heard from someone or other or indeed had not even been at the meeting at all. I think that is the very problem with Internet forums. I have been to countless Ipswich v. King's Lynn derbies over the years and they are always highly charged affairs, with the exchanges between the fans often as entertaining as the racing itself. But at the end of the meeting, everyone goes home happy, with no hard feelings and looking forward to the next encounter. Fans are always trying to think of new ways to wind up their rivals. Basically what was said on the day, stayed on the day. With the modern method of 'Internet chat', comments and situations can be regurgitated beyond all recognition from the original event.

What surprised me a tad was that I was heavily criticised by certain King's Lynn fans because my performance during the 2006 encounter between Mildenhall and King's Lynn was not enough for a local derby meeting - and reminded that the presenter is there to add to the atmosphere and build on the banter between the two sets of supporters. I have never, and will not ever, resort to some of the tactics employed by some meeting presenters in the name of 'entertainment'. I am quite simply my own man, and many of my comments are simply an extension of my personality, quick witted with the occasional double entendre thrown in for good measure.

It is such a subjective issue, that of meeting presentation and its presenters. And, of course, local fans will always back 'their man'. Many Ipswich and Mildenhall fans have spoken to me over the years and thanked me for adding a certain unique something to their meeting experience. Indeed, the very forums that offer the criticism of me will also offer up praise and appreciation of my efforts."]

Chapter 21. Peterborough: Foreigners snatch glory at the Showground

8th July

Nigel *"Who says Leigh Adams does all his work in an armchair blasting away from the start?"*

The original mid-May date for the Premier League Four Team Tournament suffered from the weather and was rearranged for another Sunday in July. Fortunately in a summer of disappointment on the sunshine front, this one dawned and bright and sunny without a hint of cloud. Though the Barber brothers have allegedly secured the exclusive rights to run the trackshops at all the *Super7even* events, just like at Somerset, they're again notable by their absence. The merchandise on display in the glass-fronted trackshop on the non-track side of the main grandstand was completely different from the range of Panthers' logoed items usually displayed on a regular race night by Peterborough (and Rye House) trackshop man Andy Griggs. Today the tables were heaving with clothes festooned with the "*Super7even*", Wulfsport or GP logos, though it takes a supreme optimist to think that anoraks will sell in bulk on a warm sultry day. Helpfully for those who'd not heard previously, Nigel Pearson explained in the programme that the *Super7even* concept was invented by Jonathan Chapman as the umbrella branding term for a series of "revamped major events" in an attempt to make them more of a highlight in the British Speedway calendar for fans and, hopefully, also the media. Not that everyone likes change or Jonathan Chapman, but one thing that had met with widespread approval was the decision to host this Premier League event on the ostensibly neutral territory of the East of England Showground in Peterborough.

I'm not sure what the opposite of subliminal advertising is, but a brief glance in the programme soon confirmed that it would have no truck with such subtlety. Nigel welcomed this choice of location, "it's great to see the Premier League Fours back at Peterborough - the traditional home of this great competition." Chairman of the British Speedway Promoters Association, Peter Toogood, noted, "it has returned to what many people feel is the true home for the event". Jonathan Chapman also saw the Showground as "the spiritual home of the Premier League Four Team tournament", while Colin Horton was equally definite that this was its "rightful home". Of all the programme columnists, only Tony McDonald and Richard Clark would resist expressing their unalloyed delight at this choice of venue. Something that everyone in attendance could definitely agree on was that the entertainment on offer would represent extremely good value for money since the afternoon was scheduled to feature 32 races and would serve up what Peter Toogood termed, "a bumper day of racing". The format had changed from previous recent incarnations at the further suggestion of organiser Jonathan Chapman to, "two semi-finals of only eight heats and then a 16 heat final. I felt this was better as in the past few years the final was only 12 heats and that wasn't enough."

Another thing that was different from usual at the trackshop was the presence of Dave Rattenberry, here to help out Andy Griggs and take a break from running his successful and (usually) lucrative mainly Midlands based speedway shops empire. This season business was such a struggle that he'd been temporarily seized by the spirit of Fraser from *Dad's Army*, "my takings are down this year to date and I'm not doing well with you - I've hardly sold a thing!" One book had only been out eight days and the other less than a month, so perhaps it was a tad early to declare them dead in the water but, that said, these things often become self-fulfilling prophesies. Nonetheless, it was worrying to hear from such a wily and experienced veteran of the speedway merchandise trade that the market was extremely tough. If the metaphorical sky in Dave's world was morosely clouded, then it was in marked contrast to climatic conditions in this part of central England. Afternoon racing often attracts problems with dust and the intense, almost tropical, heat would also make so many races strength sapping for the riders. Also the unfeasibly sultry

Trophies await

Medical attention arrives

Jonathan Chapman and off-duty
Sexy7even girls

First corner action

weather, combined with the acres of lush pasture around us, attracted unwelcome visitors in the form of a plague of flying little black insects. These tiny pests had an insatiable desire for human flesh or, at least, intensely itched your skin rather than eat it, so the afternoon was punctuated by the metronomic slap of hand on skin all afternoon. Ignoring this infestation, standing by my table in the blistering heat wasn't exactly the ideal conditions for me either and sales remained at a low ebb compared to passing conversations. "32 races for £15 - it's better than the GP - my son is under 11 and gets in free - it's a fantastic day out and incredible value!" There was rumour that the original programme provided for May 13th was about to run out, something that would have been a disaster for any spectator with 32 races to watch. I was stuck at my table but was saved by the extremely knowledgeable young (Peterborough) speedway fan, Thomas Bull, who kindly ran off, despite his half-eaten burger, to buy one for me. His father Steve was subsequently less than impressed with this delay for the family in obtaining their favoured spot in the still mainly empty grandstand.

Once the meeting got under way, the races were staged with great rapidity under the watchful eye of referee Craig Ackroyd. Though notionally a 'neutral' venue since Peterborough race in the Elite League, the sheer size and pace of the track was likely to favour any team who raced regularly at similar sized venues - places like Sheffield and the Isle of Wight. That said, riders move about so much between teams and leagues, ignoring that many also do or have raced in Poland, that you'd hope that they'd set their bikes up appropriately for the wide open spaces of the East of England Showground. The racing is consistently fast here but not always competitive since there's a tendency for the riders to get, as Dave Peet once described it to me at Hull, "strung out like a line of washing!" Even if your team wins, I'd like to think that no true speedway fan enjoys processional races, if an alternative exists. Another feature of the *Super7even* series is that you can't escape from the dulcet tones and unique presentational style of Mike Bennett, who many suspect got the gig on a buy-one-get-one-free basis because he presents at Jonathan Chapman's home track King's Lynn. In fact, descriptive duties are notionally shared with his smooth-talking and enthusiastic presentational partner in crime, Craig Saul, who works the mike to great effect at Rye House and also here at Peterborough every week. However, a number of factors (most notably, the allocation of duties, the sheer volume of races but, most importantly, the fact that yet again there's only one working roving microphone and Mike isn't by inclination a natural sharer) mean that the crowd is treated throughout the afternoon to Mike's thoughts on a stream of consciousness basis, while Craig leavens this aural feast with interjected occasional interviews. In some ways this is the structural nature of the beast since it's always going to be harder to snatch pits interviews - when the desire to rush things through and the frenetic pace of the races on the track is echoed off it in the pits.

Two teams qualify from each side of the draw for the final, and the first semi-final group pits Somerset, King's Lynn, Glasgow and Sheffield against each other; while the second has Rye House, Workington, Birmingham and the Isle of Wight competing. Compared to some meetings, there are few changes to the racecard (despite it being prepared in April for a May fixture), though the Glasgow line up almost alters beyond recognition with two changes. Predictably enough the first race is a tapes to flag affair won by Magnus "ZETTER-STRUM" that sets the tone for an afternoon characterised by some processional racing at the "spiritual home" of the PL Fours. The advent of the *Super7even* series has seen the arrival on the speedway scene of the often-admired *Sexy7even* start line girls, notable for their approachability, good humour, lithe appearance and figure hugging body suits. At first glance, it appears that Lee Dicken has also dressed for this meeting in the uniform of these girls since the design emblazoned on his kevlars echoes that chosen as the series uniform. We've ample time to ponder how the coincidence of this sartorial state of affairs could have arisen since Lee trails along at the rear of the field. The semi-finals alternate between the groups but, nonetheless, beforehand you could have predicted the winner of the next race - Tai Woffinden - though James Wright impresses with both a spectacular turn of speed and because of his comfortable low-slung off-the-back-of-the-bike racing style. You could have predicted that Andre Compton would win the next race by a country mile and thereby quickly confirm Sheffield's status as one of the pre-meeting favourites. Instead, with an unpredictability that always makes watching speedway fascinating, he finishes third to signal that the Tigers might not really roar this afternoon at Peterborough. Before the race, it's also clear that Mike Bennett's default setting is usually to endlessly chunter on about the riders he knows the best - the King's Lynn squad, big name star riders or ex-King's Lynn riders - rather than provide any real insight into the majority of riders who make up the assembled field as a whole. Consequently before the tapes fly, we're informed, "Paul 'Bruce' Lee rides for King's Lynn in this one - he was in superb form at Mildenhall last night." Ignoring the fact that he used to ride for Mildenhall, you'd expect Paul would know his way round West Row, the typology of Peterborough is very different. Consequently, 'Bruce' finishes last, but he gains an understanding of the track conditions.

On the track, this is a team event, though the tannoy pairing seems to be slightly less than telepathic. Talking about himself in the plural, Mike says, "as you know we're doubling up today with Craig Saul who is interviewing riders in the pits today". His partner doesn't expect this apparent cue and a very noticeable silence falls. "Craig?" "If you give me a minute!" replies his partner from then onwards thereby giving Mike carte blanche to either endlessly check on his availability as if he's saddled working with recalcitrant children or to hog the duties. For the fifth race of the day, there's a highly animated welcome for "Chris 'Milk it' Millsy" followed with what sounds suspiciously like a Larry Grayson type catchphrase, "well there you are!" Ritchie Hawkins is introduced with a *faux* American accent for reasons that escape me but might be known by others in the crowd. This race has actual dramas of its own, starting when Ricky Ashworth determinedly batters Craig Watson into the fence on the first bend. In the re-run with all four back, the second lap unusually finds Ashworth, Hawkins and Mills roughly neck and neck rather than playing follow-my-leader in a procession. Ricky ventures to overtake Millsy with a move onto the little-used outside line of the track. It's the instinctive manoeuvre of a born racer but, sadly, he immediately runs out of room and so smashes into the wooden back-straight safety fence at great speed. Rider and machine then dramatically tumble an inordinate distance along the remaining length of the straight. It hasn't turned out to be a great afternoon for Ricky and there's no doubt that he'll be feeling what Kelvin Tatum always euphemistically calls, "second-hand". To makes this worse, while he lies there in pain prostrate on the shale and surrounded by medical personnel who've rushed over from the centre green or who alight from the Transit-style ambulance in attendance at the Showground today - he'll be getting bitten to death by the tiny black insects that afflict everyone. To make matters worse, there's an erstwhile roving investigative reporter who also hovers above him reporting over the tannoy in a *faux* voice of sympathy. It's not going to aid your recovery or enjoyment of the situation. Doctor Mike reports breathlessly, "He has been speaking. He is conscious!" After some time Ricky gets up gingerly to his feet. This is greeted with a low roar of congratulation from the crowd and, by Dr Bennett, with a description of what we can all collectively see with our own eyes, "two main things, (a) he was conscious and (b) he could walk into the ambulance unaided!"

Seizing the rare chance to get a word in edgeways during the delay, Craig Saul has also briefly snatched back the roving mike off the good Doctor to report some important news, "If you are a BSPA member, food is being served on the first bend for you all there!" Close by, befitting the importance of the event, the traditional look of the Peterborough pits has been enhanced with the addition of two large white tents of the type often seen throughout the summer months at outdoor events, such as wedding receptions or gymkhanas. I can only assume they are there to entertain sponsors in since, even allowing for the extra riders and mechanics, the whole pits area appears way more crowded than usual. Eventually, with Ricky finally shipped off to destinations unknown but most likely A&E, the racing nearly resumes with the re-run of the third heat of semi-final one. "Once again we're waiting for Ritchie Hawkins to grace us with his presence", grumbles Mike though he fails to notice that we're also missing two *Sexy7even* start line girls. Obeying the logic of whatever can go wrong will go wrong, the delays continue - when not only does the re-run have to be re-re-run but the start gate has deteriorated in the heat of the afternoon and developed mechanical gremlins to further delay the already tardy proceedings. It seems as though the outside of the mechanism has temporarily become possessed with a diabolic force that means that only one side will shoot skywards but then refuse to stick back down in place at the base of the pole. Eventually Craig Watson wins this race and the rhythm of successive quickly run heats can again resume. Though not before the man in charge of announcing the results, the exotically named Edwin Overland, informs us over the tannoy, "unfortunately we have heard Ricky Ashworth has suffered a broken arm in that incident" before he adds the juxtaposition of a weird request, "and we're calling on Ulrich's number-one fan to come round to the pits and give him a kiss!"

A modicum of entertainment is then provided by Craig Saul warily dashing across the width of the Showground shale to wrest the roving microphone from Mike who notes, "You're right, it is like a relay race!" Breaking the uniformity of the chatter, Craig temporarily snatches back the communication device for a brief alfresco pits interview but finds himself marooned by speeding bikes before he can return said piece of equipment. As the grandstand collectively twitches to relieve the ongoing waves of insects, Craig apologises, "we need the microphone for pits interviews so unfortunately Mike's not there for the next few more heats." Seizing the moment for a few snatched words with Shane Parker, we learn, "I regard Peterborough as the home of the Fours - in the semi-finals, you only get two rides so you have to make them count!" Sadly for their fans, the Tigers of Glasgow along with the Tigers of Sheffield don't do so and are eliminated without a roar from the vital part of the competition. Given the plague of insects and the baking heat this might be a relief! Judging from the racecard in the programme, the race of the afternoon in the other section of the qualifying heats is always likely to be Heat 5 with the appearance of Woffinden, Stonehewer, Holder and Lyons on track together. Though Chris Holder streaks away by some margin, we are treated to a masterclass in the art of overtaking from Lyons and Stonehewer who exchange position with considerable determination and some stylish aplomb. Though there are no Tigers to be eliminated from the other semi-final group, the Islanders look unstoppable as a team so the Birmingham Brummies and the Workington Comets eventually find themselves going the way of all flesh.

In the final, the Islanders establish an early lead that they never look like relinquishing. It's a team performance but the rider that really catches the eye for them all afternoon is their club captain, Jason Bunyan. Unable to be spoken of or written about without some use of the word "experienced", he rides as a man rejuvenated and as a rider apparently inspired to greater levels of performance by his colleague, the 19-year-old possible star of the future Chris Holder. It looks highly likely that Jason would go through the card undefeated all afternoon, until on the last bend of the fourth lap of Heat 7 he punctures while comfortably in the lead. This loss of a 100% record prompts Mike to accurately utter, "not defeated on the track but only by mechanical gremlins." By the half-way stage (of the final) there is only ever going to be one victorious team unless severe bad luck intervenes. Someone who has enjoyed an expensive afternoon is King's Lynn's Trevor Harding who manages to seize his second engine of the day, this time without even bothering to leave the pits. Though Holder impresses out front with four immaculate wins in the final, the really distinctive rider remains Jason Bunyan. Throughout the afternoon he takes a thoughtfully different racing line round the circuit - in true Gollob fashion - to those taken by practically every other rider on display. He generates noticeable speed made all the more acute by his unusual Men-in-Black almost logo-less loosely flapping kevlars perpetually caught in the turbulence of his speedy passage up front. This made him appear slightly unworldly, like a cartoon character Dick Dastardly or possibly Batman. In the euphoria of the moment afterwards, he modestly prefers to congratulate his team on their collective performance, "as soon as we realised we had won it [with three heats to go], the pressure was lifted and we went out and won all the rest of the races at the end." Though he did acknowledge his own part in the triumph, "I know the track at Peterborough like the back of my hand and Chris [Holder] told me about a few more lines that have come to fruit recently." Looking back on the triumph, joint team manager Dave Croucher said, "we produced six race winners over the final six heats that had us finishing 16 points ahead of our closest rivals Somerset, and with more points than Rye House and King's Lynn scored between them [it was] a massive achievement for any club, at any level, but especially for the Isle of Wight. The whole day was brilliant, and I remember phoning my bride (Carol) up and telling her I was soaked to the skin, and she said 'Oh no, you're not rained off again', to which I replied, 'No - it's champagne, we just won!'"

Many fans rush away to beat the notorious Showground traffic and Dave Rattenberry tells me, "Isle of Wight only dropped 10 points all night." Though the riders haven't even come round on parade I bump into the Islanders avuncular promoter, Dave Pavitt, outside the building on the first bend that houses the club bar and the patio area that had been crowded all afternoon with fans, promoters and a smattering of riders eliminated from the competition at the semi-final stage, all keen to have a refreshing/cooling drink. As a concession to the humid conditions and the sun that beat down earlier, Dave sensibly but rather incongruously sports a flat cap that was more in fashion in my teenage years when worn by my dad on a rainy day. In fact, it was of a style too old-fashioned even for him and more probably suited to my granddad's generation. Nonetheless it's practical, does its job effectively and is almost postmodernly stylish. Pav is beaming, red faced from the sun and I half expect to see that he has a whippet with him or hear that he's off to tend to his prize pigeons. Dave appears elated with how things have turned out for his team, "we romped it! Makes you wonder why we're bottom of the league. This is the fourth time I've won it [the Fours] - I've done it with Hackney, Oxford, Ipswich and now the Isle of Wight - and it still tastes just as sweet!" Dave has ventured away from the sunshine bathed pits with a clear purpose - to celebrate the victory with a well-deserved libation or two - but doesn't quite know his way around the watering holes of alien Elite League stamping grounds like the East of England Showground.

[DP] "Where's the bar?"

[JS] "There."

[DP] "It's closed!"

[JS] "There's people inside."

[DP] "It's closed. My lot will go mad if it's not open - speedway without an open bar isn't possible!"

[JS] "The press conference is in there."

[DP] "Is it?"

[JS] "Yeh"

[DP] "I'll just have to have Coke till we go somewhere else!"[1]

8th July Premier League Four Team Tournament, Winners: Isle of Wight

[1 When I saw Dave Pavitt at the Brighton Indoor Speedway (as we now must learn to call it), I enquired about the whereabouts of his flat cap. "I've got it today in fact - it suits all weathers!" He continued, "funny story about that day - we found a pub that was open and we were all in there celebrating and the girl behind the bar knew a bit about speedway and she said 'what are you here for?' We said the Fours and she said 'who won?' We told her we did and she said 'where are you from then?' so we told her the Isle of Wight. 'Oh,' she said, 'it's a shame an English club didn't win it!' No joking."]

Chapter 22. Reading v Eastbourne:
Another new era dawns at Smallmead

9th July

Tony Millard *"We apologise to any viewer who might have seen something that might have disappointed them"*

I arrive in time to witness a new era at Smallmead under the management of new club owner Mark Legg and promoter Malcolm 'Mad Wellie' Holloway, though this would have happened a few weeks earlier if rain hadn't caused the postponement of the first two fixtures under their command. In fact, I'm there so early that I get to see trackshop history made since my arrival coincides with that of Nick and Johnny Barber as they step out of their fully laden van to inspect and clear their new premises ready for business in a few hours' time. Like Mark and Malcolm a few yards away in the speedway office, they're full of new ideas but have to get to grips with what they have inherited before they can put their own stamp on things. As a long-time Reading fan, to my mind the trackshop is a vital part of the fabric of the stadium and, most recently, has been capably run by the friendly Win Povey, mother of Andy the Bulldogs press officer and webmaster. (At least this was his position until the takeover when Swindon's Robert Bamford who inherits the Reading Speedway press duties replaced him. Andy was clearly very upset to be replaced as press officer by someone who did similar duties at another club, but has studiously kept his own counsel.) Win has also lost her job in the trackshop, though Andy has put in a good word on her behalf with Nick Barber. Both of them are Redin through and through and have followed the club through thin and thin with intermittent triumphs in between. The nature of the beast is that new brooms sweep clean irrespective of the qualities, feelings and service of those who've previously toiled long hours on behalf of the club. Change is often uncomfortable and rarely without heartache for the capable but discarded parties deemed surplus to requirements. The Barbers are genuine, proper speedway people themselves so for them this will be business rather than anything personal. However good Win is at her job or however easily she'd slot in, the likelihood is that they'll use their own contacts and people in the future at this shop. The immediate job in hand will be to assess what they find once they've gained access to the shop and then move on from there. Sentiment will play its part but, for now, the task in hand is to get things ready for the new era of fans flooding (or trickling) through the turnstiles tonight for the Elite League 'B' fixture with the Eastbourne Eagles.

Almost the first thing that the Legg/Holloway promotional team did on their return to Smallmead was change the club nickname back from the execrable Bulldogs bravely chosen by 'successful businessman' John Postlethwaite to their long-time original moniker of the Reading Racers. Quite how such a ludicrous decision was ever made really beggars belief and, to my mind, indicates how in many companies the Chief Executive surrounds himself with less capable cronies rather than those that might sensibly question their opinions. Still, the often audacious but latterly inauspicious BSI era is now over and has left its own legacy at the stadium in terms of a new lick of paint, some rather handsome tractors for track maintenance, a revamped and luxurious changing room and shower area for the riders as well as wonderful memories of snatching defeat from the jaws of victory in the 2006 Elite League play-off final. To unluckily lose unexpectedly, when really they were favourites and in such dramatic fashion was, at least, true to some of the traditions of the club. For once, the idea that events occur first as history and subsequently as tragedy or farce, had been inverted under the Postlethwaite reign, so many times that the club nearly went out of existence and, despite the stability now provided by the new promoters, still finds itself in crisis albeit of the muted variety. The sudden demise of Oxford speedway, where Colin Horton suddenly and completely pulled the plug on the club in mid-season was a wake-up call that has just about stirred the BSPA and the remainder of the Elite League promoters from their complacency about both the quality of the product on display and the possible fatal consequences for speedway if any further clubs ceased to exist. This has worked in Reading's favour since the BSPA haven't hesitated to look favourably on the pitiful situation the new promoters find themselves in and are happy to be flexible with regards to the usual rules and requirements, just to ensure that the club continues to exist as a viable entity within the Elite League for the remainder of the season.

Nonetheless, it's going to take more than the hard work of the management and volunteers or another lick of paint to address the problems created and now left behind by the Postlethwaite management era. Rumours were that he'd fallen out of love with his Elite League speedway bauble a long time ago when it was hard to manage and ate the cash in the manner of a storm drain, never mind that it didn't perform as the complementary plaything to the GP series. Never mind that it was a totally different organisational/logistical kettle of fish to run a club week in and week out at home or on the road than to stage a fortnightly series of one-off meetings in various countries dotted throughout Europe. It was as though having run a couple of successful dinner parties, I suddenly crazily decided to take over a struggling second-tier restaurant, change its name, opening times and menu - then buy the best of everything I could lay my hands on from staff to ingredients but then wonder why it didn't gel and wasn't suddenly the talk of the town with three Michelin stars to its name. In a nutshell, pride does come before a fall and though I have sympathies with the quick loss of the previous owners' tax deductible wedge they blew on the Bulldogs, it's criminal that they should have been allowed to bring the club to its knees without advice or punishment from the BSPA. Still, tonight, the past is a foreign country and another new era has dawned (though still with a forecast of possible rain) with the famous winged wheel of the Racers once again proudly emblazoned across the club tabards for all to see. Most loyal supporters will see this as a return to some form of normality, though given the guns for hire, and the slightly mercenary nature of the team assembled at Smallmead in the last year or so, it will take a while before the riders are as committed or as proud about the club as its supporters.

Back inside the Marie Celeste, aka the cramped trackshop abandoned to its own devices at the time of the latest takeover, Nick and Johnny have started to take the clothes down from the hangers or remove them from the shelves. What has been left behind is the Reading Bulldogs merchandise that failed to find an owner in the first few weeks of the season, either because enthusiasm among the fans was lower than a snake's belly or because what was left to buy didn't really appeal. Most of the anoraks, fleeces, rugby style shirts, caps and scarves are 'old' stock from 2006 when the early enthusiasm of the BSI reign led whoever ordered this stuff to hope that a nascent desire for all things emblazoned with a Bulldogs logo was about to become wonderfully rampant among the fans. Though equally, it has to be remembered that BSI planned so well after their winter takeover that they failed to have hardly any significant stock of anything with the Bulldogs brand on it until many weeks into the 2006 season. I'm sure that Bulldogs jackets will become true speedway collectibles in the memorabilia market before too long but was there ever going to be demand among die-hards for rugby style shirts in the wrong colours, even if such apparel is regularly worn in the down-market wine bars of the Home Counties where many imagine John Postlethwaite may live? However, these garments arrived here and Johnny diligently folds the unsold items and stacks them up, while Nick and I make regular journeys round the corner to the speedway office where Malcolm Holloway says we should pile it up for subsequent collection by BSI. Apparently, they claim that the new owners can buy all this surplus Bulldogs merchandise - genuinely to the untrained eye, a ragbag of mostly unsaleable remnants (pens, badges and programme boards excepted) - for a bargain price of £4000! Though they bought the club on the cusp of failing to be a going concern, the new owners haven't just come down with the rain and Malcolm takes the considered view that "they can stick it up their arse!"

With the clothing gone, Johnny empties the Perspex-covered display cabinets of everything inside. This ranges from unsold books, magazines, pens, badges, air horns and mugs to programme boards. In their capacity as speedway merchandise manufacturers - an important and lucrative sideline that keeps them very busy during the close season finding and sourcing manufacturers prepared to work at the right price and quality - the Barbers almost fondly recall that they made some of these items. "Look! The famous badges that we took three goes at doing for them 'cause they [BSI] didn't like them. Yet they have something like this!" says Johnny waving a red and black coloured cap. "Made cheaply in totally the wrong colours with stitching - look - that looks like it says 'Readino Bulldogs'! Are they Italian or someint? They really farked it up with these caps, they're awful and what's with the red and the black?" Under these caps of apparently questionable quality lurks a real treasure for the tutored memorabilia collectors eye, "blimey a 'Danny Bird Racing' cap - now that's a real collectors item" and in the corner of the shop there's another unexpected find. "Aah a farking great mushroom, probably for Jeff's salad, cowering there beside a huge pile of Ian Thomas's

Johnny Barber investigates the track shop

unsold Wheels & Deals! Nicki Pedersen's had a stomach upset these last four weeks or so, - has he been eating your cauliflower and French sausage salads then? You should invite him on Jeff Scott's F Word or whatever you're gonna call your speedway cookery programme." The brothers banter among themselves, "are you gonna just farkin sit there all day?" "I'm watching the master at work surrounded by more double-sided sticky tape than they have on Blue Peter."

Rather than get under their feet, I wander to the front gate where, under ominously dark clouds, long-time staff member and supervisor of the car park, John Rogers, tells me, "the weather forecast said Hampshire would get soaked and Berkshire would remain dry." If correct, this will cause some climatic fun where I grew up a few miles away in Tadley since a ditch there marks the border between these two counties and used to mark their respective educational catchment areas. There's a small queue of old age pensioners keen to rush in and stake out their favoured prime spots inside the stadium. Studiously walking the track lost in his own thoughts is the BSPA Chairman, Peter Toogood, who's in town to offer his moral support to the new promotion of Mark and Malcolm. With the recent demise of Oxford in mid-season fresh in the minds of fans and media alike, the last thing the Elite League or the speedway authorities need is another severe blow to the integrity and credibility of the sport. Consequently, whatever short-term help Reading speedway need to survive this period and keep going will be given. Just at the moment I watch him, Peter falls over onto the damp track in a manner that suggests he's an apprentice skater taking to the rink for the first time to practise for Holiday on Ice. It's the kind of embarrassing fall for no reason that anyone will immediately try to stave off with the pretence it hasn't happened through a deft leap to their feet and a nonchalant stride onwards. A few confident strides later in what I can only assume are smooth-soled shoes better suited to a dinner dance than a track walk (though this fall does confirm the widely held opinion that there is less grip than ever on the Smallmead track), in the absence of a gale of cackling laughter, Peter surreptitiously glances around to check for witnesses. Luckily, I'm the only one who sees his fall and when we chat a few minutes later I try to avoid any downward eye contact with the large and hugely visible shale-brown patches on his smart trousers. With attendances 29% down on 2006 when the Postlethwaite era ended and cumulative losses allegedly hovering round the half a million mark (or circa £10,000 each meeting during the BSI era), Peter is understandably cautious about predicting any immediate business success for the new promotion, "It's on its knees and starting mid-season is never ideal, so we'll see!" Genuinely but slightly naively I reply, "They just need to get a few matches on," only for the voice of experience to counter, "Well, we'll see - I hope it works."[1]

[1 as we all know the club did survive but had to cut its financial cloth to suit, so returned to the Premier League for 2008 in the close season. In the *Speedway Star* in December, Malcolm Holloway was quoted as saying, "after the well-documented difficulties of last season, we are looking to stabilise the club." In the same report Andy Povey noted this decision came, "after a turbulent 2007 season with both sets of promotions suffering huge financial losses. BSI lost a small fortune during their 18 months in charge and even after some cost-cutting by the new management duo of Mark Legg and Malcolm Holloway, the Racers were still losing a hefty sum every week."]

Though there's the usual smattering of bikes, mechanics and riders, the pits seem unusually quiet and deserted as though an air of uncertainty and an element of lacklustre but understandable just going through the motions attitude has somehow percolated throughout the team. Matej Zagar, Travis McGowan and Mark Lemon are huddled conspiratorially together in animated discussion, possibly about their immediate British speedway futures and/or surviving the transition from one promotional regime to another. The relative activity of the old lags' meeting in the Reading half of the pits isn't at all evident among the younger staff stood around on the Eastbourne side, where always ultra-professional and well turned out Morten Risager fiddles with his bike. Lewis Bridger searches noisily in his toolbox for something elusive, while 'seen it and done it all before' guest rider, Gary Havelock - dressed for comfort not style in tracksuit bottoms - leans against the edge of the pits area deep in a mobile phone conversation. With just over an hour to go until the tapes rise, the torpor inspired by the end of the Postlethwaite era still appears the dominant outlook and collectively lingers around the talent like a bad smell.

Just outside the pits gate some more white vans have just arrived and striding through the pits from the other direction is tonight's referee Chris Durno. It's a surprise to see him since it says Christina Turnbull in the programme. A glance at the racecard in said programme also shows that each club will be without their number 1 rider, Greg Hancock in the case of Reading and Nicki Pedersen in the case of the Eagles. The major difference here is that Nicki will ride again during the season for the Eagles, whereas Greg - although allegedly on a "two-month holiday" - had in reality already withdrawn from racing in England for the remainder of the 2007 season (and potentially longer). I wonder why the Eagles have Gary Havelock as a guest for Nicki and rider replacement for the also absent David Norris, particularly when the opposite would benefit them more? Chris explains, "the BSPA rules say you have to have a guest rider for your number 1 and run rider replacement for your second missing rider. Tonight both teams are without there number 1s and I fancied Eastbourne to win until I heard Nicki wasn't riding. It'll be hard to get any decent guests for either team as 10 Elite League teams are riding tonight! On paper the Eagles now look the weaker side. Watt will ride well, Bridger can do and [Stefan] Andersson is too good a rider to be at reserve and, if he finds his form, he would be dynamite but he hasn't been for a while and no longer seems to be the rider he was. Risager is a white line rider. As soon as anyone gets near him he throttles off, he's got the set up and everything but needs to get over that. That said, Reading need a win tonight to get the new promotion off to a flying start - the last meeting they had here was on May 21st so if you rush back, they're just reheating the chips for you!" Peter Toogood saunters past and stops for a few words with Chris. I take the chance to confirm he received my book in the post and to tell him that *Shale Britannia* has had some national coverage, though this amuses him, "The Big Issue! Ha ha, really!" There's no need to point out to Chris the highly visible shale-stained knees of the Chairman's trousers. After I explain how he got them, Chris notes, "it's incredibly slippery on the second bend." Somehow Peter evaded this banana skin in order to then fall on the treacherous fourth.

Back at my table I'm passed by a steady stream of fans clutching leaflets for my books kindly given out by the teenage girls stood by the raffle ticket table tactically positioned just after the trackshop on the slope down to the track that everyone has to use, even if they decide to head for the bar by the back route of the disabled access ramp. Some people stop to talk and one man illustrates the power of the local print media - well, the knowledgeable Dave Wright in the Reading Evening Post - when he remarks knowingly, "You've been coming here since 1975, I saw it in the paper!"

Never let it be said that John Postlethwaite won nothing during his time at Reading since the annual review of programmes conducted by the *Speedway Star* rightfully gave that accolade to the 2006 version of said document. They knew it well at the *Star* as they produced it for Reading that year though, I must stress the award was deservedly won fair and square. The judgement criteria used each year in the award might be somewhat bizarre (especially when you think it's speedway programmes we're talking about) and not everyone's cup of tea. But, in this respect and almost this respect alone, Postlethwaite delivered on the hyperbole of his claims to shake up, nay 'revolutionise', the presentation of speedway. Given that this application of his hard-won experience in the apparently cut-throat world of commerce nearly killed the club, just to be able to see speedway here still is a relief and to buy a programme is truly a bonus in itself for all Reading speedway fans. Another prize the 2006 season of tumultuous change could have won is an award for price inflation since the revamped document was more expensive than every other Elite League programme! However, once a precedent has been set in pricing (whether in admissions or elsewhere) others will always follow and thereby push up the overall cost of attendance for fans, particularly if looked at over the length of a season.

Eastbourne track walk

The new Legg/Holloway era version of this document looks similar if judged by the cover but there the similarities end since the use of colour throughout the inside pages has been abolished and a number of the (anodyne) features you didn't know you needed or wanted have pleasingly bitten the dust. That said, the loss of the nostalgia corner in the form of a double-page spread that looked back at years past for the Racers team (written by ex-press officer Andy Povey) is, in my opinion, the one loss from its pages that gives real cause for regret. The price has even dropped back to a more manageable and relatively customer friendly £2. Those keen to find fault could note that over 50% of the programme is now adverts (almost 11 pages) and that the content itself is somewhat spartan. However, it serves the purpose and the detailed page ("In the Opposite Corner") about the Eagles team written by Robert Bamford provides a welcome, more comprehensive overview of the visitors than the scantier detail than was provided under the previous regime. Continuing the look-alike theme started at Newport, the photo that appears of Robert could see him mistaken for a young Che Guevara, though not Stefan Andersson against whose name said picture appears. Once you start to think of the world in this way, it only takes Malcolm Holloway to stride purposefully past on his way to the pits to remind me that he looks like a dead ringer for (albeit older) Paul Whitehouse from the Fast Show.

Over the tannoy a voice from Reading's speedway past and now part of its revived future, Bob Radford, updates the crowd who've arrived with news about the team and some other idiosyncratically chosen information. Consequently, we learn that Nicki has withdrawn with "a stomach problem believed to be a gall bladder - a painful and uncomfortable condition - so we wish him well!" We then learn that it's the Racers team manager, "Tim Sugar's birthday on July 10th - I won't say how old [57] - but I will say he's back for the fourth time as Reading manager." In fact, Tim Sugar managed the team to nine trophies between 1990 and 1997 including three league triumphs! On their track walk, the six-man Eagles team manage to avoid any fallers on the hazardous second and fourth bends. As a group, they seem somewhat taciturn and reserved together rather than bantering. They're joined by team manager Trevor Geer and club promoter Bob Brimson, who appears to have tagged along at the back of the group to repeatedly and ostentatiously kick the white line that marks the inside of the Smallmead circuit. None of the riders does this and it probably serves no purpose other than the relief of nervous tension not dissipated by Bob drawing deeply on his trademark cigarette. News of Nicki's ailments has touched a chord with those gathered by my display table, "It's the lifestyle and all that awful food - think about it, the food you get at tracks and on airlines - plus riding a speedway bike can't be good for you at the best of times, never mind if you're carrying an injury!"

The comforting sense of a world that once again slowly returns to turn on its traditional axis - signalled by the reintroduction of the Racers name - is continued when the sound of "Monday! Monday!" crackles loudly through the speakers of the tannoy system and cheerfully resounds throughout Smallmead stadium (or, at least, those sections of it with speakers that work). This traditional musical accompaniment to speedway racing gets an almost Pavlovian response from me (without the slobbering) as it signifies that another exciting night of racing in Berkshire has started. The use of this signature theme was another aspect of club history sacrificed on the BSI altar of supposed progress through marketing genius. Unusually, particularly given it's not the end of the season, there's even a brief firework display. Late-season cost cutting in 2006 by BSI saw even this abandoned and the end of season dinner-dance, booked to take place at an inappropriately posh venue, cancelled. The lightness of a summer's night doesn't exactly provide the ideal canvas to enjoy the range of colours the fireworks provide but, since we've now passed Midsummer night, technically the evenings are drawing in. It's a nice way to mark the return of the Racers and certainly lets all the neighbours know we're back!

Dean Saunders, someone who I imagine is the tallest sponsor in British speedway, has come along to Smallmead to watch Davey Watt ride and hopefully draw the name of his company Saunders Surfacing Contractors to a wider audience. Dean has followed Davey from club to club as well as to the World Team Cup in Poland a few years back and has nothing but praise for the organisation, friendliness and professionalism of the man. This year he decided not to indulge himself with an executive box at the Millennium Stadium. "A corporate box at the 2006 GP at Cardiff cost £1500 plus VAT for 12 people. It's alright at £150 a person - I shared it with a mate - but four weeks before this year's event they rang to find out if I wanted it at double! They said, 'They're nearly all gone and others are keen so it's best to book now', 'Well they can have it!' I said. When I looked round half of them were empty so they've shot themselves in the foot big time."

After the bang of the fireworks, the actual racing returns with more of a whimper - this takes the form of a couple of drawn heats. Apparently gainsaying the naysayers, in the first heat Gary Havelock looks fast and competitive rather than just merely going through the motions to earn what everyone expects to be a guaranteed minimum payment on the night, irrespective of his points performance for the Eagles. The third heat that features an enthralling four-lap battle for supremacy between Matej Zagar and Lewis Bridger for second place breaks the deadlock. A sign of race rustiness or complacency (depending on which rumour you believe) compared to the kind of performance expected by him round Smallmead, Zagar is pipped at the post despite a desperate drive to the line round the last bend that the Sussex youngster does well to hold off. Despite the action behind him, Watt wins the race comfortably though the Racers immediately cut the deficit with a win in the next from McGowan. It takes a re-run to achieve this since first time out the Aussie locks up in front of the rider Bob Radford calls " Morten Riz-EAR", thereby causing a tumble and a restart called for first-bend bunching. Along with a considerable delay for repairs to the inflatable track furniture as well as a brief worry that the rain starting to spit might turn torrential and force the club to lose another meeting they can ill afford to abandon. It should have been a drawn heat because Cameron Woodward holds third place until the penultimate bend of the race, where he locks up and allows Sam Simota through for a vital point. This looked always likely to happen since Cameron has ridden the race with a level of anxiety manifested through frequent glances over his shoulder searching for his opponent.

The chance for a new broom to sweep clean at Reading speedway impacts on all aspects of the club including two-minute warning announcements. It's a subject that announcer Bob Radford throws open to a democratic decision from the Redin faithful, "we're conducting a survey on the two-minute warning announcement - do you want the US version retained or dumped? It's your choice, the George Bush [i.e. pre-recorded] version or the English one in the form of myself?" It's a big decision[1] but I'm interrupted from my reverie by a gleeful Martin Dadswell - he of Eagles trackshop fame - clutching armfuls of my discarded leaflets he's found on the floor that he delights in dumping onto my display table. "You might as well just throw them away yourself and save all the bother!" Lewis Bridger has returned to the fray with a mental note to himself to do better, if judged by the exaggerated fashion in which he leans over his handlebars on gate one, before the start of Heat 5. Though he apparently flies from the start he finds himself fourth into the first bend with Matej already off and gone after normal service has been resumed for him. Havvy temporarily holds second place but totally misjudges the corner, so finds himself shutting off close to the bend-two air fence and thereby allows Lemon through. It must have irked the ex-world champion as he proceeds to give a masterclass in how to race for the chip-shop money with your erstwhile Eagles team mate. This antithesis of team riding has Havelock and

[1 The vote eventually goes in favour of the pre-recorded American version.]

Rider parade

Bridger repeatedly get in each other's way, while the Racers riders move comfortably away in the distance. The youngster is unable to find a route past Havvy, who often slows to block the racing line in a manner that uses all his hard-won years of experience and predictive powers. Frustrated at this refusal to yield, Lewis blasts round the outside for a non-existent gap and smashes into the second-bend air fence on the last lap to stop the race. You'd expect Havvy to punch the air because of his awarded third place point but the sight of Trevor Geer and Bob Brimson galumphing the length of the track to tend to the stricken Bridger distracts everyone. By the time they arrive at his side, Lewis still remains prone on the ground. When he eventually extricates himself from beneath his machine to limp gingerly back to the pits along the back straight he benefits from Bob Brimson's consoling words. Nick Barber observes wryly, "He was down for so long, you'd think he was a GP rider!"

The differing fortunes of riders race to race shine through in the next when Morten Riz-EAR spends the heat hugging the inside white line for dear life as though magnetically drawn there. The predictability of his position encourages a rare overtake by Jonas Davidsson on the penultimate bend to secure third place. "When You-nus Davidsson overtakes you, it's time to retire, mate!" notes Johnny Barber. Immediately presented with an opportunity to prove his doubters wrong, Morten takes a rider replacement ride for David Norris in the next heat, which he wins. Though mostly since Davey Watt shepherds him home with a superb display of controlled team riding that Bob Radford mentions with some chagrin, "Travis McGowan was third, looking for the gap that never opened up." The scores have tipped back in the Eagles favour to 20-22 in a race also noteworthy because Jonas D finishes a comprehensive last. With the drizzle having disappeared as quickly as it came, it's a pleasure to finally be at a speedway meeting where it's only a thin film of shale dust that coats the crowd rather than an invasion of irksome creepy crawlies. The jackpot draw prize from a previous management era at the club has to be won tonight and the holder of the winning ticket will receive a "jackpot of £400" according to Tadley-based Paul Hunsdon. I can't see the famous jackpot prize draw boxes from my position but basically the owner of the winning ticket gets to "select a box inside of which is the main prize" or a guttingly disappointing runners-up consolation of only £10. To allay any suspicions that the UK Gaming Board might hold about the proprietary and authenticity of the draw, Andy Povey does the honours and draws the winning ticket "green 283". Its owner chooses badly so the re-draw has the frustrated art teacher in Paul reveal the newly winning ticket to be, "60 on the buff, pinkie looking colour". Its owner - Alan - has riches snatched from underneath his gaze with another incorrect selection. Paul informs a breathless crowd, "I know this is more exciting than the racing" and increasingly can't help the sound of his glee at the series of unfortunate choices that unfolds. The draw is held over until after the next race with an appeal that sounds only partially to do with the draw, "we're looking for a good-looking girl - there must be one?! - to help draw the next ticket." The imminent arrival of the riders at the tapes is heralded by the US style "you have two minutes" pre-recorded voiceover that

Bob Radford follows with a reminder about the poll enabling fans to have their say, "There were strong feelings at the [fans] forum, as I say!"

The short-lived Eagles lead vanishes when Cameron Woodward knocks into the second-bend fence to lose his third place and thereby gifts the Racers a heat advantage. The thrill of the ongoing draw temporarily abates for a few motivational words from Malcolm Holloway. With a reasonable but not exactly a stellar crowd within Smallmead, the need to sound a clarion call to rally the stay-away supporters to the cause is important, "next week if you can bring your mothers and fathers along". In marked contrast to the 'teacher knows best' (before they then screw it up comprehensively) school of 'thought' that until recently infected the club management, it's a breath of fresh air to learn that the spirit of consultation is alive and kicking again in Berkshire. "We need to hear from the crowd what they want and we'll try to sort it out and see what we can do!" There have been many losers since the BSI peremptorily upped sticks and Malcolm takes the opportunity to apologise to the "season ticket holders who lost their money". This reveals the real nature of the astonishing contempt the previous regime really held towards the most loyal Reading speedway supporters - i.e. those very people prepared to show their faith by investing their cash in the club before the season even started, despite the impact of the ongoing BSI farce of wrecking the history of the club through name changes and the like. People with honour and integrity would surely have ensured that they refunded these monies rather than anonymously slink away abrogating their moral responsibilities? Malcolm is full of hope for the future but notes the riders are a little race rusty, "our boys haven't ridden for seven weeks". He then even goes on to promise transparency with regard to rain-offs, "I like to rain them off early - I drove over from [the bright lights of] Basingstoke in the heaviest storm I've ever seen and it was sunny here which you wouldn't have believed!"

Another sign that things have changed for the better behind the scenes is the gaggle of photographers - would the collective words for this be a 'rogue's gallery' of photographers? - who huddle together chatting on the centre green: Mike Patrick, Mike Hinves, Dave Fairbrother and Dave Valentine. Under the BSI regime, the resident club photographer Dave Valentine had to pay for the privilege of his photographic access but had to vacate the centre green at each and every meeting after Heat 5. This was strictly enforced and ranks with the choice of the Bulldogs name as the height of stupidity since, at many meetings, capturing the race action is just as important during the remaining ten races of the night as at the start. A Howard Hughes like obsessive-compulsive desire for a tidy and "professional looking" centre green - just like at the GPs apparently ("did you see the superb looking centre green last night?") - allegedly prompted this edict from speedway visionary John Postlethwaite! The raffle draw continues, "66 on the white" fails to even show up to take their chance to select a winning box, though "60 on the green" does appear (the take-home lesson here appears to be only buy raffle tickets numbered in the 60s at Smallmead). Paul Hunsdon notes ruefully, "if someone doesn't win soon we'll be here 'til midnight" before he segues into a scream, "NUMBER ONE - you've won £10!" With the prize diminishing with each selection, the winners are called to account with increasing rapidity and desperation, "five on the green" comes and goes missing out on £360. "132 on the buff" fails ignominiously, while nearby the spiffing new tractors of the BSI era serenely, but industriously, circle the track. In fact, these new tractors typify their reign in a single object since they look good but only really work in the hands of skilled operators. Away in the distance, you can also see the state-of-the-art bowser parked in the pits but clearly some executive decision has been made to leave it there since the crowd would prefer (as is traditional at speedway meetings) to enjoy the atmosphere of being sprayed in a thin film of dust (rather than not).

The few people who gather by my table favourably recall Malcolm 'Mad Wellie' Holloway's exploits at the club as a rider and know that he not only understands the club's tradition but also has a genuine desire for its success in his heart. Now the club has been rescued, Malcolm (along with Mark) has hero status and only wants to look towards a rosier future that will again feature the traditional club symbol of the winged wheel, "it's 21 months since the Racers last rode." On the track, Reading move slowly ahead on points helped by a resurgent Matej Zagar who has woken from his first race torpor to hammer in a win followed by a second place behind Davey Watt. Away at the raffle draw a winner still hasn't been found although there is a loud exclamation to enliven proceedings, "argh - the Lion's just trod on me foot!"

Eastbourne promoter Bob Brimson and his brother Greg join me beside my table for the eleventh heat en route for non-alcoholic refreshment in the grandstand bar. In the first attempt to run it, Travis McGowan reacquaints Lewis Bridger with the Smallmead shale for the second time tonight when he summarily dismounts him from behind. This deservedly earns an exclusion from referee Chris Durno but, with the scores poised at 31-29, Greg Brimson nonetheless brims with optimism, "We've got a great chance now - to win the meeting let alone this race!" While he deputes his brother to queue for him, Bob confides that he's the equivalent of the Gordon Brown of speedway since he's blind in his right eye, "that's why I can't be a speedway rider!" He has endured a rough introduction into the ways of the speedway world in the few months that he's been at the helm as a promoter at Eastbourne. Rumours of mounting financial losses haven't been helped by unexpected discoveries behind the scenes, some high-maintenance staff and direct experience of some of the more unique (sometimes obstructive) attitudes to the business followed by his fellow promoters and, more importantly, the governing body. While the BSPA might temporarily treat the new promotion at Redin with kid gloves because of the recent demise of Oxford, the same level of help to smooth the way hasn't (in his opinion) been truly given to Bob, who has enjoyed an altogether more abrasive relationship. Understandably he's cynical but still, surprisingly, remarkably phlegmatic. He tells me that away in the shadows as we speak, a select 'think tank' team, chosen by the BSPA, are presently attempting to think the unthinkable ahead of the annual conference in November to prepare the ground for possible dramatic change to the structure, organisation and functioning of the sport in this country. Depending on whom you speak to, this is either in order to attempt to save it, or, at least, right some of the more straightforward and obvious ills. Americans I used to work with would call this "grabbing the low-hanging fruit". Bob puts it more bluntly, "Cook and buddies - two of them [allegedly Matt Ford and Chris Louis] - have a month on some special committee to sort things out for next year and level things out!"

The re-run temporarily distracts us - we see Jonas gate with speed and aplomb to lead Havvy who reacts shockingly slowly to the rise of the tapes and is comprehensively left trailing but, compared to Lewis, he has lightning reflexes. Bob tuts at the predictably drawn heat but, before he returns to the comfort of the Smallmead pits notes, "The track is so rough, mate - rutted up in places and really hard in others, so it's a nightmare to ride!" There must be something added to Davidsson's tea since he wins the next race too - ahead of Eastbourne's best rider on the night, Davey Watt - to record his third-best score of the season in a Racer's tabard. Australian Davey Watt provides one-man resistance against the Racers pair since Stefan Andersson suffers a first-lap engine failure. He nearly holds onto second place but a trademark Zagar pass round the outside of the third bend on the final lap stimulates the Redin faithful into a roar of congratulation and the 5-1 pretty well puts the score beyond reach of recovery by Eastbourne. The new Racers management look likely to start with the win they wanted. Dedicated, cheerful but undervalued Eagles press officer, Kevin Ling, passes to buy some hot refreshment. Unlike some others, he refuses to criticise the absent Nicki Pedersen, "he has got gallstones and, to be fair to him, they can be very painful!" Other Eagles fans are less forgiving, "lots of away fixtures have been missed by Nicki already this season. Really he should get a 7- or 14-day ban - the problem is they're so important they get away with it. You can bet he'll ride in Sweden tomorrow of course! [he didn't] Eastbourne would have definitely won if he'd turned up."

Meanwhile with a choice of only two boxes, the raffle has built up to fever pitch. Paul reveals, "Nathan from Bracknell is going to have his head shaved on the centre green". I can only imagine he's agreed to this forfeit (should he win) without any forethought or consultation with his mum. Paul is gleeful, "is there a hairdresser in the house?"

Left with a choice of boxes "two or four for £340", Nathan chooses correctly!

"Who's your favourite rider?"

"Matt -EE!"

"He's excellent [pause] with a razor!"

A drawn heat 13 fails to thrill but Bob Radford is keen to big things up so claims, "it still served up good entertainment". Talk among the Redin fans in the grandstand seats turns towards Charlie Gjedde - a rider still admired round this neck of the woods, despite his departure for the Swindon Robins. Though, as a neutral listener, it sounds as though he's damned with faint praise, "Charlie usually doesn't ride anywhere well but Redin, oh, and Oxford but they don't ride anymore, so that's no use." Bob Brimson has come back across from the pits for yet another bottle of Diet Coke and a cigarette or three on the short journey. He arrives just in time to see the last remaining possibility of an Eagles victory about to get snuffed out by a crash into the bend-three air fence by Stefan Andersson on the second lap of the penultimate race. Chris Durno awards the race as a drawn heat. A narrow defeat by a few points looks likely and, with rider replacement rides garnering 8 paid 9, Bob identifies a lack of points from Eagles reserve Cameron Woodward as a key factor in this loss. Albeit in a resigned sympathetic manner since he's only just returned from injury, "Cameron isn't quite strong enough to cope with the track conditions." If any promoter has killed a metaphorical albatross this season, then it's Bob Brimson who has seen his riders get injured on a regular basis and, but for bad luck [as the blues song goes], he wouldn't have any luck at all.

The meeting is already over as a contest since even a last race 5-1 to Eagles still wouldn't snatch a draw. In the pits Eastbourne team manager Trevor Geer decides to nominate Lewis Bridger to ride, only to be over-ruled by the referee, "because he doesn't qualify for this race." Morten is deputed in his place and celebrates with a lightning fast escape from the start line. Once again, Davey Watt chaperones him round for four laps defending second place from the challenge of occasional forays by Travis McGowan. Uninterestedly trailed off at the back is a disconsolate Matej Zagar, who barely bothers to go through the motions. Morten "Riz-EAR" celebrates the win with a punch of the air and an expansive wheelie over the line that Watt immediately replicates as he follows closely behind. Why the riders embrace a narrow defeat that could arguably have been a victory so rapturously mystifies but, at least, shows pride and spirit amongst the team. A brief firework display concludes the meeting, reminds the neighbours once more of the Racers return and marks the successful arrival of the Legg-Holloway reign at Smallmead. All that's left is for Bob Radford to accurately observe that for the Eagles, "it was too much, well, too little too late" before he appeals, "try to bring more people along with you next week and we can try to build a better future [pause] as the Racers! Good night and God bless!"

9th July Reading v Eastbourne (Elite League B) 46-44

Chapter 23. Lakeside v Swindon: Slowway racing arrives and everyone loves Alf

11th July

The famous Sky interview booth

The clash between the rejuvenated Lakeside Hammers and the widely held popular favourites for the Elite League crown, the Swindon Robins, is held on their alternative race night of a Wednesday at the Arena Essex Raceway in Thurrock. The mid-week traffic on the M25 isn't noticeably better than a Friday as jams clog the many lanes of the motorway through the irksome roadworks prior to the toll gates in one direction and, as far as the eye can see, over the Queen Elizabeth II Bridge and away to the horizon in the other. At least those stuck in almost stationary traffic on the bridge will be treated to fantastic views of this section of the always impressive Thames river and the various refineries or loading docks that crowd the light industrial estates located on its riverbanks. I have arrived so early that the pits are still missing most of the riders, the track staff are still busied with last-minute work grooming the shale and, this season's innovation of the crash barriers placed in the actual bowl of the raceway itself, have still to be fully erected on the back straight to allow the spectators to stand perilously close to the action.

Many of the staff who have arrived, but have yet to start their duties, made their way to the Café Diner located on the ground floor of the main grandstand. Inside the café, they have a flag that proclaims in large letters 'Takeaways Here', on the wall a plaque has a chequered flag motif ('1st Place Diner - Sit In & Takeaway') and, for the first time, I notice that the advertising board stood on the concourse close to the café cleverly styles itself as the ultimate destination for the hungry speedway fan on one side and for the Bangers on the reverse. The blonde, bubbly café manageress, Tracy Manning, stands outside for a brief cigarette break in the warm sunshine. "We're always popular before the meeting and throughout really. We're double barrelled - classy if you want it and common if you don't!" The programme whets the taste buds with talk of a "full menu available" as well as highlighting some bargains, "Large Tea 50p, Large Coffee 60p". Tracy is excited at the prospect of the media visitors who will again descend on her café for the next two days, "*Top Gear* are filming here for the next couple of days - they're always here - Stuart [Douglas] says he wants a signed picture on the wall in here. I have to put the prawns and the crayfish in the fridge 'cause they really love that treat. The first time they ever came into the café they kept themselves to themselves but, after that, it's been brilliant. There's no airs and graces or anything, even with the presenters, who're just normal like everyone is! I'm disappointed 'cause I've now seen how many times they have to do and re-do everything. I believed what I saw on the telly not knowing that they do that or how much they can make things look how they want. Well I s'pose I did know, but now I've seen it first hand. They're lovely to work for and very polite - we all have a laugh with them!" Cigarette over, Tracy glances at the sky before moving back inside, "the weathers been lovely here for weeks - they [Stuart Douglas and Jon Cook] deserve it after all the effort they've put in!"

Close by, Alf Weedon has parked his car with the personalised numberplate adjacent to his trackshop so that stock can be unloaded from his boot. As is traditional, he's mislaid things so impatiently shouts, "have you got the keys, Paco?" With the look of an exasperated man, Paco denies all knowledge. After much searching through the car, on the concourse and the stock-room-cum-cubbyhole, Alf finds them. With one problem solved he turns his attention to others, notably the arrangement of the merchandise in the shop. He starts to shuffle things around to his greater satisfaction while Paco hovers, "they were all nicely arranged by her 'til you messed them all up!" They're like a long-time married couple together, aware of each other's foibles and unafraid to unhesitatingly point out in a blunt manner that, to the outside listener, sounds pointed and often abrasive. Paco and the lady who works in the shop allow Alf to busy himself getting the display just so. Half an hour later when Alf's attention has wandered elsewhere, the stock has miraculously returned to where it was originally placed prior to his intervention.

Alf is only too happy to let me display my books close to his shop provided that I also display some books from other speedway publishers on my table. Stood here I'm ideally placed to watch the activity on the track and the racing when it starts. A steady flow of people dawdle by the shop to check out the merchandise or buy a copy of a magazine. One of the first people through the turnstiles is Rod Ford (aka Punch), a fantastically hard-working member of the Blunsdon Massive who form the Blunsdon track staff. Weekly as a group, throughout the year (not just during the speedway season), they toil away behind the scenes at Swindon speedway and are captured in all their glory and idiosyncrasy in the wonderful *Blunsdon Blog* written by Graham Cooke. Tonight, taking a brief but well-earned break from his various curatorial duties (and his allotments), Punch can't express himself with his customary zeal and moderates the full colour of his language because he's here with her indoors. Nonetheless, even though the soft burr of his voice sounds mild enough, he's full of strong opinions. The televised fixture that pitted Eastbourne against Lakeside featured a brief cameo appearance by Andreas Jonsson that either illustrated his commitment to the Hammers cause or, alternatively, provided a good insight to all that is wrong with the present state of the rules that govern British speedway. Punch falls into the 'that was an example of disgraceful sharp practice within the rules' school of thought, "that Jonsson just laid the bike down and then held his shoulder - he never had any intention of riding that night but just came out and did what was necessary, just so they could get rider replacement for him."

A glance at the programme confirms that the Hammers are still without their injured number one for whose rides all his team mates remain eligible. Understandably club owner Stuart Douglas takes a different perspective and explains the party line in his programme notes from "the Guv'nor". A more suspiciously minded person could think that he doth protest too much, "it was very unfortunate circumstances for Andreas, falling right on the same shoulder that had taken an absolute hiding at the Millennium, and had been worked on all Sunday to get him out for us at Arlington. Indeed, it is a testament to his resolve to prove his critics wrong and his determination to fight for the Hammers that he made sure he was there on the night. Needless to say it wasn't what any of us had in mind." Mercifully, Stuart then moves on to discuss the meeting against Belle Vue and so stops short of initiating a campaign to beatify Andreas.

Punch has also recently been to Peterborough where he was less than impressed to find that Colin Horton's commitment to environmentalism had led him to recycle their unused programme from the postponed Poole fixture and then supplement it with an insert for the visit of a completely different team, namely the Robins. The practice of adding an insert rather than reprinting the programme after a postponed meeting is a frequently aired bugaboo among speedway fans. When we all have to endure a shockingly wet summer like that experienced in 2007, this is likely to be a common grumble for fans and a problem that you can't help but sympathise with promoters about, since reprints on any scale will massively increase their costs for no real commercial benefit. That said, at least the insert usually finds its way into the programme relevant to your team rather than being applicable to that of another. "I said to Colin Horton, "I just wanna say one thing - a Swindon insert in a Poole programme, what's that about then? He said, 'you don't have to buy it if you don't want one!' Well, that's no way to go on, is it?"

Hammers announcer and incident recorder, the cheerful and experienced Bob Miller (announcing at least since Crayford in 1976), stops for a word before he heads off up the steep stairs to the control-room-cum-referee's-box that overlooks the start line here. "You should have been here last week when Geoff [Cox] said something and I said 'arse' and stopped and then I said to myself without thinking, 'why did I say arse?' not thinking it was going out over the speakers. Everyone was rockin'!" If this *faux pas* had been reported in the local paper, the headline might have been 'Cox accidentally caught in arse shocker at Lakeside'.

Lakeside attracts a star-studded audience to the raceway along with Derek Barclay who has taken a few hours off from his Internet incarnation (on the British Speedway Forum) as the Conference League advocate and serial emoticon user Parsloes1928. In this guise, he could often have an (self-righteous) argument with himself in an empty phone box. Apparently computer

Lakeside bowser in action

*Keen Academy League fan
Derek Barclay*

Alf Weedon sunbathes

programs have now been invented so that machines can interact online with chatroom users to steal vital personal information given away freely online and use it for identity theft or financial shenanigans. The sheer volume of P1928's posts would probably defeat even the most robust software, plus the usual tactic of engaging the target flirtatiously probably wouldn't work in this instance. However, any automated program that had the temerity to post any suggestion that the demise of the Conference League incarnation of Wimbledon Speedway Plc might vaguely (along with the evil GRA, of course) bear some responsibility for their 'eviction' from Plough Lane would soon get more comeback and information than they bargained for! Equally, for that matter, if said computer program was to suggest that Mark 'Buzz' Burrows wasn't the most thrilling rider ever to overtake riders half his age/experience on the uniquely shaped Wimbledon CL era track (designed specifically for pure speedway entertainment) and thereby produced racing rarely without equal in the history of mankind would also get short shrift. During its historically brief Conference League reincarnation Derek even harried the sports editor of the *Evening Standard*, probably in green biro, to buck the national trend to indifference and give Wimbledon Speedway the prominence it apparently 'deserved' (failing to realise that some London area based Championship football teams struggled for coverage in said paper) or supposedly merited based on historical precedent. Strangely, Derek writes well in the *Speedway Star* about Sittingbourne and, speaking person to person (rather than his online persona writing wholly inaccurately about me), he's charm personified with a quick wit and good sense of the absurd. His paternal enthusiasm for young fledgling riders as they embark on their first tentative steps within the speedway world is clearly sincere and heartfelt.

Tonight Derek has nipped in on his way home from work (that I gather, but don't know, involves some connection with local government in possibly, I'm guessing, the housing, planning or rat catching departments) just to watch the Academy League fixtures that they admirably stage at Lakeside prior to the 'main attraction' of the Elite League meetings. Derek studiously avoids tainting his speedway viewing pleasure with so-called upper echelon racing and prides himself that he departs without a backward glance at any of the alleged superstars of the shale. I query the economics of his approach only to learn, "I wouldn't pay to come in and do that, I have a press pass! It's on my way home from work too. It's good to see them start out - a lot of the riders I know from Sittingbourne anyway. In the Academy League meeting, you'll notice they're starting 15 metres back from the start gate tonight to avoid cutting up the gate for the big boys!" I brazenly take a photograph of Mr Barclay as he squints into the distance concentratedly gazing at the first heat of the Academy fixture until a casual fall brings it to a stop. "Are you taking a photo of everyone who buys your books then?" Little interrupts the main focus of Derek's visit, which is to absorb himself in the Academy action. The young men on display are wholeheartedly enthusiastic and entertainment levels are high, despite the inevitable stop-start nature of the proceedings. Derek does find time to share his thoughts on Oxford speedway who dramatically exited the Elite League when Colin Horton pulled the plug but, luckily, then enjoyed enough good fortune to survive as a club and reappear weeks later in the Conference League. "Oxford have only been back one meeting [in the CL] and already they're bending the rules!" he tells me indignantly, albeit without the aid of emoticons that I nonetheless recreate in my mind's eye.

Later Derek draws my attention to the lavish programme and, in particular, the owner's weekly column, "he's quite a literary writer [pause] for a promoter!" The racecard in this particular programme has suffered at the Fineprint (Sussex) Ltd studios from some inadvertent minor gremlins that afflict the Robins team listing by increasing their number to eight riders with the addition of a rogue rider at reserve - their new number seven, Adam Skornicki. Bob Miller notes wryly, "its nice to see that they're so frightened of us they have eight riders!" After the Academy meeting has finished a few interviews are snatched with the Elite League riders. Always on message but bluntly honest, Leigh Adams says, "we look okay but we need a few more wins on the road. Arena is always a tough place to come, as I know first hand, as I had two great years here." Adam Shields is a much harder proposition to interview and responds to a comparative loosener along the lines of 'how are you settling in at Lakeside?' with, "It's going okay, I've had worse spells and I've had better!"

The man to ask about double entendres in newspaper headlines would be the sports editor of the *Romford Recorder*, Peter Butcher, who stops by for a chat just after Bob left to get on with his announcing duties. Peter has bought all my books, "I like them but can you get rid of that horrible typeface - it's impossible to read but I suppose I am getting old." Like many in regional newspapers, he has reported on a wide variety of subjects and has worked for other print outlets, including my local paper the *Argus* as we must now faithfully call it to distinguish it from its other less inclusive and 24/7 incarnation the Brighton *Argus* (formerly the *Evening Argus*). In the distance the arrival of an almost empty green double-decker bus completely distracts Peter from our conversation, "Oh look! They're running the free bus again tonight. They haven't for a while. Usually six people get to travel in real style, if not comfort, to the speedway here!" The programme informs us that Blue Triangle Buses Ltd run a "free bus service to all home meetings in 2007" on a route that starts at the Romford Care Centre and travels via Hornchurch Lloyds and Upminster Station to the raceway. At one time, this brought enough fans to be considered valuable weekly revenue for the club.

The first heat of the Elite League contest is drawn though, rather ominously, Leigh Adams appears to be in superlatively fast form, "Leigh's winning time - wait for it - a quick one 57.9 seconds." This drawn heat is as close as Lakeside get to parity all night. Hardly anyone would bet against a Robins away victory, particularly given the strength of their current team, never mind the fact they have the added bonus of Charlie Gjedde at reserve (you can almost hear Kelvin saying, " a rider like him shouldn't be at reserve"). A factor in their success as a team this season will almost certainly be that they boast a high-quality point-scoring rider at reserve accompanied by Andrew Moore (and tonight, for one night only according to the programme, they have the added help of Adam Skornicki). Something that you can never doubt with Andrew Moore though is his determination to succeed and to maximise his points in every race. In fact, home or away, you always get four laps of relentless effort. His style on a bike is slightly reminiscent of the jerky movements the strings used to cause Thunderbird puppets as they melodramatically rushed off for cocktails or to save the world. The race for third place is the most enthralling aspect of the second heat since it sees Andrew repeatedly roar up close and personal to Ricky Kling's back wheel. All this roaring up behind has the cumulative knock-on effect of spooking Kling sufficiently for him to eventually wildly rush at the air fence and shut off, thereby enabling Andrew to pass. The heat advantage gives the Robins a lead that they won't surrender and effectively ends the meeting as a contest.

"Obviously we don't have Adam Skornicki in Heat 4 - it's the programme printers' error - it's Charlie Gjedde." Bob then attempts to drum up the enthusiasm of the crowd sufficiently to tempt them to come along to watch the next meeting, a *Sky*-televised encounter with Coventry. "It looks good on the telly but it looks even better in the stands. And just to let you know that Alf [Weedon] is 87 on Friday - we all love you here at Arena Alf, so happy birthday!" Heat 6 provides the race of the night, when Arena/Lakeside stalwart Leigh Lanham uses his comprehensive track knowledge gained through years of experience to hug his favoured (inside white line) racing line track and finally pass Lee Richardson, after he's stalked him for nearly four laps. With Joonas Kylmakorpi third, this is the first of the three heat advantages the home side will win on the night. In the programme Stuart Douglas highlighted the loss of AJ as a key factor and so characterised the Eastbourne away defeat as a "very tame affair, with very poor quality racing". When quizzed over the public address system about their second successive Monday night defeat on the road - this time at Wolverhampton - he changed tack to stress the work-in-progress nature of the 2007 Lakeside team,

"I've said to everyone we're in a period of transition and it's going to be tough for everyone!" After successive Elite League wooden spoons, even the most pessimistic Hammers fans would be hard pressed not to acknowledge that the club has made massive strides to reinvent/transform itself under the ownership of Stuart and expert guidance of one of speedway's brightest thinkers, Jon Cook. The interview moves into a surgical phase provoked by mention of Andreas Jonsson, "you're damned if you do and damned if you don't - he dragged himself to Eastbourne to ride for us but it doesn't work out. When he comes back he has to be fit, if not we're better with rider replacement. It's such a shame about the crash at Cardiff, but what can I do about that?"

The Lakeside incarnation of the club has gone out of its way to try to attract new fans and sponsors to come along to the speedway in Thurrock. Geoff Cox welcomes tonight's valued sponsors and their guests with gusto, "as you know speedway is growing, growing and growing!" There is also some other dramatic housekeeping news, "Mike the winner of tonight's raffle (£95) has donated it back to the club. Sadly after tonight's meeting, Blue Triangle will no longer be providing the bus service. They are a long -supporter of the club but they have been taken over so sadly this will be discontinued. And a reminder that the 18th July is the Extraordinary AGM of the AES Supporters Club - the winding up of that - starts at quarter past seven!"

Any remote possibility of a concerted Lakeside fight back that still lingered is ended in Heat 11 when Leigh Adams aggressively takes their best rider on the night, Adam Shields, out wide for a close inspection of the air fence. This thereby sends its own message to the rest of the Lakeside team but also has the benefit that it allows Travis McGowan through to claim second place. Leigh also wins his next race, Heat 13, though it will stick forever in the memory for a virtuoso exhibition of slowway riding given by the mercurial Lee Richardson. Lee rides a determinedly slow race in order to ensure - despite the best efforts of Joonas Kylmakorpi to linger sufficiently to tempt him to pass - that he finishes last. Lee is too much of an old stager to fall for that dawdling tactic and ensures that he secures the fourth place to prevent the 4-2 that would reduce the points margin insufficiently to allow the use of a tactical ride option in Heat 14.[1] Luckily, I'm here on my own, otherwise imagine how you would explain the charade of what we had all just witnessed to an interested newcomer?

Some of the supporters start to drift away to avoid the post-meeting queues in the car park. The trackshop lady shuts the trackshop too, though her departure is delayed when the lock up won't lock. After quite a struggle I manage to close it. As the crowd streams away two people stop at my table to buy copies of the "Kenny Carter book" but the news that I only temporarily displayed it for Alf before it was secured behind the metal shutters of his locked up trackshop irks them mightily now they've finally decided they want to part with their money. Both teams have operated rider replacement tonight, Lakeside got 7 paid 8 for Jonsson, while Swindon got 9 for Sebastian Ulamek so got the better of that particular bargain. Very noticeably compared to recent seasons, the fans I overhear leave relatively content and without any of the terminal grumbling that used to characterise the reaction to practically every defeat here, whether or not the home team ever had any realistic chance of victory. Tonight, against many people's favourites for the Elite League crown, the fans didn't have any realistic hope of victory. The mood of rejuvenation at the club is such that the new regime has restored enough faith within most Hammers loyalists that they genuinely believe there is light ahead over the horizon rather than just the promise of another false dawn.

11th July Lakeside v Swindon (Elite League A) 41-50

[1 in the event, Adam Shields starts that race off 15 metres but this is only a forlorn gesture to massage the final result but does create a collector's item of a race result at 4-3.]

Chapter 24. Weymouth v Isle of Wight: Battle of the hairstyles

13th July

Greg Hancock *"We can bounce back from the negative thoughts and negative press!"*

The main road into Weymouth is invariably congested so, with advice from the Wildcats official photographer and press officer Julie Martin, I'd hatched a cunning plan to take a more cross-country route to the seaside town. This involved passing Monkey World and the Bovington Tank Museum before a picturesque drive along the coast that has panoramic views of the sea on the one side and a chalk figure carved into the hillside on the other. When Gordon Brown went on holiday (after finally becoming Prime Minister), he decided to spend his time in this part of Dorset. Rather touchingly, the local tourist information office suggested that he take in the delights of Monkey World as a part of his trip. Sadly, he only had time for a day away and the obligatory photo opportunity before an emergency caused him to cut short his break. While listening to the breaking news of Conrad Black's guilty verdict in his fraud trial, my cunning plan goes well until I encounter a massive jam on the seafront road just inside the city limits of Weymouth. Afterwards I learn that this has been caused by a volleyball tournament rather than by an attack by another one of the marauding "giant lobsters" that has just made the headlines in some national newspapers. Apparently, no sooner have you dived off Weymouth jetty than such a lurking beast of the deep might attack. However, the 50-year-old lobster met its match when it bothered a 51-year-old diver called Hovard since he managed to wrestle it into his string bag and then took it to live a life of captivity at the local Weymouth Sea Life Park. Everyone is a joker in Weymouth, not least the diver, Mr Hovard of Wyke Regis, who boasted afterwards, "I managed to get it with a pincer movement," though reporters conspicuously failed to ask him why on earth he dives with a string bag.

Any visitor is clearly spoilt for entertainment in the town but, tonight tourists could do far worse than visit Radipole Lane to watch the resurgent Wildcats take on the Isle of Wight Islanders in a rare inter-league challenge meeting. It should really be dubbed the 'Battle of the Seaside Clubs' (though both tracks aren't really on the coast) - come to think of it, there's quite a few of those within speedway including Poole, Eastbourne and Workington. Typically for the summer of 2007, the sun isn't in evidence but instead there's an overcast sky with a threatening hint of dark clouds already on the horizon. I'm still rummaging in the boot of my car for my string bag when a determined Julie Martin stomps past towards the pits dressed for a heat wave attired in a t-shirt, platform sandals and fashionable shorts that highlight her deeply tanned legs. Either Weymouth has defied the poor summer weather in recent months or years of seaside living has given her the naturally darker complexion you traditionally see on OAPs sat outside their beach huts in Hove. I do raise the possibility with her that this impressive chocolate colouration might come from a bottle but don't get a reply as she scampers off to sort some last-minute tasks in the Wildcats bar perched overlooking the fourth bend. Since my last visit, the Phil Bartlett era as club promoter has seen the demolition of the old home-straight grandstand - apparently erected without planning permission and maybe even possibly seized by unpaid disgruntled builders in search of scaffolding. It has been replaced by a less architecturally impressive area, cordoned off from the wind at one end by a red fence and accessible via seven steps of a rather lonely looking wooden staircase at the other. I imagine these must be part of the fabled "noise reduction measures" the club has put in place to satisfy the local council as a condition of their licence to run speedway during the summer months. There is also more comprehensive fencing on the back straight to muffle the escaping sounds, though looking round the immediate vicinity - on my way here along busy roads cutting through what appears to be wasteland - it's so sparsely populated it would be hard to find sufficient residential properties ostensibly blighted with this weekly but intermittent engine noise.

Pav and Crouch beat the queue

An array of important flags

There's already a bustle in the pits and the majority of volunteer helpers who selflessly give their time every week at Weymouth Speedway are already here and in position or are soon about to be. The home side of the pits has seen some reconfiguration, so David Mason has now moved from the edge of the pits to be amongst the riders, "otherwise he just sits in the corner." I did hear unconfirmed reports that Dave Mason was so upset he tried to switch the name boards but contrived to hammer a nail through a power cable on the other side of the pits cladding and fuse the stadium power supply! A great story, whether true or not. It's also a pleasant surprise to bump into Craig Wright who, for a long time, was the country's youngest start marshal at Newport. Nowadays, he's mechanic for Karl Mason, "in the end I got sick of Stoney [Tim Stone not Carl Stonehewer] and wanted a change!"

If you are to enjoy success and longevity as a rider nowadays, then one of the key aspects of your preparation is diet. If you're a promoter then ensuring you have enough fuel on board to last the physical and mental demands of any meeting is also an important pre-requisite. To this end, the Two Daves - Pavitt and Croucher - from the Isle of Wight Speedway club have already made a beeline to the burger van, though apparently the lobster isn't available tonight. They have beaten the rush since the entrance gates have yet to open and so form a hungry two-man queue prepared to lead by example. They're men of the world and Double D in terms of speedway experience, savvy, personality and enthusiasm as well as girth. Dave Pavitt is resplendent in his eggshell blue BSPA (or possibly SCB) dinner jacket that cries out to the casual glance - I am in authority and part of the speedway governing body (well, it also says that on a badge on the lapel). While the other Dave of the Croucher variety - speedway's answer to P Diddy in terms of bling - wears his trademark collared short sleeved smart white shirt, despite the unseasonable chill, and comparatively modest selection of gold jewellery that wouldn't look out of place on a gypsy fortune teller or any self-respecting hip-hop artist. Dave C is in the motor trade and sells previously owned prestige vehicles. Though Tim Westwood already has the *Pimp My Ride* telly gig, Crouch really should urgently pitch the idea of *Pimp My Jewellery Box* to television executives before someone else steals the idea. As they wait for their food, with easy familiarity they discuss the race card in tonight's programme and review their tactical plans for the night.

[DP] "Use him [name redacted] if you can, he's cheaper. We don't want to run up Phil Bartlett's costs too much but we still want to win!"

[DC] "I said to Phil earlier, 'We'll win by four or five and we'll try and be gentle with you'. But, the rules are a bit different in the Conference League - we have to name our three rider replacement riders. I want someone excellent chosen in case there's a crash or we go behind and I have to put in one of the big boys in the later heats."

[DP] "Peter Oakes says it's rained off in Plymouth and it's comin' this way. I hope not 'cause it's the first time I've been here since 1982!"

The wonder of the world wide web is something else that's exercising an incredulous Dave Pavitt, "I rang Dave Tattum the next day and he said he didn't come 'cause of vandalism at the stadium that he had to put right blah blah and then he said to me, 'I watched it on the Internet last night.' I say, 'what do you mean?' and he said he watched each heat result come up almost as it happened. He even knew that someone had bent their footrest in Heat 11 - there I am sweating my balls off for about £3 per week while someone is texting away. No wonder I can't get punters through the door when they can watch it for free. I'd break their fingers if I find them. Maybe I should get a jammer and not tell anyone? That'll mess them up! Or, perhaps, I should lock them out just to let them listen to it to torture them?"

I stand to be immediately corrected but Weymouth speedway is one of the few clubs in the country that makes any kind of gesture towards saving the environment through recycling. This initiative takes the form of three highly visible, almost garish, litter bins emblazoned with a green circular logo and marked Weymouth Wildcats Speedway 'plastic bottles', Weymouth Wildcats Speedway 'glass only', and Weymouth Wildcats Speedway 'cans only' respectively. With nothing to recycle just yet, the Two Daves wander off, while the first of the fans with their garden chairs stream towards the wind-break standing area or head off without a second glance at my display of books towards the grassy banks of the back straight. Poole and Somerset promoter Mike Golding arrives for his first-ever visit to Weymouth speedway with his partner Anita, "where's the best place to watch it from?" Apart from Poole, this is the closest speedway track to his home though, tonight, he's tired after a long drive back from the Somerset away meeting at Redcar the night before. "We lost by one point last night! There was a heavy shower at Heat 7 but we managed to hold onto our 6- or 8-point lead until the tactical in Heat 14 with Havelock. We were still one point ahead in Heat 15 but lost it 47-46." In fact, it transpires that the key aspect of this turnaround Heat 14 that snatched victory from the jaws of defeat for the Redcar Bears, was the performance of Josh Auty who rode to victory off the 15-metre handicap. (His performance was such that, subsequently, he was awarded the 'Race of the Season' trophy at the Redcar Speedway Christmas party.)

Also here tonight is Howard Milton, the ace speedway reporter for the Yeovil-based regional newspaper, the *Western Gazette*. He's a keen fan of the sport and gives extensive coverage to the exploits of the handlebar heroes, at least as much as space permits. "We're in a triangle of clubs round here - Poole, Somerset and Weymouth - and this year they're all at or near the top of their respective leagues!" A clumsy man with a huge hearing aid who comes from Milton Keynes literally stumbles by my table to spill his coffee all over my pile of *Shale Britannia* books without apparently noticing what he's done. Luckily these books have been made to a higher specification with wipe clean covers. As I dry them down he tells me under the mistaken impression I'm the speedway book and magazine publishing magnate Tony McDonald, "I buy your *Backtrack* magazine, it's brilliant! I wanna get your Kenny Carter book. Did you see what happened with that American wrestler killing his kids? Exactly the same! But, years later - exactly the same! Well except a different nationality, oh, and Kenny didn't kill his kids just himself and different sport - but exactly the same really!"

Under threatening skies, the riders circle the track on the parade lorry before they hop off at the start gate to stand by their bikes for a few waves and for their individual introductions to the crowd. Club photographer, Julie Martin, has had a complete outfit change from her summer leisurewear into something more sensible and less alluring for her job - namely, long trousers, sensible shoes and an orange florescent tabard. Probably, so riders can spot her as they hurtle out of control across the centre green. Though Glen Philips is absent from the Islanders team at a long track meeting and their teenage prodigy Chris Holder is engaged elsewhere on World Team Cup duty for Australia, their line up still sounds hugely impressive. Noticeably, their equipment and clothing appears somewhat sleeker and shinier than those of their Conference League counterparts. However, in the battle of the hairstyles, there is only ever going to be one winner. The Wildcats would gain a TKO for David Mason's 2007 coiffure alone, though nowadays he sports a comparatively conservative look that you could roughly describe as 'understated', albeit with a vague hint of a Mohican motif. Indeed, his present hairstyle has echoes of Mister T, albeit in a white, less flamboyant version, rather than the wilder, punkier almost peacock-esque shapes and colours he favoured in yesteryear. Then, his choice of luminous red would be David's version of a concession to the suffocating strictures of everyday normality required on Civvie Street by The Man. Effortlessly taking on the hairstyling mantle held successfully for so many years by Mason (D.), is teenager Terry Day who models a delightful shock of hair dappled badger-like with stripes-cum-spots of blonde. This tonsorial battle between the two teams is over before it has even begun and the track remains the only arena where the Islanders can vaguely regain some vestige of street cred.

Wildcats mascot

Club photographer and press officer Julie Martin

The first leg of this challenge saw the Wildcats go down 51-39 on their travels and the Islanders top four of Jason Bunyan, Leigh Adams's cousin Cory Gathercole, the reputedly well-endowed Chris Johnson (according to authoritative sources and Chris) and Krzysztof Stojanowski will provide a huge challenge for the homesters. Rider replacement operates for the rider-now-known-as Karlis. The historical explanations for his firmly held desire for his rather lovely surname of Ezergalis not to be used to describe him aurally or in print, ranges from the much less believable "it's too long for the available space in the programme", to suggestions of premature delusions of grandeur. The explanation probably lies somewhere more mundane in between but let's hope that he does find the speedway stardom that his revised name now merits! Someone on the Weymouth promotional team has clearly visited Rye House Speedway since they imitate an old low-cost Len Silver trick, "the Clerk of the Course is going to be throwing the tossed coin into the crowd." This being the Conference League, the value of said "tossed coin" isn't revealed to a hushed, expectant and rather crowded Radipole Lane. Whereas in the Premier League at Hoddesdon, Len always makes great play of mentioning, it's a "two-pound coin" in the exaggerated manner of someone generously about to throw gold bullion onto the terraces.

The Weymouth promoter and team manager, the flame-haired Phil Bartlett clearly has a touch of the Ian Perkins about him since he has extended his duties on race night to include that of announcer too. Thankfully, he doesn't labour under the misapprehension that the crowd have assembled solely to listen to him hog the limelight and ramble interminably, but instead he provides brief, informative comment. He even kindly pops to my table to conduct a brief interview about my books and afterwards, before he rushes back to the centre green, observes, "that should sell a few more books!" Sadly his optimism fates me and sales remain becalmed. On the track the action never lets up from the off, though the Islanders reserve, Gary Cottham (in as a cost-conscious and bargain rider replacement rider), immediately feels the wrath of referee Ronnie Allen when he's excluded before the first race for "delaying the start". In what technically must be the re-run though the first running of the race never actually got started, the other Islanders reserve Harland Cook joins the fray but ends up placed, in what some speedway people on the telly rather mysteriously call, "stone last". Jason Bunyan flies from the tapes with a speed that the vast majority of the Premier League level riders emulate all night, thereby confirming the significant gulf in the standard of machinery as well as the truism that the major difference between the teams on the night will be the speed and determination in the first corner. The race is notable for a piece of really hard riding by David Mason, who takes a unique approach to team riding by diving aggressively under his partner Sam Hurst on the fourth bend of the first lap.

The second heat is also drawn and features a win for Gary Cottham who, very noticeably, immediately lined up at the start tapes without any unnecessary manoeuvring. Gathercole and Johnson imperiously win heat 3 leaving the consistently impressive (at Conference League level) Lee Smart trailing behind by some distance. Another heat advantage for the visitors is prevented in the next race by a daring overtake by another Wildcats Mason - Karl (no relation) - who threads-cum-blasts his way through the field down the back straight during the first lap and then escapes to victory. He is the only Wildcats rider to win a race all night. The next has Jason Bunyan again look like he's from a different league altogether (technically he is), while the crowd is also entertained by Lee Smart's never-say-die approach that nearly has him snatch second place on the line from Gary Cottham. To look at the way they ride the Radipole Lane track you'd never guess that many of the Islanders - often notoriously 'poor' travellers away from the Island - haven't ridden here before, let alone that the tight confines of the circuit contrasts massively with the wide contours of their home track at Smallbrook stadium. David Mason threatens to win Heat 7 and manages to entertain by keeping the fast-riding Cory Gathercole behind him for a couple of laps through a combination of guile, track knowledge, animal cunning and experience before his lack of speed finally costs him his race-leader status. The so-called 'weaker' partnership of Cook and Cottham in Heat 8 enables the Wildcats to fully explore their tactical options, when we see Jay Herne come in for Sam Hurst as a tactical substitute off 15 metres. In order to gain any benefit from this strategy, the pre-race plan will be for Terry Day to gain the lead and hold back the Islanders sufficiently for Herne to thread his way through the field to escape for double points. Things don't go to plan since Cottham escapes from the tapes and Day has to relentlessly chase him ("Terry have a look!") in order to just try to stay on terms under the close attentions of Harland Cook. To my mind, Day completely forget his team-riding instructions but the man next to me flatly disagrees with my post-race assessment, "there was no way he could shut off as the other rider wasn't far away, plus he nearly won!" Double points for third-placed Jay Herne results in a rare heat advantage for Weymouth and brings the scores to a more respectable 21-28.

By now the spits of rain have turned to steadier drizzle quickly making conditions much more treacherous for all the riders. This probably isn't a factor for Nathan Irwin who flips his bike barely a yard from the start to sustain injuries that keep him on the wet surface for some time before he withdraws from the meeting with a suspected broken foot. The re-run sees the first of successive heat advantages for the Islanders to further extend their score in the drizzle, though Heat 10 is enlivened by an ultra-aggressive ride for a lap and a half by Sam Hurst. His determination draws the eye, as does his distinctive head bobble that gives him an appearance of drunkenness or of an OAP with some form of involuntary tremens. It's clear that the riders and management of both sides are keen to offer a good spectacle to the fans, despite the inclement conditions. However, rain and speedway really don't mix no matter how willing the participants. Sadly, the inevitable happens when the rider with the most laps ridden round the Radipole Lane circuit in their Conference League incarnation, the experienced David Mason attempts to round Jason Bunyan on the second bend. He falls with considerable artistic merit and it's a crash that involves a couple of theatrical but painful bangs into the fence before he involuntarily dismounts his machine and lands in a dramatic heap. Sustaining a suspected broken hand is bad enough without the added discomfort of being completely soaked lying on the sodden shale. Sensibly, after he has excluded Mason and awarded the race, the heavy rain means that referee Ronnie Allen has no alternative but to abandon the meeting. Afterwards Wildcats away team manager Jem Dicken says incredulously (given that Radipole Lane notoriously isn't blessed with too much deep shale), "David Mason's dad says proper clubs don't put so much dirt on the track!"

The news of the abandonment is a signal to the fans to immediately rush for the exits - well, head off sharpish to the car park - and they stream past my table without a second glance. Stood on what you'd generously describe as a hillock, is a small knot of Islanders fans huddled for shelter under the single golf umbrella that Dave Pavitt has chivalrously lent them earlier. He now tries to half shelter under to get away from the torrent of rain. Stood with the Two Daves is the Islanders *uber* fan Kevin Shepherd who tries to go to every meeting home and away along with some equally keen speedway mates.[1] Anything Julie Martin can do in the wardrobe and clothes change department, Dave Pavitt can less fetchingly better having apparently brought along a dressing up box in the boot of his car. In fact, Pav undergoes more costume changes than they do at any amateur dramatic society performance and now is dressed in a sensible black autumn coat and wears his by now trademark flat cap that makes him look as though he's just about to walk the whippets.

[1 Dave Croucher told me a number of tales about the legendary Islanders "away tours", though sadly very few are printable. One that can be shared concerns Kevin. "We were on our way up country, a long way up country, like Newcastle or somewhere like that. Jason Bunyan and crew happened to spot Kevin and company in a Little Chef or something similar. On leaving for the car park, Bunyan spots a car with Isle of Wight Speedway Stickers in the windows, so he duck taped up all the door handles so the poor buggers couldn't get back in when they had finished their breakfast. That's the kind of thanks you get for being a staunch IOW supporter! Needless to say, Kevin thought it was a great honour to be treated in such a manner and still regales the tale with enthusiasm."]

Dave Mason – Weymouth Number 1

Rain fails to stop play

[JS] "How many times do you change a night?"

[DP] "Only as necessary."

[JS} "Do you have clothes with you for everything - even snow?"

[DP] "I believe I do!"

[Kevin] "It don't make him look any slimmer though!"

Dave Croucher vainly tries to make sense of the sodden ball of paper in his hand, "my programme is so wet I can't read it but I don't care 'cause we're so far ahead I can find out the score tomorrow!"

13th July Weymouth v Isle of Wight (Inter League Challenge) 32-49 (abandoned after 13 heats)

Chapter 25. Shefield v Somerset: Cuddly toy mountain hits Owlerton

19th July

The reality of promotional life during a wet summer is that with a fixture backlog you have to run your meetings no matter what alternative entertainment is on offer to your fans elsewhere. Tonight's meeting will run against the backdrop that followers of the sport might prefer to stay in and watch the World Team Cup race-off eliminator on *Sky Sports*. The fact that the WTC still doesn't really seem to capture the domestic speedway imagination allied to the fact that Great Britain have, for once, already qualified for the Final bodes well for the likely level of the crowd drawn along to watch the handlebar heroes compete live. Indeed, the Premier League encounter of the Sheffield Tigers and the Somerset Rebels at Owlerton can justifiably be called a top-of-the-table clash since both teams are presently tied on 19 points. Somerset have ridden two fewer fixtures and find themselves in third place compared to the Tigers fifth. Despite how strongly they have started this season it would be a major surprise if tonight was anything other than a home win, despite the talismanic presence of their captain Magnus 'Zorro' Zetterstrom. One of his loyal fans at Somerset, the indefatigable Di Phillips, is convinced that if I wrote a biography of the man entitled *Behind the Mask of Zorro* it would be a "best seller".

As if the rival attraction of televised speedway wasn't enough, a record-breaking wet summer and the concomitant floods in East and South Yorkshire has turned the traditional British obsession for commenting on the weather into a vocation for anyone within travelling distance of Owlerton. From Hull in one direction to Leeds in the other, nowadays it seems that no one dare leave home without calling the Speedway Office for the very latest local meteorological information from this particular part of the City of Iron and Steel. Judged by how often the phone rings while I'm stood in the doorway of the office, everyone rings at least once. Not realising how his photograph apparently stood by a boating lake of a flooded speedway track that appeared in the *Speedway Star* and the *Sheffield Star* would create a rod for his own back, Neil Machin has grown tired of this curiosity. "I'm sick of people ringing up and talking about the farking weather - I don't care if it's farking raining where they are when I tell them it's not raining here!" He's in mid fulmination when the phone rings again and he calmly reassures the next fan anxious about the threat of rain. Ever the seasoned professional, he closes every conversation with an aspirational statement that would make any true speedway fan rush along just on the off chance, "the track's lovely and I have a feeling that maybe it has enough grip on it for the track record to get beaten tonight!" It's a "feeling" that proves remarkably less than prescient but is just the sort of casually mentioned (but well practised) promotely surmise that should pique the curiosity of even the most determined stay-away punter.

GP riders - a bargain at £4.50

Rider instructions

Warm-up lap commences

I leave Neil to the sound of constantly ringing bells and head out to the car park to pick up some more books from the boot of my car. Sheffield co-promoter and centre-green presenter, the avuncular Dave Hoggart is also rummaging inside his car boot. We chat while he fastidiously unpacks four walkie-talkies, a master set of headphones and a single handheld microphone from the type of attaché case you invariably see shady assassins using in James Bond films. He manipulates the equipment with practised ease and it's yet another sign of just how organised you have to be to run any speedway club since I imagine that most fans, like myself, would expect that the broadcasting equipment would be supplied by the stadium rather than having to be brought along by the club each week. Dave is a kindly, knowledgeable man who has always been helpful to me. Speedway has just enjoyed one of its rare mentions in a national newspaper, in this case the *Daily Telegraph*, an article by the sports journalist John Inverdale that hasn't painted a rosy picture of where the sport finds itself. In fact, he rightly points out that very few people are only dimly aware that speedway still continues to exist as a sports activity in this country, never mind that even fewer could name the current (or previous) speedway world champion let alone recognise him in the street. Some speedway people have reacted badly to these home truths, particularly on the forums where the messenger has been comprehensively shot with accusations levelled at Inverdale of snobbishness, ignorance and worse. Looked at dispassionately, Inverdale is an experienced sports broadcaster who covers a wide portfolio of (often minority) sports and is well schooled in their respective popularity. Nonetheless, Dave feels that as a BBC employee Inverdale has an axe to grind, "he likes to have a dig at any sport that *Sky* cover exclusively!" Although he loves to chat, race day requires that a myriad number of tasks get done or supervised so Dave has to bustle off towards the speedway office for a brief planning discussion with Neil Machin.

Under the lee of the grandstand roof, Mick Gregory has nearly completed setting out the various tables of merchandise that form his trackshop stall at Owlerton. On the track, a battered-looking red tractor circles the D-shaped circuit endlessly and provides a steady hum of accompaniment. A significant part of the total area Mick occupies appears to have been given over to some sort of toy display. It's something I find weird until I remember that the club nickname is The Tigers and discover that Mick has one of every size to suit the depth of every pocket. Of the speedway memorabilia on display, my eye is caught by a display of rider models laid out on tin foil and housed under a transparent Perspex covered lid. Priced at £4.50 each, apparently, some rider figures are signally unpopular and Mick is reluctantly considering some form of price reduction. But, keen to find a positive, he then proudly tells me, "the Benji Compton stickers have sold out!" Not that he's had much chance to sell anything to anyone recently as the combination of floods in the area and bad weather means, "we've had no proper meeting here since June the 7th - last week's Top Gun [Individual Championship] don't count 'cause no one wanted to come to that!" The victory last week for Adam Roynon - in a field comprised of other riders from his generation who are presently serving their respective apprenticeships in the Conference and Premier Leagues - broke the run of washouts and, hopefully, changed the luck here at the stadium for the speedway club for the better. Earlier I had queried with Neil Machin the logic behind staging such a meeting when the club already had a sizeable backlog of more attractive Premier League fixtures, "We need to get rid of all the rain-off tickets before things start ticking over again for us." Mick also tries to look on the bright side, "One thing about all the rain offs - at least we'll get to run longer otherwise we'd have practically been finished by the end of August."

As a keen Derby County fan and season ticket holder at the club, Mick is also eager to highlight to me his perceptions about the idiocy of Sunderland AFC's player acquisition policy, "At least we're not spending £5 million - each - on Chopra and Richardson. I reckon Earnshaw will do really well and he's only £3 million. Up front with Howard he'll be excellent!" My reply that "Earnshaw has the teeth of an international superstar [*à la* Ronaldinho] rather than the skill" falls on deaf ears as Mick becomes engrossed in a mobile phone call. "No! No - I can't believe it!" he says loudly to end the call, "Me mate's just told me Mick Hunter's dead - he can't be any more than 60!" I nod sympathetically and leave Mick to his own thoughts.

Despite the opening of the turnstiles and the long lay off suffered by the speedway faithful in South Yorkshire, the fans only slowly trickle into the stadium. Many walk straight past the trackshop to cluster by the pits fence down on the fourth bend, while many others don't even pass at all as they prefer to watch proceedings in comfort from behind the glass of the grandstand bar and restaurant. Those that have arrived early are all greeted by the frankly unbelievable sight of the track being copiously watered by some form of crop-spraying equipment that the red tractor now tours slowly round with to deposit its load! I'm sure that this wouldn't be done unless strictly necessary, though with the back straight bathed in bright sunshine and the home straight shaded in the deep shadows of the grandstand roof, conditions under wheel are bound to be variable. The start of proceedings must be reasonably close as two youngsters - who look the part in terms of their protective gear but appear like they've yet to reach their teens - practise by endlessly circling the track on the loudest, whiniest underpowered motorbikes I can ever recall hearing. This aural irritation is exaggerated by the huge amplification provided by the empty grandstand and its high, cavernous roof. Mick isn't impressed, "I wish one of them would fall off or have an EF or someint!"

Various people stop by my stall to pass on their comments. One man mysteriously informs me, "if there's a 'Z' in it, Somerset always win if there's a 'Z' in it!" This echoes the practical advice that you should only eat mussels when the month has an 'R' in it but I struggle to fathom out what I've been told. Eventually the penny drops that this was Yorkshire wit about how poorly Somerset traditionally do (i.e. they never win) when they make their annual league pilgrimage to Owlerton. I doubt that this can be an explanation for the empty spaces in the stadium since most teams who journey here rarely put up anything like a real fight on the wide open spaces of this notoriously fast track. Each club with a huge track invariably claims that it's the fastest in the country - not everyone can be correct about this claim (made at Swindon, Sheffield and the Isle of Wight) - and it's no wonder that Neil Machin makes a virtue of this aspect to phone callers. Another man bemoans the poor standard of the Elite League, "I don't like watching it on the telly - Swindon at Arena were too processional - whereas in the Premier League there's energy and four riders really racing each other!" Out of the corner of my eye I notice Mick fussing round a larger man who tries on an anorak decorated with blue stars. Ever the salesman and clearly missing his vocation in a clothes shop, Mick says with winning sincerity, "It looks made to measure, it fits you like a glove!" Someone else stops to tell me, "I reckon you can get one more book out and then maybe stop". Another Yorkshireman dawdles and tells me, "I reckon we might lose tonight!" When I nod and say, "It would be a good result for the neutral", my suggestion that a close meeting would suit has him snap back, "What - do you mean you!" They say you can always tell a Yorkshireman - but not much.

Multi-tasking Dave Hoggart has arrived on the centre green and does the presentational honours with both teams as they line up beside their respective machines (in the deep shade of the shadow formed by the grandstand roof) for their introductions to the crowd. We also learn that "Emil Kramer is away after his crash" before I then think he said "on World Cup duty tonight" (probably riding for the back end of beyond) but couldn't be sure. We soon also find out that "Ricky [Ashworth] is not well enough to resume." Dave knows the typical speedway audience and he grabs their attention with a burst of "hands up everybody who has a red Corsa" before he pauses theatrically to then add, "if you're going home tonight come and see me 'cause I've got your keys!"

En route to the pits, Scunthorpe team manager Kenny Smith passes with his partner Julia by his side. He stops for a few words but has an incredibly husky voice that he blames on some spicy food he ate earlier in the week. Julia proffers a fuller explanation, "he had the back of his tongue taken out last week - on the 11th!" I'm not sure that I'd even be up and about eight days after such an operation, let alone going to speedway or eating spicy food! The fresh, angry scars he has on his neck confirm the story. Julia laughs gleefully to mask her anxiety, "he had salad and spring onions for lunch and he wonders why he's hurting!" I mentally try not to ask any further questions since all cancer sufferers and their carers continually have to live with a perpetual reminder of the situation when wellwishers and friends routinely enquire about progress. Even if the news is good and you are in remission, I imagine it's hard to find the respite of not remotely thinking about it and the last thing you need are questions that cause you to remember or relive events through answers to well-intentioned questions. Kenny answers one such question I haven't yet asked with practice, "I keep losing my voice but I'm feeling a lot better - thank you!" Julia holds tightly to his arm, "I keep screaming at him 'will you calm down!' but he doesn't listen." In that English way I make light of things, "with a voice like that you should be in telephone sales." Julia understands my drift, "you mean it's so sexy!"

We're interrupted by a thunderclap - not a real one but the *faux* version they blast out over the loudspeaker system that they then immediately follow with a remixed version of *Eye of the Tiger* to build up an atmosphere of anticipation. Showtime has arrived and Dave Hoggart cries out enthusiastically, "oh look at the sky - it's blue that can only mean one thing - no rain! No, it's a lovely sunny night in Sheffield for some speedway! Don't forget please support those who support us - Bradwell Skips." Later he also mentions a huge variety of other delightfully obscure heat sponsors as well as the new overall club sponsor for the 2007 season - the Sheffield Window Centre. If the meeting is to approximate anything like a contest then the Somerset Rebels team will all have to ride to the very best of their collective abilities and their talismanic captain, Magnus Zetterstrom, will have to lead by example. Sadly, his participation in the first heat only lasts long enough for him to blast through the tapes to the loud ironic cheers of the crowd. The re-run has him start on a 15-metre handicap that he fails to make up on the rest of the field. Sheffield follow up their initial 5-1 with another in the next race also after a re-run necessitated by a tapes malfunction. The mechanism sticks on the side closest to the fans, and this allows Paul Cooper and Simon Walker to escape (temporarily) until the red lights stop them. Dave Hoggart notes playfully, "It's not only the riders who are rusty but the starting gate too!" When finally run, the actual race itself is processional but the never-say-die spirit of the Premier League infects the Rebels pair of Danny Warwick and Simon Walker who - despite being distantly trailed off at the rear - vie for the reward of third place with some zeal. In fact, Owlerton proudly boasts of its reputation for speed and these two appear to be locked in their own unique private battle to find out who can get the dirtiest kevlars in the quickest possible space of time. Simon Walker gets really splattered first but then cuts aggressively across his partner for the chip-shop money on the third bend of the first lap to share a large quantity of the sodden shale with Warwick. He ends the race totally covered although his splendid dreadlocks remain in pristine condition safely concealed inside his crash helmet.

The Rebels then stage something of a fight back that starts in the next race when Jordan Frampton snatches third place on the line from a somnambulant James Birkenshaw to force the first of four successive drawn heats. The next heat is only drawn because James Cockle leaves it until the last corner of the last lap to throw away the lead to the hard-chasing Ritchie Hawkins, favourite rider of Somerset uber fan Supergran (aka Margaret Hallett). Some Somerset bad fortune then arrives in the sixth when, with Hawkins in the lead, second-placed Joel Parsons thwacks the mid point of the back-straight fence to fall and earn an exclusion for his troubles, though this is probably some form of rough justice since he appeared to completely jump the tapes. The immutable law of speedway states that whoever led the original running of the race will then suffer and, so it proves, when Ben Wilson (tardy the first time out) seizes this reprieve to blast away from the start for a tapes to flag victory.

The momentum continues to rest with the visitors who pull back a couple of the points of their deficit in Heat 7. Danny Warwick then threatened to best the unbeaten Ben Wilson by gating superbly only to be overhauled by the gifted Tigers youngster flying round the circuit with breathtaking speed and grace to record his third straight win. Sales remain poor on my stall though a passing man pointedly pats my book *Showered in Shale*, "superb book, sir!" Stood behind the nearby tables of his stall, Mick Gregory continues to sell Tiger toys to a steady stream of eager young customers. There haven't been many nights when I've been out sold by cuddly toys at a speedway meeting! Andre Compton and James Birkenshaw combine for a 5-1 to restore the

Tigers healthy advantage to 33-21. You know you're somewhere special (usually Yorkshire) when you hear the Gang of Four briefly blast out of the speaker system at a speedway meeting. Birkenshaw must have become tired by his exertions since he overcooks the entry to a bend when placed fourth while strongly in pursuit of Frampton. The race is awarded and, predictably enough, Magnus Z appears for a tactical ride in the next race sporting a black-and-white helmet colour. The first attempt to run it ends in a comedy of sorts when the wily Paul Cooper (tactically) slides off his bike in slow motion after a number of ostentatious glances further up the track towards the long-since-departed Swede. After this graceful fall-cum-lay-down of his machine, Cooper makes no real attempt to move the bike from the track. Apparently arms constructed from elastic bands have suddenly afflicted him and isn't a good combination with a lead bike weighing a ton. The referee understandably excludes him and the race has to be re-run. Far from enjoying the art of coarse gamesmanship as practised by Cooper, Mick Gregory is downcast at the Sheffield prospects in the re-run, "there's no way Parsons will beat Zorro!" Confounding all expectations, Joel Parsons gates and leads his illustrious rival who does make a couple of attempts to pass on the back straight during laps three and four. However, with age sometimes comes wisdom so the older, wiser rider decides to back off rather than be suicidal in full knowledge that the meeting is lost and that there is no point jeopardising many future high-paying nights throughout the remainder of the season with misplaced heroics. Some people contend that the fact that riders know that they will ride practically every night of the week in one country or another had reduced the average level of derring-do and almost eliminated the number of breathtakingly reckless rides you'll witness in a season. Except arguably among the younger, less experienced riders who've yet to fully realise either their mortality or the real significance of the comparative brevity of their speedway career and the earning potential of riding safely each night.

Andre Compton comfortably wins Heat 12, "that's 63 point zero - that's 63 seconds dead!" This time is three and a half seconds outside the track record jointly held by Simon Stead and Chris Holder. The feeling that Neil Machin had in his bones isn't realised. Slightly more of a Birkenshaw fan than he is a Benji Compton one, (though Sean Wilson might not agree) Mick Gregory notes, "Neil is too loyal to his riders - you can put up with Birkenshaw when he scores at home but he's not even doing that so what's the point of him?" Dave Hoggart informs us over the public address system, "if you're gonna dump your rubbish - don't forget Barnwell Skips!" With the contest effectively dead, Sheffield draw yet further away in the last few heats to massage the scoreline to much more impressive levels and would have won even more convincingly but for a confident Heat 3 fall on the apex of the last bend by a resurgent Joel Parsons. Zorro could have tried more in the last race but contents himself with a remote third - David from Slaithwaite mildly notes, "He's too fair for his own good that Zetterstrom." With the meeting officially closed, Tigers fans stream towards the car parks or the bar while Dave Hoggart apologises over the loudspeaker system, "It has been like the opening night of the season - so we apologise for the few things that haven't gone quite right tonight." What has gone right is the result for a team that (with the exception of Parsons) is an all-British one and, even more importantly, in a summer of floods, the meeting has actually taken place! Mick Gregory casts aside any morose thoughts to confirm, "that weren't a bad meeting that actually!" Though old habits die hard and - with the cuddly Tiger toy mountain smaller and a good night's takings not yet counted - he immediately worries about future prospects as further floods resurface in his imagination, "I know it's a terrible forecast for tomorrow."

As I fold up my table a man stops to tell me, "I've been coming here since I was 6 - 67 years - and the only meetings I've missed have been in the last month when we've had the rain offs." As I ferry my unsold stock back to my car, I overhear two staff members talking together as they leave about the night, "I've never seen the track prepared that badly, in fact it wasn't really raceable". If that was the case, then I can't wait to see the action here on the more entertaining raceable version!

19th July Sheffield v Somerset (Premier League) 55-37

Chapter 26. Stoke v Redcar: Mystery Chinese rider – Gwanlee – debuts in drizzle

21st July

My intended trip to the Norfolk Arena the next night falls victim to the torrential rain that Mick Gregory correctly predicted. The meeting between King's Lynn and Birmingham in the second leg of the Premier Trophy Final was called off early in the morning, thereby matching the abandonment of the first leg earlier in the week. Consequently I enjoyed another night ensconced at the always comfortable and friendly Garrison Hotel handily located within five minutes' walk of Owlerton Stadium. I waited for the rain to stop in the hope that the next leg of my mini-tour to Stoke would survive the unseasonal weather. Before I set off for the Potteries, I called the helpful Finance Director at the club, Caroline Tattum, who confidently predicted the meeting would take place ("we will be running tonight") and then reassuringly says, "when I spoke to Dave [Tattum] at the track, he said there's no standing water." The best meeting I saw on my travels last season was Stoke versus Newcastle at Loomer Road. I'd hate another abandonment, particularly because they're a Saturday night track and I've already had my complex travel itinerary wrecked by the weather. It would be difficult for me to return another night this season. That would mean the double loss of a thrilling night at the speedway and foregoing my re-acquaintance with some of the real characters you find at Stoke. In his paean to all things Northerly, Stuart Maconie, in his witty and perceptive book *Pies and Prejudice: In Search of the North*, disagrees with me and besmirches Stoke (or really the five towns that make up the 'place' known to outsiders as 'Stoke') by claiming the best thing in the town is the railway because it takes you through the place without the need to stop for a visit. I'm sure that none of these comments really apply, let alone to Stoke Speedway club which, to be exact, is located on the Loomer Road Industrial Estate so is actually in the Chesterton area of Newcastle-upon-Lyme.

When I arrive at the entrance gates to the stadium, the sky is thick with low dark cloud and to say it's overcast would be an understatement. Caroline greets me with a snigger, "What have you done to your hair - is it the Roman look?" I soon learn that the racing will go ahead and I'm told this in an incredulous manner as if my enquiry is one of the silliest questions that they've heard all season. Caroline Tattum is here with the same team of loyal, hard-working and experienced staff as she had when I called here in 2005. Her friend Gaynor has just arrived to join Torty and Gabrielle Goring. A van has pulled up close by to their vantage at the entrance and Caroline asks the others, "Who's that with the awful hair?" Gaynor doesn't know but suggests, "I bet he thinks that it looks okay!" Caroline is recently single and jovially wonders, "Does he qualify?" The assessment criteria is fairly straightforward, "35 (say 40), no children, rich, doesn't drink, possibly a smoker but he's not allowed to put on weight if he gives up, if you know what I mean!" I proudly show them their photograph in *Shale Britannia*. Torty is amazed, "I look about 12 in that!" Caroline looks at it from a commercial perspective, "how much is it then? £15! No! I'm in the wrong business." Torty is keen to produce a rival publication, "I think I might just take some photos and make a book!" Fiercely protective of her staff and keen to sing their praises, Caroline highlights that unlike some clubs featured in my photo book, she has no truck with dolly birds at the start line, "we have real girls here!"

Tonight's opponents are the Redcar Bears and one of the first people to draw up in their car at the stadium is *Evening Gazette* reporter Martin Neal accompanied by his son Tom (soon to go off to university in Newcastle to study philosophy). They want some good advice about where to go and eat locally before the meeting but only get referred to the pub down the road or the local McDonald's. Martin has a press pass but these don't find automatic favour with Caroline who reminds us that while supplied as an "official pass" by the BSPA they also have the phrase "at the promoters' discretion" emblazoned across them. "We're trying to run a business here not a charity!" she reminds Martin as though this might have been the misapprehension he laboured under, blissfully unaware that the majority of speedway clubs have to husband their meagre finances carefully. He drives off, saved by the bell, when her mobile rings. The caller is reported to be Jim, "we spoke two years ago - but now I'm single, he's back in touch," Caroline reports afterwards. With the entrance gate now officially open for business, Caroline issues some last-minute instructions to her team prior to the surge of fans they anticipate. "Girls - I want you to go balls out on the raffle 'cause it's gonna be late getting here. This week it's gonna be all the usual questions - like we know - 'but can you GUARANTEE it won't rain?' Like we know what it's gonna do! The forecast is for it to be fine!" Caroline and I reminisce about the deletions she insisted upon in my Stoke chapter in *Showered in Shale* - she still claims, "I never said the things I took out" - though, begrudgingly, she does admit to a lower tolerance for some of the promotional brethren she comes or has come in touch with over the years. Summoning up some positive memories, she's keen to stress, "I like George [English] and I like Alan Dick."

In fact, whatever the forecast, there's some slight drizzle from the impressively dark clouds. However, there's also a good wind so hopefully they'll blow past or stay away until the meeting is completed. Since the visiting Redcar Bears are from further afield, they'll be keen to get the meeting completed without a postponement. The car park is full of puddles and the track itself looks pretty sodden to the untutored eye. Stoke Speedway is that rare beast outside the Elite League - the proud owners of an air fence. This should provide some level of greater psychological comfort to the riders and actual comfort should they encounter it at speed. A slight problem with any air fence is that when you inflate it in preparation for the meeting, any puddle of water that has already gathered on its surface is deposited on the track surface. A casual glance at the track shows that, rather symmetrically, every few yards each bend has an equidistant patch of what on a golf course they would call a "lateral water hazard". On the sodden surface at Loomer Road, this surface water created by the air fence is visible but just short of an actual puddle. Inside the clubhouse that provides a bar, some catering and the chance to purchase speedway goodies from the Dave Rattenberry owned trackshop, you also get a panoramic view since it overlooks the majority of the home straight. If you're lucky enough to get there early, you can sit at one of the many tables by the windows that gives a prime viewing position from which to enjoy proceedings from the warmth and comfort of indoors. To my mind, however, speedway behind glass always kills some key aspects of the sensory enjoyment that it invariably provides - namely the noise of the bikes and the rich, pungent bouquet of the fuel. Like gin without tonic, speedway without this accompaniment is a lesser experience than it could or should be. That said, if you have to stay indoors for whatever reason, then Stoke is one of the places to consider doing it since you remain close enough to the track action (as well as overlooking the start/finish line) for it still to remain almost intimate. You also have the benefit that the sound of the engines is piped into the room via speakers so you retain the effect, albeit slightly muffled, and atmosphere of the engine noise. The ringing phone in the deserted grandstand bar is helpfully answered by John Rich, who breaks off from his duties at the trackshop to say, "Yeh it's definitely on - we had a drop of rain earlier but it's going to be fine!" He's a charming man who loves his speedway, has a curious outlook and always finds a genuinely friendly word for everyone. It's something that comes, I believe, from his love of meeting people, "Are you on another tour then? I sold one of the little ones this week" he tells me cheerily. I apologise once again for the fact that artistic considerations meant that he was edited out of one of the photographs that appeared in the final published version of the book. He's typically phlegmatic about it, "Oh well, maybe in the next one."

I search out club promoter Dave Tattum to thank him for his hospitality and to try to present him with a copy of my photo book. He's not where I'd usually expect to find him - on the track - nor is he in the pits where Wolverhampton and Redcar promoter Chris van Straaten dolefully shelters from the drizzle under a large blue-and-yellow umbrella while sporting an almost luminously bright red Wulfsport/Redcar Bears anorak. I eventually find a slightly bedraggled Dave - also dressed in a red anorak, albeit of the Stoke variety - behind his desk in the cosy speedway office. My rhetorical question, "Would you like a book?" elicits "How much is it?" closely followed by an "I'll get my money later." When he learns he can have a copy for free he brightens, "Really? Thank you. I'll look at it later - there are still some tracks I haven't been to. Edinburgh is one but any Friday track is hard 'cause I need to be here looking after things 'cause of Saturday!" Back inside the grandstand bar, countermanding her earlier "go anywhere you like" instruction Caroline suggests (in a way that brooks no argument) that I move my table from adjacent to the main doorway ("you can't stay there for Health & Safety reasons") to the far end of the room. She suggests, "why don't you give up books and

Grandstand bar

CVS with brolly in pit lane

Great racing acknowledged

buy Stoke speedway?" but before we can explore this further the phone on the bar rings yet again, "It's fine here [pause], as I said it's fine here and we're definitely running!" Gabrielle who also works at Sheffield as the green start-line girl informs me that Neil Machin has finally purchased the black-and-white tactical-ride umbrella that he'd hankered after for sometime - before she adds proudly, "we don't need one here as the meetings are so close!"

A huge contingent of Redcar fans have travelled down from the North-East to watch their team ride. They're enthusiastic followers of their speedway team and fill the bar with a sea of bright red anoraks as well as brighten the place with their bonhomie and the loud, infectious musicality of their accents. When seen in situ together, the colouring and lettering of the Stoke and Redcar anoraks look so remarkably similar that you'd think they were almost identical. I then remember that Dave Rattenberry runs the trackshop at both clubs and appears to have done away with the frippery of making each club jacket look individually distinctive. The atmosphere on the terraces appears to have improved with the arrival of the instant crowd that the visiting fans create. Away over the far side of the stadium complex, a reasonable number of cars have parked up for their owners to watch from the comfort of their own vehicles. From inside the bar you can't really be sure if the drizzle has stopped, though none of the car widescreen wipers in the distance are moving so this is probably a telltale sign that it's presently dry. Redcar announcer Gareth Rogers arrives but is spitting feathers that Caroline has refused to recognise his BSPA pass on the gate. "She's charged me and she was so rude about it. Dave has asked me before to be the relief announcer for them ("we'll pay you nothing mind") to help out sometimes, but I can't say if I will be so keen now." My table of books has attracted some interest and comment but very little custom. However, I have a superb view of the track and for the first couple of heats I can watch from the empty table with the "reserved" sign and a can of Diet Coke on it. Given how good the view is from here of the whole track, I imagine that this must be the space reserved for an important club sponsor. Some young children use the table and I perch on the end seat to fill out my programme. Just before the start of the fourth race an older woman angrily announces, "This table is reserved!" My explanation that "I was just sitting here while no one else was here ..." elicits a loud "Well I'M HERE NOW!" that causes the children with me to scatter away from the grumpy pensioner to the safety of the other end of the bar.

The meeting starts promptly ("we're going straight into it without a parade tonight") and a furious pace is kept up on the track and between races. The aggregate bonus point will be decided tonight after the first leg on Teeside was drawn. Stoke field seven riders and have Emiliano Sanchez in as a guest for Glenn Cunningham with Jamie Smith making his debut at reserve, while Redcar operate rider replacement for Mathieu Tresarrieu and also field Shane Waldron in place of the gifted but injured Josh Auty. If the visitors are to get a result, they need a big performance from their captain and ex-world champion Gary Havelock, though unfortunately to loud, ironic cheers from the home fans, Havvy grinds to a halt in the first race barely two yards from the start line. This gifts the Easy-Rider Potters a maximum 5-1 heat score. The next has the teams swap 5-1s when Dan Giffard flies away to a confident win on the track where dazzling sunshine nearly ended his career when it contributed to his horror crash only a few seasons ago. Tonight there is no danger of any sort of tan or, indeed, any sunlight. Jamie Smith only lasts until the second corner of his debut before he falls and then his bike gives up the ghost with smoke belching from his engine as though billowing from a witch's cauldron in a low-budget horror movie. In reality, the only horror on display is arguably the slippery condition of the shale surface. Chris Kerr makes a melodramatic start to his night in the third heat sponsored by "Bargain Booze" with a hopeful and artistic fall when on the outside of the pack in the first running of the heat. He manages to do so with such plausibility that the referee Craig Ackroyd gives him the benefit of the doubt on a tricky night for racing. He then just makes the restart when aided by a last-minute push-off from the track staff close to the pits gate. Justice is served in the re-run when Lee Complin rides under Kerr (but doesn't touch him) at the start of the second lap, thereby causing the American to again fall theatrically. With the rain spitting, the referee excludes him despite the interpretative merit of his demise. Stoke presenter George Andrews attempts to enthuse the riders with a call to arms, "Let's move, let's go, let's go racing!" Eventually Claus Vissing who rides in a determined but ungainly crablike manner wins the race to ensure another Potters 5-1. If he were a wrestler, he'd be known as Claus 'The Crab' Vissing but - given his brief speedway experience - would remain a lightweight (with some vicious moves) for the present.

It seems that the treacherous conditions afflict at least one rider in every race and the fourth heat has Smith again fall in true Keystone Cops fashion, albeit in slow motion, before he remounts to take the opportunity to practise at the back of the field. Shane Waldron appears to have been given a clown's bike in the next as he rides it like a drunken man slithering left and then right before unceremoniously leaving his machine - and all this before he's hardly reached the first bend. The home fans in the crowd grumble when the referee orders a re-run with all four back. Havvy wins this easily but behind him Vissing treats us all to his very own attempt to play speedway skittles with Shane Waldron who then earns himself an exclusion when he stays down for an inordinate time on the track. Vissing's all-action approach brings him second place and admiring comments, "Claus takes no prisoners - you either back off or that's it, mate! Then that's racing and it's fair." Presenter George Andrews, who is a dead ringer for David 'Diddy' Hamilton (former Radio One DJ and one-time Reading Racers announcer), grabs Rusty Harrison for a brief interview and starts him off with a statement notionally disguised as a question, "Rusty, the rain looks to have abated and the track's gonna get a lot better." Rusty tries the best he can to respond but George carries on regardless, despite the lack of a decent response. You sense that he is so professionally experienced at his job that he could probably conduct a reasonably entertaining interview with a shop dummy. George is an admirer of the fortitude of speedway riders, particularly how the breed as a whole pick themselves up after injury or falls - it's an attitude that tonight manifests itself when they uncomplainingly get on with the meeting. Indeed, the show must go on and the crowd clap Waldron appreciatively when he staggers to his feet; though the impact of his fall, his steel shoe and the sodden surface make progress back to the pits somewhat slow. "One or two footballers I know could do well to come down here and have a look!" George exclaims, though judged by the results for the professional teams in the local area last season they might better spend their time practising the skills required for their own sport rather than watching another.

Ben Barker wins the sixth by fearlessly exploiting an outside line an inch or so from the fence. It's a route round the Loomer Road circuit that no other rider has dared or had the inclination to use. The Sanchez household must be on a water meter and be avoiding too much use of the power washer (or possibly might have run out of washing powder), since Emiliano appears to be determined to keep his kevlars spotlessly clean all night. Exceptionally, he manages to escort his team mate ahead of him home without venturing anywhere near his back wheel and thereby avoids any possibility that he may get showered in shale. From the centre green George Andrews kindly promotes news of my attendance and enthusiastically encourages any reticent fans to take a look at my wares, "Browse; have a look; even buy it - that's the idea - all good value - he's the one waving at us now!" Fated by his interview with George, Rusty falls when at the back of the field in Heat 7 and Redcar take full advantage to narrow the scores to 22-20. After four 5-1s in the first seven heats, the conditions then throw up a collector's item of a race. It starts normally enough when the-rider-known-as-Karlis ("they say Len [Silver] did it 'cause they couldn't fit Ezergalis in the programme") leads Shane Waldron down the back straight of the first lap only to then make the fatal error of concentration with a brief glance to his right. This momentary distraction enables Barker to power through an imperceptible gap to take the lead. While at the rear, the Redcar pair then choose to fall simultaneously - albeit on different sections of the track - to stop the race. Craig Ackroyd then bizarrely excludes them both (rather than chose one of the two to suffer) and awards the race 5-0 to Stoke.

This is precisely the sort of good fortune that any side should seize and kick on from. Instead Stoke immediately concede a 5-1 (the seventh heat in nine where 5 points are recorded by one side or the other). Claus Vissing is unable to get sufficiently among the Bears enough to intimidate anyone and near to me the home fans implore a mystery Chinese rider I've never heard of - called "Gwanlee" - to overtake James Grieves. Gwanlee favours the exit from the second bend for all his attempts to pass since he tries this manoeuvre on laps two, three and four without success. It takes until the last lap of Heat 10 before Emiliano forgets himself and finally gets his kevlars dirty, just like every other rider on show. By now the rain is heavier and it's a tribute to all concerned that they persist with the meeting and even bother to race, particularly when visibility is so poor for them. Heat 12 showcases the battle of the hard men - yesterday's enfant terrible in the form of James Grieves versus the *terreur du jour* of Claus Vissing. The youngster wins this contest in the rain with some ease by aggressively blasting under the race leader Grieves as he enters the third bend of the first lap and then monstering him by driving him out towards the air fence at the apex of the corner. As Grieves sensibly backs off, Smith sneaks through, while the exertion of his crab-style charge causes Vissing to rear expansively almost the length of the home straight as he struggles to control his machine. He clings on, corrects himself and resumes his progress to victory.

With the points difference on the night now extended to 5, all that remains is for the riders to either insist upon abandonment or, as they collectively decide to do, rush hell for leather to complete the outstanding races. The Bears finish with a 5-1 flourish (the ninth 5-point heat of the night) to massage the score - they possibly might rue how the awarded 5-0 race cost them a draw - but victory on the night, along with the bonus point, goes to the Potters. With the meeting officially closed at 9.15 p.m., over the loudspeakers George Andrews rounds up the spectacle succinctly for the appreciative fans in driving rain, "a great performance turned in there by the Bears. We saw some excellent racing in what can only be termed inclement conditions. Congratulations to the promotion and the ground staff for getting the meeting on and thanks particularly to all the riders tonight who've produced such close racing!"

21st July Stoke v Redcar (Premier League) 45-44

Chapter 27. Scunthorpe: Big news and high drama at CL Pairs

22nd July

The recent tradition that Scunthorpe Speedway get to stage the Conference League Pairs Championship continues in 2007 and what a splendid job they've made of it in the years since the dusty, lengthy embarrassment for the sport that was the 2005 staging of the event at Plough Lane. The club in Scunthorpe remains a work in progress, but every time I visit, the strides they have made in the development of the stadium are truly impressive! There are many obvious changes and these include: an additional home-straight grandstand (to go with the one they put in last year), new entrance gates, a programme stall booth and, most significantly (apart from the fact the bar is now fully operational), for young rider development a new training track just inside the perimeter fence of the stadium. Over the past few seasons, Scunthorpe have given a wealth of rider talent its head and, without exaggeration, they can be said to have been a stellar force within the Conference League. Indeed, they have practically swept all before them and would start out as favourites to retain the trophy won last year (by their 'B' team of Paul Cooper and Benji Compton) but for the recent injury to Josh Auty. This means that the mercurial young Tai Woffinden (16) is now paired with Andrew Tully (20), another rider who has also impressed throughout the country for the Scorpions this year.

I arrive early to be greeted by a strong wind, dark clouds and a recently watered damp-looking track surface. Club promoter Rob Godfrey scoffs at my choice of attire claiming that my shorts mark me out as a southern visitor not used to weather conditions in t'north. Rob has already been here many hours with a dedicated band of volunteers that also includes his wife and son. The clouds look ominous to me so I ask Rob what the weather forecast is today, "Put it this way, we've just watered the track!" Rob's son is keen to quiz me about my impressions, "What do you think of all the changes?" he asks before pride in the infrastructure has him to blurt out, "The training track is gonna be used for the first time today!" I suggest to Rob that he must have had one of the quickest speedway educations in history when taking the club (along with his partner Norman Beeney) from an idea via humble beginnings to the enviable position it now finds itself in today. Rob modestly puts this success down to hard work, the support of others and the chance to do what they wanted on the blank canvas of these fields. The main lesson he has learnt is about the riders, "They're whiney, whingey bastards!"

Rob kindly gives me the run of the place to set up my table wherever I like. I elect not to squirrel myself away like last year at the far end of the stadium grounds in the (now fully functioning) clubhouse but, instead, to base myself on the walk down from the entrance gates to the edge of the safety fence of the main track here at Normanby Road. I do mention to Rob that on the members-only Wimbledon supporters forum moderated by Ian Perkin on Yahoo, that Derek Barclay has taken it upon himself to critique my latest book *Shifting Shale* (though he kindly damns me with the faint praise that there's "some good and well written stuff in there") as if it was primarily written as a critique of the homeless Dons. He also appears to try premeditatedly to stir up or promise some kind of confrontation with some OAPs alluded to in the last chapter of *Shifting Shale*. Derek's posts on the Internet are often characterised by strong opinions, excessive use of emoticons, late-night usage and the occasional unfunny joke. In this instance (with a schoolboy play on words) Del tenuously claimed the venue of this meeting - Scunthorpe - is a wonderfully appropriate venue/location for me to visit. [1]

Over at the training track, along with his dad, 13-year-old James Sarjeant prepares his equipment ready to christen the new training track. The Sheffield track curator Graham Trollope (pronounced Tree-low-pee) circles repeatedly to grade the surface on what appears to be the same old red tractor he also uses at Owlerton. By the time this has been completed a good-sized crowd

Bargain prices

New junior track

Engines roar

of riders and track staff have gather round to watch the inauguration. The father of Tai, Rob Woffinden, offers some last-minute sage advice, "watch out for this bit here, if he goes over the camber it'll smack him into the fence. The only way to ride it is round the kerb I reckon." After a few laps have passed without incident and the crowd has ebbed away back to the pits to get on with the preparation of their own bikes and equipment for the Pairs meeting, I snatch a few words with James's father. He tells me that this is James's second year on a 500cc bike, "he flies round Sheffield and here, so he's just going out to see how it is and to steady his nerves. He's fearless really. When he rides the big track, he really farking attacks it - goes for it so well. When we got to Brighton [Bonanza 2006] I took one look at it and said to him, 'Do ya want to go home?' 'cause it was so small, but he didn't!" Rob Woffinden has remained and intently watches James circle the mini-training track; he clearly likes what he sees, frequently yelling out words of encouragement, "spot on mate, spot on mate - not too fast!"

Man about Scunthorpe, cheerful Barry 'Bazski' Preston pops by my table to catch up and to let me know about the weather ("it's forecast to be fine"). He's helped behind the scenes at the club since it started, "crowds have dwindled a bit 'cause the crowds wanna see close racing and this year the Scunny riders have just been getting out in front and winning! This should draw them here but there's a couple of other things in Scunthorpe today - a music thing at the football stadium and someint else." I hardly see any Scunthorpe speedway anoraks all afternoon though I do see many jackets like that worn by Baz with the letters "TWR" emblazoned on them. I assume for a while that there must have been some kind of sports car rally in the area with great local cache. Later the penny drops and I figure out that this must stand for Tai Woffinden Racing. My table is ideally placed to attract passers by if they're inclined to linger rather than rush on to bagsy the best viewing positions in the stadium. The early talk of the afternoon is the drawn meeting at Radipole Lane between Weymouth and Oxford in the Conference League. Wildcats promoter Phil Bartlett tells me, "We were robbed by mechanical failure". It's an opinion shared by Oxford programme editor Rob Peasley who informs me, "We were robbed!" Oxford team manager Peter Oakes also comments on events, "It's a funny sort of

[1 Literature graduate, Derek Barclay, posted the following on the wonderful Dons Forum to supposedly illustrate - through his selection of a 'typical' single passage - the alleged many faults of the approach and style of my whole book. Below all words in bold have been deleted from the quotation by Derek Barclay as extraneous (to his argument) and all the dots (…) have been added into the version of my text presented by my 'honest' critic. "Derek Barclay **[stops by again, surveys the emptiness of my area of the hallway and]** *gloats* **[/jokes,]** "you just don't know when to stop flogging a dead horse, do you?" {(p. 333) The edited version of the quotation chosen by Derek continues **"[Uberfan of Wimbledon Speedway and, recently it sometimes seems if you judge by the critical comments he's recently posted]** about the supposedly questionable lack of "moral" integrity that my book **[Showered in Shale]** apparently exhibits… **[Ian Perkin's honorary amanuensis,]** Derek **['Del' Barclay drops by.]** He's with a group of ageing friends… **[who stand a short distance away from my stall to wait for him. They must all be fans of the Dons judged by the array of colourful Wimbledon logos that bedeck their clothing and]** one of them repeatedly waves to me in the manner of Mr Humphries from Are You Being Served? **[I wave back a few times before]** I realise that far from being a friendly gesture, the individual in question either has an involuntary affliction or takes the mickey by waving sarcastically. **[Along with Derek's subsequent comments, it's the only rather fey instance of negativity I personally encounter all day and ultimately]** it's hard to be irked by Old Age Pensioner speedway supporters who suffer whatever is the waving equivalent of Tourettes." ((pp.327-328) The passage posted quotes from two completely different parts of just one chapter from the book but in the wrong order. This quotation is 98 words long, i.e. an amazing 48% of the original text (91 words) has been deleted from the chosen passage. Worse than mere sin of editorial omission, Derek has altered the order that these words appear in my book for greater effect and, thereby, has changed meaning of the text by both omission and juxtaposition. Based on this, you can't help but wonder how accurately Derek represents the opinions of others when posting on various forums.]

robbery - a new kind, where even the most partisan of fans would have to say it was. There were three exclusions and all three went against us - two were probably okay but one was debatable to say the least!" The meeting report in the *Speedway Star* only mentions two of these exclusions by referee Paul Carrington - one involving Jordan Frampton in the vital last heat ("this sparked uproar in the Oxford pits with team boss Peter Oakes spitting fire over the phone". Peter was fined £50 on the night for 'ungentlemanly conduct', though this was rescinded on appeal) and another involving "unluckily excluded" Brendan Johnson ("despite Weymouth's Nathan Irwin clearly clipping the tapes first").

Prior to my arrival at the track, I'd called into Tesco for some refreshments and caught sight of a massive pile of the latest J.K. Rowling book *Harry Potter and the Half Blood Prince*. The pile was depleting at an astronomical rate and immediately reminded me of the unsold pallet of *Shifting Shale* I had at home. Sadly, my sales were less than brisk though a Rye House fan kindly stopped by to praise my photo book *Shale Britannia*, "it is rather abstract! Someone pointed out to me that there are no photos of any riders yet, for me, it still captures what speedway is all about." Brian Oldham also stops by to point out that I'd failed to mention his wife Celia in my latest book "you should be named and shamed - she's been to 33 British Finals and I've only been to 31, yet you mentioned me and missed her out!" Derek Barclay even wanders by with an older gentleman (I assume to be Billy) who stands silently by his side. As usual, Derek is friendly and I bravely raise the subject of the gesture from Billy and/or others I'd allegedly misinterpreted at the 2006 Bonanza and written about in my book. Like men used to speak for their wives in the 1950s, Del explains on behalf of the silent gentleman, "Billy says the gesture was a drinking one." I ask Billy directly if he has any more gestures to share with me and get a gleeful one-fingered salute accompanied by a wry smile. On the centre green of the mini training track, Tai Woffinden and some mates have started an impromptu game of football into the single set of goalposts available. I say to the man next to me, "he's probably an excellent footballer too!" Just at that moment Tai balloons a left-footed toe punt yards over the cross bar - thank goodness he has feet of clay at something.

Rob Peasley returns to my table to praise the attitude of the Scunthorpe promotion towards the CL Pairs meeting, "It's good that they don't jack up the prices massively to get in or charge much for the programme." This year the championship is split into two groups of five teams with the winner of each qualifying group seeded straight through to the final. The points scoring favours those riders who work together as a team with 4 points for first place, 3 points for second, 2 points for third and 0 points for last place. The first race of the meeting pits Cleveland against Boston and the ensuing, slightly fortuitous 7-0 for the Barracudas immediately more or less confirmed them as the likely favourites to win their group and thereby qualify for the final (provided that they see off the Scunthorpe pairing when they race them). The Boston pair features 25-year-old Paul Cooper (who recently seems to ride for a different team every year) and Simon Lambert (aged 18). They gate with alacrity to leave Greg Blair (16) and Dermot Mark 'Buzz' Burrows (aged 43) trailed behind them. However, the Cleveland pair provide all the drama when Blair rears and manages to collect his partner for an enforced tumble through the Scunthorpe safety fence. Last year, the same section was repeatedly demolished and, for 2007, the chosen section appears to have moved slightly further round the second bend. The force of the impact is such that the fence is turned to matchwood, Burrows's trusty bike (new three seasons ago) is wrecked and Blair injured sufficiently to take no further part in the meeting. In the re-run only two riders compete since Blair is excluded by referee Margaret Vardy and Burrows is unable to come back out after he suffers what Scunny presenter Shaun Leigh euphemistically calls "mechanical gremlins." Things start well for Scunthorpe in this group with an imperious tapes-to-flag win for Woffinden (aged 16) at appreciable speed, though it's over three seconds outside his own track record time. This velocity is in marked contrast to the next race won by a slow-moving Danny Warwick (aged 23) who, nonetheless, wins easily from the remainder of the field in race since they putter around behind him. Nonetheless, the Plymouth pair of Ben Hopwood (aged 16) and Jamie Westacott (aged 19) wins the heat 5-4 by virtue of having filled the minor places in a race sponsored by "Steve Butler Heavy Transport - No Job Too Big".

Before the fifth heat Shaun Leigh informs us, "Buzz Burrows has no machinery that ... huh ... basically ... yeh ... no further part, we've unfortunately seen the last of Buzz, which is a great shame! Can we just rewind what I just said? Actually Mark, Buzz Burrows, is going to ride Greg Blair's machinery 'cause he has withdrawn unfortunately - so, but we're still going to have three riders in Heat 5!" The Wildcats pair of Jay Herne (aged 22) and Lee Smart (aged 19) showed youthful reflexes to out-gate the 43-year-old Burrows, but he then stalked them before he squeezed past the wild-riding Australian to claim second place. Shaun admires this all-action style afterwards, "Jay scraped the fence on more than one occasion there, in fact I can see the seat marks all over the stuff but, then, it is his first visit to Normanby Road." Another comfortable win for Woffinden (aged 16) after he overtakes Smart (aged 19) on the second bend - he draws the eye because on his bike with his languid, compact racing style - next time out means that the 'Group One' has effectively become a two-horse race between Scunthorpe and Boston. Whereas 'Group Two' had already degenerated into a competition to see who will qualify for the third-place run-off behind the impressive Oxford pair.

The prize for the most peculiar race of the afternoon is won easily with a virtuoso display from Buzz Burrows (aged 43) and Robert Mear (aged 18). The oldest rider in the field leads into the third turn of the first lap, only for the Rye House youngster to attempt a blast round the outside on the fourth bend. It's a good idea but the execution leaves something to be desired since he clips Buzz (who summons all his strength and experience to somehow remain on his bike) before both riders proceed to clatter into each other repeatedly down the length of the home straight as though their bikes were magnetised or held together like clackers. Burrows sensibly adopts a rigid, more upright position on his machine to repel Mear who keeps bouncing onto him. It's an impressive display of control, upper body strength and skill from Burrows before the inevitable happens and the youngster bites the dust after he clatters through the section of the safety fence chosen as the primary site of all this afternoon's crashes on the second bend in front of Buzz's wife and what they call locally "the supporters' club chalet". For sheer entertainment and a uniquely protracted fall that they manage to spin out for around three-quarters of a lap, they deserve top marks. Even more impressive is how Buzz so gracefully remained mounted on Greg Blair's bike and is, I'd suggest, down to his sheer skill, exceptional balance, fantastic control of the bike and cussed determination. Shaun Leigh is as impressed as the rest of us, "They bounced into each other a few times after the initial contact - Buzz did a very good job to maintain control of his machine and deserves a round of applause, I'm sure!" Sadly I was in mid wander round to the "supporters' club chalet" at the time of this incident, so I was unable to listen to the first-hand reaction of a small but keenly interested knot of Buzz Burrows fans - Derek Barclay, Billy, Mrs Buzz Burrows and their son Max, along with knowledgeable bystander Rob Peasley ("that's what I like about speedway, the way Derek speaks to me on the forums you'd never expect that we could even meet! Let alone stand together in each other's company so enjoyably all afternoon!")

The re-run of Heat 11 has been reduced to a match race and there's only ever likely to be one winner in a battle that pits Burrows (aged 43) against Karlis Ezergalis (aged 22). I take the time to watch Derek in his natural speedway habitat - peering intently at the youngsters as they learn their trade at the Conference League racing level (with the added bonus of his favourite rider, Buzz Burrows, also on show). The contrast between this absorbed man and the horror that is his know-all, screechy, always right, always got to have the last word internet persona is quite something. There is probably a case for his family to restrict his regular late night early hours of the morning forum surfing usage so that the nicer side of their father/husband can shine through for all the world to properly appreciate. And, of course, prevent a worldwide emoticon shortage brought on by Derek's over-use of this communication feature! Paternal skills come naturally to Derek, if judged by the solicitous way in which he cares for the young man at his side. I gather that this boy is Young Burrows. "Is dad doing well?" "Oh yes, he's winning!" Derek then formally introduces me to his temporary young charge, "this is Max Burrows, he'll be world champion in 2025!"

Our concentration is broken by Shaun Leigh speaking loudly over the public address system, "we're gonna have a word with Mister Beeney - they say he has an announcement that sounds intriguing!" What can it be? Shock news that Wimbledon have relocated to the Scunthorpe training track? Or, a proposal that Scunthorpe now have to race five laps to their opponents four in the Conference League to even things up a bit? It transpires that "if our application is accepted", the Scorpions intend to race their speedway in the Premier League next season. I think everyone feels that this acceptance is likely to be a formality (especially since Rob told me earlier they'd already started to pay the BSPA their Premier League bond in instalments), not least because it's likely to be to the overall benefit of the sport if, as expected, they also continue to field a team in the Conference League as well. Exciting though this news is, Rob Peasley is absorbed in his study of the details of the next race in the accurately compiled programme, "this is the key race [Heat 13] to decide who loses to Oxford in the final!" Tai Woffinden (aged 16) wins the race sponsored by Mark Barber ("For All Your Tiling Needs") for Scunthorpe but since Boston ride strategically to ensure that they occupy the next two places, they emerge 5-4 winners and, barring disaster, look nailed-on favourites to qualify for the final from the first group to face Oxford, the run-away winners of the other one. The final races are just as much about pride as qualification and Derek forecasts fireworks from Sittingbourne's Dean Felton (aged 37) when pitted against the Buxton partnership spearheaded by Jonathan Bethell (aged 34) and ably supported by Jack Roberts (aged 16). "Dean gets a bit wound up against Buxton," Derek burbles excitedly beforehand - though he doesn't explain why to those not part of the cognoscenti that make up this particular inner circle that he's a member of - and screeches, "I told you he's a different man against Buxton!" when Felton (aged 37) holds second place behind his white Rasta team mate Danny Warwick (aged 23). Sadly, Roberts (aged 16) hasn't been informed of the script (and may well be too young to appreciate whatever animus drives his rival), so nips through a narrow gap to secure second place and deflate Derek's excitement levels back from fever pitch to neutral.

The tradition of only crashing on the second bend continues in Heat 16 when Hopwood (aged 16) and Sam Dore (aged 20) come together on the first lap. A re-run with all four back is the adjudication provided ("if fit"). Heat 17 sees Scunny gain maximum points versus Buzz Burrows - the sole Cleveland representative - who manages to finish last without turning the safety fence to matchwood. However, it's not enough for the pre-meeting favourites to qualify for the final. With a few qualification races still to go, I retreat to my table in case some disconsolate fans leave early to beat the rush from the crowded car park. A young Chloe Preston passes with her friends saying proudly to them, "my dad's in that book!" My question, "Who's your dad?" reveals, "It's Barry - Baz. I wish I was in one of those books! Have you been on the telly? We have - on Look North singing 'Amazing Grace'. It was really boring as we had to keep singing the same bit again and again so they could get different shots of us."

As expected, the final pits Boston versus Oxford and the consolation final is raced between Scunthorpe and Buxton. Before these teams take to the track for one last time, a crowd gathers to watch James Sargeant (aged 13) christen the training track with the first official inaugural ride. Sadly, he only travels two bike lengths before he falls; though he soon remounts to circle it repeatedly with practised composure. Tai Woffinden (aged 16) continues as he'd started, to remain unbeaten by an opponent on the day and with Tully (aged 20) second Scunthorpe secure overall third place on the day. The final looks like a foregone conclusion when Cooper (aged 25) and Lambert (aged 18) sweep into the lead but Frampton (aged 22) then manages to force his way into second before nearly coming to grief on the third lap. Though he stays on his machine, the opportunity for Oxford to fight back has evaporated and Boston emerge victorious, thereby ensuring that Paul Cooper is again part of the winning partnership (for the second year in succession). Afterwards, the delighted Boston promoter Malcolm Vasey highlights what we'd all witnessed at the CL Pairs Championship for the second year running, "as ever the Conference League has delivered tremendous racing!"

22nd July Conference League Pairs Championship, Winners: Paul Cooper and Simon Lambert (Boston)

Chapter 28. Isle of Wight v Glasgow: Chocolates or flowers?

24th July

If it's Tuesday night it can only really mean one thing - a trip to the Isle of Wight. Well, except of course if you're a rider who also plies his trade in continental Europe then, inevitably, it means racing in Sweden. One of the joys of the Premier League is how teams based in England, Scotland and Wales ensure the variety that the competition and the fans thrive on. Arguably, the longest journey of any season has the Glasgow Tigers travel to the Island (or vice versa). It's a journey of around 450 miles from the city of Glasgow to Portsmouth even without the ferry crossing and the final short drive to Smallbrook Stadium. If these were Premiership footballers or their key backroom staff, they'd most likely hire a plane, stay the night or, if they were slumming it, ride on a luxury coach. But, as this is speedway, everyone will try to drive there and back with only brief stops in motorway service stations to break the length and monotony of the journey. Tigers presenter Michael Max has done the journey many times and, with the voice of hard-won experience, laughs off the idea that it's at all arduous once you accept that it requires concentration and that you'll arrive back across the city limits in Glasgow after daybreak (during the summer). He also points out that many of the present Tigers team don't live in Scotland so, for some, the journey to the Island is less of a trek than the journey to any home meeting.

Given the difference in the track size and contours between that found at Saracen Park and Smallbrook Stadium, the likelihood is that the Tigers won't exactly excel round the fast, wide-open spaces found on the Island track. The peak holiday season - the weeks of the actual school summer holiday - is the time of year when the Islanders get or aim to get their biggest attendances every season. This increased revenue through the turnstiles (and bar) is essential to the viability of their business. Luckily, it's a bright evening and, despite an element of thick (white) cloud building up, there's a steady stream of people arriving, though not in the epic proportions the promoters would really like to see. After they've come through the entrance gate, the tradition at Smallbrook appears to be to turn right and head immediately up the stairs to the bar to secure an early place on the small outside viewing terrace. This allows those lucky enough to cluster there the chance to watch the racing from an excellent vantagepoint, while they enjoy the benefits of being both outside (for the noise, smell and spectacle) and close enough to the inside to avail themselves of refreshments on a regular basis. Those who don't choose the bar option, don't seem to linger long where I'm stood but prefer to crack on round to their favoured spots elsewhere in the stadium.

Some stop briefly to buy a programme and/or a raffle ticket plus tonight there's a stall selling tickets for another fundraising event at the club - a "Fun Night". This is to be held on Friday September 7 - not a race night - so those riders who live in the permanent caravans in situ at the stadium will be able to socialise and mingle with the fans. It will feature quite a variety of entertainment for an £8 ticket. The hand written notice says the cost of entry will include "BAR-B-Q-Salad Bar-Free Glass of Wine-Comedy-Karaoke". The club also depends on events like these to supplement the often meagre income (outside the key summer months) taken through the turnstiles and topped up by the taking from catering and, more particularly, the bar. As the club gains the profits from such events, it's vital that they encourage and maximise the usage of these facilities. There's a suspicion in some quarters that the club tries to exploit its remote geographic location on race night to control the time the meeting finishes by ensuring the track gets the regular attention of the grading tractor and that races aren't always rushed through as quickly as they theoretically could sometimes be. However, that said, speedway invariably attracts delays anyway through the rough and tumble of random events like crashes, mechanical failures, false starts and the like. Those who wish to head back to the mainland on the penultimate ferry sailing of the night after the racing finishes - usually the visiting team - often have to really rush to get there after the chequered flag has been waved for the final time. Those fans who're happier to relax in convivial surrounding with riders, officials, promoters and volunteers, while they wait for the last ferry sailing back to Portsmouth, provide much needed additional custom and additional revenues in the bar. Understandably co-promoter Dave 'Pav' Pavitt is fiercely protective of his club and the vital revenue stream provided by the stadium facilities, so tonight the early evening is enlivened by a very public dressing down by the turnstiles for Ken Burnett, the man who videos the racing at Smallbrook every week. "Why the fark have you been telling people that there's a 10.30 sailing when there isn't?" asks Dave in some dudgeon. Rather than throw himself on the mercy of the court and confess that he's been rumbled for inadvertently fuelling a 10.30 ferry sailing rumour to escalate like wildfire round the fans and staff in the stadium.[1] Ken initially insists he said no such thing and, then - really attacking the construction of the hole he's digging for himself - if he had said anything, it was only to one person and he wasn't sure that he definitely had said there was a 10.30 sailing anyway. This isn't what the usually highly avuncular Pav wants to hear, contradicts what he's heard and isn't what he found when he rechecked on the computer just to make sure. He forcefully reminds Ken, "there is no farking 10.30 sailing - so don't go farking saying there is! The last sailing goes at the same time it's always gone, if they listen to you they'll leave the bar early for no reason." Dave then adds a few other strong statements for good measure before stomping off in the direction of the pits. Dave is of the once said then forgotten school of argument, though a shell-shocked Ken lingers to insist to anyone who'll listen, "I didn't say that exactly!"

Fun night tickets on sale

Crouch, Chris Holder, Glen Phillips and Rose Halfpenny

Riders wait

[1 the ferry sailings were at 9.30 p.m. and 11.30 p.m. in the summer of 2007.]

'Buzz' Terry in his lair

*Shane Parker, Michael Max
and Alan Dick*

*Best coffee on the Island [provided by
Albert and Eileen Shepherd]*

After I've tried to sell my books by the programme stall, I wait until the rider parade before I leave my wheelie bag of unwanted goodies behind and rush round to the riders' viewing area by the pits. This is basically a platform made from wooden boards placed on top of a specially constructed scaffolding structure that occupies some of the sloping grassy banked area by the fourth bend end of the grandstand they have here. It provides an excellent view in all directions, particularly if you glance towards the starting gate and the vital first corner. It's popular among the riders, officials, various club staff and, at this meeting, off-duty referee Robbie Perks drinks in the atmosphere of probably his last visit to the Island before he emigrates with his family to Australia. Further along by the fencing that separates the grassed area from the rough-hewn parallel paths that run from the pits to the track gate, there is also the possibility to stand on the white winners rostrum that has been stored there. This isn't quite as popular but provides the chance to stand on the sections of the podium usually reserved for third, first or runner up. It appears that among those who stand there, everyone prefers the greater viewing height (rather than cache) provided by clustering in first place. There's a smattering of Australian riders in both teams but the one who really grabs the attention straightaway from the first race is Cory Gathercole. He entertains the crowd with his own game of dropsy on the banked third bend by falling there twice on the first and third laps. He's more malleable than some of the older riders since he bounces well and, after the first fall, remounts with alacrity. The second fall leaves referee Graham Reeve with no choice but to stop the race to exclude him and to award the result. Predictably enough, Chris Holder had by then already established a comprehensive lead over the rest of the field, so honours remain even at 3 points apiece.

In the briefly extended gap between the first two races, I snatch a few words (while he has a crafty fag on the riders' viewing area) with the always friendly and engaging Glasgow club captain, Shane Parker. The programme says he's an "honorary Scot" before it goes on to highlight, "He won't thank us for telling you, he's 37 years young now" as well as that he "remains one of the sport's great entertainers and a prolific on track scorer combining that with his position as head of the Speedway Riders' Association". I'd recently emailed him the critique of modern speedway written by John Inverdale in the *Daily Telegraph*, "that article you sent me was spot on - [speedway] is a minority sport if you look at it dispassionately!" Also here tonight with Shane is his charming wife Anji and the rest of the family, "She's here somewhere with the two kids running amok." I also manage to snatch a conversation with Glasgow co-promoter Alan Dick. He's a modest and friendly man who always manages to cut a dapper figure and somehow makes a red Glasgow Tigers race jacket look like a must-have fashion accessory. He nearly kindles a love for the Tigers that I didn't know I could have when he reveals that the distinctive red-and-white stripes of their team colours have been used from when the club was formed in 1946 because of a link (I don't fully grasp initially) between the founders of Glasgow speedway club and their support for (my beloved) Sunderland AFC. Before I can learn more, the next race has Lee Dicken handicap himself further when he has to start from 15 metres back after being excluded under the two-minute time allowance. This isn't helpful and the home pairing of Chris Johnson and Andrew Bargh cruise towards a comfortable 5-1 heat win until Bargh suffers an engine failure on the last bend. This enables the Glasgow pair of Michael Coles and Lee Dicken to sweep past to claim the minor positions for an unexpectedly drawn heat score, something that Michael Max orgasmically greets with a delighted "Whooo! Whooo! Whooo!" on the viewing platform before he scampers off to the pits for further congratulations and ostentatious celebrations. Announcer Bryn Williams remains philosophical and leans on the lessons to be gained from recent mechanical history in his summary of events, "for the second week running, disaster strikes our Kiwi when he's on a paid win. Actually he blew his engine on that last bend - it went with a bang - last week it was a broken chain, this week it was something more expensive!" A short while later Andrew is delighted to learn that his sponsors Acorn Care Services have decided to pay for this unexpected repair bill.

One drawn heat follows another with the third race of the night when the Islanders rejuvenated captain Jason Bunyan wins by some distance from second-placed Shane Parker. Jason looks quick (and stylish) to the naked eye and this visual speed is reflected in a winning time of 66.9 seconds only 0.4 seconds outside the track record set by Chris Holder in the Knock-Out Cup meeting against Workington. Stood by the winners podium but leaning slightly disconsolately against the fence, co-team manager Dave 'Crouch' Croucher - the man with an email address for every day of the week - is impressed by Bunyan, "I thought he was going a bit quick!" However, he isn't so happy with the scoreline though it could have been different if Krzysztof Stojanowski had snatched third on the line, "I can't believe we've won three races and it's still 9-all. The problem is there's not enough dirt on the outside for the five out of seven of our boys who like to get into it. After five or six races, there'll be more for them. They shut the gate on Stoj on bend two and, if he didn't get round them then, he was never going to on the last bend." Speedway is a funny business and the demeanour of the Two Daves in power here - Pavitt and Crouch - soon goes from slightly downcast to joyous with freshly beaming smiles all round, in the space of two races, after a couple of successive 5-1s for the Islanders. Crouch tells me, "It's just like London Transport buses, they always come along in pairs!" The mood has lifted so much and the confidence returned that Crouch can start to appreciate the little things in life, "it's nice to have a meeting as per programme for a change!"

The fast-fading Tigers assault then takes a brief optimistic turn when Chris Holder is relegated to fourth behind Trent Leverington and Michael Coles. The young Aussie soon picks his way past his opponents from fourth to second before he settles into the groove behind Cory Gathercole to record a hat trick of maximum heat advantages for the Islanders. With the score far from poised at 24-12, the "whoos" have long since deserted Michael Max who instead earnestly discusses the tactical options for the remainder of the races with Shane Parker, "It's either that or you do the black and white now?" The captain wants to strike back immediately, "Let's do it now!" Things don't quite work out as planned in Heat 7, when the Tigers Robert Ksiezak finds himself in the lead with Shane in third place. He tries to rectify the situation by slowing down but then nearly suffers the indignity of losing the lead to a Glen Phillips charge for the line. In the referee's box, Bryn Williams jovially informs the crowd of the race result, "If the old AB-BACK-US is working in the box here, I make the score 26-17 in favour of the Wightlink Islanders!" We then learn that there is romance in the air at Smallbrook stadium, "Today is a very special day in Ken and Jackie Burnett's life - it's their wedding anniversary! They're happily married, at least I think they are - Jackie, you're a lucky lady 'cause he takes you out for a very special night at Isle of Wight speedway, much better than a box of chocolates or a bunch of flowers!"

Already luxuriating in the likely triumph ahead, Pav has shifted further along the fourth bend and stands pit side of the perimeter fence that separates the riders and officials from the expectantly baying crowd of Islanders fans that like to watch their speedway from this vantagepoint. Well, to be more accurate, a small but perfectly formed cluster of Islanders loyalists in the form of Albert and Eileen Shepherd, who respectively sit and stand there every week on either the folding garden chair or the small wooden stool brought along for this purpose. They also come well prepared with a bag tied to the chain links of the fence that is packed with provisions ranging from a good selection of sweets and including the wonderful coffee that, along with the conversation, has once again drawn Pav to their company. "This is the best coffee on the Island - Camp coffee and full cream!" he smirks approvingly - as though we're suddenly stars of an advert - while he deftly removes the plastic beaker from the top of the Shepherd's red thermos flask to pour himself another cup. Resplendent in his red-and-black IoW anorak, Albert reminisces, "I've been going to speedway since 1951 but she started going before me - it's 55 years in September [1952] since I started courting

Post-race bike care

Lee Dicken

Hive of activity in pits

Eileen. My father was a bike pusher at pre-war Coventry for Jack Parker and we used to live opposite, so I was always going to be interested."

Pav chimes in, "Albert is one of our major shareholders."

"Yeh, I'm one of the original guys who put in £500 when the club started. It's now £4000 or four and a half, you've got to be dedicated 'cause we're not going to see anything back -apart from the enjoyment, of course, that's why we're here!" The ownership structure of the Islanders is unique within British speedway and Pav, like the many individual shareholders, is justifiably proud of the place. "Everything you see here is all done by volunteers. People like these or like Brian and Keith, who do endless hours sweeping, grass cutting and painting. I stand out on that balcony [waves at clubhouse in the far distance] and see that lovely green grass cut. It really does make me proud to be part of something like this!"

Though the result was no longer in any real doubt, and despite the differential in the scoreline, the racing remained absorbing. All the home riders, with the exception of Andrew Bargh, contributed points and excitement. We all know that Chris Holder is a unique talent and a delight to watch wherever he races in 2007 - and more so when, like tonight, he consistently gated slowly - but the Islanders are far from a one-man team. Stoj and Cory Gathercole both recovered from poor opening rides to reveal their ability on a bike, while Jason Bunyan continued to be a revelation. Heat 9 typified how he combines determination, track knowledge and grace on his machine to great effect. It was a race in which he fought his way back from the rear of the field to claim second place through a series of timely, high-speed passes. I watched this race from my favourite vantagepoint within this stadium, the high-ground scrubland that overlooks the wall-of-death type banking of the third and fourth bends. This really is a unique spot from which to experience British speedway, though surprisingly few fans appear to favour watching from here. On my way across the hillock on a rough surface strewn with purple flowering weeds, I pass Pav returning from the third bend area. "I've just been over to count the rows of cars in the car park - 12! - that's good, though I'd hesitate to guess how many people are here."

There's a jovial atmosphere in the commentary box if judged by Bryn's comments, "Hello - Graham Reeve has opened his wallet - there's a moth in the box!" Before Heat 10 Bryn confidently states, "I'm gonna lay my life on the line here and predict the winner of this is gonna be an Australian." It's an accurate if not exactly prescient observation as only Australians compete in it and it duly provides another successive 5-1 for the home team, "heat number 10: Australia One-Two-Three and Four!" Glen Phillips wins the next race and celebrates with an attempted wheelie. Bryn trots out one of his tried and tested jokes, "Can he get it up on the back straight? Oh, come on Glen, you'll have to do better than that," before he effortlessly segues into a plug for the race sponsor, "G J Aerials - for the best erection on the Island".

Throughout the summer, the stadium hosts many different motorcycling events and we get a taste of some of these with tonight's interval entertainment - sidecar racing. These bikes ride the 'wrong' way round the track (in a reverse direction to the speedway bikes at least) and the first race has barely started before the precarious lunacy of the co-riders job - to lean off the edge of the side platform attached to each bike - is confirmed when one is scraped across the shale surface of the cambered fourth bend. The co-rider soon recovers sufficiently to resume combat and entertain the fans. After quite a length of time, the interval ends and the remaining four heats of the speedway meeting are raced quickly and competitively, even though the result has already effectively been settled. We're treated to a couple of drawn heats and another couple of 5-1s (to make seven in total on the night for the Islanders). Heat 15 doesn't initially look like it might provide another maximum heat advantage for the home side when Shane Parker leads for the first lap. But, Chris Holder (lap 2) and Jason Bunyan (lap 3) reel him in, bide their time and wait for their respective ideal moment to pass him with some ease.

Like many others in the stadium who use the bus service from the ferry port that the club provide on race night, I watch the last race from the comfort of the upper deck. What you lose in sound and atmosphere, you gain in comfort from the knowledge that you'll make the (faster and earlier than the car ferry) 10.15 SeaCat sailing. This is useless for anyone with a car or a rider with a van but useful for any foot passengers. Before I got on the bus, I pass Ken Burnett at the bottom of the gantry steps he climbs to film the race action. He reminds me "Don't forget there's no 10.30 ferry!"

24th July Isle of Wight v Glasgow (Premier League) 59-32

Chapter 29. Weymouth v Wimbledon: Red lingerie arrives anonymously

27th July

SKYBALLS

Jonathan *"Could we not have asked more of British speedway tonight?"*

Given the lack of results generated by the management team of the grandiosely named Wimbledon Speedway Plc in their search for a new home, the best that Dons fans can hope for action-wise for the second successive season is to see a fixture that involves the itinerant version of their club. The side to face Weymouth at Radipole Lane has been put together by the indefatigable Nick Taylor of the Independent Supporters Club to race some challenge fixtures during 2007 and, though not ideal, to thereby ensure that the historic name of the club doesn't fade from the collective speedway memory. At least, ensure they're not airbrushed from history with the same ease with which the stadium landlords painted over the prized mural at their spiritual home Plough Lane. Wimbledon is one of the biggest-ever names in British speedway history, yet the best hope for the future appears to be that the present Plc owners of the promotional rights will concede that their protracted search for an alternative venue hasn't borne any fruit (never mind it presently looks unlikely to do so within any reasonable timeframe). Some have suggested others within speedway might be more competent/experienced than the present management to resurrect the club at a new venue or, possibly, in a new stadium. Maybe even a return to the old stadium at Plough Lane is an outside possibility, given that the stadium landlords the GRA, apparently get on perfectly amicably with speedway clubs based in the two major English cities of Manchester and, from this season, Birmingham. Some observers feel that, two years down the line, the time has come for the Plc to resurrect the club or pass the baton to others who can do so.

It's highly likely that Plc Chairman, Ian Perkin, won't be at the Wessex Stadium this evening to see this challenge meeting organised by a supporters club keen to stress their independence from his organisation (and vice versa). But then, neither will be many of the serial posters who endlessly animate the popular British Speedway Forum 'debate' on the future of the club. This lack of Dons fans prepared to travel in numbers to away tracks was a problem highlighted by Sittingbourne fans - the most 'local' away venue to SW19 - during 2005 when the club still raced in the Conference League. It's safe to say that a long journey to Dorset for a challenge meeting appears unlikely to set these loyal but stay at home and travel averse hearts racing a couple of seasons later. Leaving aside the contentious question of whether a club no longer based in Wimbledon can rightly still use the historic Wimbledon name/brand - particularly given the geographically scattered catalogue of new venues mooted during the last two years (by various sources) as possible relocation sites - this lack of travelling fans could even potentially be a sign of future problems with regard to the viability of home meetings! Nonetheless, like any genuine speedway fan, I'd be delighted to see (and support) the opening of any new track in the country. Hopefully, the present owners of the Wimbledon promotional rights will turn their ambitions into reality rather than allow the already lengthy search for a new home to become so protracted it starts to look badly bungled.

Given I saw every Dons challenge meeting in 2006 and enjoy the sight of the racing on the tight confines of the radipole Lane track, this meeting is just too good to miss out on. Sadly, the forecast rain along with the showers and overcast conditions on the journey down doesn't bode well. Indeed, for a seaside town in July, my arrival coincides with the start of light drizzle, while the black clouds over the stadium look really ominous. My last meeting here was rained-off prematurely and this one looks highly unlikely even to commence. I've arrived before the majority of the riders, if judged by the lack of activity in the pits or the absence of a phalanx of white vans from the car park. While I sit glumly in my car, track curator and team manager Jem Dicken arrives and immediately bustles off through the pits gate. Moments later a small but rather sporty-looking green Vauxhall screeches to a halt close to my car. A mystery bloke and three start line girls get out, "Whooo! Red Bull doesn't that give you a buzz? And it gives you bad breath!" Shortly afterwards, I exchange a few words with the Wildcats Commercial Manager, friendly Robin Spicer, before he leaves for some important race night duty, "I have to go and sort out me burgers!" The man on the gate doesn't hold out great hope that the meeting will go ahead, nor does he think that speedway challenge meetings ever really thrill the locals ("It's better than the sidecars anyway"). However, he is delighted that Weymouth - who were also threatened with extinction but fortunately managed to patch things with their landlords (and have now secured their medium-term future with the previously recalcitrant stadium owners following the arrival of a new promoter) - can in a small way support any struggling speedway club in their hour of need. "Clubs supported us when we were trying to get a track, so it's nice to be able to support Wimbledon as they try to find theirs!"

I wander round the pits in search of some unlikely good news about the meeting. Those people who are around either shelter in the "CATS R US trackshop", under the pits roof or stand around disconsolately in the rain. Someone who's smiling but jacketless is the SCB official referee for the meeting, Christine Turnbull. She's lived down South in Surrey for some years now (on missionary work among the heathen Sassenachs) and retains an accent - that to my ears - still sounds remarkably strong. They say that you can take the girl out of Scotland but not Scotland out of the girl and this must still hold true since Christine is the only person macho enough not to wear a coat or carry a brolly. I enquire about the whereabouts of her 'SCB Official' jacket - an item of fashion that many other refs so proudly strut about in on race night - only to learn, "they sent me one but it was too small and I'm still waiting for a bigger one!" It has taken her five hours to drive to Weymouth and the likelihood is that she'll turn right round again after a track inspection. "This rain looks set in now. I'm sure that they could race and I'm sure they would! But, the risk of injury in the reduced visibility is definitely a significant factor that I'll have to weigh up before I reach my decision - as the safety of the riders has to always be paramount. Plus, they wouldn't want any injuries - for their Northern Tour this weekend to Redcar and Scunthorpe - caused in a challenge match!"

I head off in search of shelter and club press officer and photographer Julie Martin, who I'm told might be in the 'Cats Whiskers Bar'. The only person inside is club historian Ray Collins who's sat at a table that enables him to overlook the increasingly sodden track. He interrupts his close study of the match programme to look disconsolately out of the window at Christine Turnbull and Wildcats promoter Phil Bartlett on their track walk of inspection in the heavy rain. "Because of the ridge nearby, a lot of bad weather usually passes us but equally, like today, if it does arrive it stays and this looks like it's gonna stay all night! There aren't even any clouds, just a low sky and continuous drizzle." He resumes the study of his programme, so I get mine out too.

The 'Inside Lines' notes from Phil Bartlett welcomes the "nomadic Wimbledon Dons" and commiserates with their plight. "It's been two years since the Dons waved goodbye to their home circuit at Plough Lane, and although a lot of hard work has gone into trying to re-home the club unfortunately they are still homeless … hats must go off to Nick Taylor for keeping the club alive." On another page, Julie Martin discusses the six riders named as the visitors' line up and she provides a brief but entertaining thumbnail sketch of each of them. They are: 1. BURROWS, Dermot Mark (Buzz) "well, what can you say about Buzz! … the Buzz is actually called Dermot! [He] started his career back in 1984 with Scunthorpe and has quite a few entries on his curriculum vitae. He has ridden for Edinburgh, Middlesbrough, Buxton, Stoke, Belle Vue, Glasgow, Cleveland and, of course, Wimbledon" 2. FLETCHER, Norman Stanley 3. WRIGHT, Matthew Paul "scored 15+1 in Boston's recent visit so will be confident of a good night" 4. CROSS, Andre "he represented Wimbledon in the Best pairs meeting in June. Unfortunately for Andre he ended up with a solitary point, a sore bottom and a hole in his kevlars" 5. MORTON, Raymond Paul "a bit of a surprise inclusion in this meeting … will surely relish the chance to show some of the younger opponents that there is no substitute for experience!" 6. NEWMAN, Kyle "local lad" 7. ELLIOTT, Martin John "also an accomplished Cycle Speedway rider". Even more fun on the facing page is a 'Rider Profile' of Sam Hurst who answers the "Girlfriend/Boyfriend?" question with, "Single and looking! Requirements are: aged between 17-22; slim; average height; bigger the better in the personality and chest department". Later, in answer to the 'where did you wake up this morning?' question, he also reveals his love of films when he replies, "at home, alone."

Safety notice

Spares prices

Shelter in the pits

A slightly bedraggled but still glam Julie eventually arrives in the bar and immediately rummages in the fridge for a refreshing (soft) drink. She brought along an envelope that contains a gift from a forward but slightly bashful mystery admirer. "Would you send something like that?" she asks pulling out a pair of sexy bright red crotchless knickers. The package had come to her care of the speedway club so had already been via Phil Bartlett's house - when he opened the package said garment fell out on his kitchen worktop. "He was quite shocked," says Julie laughing. We're unable to solve the mystery of male fashion sense and colour blindness when it comes to gifts of lingerie for our partners, lovers and mistresses. Apparently, there is an immutable law that insists the male of the species will always choose red and, mostly, choose tackily and tastelessly. The anonymous gift has come with an enthusiastic summary of expectations as well as with specific operating instructions contained on a note Julie waves around, "I'm to wear a short skirt and bend over by the start line. I think I know who it is - I didn't know they had such neat handwriting. It must have taken them ages!" There are more crotchless knickers here than Wimbledon fans. Sadly, before I can learn more or Ray suggests a demonstration, news that the meeting has been called off filters through to the bar. I decide it's best to head straight back off again, though as I leave the car park a few other vehicles continue to arrive and park up. These people must be supreme optimists! Some distance away at the entry to the road that wends its way past the football ground and down to the speedway, a completely soaked Robin Spicer wears a saturated Weymouth Speedway jacket, "this is another of the less glamourous jobs I have!" As we chat a steady stream of cars pull up alongside him in the by now almost torrential rain to enquire whether the meeting is going ahead. Ever the salesman and with the club commercial interests in mind, Robin greets everyone really cheerily, "yeh, it's off; but the bar is open - why not pop along?!"

27th July Weymouth v Wimbledon (Challenge) - postponed rain

Chapter 30. Coventry v Wolves: Anthem fever hits Brandon

3rd August

Jonathan	*"Coventry look really together as a team … [they] walk out together, walk back together, the pits are clean!"*
Jonathan	*"The only league team to keep the same seven - that's an interesting statistic!"*
Billy Janniro	*"We all have the same place in the pits, we take the piss out of each other"*
Kelvin	*"He he he - he's full of it, isn't he!"*
Jonathan	*"I think he meant taking the mickey, it's just his accent!"*

Jonathan [after Rory Schlein uses F word]
"We might have heard another word we shouldn't have - I apologise once again!"

Nigel [at Brandon near Coventry not NYC] *"Beautiful skyline here!"*

Kelvin [on Rory Schlein] *"This man, I must say, it's triffic for him!"*
Jonathan *"Poetic, almost"*

David Norris [after Schlein falls] *"It really could have snapped his leg like a twig there!"*

Jonathan	*"I seem to remember they kept the same team as last year except when they changed Johno"*
Kelvin	*"That was a miracle"*

Jonathan [on Coventry Bees] *"They're really buzzing - I don't raise that as a cliché"*

Nigel *"Most experts say - and I don't include me - that Coventry were in the driving seat"*

Nothing sets the local pulses racing in the West Midlands like the speedway derby meetings between Coventry and Wolverhampton, even when the likely result is the foregone conclusion that most predict it will be this season. The Bees won home and away in the 'A' fixture and since then they have shrewdly strengthened their initial squad by exiling Morten Risager to Eastbourne and cannily bringing in Steve 'Johno' Johnston, when the sudden demise of Oxford speedway meant he became available. Added to this is the fact that they have become the form side - winning their last six matches, thereby consolidating their credentials as the major rival to the pre-season favourites for the crown, the Swindon Robins. Allied to the confidence to be gained from such performances earlier in the week, they beat one of their erstwhile rivals for a top-two spot in the league table - Poole Pirates - in a home televised fixture, despite the fact that many of the team were badly under the weather but, being speedway riders, still rode. Since then Scott Nicholls and Rory Schlein have just about recovered but they were expected to use rider replacement for Olly Allen because of the recurrence of his hand injury. Olly then proceeded to aggravate his body further with a crash at Belle Vue that caused shoulder damage to add to the list of his pre-existing ailments. However, madness and

Formation tractor driving

Start girls in formation

Pre-race psychology

determination are both part of the psychological make-up required to ride on any bike without brakes, so confounding everyone, he surprisingly declared himself fit to compete tonight.

Nonetheless, in his column in the programme, co-team manager Peter Oakes talks up the likely threat posed by Wolves. "We have said before that they are always to be regarded as dangerous opponents because they have riders who are good around Coventry. It's a cliché, but still true, to say that the form book can go out of the window in any local derby, and we will be ready for them to put up a strong challenge." Peter is a man who had already done me extremely proud with a wonderfully kind and in-depth article on my books and background in the current issue of the *Speedway Star*. He'd also revealed that my previous bookselling trips to Brandon had not made this a happy hunting ground for me previously. "His worst night? That was at Coventry where the only book he sold was snapped up by security officer Kevin before the turnstiles even opened." The first person I bump into tonight, obviously enough given that he works at the entrance gate to the stadium, is the said same security man, albeit his name is Keith not Kevin! He's amiably phlegmatic about the fact that someone who works in a management position at the club should know him but not his name when he's mentioned in the *Star* for the first time. "Oh well, that's Peter," he says philosophically, though he makes a point not to even consider buying either of my latest volumes.

Someone who has read the latest book *Shifting Shale* is Joyce Blythe in the trackshop, who featured in forthright fashion, in a chapter that debated 'What is Art?' among many other topics. Smiling, she practically runs away from me when I arrive, "I'm not speaking to you again! Where's your tape recorder hidden? Show me? I said there's no way you could have remembered all that without a recorder!" Once we've established that my recall comes from my assiduous note keeping and increasingly hazy memory, we all - Joyce, her husband Malcolm along with their colleague Hazel Billingsley - chat about the prospect that Coventry will/might win the Elite League in 2007. I think that they really have some quiet confidence now - after a close season of sincere disbelief - that such a thing is possible but instead prefer to talk down their chances and mention the random nature of Lady Luck in extenuation. I don't even have the chance to look around for the new items of Bees-branded speedway memorabilia that I know will have arrived in the shop since my last visit. Joyce is always looking for ways to excite the customers and loyal fans into further impulse purchases at the shop. Tonight I notice that the tactic is to offer good discounts off the original sale price on a range of selected black-and-gold Bees items. If these garments were to be advertised on local radio there would doubtless be talk of a "price crash" and exhortations to get along and buy something "while stocks last!" Shirts are reduced to £10 for the Pits variety and to £29.95 for the more substantial "Champions" version. For £5 there are also "limited edition Bees Diamond Jubilee badges (2 colours)" along with "Golf style umbrellas" that now retail at £24.95, plus rather amazingly, "two styles of Bees coat" (anoraks to you and me) are available at half price.

I manage to resist all of these bargains but do succumb to Joyce's sales patter when I buy a copy of the *Bees Anthem 500 Miles* CD sold for charity with proceeds being split between the Garry Stead and Stuart Robson campaigns. This is a rather fantastic recording based on the famous song recorded by The Proclaimers but specially adapted to hail and worship the glorious riders who appear for the Coventry Bees. Joyce insists that I listen to the recording and even fetchingly sings (without the Scots accent) the adapted chorus and also some of the key 'funnier' lines from a pre-printed lyric sheet to persuade me that I should definitely get a copy. Though I suspect that she already pretty well knows the song by heart and it would have been tempting to ask her to belt out all of it before making my purchasing decision, I'm too reticent to do so.[1]

Before I can check if Morten Risager - exiled a round trip of 400 miles away in East Sussex - features in the song, tonight's referee Chris Durno pops into the shop for a brief but earnest discussion with the trackshop staff about the latest rumblings and grumblings from within British speedway. Malcolm Blythe has some strong opinions about the lack of loyalty shown to racing in this country by some 'foreign' so-called superstar riders and is jaundiced about the calibre of the excuses offered for their frequent no-shows. Chris isn't a fan of this pick 'n' mix attitude, "I'd throw out all the GP riders 'cause we now have a situation where 25% of the sport's income is going to 10 or 15 riders!" Malcolm is happy to advise Chris on what to look out for tonight when doing duties but cackles like a witch in a B-movie horror film when he warns, "Watch those creeping Swedes tonight!" Outside the shop I bump into keen Bees fan Jodie Lowry and enquire whether she still runs the Scott Nicholls merchandise stall inside the trackshop. "Yeh and I also sell the merchandise for Chris Harris and Oliver Allen and Martin and Rory, everyone except Billy Janniro!" "Is he missing out?" I ask. "Well, theoretically, he should have some but I reckon a pint glass would sell better and be more authentic!"

The people in this shop couldn't be kinder or more supportive of my book-signing visits. They kindly offer me my own table within the shop for tonight but, with space at a premium, I know how crowded it gets inside. So, instead, I decide to base myself adjacent to what could be called the husband's outside stall - run by Malcolm Blythe and Ray 'Brummie' Billingsley - where they sell magazines and occasional books to fans as they funnel past to various parts of the stadium just after they enter through the turnstile (and buy a programme). It would appear that many people don't subscribe to the *Speedway Star* but prefer to buy it every week during the season at the track, if judged by the muted reaction to the wonderful feature article on my book. Though someone does come up to inform me, "You look a bit different to how you do in the *Star*!" I also hear from Steve Chilton, keen member of the Leicester Speedway Supporters Club, "There's big news for Lions next Thursday!"

[1 Lyrical highlights include:

If we get drunk Billy? Well we know we're gonna bee
We're gonna be the Bees who get drunk next to you
And if we Heaver, Heaver? Jeremy is gonna be
He's gonna be the man who's dog racing it to
…{chorus}
But I would ride 500 miles
And I would ride 500 miles
Just to be the Bees who rode 1000 miles
To win the league once more na na, na na na
na na na, na na na
na na na, na na na
na na na, na na na
…
And if I grow old like Colin Pratt who's 95
We're gonna be the bees who're growing old with you
…
Scotty Nicholls
Janniro
lika lika lika lika lika la
the Rooboy
Smolinski
na na na, na na na
Olly Allen Bomber Harris
Risager
Burowski

Hearing it is believing it as they say in the adverts! Even more marvellous than the ingenuity of the lyrics and the money raised for such deserving causes is the resurgence in interest that the CD clearly stimulates in the investigative team at the *News of the World*. By the autumn, twin brothers Charlie (45) and Craig Reid (45) - the individuals who make up the small but perfectly formed band we know as The Proclaimers - are revealed as serial lotharios! "Dad of three" Charlie's alleged suggestions to "his market trader mistress, Janice Hartley" at the Copthorne Hotel in Manchester attracts the headline, "Rumpy Plumpy! Second Proclaimers' star goes all wobbly for blonde (then wants three in a bed)".]

In the modern language of political correctness, I 'person' my stall and nearby the stall I'm adjacent to is 'peopled'. Once the rider parade has taken place and we hear the sound of the engines, the stalls are almost immediately unpersoned and unpeopled (see how ugly these phrases become). I pack up my table as if I'm on a promise elsewhere in the stadium. Malcolm and Ray also start to pack away the merchandise from their stall. This takes them much longer because not only do they have more stock but they also have more takings as well as equipment like the till and the like to transport back to the trackshop. Malcolm is philosophical, "People envy me 'cause they think I see all the racing for free when really I miss the first four or five races of every meeting. I hear the scores but I don't see the racing until heat 5 or 6! Inevitably someone always comes along about 8.20 to try to buy a *Speedway Star* when everything has been completely packed away and don't understand (saying things like 'don't you want my money then?') when I ask them to come back at the interval when they'll be back out on sale in the trackshop again." Tonight, though he doesn't know it, Malcolm really doesn't miss that much in the way of excitement.

The tone for the evening's racing is set in the first heat when Scott Nicholls easily beats Peter Karlsson to give the Bees a lead that they never look like losing from that moment onwards. They stretch their advantage in the next with another comfortable 5-1, though Magnus Karlsson appears destined to hit back in the third heat until Rory Schlein somehow finds a way past him on the final bend. Wolves are reduced to sending PK out as early as Heat 5 wearing a black-and-white helmet, which he wears with some success to win the race. This brings the scores back to a more manageable 19-14, though successive 5-1s for the Bees again make the teams look hopelessly mismatched. Now based outside the trackshop, the interval produces little sales activity for me. However, I did witness first-hand the immutable Law of Speedway Merchandising, namely that as soon as the racing resumes or is just about to - you're immediately plagued with browsers who suddenly prefer to lovingly linger over your stock rather than watch the racing they ostensibly paid and entered the stadium to see. In this instance, small boys stand there vacillating over exactly which photo of which Bees rider they should consider buying. Malcolm deals with their prevarication with masterly authority, "Come on! Make your mind up - I want to watch the racing too!" An impulse sale ensues and we can all return to watch the remainder of the action.

One of the real pleasures of speedway can be its unpredictable nature and an awarded drawn 10th heat (after Allen falls and is excluded while battling with Billy Hamill for second place) has actually signalled the start of a Wolves mini-revival after the interval. This so-called fightback might merely be over-confidence from the home riders that sees complacency briefly creep into the racing equation. Whatever the root cause, the visitors briefly shade things 9-15 and this improved performance includes revenge for PK in heat 13 when he bests Scott Nicholls. They are also helped in no small part by misfortune for Billy Janniro in heat 14 when he surrenders second place (and relegates himself to last) by getting totally out of shape on the third band of the penultimate lap. Normal service resumes in the last race with another win for Scott against PK - after he passes him down the back straight of the second lap - to leave the final scores more closely poised for the return leg at Monmore Green than the action merited or than they threatened to be earlier in the meeting. The large crowd files away serenaded by the musical accompaniment of 'Who's Afraid of the Big Bad Wolf?' blasting out over the stadium tannoy system.

3rd August Coventry v Wolverhampton (Elite League B) 52-41

Chapter 31. Ipswich v Peterborough:
Eau de hot dog fails to entice
4th August

After a summer of less than ideal racing weather, a scorching hot afternoon and subsequent balmy evening greets the rarity of Saturday night racing at Foxhall Heath. This is the second year running that I have come along to watch the Ipswich Witches take on their 'local' rivals the Peterborough Panthers on a special race night. I really excel myself by arriving to find the stadium totally deserted even though the large metal entrance gates that take you through to overlook the first bend are wide open. I wander down to the speedway office and find signs of life but learn John Louis isn't expected to arrive for another 30 minutes or so. The pits area for both teams look spacious and clean, while on the track two men work by hand on the safety fence in the hot bright sunshine. Soon they walk back to the pits but rather than rest in the limited but cooling shade, they straightaway head back out on the track with the tractor and bowser. Given how hot the sun is, it seems like supreme optimism to think that the baked surface of the shale will do anything but soak up the moisture immediately. Still, I'm sure they know what they're doing.

I return where I've parked my car and unload my tables and books without, even though it has always struck me as strange, pondering the mystery of why this part of Foxhall Heath has a sandy surface. No sooner have I staked my claim to what I consider the best pitch at the stadium - the tarmac area right next to the presently boarded-up programme booth - and also the ideal vantagepoint from which to see the racing, than the Barber family arrive en masse to open up their trackshop. There is almost a full house of Barbers, namely Nick, Johnny, sister Bev and mum Molly. Everyone will have their tasks and responsibilities but it falls to the brothers to unload the merchandise from the vans and the women of the family to initially unpack and lay out the stock with casual, practised ease. Later they will be joined by father Colin who will chat and chain smoke, except when he watches the racing from a few yards away (invariably flanked by his equally avid speedway fan sons). I have gathered that it's traditional for Nick and Johnny to banter along with each other and occasionally exchange heated but brotherly words about what should or shouldn't happen or what's already been done.

They've hardly started to unload when John Louis drives through the gate in his car and parks right next to the trackshop. Already smartly dressed for the evening ahead, he too unloads a few boxes of mystery stock while he chats amiably away with various members of the Barber family. They all clearly get along extremely well and are comfortable in each other's company. In the course of their conversation, the Kenny Carter book - recently brought out by *Backtrack* publications - catches John's eye and he briefly glances through it. He reminisces at some of the photos he sees ("look at the family he had") and recalls, "I remember when I went with him to Norden. He always treated people the way they treated him. At Halifax, he said, 'they don't like me here - I could help them if they wanted but I won't'. You always knew where you stood with Kenny. I remember him crashing at Halifax [in 1981 with Hans Nielsen] and spitting his teeth into his helmet. Blood everywhere. Next week he was all wired up with a tiny gap in his mouth so he could drink all his food through a straw. Then there was the [1984] British Final at Coventry when they had a camper van in the pits for him. Everyone knew he had a broken leg but afterwards when they looked at it, the pus was horrid. I was a pallbearer at his funeral - the shortest one - Ian Cartwright was on the other corner. I didn't have it on me

Trophies in speedway office

Famous Foxhall pits phone

You are being watched

shoulder, I just held it above there. It was heavy!" Johnny Barber listens intently, "I reckon he's like Jason Crump - surrounds himself with people he knows and, if you're not one of them, you're no one to him!"

As the conversation dies, I thank John Louis for having me along at the stadium to sell my books. "You're alright so long as you don't come back again!" he smiles. After he drives off round to park his car by the pits gate that they strictly (so it says on the large notice there) don't open until 6 p.m. to admit the riders and mechanics, Johnny Barber chats as he sorts out and displays the stock. "How many promoters would come and chat like that before a meeting? All of them are usually 'phew - don't talk to me!' whereas he's just the same as ever and always has time for people. That's the kind of man he is with everyone!" It has been a difficult season for Ipswich who, before a wheel had even been turned, looked like they had a 'weak' side on paper. And, while it's a speedway truism that riders race on shale not on paper, they also had a 'weak' side on the track in comparison to pretty well every other Elite League team with the exception of Oxford (who haven't even made it to this stage of the season because of their sudden mid-season withdrawal-cum-receivership) and possibly Reading. The Witches were then really put further behind the eight ball when Mark Loram got badly injured before the 2007 racing season had really hardly started. Johnny Barber remains upbeat, "I've got an idea for a new speedway play - *Kim Jansson and the Third Bend of Doom*, well really that should be *Kim Jansson and Any Bend of Doom* but that doesn't quite sound so good. It's been a hard season here but the racing has often been good! There's talk that Martin Rempala has turned a corner - without spearing Robert Miskowiak for once - 'cause he scored 6 paid 9 against Wolves but beating Carl Wilkinson, Chris Kerr and William Lawson isn't what I'd call turning the corner. If he pops out and scores 10 tonight, it'll make me look like a right prat now I've said that."

They say that possession is nine parts of the law but, apparently, this doesn't apply at Foxhall Heath on speedway night since it's soon made clear to me by a member of the stadium staff that I haven't seen before that I'll have to move my stuff to make way for a large hot dog stall. Well, more of an open-sided tent really, that has been invited along for the evening to take advantage of the expected big crowd. With only a few minutes to go before the entrance gates open, I'm informed that limited access to one of the few electricity sockets in this part of the stadium dictates I should immediately go elsewhere. After some humming and harring, we compromise and I'm to spend the night sandwiched between the programme booth and the hot dog stand. The man in charge of it soon starts to 'cook' the bright orangey brown sausages (yummy) in steaming but far from boiling water. Wafts of acrid but ostensibly appetising fumes belch from underneath the lid and Molly Barber sympathises with the whereabouts of my pitch, "your book will smell of *eau de hot dog*!"

The renewed signs of life at Oxford Speedway - sparked by their reincarnation in 2007 as a Conference League team - is further confirmed when Rob Peasley phones Nick to sort out arrangements for the supply of air horns and other merchandise for the re-introduction of a trackshop at the stadium. They talk for ages and afterwards Nicks says, "there's some dispute over the use of "the Cheetah" - change the farking thing I say rather than bicker, 'that's my Cheetah, no that's my Cheetah!' doesn't sound sensible to me." Ipswich team manager Mike Smillie swings by the trackshop on his way to the pits to pick up his complimentary copy of the *Speedway Star* and also chats with Johnny.

[JB] "Alright?"

[MS] "Up and down."

[JB] "Have we signed any new riders yet?"

[MS] "What do you think? We're talking John Louis here! Anyway, it must be really exciting for Swindon fans to see their team score 60 every week."

[JB] "To be fair, we scored 65 against Belle Vue!"

[MS] "They were weaker when Simon Stead got injured and they had Ryan Fisher - nothing against Ryan - but they're stronger now."

[JB] "They did have a GP rider in their side - Kai Laukkanen! We gonna win tonight?"

[MB] "I hope so."

[JB] "I see you get a slagging on the forums for giving Joel Parsons his fourth ride in Heat 14 at Eastbourne, when we only needed a couple of points."

[MB] "Yeh, he'd just got a paid win in heat 9 so he deserved a kick in the balls. Anyway, Cameron [Woodward] won on the line when all we needed was a second point from the last two races. Most fans would want to see that every week not 60 point wins!"

[JB] "When you go on the forums you realise why most fans don't become promoters."

[MS] "I've banned myself from looking 'cause I get so wound up!"

[Nick] "Half of them don't even go to the meeting but still have an opinion!"

The relocated position of my stall is such that I get to watch the majority of fans as they amble by. Peterborough team manager, Trevor Swales stops for a brief word, "It's nice to see some sunshine 'cause everywhere I go it's pissing down! If you're gonna come to ours - versus Coventry would be best. It's provisionally on Bank Holiday at 2 p.m. but we're waiting on knowing what the Polish play-offs are - which riders are where - and seeing if we can get them back. Should know tomorrow. If it's not then, I don't farking know when it'll be!" The friendly and quick-witted Witches presenter, Kevin Long, drops by to banter at the trackshop, programme booth and my stall but isn't tempted to eat one of the sausages this early on a work night. Given how hot it still is, despite being old-school theatrical in his approach to his duties, Kevin eschews his usual jacket but still dresses dapperly enough to wear a tie with his orange shirt. His head is newly shaven and as smooth as his conversation. He briefly updates me on news from Mildenhall, "We've all been taking the mickey out of Shaun Tacey's new dating website. You should see some of the girls on there! He did tell me, 'It's for everyone except your sort!' We had some Scotsmen dressed as Blair, Bush and Saddam and I thought I must interview the half-pissed Saddam. He offered me a drink from his whiskey bottle - 'take a swallow' - and I jus couldn't resist saying, I've just been offered a swallow by Saddam Hussein!" Nearby, John Louis also mingles leisurely with the Ipswich fans in the crowd and appears to really enjoy the opportunity to talk speedway at length with many followers of the club.

Colin Barber has just arrived and, since his sons now run the trackshop at Reading, he tells me all about his impressions following his first trip to Smallmead in many years. Though this is the latest outpost to be added to the Barber speedway merchandising empire, Colin actually really associates the trackshop at Reading with Alf Weedon. He tells Johnny, "Alf is in a bad way!" Johnny nods concernedly but perhaps slightly prematurely says, "Sad we'll not see him again!" Colin continues, "Alf said Malcolm Holloway hasn't got a pot to piss in but what he's doing at Smallmead is excellent. Or will be when the track staff figure

Yummy hot dogs

Track shop

John Louis chats to fans

out how to prepare a track properly - the bowser piddles out water as quick as I pee. That said, it always impresses me when a promoter rolls up their sleeves and helps with the track, like Malcolm does! Plus, he wanders round and chats to anyone and everyone. Their crowd was 15 to 16 hundred - there's more there than here [at Foxhall] - I was really impressed and it's definitely on the up!"

This meeting was originally scheduled for a Bank Holiday Monday on May 7th but was called off because of heavy rain. The programme we all use for this rearranged meeting is the original one plus an insert though, unusually, both team have exactly the same line ups in exactly the same race jackets except for the Witches guest Craig Boyce being replaced by Jesper B Jensen. Sadly, one rider that hasn't made it along to the pits is Lukas Dryml for whom the Panthers have provided a seven-day doctor's certificate because of the recurrence of a shoulder problem.[1]

The vexed question of the outstanding transfer request of Ipswich asset Danny King (on loan in 2007 at Peterborough) also contributes to the ongoing poor relationship between the team management staff, "Maybe if Ipswich didn't wait until March to start team building they wouldn't be in the position of having to have some digs at a team that beats them home and away."] When the riders are introduced Kevin Long playfully asks, "Who is cheering for Danny King tonight?" Michael, my favourite young fan from Mildenhall is here and rushes up to my table to tell me, "Look! You're in the *Speedway Star*!" but declines my offer of an autograph. Over the loudspeaker system, Kevin Long kindly tries to drum up some interest in my book stall: "Don't worry that it has got Scary Sheila on the front and please don't let that put you off this unique photo book - a word of warning, read the first two pages at the start of the book to set the scene." Despite the fact that the smell has been intense, sunshine and hot dogs appear to mix as well as sunshine and speedway books tonight. My impression is that hot dog sales have barely outstripped book sales, "it's been crap - dunno why they made me stand outside rather than indoors? At the stock car weekend I took £2500 but here it's been farking awful!"

The evening starts promisingly for the Witches when ex-Ipswich rider Hans Andersen falls on the first bend of the first lap of heat 1 (this is later attributed to a damp patch of track) to loud ironic cheers from the home fans. He eventually trails in last, nearly half a lap behind. The heat is still drawn since another ex-Ipswich rider, Danny King won on a rider replacement ride for Lukas Dryml. Indeed, the facility granted for Dryml gains 9 points in four rides for the Panthers on the night, something that the local fans inform me is many more points than Lukas ("he's dismal Dryml round here usually") traditionally scores when he bothers to struggle round the Foxhall circuit. After another drawn heat,

[1] After the meeting Mike Smillie would write to the Speedway Control Bureau Administrator Graham Reeve "putting on record his disgust" (as the *Speedway Star* termed it) that, despite this ostensible injury, Dryml rode the next day in Poland and for the Panthers at Swindon the day after. Smillie noted, "We have kept on eye on the situation and have noticed that Lukas rode again on Monday … Lukas can explain riding on Monday - within the seven day medical notice - by saying that he was riding against doctor's orders. This is something that does the image of speedway no good and I think the public are likely to jump to their own conclusions." The Panthers team manager Trevor Swales saw the situation somewhat differently, "It seems to me to be a blatant attempt to deflect the attention away from a home defeat. Rather than coming out and speaking honestly about a poor performance, they have instead chosen to accuse my team of foul play which is not something I appreciate … Ipswich are nothing more than a bunch of whingers and if they want an argument, bring it on!"]

the initial running of the third race looks likely to result in a 5-1 for the visitors until ZI-BEE SUE-CHECK-HEE intervenes. Bossed out of the way on the first bend by Iversen he pootles around trailed off at the rear until he spectacularly smashes into the third bend air fence on his second lap. You would suspect that this was a 'professional fall' if it had involved some other cannier riders but, in the case of Zibi, you can only conclude that it has happened because of a lack of control. Rather than award the race, referee Phil Griffin decides on a re-run with only three riders after the exclusion of Zibi as the primary cause of the stoppage. Su-check-hee eventually staggers to his feet, something that delights Kevin so much that he gets his senses confused, "Zibi's up on his feet - which is good to hear!" The re-run doesn't last long since Piotr Swiderski unluckily misses the second bend air fence and instead massively wrecks the wooden fence that follows it. The fence is totally shattered and Piotr eventually, somewhat groggily, staggers back to the pits (apparently oblivious to his exclusion). Here at Foxhall as a spectator and stood in the crowd with a knot of other Panthers fans overlooking the first bend, Peterboroughs Dick Swales isn't happy with what he's just witnessed, "This farking track should be farking shut down and it's all prepared for that farking twat there! I don't like Chris Louis, I must admit. That farking bend two is farking something else. It suddenly just lifted on him [Swiderski] without warning. They all know what to do - so, you have to ask yourself, what is happening? Loram and Henning - both experienced, both bend two - there must be something! Sully would always be first out to the start, no practice laps." With the re-re-run reduced to a match race, Chris 'FT' Louis misses the gate but executes one of his trademark cut backs to head Iversen out of the second bend before he powers away to victory and gives the overall score an unbalanced look at 9-8.

Ipswich retained their lead for the next couple of races. Not that they were helped in this by Robert Miskowiak's flamboyant starting technique - basically he rears massively at the start line before he recovers his composure sufficiently to gain third place in a race won by Tobi Kroner. Hans Andersen wins the next race but doesn't get support from Danny King who runs a surprising last. Zibi gets paid for 2 points when he finishes behind FT Louis, no doubt driven onwards by the hugely enthusiastic lady near to me who bellows, "Go on, Zibi!" throughout the race. I watch quite a few heats with Nick, Johnny and Colin Barber since they stick to a tried and tested rhythm that sees them (with the exception of their father who can wander around more casually as he pleases) dash from the trackshop just before the tapes fly and then dash back again as the race ends. This way they maximise sales in the trackshop - guarded throughout by Molly and Bev - and their enjoyment of the speedway. I ask Johnny - who has always been an enthusiastic and encouraging man about my speedway writing - for his advice on what my future books should cover. "Interviews with the promoters is no good. They'll just tell you the rubbish they say in the *Star* every week - money's no problem, the racing is excellent, the crowds are wonderful and there's no problems anywhere. That sort of thing just isn't gonna get people excited. I like reading what everyone else says - that's much more interesting and honest!" The result of the sixth heat causes Johnny some consternation. The bare bones of the thing features another good ride from Danny King who picks his way from the back of the field past Jesper B Jensen on the outside on the third lap before almost immediately passing Kim Jansson on the inside line as they exit bend two for the last time. This ensures a 5-1 for the visitors. "Anyone would think JBJ is lowering his average to around 5 to go to Peterborough next season. Ask yourself, would you sign him on a 9-point average or 5 and a half? I like Danny King - don't get me wrong - but overtaking JBJ like that - come on!"

Before Heat 7, with the scores poised at 17-18, Kevin Long is keen to talk up the drama of this notionally evenly matched contest, "Can the Panthers retain that slender lead?" The answer is no - if judged by the fall and retirement for Iversen that gifts the Witches pair of Miskowiak and Rempala a heat advantage. The home side then cling onto this lead until another Bjerre/King maximum over FT Louis/Suchecki gives the Panthers a wafer-thin advantage they never quite surrender. Heat 10 sees JBJ forget his alleged average manipulation to win the race (or deflect further suspicion about this by the win). The next race sees the Bjerre/Andersen duo power imperiously away from the tapes to lead - the win is so easy and straightforward, Hans forgets himself and is nearly caught by a determined Robert Miskowiak. With 8 points from three rides, the impressive Kroner runs a last in the race because of his burnt-out clutch. Normal service resumes from him in the next heat which he wins, albeit under close supervision and guidance, from Foxhall expert Chris FT Louis who gives an exemplary display of team riding throughout to ensure that (despite constant pressure) Iversen is unable to find any route past them. Tantalising their fans and flirting with the possibility of a home win, Ipswich then draw heat 13. There is drama off the track when my table collapses, while on the track Tobi Kroner falls heavily but is surprisingly allowed back in the re-run by referee Phil Griffin. Dick Swales isn't impressed ("farking hell") with the 'all four back' decision but, in the re-run, justice of sorts is dished out when Kroner is ridden hard towards the fence before he falls (on borrowed equipment from FT Louis). With the scores poised at 40-43, Ipswich could win the meeting with a 5-1. Although FT Louis does win, the Panthers top notch pairing of Andersen and Bjerre are content to ensure victory by relegating Robert Miskowiak to the rear. The large crowd slowly funnels away, though one person stops by my table to bizarrely berate me about the collection being held for Mark Loram, "Why have a collection for Mark Loram - he's a farking millionaire so another £500 isn't going to make no difference to him!" The FT departs without listening to my sharp reply. Showing his liking for a track he left in controversial fashion, Danny King stars for the visitors with paid 14 points, Chris FT Louis (narrowly) heads the Witches race card with paid 12 though mechanical problems and falls hold Tobi Kroner's score to a still creditable 11. While Robert Miskowiak arguably further turns his own metaphorical corner with some notable scalps in his haul of 7 points from four rides (though this becomes five rides, after he blots his copybook with a last place in the nominated race). In the final analysis, the 9 points gained through the operation of rider replacement for Lukas Dryml (on a track he has struggled with in the past) proves a decisive difference between the two teams.

4th August Ipswich v Peterborough (Elite League A) 43-46

Chapter 32. Sittingbourne v Oxford:
When 8 become 7

5th August

SKYBALLS ON PAPER

Jonathan *"A night like tonight when you've got two very strong teams on paper"*

It's always a pleasure to find yourself driving down Raspberry Hill Lane because you know that you're only a short distance away from another meeting at one of the country's true grassroots speedway locations - The Old Gun Site - home of the Sittingbourne 'Spray-Tex' Crusaders. The final hurdle to getting there is the obligatory slow drive (via a rutted track over the farmer's land) before you park up. In the baking heat of an August day, this track is dry enough to only leave the odd major pothole to really worry about though, just like policemen get younger, this route gets rougher and more rutted each time I drive it. Still, at least, the club continue to have permission to traverse the short stretch of private land required to access the stadium.

The meeting against the Oxford 'LCD Publishing' Cheetahs symbolises a clash of the two cultures that uneasily exist in the 2007 Conference League. If this were television, then the Crusaders occupy the *Blue Peter* corner since they have constructed their homemade team with love, dedication and sticky-back plastic. Whereas the Cheetahs - though equally filled with young riders who have also only progressed in their chosen sport due to application, perseverance and the support of loved ones - are much more *Dragons Den* since they are bankrolled by speedway enthusiast and self-made businessman Allen Trump. He is the man behind the campaign to reintroduce Exeter Speedway in Devon and is frequently spoken of as a millionaire businessman in the *Speedway Star*. Whatever the truth or otherwise of this claim, there's no doubt that he loves his speedway, the memorabilia of our sport and that the authorities in the form of BSPA think highly of him, since he was neither the highest nor the most-experienced bidder for the Oxford promotional rights when they suddenly became available earlier in the summer. Though his reign at Cowley is only in its early days, the club has hit the ground running, built a strong side and have so far won all (four) of their home Conference League fixtures (but have yet to triumph on their travels).

Even though I've arrived close to the noon start time, my favourite place on the grass by the disabled access ramp that leads up to the Sittingbourne clubhouse-cum-tearoom is still free. It provides an excellent view of the track (the same can be said of anywhere you stand to watch here) and the staggered start and finish line that they operate. I've had no time to go to the shops, consequently I'm still stuck with my table sagging badly in the middle. They say necessity is the mother of invention, so again I try to prop it up by placing boxes (of unsold books) underneath to support it. Pits marshal Dick Jarvis stops to admire my handiwork and asks, "Is that your BSPA table?" Another person to wander by is young rider Rhys Naylor, "I rode at Ipswich last night. I really enjoyed it - my best ever, I thought it was lovely! There was a bit of a soft spot on the outside of bend two but I didn't mind!" While grabbing some more stuff from my car, I bump into the friendly, witty and chain-smoking Bryn Williams who's moving at a snail-like speed towards the business area of the stadium. He's one of the many unique characters in speedway - described in the programme as "one of the real unsung heroes in bringing on and encouraging young talent" - but hasn't enjoyed the best of health in recent years and sports an impressive open cast on his foot that should enable his toes to get a tan today but, judged by how painfully he hobbles along, is a source of considerable discomfort. A student nurse (or someone with post-modern artistic leanings) has apparently done his dressing since it looks more like a burst sofa than a medical intervention. Not that he's a man to complain or slack off on his speedway work that sees him extensively involved at both the Isle of Wight and Oxford speedway clubs. Over by the entrance to the pits, referee Phil Griffin is looking somewhat harried. Like me, he was at Ipswich last night and has enjoyed roughly 14 or so hours since the end of the last meeting and the start of his next. Within that time he's had to catch some sleep, travel the highways and byways of the English road system and, in his case, complete one set

Hot day

Rider parade

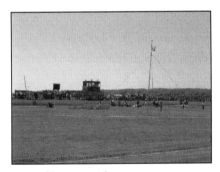

View of home straight

of mandatory SCB paperwork for the Ipswich meeting and prepare another set for Sittingbourne. When you're tired errors can creep in and, sensibly, Phil waves his programme and interrogates Bryn.

[PG] "It says you're the team manager today - is it as per programme?"

[BW] "I think so. I'm not wearing a tie today it's too hot!"

[PG] "That's a £50 fine and £50 for no jacket."

[BW] "I haven't been issued with one so it's hard to wear it!"

Recently, there's been an inordinately long time elapse between Conference League meetings at the Old Gun Site. There were none at all during July, though this was solely a result of a postponement due to a waterlogged track at the start of the month on the Sunday immediately after the Cardiff Grand prix meeting. In fact, this was the first rain off they had suffered at the track since 1994 - something of an enviable record that other promoters would be delighted to emulate. The programme states the home team "are desperate to break our duck of no wins in the league this year", though Sittingbourne did indeed triumph in a Conference Trophy meeting at the Old Gun Site in 2006, they haven't won a league meeting at home since 1996 when they beat Ryde. This would have been a hard feat to achieve in the years when they didn't enter the league and, thereby, found it really difficult to win anything. They do also have some previous since they drew their 2005 home encounter against Oxford (and even won away at Newport that season).

The riders line up by the flags on the centre green and are introduced to the small, perfectly formed but expectant crowd. It's the first-ever visit by Oxford to the track in their 'LCD Publishing' Cheetahs guise and the visitors include some august riders in their ranks with oodles of Conference and Premier League experience along with someone announced as "Les Smethills" (the rider formerly known as Lee). The dulcet tones of the announcer aren't those of serial British Speedway Forum poster and emoticon user Derek Barclay, so I can only assume the disembodied voice booming out over the loudspeaker system belongs to the John Strong named in the programme. From the vantagepoint of the referee's box, which also houses the broadcasting equipment, we're treated to a continuous blow-by-blow but breathless commentary on the sheer excitement and spectacle of the coin toss for gate positions. "Debbie has just divested herself of the coin; [long pause] come on, could someone tell us who won the toss and what gate positions they're taking?"

Viewed from an angle ahead of the starting gate, the meeting starts with a competition between Danny Warwick and Les Smethills to see who can touch the tapes the quickest. Phil Griffin adjudges Smethills the tape-touching contest winner to the delight of an over-enthusiastic middle-aged fan nearby my table who celebrates this decision as a wondrous triumph, "Go on son! That'll do us!" An indication of the calibre of the team Sittingbourne actually face this afternoon is provided when Danny Betson wins for the Cheetahs and Smethills finishes third in the re-run race, despite his additional 15-metre handicap. In the next race, George Piper appears to have misunderstood the exact nature of rules governing speedway since he appears to be on a one-man campaign to fall every time he reaches the first bend. To his chagrin, his second more painful-looking fall sees the race stopped (and awarded) since it appeared that he wouldn't be able to clear the track in time. The third heat is drawn but featured a fourth bend fall for Matt Bates, who then returned to the pits complaining of dizziness. The fourth is both a collector's item and typifies the rough and tumble, needs must, the-show-must-go-on attitude that is one of the enduring appeals of speedway racing at the Conference League level. The initial running of the race has Brendan Johnson knocked off on the first bend and a re-run called by the referee for first-bend bunching. Brendan takes some time to right himself, pick up his equipment and, escorted by his dad, wander slowly back to the pits. It would be safe to say that he appears not to be at all happy and, though normally a placid young man, it should be borne in mind that he does have martial arts expertise. Brendan fails to appear for the re-run and is replaced by George Piper who falls twice on the first lap - first on the third bend (where he remounts) before he then falls again on the fourth. The race is awarded but, with hindsight, it appears that referee Phil Griffin fails to log the first, albeit brief, appearance by Brendan on the track as the "frustrated ride" that under the regulations of the SCB rulebook it is.[1] Though equally commonsense or pragmatism would dictate that this could be seen as not having been a ride[2] (but more of this later). In the re-run James Theobald suffered an engine failure to reduce the contest to a match race won - after the referee awarded it - by Jordan Frampton ahead of Jerran Hart, thereby moving the cumulative score to 11-12.

The next race also features an engine failure, this time for Danny Betson. Upon his return to his stall, it's livelier in the pits area than it ever was on the track since he proceeds to throw his tools and equipment around with some abandon as well as blame his mechanics and Uncle Tom Cobbley for the gremlins that afflicted his machinery. Next up we witness a fall and a remount by George Piper as well as a spectacular fourth bend fall for Jordan Frampton during the course of which he narrowly fails to T-bone Danny Warwick, who escapes collection for an enforced crash by the merest fraction of a millimetre. Frampton then remounts to display a stunning turn of speed so great that he nearly caught up with Crusaders number 8, Jon Stevens, who despite having had a lead of almost a lap at one point nearly fritters it away. Jon potters round the circuit in a carefree manner that could possibly soon lead him to gain the soubriquet 'Stuttering' Stevens. Another faller is the luckless George Piper who retires from the race but then subsequently spends a considerable amount of time receiving attention from the paramedics while we collectively wait for the arrival of the County Ambulance. The announcer advises everyone to "Enjoy the sun - enjoy the facilities" and during the forty minutes pretty well everyone (except the paramedics and George Piper) does so without a hint of complaint. In fact, someone goes out of his way to tell me that the club at Sittingbourne "is run on love!", though I personally fail to get a hint of a snog all afternoon. Rumour has it that Piper has suffered an ankle injury and, a short while after the arrival of the ambulance, we learn that the Cheetahs line up has been decimated, "Matt Bates [headache] and George Piper have been withdrawn from any further part in the meeting." I snatch a brief conversation with Adrian Kearney from Arena (sorry Lakeside) who's proud of how things are turning out there under the new regime and brooms of Stuart Douglas and Jon Cook. "We're fifth now and have proved a lot of people wrong - if we hadn't thrown away a lot of silly points we'd be in the play-offs by now!"

Speedway *über*-fan and Reading Racers aficionado, Arnie Gibbons, also stops by for a chat and to praise the flexible attitude taken by the BSPA towards his team in their hours of darkest need around about the time of the takeover by Mark Legg and Malcolm Holloway. In the trickiest hours for the Racers immediately following the takeover, it was possible that the potentially bitter aftermath of the disorganised inheritance passed on to his successors by the bungled Postlethwaite Bulldogs reign could have led the club to 'Do an Oxford'. The fact that they haven't gone the way of all flesh and survived is a credit to the hard work and cussedness of the new promotion, the rejuvenated enthusiasm of the Reading fans and the enlightened decision of the governing authorities of the sport to "grant them leeway to make the end of the season". This flexibility must also be with the

[1 The relevant rules are: 18.8 A Rider is subject to both a "minimum" of 3 rides and "maximum" of 7 rides in a Meeting. For the purpose of achieving the "minimum ride rule, "frustrated" rides shall not count, whereas **in calculating the "maximum" number of rides taken "frustrated" rides shall count**. 18.8.2 A "frustrated" ride is one, whether programmed or not (i.e. nominated as a Rider Replacement, Reserve Replacement, TR or TS), which results in an exclusion for a Starting Offence **or for any reason whatever is unable to take part in a re-run AND is replaced by another Rider**. If no replacement is made it is a "compulsory" ride. Afterwards, Crusaders Pits Marshal Dick Jarvis says they were fully aware of the infringement but remained phlegmatic about it. "We asked and there was lots of debate in the pits. Technically it was a fall and a non-start but was treated like he'd been replaced by the other reserve." I pointed out to Dick that the club would have had good grounds for a subsequent post-meeting appeal if they'd lost, "we'd already thought of that but didn't 'cause we won fair and square anyway!"]

[2 Rob Peasley also commented afterwards: "Incidentally, during the gap in proceedings for the Sittingbourne v Oxford match during Heats 6 and 7 while the wounded were being tended to, the referee was asked regarding Brendan's ride in Heat 4 and he said we could still give him another 6 rides. So we did! … I was helping out Bryn that day, and I was keeping a close eye on Brendan during his 'four on the trot', as his wrist was still a bit painful following his fall. Had he needed a rest, he would have got in Heat 9 (a race where he didn't score). So it was actually immaterial that he was given an 'eighth' ride."]

Danny Betson leads Danny Warwick in Heat 1

The busy Brendan Johnson drops his bike

Victory parade

tacit agreement of the other Elite Leagues clubs and is a sensible business decision, particularly since to lose one club is to carelessly damage the reputation of the league but to lose another would be disastrous and damage it irreparably. "We've now had two months without Hancock - he's clearly not withholding his services as he only ever had a short-term contract, so we should be required to name another rider to replace him. But, instead, we're still allowed to use guests. Zagar often doesn't bother to turn up but we continue to get rider replacement when we shouldn't. I disagree that the BSPA are allowing us to 'cheat' - it's too strong a word to use - they're being very generous, it's sensible for everyone!"

After we've all topped up our tan, the seventh race has Brendan Johnson ride for the third or second time depending on whether you are the referee or not. Despite the heat and the stress on his equipment, Brendan rides successively from heats 7 to 10. On the third corner of the first in this sequence, he executes an effortless 360-degree turn before he falls. Giving people the chance to tidy his area of the pits back up while he's on the track, Danny Betson more or less pressures race leader Danny Warwick throughout. The noise of the bike close behind him must have upset Warwick's equilibrium since, without any obvious real reason, he brays the fence at the apex of bends one and two at the start of his second lap to gift Betson the win. The announcer tells us what we can see with our own eyes, namely there's another short delay for what he calls, "brief safety fence maintenance". Referee Chris Durno and his MUFC-supporting son Thomas have journeyed down from the Midlands to watch the meeting but now have to leave before it has ended to go onto Mildenhall for their 2 p.m. start time. "It's taken two hours for nine heats - they should have run more than that!" One of the terms and conditions of speedway being allowed to be raced at the Old Gun Site is the dust-prevention measures that require the track to be watered every four heats. Chris believes that they could integrate this into the warp and the woof of the meeting more effectively. "They don't help themselves by watering after they've taken off the injured rider - they should do it then. It's doubly bad as the riders then slip off when it's wet and cause yet more delays!" You notice the delays more on a day of blistering sunshine, particularly when the meeting is run at a leisurely pace by Phil Griffin and where - because of noise restrictions - the usual distractions of rider interviews and music over the tannoy are notable by their absence.

Mostly in place of his absent colleagues, Brendan's four races have only garnered him a single point but have provided invaluable experience and showcased his determined race attitude. Always combative on the track today, from the tapes Danny Betson wins heat 11 but spends the last two laps pointedly looking at the main grandstand and referee's box as though he's just about to win the Grand Prix series or something similarly prestigious. With Les Smethills second and Aaron Baseby snatching third place on the line from his team mate James Theobald, Oxford find themselves back with the slenderest of leads at 32-33. Having thoroughly acclimatised to the track, Brendan gets a paid win in the next when he partners New Zealander Andrew Bargh for the

Cheetahs to a second successive 5-1 to extend their lead. Given the Sittingbourne traditional preference to blood young riders rather than operate a win-at-all-costs attitude to their speedway, a 5- point gap with three races to go would usually signal that the metaphorical end to their victory ambitions was nigh. There's drama before the start of the next race when James Theobald is excluded under the two-minute rule, though we learn, "he has to have three rides so he'll start off 15 metres - I hear he's changing a plug in the pits, oh, he's coming out on a replacement bike!" James is mounted on said bike and, under blazing sunshine, two mechanics slowly push the machine in true Keystone Cops fashion without success before he's again excluded under the two-minute time allowance. Creditably the only Crusaders rider on show in the race, Danny Warwick, wins but the drawn heat still leaves them five points adrift at 36-41 with two heats to go.

The penultimate heat sees Brendan take his eighth ride (or seven in new money) of the afternoon as the sole representative for the Cheetahs since he can't simultaneously take his own scheduled ride and also replace the absent Matt Bates. A good start from the sole Oxford representative is essential if he's to prevent a possible last-gasp Crusaders revival but, sadly, he's excluded for touching the tapes (subsequently put down to a "slippery clutch"). In the re-run he soon makes up the additional distance of his 15-metre handicap but finds his route to second place repeatedly blocked by the experienced Dean Felton who continually slows and parries him on the corners. This appears to prevent a full slide from Johnson and, since he sticks rigidly to the inside racing line, the youngster finds himself locked down and unable to pass while upfront Aaron Baseby wins. The woman near to me says, "He's gonna be so pleased" and, indeed, he really is! This Sittingbourne heat maximum takes the score to 41-42 and takes the meeting to a last-heat decider. A drawn heat would suffice for Oxford but things immediately take a turn (or lack of one in this case) for the worse when on the outside of Warwick, Bargh lifts, loses control and then crashes heavily into the wooden fence on the second bend. The St John Ambulance staff on the centre green appear to have been affected by the heat since they wander over to the stricken rider in the manner of curious ruminants. While the excluded Andrew Bargh is treated on the track for his suspected broken ankle, Brendan Johnson and Rhys Naylor prepare his start gate with an enthusiasm that could lead you to think that they were in search of buried treasure. Their gardening in the sunshine fails to pay the full dividends you'd expect from such hard work since Danny Warwick wins and, with Jerran Hart third, their 4-2 ensures the narrowest 45-44 victory for Sittingbourne before the meeting officially closes at 3.20 p.m. After a decade without such a triumph, you'd expect exultant celebrations but instead - typical of the community basis of a club that prefers to welcome all abilities and to compete to improve rather than to win - the delight is understated, modest and tempered by an acknowledgement of good fortune. It's a pleasure to have witnessed history being made! While seeing it celebrated in typical fashion for Sittingbourne Speedway (in almost exactly the same good-natured way that they also take defeat here) with an insouciant and matter-of-fact shrug.

5th August Sittingbourne v Oxford (Conference League) 45-44

Chapter 33. Birmingham v Redcar: Firm management on display at Perry Barr

8th August

I'm excited by the prospect of finally getting to visit Perry Barr Stadium, the home of the Birmingham Brummies and the newest club in British Speedway under the ownership of 'Kidderminster based businessman Tony Mole' (copyright Nigel Pearson) and the management of Graham and Denise Drury. Without speedway in the city since its closure in 1986, the re-opening of the club has really caught the imagination of the fans in England's second city and, by all accounts, the quality of the Premier League racing on offer has enticed a loyal following to pack the bars, terraces and grandstands practically every week. Birmingham Speedway has a rich history since the club was founded in 1928 and, uniquely, in its history has had different stadiums all located in the same road! The club hasn't always run continuously and has been beset by interruptions and events such as World War II and less dramatically but much more effectively intrusive events like stadium closures. Or the unfortunate death of Alan Hunt in South Africa in 1957 which directly resulted in the Brummies closure and not racing again until the early 1970s.

The stadium is accessible by public transport since Perry Barr railway station is only a short walk away and the area is regularly served by a number of bus routes. Given its central geographical position in the country and its rich industrial heritage, Birmingham was a city that threw itself into post-war town planning with gusto. It fully embraced the benefits of the modernising obsession with road building and has reaped the rewards as well as become a confusingly sprawling conurbation for casual visitors. The stadium owners clearly expect that the majority of visitors will arrive by car since they have a wide choice of adjacent car parks, namely of the Stadium, VIP and, most recently (with the inexorable rise of car ownership and superstore shopping countrywide) the One Stop variety. The tide of selfish behaviour that afflicts contemporary life seems to be particularly prevalent among car drivers, if judged by the "polite request" printed in the programme for drivers who shun the enviable variety of car parks on hand here. "We have been made aware that there have been complaints made to the Council from local residents about speedway fans parking their cars inconsiderately in residential areas. As fans, we campaigned long and hard to get the Council to grant planning permission so the one thing we DON'T need is the Council getting upset with the Speedway. Please avoid parking in roads close to the stadium. There is free parking available at the One Stop Shopping Centre, and it would be appreciated by all concerned if this could be used by fans."

The drive from the dreaded M6 motorway takes you three miles along a section of the A34 that feels like a throwback to a less pressured, much more straightforwardly human scale era of urban planning and road construction. Though you ostensibly travel towards the city centre, the tree-lined road is wide. It has a section where the central reservation is made of grass not concrete and is mostly lined by a comfortable mix of residential housing (with gardens) as well as intermittent low slung parades of shops intermingled with some 1950s-looking light industrial factories with whitewashed walls. All of these were built at a time when the optimism surrounding the impact of the "white heat of technology" promised an efficient and trouble-free future for everyone. After I pass a few factories that advertise they're making 'fastenings' and the like, I arrive at some traffic lights adjacent to the stadium itself. In front of me are some buildings (probably the Halls of Residence) for an outlying part of the University of Central England or Birmingham Polytechnic in old money. The rise of the new university and the inexorable spread of the polytechnic started in the 1950s and really ramped up throughout the 1960s and 1970s and was a rising cultural phenomena at one time on a par with speedway. Its popularity and importance has continued to increase in the successive decades since then, whereas the locations that run and the numbers that follow our sport has gone into decline. The Perry Barr stadium looks much more contemporary than the university buildings that are built in a style of construction that reveals it's an architectural child of its time.

The halls of residence appear boxy and functional rather than elegant while, in contrast to this somewhat soulless look, Perry Barr stadium is a two-storey triumph of glass and red brick that enables the punters to overlook (in some comfort) the primary piece of real estate that they primarily turn up to see - the dog track. This thereby provides the Birmingham speedway fans with enviable surroundings and, since first impressions count for a lot, mine is that this must be one of the top locations in Britain that now stages speedway based on the quality of its stadium facilities. It is owned by the GRA and, under Tony Mole and Graham Drury, the Birmingham Brummies presently enjoy a warmly supportive relationship with their landlords that contrasts to that experienced at some other GRA-owned stadia. This harmoniousness gives the lie to claims that the GRA organisation has a 'hatred' of our sport or a strategic plan to deliberately rid themselves of involvement with shale. Like the clubs at Newcastle and Wolverhampton that are tenants in (Ladbrokes owned) greyhound stadiums with similar aspects, the majority of fans will watch the race action either from inside the grandstand building itself or from one main section of terrace that runs along most of the length of the home straight and thereby overlooks the start/finish line. At Perry Barr stadium, fans can also watch from the first bend and have a choice of two roofed structures that are across from the pits area near to the opposite bend.

I'd really looked forward to my first visit to see the Brummies but had to postpone my original trip earlier in the season. I arrive early at the locked and deserted stadium gates and fortuitously find experienced promoter Graham Drury has also just turned up. His greeting reminds me I'd forgotten to reconfirm the date we'd arranged for my book display at the club, "You didn't email to say that you were coming?" Though he has many things to do in the five hours before the tapes rise on the encounter with the Redcar Bears, he's happy to chat about progress so far for the club. "It's going excellently! I always say in the first season it's best not to do too well! I said we could do with a good cup run - which we've had - and we were aiming for the top half of the league. If we win tonight, we're third but I'm not counting any chickens, so we'll just see how the rest of the season unfolds. I'll probably get a bit of stick tonight over the sacking of [Ulrich] Ostergaard but the days of me being dictated to by riders is over! If he wants to go to Denmark to sit in the pits [as a non-riding reserve], then he can as far as I'm concerned - good luck to him! We've got Henning [Bager] now and I've got a speedway club to promote - one that has exceeded expectations with how well it has gone!"

While I wait on the flat terracing in front of the grandstand for Nick Barber to arrive and unlock the doors, I take the chance to study the track. As you'd expect at a speedway club run by Graham and Denise Drury everything is already prepared many hours before the scheduled start time. The red shale glistens having clearly been recently watered, the selection of flags required at any speedway meeting are ready and wait for the start marshal by the start line, while the inside white line looks bright and recently painted. The tarpaulin that covers the greyhound track to protect it from flying shale is battened down and secured into position. Away in the distance on the third and fourth bends an impressive display of four tractors have been parked up in orderly fashion with military precision.

Though I can't say that I'd really been that aware of it before I arrived at the stadium, the talk is indeed mainly about the Ostergaard sacking directly after the Birmingham away win at Mildenhall, where Ulrich had played the starring role. Typically on the British Speedway Forum, Graham Drury gets short shrift for the manner and timing of his decision, plus we also learn from other outraged posters (who apparently know the rider) that Ulrich was upset in the pits at the shock of the news. The timing of the decision to dispense with his services with immediate effect might have been unexpected but there were already some warning signs in the past that some issues were building up between Ulrich and Graham Drury, so perhaps he shouldn't have been quite so shocked. Nick Barber explains to me, "Ostergaard seems to pick and choose his meetings. He missed a Sunday meeting at Newport in the KO Cup and he also missed the home leg - which Birmingham lost to ruin any chance they had - of the Premier Trophy final against King's Lynn. That was after he'd rode for the club on the Wednesday (at Birmingham), the Thursday (at Redcar) and the Friday (at Edinburgh) but then flew home to Denmark from Peterborough before he was 'ill' on the Sunday with a bad back. He had no intention of coming back from there - he's just moved into a new house and has a young baby - but

Modern facilities

Bill Gimbeth and Bev Barber in anorak heaven

Good crowd

did return for the Wednesday. The last straw was he wanted to miss the Sunday meeting at Mildenhall last weekend 'cause he was originally second reserve - though that soon became first reserve - for the Nordic Final [UEM European Championship semi-final] that Henrik Moller has already qualified for. So, rider replacement wouldn't be available for two Birmingham riders, if Ulrich missed it too! Graham Drury rang Jan Staechmann to find out the situation and he said he was unlikely to ride in the Nordic Final so he'd have been there for nothing really. Graham pleaded with him at the Isle of Wight to ride at Mildenhall (he did finally). So it's complicated but he's brought it on himself! Though, that said, he's at Workington now so he was only out of work a day. Long term, Graham has done British Speedway a service by standing up to riders who just want to pick and choose their meetings to suit themselves! If only more promoters would do so we wouldn't be in the mess we are again this season with riders missing meetings whenever they choose."[1]

When the fans arrive the departure of Ostergaard remains a hotter topic of conversation than the pending meeting against Redcar, particularly since the likelihood is that this will be a home victory to go with the away triumph (42-53) already enjoyed by the Brummies on Teeside 13 days previously. One fan tells me that he's going to start a petition and another that he will write a letter of complaint. A member of the ground staff looks at things from a practical point of view, "They only just took a team photo last week and now they'll need another!" The still-reigning Miss Fina Invader (from the now-defunct Long Eaton speedway) - aka the bubbly Wendy Jedrzejakski - is also outraged on Ulrich's behalf, "He won the meeting for them and then gets sacked! Alright he wasn't gonna ride but he did - when he told me he had a tear in his eye. Funny how 24 hours later he's at the other track [Workington] that Tony Mole owns. It's Birmingham's loss as far as I'm concerned."

Securing the trackshop concession at Birmingham has been a shrewd move for Nick Barber's speedway merchandise empire as the space given over within the grandstand bar is considerable enough to run two separate stalls in these pleasantly plush surroundings. Arguably, it's the fanciest trackshop space in the country and tonight Nick runs one stall while by the doors that lead to the track side, the other is run by his friendly sister Bev who is joined tonight by the affable Bill Gimbet. Because so many fans pass through the bar and catering area on their way to watch the speedway (or return periodically throughout the night), everyone notices the stock on display. Enthusiasm for all things coloured

[1 A statement on the Birmingham speedway website prepared beforehand but released after the Mildenhall meeting (5th August) said: 'The decision has been taken as a result of Ostergaard's reluctance to commit himself to racing for the Brummies ... Promoter Graham Drury explained, "Before I agreed the fixture change with Mildenhall to go to West Row on Sunday, I spoke to all the riders who confirmed they were available. Three weeks ago Ulrich informed me that he was second reserve for the European Championship meeting - but I could not believe that he wanted to sit in the pits there rather than ride for his club, and I checked with (Danish manager) Jan Staechmann that he was not required to attend that event. He then reluctantly agreed to ride at Mildenhall, but then a week ago he informed me that he was now the first reserve and wanted to go back to Denmark. This was not acceptable to Birmingham Speedway, and I double-checked the situation with Jan again. We would have had a facility for him, but that's not the point. We give riders so many meetings in England, and I could not accept him being there just as reserve rather than riding for us. As late as Thursday night after the Isle of Wight meeting he was adamant that he was going to Denmark, and I gave him the ultimatum that if he did so, his services would be dispensed with. It took over half an hour to convince him to ride for us today, but on the ferry back I came to the decision that I would not allow Birmingham Speedway to be held to ransom, and therefore I would make a change. I would like to thank Ulrich for his contribution, he is a terrific rider who has always given 100 per cent, and I will help in any way I can to get him fixed up elsewhere. It's been a far from easy decision and I realise how popular Ulrich is, but I hope the fans will understand why I have made this move. We should not even have been discussing the possibility of him missing a Birmingham meeting to be a reserve elsewhere."]

in the red and yellow of the official club colours is incredibly strong, if judged by the sheer number of people who sport race jackets, scarves, track-suit tops, T-shirts, caps and other garments with the Brummies logo emblazoned on it. The terracing is awash with these two bright colours (sunglasses should be issued) and they are set off by the warm sunshine of the evening that bathes the terraces as it slowly sets during the course of the meeting. My display table of books allows me to just about watch the racing through the window. It attracts much attention but people stop to gossip rather than purchase books. I'm delighted to see the diligent but modest Tim Hamblin who used to so intelligently and articulately report on Wolverhampton speedway for the local Express & Star newspaper until the sports editor was seized by sufficient stupidity to fail to reappoint this gifted reporter. As Holden Caulfield notes in *Catcher in the Rye* "people are never too old to find new ways of being stupid". A couple of Stoke speedway supporters stop by to praise my book *Showered in Shale*, "We really enjoyed it but the only unrealistic bit was about Stoke our local track - Caroline Tattum must have been putting on a show for you to appear that nice!" I insist that throughout the book I spoke as I found and always related what I found on all my visits. Keen Freddie Lindgren fan Kayleigh Jones, whom Dave Rattenberry has taken under his paternal wing at Wolverhampton, informs me that unfounded malicious gossip has caused the Swede's mechanic marital difficulties.

Everything about the promotional set up at Perry Barr Stadium on speedway race night cries out the words 'professionalism' and 'experience' - whether we're talking about the riders, track staff, promotional team, owner, trackshop merchandiser or even the presenter, who is Peter York - the thinking man's Mike Bennett. Though this is the Premier League, they've also had the foresight to invest enough money into various aspects of the stadium infrastructure under their control to ensure they guard as best they can against mishaps. Consequently, they have a double set of tapes that ensure that, should there be a malfunction, the entertainment on offer won't be needlessly interrupted for some dull but routine maintenance work. However in the warm August sunshine with all the chatter and angst about Ostergaard, all eyes are on his replacement in the team (and ironically also his housemate in this country), Henning Bager, who marks his debut for the club with a shockingly poor start. This must have blindsided the Redcar pair of Gary Havelock and Byron Bekker who both succumb to Bager before the third bend of the first lap. The resulting 5-1 maximum heat advantage hammers another nail into the possibility of a wonder performance on the road for Redcar. Their cause on the night is further hampered by the absence of the injured Josh Auty their not-so-secret-weapon. He's a youngster who would be the most mercurial speedway 16-year-old in Britain but for the existence of Tai Woffinden. A drawn heat is then followed by a comfortable win for Jason Lyons who, I imagine, given he was fired a few years ago from his team in Sweden for smoking, must either be really suffering with the effects of the ban or have dispensation to have the odd crafty puff between races. Someone who looks on fire on his first outing is heat 4 winner Mathieu Tresarrieu - that rarest of speedway breeds, an exciting and skilful French rider - who confuses the Brummies programme editor enough to misspell his name throughout the racecard.

By heat 7, to a neutral like myself, the meeting looks over as a contest but the crowd enthusiastically greet each Brummie heat winner in an exuberant manner that suggests they'll lift the roof off the place if they win a trophy. The sight of Emiliano Sanchez excitingly threading his way through traffic to win is definitely worth the huge cheer that it gets. Manuel Hauzinger is in the wars at the start of the next race when he falls heavily on the apex of the first corner. He was helped in no small part by the attentions of Jack Hargreaves who manages to make it round to the second bend before then leaving his own mount. News that there is to be a re-run with 'all four back' doesn't please the home faithful who have quickly picked up on the speedway tribal art of booing unpopular refereeing decisions. Peter York comes over all Watergate when he interviews Graham Drury who, under difficult questioning ("is it all over for the Bears at 35-19?") is forced to admit, "it's never over til it's over!" Stuck as we are on the opposite side of the track from the pits, we're unable to see if the proverbial large lady is about to warm up her vocal chords. It's probably best she hasn't and sensible that Graham is instinctively cautious since, after another 5-1 has stretched the scoreline further, the Redcar Bears then cast off their collective torpor and embark on what looked like a small spirited fightback. This takes the form of a couple of drawn heats and a couple of heat wins that spark their impressive away support into life sufficiently for me to be able to finally notice a rather large contingent of them proudly wearing the Redcar red and black cunningly disguised among the (until then) voluble sea of red and yellow speedway branded items of clothing. The pick of these races was heat 11 when the confident and exhilarating Lee Smart held Havvy - on a tactical ride - at bay for three-and-three-quarter laps until a last

Sunny night

Brummie celebrations

Jacket required

desperate dash round the outside saw the ex-World Champion home. The effort of drifting wide to fail to block Havvy also allows Sanchez to sneak up the inside, though the disappointment of this further loss of position is tempered by the fact that he is a Brummie teammate. Weirdly, this race excites the Birmingham fan in front of me to scream into his mobile, "I think we are GOING TO BE THIRD! Is it top two who go up? Oh …"

The next race features a complete flier for James Grieves that Jason Lyons nearly nullifies on the line and, to further jubilation from the fans from the North-East, the next race has the Bears pair fly from the gate to win but still left the scores at 45-36. The last throw of the dice by Redcar team manager Brian 'father of Havvy' Havelock sees the flying Frenchman Tresarrieu sent out in a black-and-white helmet as a tactical substitute off 15 metres. To gain full effect, Chris Kerr will need to clamp down on Henrik Moller but fails to do so after he made the gate, though the double points window dresses the heat score 3-5. Despite the foregone conclusion of the meeting result and destination of the aggregate bonus point before the nominated final race, Peter York uses his many years of presentational experience to work the crowd up with a few well-chosen phrases. For good measure, he then twice mumbles the details of the Redcar riders inaudibly. Whoever they are, they ride anonymously and suffer a 5-1 reverse. The meeting ends and the buoyant fans flow happily from the stadium having seen the Brummies win home and away by exactly the same score of 53-42 with exactly the same team line up except for debutant Henning Bager who scored paid 10 (compared to paid 13 for Ostergaard on Teeside). Tim Hamblin then kindly stays with me to help with my own unofficial 'Keep Britain Tidy' campaign, when we search the stadium together for discarded leaflets advertising my books Then, furthermore, he helps me to my car with my stock and equipment.

8th August Birmingham v Redcar (Premier League) 53-42

Chapter 34. Redcar v Mildenhall: Family feud fever hits Teeside

9th August

The second season since the reintroduction of speedway on Teeside proves that you don't need the latest in luxurious facilities to attract and retain the interest of the fans, just a team that excites them on the track! This isn't to say that there haven't been some infrastructure developments since my last visit; the most notable of which is the addition of a sponsors' lounge-cum-portacabin with a wooden balcony overlooking the apex of the first bend. The grounds of the stadium still retain the rough-hewn charm of its genesis on a previously neglected area of industrial land near to the Tees River in Middlesbrough. Nearby to the speedway track is a mini Formula 2 motor racing circuit and the atmosphere of the surrounding catchment area is resolutely industrial as befits this hard-working town. Once the novelty aspect has died away at any newly opened (or constructed) track, there's always the business risk for any promoter that crowds may plummet to uneconomic levels. By all accounts, the Premier League version of the speedway club at Redcar is definitely profitable to run, though the Conference League side of the operation - the Cleveland Bays - like so many other clubs at that level, will probably be a net drain on financial resources. Just to illustrate that ultimately speedway is a business, Chris van Straaten - the experienced club co-promoter - surprisingly let it be known over the winter close season of 2006 that he would listen to sensible offers for his share in the business. While new promoters buying their way into existing clubs come and go - almost before they have dug their new broom from their cupboards and with their revolutionary 'marketing' ideas either untested or looking pitifully misguided - none of these ambitious individuals have ventured north beyond Coventry in recent years.

The fixture between Redcar and the Mildenhall Tigers has been given additional spice beyond its significance for the Premier League standings since it is also the 'Clash of Two Speedway Brothers' as *Sky* might style the meeting in their shouty adverts if this were, say, boxing. Tonight pits Redcar Director of Operations, Gareth Rogers against his brother Laurence, who is team manager at Mildenhall. Given how avuncular both men are normally, there will be no needle but there could be loss of pride and endless banter (even though most bookies would have this down as a home banker). That said the loose talk in the *Speedway Star* was of a "family feud" and there was also a reminder that Mildenhall narrowly triumphed in the clash at West Row in a "controversial meeting". No doubt all this is mentioned in the hope that all this talk of 'honour' and 'family pride' at stake might further fan the embers of interest locally and thereby swell attendance. There's some longevity to their rivalry which stretches back memorably to 1980 when they were then involved with two great name tracks (sadly now defunct) since Laurence managed Cradley Heath and Gareth announced for the Hackney Hawks.

Gareth Rogers and Dave Peet eat early

Packed home-sraight grandstand

Mildenhall have recently lost at home for the second time this season to effectively end their challenge for a play-off spot. Reviewing the performance of his team so far, Laurence identified that reserve rider Tomas Suchanek and Kyle Legault had both improved their averages, whereas the rest of the team had been plagued with inconsistency. Indeed, Kyle has apparently relished the challenge of pastures new so much since his move from Sheffield to the Fens that he finds himself one meeting away (in Vojens) from a surprise qualification for the 2008 Grand Prix series! A glance in the programme at the Redcar team illustrates the difficulty of the task facing them since Josh Auty returns from injury to occupy the often difficult number 2 team position and Jack Hargreaves returns to Redcar - indeed, the cover of the programme pictures him and has the caption "welcome back to Jack Hargreaves". In fact, he makes his 2007 home debut for the club at reserve following an extremely brief retirement from the sport that hasn't left his previous employers Stoke exactly happy with the situation.[1]

I've kindly been allowed the freedom of the Tees Motor Park so I can set up my bookstall wherever I feel it would attract the most attention. I decide to base myself equidistant between the imaginary triangle on bend 1 formed by the home-straight grandstand, the burger van and the toilet block. Pretty well everyone who comes into the stadium is likely to consider using one of these or will pass by as they wander down to the fourth bend where you can see into the pits area and visit the trackshop. The catering offered by the burger van must be acceptable since Bears Clerk of the Course, Dave Peet, and Director of Operations, Gareth Rogers, both avail themselves of the fare on offer before the gates open to allow other fans to join their queue. Gareth thinks I've chosen my pitch sensibly, "Very sensible you get both ends of the equation standing there - they're either attracted to the food or come to the loos!" The man in the burger van, Richard McGlade, is curious about what I'm doing stood with a pasting table of books near to his catering outlet. When he learns I'm the author he tells me, "I've written a book, well part of a book - *The Brick* - about the hooligans who used to follow Boro. I've written one story in the book ('Away at 'Ul') - it was my mate who done it really. Just fell to his death. He worked in scaffolding. Yeh, I used to travel home and away with Boro for about eight seasons - never missed a match. The things that used to go on you wouldn't believe. I've moved

[1 Dave Tattum commented, "Jack needs to sort himself out. We have been more than right with Jack and helped him as best we can. Taking time out wasn't ideal for us but we had to run with it, yet within two or three weeks, he wants to ride again and has now joined a rival club. Last season, Jack was saying that he didn't particularly get on with Brian Havelock and the travel to Redcar was affecting him. Maybe they have moved Redcar for him, I don't know. The other thing is that recently I received in my post a letter addressed to me and Jack. I opened it seeing as my name was on the envelope and inside was a cheque for Jack for £1000. There was no name from the sender, only a note saying, 'I hope this goes some way to making your engine a little faster'. We really don't know who sent it, but if it was someone from off the Stoke terraces who sent it in the expectation it would benefit Jack as a Stoke rider, that is dreadful for them. Our thanks go out to whoever it was - it's just a shame that Jack won't use it to score points for us." At the time Jack responded, "I need racing because I'm not working … I'm still having counselling and I know I need to sort myself out. But I need to race to earn and I'm very grateful to whoever it was who sent me a cheque for £1000. My debts are still not cleared but it is a big chunk taken care of." Looking back with the benefit of hindsight in the winter of 2007, Jack maturely commented, "I look around at other riders of my age group and I can see now that I need to change some things in my life otherwise I'm going to miss out on where I want to go in the sport…there were highs and lows last season, but the bottom line is that I came out of it well and I have now finished the treatment I was having for depression and feel much better and focussed in myself … I've got two jobs on the go - one in a shop and the other at an Esso 24-hour garage where I can have as many hours as I want almost. The plan is to sell my old equipment and invest in new stuff and then get myself fit and organised after Christmas. I'd like to think that I have learnt a few hard lessons. But it's also important to acknowledge that I am only 19 and hardly over the hill. Having said that, though, I do accept that I have messed about too much and I do regret some of the lost opportunities."]

on now. I do this all through the summer and then you're off in the winter. I do alright here but mostly I go to the races, and all over - Thirsk, Ripon, York."[2]

Over in a trackshop heated to almost sauna-like temperatures, Bill Gimbet and Dave Rattenberry are in the process of unpacking the stock from Dave's Renault and arranging said merchandise attractively. 'The Rat' is a man who also travels round the world to watch football, though he's what they call a 'ground hopper' not a hooligan! He's not quite his cheery self in the warmth of the shop and his usual get up and go appears to have got up and gone until he tactically perks up with the arrival of Chris van Straaten. Chris has come to pick up a copy of the latest edition of the *Speedway Star*. He thumbs through it while he chats and reveals a sharp wit (that I'd never been with him long enough to notice before) when confronted with a photo inside of Gareth and Laurence gurning together for the cameras to promote tonight's clash, "they say the *Star* isn't for sale to the under-18s this week!" Also in the Premier League news section is the (premature) delight of Berwick's promoter marvelling about the astonishing 16-point margin of his team's away victory at Newport, due in no small measure to the five-ride maximum from Lee Complin the guest he booked as a replacement for Jacek Rempala. Rat asks, "What about Complin then?" CVS is nonplussed at the situation, "Peter Waite was told when he decided to sign two Poles [Sebastian Truminski and Jacek Rempala] that he wouldn't get a facility when they went back. They both signed a piece of paper saying they would always be available on a Sunday but, as soon as it's just before the Polish play-offs, their [Polish] clubs ask and they go back! That said I don't understand why Peter Waite decided to book Complin as a guest away? At home I can understand it - you can say after you've won the score had to be adjusted - but away! I really don't understand it all." Rat has nodded in agreement throughout but interjects to advise me, "If only more promoters were like CVS. He knows everything there is to know about speedway!"

Later when I take the chance to hand Chris his copy of *Shifting Shale* in his office ("another one!") he politely tells me my photo book has "some quirky photos". I ask his permission to return to Monmore Green Stadium - the home of his other club, Wolverhampton - to try to sell *Shifting Shale* at the double-header Eastbourne/Poole Bank Holiday meeting. "I'd come to Coventry on September 3rd - they'll all have spent their money on the double header [because of the slightly increased admission charge that night] before they get to you!" Sadly other pre-arranged commitments dictate I can't take Chris up on this kind offer, so I miss out on another night savouring the unique atmosphere created by the Wolverhampton home-straight crowd that invariably makes it a popular speedway venue in this country.

Stood by my table I finally get to meet the author of the brilliant Mastermind quiz that used to grace the 2005 season Mildenhall programmes. They were my favourite feature in any club programme that season. I failed to catch the bloke's name so I only know him as the 'Mildenhall Quiz man', "I spent that Christmas ringing people saying I was in your book! I sent you an email but you couldn't be arsed to reply." Sadly, this email never arrived but my apologies didn't seem to be believed even when I stressed how I always reply to anyone (unless they're abusive) who takes the trouble to email.

[2 That night's issue of the *Evening Gazette* carried the story of the death of Paul Debrick. "A bodybuilder and former football hooligan who wrote a book about his violent exploits with the Boro has died aged 42. Middlesbrough man Paul Debrick, who earned the nickname 'The Brick', was found dead at his Teesville home on Monday this week. The 18-stone self-confessed hooligan had been a member of one of the UK's most feared mobs, the Middlesbrough Frontline." His brother Mark, 43, expected about 3,000 people to attend his funeral including "big names from the football scene" coming to say goodbye from all over the country. "Paul was a hooligan but then he was honest about that. We are gutted about what's happened. We don't know exactly what went on but we think he may have fallen at the top of the stairs and hit his neck. I always expected something to happen to him because of the way he was but I thought he would have been shot or stabbed … the thing about Paul was that he could also be a gentle giant at times and he had four boys. He would do anything for you. A lot of people knew that side of him. The fighting was all part of a lifestyle and it was something that happened back then." The reporter Will Sutton noted, "his book famously claimed he had been 'shot at, glassed, stabbed, arrested and jailed' during his 20 years as a hooligan." The book written by Paul (one of the Mr Universe contestants of 2004) - *The Brick* - is a candid, matter of fact account of his life that features accounts of the various fracas and fights he chose to get involved in. It's an era when following football necessarily involved some element of hooliganism inside the ground but, more often than not, outside the grounds. The organisation involved is staggering and this part of our shared cultural heritage is vividly drawn. In the introduction Paul writes, "Personally I couldn't give two ****'s about Middlesbrough Football Club, never have, never will. The truth is I used Middlesbrough as an excuse to vent my violence on anyone we played. Why? Because I love a bit of violence, and football was as good an excuse as any … I can honestly say in my twenty-odd years of travelling with the Boro 'Casual Firm', at any one given time I couldn't name the team. It took me two years to learn the offside rule, but who gives a ****?" In the concluding chapter of the book, thereby echoing how he lived his life, Paul remains defiant and true to himself (as well as speaking for many authors), "I'll probably get some good reports for writing this book but I will also get some **** as well. Either way I'm not arsed. It was how I saw things through my eyes. People might have seen things differently. No two people's minds are the same and opinions vary. All I can say is you're entitled to your own opinion, as I am mine. Anyone who thinks what I have written is *****, then all I can say is stop criticising it, get off your lazy lard-arse, spend month after month researching and writing, and write your own ****ing book."]

One lap to go

The warm night on the Costa del Tees attracts a large crowd keen to pack every available space in the stadium, thereby visually confirming that they're really mad for it in this particular part of the North-East. Just before the teams come out on parade, Bears announcer, Keith McGhie (who looks a dead ringer for my dentist) interrupts Gareth on the centre green in mid flow with a plaintive, "Can an electrician come to the announcer's box?" Panic request for an emergency visit by the club sparks now over, Gareth effortlessly resumes his patter finessing last night's defeat at Perry Barr for local consumption, "Havvy had to withdraw from the last heat at Birmingham with hay fever" he earnestly informs the credulous faithful. Keith butts in with some banter about the significance of the Redcar versus Mildenhall clash for the Rogers family, "Laurence tells me he's the better looking one of the two!"

Once the meeting starts, Josh Auty's return to action lasts just long enough for him to get excluded for a tapes offence and to be replaced by Hargreaves (who Keith welcomes but occasionally calls 'HarGRAVES'). The first two heats are drawn before Gareth rather presciently notes of the Tigers pairing of Legault and Fry - as though he's just caught sight of someone else's prize livestock - "another very solid pairing!" So it proves with a win for Fryer and a third for his partner to give Mildenhall a slight but early advantage, "a little bit of a pendulum swing to the Tigers there." The flying Frenchman Matthieu Tresarrieu looks totally unstoppable when he wins the next race, but when Suchanek overtakes Hargreaves with a pass round the outside on the first and second bend of lap three, the heat is drawn. A short while later, Gareth diligently pinpoints the problem for us, "They've just taken the cover off Jack Hargreaves's bike and there's oil everywhere and the feeder pipe's askew!"

Part of the fun for the first half of the meeting is to watch Laurence Rogers run back and forth from the pits to the centre green and vice versa. Each race he waits until the riders are pretty well under orders before he gambols down the slope that connects the two locations in the determined manner of someone no longer used to running on a regular basis. Then, as soon as all four riders have crossed the finish line, programme flapping like the baton in a relay race, he purposefully scampers back up the slope to breathlessly offer words of advice and encouragement to his troops or heartily slap his riders on the back. After a maximum for the home side in Heat 5, the next race has Mark Baseby appear to be about to lead a fightback for the visitors when he overtakes Havvy and Josh Auty on the second bend of the second lap. However, though leading, Baseby starts to wobble slightly out of shape towards the end of the penultimate lap, thereby enabling Havvy repay the favour of a second bend overtake and by the final corner Baseby is left battling his own machine as much as the opposition. Josh Auty completes the formality of his own overtake while Baseby struggles to retain his mount. The successive 5-1s for the home team punctures the mood of optimism among the few fans that have made the journey up from the Fens, while simultaneously rousing the quiet Bears fans into a greater noise level much more appropriate to their significant numbers. Once awakened, clearly schooled in the chants and mores of football much more than speedway, the home crowd collectively finds its vocal chords to yell praise, make ribald but anatomically impossible suggestions to the Tigers riders or generally appreciate the exploits of their own handlebar heroes.

Over the tannoy, Gareth updates us on the injured Greg Blair, "his mouth wound that caused such a loss of blood last week has improved," and then welcomes the lesser-spotted Bennett who has briefly deserted his Norfolk lair, "one other 'hello' to one of the top presenters in our sport on holiday in this part of the world - Mike Bennett!" Sadly, Mike walks past without any acknowledgement with his nose stuck in the air as though he's caught a sudden whiff of a bad smell. The solid pair of Legault/Fry flatters to deceive with an early lead before Dan Giffard bravely and rather thrillingly flies past them both on the back straight of the second lap with some confidence. If I were a betting man, I'd be surprised to find Tresarrieu stuck at the back of this particular field and, even though he tries hard, he's totally unable to find any route past his rivals. Gareth is jubilant, "I said earlier to Mike Bennett and Philip Lanning that we often have three abreast racing - that must be one of the races of the season!" When James Grieves and Chris Kerr combine for another 5-1 in heat 9, particularly given the strength and confidence of the Bears riders round their home circuit, the meeting looks over as a contest at 32-22. Not that this stops Havvy briefly taking on the role of tour guide for (the rider Keith McGhie knows as) "LegALT" who he runs close to the second bend fence on the first lap. Gareth Rogers coos approvingly, "the skipper emerging and stamping his authority on that heat."

Keen to corner the market on the exciting race action, Dan Giffard rides at high-speed millimetres from the safety fence to pass both Tom P Madsen and Shaun Tacey at the start of the second lap of the next race. Not content with the derring-do of his fence hugging, Dan adds a flamboyant twist every time he exits the fourth bend by flinging his right leg away from his bike. It's a weird sight (though one I've noticed for a few years now) and it's a unique part of the inimitable Giffardsson style. With a lack of opposition to best, Dan decides to thrillingly ride neck and neck with his teammate Tresarrieu to delight and excite the appreciative Bears crowd. Though it's now dark, Gareth is delighted enough to try out his latest 'lights' analogy when trying to describe Giffard's performance, "suddenly the switch is switched on, he's turned the corner - he's back - superb!" Mildenhall finally use one of their tactical options when they send out Kyle Legault for double points. He has a no-holds-barred and no-quarter-given close encounter of the speedway kind with James Grieves, whom he bravely (some would say foolhardily) squeezes past close to the fence on the fourth bend of the first lap. Another Tigers heat advantage follows in the next to bring the scores back to a more acceptable margin of 44-37. The Bears reply in the next - an extremely close race that afterwards has Gareth observe, "You could have almost thrown a blanket over all four riders!" In the final race of the night, Paul Fry wins an exclusion when he showcases one of the most spectacular dismounts of the season. He arrives third into the first corner so, using his years of hard won experience, rather cannily he tries to lean on the other riders but instead comes spectacularly unstuck with a 360 degree turn prior to spectacularly looping over the bike. This causes his machine to somersault and then hit him on the head before - as though suddenly possessed - it flashes off to get hooked up in the safety fence. In the re-run all looks lost for Mildenhall until Kyle Legault swoops round Chris Kerr on the third bend of the third lap and then, from the same place a lap later, sweeps inside Havvy to thereby go from third to victory in the space of a lap.

As a neutral, I've found the meeting absorbing with some thrilling highlights, while the track has held up so well that the meeting has remained dust free, despite the heat of the afternoon and evening. Newcastle promoter George English stops to enquire if I've seen "the Redcar announcer go past?" I haven't. "I stayed until the end to see if that announcer might mention the fact that Redcar are at ours on Sunday night. I listened out but what did you hear? [No mention] I've just been and had a word with CVS about it. The racing was like it always is here - three riders close together but little or no passing. It always looks good but people rarely get by! The banked bend looks the part but it serves no real purpose as you'd think it would from looking at it." A jubilant Bears fan was appreciative of the competitive spirit of the meeting, "there was a good feeling between the two sides - something that's not always the case here - the Mildenhall riders came out to applaud ours as they got on the truck for their victory lap. Matthieu Tresarrieu was poor at the start of the season, got injured but, since he bought an engine from Havvy, he's been flying!" A Monarchs fan stops by shortly afterwards to embark on a lengthy denunciation of the entertainment offered here. I wonder why he bothers to come if it's that bad as he angrily repeats himself for the third time, "That was an awful meeting. It was nothing special until Legault passed them in 15!"

The large crowd departs so quickly that I assume that they're on a collective promise somewhere else in town and I soon find myself isolated and packing away on my own. Meanwhile, suddenly, the air is filled with a strange but pungent rotten-egg smell that I can only associate with the brightly lit industrial estate in the middle distance - with it's impressive array of chimneys that I suddenly notice belch copious plumes of smoke. I say goodbye to a distracted Bill at the trackshop who attentively helps a blonde Polish lady visitor and, afterwards, stop by the speedway office to thank CVS. Invariably managerial, I find CVS sat behind his desk while he chats with Sheffield announcer Shaun Leigh stood in the doorway. CVS is amazed at the reaction of the Edinburgh fan, "Not sure what he was watching - Philip Lanning hadn't been before and he couldn't believe what he was seeing!" Shaun is equally appreciative of the quality of racing on display at Redcar and singles out Dan Giffard's rejuvenated performance for particular praise, "Last night he struggled to score nought!" CVS confirms the crucial part played by psychology in speedway, "When we went there [Weymouth] Lewis Bridger came and rode on his usual line round the outside and set a track record. In every other heat it was like a different track - everyone struggled. It was rough but it just shows that confidence is everything!"

9th August Redcar v Mildenhall (Premier League) 51-42

Chapter 35. Workington v Somerset: Talk of Mr Woo, birthdays, Speedway Regulations and Graham Drury

11th August

I dash to Workington speedway from the early kick off at the Stadium of Light where Sunderland have (unusually it subsequently turned out) won their first game back in the Premiership 1-0 against Spurs. The Comets are up against the Somerset Rebels and the drive to work at Derwent Park for any rider is a long but beautiful one. The first cars have already arrived in the car park by the time I set up my bookstall outside the entrance gates. I snatch a few brief words with one of my favourite promoters, Ian Thomas, "look at the farking sky - it's farking bad enough running on a Saturday against the GPs without that!" Prospects also don't look great with the talismanic Comets rider Carl Stonehewer - the "comeback king" as he's rightly hailed by Workington team manager Tony Jackson - out of action for the rest of the season with a broken vertebra sustained in a crash the previous week at Edinburgh. Consequently Ian has almost immediately signed Ulrich Ostergaard, who presently is as popular as a rattlesnake in a lucky dip with Birmingham promoter Graham Drury. With some understatement Ian notes in his 'This Is It' column in the programme, Stoney's injury is "not good but it could have been a lot worse". Luckily for the club with a series of important fixtures ahead that will define the success or otherwise of their 2007 Premier League campaign, Ian "heard a whisper on Saturday night that Danish rider Ulrich Ostergaard was going to get the sack after Birmingham's visit to Mildenhall". The Dane fell out of favour at one club and back into another within 24 hours, a change in affairs that is remarkably quick even by the standards of speedway circles.

However the signing that has got Ian really excited isn't Ulrich but "Mr Woo - not a speedway rider but the World's Greatest Football Entertainer!" Once show business is in the blood, you're forever an impresario and salesman. In reality, Mr Woo is the World Keepy-Uppy Champion (!) who'll make his speedway debut at the stadium before the August Bank Holiday encounter with Berwick. "I'm his agent but it's difficult to communicate as his English isn't that good - he's from Korea - and already has the football market sown up! But I can bring him to speedway (here and at Sheffield and elsewhere once they hear about him) as well as night clubs, country fairs and the like." I need no second telling since I've already seem him in half-time action at a Sunderland away game at Carrow Road (Norwich), where wags in the crowd suggested we should immediately sign him. Ian's patter is never far away, "he used to play for Stuttgart, dunno how good he was but the only autograph Ronaldinho has ever asked for is Mister Woo's and that's good enough for me! He's performed everywhere - the Olympics, Pele's birthday, done TV adverts, the lot and now he's coming to Workington!" It's certainly a rare skill and one that, hopefully, will capture the collective imagination in this part of Cumbria, though I worry that in nightclubs the height of the ceiling might be an issue. Whatever my anxieties, Ian has no doubts, "former England captain Bryan Robson says, 'he's unbelievable' and he's never seen anything like it!" Given he now manages Sheffield United that sounds an entirely plausible reaction.

A steady stream of fans trundle past my table and through the turnstiles ready for the 7 p.m. start time. The cost of admission at Derwent Park to see the Workington Town Rugby League club play is £10, whereas adults pay £13 to get in to see the speedway. Children aged under 16 usually pay £5 but the summer special offer allows them to be "admitted FREE when accompanied by an

Turnstiles

Emil Kramer, Ritchie Hawkins and Stephan Katt watch studiously

Track staff mark their programmes

adult or senior citizen." Quite a number of the local kids have knowledge of this offer and plead with passing adult strangers to be allowed to go into the stadium with them. First we have guest riders, now we have guest children at speedway! The girls on the programme stall next to my table clearly have some previous experience with these particular boys and do everything in their power to shoo them away. Their language and behaviour indicates to me that this is a sensible decision since indications are that they probably will run amok inside, if unsupervised.

By the time I get inside the stadium, the first race against the Rebels is about to start. Ian Thomas has welcomed the visitors in the programme and especially "the new Somerset promoter for 2007, Mike Golding. He also co-promotes in the Elite League at Poole with Matt Ford. I have a lot of time for Mike, who is a very nice guy, which is more than I can say for his partner at Poole." Ritchie Hawkins makes his first return to Workington since the season-ending injuries he sustained riding for the Comets against Glasgow in the summer of 2006. He's an enthusiastic and combative rider, who tonight sports closely cropped dyed blond hair to celebrate his return. His never-say-die approach has made him a crowd favourite at both of these clubs and his long-standing number one fan, Supergran Margaret Hallett, confidently tips him for eventual Elite League success. I'm just in time to see Ulrich's debut in a Comets tabard when he finishes second behind Somerset star rider and captain Magnus Zetterstrom. He's clearly been interviewed over the phone ("can I say here and now that I enjoyed riding for Birmingham") for the programme and inevitably covers the recent events that unexpectedly brought him to the North-West, "let's just say that I did not see eye-to-eye with Graham Drury on one or two things, although the axe was a great shock when it came." Nonetheless, he looks forward positively to the challenge of a new club since he's heard about the "very god team spirit" (I didn't know that religion was such a factor for Ian Thomas and his riders). Ulrich also informs the home faithful that long-distance travel isn't a problem for him, "I am based in Denmark and fly in and out of Britain for meetings" plus he knows the packed fixture list next week (IoW and King's Lynn) will mean at his new home, "I'm not going to get much painting done".[1]

I watch the first few drawn heats from the rider and guest viewing area a short walk away from the pits. From here you get an excellent view down towards the start line and can watch the riders race from the grandstand area towards the sharpish corner of the all-important first bend. Because the track surrounds the Rugby League pitch, the straights are long and narrow, while in the far distance the track boasts one of the few truly banked bends seen in British speedway (all of them in the Premier league at Berwick, Isle of Wight and Redcar). It makes for exciting passing manoeuvres and also allows riders more used to its contours to dramatically sweep past their opponents and rush for the finish line.

[1 Interestingly the question of Ulrich's availability would rear its head later in the season. In the semi-final of the Young Shield Workington went to Redcar and only lost 50-40. But, in the return leg on the 20 October, Ulrich didn't ride due to a prior engagement in Denmark (painting duties) and Workington subsequently only won by four points so were eliminated. This defeat cost them their Cup Final clash with Birmingham.]

From here you also overlook the access route back and forth from the pits to the trackside gate. Ian Thomas bases himself in a prime position towards the left-hand edge of this viewing area, thereby enabling him to see everything of any significance during the meeting within only a few short steps (except for the away pits roughly thirty seconds away). He's clearly in his element as he watches each race intently, barks instructions, chats amiably or carefully studies his programme. When he learns my book sales haven't been that stellar, he suggests practical measures for me too, "You can walk round trying to sell them if you like!"

At Derwent Park, they have a proper old-fashioned grandstand that directly overlooks the start line and home straight (and another more compact version of the terraced grandstand on the back straight). There was a time when the speedway was so popular at Workington that you'd never have even got a place to sit in the main grandstand unless you arrived really early. But times have changed since the recent glory days when Carl Stonehewer - everyone's favourite speedway son locally - used to compete in the Grand Prix series and fortnightly put himself, the town and the Premier League on the map. Tonight, despite the fact that the meeting has started, I have a wide choice of seats. Workington is one of a dying breed - one of the few true speedway towns - but, even here, the enthusiasm for this sport appears to have waned. Those that do come have taken the first home defeat of the season badly enough to complain vociferously. According to the experienced track curator at Derwent Park, the taciturn Tony Swales, "last week Stoney was injured on Friday, on Saturday Ian Thomas had a new rider. But, after we lost to the Isle of Wight when he had rider replacement [for Stoney], the more vocal fans started effing and blinding saying 'why doesn't farking Thomas put his hand in his pocket?' Bearing in mind he had signed a rider and the IoW are unbeatable at present and any team would struggle against them, you just can't win!"

I've barely taken my seat when I hear (Glasgow based) presenter, Michael Max, say from the centre green, "a good friend of mine - Jeff Scott, author of *Showered in Shale* which has sold three or four copies by now - is here tonight with his latest book! It would make the perfect Christmas and birthday present and is a good, good read all about speedway." Michael is in good form over the loudspeakers and even finds time to consider the messages he reads out philosophically, "there's a birthday request that doesn't give too much away 'happy birthday to Helen from everyone'. Is that everyone in the stadium? Everyone in the world?" He welcomes southern-based referee Dan Holt to the stadium, "not quite sure if it's his first visit here but it'll be one of his first," before he optimistically tries to drum up a hint of some atmosphere from the visiting fans (that I singularly failed to spot troop in through the entrance gate having been stood outside for over an hour), "come on you Rebels fans - have you got air horns or cheering voices among you?"

Tony Jackson wrote in the programme that last weekend against the Islanders James Wright "went down with a virus during the meeting and had to withdraw before the end" and his mum Lynn confirmed he'd been under the weather all week. There was no sign of this at all in heat 5 when he beat Zorro by the proverbial mile to thereby ensure the Comets enjoyed their third successive 4-2 heat advantage to stretch the scoreline to 18-12. Michael Max likes what he's seen, "I did say that Magnus Zetterstrom is - by general consent - the best rider in the Premier League and James Wright has just blown him away!" Heat 6 has Ritchie Hawkins properly announce his arrival back at Derwent Park with an aggressive dive under British Speedway's only Italian rider, Mattia Carpanese. Though he falls heavily, he's soon up again quickly in one piece though the same can't be said of his badly damaged equipment. Michael quickly confirms the evidence of our own eyes, "the verdict of the referee is that Ritchie Hawkins is excluded for foul riding". There is the excellent story that Carpanese was put up in the Branney household where mutual language difficulties made communication difficult. Craig Branney felt sorry for him so got up early one morning and attempted to make him feel more at home by cooking Heinz spaghetti on toast.

There's an 11 minute and 30 second delay between the running of the heats that allows Michael Max to pursue his hobbyhorse-like obsession with the Berwick Bandits, who clearly form some sort of irksome element in a mental triangle involving his present speedway clubs, Glasgow and Workington. The mere thought of their arrival on the Bank Holiday provokes him, "The Berwick Bandits or, to give them their full title, the bottom of the table Berwick Bandits." Fortunately the need to fill the delay soon distracts him from the playful denigration of all things Bandits, "Ian Thomas signed a rider that no one had ever heard of - Mattia 'CAR-PAN-NAY-SAY' - he's not had the best of luck with injuries, equipment and his form but he's kept on battling his corner. So

Ian Thomas plots victory

Push off from pit lane

Michael Max charms the crowd

let's hear it from him [appears through pit gate] oh dear, his bike has given up the ghost." Craig Branney's bike is quickly thrust into service before the two-minute warning expires. At the start line the Workington start marshal takes it upon himself to try to swing the odds even further in the Comets favour by hassling the only Somerset Rebel in the race, Jordan Frampton, while he's under the orders of the referee. Despite these attentions Frampton finishes second behind Ostergaard who wins his first race in Workington colours (and would end the season with an average of 8.83 for Workington compared to 8.80 for Birmingham).

The next race features a lightning start from Charles Wright and behind him on the first lap the shrewd Kauko Nieminen rides the chasing Stephan Katt (2006 European Grasstrack Champion, fourth in 2007 World Longtrack Championship and brought in mid-season to replace Tomas Suchanek) hard to the fence on the second bend and at the apex of the next corner. Having marked his territory, Nieminen settles in to give a textbook example of team riding as he shepherds his young teammate home. Charles Wright delightedly punches the air as he crosses the line and the crowd reacts with a much louder roar of approval than the comparatively tepid way they greeted Ostergaard's victory the heat before. Mr M. Max views the win as a modern speedway parable to fortitude and resilience, "that's good to see - [team manager] Tony Jackson just said to me Charles Wright was really struggling with his confidence after his injuries and poor form, particularly since his smash at Glasgow." According to his mum Lynn Wright, functioning equipment has also been quite an issue for him, "he's had 10 engines blow already this season - it's killing him at £650 a throw!" Once you've endured such a run of mechanical misfortune, everyone starts to pay attention to the smallest changes in engine sounds that otherwise they might ignore, "[his] engine sounds sick, I reckon it's gonna blow!"

With the score already problematically stretching away from them at 27-15, Somerset team manager, Steve Bishop, brings in Magnus Zetterstrom 15 metres back as a tactical substitute and replaces the uniquely coiffured Danny Warwick with Jordan Frampton. Tony Jackson also rings the changes to his line up when he brings in Wright (C.) for Mattia Carpanese. On the fourth bend Frampton skittles the original programmed starter, John Branney, off his bike when he tries to move/force him off his racing line but instead clips his back wheel. Like crowds everywhere, the Workington faithful can be as one-eyed as the best of them, so what could be seen as a racing incident is definitely viewed by them as malice aforethought. The crowd boo, jeer and expansively gesture in Frampton's direction who, while he trudges back to the pits, signals his disapproval to the grandstand with a shake of his head and a gesture that indicates Branney 'locked up' in front of him. Though Frampton is excluded, Branney remains prone on the track for some time with Michael Max (as is his wont) hovering attentively close by, carefully watching every move of the medical team in attendance. A Glasgow fan familiar with his post-accident centre-green gait and stance told me last season, "he's not a mastodon - he's much more of a predator, always curious. Look at the way he holds his head to one side, always inquisitive but slightly ghoulish." We're treated to a running commentary, "John took a hefty tumble there … he's on his feet and I would say he's very pale but he's always very pale and I would ask him how he was but the grimace on his face says it all!"

While Branney freshens up, Michael Max snatches a few words with Ulrich Ostergaard. It's soon clear that the crowd and Ulrich hold ex-Workington promoter Graham Drury in roughly the same esteem. Quizzed by Michael on his feelings about the situation that led to his switch from the Brummies to the Comets, we learn "Aaah, I don't want to say too much [pause] I just don't like that man!" This gets the second loudest cheer of the night but, with serial Drury appointer and owner of both clubs Tony Mole listening in the audience, the subject is immediately and sensibly changed by Michael Max with a question about the delights and appeal of Workington. However, Ulrich isn't going to be diverted that easily, "Well I was top scorer and we won our away meeting in a last-heat decider when I had turned up and I was sacked. I wasn't happy about it - most strange!" Looking to the future, the Dane prefers to talk transport rather than confirm that he will definitely be back with the Comets again in 2008, "it's a four- or five-hour drive here and I'm used to long drives but you never know what's going to happen." The re-run of heat 8 has Charles Wright gate with incredibly sharp reaction to stretch his initial 15-metre lead over Zetterstrom even further into the first corner. Normally, you'd expect a rider with Zorro's pedigree and stature to soon catch up then blast his way past the younger Wright brother. However, Charles hasn't read the script, so rides the race of his life to beat his illustrious rival in a comprehensive manner that has the crowd leap as one to their feet to cheer ecstatically. The man behind me shouts, "that was incredible" above the noise and, on the centre green, Michael Max concurs, "that was something really, really special indeed - the night is getting better, better and better!"

The result of the meeting is already beyond doubt but there is still the matter of the aggregate bonus point to consider since the Rebels won at the Oak Tree Arena 52-41. Another key consideration is the weather, "there are some very nasty black clouds close to the stadium!" The riders, management and referee - starting with heat 9 won by Wright (J.) - rush through the remainder of the meeting. The possibly decisive heat to decide the whereabouts of the bonus point looks likely to be the 10th when, in last throw of the dice territory, Emil Kramer gets sent out in black-and-white as a tactical substitute. It turns out to be an inspired decision since Ostergaard suffers an engine failure on the start line and Kramer enjoys a tapes-to-flag victory though, creditably, Carpanese finishes second on borrowed equipment. The Rebels 7-2 takes the score in the meeting to 41-30 and thereby levels the aggregate scores. This adds extra excitement to the closing five races and raises important methodological questions. "Ian Thomas has just asked me what happens - if the meeting is abandoned - to the bonus point? Well, it would go to the team with the most 5-1s, then the most 4-2s and, if still not decided, I have no idea!" A couple of drawn races follow before Hawkins and Ostergaard have a ding-dong encounter in heat 13, where they take it in turns to ride the other hard for a close inspection of the safety fence. Far ahead of their mini-battle, Zorro wins comfortably and the Rebels also take a heat advantage. Sparked back into life and contention, they repeat the medicine in the penultimate race of the night prompting the man behind me to observe, "rather than spend money on fireworks why not spend it on a farking number one?" In the best traditions of speedway, the contest boils down to the last heat, where the Comets will need a 5-1 to take the bonus point. Having been bested twice already, Zorro is in no mood to continue this surprising pattern and, instead, reels off his third successive race win to end home hopes of aggregate victory. I don't savour the full glory of this race since by now I've set up my table next to the metal sea container that doubles as the trackshop at Workington. The disgruntled spectators exit the stadium with some speed and the majority flow past towards the car park without a second thought about speedway memorabilia let alone my books. Some people do linger to thoroughly consider whether they want to lash out some of their hard-earned money on a badge or a model of a rider. Friendly, knowledgeable and genuine speedway people run this far-flung outpost of the Barber trackshop empire - namely, Liz Fleming along with help from partner Gary and son Scott. Like the majority of people here tonight, they're keen to get away before it lashes down but have to painstakingly recount the (unsold) stock they have carefully arranged on the tables inside the sea container.

Back at the speedway hotel in Workington - the Waverley Hotel - I quickly discover the whys and wherefores of the new smoking ban regulations. Initially I'm mystified as to how come my room smells like it has been the location for a lengthy protest smoke in. Though the ashtrays (!) are empty the fug and stink of cigarette smoke still remains in full effect, despite the room having been ostensibly cleaned since the previous (I estimate) 100-day resident. I leave all the windows open and so get to enjoy the karaoke held downstairs until around 1 a.m. that is then followed by some drink-fuelled high jinks in the street.[2] A regular guest at the hotel is Comets owner Tony Mole and, the next morning, I listen to him get earnestly questioned about the events of the previous night while he queues at the self-service section of the breakfast bar. Mr Mole is of the opinion, "we would have won the bonus point if Ulrich hadn't lost a chain." Talk ranges widely but I still gather "the floodlights have had it" and, when told that the speedway fan he's talking to is just about (like me) going to drive over to Brough Park says, "Newcastle has a nice stadium though it's a bit of a home track!"

11th August Workington v Somerset (Premier League) 51-44

[2 The next morning when I question the helpful lady on reception, she confirms that smoking has indeed been banned in public places - even in Workington - but under the law as it applies to hotels, I have in fact "hired a private room." Unluckily having failed to specify I'd like a "no smoking room" I've been assumed to be a nicotine fiend and given one of those designated for the newly oppressed, "so smoking is permitted in this room". Any smoking speedway fans should, when they rush to the North-West of England to visit this historic coastal town, immediately note down the phone number (01900 603246) of the Waverley since there is a whole floor of these smoking rooms still available! Hardened non-smokers should beware of the fine print of the regulations that apply to hotels.]

Chapter 36. Newcastle v Redcar: Irene, George, the "Official Club Magazine" and Redcar All Impress

12th August

Despite briefly losing my way in Carlisle and again near to the stadium in Byker, I arrive so early at what they now call Newcastle Stadium (rather than its original designation Brough Park) that the only cars in the muddy pits car park are those of the track staff. They have to fit their work round their full-time jobs and the restricted access they have to the stadium during the week when its main preoccupation is the greyhound racing they stage here. Race day on a Sunday gives the volunteer curatorial team the chance to turn up at sunrise (if they wish) to give themselves the maximum time to make all the necessary preparations before the earliest scheduled evening start time in British speedway at 6.30 p.m. I've hardly pulled up in the car before the jet-black clouds - they're so fanatical about the Magpies (Newcastle United) up here that even the clouds are correctly coloured - do what they've been threatening and douse the area with some impressively torrential rain. These monsoon-like downpours typified the early months of the summer and, thankfully, this intense rain is short lived. Nonetheless puddles have appeared all across the car park and the track now has a sheen it didn't have a few minutes earlier. The track staff had briefly sheltered away from the deluge but, as soon as it abates, they're straight back out onto the centre green, working on the safety fence or on the shale surface. Rather notably, there's also a lady member of the curatorial team here who works in a way that indicates that she is a regular and accepted part of the gang. George English is justifiably proud of his volunteers whose contribution to the club really is essential to its longevity and livelihood, given that they "operate in one of the most expensive stadiums in the sport and receive no additional income from catering or bar sales."

I've always found Newcastle's speedway co-promoter George English friendly and welcoming while his mother, Joan, is one of the true characters in the sport. No pun intended, she's a real diamond who loves her club and enjoys her long-time participation in the sport. As usual on race day, they're both here early and although there's a lot to organise, people to greet and things to be done - they always take the time to chat. George does have the odd cross to bear since he's a Newcastle United supporter and he wastes no time in highlighting that Sunderland's unexpected 1-0 win against Tottenham had a Magpies flavour, "it took an ex-Newcastle player [Michael Chopra] to score for you!" We're in his office and invariably people ring up to enquire about the weather, "Yes, it's fine here - we're watering the track!" he assures an anxious caller keen to tell him about the conditions where they're calling from. "I'm not bothered if it's raining in Teeside," he tells me after he's hung up. Joan is equally definite in her meteorological forecast about the dark black clouds that still dominate the sky, "they're heading out to the coast!" If she ever decides to give up at the speedway, Joan should go into weather forecasting as the evening turns out to be a lovely sunny one. Indeed, despite an awful summer of wet weather, Newcastle would only have to postpone one meeting all season in 2007. This was unusual compared to most other tracks and unusual for them given that their 2006 season saw umpteen rain-offs. Naturally as a result, while 2006 was a "financial struggle", this season the club has been on a straighter path tracking a side in 2007 more cut to their own particular financial cloth. This team is one that has also managed to excite the Tyneside public enough to attend in slightly increased numbers than previously.

Tyre heaven

Early arrivals

In the passageway outside the speedway office is the small kitchen manned by volunteer Mrs Irene Best who looks after one of the key tasks at the club - making the tea and coffee! Traditionally, you've barely arrived in the building before she kindly enquires if you'd like any refreshment. "I'm a lifelong supporter of Newcastle Speedway. I came along as a child before the War - I can't really remember it. It must be raining the way that phone keeps ringing off the hook! I just took to it - I lived locally at the bottom of Fosse Way. There was the war in 1939 and in 1946-47 we had Ken Le Breton - the White Ghost. My husband was more into grass tracking. I've never followed any other sport. Of course, our only child has come all his life and doesn't know any other. He's a man of 46-47 now, Robbie - he's the Track Manager. Of course a lot of people give him a lot of help, I mean my son works full time as well as doing that. Monday was always our race night. The promoter I remember the most was Johnny Hoskins in the 1940s and 50s. I've seen some good riders come and go over the years. In the 60s there was Mauger. Of course we had the young Kenny Carter - we had Ole Olsen and Anders Michanek. All told we've had six or seven World Champions. Apart from my family, it's my one and only love! And I've made some good friendships over the years. And the Owen family - Tom Owen, not Joe, is my favourite all-time rider. He's a gentleman - and still keeping in touch with me!" At that moment we're interrupted from our brief trip down memory lane by the arrival of one part of the club presentation team (and club Finance Director), Andrew Dalby, and also by George English who happens to open the door of his office at that moment. "Ee, George, the place is crawling with Sunderland fans! What's happening here?" George rolls with the punches in life and speedway, so a few more Sunderland fans is just something you have to take in your stride, "I can't blame him he doesn't live here but this one [Andrew] does!"

Once Irene has ensured that I have my cup of tea, I retreat to one of the nearby benches to study the Newcastle programme that this year has transmogrified into an "official club magazine" with colour throughout. It really is a quite magnificent document and, would if there were justice, win the *Speedway Star* 'Programme of the Year' award though (based on what I've seen on my travels) I suspect this is likely to go to Lakeside. A case could be made either way - if you leave aside the argument that surely Elite League clubs should produce elite materials - but arguably this should still really go to Newcastle for the sheer variety of the content inside this document as well as upon grounds of value, given the fact it only costs £2. The big news of the week at the club is one of the headlines on the cover of today's issue of the magazine, namely that Ross Brady has been sacked from the club and replaced by Paul Clews. In his column, George uses the euphemism "parted company" with the rider before he explains his decision was based partly on Brady's poor performance against his old club Edinburgh at Newcastle Stadium the previous week. It was a showing by the rider that "was not acceptable to the spectators, the management or indeed Ross himself. Ross was so disappointed last week but that meeting was really only the final straw after a series of mystifying rides that have seen him lose, what looked like safe points, to inferior riders … he is just not the same rider [as the early months of the season] and as our team is set up for solid performances from all, not top heavy, we have been riding meetings with first six then five riders only scoring points, and that is no good to anyone, not least the struggling rider." George's column is wide ranging and, like many features in the match-day magazine, both entertaining and a delight to read. George covers recent events with wit and some feeling. Though defeated 57-36 at Birmingham, the club had taken along a "large contingent of Newcastle supporters" and the meeting had apparently been "enjoyable" to watch except for an "abysmal refereeing decision [by Dave Watters] in heat 8 which left Carl [Wilkinson] absolutely spitting feathers and everyone else totally dumfounded. I know today's visiting promoter, Chris van Straaten, has had plenty to say about refereeing decisions this season but I have to doubt whether any of those that he has witnessed or indeed the ones that he didn't see as he had comments to make about a match here and he wasn't actually in attendance that day, were as bad as that decision at Birmingham." There are too many new features in the programme to do justice to them here, though it was pleasing to learn from guest columnist Keith McGhie (the Redcar speedway announcer), "George is a regular visitor and invariably made welcome at South Tees Motorsports Park every Thursday - especially by the burger van, as he religiously follows his latest health food diet."

The local derby clash with Redcar is something to set the pulses racing for Diamonds and Bears fans as well as club co-presenter Andrew Dalby. "The sport needs passion and feeling - so long as it doesn't get silly - increased tension is what keeps the crowd and the riders, let's not forget, engaged." Though he's got limited time on any race night, I pop in to see George to thank him for his kind hospitality when I return my mug to Irene's small kitchen area just outside his speedway office. Team changes are on his mind, "though [Paul Clews] hasn't ridden all season just by showing up he'll please the fans a lot more than Ross has recently. That said he scored 8 at Edinburgh - we needed the away win - and, after the meeting, I had to tell him that he was sacked. You have to declare your team three days before any meeting - it's not pleasant but it's part of the job." I congratulate George on the new-look programme and wonder if he'll win the aforementioned *Speedway Star* Programme of the Year Award. "The person [Howard Jones] who judges it has an agenda as he used to do the programme here. We're very pleased with what we've done and we've already won it four times, so I'm not really bothered, as we know it's good! Though someone did ask for a programme not an official match-day magazine without a racecard until we pointed out it was in the back!"[1]

The highlight of my night, indeed my season was finally meeting George Grant again - the man who took me to my first-ever speedway meeting and, as a result, fired my love for the sport! Though only a friend of a friend (as well as a guitarist in the Tadley band), George typified the speedway attitude and ethos when for many years he faithfully took me to the speedway at Smallmead without charge or complaint. He's always been a Newcastle speedway fan but his work had taken him down south and his need for a regular fix of his speedway led him to watch his local clubs - in this case, the Reading Racers. George now lives in Valencia with his wife Betty for the majority of the year but, whenever he's back in the North-East, his pilgrimage to the speedway is regularly difficult to resist. Things have changed but he can still fondly remember and vividly recall many aspects ('it's remembering the 80s that I struggle with not my childhood') of the Brough Park of his youth. "I went first of all with my parents - George and Jean - in the mid 40s when it started again. I was only very young - six or seven - but I can still remember the big crowds and some of the riders. People like Norman Evans, Alec Grant - Rob Grant's granddad - Ken Le Breton, Sunny Mitchell, Don Carson, Herbie King and the like. Derek Close was my favourite because he was a good rider and won a lot of races! Of course, we got to see all of those who came there - we were in the Second Division then - and I liked Alan Hunt who was more of a Peter Collins type rider and also Jack Young who was most exciting and a good gater, say, like Ivan Mauger. I think it closed down in about 1951 and in 1954 we moved to Tadley 'cause me parents got a job at the Atomic Weapons Research Establishment in Aldermaston. I didn't go again until the early 60s when we went to Swindon, which was virtually our nearest track at that point. They had riders like Bob Kilby, Mike Broadbanks and Barry Briggs, who was my favourite. When Reading opened in 1969 it was much closer and I started going there with friends. Reading was more exciting to watch because there were junior riders learning and having a go, plus there were older riders in the late stages of their career. It was a nice mix."

[1 In fact the programme was judged to have scored 960 out of 1000 by the 'anonymous' judge of the award. However, some of the criteria remains ludicrous as illustrated by the comments, "the paragraphing isn't perfect" or "while some of the background shades and tints might not be everyone's cup of tea, the content is first class." I have to say that like 99.99999% of fans I always buy my programmes to do a job and provide information and entertainment along with a racecard rather than fulfil some arbitrary style criteria or meet someone else's essentially unquantifiable acceptability.]

Racing and gymnastics

"Michanek along with Dag Lovaas and Geoff Curtis came to Reading in 1971, I think, when Reading took over the Newcastle licence. Geoff Curtis was one of the riders I really liked watching till he died in a crash in Australia in 1973. That was the year Reading won the league (the First Division) and then it closed down when they had to move from Tilehurst. In 1974 I went to Oxford to watch - that was the year Anders became World Champion, of course - and then it was back to watch Reading at Smallmead in 75 when that opened. After we had Anders we had Dave Jessup who was a great rider except he always had engine trouble, something that I think cost him the World Championship in 1978. When I went to Reading I would always go and see Newcastle whenever they were in the vicinity. I was always a Newcastle fan, even though I lived away. We moved back from Tadley to Newcastle in 1986. The team they had then was very poor. Since I came back we've had loads of really good riders like Nicki Pedersen, Bjarne of course and Kenneth Bjerre. In the past Dave Bargh used to go very well there and Thorpe, Mark it was, and Rod Hunter. We moved to Spain last year, near Valencia and we come back in the summer 'cause it's too hot for me so I get along every week when I'm back. Nowadays they don't rely so much on skill as on engine power and, in the old days, we had deeper tracks with more than one racing line. It wasn't first out of the gate and, with the lay-down engines, they have more problems with the chains breaking off than they did in the older days. A lot of it is down to the tuning of the engines now - the higher the rider the more money he spends on getting it tuned. I don't see how the youngsters or those starting out have a chance when they don't earn much points money. It's harder to make it pay and it costs so much to get the engines tuned. It used to be more even before. And with more shale on the tracks there were less postponements. At Reading after the rain it would look unrideable but often they still raced and the racing was good!"

"Something I don't like nowadays is they keep on changing the rules and I think this tactical rides with the double points is silly. The old system was better and you have to say that Reading were robbed by Peterborough using those double points in the Elite League Final last year. It wasn't right. I watch the Elite League on *Sky* - I don't care who the teams are, I just like to see a good close meeting. There haven't been many of them this year and they keep saying it's good but anyone who hasn't been to speedway before will get a bad impression, if that's what they judge it on! The Grand Prix was excellent this year - really exciting on the telly - the one thing I really miss living in Spain is the speedway. We were awful in the World Team Cup and I worry we haven't got anyone of any quality coming through. They didn't have the engines tuned right, which amazes me given most of them ride there. I don't think any current British rider is a decent gater and you need that, especially in Poland 'cause in the sort of climate that we have now you need to gate or, at least, be on equal terms in the first corner as it's so hard to get back otherwise!"

Sadly for the good-sized crowd of fans who turn up to watch from throughout the North-East region, the entertainment served up on the night is variable. However, it is enjoyed by a voluble contingent from Redcar since from Heat 3 onwards there is clearly only ever going to be one team in it to win. One of the many speedway truisms concerns the need to avoid running last places in a team meeting, if you are to succeed. This is amply illustrated by the fact that by the end of the meeting Newcastle only manage this three times, while none of the top five Redcar riders runs a last place all night. Not that this is solely the decisive factor as collectively the Bears show much greater determination all round but particularly in the first corner, something that is often decisive on the night. Though things are hopeless at a very early stage, the home fans do rouse themselves at the start of heat 8 when Carl Wilkinson is bizarrely excluded (rather than punished with a 15-metre penalty) by referee Dave Dowling after a tapes infringement. Diamonds presenter Barry Wallace - a man with a sing-song, soothing accent and, so the programme tells us, a green bedroom carpet - can barely hide his incredulity, "Carl Wilkinson is excluded for not being under power at the start of the race - I'm repeating exactly what was said, so there you are!' Moments later a bemused Barry is back on over the tannoy again, "under the rules Carl can't go off 15 metres so will be replaced by Sam Dore - it's a strange business indeed, strange business!" With the scores already at 17-25 prior to this race, this wouldn't have made any material difference to the end result but definitely increases the noise levels. Afterwards Carl Wilkinson wryly notes, "I'd love to know how I managed to touch the tapes with a bike that wasn't under power, considering that it was the clutch that dragged me there." The re-run of this contentious heat sees Josh Auty gate with Sean Stoddart relegated to third place until he blasts under his teammate, Sam Dore, who's then scattered off his bike. The referee stops the race and orders another re-run. Auty doesn't emerge victorious from the re-run since Sean Stoddart wins instead but, nonetheless, his motorcycling skills still impress after he somehow manages to stay on after rearing massively. Close by to me, one Diamonds fan says appreciatively, "He's awesome, isn't he!" while another shouts, "You didn't roll enough, Auty!" I would have to say that there was often movement from the youngster at the start line as he tried to predict the imminent rise of the tapes, but equally he wasn't alone in that respect.

Someone with something to prove on the night is James Grieves, who spent a couple of seasons with Newcastle. He looks imperious and only drops a single point all night. But, then again, many of the Redcar riders look so comfortable you'd have either thought they were the home side or had ridden at Newcastle Stadium on a regular basis. On his debut, newly minted Diamond Paul Clews shows glimpses of the all-out action-racing style that has deservedly won him so many admirers (including myself) in the past. The ninth heat is a case in point where numerous times he tries the (dusty) outside line in order to try to pass Jack Hargreaves only to not quite manage it. Clearly the old instinct doesn't leave you but his race rustiness, having sat out the season to this point - after Stoke gave him his testimonial last season but were unable to find him a team place this season - proves too great a handicap to overcome. If Ross Brady had raced to a lacklustre zero last week, Paul Clews races to a determined zero this week! He would have 65 rides for the club to return an average of 4.80 in the 2007 season. The margin of victory could have been greater but is still an impressive 38-55 to the Redcar Bears. This is the first home defeat suffered by Newcastle in three years, despite flirting with disaster the previous week against Edinburgh. The only home rider to emerge with real credit on the night is the indefatigable Diamonds reserve Sean Stoddart who in 2007 has finally really blossomed into the kind of successful rider you would hope that his long hours of dedication (and sheer pleasantness as a person) would have achieved. Beforehand George English had told me "it's going to be tough against Redcar" and, in retrospect, I realised that this must be some kind of coded language occasionally used by promoters when they know they're likely to get tonked. In the media, George doesn't dress things up at all, "The better side won, and from our point of view it was hard to say which performance was worse - our team's or the referee's. Apart from Sean Stoddart, who was magnificent again, we didn't have a lot to offer."

The last race has barely been completed when George kindly but unnecessarily apologises to me, "Sorry it was such an awful meeting for you to come to here!" In fact, I enjoyed what I saw but the real pleasure for me was, once again after nearly three decades, being reunited with George Grant. Despite the result, he enjoyed the meeting and can still fondly remember many things about Brough Park including, "when we used to have an outside line or riders who could use it!"

12th August Newcastle v Redcar (Premier League) 38-55

Chapter 37. Edinburgh v Glasgow: 13 years of hurt ends

The lure of the local derby clash between the Edinburgh Monarchs and the Glasgow Tigers is a difficult one to resist travelling to Scotland to see, particularly when you can also then see the return leg at Saracen Park in Glasgow on the Sunday. After you get past Newcastle, the train journey to Edinburgh Waverley station allows you to take in a beautiful stretch of coastline as the train track runs parallel to it. Without a car, humping my books to the stadium at Armadale would be difficult to do without access to the Monarchs supporters' club bus that runs every week from the city centre to the stadium. Indeed, its popularity appears to have increased and, as ever, Ella MacDonald runs this service with firm but calm efficiency. I've brought along my books more in hope than expectation since my track record of sales hasn't been what I would have expected at Armadale, never mind that the supporters' coach arrives with only a short time to go before the racing starts and thereby minimises the valuable selling time available to me. The invariably cheery Edinburgh co-promoter John Campbell passes my pitch, so I enquire whether there's ever an interval here, "Nah, we don't make anything from the food and bar - plus it's forecast for heavy rain tonight!"

Before the light fades I study the programme and notice that the Monarchs are somewhat depleted without their number one George Stancl who remains injured and it's an absence that's rather euphemistically called in the programme "a bit of a disaster". That said when he did ride last Friday in the home defeat against Newcastle, he had something of a jinx with his and everyone else's equipment. First he blew his best engine while leading heat 1, then he borrowed Jason Lyons's second engine and blew that up on his stand in the pits before he then borrowed Matthew Wethers's bike and bent that badly in a crash during heat 6. According to John Campbell in his programme notes (where he rather wittily catalogues a rich seam of mishap and disaster), this crash forced Matty to race the remainder of the meeting against Newcastle with "his second, not quite so suited to Armadale, bike." It was a week in the wars for George who was also involved in crashes at King's Lynn and Sheffield. Another rider we won't see tonight is that rarest of breeds in British speedway - an Italian speedway rider. After his Heat 13 fall in the close meeting with the Diamonds, Daniele Tessari's season has ended prematurely with damage to his knee and subsequently this has been diagnosed as an injury complicated with "water on it". Derek Sneddon ruined a bike at King's Lynn and then the next night also fell sufficiently heavily at Sheffield to require a trip to the first aid room and the hospital. But though injured, Derek still returned to the stadium in double quick time to see a race win in Heat 14 for Kalle Katajisto at Owlerton. This landmark race win was described as a "big talking point" by his promoter John Campbell, "he missed the gate, as normal, but then produced the ride of his life to pass all three riders in front of him to produce his first win for us. A thrilling ride by a young man who is getting better and better with each ride." Such occurrences are so unusual that the programme includes a photograph of three riders captioned with the words, "Kalle makes a start!" While by his taciturn standards Alan 'Doc' Bridgett - track curator extraordinaire at Armadale as well as General and Team Manager - gets carried away with the heady triumph of it all and, somewhat prematurely, predicts, "We saw Kalle showing signs of progress." Kalle has also now graduated enough in race wins and language capabilities for Scott Wilson to interview him for the first time, "I asked him how he was, and he touched his knee and said, 'My elbow is really sore!'"

In fact the majority of the Monarchs have been plagued with injuries, falls and mechanical mishaps over the last few weeks. Scott Wilson is convinced "somebody has broken a mirror somewhere." Whereas John Campbell suggests we try to empathise with Derek Sneddon's feelings after trashing his bike at the Norfolk Arena through a visualisation exercise, "picture screwing crisp £100 notes in a ball and setting them on fire and see how you would feel about that." I already knew that Scottish currency looks exotically different to that in England but I didn't even realise that such a large denomination existed!

Tonight sees the 288th ever speedway meeting at Armadale and one that local pride dictates you must at all costs strive to win. My arrival isn't seen as a good omen by Dougie Copland who, when I join him overlooking the second bend at the spot equidistant between the fabled Monarchs' hospitality area and the grandstand, greets me with, "We lost the last time you were here!" Things start promisingly for the Monarchs when Derek Sneddon roars away from the tapes with a speed that you'd usually associate with someone driving a vehicle taken without consent. Andrew Tully enthusiastically tries to pass the experienced Craig Watson and presses him determinedly for a couple of laps until the wily old stager deliberately slows into the fourth corner on the second lap. Tully is caught unawares by this unexpected manoeuvre and trapped behind Watson has to shut off to avoid crashing into him. This enables the much improved and highly thought of Tigers' rider David McAllan to nip past to gain and, ultimately, retain third place. The drawn heat is as close as the Monarchs get to a win all night. The scale of the mountain the Monarchs will have to climb if they are to put up a fight is revealed in the next race won easily by veteran Michael Coles, who now rides at reserve for the Tigers. Dougie isn't happy, "You know your luck is out when Michael Coles can win a race!" Fresh from his call-up to the Scandinavian Grand Prix the previous weekend, Kaj Laukkanen can only manage a disappointing third place behind the Tigers' Australian pairing of Shane Parker and Robert Ksiezak. Dougie accurately comments, "That was a piss-poor effort for a GP rider!" Stood next to him is Steven Brykajlo along with Jim his moustachioed Berwick-supporting father, who also isn't impressed with the, "man who asked for more dirt on the track and he canna ride it!"

Jim is a speedway fanatic with a rich fund of stories from the shale and an even greater variety from his travels on the road as an Edinburgh taxi driver. It's a job that has him brush with famous people on a regular basis, "I was on George Street and I saw David Walsh across the street and I was just about to call 'Walshie!' and then [the really unfunny comedian] Jimmy Carr got in it. I thought 'fark off!' but took him to the Marchmont where he's staying for the Festival. He's a crap tipper he only gave me 50p!" At least Jim knew who this passenger was, unlike the time when "this bloke got into the cab with a dolly bird young enough to be his daughter and on the journey said, 'Do you know who I am?' I didn't. So then he asks 'Do you like country music?' and I tell him no it's crap! So he says 'I'm Willie Nelson' and I say 'I've heard of you'." By now the riders have appeared at the tapes for the start of the fourth race and Dougie poses one of the great unanswered philosophical questions to confound us on the night, namely, "How long before Cockle falls off?" We soon learn the answer when he almost immediately tumbles from his machine on the first corner. Though, to be fair to him, he did earlier manage to finish second in heat 2 without doing so.

If in the pits the Edinburgh team carries many injuries, then the same holds true for Jim in his taxi, "I'm gonna take painkillers for my sciatica though the medication is clashing with my diabetes. The doctor told me don't stand at the speedway or drive your cab - he said, 'I'll sign you off for a month' and I said 'thanks a lot I'm self-employed'. Basically he says I can't stand or sit!" Out on the track Edinburgh prospects improve with a win for Laukkanen in the next race apparently because he appears on his second bike rather than following the advice of some of the crowd stood by me to get stuck into the vodka. The forecast that "we're going to get a Tully special round the outside of McAllan" fails to materialise. In the next race, a superbly executed pirouette by Trent Leverington on the first bend ensures that the Monarchs combination of Sneddon and Laukkanen definitely gains the maximum points from the race and narrows the scores to a much more competitive 17-19. Next up, a fired-up Shane Parker shows how much the win means to the Tigers by his treatment of Matthew Wethers. On the first and third bends of the first lap, Shane rides really hard underneath his fellow countryman to send a clear message about his own determination and the level of foolhardiness or bravery that would be required to attempt to pass him. On the centre green, over the tannoy Scott Wilson asks, "Matty shut off - what did he shut off for, George?" only to hear in reply "Otherwise he was in the flipping fence" or words to that effect. Jim remains calm about the forceful racing, "Aye, Shane was a bit hard there" but he feels the deliriously ecstatic celebrations [for a 4-2] of the Glasgow Tigers fans who've come along to watch to be both slightly over the top and an embarrassment, "They're like vultures the Tigers crowd!"

Crowds gather

Riders wave from parade truck

View from centre green

A 4-2 for the Monarchs - that again narrows the cumulative scores (this time to 26-28) and temporarily silences the Tigers fans - arrives after the previous drawn heat featuring James Cockle who manages to complete all four laps without mishap. Every time he appears tonight, it seems that Tigers captain Shane Parker will power to victory and, once again, the 10th heat is no exception. The mystery of why Michael Max referred to the "bottom of the table Berwick Bandits" is put into some context when I hear about an infamous Glasgow versus Berwick encounter at Saracen Park. At the time, Michael was the presenter at Berwick on the Saturday and Glasgow on the Sunday but was "sacked on the centre green at Glasgow by Peter Waite after he ran over to the start line to highlight to the referee - who hadn't noticed till then - that Adrian Rymel was wearing the wrong helmet colour. Peter wasn't happy - not that it mattered really 'cause we won on aggregate and Carlos Villar came out and won the race anyway!"[1]

Edinburgh do appear to have a chance of a change in fortune when Parker misses the start of Heat 10 but - with Derek Sneddon taken on a long route to inspect the fine detail of the wood panelling of the safety fence by Robert Ksiezak - Shane is able to cut back and power under Matty Wethers (once again) for the lead as they come out of the second bend. Shane then rides off into the distance to preserve his possible maximum. Another maximum man on the night is Kalle Katajisto, albeit his is of the unwanted variety that he completes with another well-deserved last place in Heat 11. Kalle was to have another programmed ride in the Heat 14 but his programmed ride is taken by James Cockle, undoubtedly the better of the two Monarchs reserves on the night. By this stage of the meeting, Cockle has succumbed to his own traditional demons but makes it to the fourth bend before he again falls and retires in Heat 14. This cameo display goes with another similar happening two races earlier in Heat 12 - a race that features a third place for Michael Coles "seven points for him - he'll be able to pay for another divorce soon" - thereby taking the cumulative Cockle fall count on the night to an impressive "three bloody falls" in five rides. The final fleeting chance of a concerted Monarchs fight back comes in the 13th when Sneddon and Wethers lead only to be called back after Watson gets into a tangle and unceremoniously clatters his own teammate Leverington from his bike, thereby resulting in his exclusion by referee Barbara Horley. Predictably enough in the re-run, Trent splits the home pair and keeps Sneddon back in third to minimise the possible damage to the Tigers lead on the night. The apparently inevitable Tigers victory is assured (technically confirmed when Ksiezak crosses the line) before the final race of the night is won by Shane Parker to complete his maximum. The visiting

[1 Dougie tells me later, "On the 11th May 2003 Glasgow versus Berwick was abandoned at 42 apiece after 14 heats. Carlos Villar (on only 1 point) came out on Claus Kristensen's bike in a monsoon and defeated the then Tigers number one James Grieves to send the Bandits through on aggregate by 6 points. It was possibly his greatest win as a Berwick Bandit in his short, but exciting British career that promised so much. Sadly, Carlos was paralysed from the waist down after an innocuous fall whilst leading a race against Newport at Shielfield in the last match of that season. The meeting itself was full of gamesmanship from Glasgow officials throughout, terrible really, especially Michael Max who was nothing short of a disgrace and an embarrassment to Glasgow speedway. Not for the first time either, he can't seem to help himself though. In the end Tigers got what they deserved - a knockout punch."]

Glasgow fans fully savour their first league win in Edinburgh for 13 years and, understandably enough, celebrate the final two heats in ecstatic fashion. They linger slightly longer than many of the Monarchs fans who rather quickly but disconsolately stream out to the car park muttering about their weakened team. While collectively clinging to the fragile consolation, "that's the first time they've beaten us in the league since we came here!"

17th August Edinburgh v Glasgow (Premier League) 41-49

Chapter 38. Glasgow v Edinburgh: Afternoon of passion and pantomime reactions

19th August

SKYBALLS - JASON CRUMP

Jonathan	*"That's what I like about him - he wears his arm on his sleeve and tells you how it is!"*
Troy Batchelor	*"It's awesome, Jason's awesome, everyone's awesome!"*
Jason Crump	*"We're racing in a league match - we're not going to do anything stupid and, hopefully, the crowd enjoyed it!"*
Jonathan	*"Interesting words from Leigh Adams".*

After a trip to Wigan to see the Black Cats prove the adage that it isn't over until the fat lady sings (although in this case it was a bloke singing opera before the match), I took a corporation bus in the rain to Penicuik on the outskirts of Edinburgh. I was to be driven to the return leg of the derby meeting between Glasgow and Edinburgh at Saracen Park by speedway supporting taxi driver Jim Brykajlo in the company of his son Steven and cousin Dougie Copland. After getting over the surprise that we wouldn't actually be travelling in his black cab, I settled back and enjoyed the drive in the drizzle and the easy flow of the mostly speedway-related conversation. After we'd discussed matters such as rumours surrounding various riders, matches and teams, I quizzed them about what changes they'd make to the sport to improve it. Jim belongs to the school of thought brought up on the traditional virtues and mostly wishes it was still as it was in the 1960s (when I imagine he first started going). "I'd kick out all the GP riders, bring back white helmets and get rid of the tactical-ride rule," he says without any hesitation although he'd already worked out his speech outlining a master plan to resurrect wide-scale interest in the sport. Dougie echoes some of these recommendations and then wonders rhetorically, "How can you justify using a tactical ride at home when it was brought in to help the away teams?"

Just like we used to go to work on an egg or expect a fair day's pay for a fair day's work, Dougie believes that rider development in this country (the United Kingdom not just Scotland) would be helped "when we had the rule that the two reserves have to be British teenagers - well, under-21s. Then the problem was you mostly had home 5-1s every week whereas it would be better if heats 2, 8 and 14 were guaranteed just for reserves. Reserves must be of the same standard or as close as at the start of the season. There is another argument though. With adding more youngsters to the teams this can lead to the product being watered down and the racing not so good. Premier League is still the best for racing without a doubt."

Dougie continues, "I believe speedway's problem lies in its youth development system. The Conference League was a great success a few years back but the lack of tracks (and of course fans) has caused the number of emerging talent to drop dramatically. Premier League tracks are still benefiting from the good days when the League was strong, off the top of my head, Rye House and Edinburgh. They invested in the Conference league racing while others didn't. John Campbell tried in vain to keep the Dale Devils racing, we'll never know how many more he could have brought through. Although not a great lover of the old Rockets and Uncle Len I take my hat off to him for what he's tried to achieve. There seems to be a new superstar at reserve every season; brilliant!"

Symptomatic of the malaise sparked by not bringing young riders through the ranks is the present situation at the "Glasgow Tigers who have two experienced riders with 10 years' experience minimum each." As an ostensibly 'neutral' Berwick supporter, Jim interjects his agreement about the iniquity of the situation, "Lee Dicken and Michael Coles - that is bloody nonsense!" Clearly used to such interruptions from Jim, Dougie continues, "We need a 45-points limit where anyone can ride and where, every month, the bottom two riders are at reserve. We should start the season with league racing to stop the fiddling of the averages. Peter Waite was doctoring the averages to bring in foreigners for the league but, 'cause of the rain-offs, it backfired on him. He tries to do this every season in the Premier Trophy which should be outlawed (especially in Bandit country!). He wonders why nobody goes to watch his team or why the authorities don't give him any sympathy. Sign seven riders and get on with it, man!" In Jim's opinion another area to be looked at should be track preparation, "There's too much doctoring of the tracks nowadays - why not say track preparation isn't allowed once the meeting has started?" As planned we arrive outside the stadium in sufficient time to obtain one of the limited number of spaces available in the secured car park outside the Saracen Park stadium buildings. "It's best to be careful" Jim notes sagely before he nods over towards the fenced beer 'garden' of the drinking establishment that borders the car park and the stadium, "how many pubs do you see where they fence the customers in the garden?"

Practice start for Shane Parker – King of Saracen Park

Once I've finally persuaded the man on the pits gate that I haven't concocted an elaborate story about selling books in the stadium to hoodwink my way past him, I set out my books upon my wheelie case in prime position on the stepped lower terrace of the main grandstand that overlooks the start line at Saracen Park. The stadium is home to the Ashfield football team and, surrounded by a damp looking track of deep red coloured shale, their pitch looks luxuriantly green after all the recent rain. In fact, the cloud filled sky looks likely to provide some more rain before too long - though the forecast is for it to remain fine, albeit with the threat of showers. The Tigers fans are a fanatical bunch about their speedway and draw their support from a wide cross section of the various communities that make up the rich tapestry that is the city of Glasgow. From what I'm given to understand of the background of those who sit in the main grandstand, it's likely that Glasgow speedway would perform very well should there ever be a Mastermind competition drawn solely from supporters of our sport. I invariably enjoy the enthusiasm and commitment of the fans here, something that contributes to the atmosphere already enhanced by how close we can all actually get to the action on the track. Though old fashioned and very much of its time, in this compact stadium you get an excellent view from wherever you base yourself in the grounds - whether outside or inside the bar that overlooks the fourth bend. There's also the option to watch undercover on the home straight - in the grandstand or on the terraces - or, instead, stand exposed to the elements on the first and third bends as well as the accessible sections of the back straight. I'm in an excellent position to attract attention from fans who pass by to access other parts of the stadium as well as to chat with the people who like to position themselves in this particular section of the grandstand. I finally get to meet the friendly Alison Chalmers from Lenzie who has bought all my books and who's here this afternoon to watch her beloved Tigers win along with her daughter, Lauren. Though we've often been at the same major meetings, it's also the first time this season I've finally managed to

Last minute adjustments

Racing under dark skies

Tiger mascot poses for photos

Joy abounds

Vital St Andrews Ambulance staff end their duty

catch up with Kirkintilloch based Glasgow Tigers season ticket holder and knowledgeable long-time Tigers fan, Ian Maclean.

It would be safe to say that the result today is expected to be a foregone conclusion but local pride dictates that the Tigers fans fully savour the glory of the moment anyway. Chief cheerleader in this respect is Michael Max who welcomes the home team on parade with the words, "There are the guys who helped us to our first-ever league win at Armadale!" It's a theme he really warms to and I lost count of the mentions of this fact after I'd heard it at least five times during the introductions. The darkness of the cloud cover is such that clearly the races will have to be run quickly with one eye on the weather by referee Barbara Horley, someone who Michael describes as a "virgin". The first heat starts with a win for Derek Sneddon and results in an unexpected 5-1 for the Monarchs when Matty Wethers finishes second. Derek has his own 'special' relationship - that mixes pantomime and tribal hatred - with the crowd at Saracen Park, "Derek Sneddon is always keen to do well here!" In the programme I'm described as the "token Englishman" alone among the Scottish speedway public and Michael even invites me onto the centre green during the meeting for a brief interview to plug my books. Say what you will about any presenter, just talking into the microphone takes some getting used to particularly with the distraction of the fractionally delayed sound of your own voice booming through the stadium loudspeakers. I invariably get breathless and can't get anywhere near the effortless facility with words achieved by Michael. Clearly to do well as a presenter you have to like the sound of your own voice and have no anxiety about performing in front of crowds. The fans inside Saracen Park are welcoming and I receive a "warm Glasgow welcome" in the form of a round of applause.

On the track the Tigers, if judged by the consistency of their scoring, merit only applause from the crowd for the next nine heats. They overcome the initial points deficit to slowly but inexorably pull away from their local rivals with a team performance that sees every rider contribute. To be fair, James Cockle wins his first race in the second heat but, after that, the only real opposition effectively comes from the three-man Monarchs team of Derek Sneddon, Matthew Wethers and Kaj Laukkanen. Heat 8 features a very impressive ride from the man the crowd love to hate, Derek Sneddon, who survives a combative first corner where David McAllan batters Snazza's vigorous elbow with a mudguard to escape. Undeterred Snazza chases him determinedly and finally stalks past his rival on the back straight of the fourth lap. He celebrates his win with a clenched fist as he crosses the line and then proceeds round the circuit for a celebratory victory lap that involves said fist repeatedly on display in a constant pumping action. Snazza gets the predictable response from the Glasgow faithful and, I think we can say all parties enjoy their own participation in the celebrations. Sadly from an Edinburgh point of view, this sterling performance only produces a drawn heat that still leaves them somewhat adrift at 27-21. Michael Max decides to ignore the last win by, instead, striking a more cheerful note about the line up for the next heat, "here comes super Shane!"

It was always going to be a question of when, not if, the Monarchs use their tactical options though it takes until the end of the 10th heat before the deficit is sufficient for us all to get to see a black-and-white helmet colour. It's to be worn by Kaj Laukkanen though Michael Max isn't a fan of such fripperies. "One of the silly rules in the sport - but one we have to accept", he notes ruefully. At one time maximum points seem a possible outcome for the visitors when Snazza led from the gate but, sadly, he either falls asleep or misjudges the speed of his opponent Trent Leverington. Whatever his thinking or lack of it, Snazza slows on the second lap and finds himself going backwards down the race positions from first to third in the space of just a few yards, though thankfully for the Monarchs, Laukkanen wins. The Tigers fans express considerable disappointment that, after his third place, Snazza immediately retreats to the pits, "Come round Sneddon, come on - that's not very sporting." The affable Jim Henry notes, "He didn't do very well there" before he wanders away to the open spaces of the first-bend banking for yet another cigarette. Edinburgh speedway director Mike Hunter ambles past, "He thought about letting Kaj through too early - two laps too early - and let them through. Derek's riding with a lot of passion; he's not the most popular here! Think, if we had a proper team, we'd really be giving them a run for their money!"

Until this point in the meeting, it would be true to say that the Tigers had been comfortable though, perhaps, the anticipation of an easy victory had dulled their competitive edge. Instead they finish with four heat advantages to change the points deficit on the afternoon from a relatively close 5 points to a comprehensive 17 though, that said, the racing still provides some excitement (at least from a Glasgow perspective). With the result almost a foregone conclusion, Michael Max talks up the drama, "if you thought you'd seen the last of the Monarchs captain [Sneddon, D.] you haven't 'cause he's out in heat 13 for a rider replacement ride - he's been high entertainment value all afternoon!" It appears that Trent Leverington must have some sort of hex over Snazza since he again translates his earlier psychological advantage into yet more race points when he passes him on the fourth bend of the first lap to relegate his rival to last place. It's a circumstance the Glasgow fans verbally draw to his attention as they welcome him past the finish line with an almost beautifully choreographed sea of single finger salutes. They also loudly suggest that they definitely think another lap of commiseration would be the done thing.

Though the Monarchs roll the dice with a tactical substitute ride for Matty Wethers off 15 metres, the win for Glasgow is confirmed in the 14th heat when Robert Ksiezak takes the chequered flag. Michael Max is delighted with the synchronicity of it all, "for the second time in three days Robert Ksiezak gets the honour of crossing the line to ensure a Tigers victory!" Like Friday, the man of the match is their inspirational skipper Shane Parker who has taken 30 points out of a possible 30 over the two meetings, "you know what happens when you get a maximum - you go up in the air!" The bumps are duly administered and the Glasgow riders congregate on the centre green after their lap of honour for interviews, while, on the track under jet black skies, the Lakeside mascot Rhys Naylor (aged 13) has a couple of exhibition races (on 250cc machines) against Marc Owen (aged 12). Earlier Rhys had told me, "I was at Berwick last night for the [restaged] 40th [anniversary meeting] - my bike's going well but I'm not at the moment!" Judged by the couple of races we get to see at Saracen Park, the main difference between the two riders appears to be their noticeable difference in speed from the gate. Michael Max praises Marc Owen as having a "lovely style" after his first race win and, after his second, he's welcomed back with the observation "gating is so important". Though they may be the stars of the future, the home crowd only really have ears for the interviews and eyes for the Tigers riders. Touchingly, Shane still believes in the outside possibility of success in the league for the Tigers in their 2007 campaign, "we're climbing up the table to leave us with a chance of a top four finish but we need a couple of away victories!" Whatever the future holds, this evening the fans enthusiastically swarm round the riders as they make their way with their kitbags (via the gate by the start line) to the changing rooms deep inside the main grandstand. Typifying the closeness of the speedway community and the connection that exists between the stars of the shale and their fans - all the riders who pass by make a point of stopping to chat, pose for photographs or sign numerous autographs. Afterwards many of the fans, and some of the riders, carry on their celebrations in the bar.

19th August Glasgow v Edinburgh (Premier League) 55-38

Chapter 39. Isle of Wight v Mildenhall: Girl power nearly overwhelms Smallbrook

21st August

On my journey to the Portsmouth to Isle of Wight ferry, Clive Everton, the snooker sports journalist is on the radio to promote his autobiography. Something he says sounds wonderfully applicable to the ongoing decline of speedway from its recent heyday, "a sport only gets to go on honeymoon once!" Well, this isn't quite true for speedway since it has had bouts of mass popularity but the days of large crowds and regular media attention seem long gone. That said, on Wall Street the concept of a brief but illusory resurgence - known as a "dead cat bounce" (i.e. if you drop a dead cat from high enough it will always bounce) - often enjoyed by stocks in terminal decline has long been acknowledged as a last-gasp blip rather than as a signal of recovery. We'd all like to think that speedway has a long way to go before it reaches that desperate stage even though its demise has often been both forecast and lamented. How far we have fallen during these years of decline is signalled by the comparatively big, breaking news that the BBC will be at the speedway tonight on the Isle of Wight. Sadly this isn't the BBC Grandstand cameras but the latest leg of the local regional radio station - *BBC Radio Solent*. The broadcaster is on a countywide tour to promote the nationwide BBC RaW (Reading and Writing) campaign and the local station handles this particular regional event. This laudable initiative aims to develop the reading and writing skills of young people throughout the country by engaging them at various 'exciting' events (like speedway) - rather than the normal channel of school. The hope is that they might enjoy attending the speedway (or similar event) and this might obliquely and stealthily encourage them to view the acquisition of these basic but important reading and writing skills as somehow cool and essential to their lives.

As usual, the Wightlink Ticket Office lounge is a veritable Who's Who of Speedway as they come to visit the Imperial Royal court of 'The Daves' - Pavitt and Croucher. It seems I've missed the traditional pre-ferry crossing ice-lolly but the banter and the bustle with the riders, mechanics and helpers continues with nonchalant ease. Dave Pavitt is at the nerve centre of operations, something that is basically indicated by the fact that, as ever, he has his smart but slightly battered executive briefcase open (and mobile phone at the ready). It's the kind of briefcase that would control the codes to the nuclear trigger, if he were an important high-ranking official in the Ministry of Defence but, instead, it contains vital SCB paperwork and the like along with an impressive bundle of the ferry tickets for the various speedway people who have yet to arrive to make the crossing. Apparently, many of the Mildenhall team have already sailed on the earlier boat. Shortly, we'll all rush back off to our cars and vans to drive in single file onto the lower car deck of the roll-on roll-off ferry, where the bored staff will carefully cram all the vehicles together. Many people treat this journey with the studied boredom of a regular bus journey, but I'm always excited by this most exotic of speedway trips which requires that we all briefly take to the water. Dave Croucher has kindly volunteered to drive me to the stadium in one of his never-ending stream of executive motors that he fastidiously road tests from his car business. This afternoon he has his son Alex with him - a man who's clearly well used to Dave's company and affable story-telling - since he sits quietly in the car absorbed in his Sudoku puzzle book.

Before we board, like a younger Lear and an older, sex-changed Cordelia in *King Lear,* the Two Daves casually discuss various pertinent administrative details with the riders when they briefly pop into what Wightlink grandly calls the 'departure lounge'. If no riders are to hand, they generally just catch up on the latest comings and goings in the speedway world. This afternoon they're joined by Peter Thorogood who every season has a short sojourn on the Island - possibly staying in one of the on-site caravans (though I don't actually check this) - to give the track a bit of mid-season tender loving care and an essential general overhaul. He also contentedly lolls on the departure lounge chairs like the Daves do. Chris Holder pops in and is quizzed about his performance at the Berwick 40th anniversary meeting on Saturday. Having continued the rich vein of form he's been in all season (so far) at Shielfield Park and won every qualifying heat, he cheerfully tells us, "I farked the final!" Like so many things in life, confidence plays a key part in success according to Dave P, "unless they're winning the races they're not earning the money and investing and therefore winning more - success breeds success when they're winning!" The man who I think runs the spares van on race night for the Islanders, Max Richards of 'Pegasus Speed Needs', regales the assembled Islanders senior management and their esteemed guests with his impressions of the previous night's racing at Smallmead. "It's the best I've ever seen it at Redin' - no blue line, four riders abreast, lots of different racing lines - it's still Dougie doin' it but, last night, he had it RIGHT!"

While we continue to wait for stragglers, talk turns to the attendance of the BBC people and the plans in hand for the night. Basically, they'll have their own tent of books and leaflets on the grass banking that overlooks the first bend plus there will be a 'star' guest appearance by the Radio Solent presenter Charlie Crocker (a lady) who will meet and greet 'her public' in their stall-cum-tent. Unless they're devotees of the local station, most people will probably be mystified as to what the goodness is going on, never mind who on earth this famous lady actually is. The BBC liaison person and harassed organiser of this particular initiative at the speedway on the Island, Roger Hammett - who goes under the grand title Learning Project Manager, though he really comes from the Newsroom at BBC Radio Solent - pops by to collect the tickets for the BBC staff for their ferry crossing. Dave Croucher and he have been in regular touch and it's revealing to watch Dave ooze charm, bonhomie and display nonchalant but careful attention to detail. Once Roger has rushed back out to the car park to ensure he doesn't miss the sailing (while the experienced Islanders crew sit calmly inside knowing there's still longer to wait before they amble out to their vehicles), Dave says, "I misread the email thinking we were getting Richard Hammond [the high speed crash bloke from *Top Gear*] otherwise he wouldn't have got so much as a cheese sandwich!"

Australian Cory Gathercole arrives at the last minute and genuinely seems to have the laid back almost catatonic manner that cliché would insist is the default attitudinal setting for those from Down Under. Cory regales his attentive audience with a brief update on his recent racing activity and comes out with the immortal line, "I went from the penthouse to the shithouse in one race". He's clearly a fund of such memorable one-liners as earlier Dave C had said, "I've got a title for your next book - something Cory said last week] after he'd had a big crash at Glasgow, and I asked him if he was OK to take part in the re-run [affects an Australian accent]: 'Yeah, no worries, I've had me concrete for breakfast, Crouch!' He's a lovely kid and so laid back it's untrue, even by Aussie standards!" Dave Croucher retrieves a piece of paper and ostentatiously hands it Cory who glances at it but mostly nods while he's given some last-minute instructions. "I don't want anyone doing anything silly tonight 'cause we've only got 8 or 9 points to make and that should be no trouble. Tonight's not crucial but the weekend is and the next meetings are critical - Friday at King's Lynn and Monday at Rye House - so nothing silly tonight!" After he's enthusiastically nodded his agreement throughout, Cory is about to scoot off again and leave Dave to wave his pre-printed information sheets and ponder the meaning of life, "I dunno why I bother to print these up - you just screw them up and put them in your pocket. When he rode here, Steen Jensen said to me in August 'do you have Boycie's number?' and I said it's been on the piece of paper I've given you every week since April, you obviously haven't read it! Anyway, Cory, you want to get a few more curries down you - it'll make you quicker."

We're soon out to the vehicles to queue to board and I squeeze my wheelie case of books into the boot of the Jaguar Dave Croucher has brought along this week. Inside the boot is a box full of plastic-wrapped silver trophies (well they're more like goblets) and a set of Islanders race tabards. While there is an unexpected delay to board, I quiz Crouch on some of his other

Boot full of trophies and tabards

Big queue big enough to love

business activities, most notably the revolutionary mud that he has invested in with an eye - should it be successful - to the creation of a healthy pension nest egg for his retirement. The level of his investment already would mean that he could have paid the Hans Anderson transfer fee twice over. "The mud has now been called two things, but I have always referred to it as simply 'the Mud'. As the product has developed, we have moved along with the companies who have taken the process forward, and we are now effectively selling *Mud MkV.* [They say, where there's mud there's brass] The company who owned the worldwide rights to *Mud Mkl*, and had all the patent agreements in place, had none of the marketing strategies or rights to improvement. The chap who originally invented it has gone to another company to develop an advanced product based on it but me, and another investor, through our company now own the rights to sell it worldwide. Basically the magic mud retains water and propagates growth. Say a tomato plant took ten weeks to grow ten tomatoes then, with the mud, it will now take seven weeks to grow 14 tomatoes. There's a top-secret fluid - I will have to throw you from the car if I tell you about it - that goes into the mud that gives it incredible retentive properties. With this mud, things will grow in salinated and toxic land, in bad areas where the land isn't usually suitable for farming (not just West Africa). It reverses desertification so, with assistance from the World Health Organisation and the World Bank, countries that don't have enough food will be able to grow it for themselves! It's made up of seven types of volcanic rock and 'cause it boosts growth and retains fluid, you'll also need to use less fertilisers 'cause of the nutrients it has. They've already built a golf course in Saudi Arabia with it; well it's only a green and half a fairway - about 100 yards of it. But the commercial applications are endless: golf courses, racecourses, anywhere they need grass really. Some greyhound tracks are interested and a number of polo clubs. For example, they have big problems with water at the polo ground at Cowdray Park in Sussex. They take 140,000 gallons out of the river there twice a week during the summer and three times in a dry summer. They have Moses Rights but that won't continue long term as the government won't allow it if everyone else has a hosepipe ban and can't even wash their car. It would even work at speedway - if you mix the mud in with the shale, you'll retain the moisture in rather than have it disappear over the fence and go home on everyone's car as it does at present! The retentive properties, the fact you can take it anywhere, along with the way it exponentially propagates growth, is really exciting and many people are going to be interested in the commercial applications!" That said Crouch doesn't exactly warm to my suggestion that cocaine and cannabis farmers immediately come to my mind as the most needy, readymade and lucrative markets with endless demand for the commercial benefits that the application of such a wonder product could provide! His business plan focuses exclusively on more traditional commercial opportunities for *Mud MkV*, "once we get the final details sorted."

On the ferry journey across to the Island I'm privileged to sit at the same table as the Two Daves (Pavitt and Croucher) and Pete Thorogood. They have well over a century of speedway experience between them and so, to sit there, is a bit like the speedway equivalent of being invited to the top table at Oxford, albeit we only have coffees and doughnuts rather than vintage wine, port and *haute cuisine*. The conversation ranges widely in a low-key affable fashion that indicates everyone is extremely comfortable in themselves and with each other's company. Crouch explains to me, "There's just as big a gulf from the CL to the PL as there is from the PL to the EL - Tom Brown got 14 at Rye House in the CL but only got 1 in the PL - not through lack of effort I hasten to add!" They casually discuss recent events and riders they've seen, Pav thinks, "Jay Herne - he doesn't want to be a speedway rider, he just wants an excuse to be here." Crouch moves onto Eric Boocock who has returned to the sport as Belle Vue manager, "It's like a rider getting back on a bike [after injury] and finding he's not good enough." I've noticed before that they unconsciously bicker like a long-married couple, oblivious to others around them. Naturally, Pav doesn't agree about Eric Boocock, "That's not fair, he can't help the side he has!" Crouch clarifies, "Nah, fair enough, that's not what I meant." Talk moves on to Workington and Pav mentions to Pete, "Ian Thomas asked us if we'd go easy on them when we were there - course we didn't, we got as many as we could!"

One political hot potato in speedway circles nowadays is the poor relationship that exists between the Polish and British speedway authorities. Co-operation appears to have collapsed at the same time as the vast majority of 'foreign' riders have generally downgraded the importance they attach to racing in this country. Consequently, many have become increasingly selective about when they 'choose' to ride here. Symptomatic of this situation, this season there has been an epidemic of no-shows in the Elite League for often barely credible reasons. Pete Thorogood highlights the huge demands of all the other alternative sources of employment (or distraction): the Grand Prix series; the race nights of the other major leagues (Poland on a Sunday and Sweden on a Tuesday) and the emergence of Russia, not to mention other intermittent complications like the World Team Cup, the GP qualification rounds and the Under-21 World Championship. All in all, this adds up to a nightmare and totally demanding schedule for any capable rider, let alone the really gifted ones. Something is bound to give! In the present case, loyalty to the demands of the British speedway season is non-existent among some riders. Pav bemoans the latest development in the Premier League, "It's starting to happen in the PL now - Zorro is missing some Somerset meetings to go to Sweden for some cup final or other [and ride in Poland]. He ain't gonna be popular among the fans for shitting on his team! We're third behind Sweden and Poland now." Pete nods his agreement, "I was at Arena recently and asked where their Pole [Kasprzak] was and they said 'He's at a victory parade for winning the World Team Cup' - what the fark's that about?" Plans are in hand during the winter for the rules that apply to this situation to change, "Next year it'll be a month ban - that'll mean that any promoter that's gonna sign a dodgy rider - who you know will mess you about and be unreliable - will know the consequences when the season starts!"

Pav has been so long in the promotional game that he's become inured from any residual excitement that crowd-pulling initiatives might create among the less battle-hardened. Consequently, he's not holding his breath about the impact of the arrival of the local BBC Radio station and their tent in his stadium to promote the RaW campaign. At the height of the holiday season, crowds are big throughout the Island so, like many other seasonal businesses, the speedway club feels the benefit of the increased passing trade. In reality, the benefit is likely to fall to the BBC (rather than the speedway club) since a far greater number and variety of people will now be exposed to the various uplifting messages contained within the red RaW tent or their free promotional materials than otherwise might be the case on an average race night.

With its unique ownership structure (I can't say that I've ever seen the Two Daves as proto-Marxists or Communists but it's definitely more 'for the people by the people' than free-market capitalism on the Island), the speedway club operates on a shoestring basis and depends for its financial health and long-term survival on some big events that aren't speedway related. Pav proudly tells me, "We get loads of Mods on scooters driving over for the Scooter Rally, it's heaving - the bar takes £25 grand and it serves them breakfast and everything, there's never any trouble neither!" Speedway initiatives that he's been involved with haven't always been similarly successful, "when I was at Hackney we did 40,000 free leaflets all round the place - campsites, pubs, shops, everything - with loudspeakers going about. Not only that, you got a free burger and hot dog. Brent Walker brought in a thousand extra hot dogs but only 10 were redeemed!" Everyone round the table nods agreement and they nod even more at the statement that the time involved in staging any normal, run-of-the-mill speedway meeting is fixed, " there's no more extra work goes into staging a meeting for 200 or 2000!"

Large crowd with BBC RaW tent in the distance

The weather in Portsmouth usually bears no relation to the climatic conditions you can expect on the Island. Sniffing the air like a seasoned sailor (though we're inside near the coffee bar) and glancing upwards at the slightly overcast sky as the ferry pulls into port to dock, Pav contentedly notes, "at least they won't be on the beaches - it's too cold - they'll be queuing up to get into our place!" With the world a slightly better place, I get back into the deluxe Crouchmobile for the journey to the stadium. I gather from Alex that he sometimes accompanies his dad on the road trips to some away meetings at places like Redcar. The team spirit is excellent among the riders, mechanics, fans and staff with emphasis put upon professionalism at the track and enjoyment off it. A revelation this year - and one of the secrets of the club's success - has been the inspirational form on the track of Jason Bunyan and off it in his role as team captain. Jason's mechanic and girlfriend New Zealander Rose Halfpenny is also honorarily one of the lads and seen as an influential factor behind his success. I gather that they live the dream at the track together and that Jason works as her mechanic when she pursues her passion for driving stock cars in New Zealand during our winter months. Something she does well by all accounts, despite her youth (21, five days previously), "She said to me recently, 'Crouch, I'm not really the ladies New Zealand stock car champion like you keep saying' - I knew that, she didn't start out as a stock car driver: she just went to the shop!" In fact Rose has an illustrious stock car racing career - she was third in the NZ Champs Grand Slam in 2005, second overall in Feature in 2006 and in 2007 qualified for the North Island Stockcar Champs prior to her sojourn in British speedway with Jason.

The talk in the pits concerns the rather racy dating website that Shaun Tacey has recently sprung on an unsuspecting world via the web. The chance for lonely hearts to potentially get together because of a shared mutual interest in speedway is obviously one factor, while the opportunity to meet or look at some lascivious girls is another. Shaun asks me about what I think of things, "Didn't you see it? There's a girl from Eastbourne posing in knee-length boots and black knickers that didn't go down very well 'cause you could see everything, really." Inspired by the attention and the website, apparently some girls will be coming along tonight all dolled up to have a photo shoot inside the speedway stadium. This has the blessing and approval of the riders, at least in the Mildenhall area of the pits where I am, but has blood pressure rising elsewhere among the Islanders' management staff for entirely different reasons. Luckily, there are no girls around at present so the topic of conversation can turn to other topics close to the heart of any rider - rates of pay. Kyle Legault regales Shaun with tales of his own unique negotiating tactics on the phone with Graham Drury during the winter when the chance to ride at Birmingham had presented itself. Shaun is mystified at the reported offer since in 2005 he used to ride for Graham at Workington and found him to be a careful but fair-minded man in negotiations. "I got £50 a point, double petrol money - it was a really long way there from where I live - and free tyres. Given they're at least £28 plus VAT each that adds up to £1500 during a season". That said, he does know that Paul Fry took umbrage when he discovered that he'd been offered a lower rate of pay to guest for the Brummies than someone else who had earlier been unable to take the suggested booking. Discussions continue among the riders - as they prepare their equipment for the racing ahead - about the foibles and negotiating tactics of various other promoters and it would be safe to say that it's a complicated, varied and mysterious world.

Elsewhere in the stadium modern sexual politics and the supposed contemporary empowerment of young women in the Noughties isn't so warmly welcomed. Bryn Williams smokes one of his many cigarettes of the night outside the officials' box that overlooks the start line, "They caused a bit of a stir when they posed at Mildenhall 'cause they were topless - on the forums they went mental 'cause of the families and young children present!" Sadly I learn no more because a holidaying Mike Bennett has shown up for some much-needed *ad hoc* training, "I thought I'd come and see a professional at work!" As I walk back round towards the entrance gates, I pass the young women in question - three of them with a minder. Subtlety doesn't appear to be a strong suit collectively and their *décolletage* is eye catching. However, in my opinion, the trainee-porn-star-meets-lady-boy look they sport isn't likely to catch on that widely on the Isle of Wight. Over by the trackshop, Dave Pavitt is weighed down with the responsibility of the situation and is in a lather that he solves by electing Alex Croucher for the job everyone wants but doesn't ask for, "You go and watch them and make sure they don't do anything silly!" It's a question of image and, given the huge queue of holidaymakers and fans that stretch away into the distance all the way to the main road, common sense suggests that (even more than usual) such things will be important to get right tonight. With no disrespect to the visitors or the club, clearly the crowds are drawn to this speedway meeting by the mere fact it's on! While they are on holiday and look for things to do and ways to distract/entertain the kids, this definitely fits the bill and isn't killingly expensive. I'm stood in a prime position with my books but the numbers of purchasers are small, though the questions about where to go, whether to get a programme or, once purchased, how to understand the scores, fill them out and generally understand the mechanics of the racing are numerous. Dave Pavitt acts like a dog with two tails, as he gleefully clasps his hands together while he wanders up and down proprietarily alongside the fence inspecting the volume of fans waiting to enter the stadium. "We haven't had 500 paying adults all season!" he chortles as he heads back towards the stairs that lead to the speedway office and bar area.

BBC Radio Solent have been well advised by Crouch and, since the weather has been kind, they've picked a great evening to attend the speedway to showcase their campaign in a small red tent-cum-gazebo on the grass banking of the first bend. When I pop in to find out more, the staff were distracted setting out onto tables what appears to be the well-used and slightly battered library books they'd borrowed from the Isle of Wight Library Service for the night. They say you can always quickly tell when strangers are in your midst and rather effortlessly the staff have that awkward air of people who've vaguely heard about speedway (probably about the noise and the dirt) but are not quite sure what to expect of the event or the allegedly working-class fans, never mind quite how to best comport themselves among the natives to appear relaxed. No one has an unduly posh accent but, nonetheless, a hint of middle-class propriety and complacency exudes. Still, we all like something for free and those parents who are prepared to publicly admit that their children might struggle to read and write or might not have progressed at the speed of their contemporaries, can get a free spiral-bound book. On the blue cover a brightly coloured tent motif shouts *Max and Lara's Amazing Travelling Space Circus: A family guide to developing better reading and writing skills*. From my time in publishing I'm familiar with the gentle pedagogic style of presentation taken by many schoolbooks. Such books seek to excite and interest the young reader and the material contained in this book very much comes from that tradition. Inside the pages of the *Space Circus* book, the curious young reader is invited to "look at the pictures, read the story headings, read the story in full or do the activities". Plus, a couple of pages of stickers at the rear should encourage some interactivity from even the most reticent user. It's a laudable campaign and, even if the circus theme is wildly misplaced tonight, the leaflets that advertise the Writing Competition sensibly have as their focus some questions actually related to the speedway. There are three prizes to be won and one of them is my photograph book *Shale Britannia*. As well as the chance to leave their name and telephone number, in order to enter, the young person has to submit a short piece of writing based on their answer to the following questions, "choose one of the following and tells us what makes it special for you: (1) My favourite rider; (2) What I like best about this track; (3) The best race today; (4) My favourite motorcycle."

Closeby to the stall I bump into speedway's most popular referee - Tony Steele - a man of intelligence and great modesty. Either internecine politics or bungling by the F.I.M. over referee selection for the 2007 Speedway Grand Prix series has ensured that the overall standard this year has suffered as a result of his absence. He's too polite to talk about it. Like all referees, Tony knows before every meeting he officiates at that the job is basically performance driven as at every meeting you're judged anew and, "You're really only as good as your last meeting!" One question that tonight could be added to the list is 'Do I want my daughter to go to the speedway heavily made up and in her underwear?' I meet with Wendy Jedrzejakski, the reigning 'Miss Long Eaton', who's been savouring the heightened, somewhat enervated atmosphere that applies to the Mildenhall area of the pits this evening at Smallbrook Stadium. "Tomas Suchanek's girlfriend has been asked to leave the pits, while those girls are lying all round the place! She said to me 'Often his dad doesn't take me to meetings so Tomas can concentrate but, tonight, what about their concentration?' She has a point. They didn't go topless or anything but the way she bent over the bike left nothing to the imagination! Another one took off her knickers and put another pair on - nothing wrong with that - it was just the way she did it, you could see everything!" The never-ending queue outside the stadium is still there and might even be longer, should news of the seductive wiles of the knicker-changing girls in the pits become common knowledge. The exceptionally long queue is definitely not an optical illusion and even the programmes have sold out. I reckon it's news of the handsome advert placed by Mick Cave to promote his 'Grab & Tip of Burgess Hill' services that have caught the collective imagination of the holidaymakers. Their desire to purchase a programme momentarily increases interest in my wares until they discover I'm only selling boring books on speedway. Rather than stand around not selling anything, I decide it would be important in the interest of research if I abandon my sales efforts to check on the sterling job Alex Croucher is probably doing to keep a watchful eye on things round by the pits area.

He's nowhere to be seen but then neither are the girls. Perhaps he has abducted them? I ask a man who'll know - Shaun Tacey - but he professes to have no idea. Then again it is only a few minutes until he has to work "I haven't gone well here for four or five years - I rode here when they opened in 1997 and rode well here for a few years afterwards." Sadly for Shaun his recent form was to continue. If the meeting was expected to be a close contest that idea was soon dispelled by the comfortable maximum heat advantages that the Islanders gained in the first two heats. The second race also showcased the start of a night of torment at Smallbrook for Mildenhall guest Jay Herne who fell and was excluded from the re-run. Arguably this was as good as it got for him since he followed this with a last place and two retirements in his allotted four rides. However, he did gain valuable Premier League experience that will stand him in good stead when he rides for Weymouth in the Conference League. Paul Fry provided some vim for the Tigers when he won the third race of the night, thereby giving Bryn Williams the chance to delight the bumper crowd with one of his well-worn standard phrases: "42 years young still going strong - he seems to mature with age!" News that there is some illegal photography going on in the stadium then enables him to counsel the hordes within the stadium about the perils and problems caused by "flashers".

A contented and beaming Dave Pavitt has stopped to watch the racing on the fourth bend by the perimeter of the pits fence where he can join Albert and Eileen Shepherd, who occupy their traditional, favoured spot in the stadium. Dave is already in mid-coffee ("the best on the Island is from Albert!" he invariably tells me whenever I catch him in mid-cuppa) and happily chats away about future prospects for the sport. "If we got promoted as champions we'd have to get some serious sponsorship onboard or win the Lottery. What a lovely thought though, eh!" Rather than hypothesise, Pav is happy to continue to luxuriate in the delight of tonight's extremely healthy attendance, "I love queues - I take photos of queues - and now you've told me we've sold out of programmes that's the second best news of the night I've had. I'm so happy I'm gonna go and talk to someone!" Albert and Eileen have lived on the Island since 1975 when they moved here from Coventry. It's a significant year for them as they recently celebrated 55 years of marriage ("it's an emerald anniversary") with a "party for 25 people in our favourite restaurant - Mojac's in Cowes, it's lovely [and known on its own website as "Mojac's A La Carte Restaurant"] - where they have an ex-chef from the QE2!" The lure of the coffee is irresistible and it's not long before we're joined by Dave Croucher who's also keen to sample Albert's highly sought after dark brew. Unlike everyone else - who has, apparently, been outraged by the sight of scantily clad girls with an interest in speedway (or speedway riders) - the sight of Shaun Tacey on the track has shocked Albert. "I can't believe it's him - he's a shadow of himself - he used to go so well round here, like a train! He was the best until Shieldsy came along!" Crouch is keener to talk about the girls, "The difference in start-line girls is amazing. Some places we go, the riders want to take them home, and at other tracks, they try and run them over. They had a Miss Mildenhall contest with this lot in it and they all came second. Nobody won!" This somehow prompts Albert to tell the most disgusting joke of the season (in front of his wife Eileen), "What do you call the bit of fat round a clitoris? A Woman."

Before Albert really gets going, I head back round to the grandstand to set out my books on my wheelie bag in the hope of sales that don't come. There isn't too much to write home about with regard to the racing but, as I rush back from the toilets to watch the start of heat 11, my eyes are drawn to the frequent flicker of flash photography as the bikini clad girls take advantage of the distraction provided by the racing to theatrically gurn and grind away together in faux Sapphic pleasure on the bonnet of a yellow mini! As it turns out, they're missing the race of the night as Tom Brown excitingly fights his way through the field from fourth to an eventual second place to ecstatic cheers from the crowd. As we're well past the height of the summer, the evenings have started to draw in and the light inside the referee's box reveals all its occupants. You'd expect to see announcer Bryn Williams, incident recorder Chris Golding and referee Tony Steele on duty in the box but they're also joined by Paul Fry. They all enjoy a laugh and a joke together.

Just as the interval gets underway Bryn has his obligatory fag on the steps of the terraces just outside the box - so far so addicted, though tonight he has woman trouble all of his own to contend with. In this case not of the salacious young strumpet variety but in the imposing form of *BBC Radio Solent* star presenter Charlie Crocker. She's a well-kept and smartly dressed woman of a certain age who looks and sounds supremely well suited to radio work. Her dress sense indicates that she thought a speedway meeting might have something in common with a film première. Though Bryn manfully tries to conduct his interview with his customary wit, professionalism and insouciance, nonetheless he still betrays some unexpected nerves when thrust into close proximity to Charlie within the intimate confines of the referee's box where he haltingly conducts his interview. Charlie has a luxuriant come-hither voice that playfully caresses your ears in a manner I imagine would work better on premium rate phone lines than it already apparently does on local radio in the Solent area. Bryn decides to quiz Charlie on her first impressions of speedway since she's never previously had the honour. Her statement "I've been in leather all weekend!' causes Bryn's capacity for quick-fire questions to temporarily go on the fritz. Ever the professional Charlie fills the pregnant silence, "I think I'll have to lose some more weight as I won't be able to get my leg out that far - can I?" With his mind in mental discombobulation as he conjures with the image of a leather-clad Charlie stretching her legs wide (or even akimbo), ever-gallant Bryn murmurs, "Er ..." pauses for what seems like an eternity and blurts out the best immediate answer that springs to mind, "I dunno!" From this distance I'm unable to see if she's gap-toothed but judged by how Charlie is consumed by the incongruity of Bryn's shy response at that moment, her laughter sounds Chaucerian in its spontaneous raucousness. It's also gleeful in a way that all at once somehow manages to combine wholehearted and sensual. The whole stadium echoes with her amusement over the loudspeakers "Ha! Ha! Ha!"

21st August Isle of Wight v Mildenhall (Premier League) 60-33

Chapter 40. Sheffield: A night to remember

23rd August

There are some days when your faith in the kindness of humanity is refreshed through the cumulative effect of a myriad of individual gestures. One such day dawned sunny in Sheffield as the weather gods looked down favourably on the city for the major event of the 2007 speedway calendar - the Garry Stead Benefit Grand Prix. Forget your over-hyped invariably processional Cardiff Grand Prix, the manufactured saccharine excitement of the so-called 'cliff hangers' of the various play-offs or even the random meetings you saw that thrilled you - this night in Sheffield, when the speedway family got together to try to look after and pay tribute to one of its own, stood out above all of them in 2007. The talk in the weeks and months beforehand among the fans, riders and volunteers built up the anticipation along with the articles in the press as well as the various collections and the sale of the fund-raising wristbands at practically every club in the country you went to. All this preparation and anticipation still didn't prepare me for the atmosphere on the night. Sure we often read from cheerleaders with vested interests about what a brilliant meeting - usually a Grand Prix it has to be said - that we just missed going to actually was. Often the reality of the experience is as predictably dull as ditchwater. Never mind that the default setting on the *Sky Sports* television coverage requires all and sundry among the presenters to see the King as fully clothed and to relentlessly exaggerate the thrill of the spectacle, irrespective of the sometimes execrable quality of the product on display. But then, though the racing served up tonight was absorbing, it was only really so because of the chance to take part in a tribute to the injured Garry Stead rather than for the fine detail of the final results.

When James Blunt sings about 1973 - vaguely evocative though some of the sentiments are in the song (and video) - you know that it's just part of some marketing person's version of false-memory syndrome. Many people of a certain age (including myself) in the speedway community have fetishised the 1970s (or earlier) as an era when men were men, speedway riders were speedway riders and the racing was always closely contested and consistently thrilling on deep shale tracks without the namby-pamby accoutrements of dirt deflectors, lay downs, double-point tactical rides, yellow helmet colours, abandonments for soggy conditions or kevlars (to pick some *bête noires* at random). Even more importantly, crowds were bigger and, at least in recollection, the atmosphere always top notch. That's mostly the air-brushed version of how I remember it anyway, even allowing for the romanticism and nostalgia for a simpler, less complicated time in our lives compared to the modern stresses and strains of living in the Noughties. Watching what speedway has now become in the twenty-first century is still addictive but harder to square with what it once was. Nowadays it's a minority sport served up in often decaying and poorly equipped stadia (part of its real appeal in my opinion but that's another story), thereby resolutely setting its face against the contemporary demands of commodification and the ersatz comfort of the 24/7 mass-market culture with a strong element of a chip on our collective shoulders about how the world has passed us by, in the pursuit of glitzier and transient consolations. However, tonight in Sheffield, something special has been spontaneously recreated (albeit with a lot of careful planning and hard work behind the scenes to ensure it was just so) and with it there is a querulous feeling that we have all somehow stepped back in time for a brief few hours into the 1970s.

Not wishing to slop the whitewash around with the gay abandon I chastise others for when they do it in print and on the telly, the general mood and atmosphere really was one of celebration - tinged with sadness - as a British community came together to pay tribute to one of the nice guys that make the speedway community what it is! It's a broad church and many of the varied representatives from its eclectic congregation have turned out on a weekday night in South Yorkshire to join in celebration with one of the temporarily fallen. One who, in characteristic fashion (of himself and speedway), has already set out on the long road to pick himself up and put his life back together, albeit within the context of dramatically changed circumstances. Indeed there's an earnestness and gaiety to the large crowd that you don't get to feel any longer at speedway. It's not just the volume of people or an attitude I'm projecting on them, but a genuine sense of belonging mixed with a common humanity and sense of subdued outrage at how the quirks and foibles of our lives can often change things so cruelly in a split second. We all share this fragility yet so few - the bloke next door, our sons and brothers, somebody's actual son or brother - test out that essential risk on a daily basis in their work. It's a living which, when you come down to it, exists to entertain others by endlessly racing round in circles on high-powered machines without brakes in the full knowledge that at all times a clear and present danger hangs over their competitiveness or talent. We all know the riders choose to take part in this paid pastime and that the risks they take is part of that decision. Whether or not they factor it in every time they arrive at the stadiums and tapes, let alone explicitly consider all its ramifications, implications and practical details is another matter. It's also part of the pact and unspoken contract that the supporters share when they watch the spectacle of these handlebar heroes on a weekly or occasional basis. Well, that's the way it feels to me and also a great many other people, if judged by the size and attitude of the turnout at Owlerton.

After the endless stream of fans have made their way through the turnstiles, many then dawdle by the programme stall where a framed copy of the original artwork for the truly unique looking programme cover rests casually against a yellow litter bin. It's been designed by the wonderfully named Elvis Jones and signed by every rider who took part in the 2007 Cardiff Grand Prix. On the basis of the image alone it would be a sought-after collectible and the interest it creates is considerable, though eventually it will be auctioned on eBay. Tonight there are no specific details about the whys and wherefores of the sale other than the minimum expected price of £1000. By the steps that lead upstairs to the grandstand bar (technically known, because of the quality of the views it provides across the track and stadium, as the Panorama Room), Joan English, the mother of Newcastle co-promoter George, uses her well-developed skills of persuasion ("there's only limited numbers") to get people to purchase in advance the wristbands they will need to gain access to the post-meeting entertainment. This post-meeting bash will continue the retro atmosphere of the overall event since the band - billed beforehand to be that of World Superbike champion James Toseland and friends - are almost themselves a blast from the past and come squarely from the cock rock, heavy metal genre that dominated the 1970s. This era of music always typifies the sounds and songs that make up my recollections of the traditional soundtrack of my speedway youth, never mind the badge-festooned garments, long hair, tattoos, leather jackets, Doc Martens and jeans that were apparently also always *de rigueur* at any speedway track of that time.[1]

So many people have willingly given their free time to the organisation of this event it would be invidious for someone like me who knows so little about it to single out anyone for mention or praise. One thing I do know is that the commitment has been absolute and unstinting from everyone. The people I have spoken with most about it have been the indefatigable Julie Reading and Stephanie Babb whom I've seen at tracks everywhere throughout the country. They have clocked up a huge number of miles spreading the message, selling the wristbands as well as morally supporting other fund raising activities elsewhere. They have a

[1] in fact, sadly, James Toseland was unavailable on the night. Afterwards Dave Hoggart explained the situation to me. "James Toseland was originally free that week but the Formula 1 guys ripped up the track at Magnys-Cours and the whole racing circuit had to be resurfaced. This created a massive safety risk to the other motor sports so the Superbike organisers organised a week of testing for all of the race teams so that they could assess bike set-ups, tyre compounds and so on. James still hoped to fly back for the Thursday meeting but his team would not hold up testing for 24 hours and we got the call a few days beforehand. The band (Shrine of the Monkey) who played had planned to back him anyway and they were local musicians put together by Kevin Lee, one of our brilliant fans. Kev played the drums."]

Poster for auction

Garry with fans

Graham Beck with his badges

justifiably deserved reputation for superbly organising rider-testimonial events - no mean logistical feat in itself - while retaining a warmth and friendliness when the rational reaction would be to lose your sense of humour. Sheffield co-promoter Dave Hoggart is also someone I've regularly heard from concerning this event and, though an understated but knowledgeably intelligent man who likes to hide his sensitivity and perceptiveness behind his slightly cynical wit, he appears to have channelled his deep upset about the accident to his friend Garry into a passionate commitment to ensure that everything to do with the night goes off magnificently. Until now my favourite all-time programme was the Stoney testimonial one but Dave has achieved what he set out to do with the souvenir programme for this event - to produce something really special! It's a document to treasure from a production values point of view but also it does something else significant in that it simultaneously celebrates Garry and his achievements, and demonstrates the love and high regard he's held in by so many diverse speedway people while still telling a difficult human story without being mawkish (while also remaining positive and upbeat about the future).

With so many demons to face that I can't really possibly imagine, Garry is by all accounts determined and positive. Though it's his big night it would be understandable and only human nature if the idea of attending his own Benefit meeting would be a step too far so soon after the accident. I understand that he was offered the option to cry off or cut things short if it all got too much for him at any point during the evening. You would never guess that such an anxiety had ever been discussed if judged by the modest, wry way he held himself when he appeared amongst the fans 60 minutes or so prior to the scheduled time for the tapes to rise. In fact, such was the electrifying buzz of delight and warmth in the crowd, I gathered he must be close before I actually saw him lost in a throng of people offering kind words, handshakes and capturing the moment for posterity on their camera phones or digital cameras. Like some other speedway riders, he has an easy, natural connection with the fans. He was happy to pose patiently with anyone who wanted their photograph taken with him. Great with the children and capable with the star struck, he was modest and unassuming but somehow slightly shucksy about being the centre of attention. He's surrounded by friendly faces and his friends - David, Julie and Stephanie (along with Neil Machin in a bright white perfectly pressed shirt prominently emblazoned with the Sheffield Window Centre logo of the Tiger's 2007 team sponsors) among others I don't know or recognise so can't acknowledge [sorry] - hover close by while the metaphorical waves of compassion bathe the area as strongly as the bright evening sunshine. What anyone might give to turn the clock back but, instead, the harsh reality is that Garry is where he finds himself and, despite his own intellectual and emotional struggles, he plays his part to the full to ensure that the show goes on and the warmth of the feelings expressed are properly acknowledged. As a child it's a mystery what it really means to be grown up or act like a grown up, maybe this equanimity and fortitude in the face of adversity when life has dealt you a cruel hand is part of that calculus?

A pretty high quality field of riders have willingly given their time to this event for nothing. They say it was oversubscribed because Garry is so popular among his colleagues. The mechanics, numerous other speedway people and all the many volunteers that oil the wheels of any speedway night at Owlerton Stadium in Sheffield (just like they do on race night at any track around the country) during the season all give their services for free too. The crowd is here in numbers because they want to be part of the loose grouping that we can, perhaps, call a speedway 'family'. As well as, obviously, enjoy the spectacle and play their own small part in a unique speedway event that really should be seen as a celebration of a career rather than the commiseration of its enforced and sudden end.

Invariably life goes on and stood at my stall I can overhear the chatter as people bustle by or offer their thoughts on the latest speedway intrigues. Hard-working and friendly Scunthorpe press officer, Richard Hollingsworth, stops by for a few words. I don't catch where exactly he's talking about but he tells me earnestly, "they didn't make much of a thing about Tai being within a tenth of a second off the track record!" I agree they really should have but we've hardly said a few words before a couple of know-all speedway types wearing the rare but apposite T-shirts that signal their long time allegiance to the speedway cause stop to loudly tell Richard what's what. I gather they must go along to Hull and realise they belong to that select cadre of *über*-fans of the shale who know everything about everything. They hold forth on a variety of matters, particularly a paunchy bloke who says, with an earnestly straight face as though he's privileged enough to be bringing the tablets down the mountain to us for the first time: "Agreements count for nothing in speedway!" Blimey - hold the front page! I reel from the shock that promoters (and riders) might not be as honest as the day is long, let alone the suggestion that rules can be bent and results gerrymandered! Apparently, if he were Tai Woffinden (or his family and advisors) he'd metaphorically kick that spritely 76-year-old Len Silver in the knackers and immediately tear up his contract to ride for Rye House in the Premier League to stay with Scunny in 2008 when they make the step upwards. "He owes Len Silver nothing - what's he gonna do? Think about it, what can he do?" Given Len has forgotten more than most people know about speedway, let alone that once your word counts for nothing it stays devalued a long time, I'd suggest probably Tai wouldn't want to really find out what either Len or Hazel Silver might decide to do. Standing there completely blocking my stall from prying eyes for nearly 30 lengthy minutes, these revelations *apropos* of nothing just keep coming from Mister Paunch - the Pope is Catholic apparently, bears treat wooded areas with contempt [2] and "they don't have to pay VAT as it's a testimonial - it's all part of their thinking!" At least someone is thinking. I'm not quite sure who this "they" is or even what the issue has to do with the price of eggs or this Benefit Grand Prix as I can't imagine anyone is charging for their services, let alone levying VAT. Thankfully all things eventually pass and, even though I couldn't escape sharpish like Richard sensibly did, the *über*-fans finally wander away to pastures where their authority will be appreciated much more than I could. I marvel at Richard's cheerfulness if he has to put up with such nonsense every week. Later he lets me into the secret of his diplomacy: "it's either nod politely or have a blazing row!"

With the stadium closer to bursting at the seams than it has been for some time, the rider parade displayed an impressive roster of talent who're all keen to ride for Garry. Though here to put on a show, the raw emotion of the reason for the meeting came to the surface when a humble Garry thanked everyone for coming particularly when, with his voice breaking, he sincerely thanked the St John Ambulance team - the men "who saved his life" at Somerset. There's a surprise presentation of a signed photo and Garry even gets to meet the medical people who helped him that night. It's a poignant moment on a night where the emphasis can't help but occasionally stray away from celebration to tearful contemplation since life and fitness are fragile things that can be lost or taken away forever in seconds.

The racing is keenly contested and thrilling as the assembled riders put on a sterling show for the crowd who collectively seem determined to enjoy themselves. Initially it's a bit of a stop-start affair. Dave Hoggart tells us, "he said he'd never ride again but Moggo [Alan Mogridge] has decided to make a comeback for Garry's meeting!" In his case, this is in the 'veterans' race that also features Sam Ermolenko (strange to think of him as such), Les Collins and Alan Grahame. As the riders line up at the tapes, a man nearby says, "It's the old man's race". Sadly Moggo's comeback doesn't last too long before he demolishes the back straight

[2 Actually, technically, since bears hibernate for six months of the year and half the world's bear population are ice-bound polar bears without sign of any vegetation, they don't go into the woods as often as it's commonly held]

fence after Ermolenko touched him. There's a slight delay for repair works but Sod's Law then intervenes (as it can at such events) when Richard Hall has a bad crash that sees him smash the fence on the exit from the second bend on the first lap of the third heat. There's a huge delay and talk on the terraces indicates that, unfortunately, his leg is severely broken. Tonight of all nights really doesn't require any further reminders that the riders risk life and limb every time they throw their leg over a high-powered bike without brakes to make their living. The show must go on and announcer Dave Hoggart fills in time with an extensive number of thank yous, brief medical updates and news that "we'll have a short delay while we rebuild the fence". Despite his professionalism and the faux excitement in his voice, you can't help but notice that tonight Dave isn't quite his usual carefree ebullient self on the microphone.

One of the most exciting riders of the season (along with Chris Holder) has been Lee Complin who has ridden in resurgent fashion practically everywhere in his comeback season in the sport. Whenever I've seen him he's shown determination, bravery and much stylish skill on his machine. He looks well up for it tonight at the Sheffield track that invariably sorts the men from the boys with the way it demands you open your throttle fully in order to effectively master this lengthy track. The delays caused by the crashes and repairs to the stadium furniture cut short the schedule of races, "because of the 10 p.m. curfew we're taking out races 17 to 20 after consultation with the meeting referee and riders, so we'll go straight to the semi-final and final!" The atmosphere is driven by the size of the crowd, and with packed terraces, it truly feels just like old times. Some races stand out - Alan Grahame wins a veteran's race in a time of 66.5 seconds ("so, eh, not too bad, eh, you be careful!") and Steve 'Johno' Johnston excites when he superbly passes Paul Cooper at great speed on the third bend of the third lap of heat 13. That said, Lee Complin is the rider that most catches my eye. With time pressing and before the semi-final races, the fireworks are set off early on the centre green before causing the start line girls to dash with great speed from their seats to safety just before the blue touchpaper is lit. Though the "riders have given their services free of charge", the final itself is contested for a glittering array of donated prizes "the rider that finishes in first place will get a Ferrari laptop [I knew they made cars but this is something I'd never heard of until now] worth £1700 and second prize is a kevlar race suit worth £475!" When the tapes rise it appears Freddie Lindgren is keener to surf the web than Lee Complin since he blasts round him with some ease on the second bend. However, Lee gradually reels him in and returns the favour three laps later, somehow squeezing past Lindgren through the proverbial non-existent gap between him and the safety fence.

The crowd roar their approval at the win and they then stay to see the riders shower each other in 'champagne' during the presentation ceremony, while Garry looks on patiently from his wheelchair. By the time I've packed away my stuff, the Panorama Bar is heaving and, above the hubbub of chatter, the band is in full voice; well, in the middle of a pained guitar solo, if judged by the bulldog chewing on a wasp expression taken by the guitarist, on the specially set-up stage by the windows. Dave Hoggart goes out of his way to introduce me (with some kind words) to Garry, who's diffident and politely welcoming, despite the fact that a constant stream of admirers and well-wishers have sought out his company for the past six hours or so. It's humbling to meet someone ostensibly so adjusted to their enforced situation and a pleasure to have been a part of something so big that represents all that is so decent and good about the tight-knit speedway community.

23rd August The Garry Stead Benefit Grand Prix, Winner: Speedway

[3 Here are some of the comments from the souvenir programme which I reproduce with kind permission. The first is from Garry and the second from Sheffield speedway co-promoters Neil Machin and Dave Hoggart who staged the event at Owlerton Stadium.]

"Speedway has always been my love. All I have ever wanted to do is race motorcycles and of course I didn't plan for my career to end like it has done. But I can get through this.

My injury is not something you think about when you are racing, you always know in the back of your mind that this can happen but if I could wind the clock back to even five minutes before the accident I wouldn't change a thing. I've loved every minute of it.

It's happened but I will be back at speedway in the future being a part of the racing atmosphere; helping out where I can, doing what I can. Rehabilitation will take some time, I am hoping to be out of hospital in less than two months from now - but that is my personal objective and not a timescale given by my Doctors. Lol (Hare) has told me he was in hospital for over 200 days so I know it can be a long job. I'm still determined. I'm devastated that this has happened, but when I started racing I knew that something like this could happen. But I'm sure I'll still see everyone around and the meeting I'm going to have is really a testimony to what people have done for me. I know it's going to probably be the biggest thing I've ever done. Believe me, it's going to be hard but once I get to the track I'll be OK and I'm really looking forward to it. All my mates will be there for me. There are a lot of people that I've not seen for a while. Guys like George Stancl who I haven't seen for some time but did quite a lot for me in the early days. There are so many people coming out because of what's happened - riders, friends, supporters - and I can't thank them all enough. I've enjoyed every minute of my career.

If I had a favourite track it had to be at Hull. That was the main place I rode at and I loved the place and the people there. I was one of the chairs in the cupboard at Craven Park! I would still have been there if Hull had kept going. But after that I really wanted to go to Workington and loved it there as well. Unfortunately I didn't get the chance to go back there this year as I went to Stoke, where I started my career. I always got on well with the promoters at Loomer Road and I've ridden for them loads of times as guest and thought maybe I'd see the rest of my career out with them. I actually started at five as a junior grass tracker and progressed to speedway when I was 15, riding at different tracks here, there and all over the place. I started in 1988 when I rode for a season at Cradley and went along to Stoke, had two or three years there and in 1990 I rode full time with Stoke. I liked the time I had with Bradford. It was a shame I didn't go a bit further forward but I didn't really have as much help as maybe I could have had at the time. Bradford closing didn't really help either!

I really thought I could have been a better rider than I was but I ended up going into the second division and I think I've been at the top end of the Premier League riders in the country over the last ten years. I maybe wish I could have gone on for another three years or so. But my years as a speedway rider have been great and I've been all over the world and made so many friends. So many people have helped my out. It's been good, it's all been really good.

I've enjoyed ever minute of it...and I don't regret anything. Garry." Good Friday was April 6th and Sheffield were at Birmingham in our Premier Trophy group, we'd had a good night, lost as usual, Neil and Hoggy were in the bar socialising with our travelling fans. It was Ricky who said he'd had a text message that Garry Stead had taken a knock riding for Stoke at Workington, gone over the handlebars and was at the hospital being checked over for a head injury, but there was no further news.

Now Garry Stead was the guy Hoggy had just spent a season with at Workington, they'd gotten on well (particularly as David was the man who paid for half an engine for Garry when he rode at Hull!), they'd been out on the lash together a few times in 'Dodge City' and David was naturally concerned. Garry replied to Hoggy's text at 1.30 a.m. on the Saturday "I'm fine mate, bump on the head'll do me good, thanks anyway." No worries there then.

Friday May 18th was a similar but different story. Sheffield were at Redcar, same drill, good night ... lost as usual Hoggy was in the bar (where else?) socialising and Neil had left with Andre. It was Stoney (also in the bar and guesting for Gary Havelock) who got the text this time from Sean Wilson. "Steady's taken a knock at Somerset, sounds bad, meeting's been abandoned."

Hoggy's thinking no worries there then, particularly as two other riders had been taken to hospital two races earlier. They must have ran out of ambulances. Little did any of us know just how seriously hurt Garry was, the duty BSPA Press Officer had inkling from the track correspondent and when Hoggy spoke to Garry's partner she was already on her way. Garry's parents had been summoned too. This was looking pretty grim …

The events of the next few days are a testimony to the expertise and skill of every member of the medical teams that came into contact with Garry. The St John Ambulance team at Somerset, who repeatedly resuscitated him, the surgical team at Weston-Super-Mare who took him from "less than a fifty per cent chance of survival" to "the operation went well and he is as comfortable as can be expected" and the specialist spinal teams who operated with such great optimism that they believed they could salvage some of his lower spine and reinforce his torso to give him some kind of life. From the track paramedic to the helicopter pilot, those people were doing their job and some of them may never meet Garry again but we know just how much he really does appreciate each and every one of them.

This meeting is not only for the benefit of a great sportsman but also a tribute to the ladies and gentlemen who have worked - and those who are working - so hard to give Garry his new life. We are sure you will join us with a very, very sincere thank you to them all.

Have a great evening and "dig deep".

Neil and David

Sheffield Speedway.

Sponsor Thank yous

RIDERS: 1 Tai Woffinden; 2 Lee Complin; 3 Carl Stonehewer; 4 Magnus Zetterstrom; 5 Andre Compton; 6 Freddie Lindgren; 7 Robbie Kessler; 8 Rusty Harrison; 9 Tomas Topinka; 10 Chris Kerr; 11 Simon Stead; 12 Steve Johnston; 13 Ricky Ashworth; 14 Gary Havelock; 15 Joel Parsons; 16 George Stand; 17 Paul Cooper; 18 Ben Barker

VETERAN RIDERS: Alan Mogridge; Peter Carr; Les Collins Alan Grahame

RACE SPONSORS: Scunthorpe Scorpions Speedway; Claire Perkins; John Elliott Limited;Glyn Taylor; Anne Shilton; AKN (Andre Compton); Jim Barrow Motor Factors; Visual Blinds; In Memory of John Jervis; Wolverhampton and Redcar Speedway; SF Racewear; Disease Gear; Foregale Limited; N D Racing; Ian Cartwright and all at Robert Thompson (Mouseman Furniture); Mike Hunter; Coy Comp Track Sales; Joe Hughes Racing

TYRE AND FUEL SPONSORS: Mildenhall Fen Tigers Speedway; Gary Lough - Go Steady Go; Tweedside Commercials; Just Diesels; Teesside Autodrome; Paula Rogers; Auntie Sue; Allparts Motorquip; Newport Wasps Speedway; Joy Perkins; Newcastle Diamonds Supporters Club; Travel Plus Tours; *Speedway Star*; Travel Club; Hanley Collectables; Scott Richardson; Just Diesels; Jane Winthrop; Monarchs Fans, The Jacket, Merlin and the Lads.

RACE SPONSORS: 1 George Metcalfe and the Workington Comets Fans; 2 Poole Pirates Speedway; 3 Somerset Rebels Speedway; 4 Birmingham Brummies Speedway; 5 Workington Comets Speedway; 6 GRT Media; 7 GRT Media; 7 Rye House Rockets Speedway; 8Auntie Sue; 9 Newcastle Diamonds Speedway; 10 The Speedway Riders Association; 11 Arthur Doodson Insurance Brokers; 12 A&S Leisure; 13 Swindon Robins Speedway; 14 Isle of Wight Islanders Speedway; 15 SJP Products (Race Jackets); 16 Stoke Potters Speedway; 17 Tony Marsh; 18 www.unofficialcomets.co.uk; 19 Kings Lynn Speedway; 20 Sheffield Window Centre; 21 Steel City Bearings

Michael Lee - SPONSORED BY Coventry Bees, Eastbourne Eagles and Newport Wasps

Chris Morton - SPONSORED BY Joe Hughes and Christian Hefenbrock

MATCH RACE SPONSORS: 1 Elvis Jones; 2 www.garybooth.co.uk; 3 Wolves Fans

VETERAN RIDERS SPONSORS: "Potters Power" Stoke Fans; Pegasus Speed Needs; Wulfsport; Andy Smith; Mark Sawbridge & Sally Knight; Dave Walsh; Sittingbourne Speedway; The Armadale "Emmerdales"; Gerry at GBM

DEMONSTRATION RACE SPONSORS: Plymouth Speedway and Lakeside Speedway

ACKNOWLEDGEMENTS

Today's event could not have taken place without the support and contribution of so many and we wish to sincerely thank, on Garry's behalf, each and every one of them. In no particular order then:

Julie and Steve Reading; Steph and Lisa; Claire Perkins; Easy Rider Motorcycles; J Edgar and Sons; Sharp Retail Systems; SJP Products; SF Racewear; Andy Smith; Tony Royston; Bert Harkins Racing; Ozchem; Wulfsport; Joe Hughes Racing; Coy Comp Track Sales; A& S Leisure; Craig Ackroyd and The Association of Speedway Referees; Graham Reeve and The Speedway Control Bureau; Bernard Crapper, The Speedway Riders Benevolent Fund; The Speedway Museum; The British Speedway Promoters Association; Members and Management Committee; Yorkshire Television (Calendar News); Vicky Locklin; BBC Look North; BskyB; Suzi Perry; Members of the Local and Regional Press: *Huddersfield Examiner, Halifax Courier, Hull Daily Mail, Workington News and Star, Middlesbrough Gazette, Sheffield Star, Stoke Sentinel, Yorkshire Post, Manchester Evening News*; The "Shared Event Media Team" Paul Rickett, Nigel Pearson, David Rowe, Peter Oakes, Tony Macdonald, Neil Evans, Brendon Smurthwaite, Mike Patrick and Richard Clark; *Speedway Star*; Peter York; Michael J Beck; Nigel Hinchliffe; GRT Media; Andy Garner and Chris Spires; Hywel C Lloyd; Shaun Leigh;

Reel to Reel Television and Video Productions; Shiffa and all at Potters Power; Sheffield Window Centre; Foregale Limited; Sheffield Speedway Trackstaff; Stoke Speedway; Matej Zagar, Hans Andersen, Joe Screen, Chris Harris, Greg Hancock, Billy Hamill, Laurence Hare,

Nicki Pedersen, Leigh Adams; Chris Van Straaten; Barry Campbell and the P45s; Danzell;

Simon Clegg; Jim Blanchard; Jeff Scott; Mike Golding; Mick Gregory and Dave Rattenbury (Sheffield, Stoke, Redcar and Wolverhampton Trackshops); The British Speedway Forum; Dr Jim Nelson;Gary Booth; Steve Johnston; Paul Puttnam; Dave Watson; Keith Thompson (STAARS)

"My school have organised a Fun Run especially for my Dad" - Lewis

Thanks to you all ... Easy-Rider (Europe) Ltd]

[4 With his usual casual understatement Sheffield co-promoter Dave Hoggart updated me on Garry's progress in January, "Garry has had a pretty rough winter and is back in hospital, I won't go into the gory details but there is a healing problem. Garry's website is still the best place for fans to follow his progress."]

Chapter 41. Reading v Swindon: Battle of the tactical doctor's certificates

31st August

Trevor Swales [to referee Phil Griffin]

"No, no, no I asked you the question - who's fault is it? [No answer] At the end of the day I think you've made a terrible, terrible mistake there, everyone standing here - Middlo, Terry Russell - thought it was an odd decision!"

Trevor *"These refs are going to ruin the sport before we're done!"*

Jonathan *"I've just heard from Sarra - Trevor Swales is talking it up like we are!"*

Jonathan *"We saw Trevor Swales standing there not making a move to make a move"*

Many people hold that it's the playing that counts and not the winning. For Reading fans, the fact that the club even survived the initially enthusiastic but ultimately bonkers business practices of the reign of BSI Reading supremo John 'I'm a speedway business visionary, me' Postlethwaite is cause enough for ecstatic celebration without need of results on the track. Interestingly, the Benfield Sports International website claims John had "senior level commercial and marketing roles at the Benetton Formula One team, Pepsi Cola International and Nabisco Group." Based on his approach to things at Reading, it's amazing that these companies still survive. It would be churlish not to acknowledge that Reading were 'robbed' by the near miss of the narrowest of points margins and the rules of the sport in the Elite League Play-Off Final in 2006 against Peterborough. If they had won on the night, history would have been rewritten and Postlethwaite would still be lauded as a hero. Without such an outcome to paper over the cracks, the club quickly assumed the status of an expensive and dispensable plaything in his eyes. Some of the expensively assembled on- and off-track talent also proved to be more of the Goodtime Charlie school of commitment - happy to bank the cheques but reluctant to stick around when the going got tough. The figure allegedly invested varies but the consensus says it was round about a cool half-million pounds. That 'investment' of £500,000 roughly represents a thousand pounds for every fan who regularly passes through the turnstiles at the bitter end of the Postlethwaite era. The phrase "you might as well glue your money to a dog's arse and watch it run off into the distance", attributed to the plain-speaking hair-lipped Sheffield singer Richard Hawley springs to mind.

The return of 'proper' speedway people to the club has occasionally seen things be a little bit wee and a little bit woo, but there's absolutely no doubts about the commitment to the club of Malcolm 'Mad Wellie' Holloway and his promotional partner Mark Legg. They've inherited a difficult hand to play with some inflated rider contracts and something of a train wreck of an Elite League team - expensive to run and often unlikely to hold its own against superior opposition at home, let alone away. Coupled with a fixture pile up brought on by the poor summer weather and the interregnum forced on the club during the sale process itself, minimising losses and survival to the end of the season is the name of the game. Interestingly, crowd levels have picked up, the track and entertainment levels offered are reputedly much improved while greater optimism is the *lingua franca* of the supporters. The return of the winged-wheel logo of the Racers to replace the ill-fated Bulldogs sobriquet with its childishly condescending dog-on-Prozac motif has also been widely celebrated among the Smallmead faithful.

Still, necessity is invariably the mother of invention and Reading have been forced to catch up their fixture backlog by running meetings twice a week on Mondays (the long-time race night) and Fridays (the newly chosen race night as part of the Benfield revolution at the club). This is bound to stretch the finances of even the most die-hard and committed fan. The prospect of a contest against the high-flying Swindon Robins as they aim to fulfil the widespread pre-season predictions that they would emerge as Elite League champions at the end of the 2007 season is likely to only have one outcome (though, of course, for many years until recently this would always have been a Premier League fixture). Even when they had a notionally stronger team earlier in the season, Reading were comprehensively humped at Smallmead and a repeat dose of the medicine definitely looks to be on the cards. Not that you'd ever guess this if you read comments in the press from team manager Tim Sugar, "We will not lay down and we will make them battle hard for every point." Malcolm manages to illustrate exactly why promoters are called promoters when he also talks up the prospects beforehand, "It has all the makings of being a tremendous derby clash and we are all looking forward to it. We are expecting our biggest crowd since we took over here and, with that in mind, have decided to open the gates half an hour earlier than usual at 5.30 p.m." The task of enthusing the public about the meeting is particularly peculiar for speedway historian, statistician and bestselling speedway author of his generation, Robert Bamford, since he's the press officer for both Reading and Swindon. Should he ever feel the need to coordinate copy with his opposite number then the Racers versus Robins meeting involves a conversation with himself! Luckily while Colin Horton owning both Peterborough and Oxford raised more than a few eyebrows during the close season (except at the BSPA), Robert's multi-tasking is welcomed due in no small part due to the respect for his hard-working and diligent approach. The press pronouncements of Alun Rossiter would present any press officer with a unique challenge, since to vaguely control them or rein in Alun's natural passion for the sport, never mind translate them into more fluent and readily understandable English, requires constant alertness. For a fixture that is a foregone conclusion in his mind, Rosco studiously avoids comment in the press on the meeting with the Racers and, instead, he prefers to look to more important matters like the play-offs. He treats us all to some Zen-like philosophical insights to guide the less initiated through the thicket of complexities of the whole process involved, "The final is over two legs and you have to be in it to win it." The Racers are unlikely to delay the part of the process that requires qualification, particularly given the comparative strength in depth that the Robins boast in their team.

You wouldn't bet against a Leigh Adams victory in the first heat and this would have been a sensible decision. Matej Zagar for Reading returns having recovered from yet another "illness" that caused him to miss the 56-37 defeat at Belle Vue. With some élan, he finishes comprehensively last, while Jonas Davidsson shows some real fight to pass Tomasz Chrzanowski to secure second. Having quickly got the measure of a smooth-looking and seemingly shale-free Smallmead circuit (though what shale there is billows off the surface in eddies of dust cloud), Jonas then goes out and wins the next race and, with Chris Neath third, the 4-2 brings the scores level at 6 points each. Before each race Bob Radford advises the crowd over the tannoy that the two-minute warning has sounded, thereby confirming that the advent of democracy in action at Smallmead has seen the awful pre-recorded insistent but faux enthusiastic American-accented noise pollution - much better suited to warning of a nuclear attack ("you have two minutes! You have two minutes!") - has been consigned to the dustbin of history by the incoming promotion. Sadly, what appeared to bode well from Davidsson's battling performances and raised the possibility of a fight from the Reading Racers, immediately disappeared with three successive maximum heat advantages for the visiting Robins. These successes came in dusty race conditions and stretched their lead to a comfortable 9-21 by the end of Heat 5. Indeed, the home faithful have to wait until the 10th heat to see another rider in a winged-wheel tabard cross the line first. With poor home form, as a Reading fan you're always to see the early use of the available tactical options and, so it proves tonight, when Zagar comes out in a black-and-white helmet colour for Heat 6. Though Matej manages to start with greater alacrity from the tapes than first time out, Sebastian Ulamek shoots away even quicker to win comfortably to create that always odd-looking heat scoreline of 4-4. With the search for points proving difficult, roving colour man Paul Hunsdon decides to restore some local pride by baiting the healthy contingent of Robins fans who've turned up to savour the away win. "Any Swindon fans here who went to the ELRC at King's Lynn last night? Come on - don't be shy! You could have given Lee Richardson [who 'broke down' en route] a lift is all I'll say!" with time to fill while the track is watered, Paul playfully explains, "We're watering the track for the Swindon fans [ironic cheers] so you can see your boys disappear into the distance."

Paul then embarks on a quest apparently harder to find than a decent marketing idea during the Postlethwaite reign at Reading, namely "are there any attractive female fans from Swindon here tonight? Ah, there is! Oh, it's Rory the Lion." Desperate times on the track call for desperate entertainment measures off it, so Paul widens his search though, as a long-time regular at

Smallmead, he must already know that his search is optimistic, "have we got a buxom, young woman who'd like to make the draw for us?" Our return to the chauvinism of a different era when speedway ruled the sporting roost is temporarily suspended by the arrival of Heat 7. I mark this in my programme as yet another heat win for the Robins (2-4) after an exciting battle on the line for third place between Davidsson and Charlie Gjedde that I would definitely have given to the Robins rider. However, referee Dale Entwhistle without much, if any, controversy to really adjudicate on throughout the night is the man in charge and he rules in favour of the Racers to thereby make a mess of my programme racecard. To distract from the paucity of the home performance on the track and to regain some minimal vestige of local pride - after having barely obliquely criticised Wiltshire womenfolk - Paul Hunsdon broadens his critique of all things Swindon to cover the parenting skills of the travelling Robins fans. The smoking gun that forms his damning evidence is the highly enthusiastic scramble of children keen to take advantage of a giveaway of gifts to the crowd "I don't think the parents in Swindon give the kids anything - I've never seen 25p horns be so popular!"

Heat 10 sees the keenly anticipated 'Battle of the Tactical Doctor's Certificates', otherwise known as Matej Zagar versus Lee Richardson. The Slovenian wins with ease and, as ever, looks comfortable up front and the heat is drawn when Richardson ensures he keeps Davidsson relegated to last place. The most exciting race of the night is heat 12 and this initially features what appears to be a comfortable win for Janusz Kolodziej until Lee Richardson remembers his experience round Smallmead to put in a sizzling last lap to win the battle for first place on the line. In the referee's box, presenter Bob Radford informs us, "they say he can't pass but he did there - Sebastian Ulamek - oh, er, Lee Richardson, I mean." With the meeting result beyond any doubt, I think the riders and the majority of the fans (except for those Swindon fans who like to fully luxuriate in the thrill of this foregone conclusion) are pleased to have seen the meeting run in brisk fashion (except for necessary track watering). However, the likelihood of a swift end to the fixture disappears in the dramatic first corner of the initial running of heat 13. In a congested first corner Leigh Adams gives Zagar a massive shove that forces him outwards and thereby causes Ulamek to move over to leave Travis McGowan with no room at all. As a result of this, he smashes into the air fence at the apex of the bend and, though up on his feet straightaway, the fence has been punctured! We're then treated to a lengthy delay for a bout of repairs (and an answer to the question of how many track staff it requires to mend an airfence ["inflatable barrier", © SCB] puncture) before the meeting can recommence on its path to the inevitable conclusion that history will show as a 35-57 defeat for the Racers (thereby equalling the worst-ever Elite League home defeat). One man who can ill afford to hang around for any length of time is Alun 'Rosco' Rossiter who fulfils his team management duties on the night despite the fact "his wife is in hospital waiting to be induced!" In the meantime, Malcolm Holloway says a few heartfelt words. "Thank you to all the Swindon fans for turning up in their numbers tonight. It's just a shame that we can't keep up with them - they're a class apart at the moment! Being Swindon born, I wish them all the best - I can remember the last time they won the league, believe it or not!"

31st August Reading v Swindon (Elite League B) 35-57

Chapter 42. Belle Vue v Swindon: Unofficial 'Keep Britain Tidy' campaign starts

3rd September

The lure of the Buxton versus Stoke local derby in the Conference League led me to schedule a few days in the North-West so that I could take in a football game and a trip to Belle Vue with my good friend Stefan Usansky. He used to go to Hyde Road in the glory days and his speedway re-education as a returnee to the sport in the twenty-first century has previously taken him to speedway meetings at Arlington and Wimborne Road. Every time I visit Manchester it appears rain is compulsory and, though the journey to Buxton speedway is beautiful, only blind optimism made it likely that the meeting would be on after a journey there in continuous rain. When we arrived at a windswept track there were still a substantial number of volunteers present, though they were sensibly sheltering in the sea container in the pits that serves as the lair and tearoom for the track staff. While in the referee's box, a damp but cheery Jayne Moss told us that they had hoped to run the meeting but the heavy rain that swept in during the morning (when she was at football with her son Josh) had reluctantly forced her husband Richard's decision to postpone, despite the fact that pretty well everything was already prepared for the meeting. A chirpy John Rich and 'Mushy Pea' (ICA Crook) were just about to depart the scene too having recently unloaded the car of speedway merchandise into the trackshop, only then to reload it again. The slightly desolate walk from the car park to the stadium and back in cold winds and lashing rain wasn't exactly ideal conditions for Stefan, with a hacking cough to indicate that his remission from lung cancer perhaps wasn't all that it was claimed. After the long drive back we dined early evening in a Greek restaurant in Sale where, towards the end of the meal (after dark), the waiter cheerfully told us, "You wouldn't believe it round here on a Friday and Saturday night!" Apparently the place where we had chosen to eat was located in an area known as a knife crime hotspot far worse than places you'd automatically think would fall victim to this lawless behaviour. Even though it was a Sunday night, it's never good to accidentally find yourself after nightfall in an area notorious for unprovoked knife attacks. Perhaps the restaurant management could feature this as a unique selling point in their future adverts?

The next day saw the weather gods look kindly on the Belle Vue fixture with Swindon and the sky is almost cloudless. Later we'll all be treated to a lovely crimson and blue sky that supposedly indicates that the shepherds in this area will be delighted. A difficult campaign for Belle Vue speedway from the outset of the season has supposedly been reflected in the crowd numbers but, whatever the truth or otherwise in these rumours, it's the kind of foregone conclusion of a meeting that any promoter would dread and surely would (particularly during a season like the 2007 one) only attract the hard core of die-hard Aces fans along to watch.

Earlier in the season, the 'A' fixture had seen Belle Vue lose 38-54 though tonight the often injury-ravaged Aces are arguably stronger since they have Simon Stead rather than a guest replacement, plus they have notionally been improved by the mid-season addition of Antonio Lindback in their side. Stead was injured (for the first time in an injury plagued 2007 season) on my last visit here for the meeting versus Eastbourne on a bitterly cold night when Nicki Pedersen reinforced his hate figure status among some sections (well, the Manchester Mexicans plus some other randomly aggrieved parties) of the Kirkmanshulme Lane

Bike display

Stef hands out leaflets in reception

One lap to go

crowd. Stefan had come along that night too and taken quiet satisfaction in the Aces 50-43 victory, while being the only person to wear a Manchester United bobble hat (minus the bobble) in the pits. That night the famous guitarist from the heyday of The Smiths - Johnny Marr - had attended as a guest of Bob Brimson the Eastbourne co-promoter with extensive music industry connections. Though we stood next to him, I regret not taking the opportunity for a brief word. Stef also noticed Johnny but only really because of his long hair rather than any real idea of who he was. Now that we're back inside the stadium via the pits gate, as guests of the Belle Vue promotion, it's clear that this whole area has been further remodelled in the five months since April 2nd. The most notable additions to the pits area aren't any of the permanent changes but the green awninged sideless tent erected in a prominent position parallel with the first bend under which to display a sparkling array of vintage speedway bikes. Like shoes on an army parade, everything about these machines glistens (including the huge pride of their owners), despite the lack of sunlight. Always curious about his environment and keen to meet people, Stef soon has the owners explain to him at great length the technical and maintenance aspects of their respective pride and joys. The copious technical detail soon loses me. The bikes do look lovely and with the metalwork burnished so brightly, these JAP bikes look magnificent. Stef marvels at the display of these machines since they immediately take him back to his youth and allow them all to reminisce about the privilege of the experiences they regularly had on race nights at Hyde Road.

They're all friendly men who're quickly mutually enthralled, though I have to drag Stef back from down memory lane for the short walk towards the main grandstand where I've been invited by Gordon Pairman on behalf of the Directors of Belle Vue speedway to display my books. I have their permission to base myself wherever I like to sell and display them, so again I choose to locate myself at the open plan area that's located just inside the turnstile entrance. From here all Belle Vue fans who enter the stadium have to pass either Stefan or myself. Those fans on their way upstairs to watch through the giant windows of the home straight grandstand, encounter Stefan handing out a leaflet cum postcard about my book. Since the upstairs has been developed to appease the demands of greyhound punters and liberate them from their money in some comfort, you definitely get a panoramic view of the track and a good selection of tables to sit at. That said, in my opinion, speedway isn't a sport to watch indoors, never mind behind glass, unless you have no choice in the matter. The alternative route for the fans is to stream past my small display table of books by the double doors that lead through to the rather dingy bar area that, after yet more fire doors, eventually leads out into the open air. From there, the choices are to remain on the concrete stepped terraces of the home straight under the lee of the roof or head off to take your chance exposed to the elements and stand on the fourth, third or second bends.

Completely thoughtlessly, I've already made a subsequently significant error of courtesy. I'd already been given express permission to display my books by

Gordon Pairman (one of the Belle Vue promoters) but forgot to alert the trackshop owner of my intentions prior to my visit. Fortunately, I had previously agreed some comparatively usurious terms of trade for book sales on these premises with said owner of the speedway trackshop concession at Kirkmanshulme Lane, Mr John Jones. He's a territorial man and, like so many other people who've made his acquaintance, we've not exactly been bosom buddies - indeed he studiously ignored me at Cardiff and Newport, despite my attempts to be cordial - since our last encounter here in 2006. Nonetheless, common courtesy cuts both ways and dictates that I should have had enough professionalism to apprise him of my visit before I began to hand out my leaflets to the incoming fans.

Giving the lie to claims on reduced numbers through the turnstiles, an endless stream of Aces fans wend their way past us. Despite his 42 years in the book trade (32 in publishing sales and a decade in bookselling), Stef had never had the often soul-destroying experience of trying to pass on a leaflet to passing strangers who are often insulted, disquieted or suspicious of receiving such 'gifts'. I put this down to the fact that when you're handed something in the street you almost definitely never use the service or product advertised and view any product claims made with the utmost suspicion. Though my leaflet is the exception that disproves the rule, in this context we're really as welcome as a vegan in a crowded late-night kebab shop. Repeatedly saying the same phrase ("would you like a leaflet?") soon dries the mouth and saps your energy, though Stef approached it with his usual friendliness, vim and vigour. In fact, he started his own one-man campaign to test and record the limits of civility on a Monday night at Kirky Lane by being even more ultra-gracious than usual. This increased unctuousness soon has him amass (and record) a much larger number of "thank yous" from passing fans than I manage in the same time period. As the new boy to the discipline of smiling like a synchronised swimmer at a speedway meeting (often in the face of deliberate or unconscious abruptness), his enthusiasm levels are high but his energy levels are low. Though we soon swap places so he can hand out the leaflets sitting down by the book table, nonetheless, his volume of "thank yous" continues to increase, thereby indicating that it's his warmth and showmanship that elicits the response not the position of the pitch. Stef believes that people in the North are significantly friendlier than in the South and feels that this vindicates his feeling that Manchester people confirm this geographical divide. Allied to this affability is his innate (and almost blood-conscious) salesmanship that soon has book sales increase exponentially. Well, technically sales increased by infinity as I'd achieved none and he soon had sold two as well as nearly making me almost want to buy one as a result of the earnest, sincere and loving way he spoke about them. It's a rare skill and on my extensive travels only Alf Weedon and Johnny Barber have exhibited this potent combination of enthusiasm, plausible genuineness and killer sales instinct.

We barely make it round to the pits to stand in the new viewing area for visitors and guests ("you can see everything but the track" Jonathan Bethell notes standing by me - something forgotten in the pits whenever the decision of the sight-challenged referee perched high in the grandstand is queried) before Leigh Adams fires off from the start gate and disappears into the distance, comfortably ahead of Simon Stead and James Wright. Though the race is drawn there was such a huge distance between the Aces and the Robins captain at the finish that this really doesn't bode well for the remainder of the meeting. As if to emphasise the gulf between the teams, Andrew Moore wins the next race from the gate. He shows considerable delight when he crosses the line, though his victory lap of celebration only gets as far as the first bend before he falls (conveniently) in front of the pits gate to loud, ironic cheers from the Belle Vue fans on the terraces. The next three races all result in heat advantages for the Robins and, consequently, Simon Stead appears out in the sixth heat on a tactical ride. It's an inspired choice by joint team managers Eric Boocock and Chris Morton since not only does Stead win but James Wright follows up his rear for an 8-1. This brings the scores back to a much more manageable 18-21 and the delighted announcer informs the assembled faithful, "That's more like it!" And it briefly is until Charlie Gjedde and Lee Richardson combine in the next race with an immediate 5-1 reply for the Robins that silences the crowd except for a small section of (so-called) Aces fans on the grandstand terraces, who loudly barrack Antonio Lindback and doubt his parentage because of his inopportune engine failure.

With the interval approaching, Stef and I rush from the comfort and safety of the pits back towards the grandstand where I intend to resume trying to sell my books to the Aces faithful. At the last World Cup the Japanese fans were a real hit with the stadium owners after they stayed behind for an hour after the game to clean their section of the stand. They always left it tidier than they found it. Increasingly nowadays people throw rubbish and litter wherever the fancy takes them. It's one of those tiny but extremely visible signs of selfishness that seems to characterise the use of public spaces everywhere you look in Britain. As previously explained, whenever I travel to speedway tracks round the country I try to entice people to think about buying the books I've got on display by handing them a leaflet. Some people are very reluctant to take it, some immediately tear it into shreds and others actually say "thank you". Handing them out at the home of Belle Vue speedway I reached 43 "thank yous" and so narrowly lost to my friend Stefan who'd got to 48 when he stopped counting far earlier than I did. Once the speedway bug for statistics has bitten it's hard to shake!

Everywhere I go, after the meeting, I try to find as many of these discarded leaflets as I can and place them in the bin provided or take them home again to throw away. I do this partly so as not to irk my hosts or the stadium owners with my additional litter but also, more selfishly, I'm vainly trying to preserve some residual cache for my books by attempting to make them look valued. Belle Vue trackshop merchant, John Jones obviously takes a territorial pride in his workplace and, unbeknownst to me, during the early heats of the meeting he'd kindly taken it upon himself to conscientiously pick up all the dropped leaflets he could find scattered around the bar area and meticulously shredded them for recycling. I admire any example of environmentalism but didn't expect to find such a committed and avid eco-warrior in the speedway merchandise community. Sadly I didn't know that I should thank him for this service when I bumped into him, just before the interval of the Elite B fixture against then league leaders Swindon. I said, "Ah, John, how are you?" They say cleanliness is next to godliness and the extremely territorial Mr. Jones clearly doesn't have much truck with litterbugs like me promoting their books on his chosen patch. With admirable passion for the environment, he replied angrily.

"You've got a farking cheek you Farking **** showing your face here. You can fark off! Don't you farking call me a 'Freaking Professional'[1] I didn't farking expect you this week. I hope you're farking coming 'cause they're farking booked! I've got a farking bag of confetti for you [calls to wife 'where's the bag for the ****? His farking confetti!'] 'There you go you farking ****!' There's your farking confetti [hands over the plastic bag of ripped up leaflets he'd kindly picked up. You've got a farking cheek. Fark **** - your solicitor's letter is on its way. Don't you farking 'freakng professional' me. Farking writing that - think you're so farking clever. I'm demanding a farking apology from Philip Rising[2] You **** and, if not, you're farking for it, you're dead, the farking solicitor's letter is on its way and I want every farking penny commission from tonight. Every farking penny you ****! Showing your farking face. If you print a farking word, you're dead! Fark off you ****!"[3] who the fark do you think you are, you ****. You're getting a farking solicitor's letter you ****. I was hiring two farking blokes to sort you out farking properly for next week [the visit of Eastbourne on September 10th].

Quite what you do after such threats isn't easy to decide when you're shaken by the ferocity of the conversation itself. I subsequently learnt that the SCB official in charge of a meeting has the powers to exclude anyone they choose from the stadium whom they deem to be behaving detrimentally towards the safe running of the meeting. These powers apply to anywhere within the stadium so this includes the fans just as much as the riders, officials and mechanics. The natural inclination in the face of threatening behaviour that you take seriously - which I did - is to report it to the police. We all know that policemen are not required at speedway meetings and this remains a genuine source of pride to us all within the speedway community. Equally going to the police station afterwards in a city you don't come from is bound to complicate things and, anyway, it really doesn't seem sensible to run the good name of the club and speedway through the mud because of the reprehensible attitude of one peculiar individual. On top of that everyone at the club has been unfailingly friendly. When I get back to the pits I explain what has happened to the head of security who tells me that John Jones is all hot air and should be ignored. He insists that I should attend the next meeting at Kirkmanshulme Lane when Eastbourne are due to visit and I'd come along as part of my Writer in Residence

[1 See pp.97-98 of 'Shifting Shale' for details of our first encounter at Belle Vue]

[2 Editor of the Speedway Star. I subsequently learnt that John Jones had written a letter objecting to a brief mention of his behaviour in my book in an article by Peter Oakes that appeared in the magazine. It's probably always best to avoid unnecessary legal action but quite why an apology was required for alluding to his original poor behaviour written in my book remains a complete mystery to me.]

[3 This conversation with John Jones, trackshop man at Belle Vue speedway, took place at 8.20 p.m. on September 3rd 2007. This conversation comes from my contemporaneous (shakily) hand written notes composed immediately afterwards in the grandstand bar though I didn't really take in the panoramic view. Throughout his tirade, Mr Jones stood extremely close to fulminate and threateningly jabbed a finger at my face repeatedly - he appeared to struggle to restrain himself from hitting me. I said nothing at all in reply, though my guest, Stefan Usansky witnessed the whole event and frequently interjected with "what disgusting language" a number of times, but to no avail. Afterwards Stefan said incredulously, "I've never come across anyone like that in my life!" More importantly, he couldn't believe that such an ostensibly family-oriented sport as speedway could harbour such a repugnant individual in any position of responsibility, let alone in charge of the trackshop of the club he's followed since his youth!]

duties. This is easy for him to blithely say. I'm reluctant to tempt providence or John Jones's temper but he reassures with "don't worry if he starts anything some of mine are itching for the excuse to sort someone out!" Without wishing to interrupt their enjoyment of the meeting, I also briefly explained the conversation and threats to Gordon Pairman and David Gordon (whom I met for the first time). They were shocked and apologetic on behalf of the club but pointed out that when they completed their takeover at the club many other matters directly relating to the actual functioning of the speedway club took their immediate priority and attention. The relationship with John Jones and the fact that he was in charge of the speedway franchise at the club wasn't their choice but an inheritance from the previous Tony Mole regime at Belle Vue. Also, technically, Jones is really a franchisee at the stadium on speedway race nights who rents his pitch from the stadium owners the GRA. So, ultimately, responsibility for his supervision and behaviour falls under their jurisdiction. Not that the Belle Vue promotion were washing their hands of responsibility and they assured me that they would be having strong words with John Jones at the earliest opportunity to highlight their displeasure and concern as well as identifying to him what they consider to be the professional standards of behaviour they expect from anyone concerned with Belle Vue speedway club.[4]

I must say that EVERYONE I met throughout my night as a guest of Belle Vue speedway (with their full permission to attend and sell my books as well as describe this incident in my book) were charming, friendly and affable or couldn't have been more helpful and supportive.

Though I watched the races and noted down the scores, the remainder of the meeting passed in blur as I sipped a hot strong cup of tea in the pits. It was Swindon's second away Elite League win at Kirkmanshulme Lane in 2007 and the final score at 35-58 was one point more than that achieved in the 'A' fixture. It was a record-breaking night for all the wrong reasons since this 10th home league defeat of the season set a new (unwanted) Aces record. In the 20 years the club have spent at Kirkmanshulme Lane, Swindon became the first visiting side to track three unbeaten riders during a meeting and it was the second heaviest loss ever at the track (after the 32-58 defeat by Poole in 2001). For reasons of tiredness, my friend Stefan wanted to leave the stadium without hanging around to try to sell more books by the stadium exit doors. My stubborn streak dictated that having come all this way I would persevere and I was rewarded with an additional sale and a charming conversation with the security people who, like so many others involved in the sport, had their own stories to tell about John Jones's irascibility that don't reflect well on him as an individual.

3rd September Belle Vue v Swindon (Elite League B) 35-58

[4 Afterwards Gordon Pairman wrote to me copying Chris Morton and David Gordon to say, "can I apologise for that man's appalling behaviour, please? I spoke to him after we spoke - actually it was closer to me shouting at him - and David, Chris and I discussed the incident at our board meeting on Tuesday. Although it is true that he is not an employee of Belle Vue, simply a franchise holder, we take our responsibilities seriously, and his attitude is simply unacceptable. I will do my utmost to ensure that your next visit is not marred in the same way."]

Chapter 43. Edinburgh v Rye House: New martial art hits Armadale

14th September

Worried that I would miss the regular 6.30 p.m. Friday night Edinburgh 'Scotwaste' Monarchs Supporters Club coach that leaves from Waterloo Place to go to Armadale, I arrived early. The bus was late so I had a few additional minutes to drink in the pre-meeting chatter among the good-sized group of regular die-hard Monarchs fans who gather here every week prior to their weekly dose of speedway medicine. I always feel youthful in this group, despite already being middle aged. There's talk of the wonderful, roll-back-the-years performance by Tomasz Gollob on his home track of Bydgoszcz - pronounced big-gosh by the speedway cognoscenti (it's funny how the sport improves your vocabulary and geography) - during the recent Polish GP. Talk soon turns to the results the Monarchs require from their remaining fixtures in order to finish 12th in the Premier League and, thereby, qualify for the Young Shield (a trophy named after Edinburgh's first and original legend, Jack Young, who won the World Championship when a Division II rider). Destiny is mostly in their own hands, though an away win for the Tigers at Mildenhall would help matters. According to these fans, it's imperative that this mini-campaign starts tonight with a win against the in-form Rye House 'Silverski' Rockets. Optimism, if it exists, is tempered by the caution borne of many years' experience and, instead, many fans grumble about the late arrival of the bus and speculate upon its whereabouts. Though this is apparently a widely and sincerely held complaint, strangely no one ever appears to bring this up with the trip organiser, Ella.

Clearly standing out as an interloper - spatially and sartorially - from the group of Monarchs fans (in his Rye House logoed clothing) is a diffident man named Gary (42), who has flown up especially from Stansted to see this fixture. He travels widely - domestically and internationally - to watch speedway, though "because we're a Saturday track, I have to miss some home meetings - not that many, though - to go away elsewhere. It's funny looking at the people who go on these speedway tours - they're all of a certain age, at least 50, and many of them are much older which just shows that the sport has future problems stored up 'cause we're not attracting the interest of the younger generation. In fact I'm one of the youngest usually." Like the assembled Monarchs fans, he's reluctant to forecast a definite win for his team tonight but does venture the opinion that Rye will race against King's Lynn ("I think we have the beating of them this year") in the play-off final that now determines who are the Premier League Champions. He ignores the small matter of a top-four finish and the need to progress past the two-legged semi-final round. "After that win on the telly, no one is going to relish racing at our place now they've seen what we can really do!" Gary has read my *Showered in Shale* book ("twice") but claims not to have sufficient money to purchase the follow-up volume due to a lack of funds brought on by his recent spend on speedway travel. I ask for his comments on the book, "You capture how many of the places where speedway is presently staged are somewhat run down," and "I liked reading about your meetings with the promoters - it struck me that the promoters you spoke to were very territorial, like animals marking out their territory by pissing everywhere!" For some reason, the talk turns to Birmingham and Gary remarks that co-promoter Graham Drury is a "robust" man, "though I'm not really sure whether he or Denise wears the trousers." Whenever I have seen Denise, she invariably wears a business smart trouser suit.

The advantage of the coach journey is that my trip to Armadale Stadium is comparatively relaxed and hassle-free compared to driving myself. It does mean I arrive only a few minutes before the start time. Sadly by then, the majority of the crowd have already passed through the entrance gates and taken their favoured places in the stadium. Consequently, they're unable to even consider purchasing any of my books that I set out - rather forlornly - on top of my wheelie travelling case. This had attracted some comment from the queue as we waited to get on the bus ("are you planning to stay the night?") and I had joked to one man with an Alex Ferguson-esque red and bluey coloured nose that it contained "my books and a bottle of whisky". Consequently, he attentively spoke to me at every opportunity for the rest of the night, "we'll need to drown our sorrows with some if we lose later".

By this time of the year, and when you venture this far 'north', the evenings have started to draw in and the few stragglers who dashed past were only really likely to notice my book display if they accidentally fell over it. I could already hear that the usual Monarchs presenter - the ebullient Scott Wilson - was absent (at a wedding) so I asked the always friendly Monarchs co-promoter John Campbell if his replacement could mention my attendance (sadly this mention produced no sales). Never one to shy away from conducting market intelligence, John thoughtfully enquired about my journey as well as the talk/atmosphere on the supporters' coach. I reported grumbles about the tardiness, "I bet no one complained about the prices [it's a bargain £5 return!] as you get right here and it's £6.75 to Bathgate station, if you come on the train". Unaware I'm also going to Sunderland in my hire car (rented because of railway engineering work between Edinburgh and Newcastle) John also enquires how I'll get to Berwick tomorrow night. He kindly suggests that I should have told him so he could have arranged a lift in George Stancl's van. Thoughtlessly, and confusing the reputation of George's bikes with his mode of transport, I blurt out, "I wanna get there, not break down!" John reassures me, "You'd have been fine, [pause] though his van did break down outside my house once!" Jonathan Chapman often gets a lot of recognition for his personal meet and greet strategy to welcome the fans as they pass through the turnstiles at the Norfolk Arena. This is something John Campbell also does on a more low key basis at Armadale. His approach is slightly different in that there's fewer numbers as well as the fact that he's much more naturally taciturn than Jonathan but, nonetheless, my experience is that he's still often available for conversation with his paying public.

As the rider parade has already taken place and the two-minute warning sounded/lit, I make my way round to my traditional place - the lee between the bend one grandstand and the terrapin hut with concrete balcony that serves as a corporate hospitality area. Edinburgh speedway boasts two corporate entertainment areas. One is the George Hunter Memorial Lounge (according to the programme, the package costs"£650 + VAT" to include "free bar(!) buffet, admission for 25 guests, programme & p.a. advertising and superb view of the action") and the other is the Champions Lounge (ditto but no programmes, p.a. advertising and five less people for £550 + VAT). I'm never quite sure which one I'm stood next to. Whenever I'm here the sponsors always appear to enjoy a brief trip to the centre green - a wonderful vantagepoint and experience at Armadale (as it is at any track) - and I expect the raised area of the corporate terrace provides a slightly better view over the safety fence. Stood where I am, you get a superb view over the majority of the track, though the nearby wooden safety fence slightly obscures the enjoyment of the exact, detailed minutiae of the action as it happens on the apex of the first bend.

However, I stand here for the company of the people rather than for an uninterrupted view of the first bend. Bill Copland has arrived already but the rest of the Penicuik Massive - in the form of his son, Dougie (who William rather formally refers to as "Douglas"), and Jim Brykajlo (the Berwick-supporting Edinburgh taxi driver who, with a name like that, should really be a speedway rider) are elsewhere. They're indulging their obsessive passion for collecting speedway programmes (the sport of speedway's equivalent of truffle hunting) and, apparently, are "over in the grandstand stood by the programme stall there." Jim would usually attend with his son Steven, whose ambition is to become a journalist, but he's away at a Richard Hawley concert rather than at the train-spotting event I incorrectly guess might have called him away tonight. Bill usually lets everyone else do the talking but tonight we get the chance to chat and he tells me, "John Campbell says in the paper we'll finish 12th". When I glance upwards and scoffingly ask - based on the comments I've heard this season from Monarchs fans, never mind the variable form shown in 2007 - "Is that a pig flying by?", Bill quickly retorts, "You've got to have faith in your team!"

Despite the alleged similarities that supposedly exist between the Rye House and Edinburgh tracks, the Monarchs start proceedings with a comfortable 5-1 from George Stancl and Derek Sneddon ("our 5-1 pairing"). When the rest of the Penicuik Massive arrive - Jim Brykajlo and Dougie Copland - I quickly gather that they don't hold Rye House in the greatest respect for the perceived gamesmanship of their antics at Armadale during previous visits. This makes them particularly fervent tonight in their desire for a Monarchs victory but doesn't blind them to the skill and quality of the opposition riders. A long night ahead looks in prospect for the visitors when George Stancl and Derek Sneddon power away to a comfortable 5-1 in the opening race of the night. Before Heat 2 Dougie bats off talk of a win with, "It all depends which team turns up tonight for the Monarchs - the good one or the other one!" Heat 2 is traditionally viewed as the reserves race. The home side field the powerhouse combination of their experienced guest Michael Coles, a great rider in the twilight of his career, and (taking his first tentative steps in the sport à la Bambi) Kalle Katajisto, who has yet to show sufficient form to acquire the traditional "promising" soubriquet. I've listened enough to Dougie to now know the correct pronunciation, "Cally Cally-jis-TOE" albeit I can't replicate the subtle singsong burr of his Scots accent. To my mind, Cally-jis-TOE sounds like a martial art that should sweep the country as the latest in the long line of exercise crazes that appeals to metropolitan types excited by fads that combine delicate bodily control, simmering violence, a strenuous work out and a hint of Eastern mysticism. I've yet to be convinced by what I've seen of Kalle, even if I make allowance for his youth, and (if speedway was a martial art) he'd definitely still be lucky to hold onto a white belt. But, they've taken him to their hearts in certain sections of the Armadale crowd - I imagine in the way abandoned animals usually pluck the emotions - and they're only too keen to accentuate the positives. "He won his first race here last week! If he makes the starts he's great, [pause] though his gating is a bit of a problem." With all due seriousness, I overhear them say as though this is even news or a possible shock, "He needs a good performance shortly or he won't be in the side next year!"

The Rockets look likely to launch an immediate reply in kind and Dougie soon notes of the race leader, "Adam Roynon's really come on," only for him to then immediately suffer an engine failure ("well that fated him") to ensure a drawn heat. The next heat is also drawn, though only after the referee Dave Watters awards the race and excludes flame-haired Tommy Allen for crashing into the fourth-bend safety fence straightaway after he'd been passed by Andrew Tully. There is only ever going to be one winner of the race itself, whether awarded or completed in the traditional manner, and that is Tai Woffinden (who looks to be a class apart from the rest of the Rye House riders on display). Dougie is quick to praise the 'British' youngster, "Tai looks fantastic - we were probably lucky there as Laukkanen had given up!"

There's a spate of re-runs ("he had to call that back as Edinburgh were on a 5-1") and one of these false starts featured a smart piece of riding skill by Matthew Wethers who showcased his wonderfully quick reactions to avoid the fallen Adam Roynon before the fourth heat eventually got away to conclude in another draw. When the race cruelly billed as "it's Matty against Fatty" finally gets under way and completed, Steve 'Fatty' Boxall wins but spends considerable time glancing over antagonistically at his erstwhile rival. "What's Fatty looking at? It was him that clamped down on Matty not the other way round!" Though trailing 14-10 after four heats, the Rye House Rockets had already managed to provide three of the four race winners. A keen student of speedway history with a long memory to boot and mixing irony with a hint of bitterness, Dougie wonders rhetorically, "How many heats before they scrape the track? [Pause] Probably when Len asks them to!" The riders come under orders for the fifth heat but the referee then holds the tapes for an inordinately long time causing Jim to ask querulously, "Why are they holding the tapes tonight?" The initial attempt to run the race is stopped for the fallen Luke Bowen to be excluded by the referee, while Tully escaped similar punishment for his fall and survived to race again. While we wait for the recommencement, Dougie fondly recalls the exploits of Andrew Tully during his Dale Devils incarnation. "I remember when Andrew Tully threw his bike down and was half way back to the pits before he realised he'd have to trudge back and get it himself, after his dad refused to help collect it - 'you threw it down, you get it!' Lee Howard the Stoke Conference League rider was another - he was hopeless and whenever he fell off, he'd get up and remonstrate but no one was ever anywhere near him 'cause he usually fell off on his own!" Laukkanen led first time out but Tully wins the re-run thereby reminding Dougie of another perceived injustice, albeit one from the 2007 season, "Tully has the highest average in the Conference League for Scunthorpe, so Peter Morrish picks Auty and Tai for the Conference League Riders' Championship 'cause they're the big names."

Heat six has Stancl and Sneddon arrive at the tapes for the Monarchs and Dougie has barely uttered the words "It's our 5-1 pairing" before events of the first bend confirm, "That's fated us!" Sneddon is relegated to the rear though Stancl has escaped ("it helps when Boxall takes everyone to the fence"), though he's soon joined in a battle royal with Adam Roynon for first place. His progress is slowed by frequent anxious glances to his right to establish the present whereabouts of the hard riding youngster. The exotic sounding Cally Cally-jis-TOE has another outing in the next and rides the track so tentatively that it appears as if he's refused on principle to overtake the plainly out-of-sorts Tommy Allen for third place. Eventually the Rocket is going so slowly that good practice dictates that he should try a passing manoeuvre though, sadly, this goes badly awry when Cally tumbles spectacularly on the second bend of the third lap before he smashes heavily into the safety fence. While Cally remains on the deck for some time ("it's 'cause he takes half an hour to get into a coma"), the referee causes further consternation among the home supporters by ordering a re-run rather than awarding the race. "It's not Dan Holt is it? They usually bring their own ref up with them! Dan Holt was bullied by them [Rye House], so they scraped all the dirt off the track to make it like a billiard table! We were treated to the sight of Danny Betson - with all his many years' experience - telling Alan Bridgett how to prepare a track!" Once again, Tai Woffinden finds himself as effortlessly at the front of the field in the re-run race as he did first time out. Behind him Wethers is comfortably second though Tommy Allen battles with his own self-imposed demons when he rears massively ("he's a scary rider") on the fourth lap as though he's suddenly woken from a dream and found himself on an undulating motocross circuit instead of on a speedway track. The bucking bronco effect happens right in front of us but, somehow, Allen still remains on his machine to claim the point that gives the Rockets their first heat advantage of the night.

Tommy Allen is out again in the next race as rider replacement for Stefan Ekberg but even this rankles. "Ekberg is riding in Sweden but because they'd arranged it weeks before they can use r/r but any other team has to have a Conference League rider." The tapes fly as so does Michael Coles, "Oh my God, Coles has gated!" exclaims a shocked Dougie before normal service resumes. Though, that said, Coles tries to frighten his way past the third-placed Adam Roynon but can't quite catch up with him enough to intimidate him ("Coles nearly beats him with 'trackcraft' - i.e. tries to take him off!"). One possible but unlikely explanation for his failure to muscle his way past is the fact that Michael Coles no longer sports "his old leathers - the ones with 'I'm the only gay in the village' on them". Though far from potent or, indeed, ideal, the consensus is that the Monarchs reserve pairing of Coles and Cally-jis-TOE is preferable to what could take its place in 2008 if a proposal (attributed to Peter Oakes) is passed at the BSPA Annual AGM conference in the winter. Namely "Peter Oakes wants British riders at number six and seven in the Premier League next year - it's okay in the South, where they're all based, but a nightmare for any of the teams in the North!"

With Jim and Dougie around, the conversation is never far away from some discussion of the Berwick Bandits. I'm going to be there for the visit of Edinburgh tomorrow night and Jim warns, "If you get there at half five, Peter will have you in the team!" Berwick speedway has been big news this week in the national press - not for the long since abandoned film but for "Kus banging his head and talking English." When I read the English edition of the *Sun* newspaper in the comfort of my University of Edinburgh Halls of Residence, I quickly discover that not only has speedway hit the headlines in the main section (well page 27) of the paper but a smiling photo of Peter Waite - dressed in his smart, bright black-and-gold Berwick 40th anniversary anorak - noticeably looms out of the page! Matej and Peter keep august company as also pictured on the same page are James Blunt and Pink Floyd. While this is the main story on the page they also have to share with news of a six-year-old girl who was raped and strangled in her garage in America ('Horror of rape girl hanging') and news of the premature birth of a baby at home "two weeks early in Bridport, Dorset" ('Arrival Lounge'). A speedway person hasn't attracted such attention in the country's best-selling newspaper since the Scott Nicholls and Sophie Blake relationship 'furore' [headline 'Sleazy Rider'] or, even more weirdly, when an inaccurately colourful account of some details drawn from Ian Perkin's industrial tribunal resulted in his distinctive headshot appearing on one page along with a pithy comment in 'The *Sun* Says' leader column on another. The headline in today's paper says 'Fast Learner - Czech speaks English after bike crash' and is the tabloid story about his crash at a Bandits away fixture at Glasgow. After the headline draws you in, the story continues, "Matej Kus, 18, could barely speak a word of our language before coming off his bike and having another rider drive over his HEAD splitting his helmet. He was out cold for 45 minutes then came round and asked paramedics where he was and what had happened - in a posh English voice. Stunned team boss Peter Waite said: 'He sounded like a newsreader. He was speaking perfect English without any sort of an accent'. Matej had arrived in Britain only days before … he lost his memory for 48 hours - and as soon as it returned, he lost the ability to speak English." What a strange and disconcerting period this must have been for Matej (if the story is true), suddenly gifted with a different tongue and labouring under the misapprehension that the Berwick Bandits were a championship-winning team. Wars and major political upheaval get short shrift in the *Sun*, but this sort of incident requires immediate investigation and, whatever resources it takes to verify things, will be instantly available. Consequently, the paper interviews Matej through an interpreter "back home in Pilzen in the Czech Republic" to learn, "there must be some English deep in my head but obviously I needed a bang on the head and a crash for it to come out." Apart from finding success on the track, Matej's ambition is to master English and, if he spends long enough at Berwick, he should soon be smiling and speaking like the perpetually cheerful Peter Waite. Refusing to leave any stone unturned in a major story like this one, the *Sun* then explores the medical ramifications of the incident and discovers, on behalf of its worried readers, startling information about the "extremely rare Foreign Accent Syndrome". This complaint is so serious that they have to give it capital letters for emphasis in the article and briefly refrain from making things up, though my suspicions are aroused by their use of the phrase "doctors say". The one 'doctor' who is actually named in the article - "Doctor John Coleman of Oxford University's phonetics lab" - doesn't actually practise medicine and isn't directly quoted - though clearly he does, at least, have a PhD from closely studying language. He confirms the mystery of it all, since "he had never seen a case of someone speaking a foreign language before." Perhaps he should leave the laboratory more often or read the *Sun* on a regular basis as they have quite a track record for 'discovering' Foreign Accent Syndrome incidents. "Last July [2006] The *Sun* revealed Geordie Linda Walker, 61, of Westerhope, spoke with a Jamaican accent after a stroke". To generalise massively, it's safe to say that something called a 'syndrome' is likely to be all the more tenuous (and arguably less serious) than something medically classified as a disease. A syndrome relates to disease in the same manner that some contemporary promoters relate to the word 'promotion'.

The 10th heat gets the juices flowing on and off the track, though mainly on it where a slightly wild Tommy Allen makes a couple of flamboyant attempts to take Derek Sneddon off his machine, albeit without success. However, he does succeed in nearly 'fencing' one participant, his own teammate Tai Woffinden, who has to suddenly throttle off to avoid disaster! Dougie admires Snazza's skill and composure, "That's a brave race 'cause Allen tried to fence him twice and then he nearly fenced his own rider on the last bend!" In fact Dougie has spoken too soon since Sneddon waits to discuss the race on the warm-down lap and as Tommy Allen draws alongside him, Snazza shoves him in the face - well, the part of his face visible when wearing a crash helmet - and they then proceed to discuss life animatedly all the way back to the pits gate where they grudgingly shake hands.

Knowledge of the rules and the race card is essential for the success of any speedway team manager and, before heat 11, Dougie isn't convinced that Rye House Rockets team manager John Sampford is quite up to the demands of the job. "He said in the *Speedway Star* recently that he doesn't mind that Len often tells him what to do! What sort of team manager puts up with that? Now they've messed up 'cause they brought in Allen in heat 8 so, now, Neath can't come in [for a rider replacement ride for Ekberg] and ride with himself in heat 11. I'm trying to figure out the Rye House tactics!" These tactics turn out to be the strategic masterstroke of introducing Tai Woffinden as a tactical substitute off 15 metres. With Matthew Wethers ahead of him in the race, there's clearly a lot of potential ground to recover, though Tai helps himself by obviously rolling at the start. The referee must have deemed this acceptable since he conspicuously fails to call back the riders. Tai has soon caught up with Cally Cally-jis-TOE who immediately loses control of his machine ("he just got nervous and fell off like he did last week").

Before the next race we've just got enough time for Dougie to express his reservations about the Mike Moseley column in the Berwick programme. "He always writes 'if I don't see you before, I'll see you here' though really it should be 'Mike Moseley - have no fear I'll not be here!" It's bollocks, actually, no, read it - it's brilliant - it's my highlight of the weekend. I've looked for him for years and not found him. It's not like he could get lost in the crowd. It would be like me writing about Eastbourne in the Eastbourne programme but staying in Penicuik!" Talk of speedway notables segues the conversation onto Ken Burnett and they wonder if I've ever enjoyed the full glory of a Burnett speedway commentary ("he thinks Ales Dryml is Adrian Rymel's father"). Luckily heat 12 arrives but is only really enlivened by some good skill shown by Adam Roynon after "Colesy just turned left on him." With the Edinburgh Scotwaste Monarchs ahead by 41-33 with three heats to go, I'm pretty confident that they'll win though I'm in a minority of one on this matter ("we can do anything"). The possibility of last-gasp defeat recedes massively after a Monarchs 5-1 in the next race won by Wethers with George 'eyes right to glance behind me' Stancl second.

With a Rye House victory now mathematically impossible unless the Edinburgh riders somehow manage to contrive not to finish both remaining races, the Rockets bring out Adam Roynon in a black-and-white helmet colour on a tactical ride to add some vague tension. Dougie fancies a Cally-jis-TOE win, "If Cally-jis-TOE gates he can hang on - that said he's only gated once all season - I live in hope!" Jim isn't pleased with the referee, "he's held the tapes so long they'll get an 8-1." Personally I'd have said that Dave Watters perhaps could be criticised for his eccentric control of the track lights, which he apparently decided to flash on and off under the impression he was at a school disco. Dougie is equally outraged but, in his case, at the antics of Tommy Allen, "he's just tried to fence Tully!" This saves up some bad karma for the Rocket since he then endures an engine failure when well placed. The degree to which Cally-jis-TOE has to still improve at this standard of speedway is illustrated by the fact that he struggles to make up the half lap he was behind (at the very moment of mechanical failure) or overtake a rapidly slowing bike as it coasts to a stop! Before the Rockets massage the final scoreline with a last race 5-1 founded on Tai Woffinden's fourth win of the night, I again get the chance to ponder the almost complete absence of litter bins - except for the one by the burger van - within the stadium at Armadale. "We're sponsored by a recycling company but there's never any bins to put your rubbish in here!" Victory keeps the Monarchs outside hopes of Young Shield qualification alive until their next must-win meeting at Berwick tomorrow night. Interviewed afterwards over the tannoy, John Campbell says, "We've had some luck here tonight. Come along and support us at Berwick tomorrow - we need an away win and a win against Somerset next week to get in the Young Shield. Tonight, we've beaten one of the best teams in the Premier League!"

14th September Edinburgh v Rye House (Premier League) 50-45

Chapter 44. Berwick v Edinburgh: 'Only Gay in the Village' turns back the years

15th September

SKYBALLS ON WORLD TEAM CUP

Middlo *"I said to Scott afterwards 'you really wanted that' and he said, 'yeh'!"*

Nigel [after a Russian rider wins]
"That's a surprise - who could have predicted that? I did say earlier - don't take these Russian guys for granted!"

Kelvin *"The boys are really squabbling over themselves"*

Kelvin *"This race was all about second, third and fourth"*

Jonathan *"Keep that head on and take it to Poland for us!"*

Nigel *"There's the Russian team manager - he'll be mildly satisfied"*

The best-laid plans often go awry. When I planned this trip to Scotland and the North-East ages ago, I would have got to see the Scottish Cup Triangular Tournament featuring Edinburgh, Glasgow and Berwick for three consecutive days. I imagined it would excite the local imagination and generate bigger than usual crowds to buy my books. A summer of rain and postponements has ensured that the tournament was summarily abandoned while all the teams tried to cram their outstanding fixtures of the season into the few remaining weeks though, in the case of Berwick, this will be their penultimate meeting of the season! Cunningly, I'd also thought I could sneak off between speedway meetings to see my beloved Sunderland play Reading in the Premier League, though I must admit that it still seems incongruous that Reading no longer play in the (old) Third or Fourth Divisions as they did perpetually throughout my youth.[1] It's in the nature of our frankly laughable transport system that engineering works intervene on a regular inconvenient basis so that I'm forced to hire a car to travel between the exotic triangle formed by Edinburgh, Sunderland and Berwick. This deprives me of the always fascinating view from the train window of the beautiful North-East coastline as well as making it quite a rush to get from the Stadium of Light to Shielfield.

When I arrive, the car park is already crowded and there's quite a queue of fans waiting in line to enter through the rather quaint turnstiles of Berwick Rangers Football Club, who own the stadium that the Bandits call home on Saturdays during the speedway season. Not only is there little time to excite any interest in my books before the prompt start of proceedings at around 7 p.m. (invariably the case with a strictly adhered to 10 p.m. curfew in operation) for the Bandits versus Monarchs fixture but, being a soft English southerner, I can't help but notice that less than 100 miles north of Sunderland winter appears to have arrived early! In fact there's a strong cold wind blowing and, even sheltered from the elements, the markedly cool ambient air temperature is invigorating enough to make the stadium psychologically appear much more exposed than usual. This fixture was originally scheduled to take place on May 19th but was postponed at 6 p.m. after a couple of heavy downpours during the afternoon led the track to become waterlogged. This late deluge prompted Peter Waite to say, "it never rains but it pours! It had been dry in town until well after 3 p.m. … and again at about 5 the rain was stotting off the ground and bouncing some distance back up again!"

[1 A rare 2-1 early season win that saw our new talismanic striker Kenwyne Jones languorously score his first goal - a header - for the club. However, the game was much more significant for a celebration of Ian Porterfield's life that reassembled the 1973 FA Cup winning team and had spontaneous chanting erupt mid-way through the second half for well over 10 minutes. Emotional and genuinely uplifting stuff!]

Typically, later, at the scheduled start time, the skies were blue and the stadium bathed in sunshine. In fact, reports in the

Speedway Star had it that the Berwick team were prepared to race "but the visitors, to a man, were adamant that they would not ride". Given the lateness of the season and the Monarchs chance of qualification for the Young Shield, tonight both teams of riders will definitely be prepared to ride to ensure that this meeting is completed.

The programme from the original fixture is brought back from the storeroom and put on sale along with the traditional insert of the race card relevant for tonight's meeting. This practice is a regular bone of contention between promoters and fans, with the paying public often feeling aggrieved and short changed at being fobbed off with out of date and superseded material. While, at a club like Berwick (and many others round the country), finances are always tight and the need to account for every penny means that promoter Peter Waite can ill afford to waste a perfectly usable document and bear the cost of printing another more 'relevant' version just to create a feel-good factor among his loyal band of regular punters. However, where the fans do have legitimate grounds for objection is the sheer price of the Berwick programme which, at £2.50, makes it the most expensive such document in the Premier League and, almost, in all of British speedway. Reading in their Bulldogs incarnation charged this price in 2006 for a programme printed on high-quality paper with the use of colour throughout and this season Lakeside have produced a stunning-looking souvenir quality style magazine in full colour and in a big format at this price. Comparatively, both of these arguably represent value for money, whereas the normal Berwick offering does not. This is definitely the case when the 150 copies of the insert printed as an update for tonight's meeting almost immediately sells out, leaving the remainder of the fans to purchase the 250 programmes still available from the original mid May attempt to fulfil the fixture. Given that a speedway fan without a programme is like rum without Coke, then some of the grumbling I hear when standing by Davina Johnston's programme booth with my books display is wholly justified (though she does, it must be said, counter objections very sweetly). The mathematics of the situation indicates that 400 programmes sold at £2.50 each will generate a gross revenue of £1,000 for the club less the production costs of said programme along with the additional expense of printing 150 inserts. Given the legendarily delicate finances of the club, the handsome profit this clearly generates wouldn't (I'm sure) be begrudged by anyone provided that they felt they got value for their money! Having historically railed against the iniquities of the Internet, perhaps this indicates that Peter Waite has now become a convert and is conducting an obliquely subtle campaign to force people to eliminate the expense of programme purchases for any meeting during the season in favour of using the programme generator software provided free on the excellent and always interesting www.speedwayplus.com website?

For those quick off the mark enough to secure a copy of the programme insert, one area where value could be obtained is from the comparison between the Berwick team that would have ridden that night and the one that will take to the track this evening. The differences are hugely indicative of the troubled (and often woeful) season endured by all associated with the club. Only one rider - Jacek Rempala - who was scheduled to ride for the Bandits in mid-May has managed to survive a mere four months later to keep his place in the team and so take part in this meeting! Even he has had a minor transformation as his name has changed in the programme from a more carefree "Jac" to a more formal and serious "Jacek". As with speedway teams everywhere, changes are forced in the team line-ups due to injuries and (particularly for Saturday tracks) international racing commitments elsewhere. Typically promoters react to poor results by sacking 'out of form' riders willy-nilly in the hope that bringing in so-called 'fresh blood' or 'talents for the future' will staunch the run of poor performances and, usually, the loss of fans through the turnstiles unenamoured with their association with a losing team. In the case of Berwick, most years Peter Waite traditionally likes to indulge in brinkmanship almost until the season starts in order to keep a strong air of mystery about the actual team line up until practically the night before the first meeting. This also forces riders left without a team into a much weaker negotiating position with regards to payment levels. In 2007, he's been keen to keep the team line up a mystery every week! The comings and goings are all too complicated to go into the specifics, particularly the whys and the wherefores of the epidemic of injuries suffered by the riders so, instead, it's easier to conduct a roll call of the now missing riders who appeared in the original line up for this meeting against the Monarchs. Namely: Michal Makovsky, David Meldrum, Stanislaw Burza, Andreas Bergstrom, Benji Compton and Jamie Robertson. To my untutored eye, this appears a strong line up. Tonight the Bandits take to the track with a much more make do and mend appearance to their team with Carl Wilkinson (guest), Arlo Bugeja, rider replacement for Matej Kus, Ritchie Hawkins (guest), Sam Martin and Byron Bekker (guest). The only consistent elements from May to September is the appearance of Rempala and the fact that Berwick were anchored at the bottom of the Premier League table then and now! That

Programme queue

Tractor access route

Under orders

said the Edinburgh line up hasn't exactly been a stable one either and, possibly, this is also indicative of a season of struggle. The riders missing for the Monarchs tonight, but programmed to ride in May, were Ronnie Correy, William Lawson, Henrik Moller and Daniele Tessari. In their place, they have George Stancl, Kaj Laukkanen, Cally Cally-jis-TOE and Michael Coles.

Many Bandits fans will tell you that most of these changes to the Berwick line up have been wrought through the sheer capriciousness of Lady Luck, Peter Waite having apparently run over a pack of black cats. Equally we all know speedway is a dangerous sport and its performers hardy. None more so than Stanislaw Burza, who we're informed over the tannoy is "here tonight - he's wearing a full body brace would you believe! He's in a bit of pain." Traditionally many riders come back from injury far too early and then ride through the pain for the club. At Berwick, even the track staff take the same hardy, never-say-die attitude since tonight marks the return of Bob Johnston for his first meeting back in harness since his hernia operation nine weeks ago. The smart money - if there is such a thing when it comes to gambling - would have definitely been on a comfortable Monarchs away win but, during the early heats, we're treated to some all-action racing, eventful falls and an evenly matched scoreline. The third race of the night has the high hopes of the Bandits faithful in guest Ritchie Hawkins dashed by the second bend of the first lap when he falls from his machine. When I say fall, it's much more like a wrestling match with his bike in the style of a lion tamer teaching the recalcitrant beast a lesson. Ritchie soon remounts, rejoins the race and then leads by the proverbial street only to fall again in more or less the same spot on the third lap. Amazingly he remounts and still gets third place, though this is in no small part due to the fact that Andrew Tully had also fallen and remounted earlier in the race and then trailed off by such a distance that Hawkins had time to fall, clean his bike and kevlars, make a cup of tea, remount and still pootle round for third spot.

Next time out Hawkins gets a big fat zero when he again falls and is excluded by referee Jim McGregor for his troubles. The re-run of the fifth race features an enthralling encounter that has Sam Martin bravely hammer past Derek Sneddon on the banking of the fourth bend on the second lap and then duel with Snazza for the remainder of the race for the honour of second place. The determination of young Sam Martin even sees him try to win on the finish line with a last-ditch attempted burst past Stancl, who'd obligingly locked up on the last bend when - inevitably - checking over his shoulder for the big bad wolf. It was obviously a manoeuvre that Sam had gained a taste for since, in his next outing in heat 7, we again see him bravely fizz past Andrew Tully in the race to the finish line for third place. Unfortunately for Sam, he generates such speed that it subsequently causes him to crash spectacularly into the fence on the first bend of his fifth lap! It was a brush with the stadium furniture that took its toll on his later points scoring as well as his vim and vigour. However, this desire to race until the very end for the best final position shown by Sam Martin is part of the rich tapestry of speedway as the daredevil spirit of youth endlessly renews the sport through the brio of their enthusiasm - really something to be admired and always uplifting to witness.

The Monarchs fans near me have high expectations and, given their own riders don't emulate (or even approximate) this passionate will-to-win, aren't at all happy with what they saw in either race, but particularly heat 5. "That was Edinburgh riding like a bunch of amateurs - pathetic - I suppose I shouldn't be surprised 'cause we've been riding like w***** all season. Stancl's always looking round too much and Sneddon should hang his head in shame getting passed by a Conference League rider!" The unexpected crash at the end of the seventh race hasn't improved the mood of the visiting fans either since the overall scoreline has both teams still locked together on 21 points apiece. Given the patched up nature of the side they have tracked - never mind the recent poor home and away form of the Bandits - to be still within a shout of their local rivals (let alone on equal terms) is, in itself, no small achievement. Inevitably on such occasions, the talk on the terraces turns to other speedway matters and Dougie Copland highlights the limitations of the present system to choose the eventual Elite League champions. "That's the fiasco of the play-offs, Leigh Adams gets injured - the most professional and consistent Elite League rider of his generation in my opinion - and that wrecks Swindon's season!"

Wrapped up like a polar explorer against a fresh wind that verges on the howling, I watch the race action from the exposed section of terracing on the back straight with a large knot of Edinburgh fans. Conversation is almost impossible and the vagaries of the wind tonight are such that the few loudspeaker announcements that you can hear by straining your ears excessively are invariably blown inaudibly away into the distance. Sadly this means we miss many bon mots uttered by the evergreen Dick Barrie (listed in the programme as in charge of "Centre Green Presentation") as well as those of his partner-in-crime, Dennis McCleary, whose job title of "Announcer/Timekeeper/Incident Recorder/Programme" would require a business card the size of a Cornflakes packet should club finances ever extend to indulging in such fripperies. The lack of any detail or post-race commentary has the consequence of heightening your concentration on the race action, thereby further exaggerating the natural intensity of the senses invariably brought on by watching speedway under floodlights. With the lights brightly illuminating the dramatic glistening green of the pitch, Shielfield Park would be the ideal place to watch speedway during the hours of darkness but for the minor flaw that the lights are positioned to highlight the action on the pitch rather than on the shale track that surrounds it! Occasional words do percolate through before they're swiftly flung away on the wind. In fact, when some words finally do beat the elements and sound system to become vaguely audible, I register the hint of exasperation in Dick Barrie's voice just before his words finally sink in, "For the third and last time of asking for the speedway author Jeff Scott - who's in the stadium tonight - come to the starting gate so I can do an interview!" As I wander round from one side of the stadium to the other, the re-run of heat 9 has the luckless Ritchie Hawkins suffer an engine failure on the fourth bend of the second lap while leading comfortably. This enables Kalle Katajisto to salvage his only point of the night - all this despite the mandatory 15-metre handicap he had inflicted upon himself as a result of his earlier tapes offence - and take the Monarchs overall lead on the night to 6 points at 24-30.

It's typically professional and hugely kind of Dick Barrie to go out of his way to try to boost the interest of the crowd in my wares on a windswept night in the Borders. Having made sure that the riders and the tractor had already circled past the starting gate area, I scamper across the damp shale to the brightly lit grass of the centre green. Interviews aren't something I particularly enjoy or relish, especially since I get distracted by the distant echoing sound of my own voice played over the loudspeakers but, also, the mere sight of the microphone and my keenness to answer the questions quickly induces breathlessness when in the torrent of words I forget to breathe properly. With donkey's year's experience, Dick ensures the questions are entertaining and that my breathless replies are quickly summarised in a more appealing fashion. It's over before it's hardly begun and I decide to spend the rest of the meeting with my books stood in almost complete darkness next to the programme booth. Inside, Davina watches the rest of the speedway meeting unfold from her fantastic vantagepoint on the first bend and, between races, she uses the flashlight she's very sensibly brought along to light and mark her programme. The arrival of heat 12 finds the Bandits trailed off by 10 points at 28-38, so their last fling of the dice sees Ritchie Hawkins take to the shale in a black-and-white helmet colour for a chance of double points as well as to atone for his previous troubled rides tonight in the apparently jinxed Berwick race tabard. Predictably enough, when second in the race, he again fails to finish after he locks up, struggles with his bike as it straightens (snaking all over the track as though it were suddenly made of rubber) on the downhill section of the fourth bend before exiting the race by crossing the white line that separates the shale from the hallowed turf of the centre green. If the football club are more than happy to have the Bandits as tenants, the one thing guaranteed to put a spanner in the spokes of this comfortable relationship is any damage to their sacred pitch. Along with his numerous metaphorical hats worn every week for the speedway club, Dennis McCleary is also Club Secretary at Berwick Rangers Football Club. However, he eschews any mention of the damage to the turf inflicted by Hawkins but, when Matthew Wethers from Edinburgh, also graces the hallowed turf astride his steed, he admonishes-cum-promises him, "And that's Matthew Wethers about to get a bill from the football club for disturbing the pitch!"

Between the later races, Dick Barrie attempts to entertain the crowd with Sarah, the next interviewee, who's "off to London for a degree in Adult Nursing!" Ever the optimist and conjuring an image the less fainthearted in the crowd will probably ponder late into the night, Dick asks, "Can you give me a bed bath when I get older?" As familiar with bed baths as she is with enemas and barium meals, Sarah politely declines the suggestion. I gather Sarah must be some sort of local celebrity fan but, when I ask Davina for insight, she says she has only half-heartedly listened and instead has been distracted by events on the track, "It's been a disaster again tonight," she replies. [2]

After they'd just about held their own until heat 7, the Bandits are (again) put to the metaphorical sword and we're collectively treated to what is nowadays the reality of Elite League racing - two races in one! Or, if you want to try to be positive about the gulf in class in a single race that often leaves a couple of riders trailed way off at the back of the field competing for the 'chip shop money', two for the price of one. Ritchie Hawkins finally wins a race but, since it's heat 14, it's too late by then to make any real difference. Dennis McCleary offers words of encouragement: "Ritchie Hawkins has ridden well enough for 10 or 11 but has 4 points." The star turn of the night is really Michael Coles in his 'only gay in the village' leathers who turns back the tide of time to score 12 (paid 16) from six rides. Some skilled straw clutching comes into late play over the tannoy and away from it. Dennis McCleary attempts to drum up a huge crowd for the final meeting of the season at Shielfield - the mouth-watering prospect of a clash between Berwick and Mildenhall (who hover one place above the Bandits) with the added dimension to the night's entertainment provided by the visit of Kyle Legault, "the biggest mistake of the season - Sheffield getting rid of Kyle Legault." Dick then informs us as the Monarchs come out for a victory lap of celebration, "I think it was a much more encouraging showing - I predict it will be the Bandits on that truck next week!"[3] A kindly stranger stops to buy a book and tells me, "I won't read it mind, I just think it's a shame when folk put themselves out and get no interest!" After the crowd has pretty well deserted the stadium, I snatch a few words with Peter Waite - a man whose default setting genuinely appears to be set to cheerfully ebullient - about this meeting and the season in general, "you've just got to keep on! Last year we were second and everyone said we'd be champions this - and, look at us, at the bottom!"

16th September Berwick v Edinburgh (Premier League) 35-55

[2 Sarah the trainee nurse had actually been taken to Berrington Lough (the previous home of the Berwick Bandits) as a babe in arms, and had been a regular every-week attendee for all her 18 or so years.]

[3 It was 45-45. The only draw Berwick had home or away all season.]

Chapter 45. Swindon v Coventry: Night of song, consistency and inaccurate times

24th September

Rosco	*"That was very poor decision, mate"*
Jim Lawrence	*"It's a shame you think that Alun, 'cause I think it was a rather good decision because yellow was out of control"*
Rosco	*"That's the worst decision you've made in my whole life that I've seen"*
Jim	*"It's a bit early to say that?"*
Rosco	*"Having said that he never came off, he did not crash Jim!"*
Jim Lawrence	*"So, are we going to wait til they crash before we deal with it?"*
Kelvin	*"I think Alun's a bit emotional … I think Jim Lawrence has made a brave decision - a refreshing one! It may not please Mr Rossiter in the pits but it's the completely correct one."*
Jonathan	*"We've seen motivation in motion!"*
Nigel	*"We love Alun Rossiter - he's a great guy to listen to. I've admired him for many years!"*
Norris	*"To me, Rosco was a speedway version of David Brent"*

After all the hype and a season where only three or four Elite League teams came along to the party, the 2007 campaign ends with the Play-Off final everyone expected - Swindon versus Coventry. Coming into the fixture the Bees are the form team and have replaced Swindon as the bookies favourite to lift the trophy. Ignoring relative team strengths, whoever has their home leg second probably has the edge and this honour also falls to Coventry (who got to choose by finishing top of the Elite League qualifying table). When I arrive at Blunsdon, everything in the stadium looks almost picture-postcard perfect for this blue riband event. All around the stadium last-minute adjustments are being made in the pits, on the track, in the grandstand bar and to the huge variety of speedway merchandise being set out on the trackshop tables.

It's late afternoon and although the turnstiles are still locked, there's quite a queue of fans lined up already and the car park has started to crowd out, albeit with many people relaxing inside their vehicles to have their sandwiches and a cup of something hot from their flasks. The trackshop is located underneath the lee of the home-straight grandstand roof by the steep stairs that lead to the toilets and the bar. It's a natural stop-off point for a brief conversation for anyone who passes. In-demand sports commentator, Nigel Pearson, fiddles with the *Sky Sports* security badge attached to the lanyard he wears round his neck while deep in conversation with Nick and Johnny Barber. He's knowledgeable and practised enough that he will require little additional preparation for the two hours' work ahead, but he's professional enough to arrive early to do it anyway. On this basis, Jonathan Green should really arrive the week before to iron out the gaps in his understanding and to prepare some simple notes for use on the night in crayon. I continue my education into the highways and byways of live sports broadcasting when I overhear Nigel say, "I had to re-voice the [GP] Final 'cause of a Tony Millard mistake saying Nicki Pedersen is stone last." Like many people, you have to wonder how many major and minor errors Tony Millard can make every time he commentates before *Sky* finally decide that he has embarrassed them enough. Though, that said, any organisation that can have Jonathan Green on their staff, let alone in a key position, clearly has superhuman tolerance levels and less emphasis upon accuracy rather than 'entertainment' in its broadcasts.

Nigel Pearson with Johnny and Nick Barber

Crowds gather

Robins logo in flame

A keen student of the catering at speedway tracks and sports stadia throughout the country because of his commentary work, Nigel gestures towards the doorway a few yards away from the trackshop and tips me the wink, "If you wait a few minutes, they'll be selling hot dogs!" Diffident Swindon press officer and the most prolific speedway writer of his generation, the moustachioed Robert Bamford joins in their group discussion but studiously avoids any predictions when I quiz him on the likely outcome. He's too long in the tooth, and superstitious to commit, other than to state the obvious, "This is the BIG one tonight!" Rob is far happier talking about another track he knows elsewhere, "The whole stadium is a tip: they don't need bins!"

A vital member of the hard-working track staff team here at Blunsdon - justifiably made more widely famous through the exploits related on the always insightful *Blunsdon Blog*, written by Graham Cooke - Shirley Jessen ("I have Danish ancestry") stops by to inform us, "I saw and touched the trophy today and touched it in Terry's [Russell] office when I went in to clean up!" Rob shifts from foot to foot and issues what I assume is his version of saying 'no comment', "I'm not saying any more!" Shirley would like to be able to see the trophy on display at the stadium every week next season. In the absence of wood to touch or a cross to hold, Rob says, "You're getting me flustered now!" As if on cue, the diminutive Alun 'Rosco' Rossiter swaggers by with said trophy and clearly doesn't suffer from any superstitious anxieties about fate or bad luck from over-confidence or predictions of likely success. Shirley remarks, "it looks much bigger when he holds it!"

I make a point of nipping down the slope that runs towards the turnstiles and the programme booths at Blunsdon to pop into the speedway office to thank the affable Wayne Russell for his kind permission to allow me to display my books at the meeting. As I arrive, he walks the other way towards the pits to check on the myriad of last-minute details that invariably crop up on any race night, let alone at such an important meeting as this one. Contrary to popular belief on the Internet, significant work goes on behind the scenes into the planning and co-ordination of the complex logistics involved in the staging of these blue riband events. Particularly ones that will be broadcast on national television since the speedway promotion has to keep everyone in the stadium happy - riders, sponsors, television people, staff and fans - and also ensure that the spectacle seen by the armchair audience also puts the best foot forward for the club and the sport in general. There's a business truism that you shouldn't sweat the small stuff but, when you're in Wayne's position, if you don't you can guarantee that something will jump up and bite you on the arse. Despite all this possible pressure, Wayne is invariably calm, welcoming and understatedly knowledgeable whenever I've had the chance to speak with him. He's proud of the pre- and post-meeting fireworks planned to go off on the centre green but the decision to invite operatic tenor Martin Toal to provide the pre-race entertainment is an even bigger source of pride. "He's gonna do that famous one - you know, what's it [*Nessun Dorma*] - to build it all up for ten minutes after the parade and before the first heat. It's something different for speedway that'll go down well and get everyone pumped up!" Martin clearly specialises in performing at incongruous venues for his art since tonight he's here at Blunsdon and only the other week, I'd seen him perform in torrential rain at the JJB Stadium prior to the Wigan Athletic versus Sunderland game. I must say that he's a true professional (or honorary Northerner since he sang throughout in a conspicuously thin, non-waterproof jacket) with a powerful and affecting voice that, in Wigan, almost silenced what you'd imagine to be a difficult crowd to entertain. You don't often get to listen to an operatic greatest hits medley crossed with the theme music from adverts you instantly recall except don't quite know what product was being advertised (well, except for British Airways, of course).

This was my first chance to discuss my incident at Belle Vue where I encountered the abrasive trackshopman John Jones with Nick and Johnny Barber - people in the industry who are in the know about the man and his idiosyncrasies, plus they also work in the same line of business so can empathise with his perspective. Nick told me, "I can see John Jones's point of view. For years his payments helped to keep Belle Vue going really, especially through the John Perrin era, and what thanks has he got for it? In fact, he's got nothing to show. He's an old-fashioned trader - cash up front, he would pay his two or two and a half K at the start of the season - and all he's seen is people invade his patch and take the piss! Simon Stead and James Wright sell their stuff out of the back of a van - in his patch - just like Kenneth Bjerre and Jason Crump before them, without anyone saying or doing anything! He's defending his patch, as no one else will do it for him. I think he's had enough - partly 'cause Belle Vue have had a couple of really disastrous seasons, so I can't imagine the trackshop pays. If they were second or could finish second next year, he'd still be here but he's retired to Portugal - he has more than enough money - 'cause he's sick of it. If John Jones likes you, you're fine - but, if not, it's a nightmare!" When I catch up with Johnny I learn, "I should have warned you not to go - sorry! He's a thug, isn't everyone from Manchester? You went on his patch and, like all bullies, he threatened you. If you'd gone to the police or posted it, you'd have given him the excuse to take it further. Pride would have dictated so. But now, he's said his piece - threatened you and protected his patch and moved away, so I wouldn't worry about it!"

I've set my table up on the other side of the stairway because tonight the area regularly covered by the trackshop has massively expanded in anticipation of a bumper crowd. So rather than perch next to them as usual, I find myself isolated on the opposite side of the access area conscientiously patrolled by the stadium stewards and marked out as a safety zone by yellow hash lines on the floor. Because of the topology of the stadium at Blunsdon, my position is ideally located for an excellent view of the start line and first bend outside of the glass-fronted room that used to serve as the trackshop a few seasons ago on the raised but flat section of the home-straight grandstand terrace. If the stewards are zealous in their attempts to keep the bottom of the stairs completely free of human obstructions, then the old age pensioners who have stood in the spot occupied by my table are even more territorial. Or so Darcia Gingell (one of the knowledgeable and friendly stewards on patrol here on speedway race nights) and her steward friend warn me beforehand, after their experience trying to raise money by selling raffle tickets in this very spot. It's worth noting that Swindon has a deservedly high reputation with regard to their staff training and their thorough and conscientious safety planning for stadium incidents. Many other tracks should be envious of this professionalism. Like every Swindon Robins fan, in their hearts they know that the team have to win handsomely tonight ("10 or above would be wonderful!") to stand any chance of victory over the two legs of the Play-Off Final. However, I'm sure that many fans in their heads already realise that the season looks likely to end in the frustration of getting so near and travelling so far, but without the ultimate satisfaction of triumph in the end. If the lyrics of the 'Three Lions' song speaks of "30 years of hurt" suffered by England football fans in the wait for glory (though, obviously, there has now been a much longer period since the song was written, let alone that ending this trophy drought looks unlikely in my lifetime), then a song composed to cover the trials and tribulations of being a Robins fan waiting the pursuit of further glory over these past four decades would be far more wistful and mournful affair.

Even the text of the attractive full-colour rider review "through the lens of Les Aubrey" in the programme can be read two ways - on the one hand as an optimistic summary of the 2007 achievements of each individual rider. Or, on the other, after duly accentuating the positives as a coded acknowledgement that at the last hurdle of the season the game was up, the team would stumble and, ultimately, all grounds for hope were lost. We learn Leigh Adams is rightly seen as "Captain Fantastic" and "an inspiration to everyone at Swindon again this year", while Andrew '007' Moore has "grittily battled away this year" for a total of 144 points. Cory Gathercole has shown "great style in his limited outings" and "darling of the Blunsdon crowd" (and some club sponsors) Charlie Gjedde has been in "dynamic form over the last three months or so". Tomasz Chrzanowski "made great strides" as the change in his average from 4.25 to 7.15 testifies, while despite a "season disrupted by a couple of wrist injuries", the "always immaculately turned out Polish stylist" Seba Ulamek "solidly" averaged 7.74 from 28 appearances. Though absent from the end of the season through injury, Mads Korneliussen is mentioned in despatches and, something I think I'd pay good money to see, we're informed that ever-present Lee 'Rico' Richardson's "aim at the beginning of the year was to rise like a phoenix and, broadly speaking, he has achieved that goal." Well, given the phoenix is usually seen as either a bird that never dies from Egyptian mythology that lived in the desert for 500 years and consumes itself by fire in order to rise renewed from the ashes (with the appropriate ambiguous doctor's sick note in its beak), or is a person of unsurpassed beauty and excellence (a paragon), then this is a hard concept to grasp as there is only one Rico and there can only ever be one phoenix. Fortunately, there's the distraction of Alun 'Rosco' Rossiter even though I'm not quite sure what mythical beast he would be? Still, the programme notes he has "enjoyed a very good season as team boss", managing his "charges" to ensure "perhaps, most importantly, the side maintained a 100 per cent record at Fortress Blunsdon for the first time in senior league racing since 1967!"

Just as Wayne surmised and planned, the pre-meeting fireworks were something that had been seen many times before at speedway meetings. Though those used on the centre green weren't the colourful ones you'd expect but were more in the fashion of the distress flares you fire into the sky when your boat is sinking. This approach to presentation was definitely an unexpectedly different touch and, as is traditional, were let off as the riders took to the track. Before the spectacle of the distress flares, the performance by tenor Martin Toal really stood out as something completely unique. In my opinion, speedway meetings are a difficult gig to play. At best, you have the status of support band where everyone wills you to just get it over with so that the main entertainment they've come to see can finally commence. Or, the fans just ignore you as they chat with their neighbours or hunt out that ideal vantagepoint inside the stadium. The territorial OAPs I'd been warned about had arrived as promised and made no attempt to hide their disgust at the position of my table. After they'd paid to get in for the most important meeting here in many long years, I can understand and sympathise with their annoyance when they found their favoured spot occupied by an interloper. They say advanced age brings either contentment or belligerence. Disappointed at my answer to a blunt question ("Can't you go away?"), I suggested we share the space behind my table, except for the space I stood in. Clearly the idea of sharing this area wasn't compromise enough since it was patently obvious they considered I should fark off elsewhere and leave them alone. There was a cacophony of tuts, loud exhalations as well as an ongoing but unspoken passive-aggressive campaign to move my books aside and/or cover them completely. Still, we almost rubbed along together and, once the meeting started, they seemed content enough to loudly grumble about the performance of the Swindon riders all evening and thereby studiously avoided any conversation with me. The size of the crowd was such that there was little passing trade since, once you found a spot in the stadium, you stood there immobile - except for occasional but necessary refreshment or comfort trips.

Facing one direction, looking over the sea of heads in a bumper crowd I can see the action on the track as it unfolds while, if I turn round and look through the window into the room behind me, I can see the replay of each race on the television. This is the best of both worlds since you get to see replays of the contentious bits of the action and silence is arguably the ideal way to experience the work of Jonathan Green. Elsewhere in my writing, I've sometimes expressed reservations about the structure and style of some of the *Sky* coverage, particularly the relentless hyperbole.[1] Tonight, however, I was able to accidentally discover that, if they behave similarly at all outside speedway broadcasts, *Sky Sports* consistently misrepresent some key factual information about every single race - namely the time! Speedway as a sport (and many of the fans as a breed) places great emphasis upon recording the numerical minutiae of each race to better enjoy and understand it at the time as well as for comparisons of riders and teams in the context of history. For some this particular aspect of our sport - numerical records and the tabulation of said same into tables of performance by team or rider - is both a passion and an obsessive delight. Imagine my horror (on their behalf) to discover that the race times given out to the armchair audience are completely fallacious! An audience the *Sky* publicity office lead us to believe they delight in enthusing and educating that, like the universe, is ever expanding. Rather than wait a moment, the increasing McDonaldisation of our culture, not to mention television representations of it, requires instant

[1 though equally, I've also given out praise when praise is due. Never mind the obvious caveat that practically all speedway fans are delighted to enjoy the regular oxygen of publicity that satellite television provides.]

and immediate gratification - in this instance, with a race 'time' to promptly appear along with the standard *Sky* caption of the result. To pick three examples at random (though it did become quite obsessing for me):

Heat 3 Sky Time: 65.54 Official Time: 66.02

Heat 6 Sky Time: 66.66 Official Time: 66.58

Heat 12 Sky Time: 66.27 Official Time: 66.83

We can all make allowance for human error (and clearly the times given out by *Sky* suffer from this fallibility too), but surely to pass these times off as accurate betrays real contempt. It illustrates better than anything else that *Sky Sports* really views speedway as an easily manipulable entertainment rather than as a sacrosanct sport. Surely, it's a reasonable question to ponder, if they wouldn't make up the important fine detail of a cricket match and pass it off as fact, then why do they do this for speedway? Indeed, not only does speedway historically record track records (never trust news of a track record being broken if you're told it has been during the live broadcast of a speedway match on *Sky* until you, at least, have independent confirmation) but also many people like to record the fastest times of individual riders. For those of the anorak persuasion, at King's Lynn, they have advanced things so much that they even have the innovation - with the use of tracking technology - to record the individual lap time of every rider in each race.

Though it was only nine days since his painful accident at Smallmead, Leigh Adams had already ridden in the Grand Prix at the weekend and, though still hampered by his injuries, the talismanic and inspirational Robins leader was back on track when it mattered for his team. Unusually without a guest in sight for either team, the Bees once again operated rider replacement for the injured Olly Allen, even though some Swindon fans had it rumoured that he could have ridden but the tactical use of rider replacement was too good an opportunity for the Bees to miss (particularly at home). Sadly for the biggest Robins crowd in a quarter of a century, their riders never really established the home-track advantage that previously had held them in such good stead throughout the 2007 season against the majority of teams, even at their bogey track of the Abbey Stadium. The omens didn't look good for the Robins when the highly rated reserve pairing of Steve Johnston and Billy Janniro gained the maximum 5-1 heat advantage in the second race. After this initial triumph, the performance of the Coventry reserves wasn't the decisive factor that the expert pundits predicted it would be beforehand. However, the all-round team performance of the Bees would be decisive in restricting the Swindon team from ever gaining a decisive enough lead to take with them to Brandon. In the early stages, it appeared that you could only win a race if you started from gate 3 and it wasn't until Heat 7 that a rider from another gate won, when Chris Harris shot from the inside to win comfortably to leave the scores at 26-22. Though the eighth race winner was also to come from gate 3, the other starting positions became a factor from that point on in the contest.

It wasn't really to be a night to savour for the Robins faithful packed into every available nook and cranny of Blunsdon and the muttered collective groan of anguish, when Smolinski and Nicholls combined in Heat 11 for a 1-5 to level the scores at 33-33, signalled the point at which even the optimists conceded that any real possibility of championship triumph receded back to pipe dream status. A couple of maximums in successive heats for the Robins (what appeared to be a real roller, viewed with the naked eye, for Adams in Heat 13 didn't appear so on the television replay) restored pride but merely massaged the scoreline to a more respectable 8 points advantage. A fall in the last race by Lee Richardson definitively ended the night with another groan for those of a Wiltshire persuasion, particularly when television replays showed the cause to be Rico trying too hard rather than any interference by his rivals. The re-run saw Leigh Adams drop his only point of the night when Scott Nicholls temporarily clamped him down to thereby enable Chris Harris to escape. On the night many of the Robins team only showed consistency in preference to brilliance and, if fingers had to be pointed, then Leigh Adams and Damian Balinski were definitely exempt while Seba Ulamek might have looked the part but didn't produce the goods when most badly needed by his club.

24th September Swindon v. Coventry (Elite League Play-Off Final, 1st Leg) 49-43

Chapter 46. Swindon: More traffic chaos hits the *Super7even* series

30th September

Alun 'Mister Motivator' Rossiter [names heat 15 line up]
"It's gunna be Andrew Moore , nah, huh huh, it's Leigh Adams"

Rosco   *"I'm not saying anything about the ref - I was very disappointed with him"*

Rosco   *"My Poles should have stayed in Poland tonight"*

Rosco   *"Probably everyone will be opening their eyebrows"*

The final round of the *Super7even* series sees the Premier League Riders' Championship held at the neutral track that everyone has banged on about for years, in this instance Swindon. Inevitably there's talk that the long fast track will 'favour' certain riders, most notably those from Sheffield and the Isle of Wight where week in and week out the home riders have supposedly acclimatised to the demands that greater speed places on man and machine. It will also possibly favour those longer-in-the-tooth riders who enjoy some additional longevity for their careers at the Premier League level as it won't be that long ago since they'll have ridden at Blunsdon in league meetings. That said, you wouldn't be part of the field unless you excel on the shale and, given that they make a living at this activity, you'd expect riders to be able to adapt and prosper no matter where they ride, irrespective of the track size and shape. The low hum of often irrelevant grumbles is a constant on the Internet so we should ignore them and, not wishing to sound like I'm reading from the *Super7even* press releases, there's no doubt that the blue riband events of the speedway calendar have been reinvigorated. Credit here must go to Jonathan Chapman for realising his vision to re-brand these disparate events under the umbrella of the *Super7even* banner. Like most marketing activities, overnight success isn't sensible or desirable to expect but the overall impression created by the series should be seen as work-in-progress where pitfalls and defects that arise are rectified by the lessons of experience. There's no doubt that there has been a massive improvement on the past although, clearly, the promised renaissance hasn't yet quite materialised. And equally, there were grumbles during the winter that the increased marketing spend set in train by Jonathan to prettify the series concept dented the overall shared profits divvied up to the clubs, despite the increased crowd numbers.

The series has suffered from the weather, track preparation, absentee riders and, impossible to predict or plan for, traffic chaos! The Somerset event attracted an almost surreal number of accidents in a short space of time on the roads (rather than the track) in the general geographic area of the stadium, something that quickly brought gridlock and frustration to every vehicle not already there. The traffic gods have definitely continued to be upset since, almost bizarrely, a couple of accidents have practically cut off the Blunsdon stadium in all directions. Traffic delays are an inevitable part of the contemporary driving experience as throughout the country car ownership expands exponentially to fill and exceed all the available space on the tarmac and streets. Road rage and aggression aside, everyone usually rubs along together until a random blockage caused by an accident disrupts the flow and chaos often then quickly ensues. Nonetheless, it's bizarre that every *Super7even* meeting appears to cause the road infrastructure to break down! Swindon steward Darcia Gingell - who tells me that she along with many other of her Swindon speedway friends will be sporting "red hats and red hair dye for Monday at Coventry" - is the speedway equivalent of the 'flying eye' actually able to report on what she saw rather than repeat third-hand exaggerated rumours of what's going on. "The M4 is shut at both Swindon junctions - 15 and 16 - and the A419 is blocked as a lorry has overturned at the roundabout quarter of a mile from here. How it did I don't know! If you're coming from Gloucester you're fine but, otherwise, if you're coming from the M4 direction everyone is really stuck!" Given you'd expect that the speedway hordes drawn on a Sunday to watch the cream of Premier League speedway don't all live in the vicinity of the Gloucester area or are naturally drawn to travel through it from other speedway 'hotbeds', then the *Super7even* transport jinx, once again, appears to be in full effect.

These early eyewitness reports underestimate the massive cumulative impact that motorway closure can have on a busy Sunday evening as vehicles hurtle along the main London to Wales and the South-West transport link. In the westbound direction, there's a 30-mile tail back at one point and, even after the meeting, when I drive in the opposite direction there's mile after mile of stationary or incredibly slow-moving traffic. Sod's Law also applies since the careful pre-season planning of the events completely failed to foresee (!) the possibility that bookies' favourites for the Elite League crown, Swindon, might actually qualify for the Elite League Play-Off Final. So, despite the notional attractiveness of staging the event at a 'neutral' venue where crowds have been consistently high since talk of the stadium closure started, it perhaps wasn't the brightest move to stage the PLRC between the two legs of the play-offs. Let alone on the night before the most important night in the history of Swindon speedway for 40 years! Speedway fans aren't generally blessed with the deepest pockets, so it's definitely the case that optimism has trumped pragmatism or that the obvious implications of three premium-priced showpiece events in one week would ensure that the Wiltshire-based public would have to make 'difficult' zero-sum choices about the meetings they decided to attend. If one of the three meetings in a week had to be missed, then the sacrifice was always going to be the PLRC where the riders were effectively strangers and the standard of racing often (inaccurately) seen as 'lower' than the so-called Elite level. Locally, this ignores the fact that the promised land of *Sky* and the appearance of 'superstar' riders from the GP isn't an arena that the Robins have always regularly graced.

Another problem that has historically beset BSPA shared events is the last-minute absence of riders through sudden 'injury' or peculiar circumstances that frequently strain credulity. Given that riders regularly return from serious injury with great alacrity or continue to ride with injuries that would ensure lesser men took time off, it always seems peculiar that so many of the species suffer from these sudden, intermittent, strategic and incredibly short-lived debilitating sicknesses. So while on the track we have tactical riders, off the track we have tactical injuries! This will-to-doctors-note has been officially re-branded during 2007 as the 'Matej Zagar Effect' in honour of its most shameless and brazen practitioner though, to be fair to everyone's favourite Slovenian, there are other equally capable exponents of this dark but increasingly prevalent art. While in the speedway press the honour, lustre and prestige of these championships are talked up as if they are established facts, the reality is somewhat different. During an intense and lengthy speedway season (particularly towards the tail end of it), the riding talent has become careworn and jaded at the thought of yet another meeting rendered more meaningless in their minds by the low rates of pay allegedly offered at any BSPA shared event. So physically and financially, there's a disincentive to attend and, if you do turn up, unless your competitive instincts naturally kick in as soon as you don a crash helmet, then human nature will dictate you'll probably ensure that you get to ride at the other more lucrative meetings that remain in the season. Particularly after an initial poor ride or two, common sense and self-preservation is logically going to make you think about the need to fight another day. A glance at the lavish "Official *Super7even* magazine £3" reveals that only three riders are absent from the programmed field at the time the programme was printed. Of these absentees, it would strain belief for the absences of Shane Parker and Glenn Cunningham to be anything other than totally genuine, though questions remain about the third man Gary 'Havvy' Havelock. When I say to Birmingham promoter, Graham Drury, "I see Havvy has withdrawn with a suspected wrist injury," he pauses for dramatic effect with a skill that would suit a career on the stage before he utters an extremely expressive "Well!" At the trackshop, Johnny Barber had watched the mix of retired footballers and 'personalities' that make up the sides that compete in the indoor Premier League All-Stars on the telly (*Sky*), so has some pertinent questions too, given Havvy is a mad keen Boro fan and was part of the tournament, "Do you think he hurt himself playing football? Middlesbrough have won through to the semi-final and that's tonight![1] I wonder if a doctor will confirm it's broken?"

[1 versus Sunderland and won by eventual champions the Smog monsters with a couple of goals from Bernie Slaven]

Stewards Julie Freeman and Darcia Gingell

Lynn Wright always watches her sons ride

Table obstruction proves handy

Another unexpected absentee is Jonathan Chapman, whose drive, enthusiasm and distinctive hair styling has become so much a part of the fabric of the *Super7even* series. Not having him around is a big miss (albeit less of one than if the Sexy7even girls didn't show up) and scanty details from his dad, Buster ("Jonathan's ill"), doesn't completely dismiss the idea that tonight JC is the Matej Zagar of the promotional world, so will definitely pop up right as rain at the next King's Lynn meeting. Reading's Malcolm Holloway passes and calls out, "Who's your money on?" only to learn from Buster "I don't bet!" It's widely acknowledged that the Elite League has had what can bc euphemistically described as a 'difficult' year. Partly self-inflicted through the structural diversity of team strengths (and what was described to me as "the blind willingness [of promoters] to pay inflated superstar pay rates despite meagre attendance incomes") coupled with unpredictable rider absences but also through the ongoing and hugely deleterious effect of the GP series, the interruption of the 'meaningless' World Team Cup as well as the demise of Oxford and the rockiness created by the abandonment and sale of Reading by experienced 'businessman' John Postlethwaite. While frequently praised as the ideal model for speedway league racing in this country, the Premier League has also had its issues even at a successful club like King's Lynn that boasts dynamic promotion, a loyally fanatical fan base, excellent stadium facilities as well as regular trophy success over recent years. Buster tells me, "People haven't got any money - it's the economy - but our crowds are up! Amazing we could increase the admissions when you think about it but the bar and food takings are slightly down. But when people are short, they economise. We're very pleased with the FIM stock car event we held at the stadium. We were being bad-mouthed beforehand at the other events and on the Internet - some people were unhappy we had it, Coventry really - but people decided to come and see for themselves! It was amazing - we had 10,000 and there was still loads of room. I can't tell you about the bar takings! On the Internet afterwards, we've had page upon page of praise saying it was the best stock-car meeting they'd seen in 25 years! There was a bit of a delay before the final - the drivers asked we grade the track before the final - but the moans stopped when they saw the difference it made. Everyone was happy!" Many seasoned speedway observers were surprised when the King's Lynn promotion chose a harder tie against Sheffield rather than the 'easier' one against Isle of Wight in the semi-final of the Premier League play-offs. Buster explained the logic behind this decision, "on purely commercial grounds we chose Sheffield 'cause they will attract a big crowd and they'll bring fans whereas the Isle of Wight don't have a group of travellers. Then, if we go out, we've had a big night!"

Some fans like to leave early and make a day of the trip to the speedway. This is true of some families but particularly so for the older generation who travel with their flasks, foil-wrapped sandwiches, cakes in Tupperware containers and garden furniture. The initial queue of these reconstituted teenagers have just come through the recently opened Blunsdon turnstiles and immediately lined up again at one of the two programme booths to purchase their copies of the "Official *Super7even* magazine". Something they don't like - no matter how high quality the paper, colour and production values - is price inflation, "Three pounds! Three pounds! At that price I'm definitely not getting one!"

On the subject of programmes I bump into Ipswich presenter, Kevin Long, who's here to conduct some pithy pits interviews with the riders for the Re-Run Videos extravaganza on the PLRC. In his hand Kevin has his secret weapon and a revolutionary tool for programme changes - *Tippex* correction tape. "This is invaluable and very conveniently they manufacture it at just the right width for speedway programmes, though they could do it in different colours! You don't even have to wait for it to dry." He lends me his to alter my glossy PLRC magazine and, I must say, it's amazing stuff! I tell Kevin I'm thinking of coming to Mildenhall on a Tuesday night to watch the Young Shield clash with Birmingham, "Are you that desperate for sleep? I'd save your money if I was you!"

I've again placed my table on the other side of the yellow safety markings at the edge of the giant area occupied by the Barber trackshop. I'm sure that I'll get another frosty welcome from the territorial old age pensioners disgusted to find their favoured position cluttered. While we wait for the occasional car to intermittently wend its way into the car park from the almost-gridlocked traffic jams surrounding the stadium, I can watch the world go by from behind my table. The friendly and redoubtable Joan English from Newcastle speedway passes so I mischievously enquire about her son who is a Newcastle season-ticket holder: "Is George coming over to Sunderland for the big game? It's a lovely city!" Joan gives me an incredulous look as she tries to figure out my sanity, "You are joking, aren't you?"

Jo Lawson, who cut her speedway teeth at Blunsdon before she moved onto Somerset, lives reasonably locally and has also taken the opportunity to catch up with old friends as well as watch the action. I haven't seen her in ages and she proudly informs me her baby Chloe is "now nine months!" Motherhood obviously suits her. She has a soft spot for Lee Complin - one of the pre-meeting favourites who has been in rejuvenated form since his return to the track this season after his brief but premature retirement, "he was always a stylish rider, so the idea that he could be lost to the sport was tragic. His photo in the *Star* made him look like Leonardo DiCaprio, which can't be bad!" Also scuttling by at regular intervals is Swindon Press Officer, Robert Bamford, as ever attired in his distinctive Robins red anorak and sporting a luxuriant moustache. Glad-handing the public isn't something that he views as part of his remit and, by virtue of moving about the place quickly as he can, hopefully, mostly elude them. We briefly discuss how his work on the forthcoming *2008 Speedway Yearbook* is progressing but the mere mention of this, with the implied pressure of deadlines, isn't music to his ears. "When you get to my age [45], you don't need any more stress," he says dolefully as though the cares of the world weigh on his octogenarian shoulders. He briefly lingers then does nothing to dispel his alleged similarity to Major Major in *Catch 22*, when he tells me conspiratorially, "I'm trying to avoid everybody and I'm gonna go round the back and sneak up to the ref's box that way!"

There are fewer of the old age pensioner regulars to take umbrage at the positioning of my table by the time the meeting gets underway, thereby confirming that expense trumps proximity even for most dedicated speedway fans when it clashes with the high point of their season. However, those that have ventured along soon pointedly spread their programmes, bags and possessions over my books in a gesture I would describe as passive-aggressive without the passive. When the meeting gets underway, there's a good-sized but not exactly spectacular crowd inside the stadium. I can't imagine the remainder you'd have expected to see are all in the "30-mile tailback westbound to Bristol" we hear about over the tannoy and collectively we thank our lucky stars not to have the joy of experiencing it first-hand. Mildenhall rider Jason King was unlucky enough to get caught in the chaos and missed the meeting, as did a coachload of fans from the Isle of Wight. When the changes to the programme are announced yet again, the news that Gary Havelock is missing because he was "injured during the week playing football" gets ironic cheers that I suspect comes more from disbelief than surprise that he can survive the danger of speedway but not football. With the absence of Havvy and Jason King, the problem of rider development within British speedway is there for all to see since I can only count four British riders in the main field (though there are five if you count meeting reserve Chris Schramm).

The tone for the meeting is set from the outset when James Wright beats the meeting favourite Chris Holder in the first heat, while a win for Jason Lyons in the second caused the large contingent of Birmingham fans in attendance great delight. Earlier, Birmingham promoter Graham Drury had been by to talk turkey with the speedway trackshop franchisee at Perry Barr, Nick

The dapper Kevin Long

Shirls displays her authographs

Rider parade

Barber. Displaying the diplomatic skills that appear to come so naturally to him and all skilled politicians, Nick enquired about planned contingencies should the Young Shield campaign not end in triumph for Birmingham: "If the unthinkable happens and you do go out - have you got any plans to have those meetings anyway?"

"Yeh - Belle Vue might visit."

Graham says hello and I show my ignorance by asking whether the Brummies have suffered from many rain-offs, "Six! It's been a nightmare. They say it always rains in Birmingham." The weather has also played its part in their failure to complete their fixtures in the run in for qualification for the Premier League play-offs, "Yeh, we were beaten by the cut off. Glasgow did everything to try to persuade Stoke to change it - if you get that support from another promotion you can't ask for more than that - we would have definitely had the bonus point and, with that, we'd have been in the play-offs. If we win our outstanding fixtures we'll finish second!"[2]

If the shock of Chris Holder's second place in the first heat wasn't enough, then a win for reserve Chris Schramm in Heat 4 (in place of Jason King) with Lee Complin in third has the pre-meeting form book in disarray from the get go. In Heat 7, Daniel Nermark gives Chris Holder an almighty shove in the first corner for absolutely no effect whatsoever. James Wright wins his second race of the night after a re-run in Heat 8. With Complin having two rides on the trot there's a bit of a delay that allows me to chat with Reading *über*-fan Arnie Gibbons. He sings the praises of PLRC referee Tony Steele, "some referees take the approach 'I'm the ref - I'm laying down the law - you're bloody lucky I'm even allowing you to shout at me'. Whereas Tony Steele knows the rules but, more importantly, he knows how to manage people. He explains afterwards to riders 'I'm sorry I had to exclude you but I saw it like this'. That said he wrongly excluded Phil Morris at Arena, in 2002 (I think), it was outrageous and there is a school of thought that when he excluded Tony Rickardsson in 2000 - I can't recall it, but a friend of mine always goes on about it - that cost him the World Championship!" Arnie's a proselytising fan of the PLRC, "it's a good field, reasonably evenly balanced plus it's wide open with several favourites - much more so than the ELRC or even the CLRC!"

The return of Lee Complin onto the shale briefly cuts short our conversation (as do any announcements over the exceptionally loud speakers with the volume apparently cranked up to deafening in anticipation of a crowd of old age pensioners with hearing difficulties) long enough for the race to run a couple of laps before being stopped. On the third bend of the second lap, with Jason Lyons way out in front Complin powers to press Jacek Rempala but has to bail

[2 Birmingham did finish second in the final Premier League table but didn't take part in the play-offs. Like other recent times when all teams haven't completed their fixtures, this makes the professionalism and administration of the sport look like a joke to the casual observer and, should anyone be looking, in the media. No wonder we continue to struggle with an image problem when we can't get the basics right on the one hand and, simultaneously on the other, *Sky* hype their televised meetings up out of all proportion to the entertainment actually offered and often represent the sport in a manner that suggests that it's merely some form of glorified monster truck racing.]

out when the Pole moves over. Lee is excluded for his fall and we get a two-for-one exclusion with Chris Kerr also thrown out for not being under power at the time of the incident. Inevitably in the match race of a re-run, Jason Lyons is deprived of his victory with a second place (or last position). Before the next race, Arnie takes delight in the recent wit of the Brummies management and press team regarding team strengthening, "Birmingham's teaser was funny when they signed Phil Morris - 'we've signed a new rider and he's not English' - who's definitely Welsh." An avid researcher of all things Reading, Arnie recalls his delight upon noticing that the (excellent) www.speedwayplus.com website archive contained news that for the meeting versus Oxford, rider Danny Bird might be the key rider for Reading but this depends "if he flies high this season". It was only a short while later that Danny received a two-year ban from the sport for failing a drugs test, allegedly for recreational cocaine use.

While, the OAPs by my table continue to be afflicted by a form of territorial Saint Vitus dance, BSPA Chairman Peter Toogood glides down the adjacent stairs with his hands out in front of him as if he's a magician adjusting the rabbit up his sleeve. It turns out that he's not the interval entertainment, "I hate those driers - can't be bothered with them!" Heat 12 sees James Wright enjoy the kind of good fortune that victory in life or speedway often depends on, when Kaj Laukkanen gifts him second place with an engine failure. This was to prove significant and let Wright off his totally shocking gate that had deservedly relegated him to a distant third place. Temporarily between interviews, Ipswich presenter Kevin Long passes by and shares a few words on King's Lynn presenter, the inimitable Mike Bennett, "at the Premier League Fours he mentioned King's Lynn loads of times, he even mentioned their sponsor but no one else's. Bad when you think it's a shared event and every team has one and would welcome the plug!" After he's left some teenage lads come up and ask a series of quick-fire question that have clearly been playing on their minds (and hormones), "When you wrote your books did you get to meet the start line girls? They're models aren't they? What are they like?" I go from hero to zero in their eyes almost instantaneously when I reveal that my investigative skills as a writer haven't extended to a level of any great intimacy with these girls.

Bizarrely, particularly for someone who flies round the Owlerton race track every week with confidence, dash and brio, Andre Compton seems out of sorts at Blunsdon and reluctant to leave off from hugging the inside line during every race he participates in. Innate competitiveness has Compton blast from the tapes in Heat 14 sufficiently quickly to relegate an also out-of-sorts Tai Woffinden behind him, but the fatal flaw of his overwhelming desire to ride the white line sees Chris Kerr exhilarate the crowd with an outside dash round him on the last bend of the second lap to gain the lead and subsequently power to victory. Swindon steward Darcia Gingell passes to praise the riding, "finally a race worth watching" without apparent irony, given the number of follow-my-leader races regularly served up at Blunsdon on a weekly basis when the home riders often cruise to victory. "I don't often see the Premier League riders - they look really fast but the times are really slow: but then the track is a bit rough!" Occasionally, absorbing though the PLRC action is, the thought of tomorrow's vital clash at Brandon isn't ever really far from her thoughts, "if I was the Coventry manager, I'd be paying Olly Allen not to ride 'cause rider replacement is good for them there!"

Also here tonight is a man of great generosity and humanity, proud Scotsman Ian Mclean who takes in the PLRC with his southern-based son Alan. Ian is invariably scrupulous in his comments and is keen to correct a misapprehension he'd informed me of via email about the culpability of James Grieves for unseating Shane Parker at Saracen Park recently. "I spoke to Shane about it and I owe James Grieves an apology because Shane had a puncture." Like his father, Alan travels around the country as much as work permits to watch his beloved Glasgow Tigers but also travels to occasional overseas GPs and visits other tracks that the red-and-white army don't reach. "I went to a really dire meeting at Eastbourne against Arena. The highlight of the meeting was seeing Scott Nicholls feed his baby in the bar! Nicki Pedersen was on a different planet that night."

The indefatigable Norman 'Nobby' Hall is also here tonight having ventured away from Cowley Stadium for some relaxation after another eventful season and his endless hours of hard, unpaid work there. Like many genuine Oxford fans, he didn't have much time for the people involved in the Colin Horton promotional era prior to the debacle that nearly saw the club go suddenly out of existence. In comparative terms, the arrival of Allen Trump had quickly illustrated a key difference between the two promotional regimes, "He's a gentleman - when we came in, me and Mike, he rushed downstairs [from the bar] and said 'I just wanted to say hello' which isn't something that would have happened before." Away to our left the riders are up at the tapes for Heat 17, in yellow on the outside gate Kaj Laukkanen twitches nervously causing Andre Compton in blue to flinch slightly - this mere hint of additional movement, then immediately causes Kaj to completely annihilate the tapes. With a hint of understatement the announcer informs us, "Kaj Laukkanen is excluded for touching the tapes." Oxford programme editor and all-round good bloke, Robert Peasley sails past where we stand, "He's in a world of his own, that lad!" says Nobby affectionately.

The completion of the 20-heat qualification process that forms an inevitable part of almost every individual speedway meeting nowadays (something I still instinctively object to as inequitable, never mind that it's symptomatic of the continued creeping influence of the Postlethwaite-era Speedway Grand Prix series) sees James Wright and Jason Lyons seeded straight through to the final on account of their points totals. The "last-chance qualifier" results in Jacek Rempala along with winner Daniel Nermark qualifying at the expense of Chris Holder and Tomas Topinka. There's a large contingent of Birmingham fans congregated by the start line and, ignoring the fact that nearly all of them proudly wear various items of red-and-yellow clothing emblazoned with a large capital letter 'B', they leave no one in any doubt about their spelling abilities or their collective desire for a Jason Lyons victory. They chant as though they're the speedway offshoot of the Hare Krishnas, "give us a B, give us an I, give us…" loudly and delightedly. "You don't often hear that anymore," says Nobby wistfully. All we're missing to complete the tableaux are the riders. The announcer explains the delay, "Under the rules, the riders are allowed a short break before coming out to choose gates." This isn't music to Nobby's ears, "Oh no - we're all bloody freezing!" As if the drama of the night hasn't already been spun out long enough anyway, the choice of gate positions by the riders takes an inordinate length of time to get under way because the riders are all allowed to fit new tyres for the Final. The announcer throws himself diligently and almost breathlessly into his hushed, slightly reverent commentary - obviously modelled on the obsequious manner and style of a particularly fawning journalist at a meaningless wedding of minor Royalty - "He comes out over the tapes to try to find a rut that will propel him into the corner!" before he spoils the effect with, "I should remind him, he's choosing a gate not a girl." Once the faux anticipation we're all supposed to feel (but I suspect don't at all) while we watch the alleged 'drama' of gate selection is over, James Wright takes command from the outset and triumphs in some style from his nearest rival in the race and on the night, Jason Lyons. As ever, at speedway meetings that feature either of her sons (James and Charles), Lynn Wright attends and proudly sees her eldest storm, on this occasion, to a well-deserved victory. The top three riders take to the podium for the presentations and, afterwards, give their thoughts to the remnants of the crowd who have lingered on a bitterly cold night to experience the conclusion of the event. Jacek Rempala tells us, "I'm very happy! Berwick team not good this year." The soothing strine of the laconic Jason Lyons booms out over the loudspeakers; first he discusses the meeting at hand "I made a dreadful start off gate four" before he elicits further cheers from the Brummie faithful pressed close against the perimeter fence by the start gate by confessing, "I'm loving it at Birmingham!" Even James Wright - who usually prefers to let his exploits on the track speak for him rather than his interviews - appears seized by the giddiness of his moment of triumph and departs from his usual somewhat reticent interview style to celebrate his victory. "I started out with a heat win and, after that, everything fell into place. And, what with Kaj breaking down, I got some luck too. I'm over the moon - I can't believe it! I've got a brand new bike to go home with too!"

30th September Premier League Riders Championship, Winner: James Wright

Chapter 47. King's Lynn v Leicester: "I know it's great for you guys just to be here, getting racing again!"

3rd October

With the exciting news that the successful promotional team of Buster and Jonathan Chapman would be the experienced backers adding their expertise to the long-running campaign by the Leicester Speedway Supporters Club to resurrect the Leicester Lions in the city, it was only a matter of time before a challenge meeting at the Norfolk Arena took place to celebrate this partnership. With a coachload of enthusiastic fans making the journey cross-country from England's sixth biggest city to Norfolk, all the omens were positive for the encounter of King's Lynn versus the itinerant Leicester Lions. The doyen of British speedway referees, Tony Steele, had agreed that he would officiate - something that added to the poignancy of the event given that he was inspired to take an interest in the sport as a direct result of his curiosity being excited by his initial sight of the Blackbird Road stadium roof from the upstairs of a passing bus in his childhood Leicester. Indeed, there would be widespread celebrations throughout the whole of speedway if a traditional, sadly defunct club like the Leicester Lions could once again take to the shale.

The only metaphorical cloud on the horizon is the complex process that local government planning and environmental approval requires any new sporting club to complete successfully. But with these battles yet to be fought, inside the locked turnstiles of the stadium the only clouds on the horizon were literally just that - floating overhead in the sky and also away in the distance as far as the naked eye can see, all around the vicinity of King's Lynn. With a dark, troubled expression, Buster Chapman wonders rhetorically "Why does it farking always rain on Wednesday?" Sensibly no one answers before he continues, "It does my farking head in!" In our group of amateur weathermen gathered outside the trackshop, Mike Moseley morosely glances to the horizon (where we can all clearly see the dark haze of not-so-distant rainfall), "It doesn't look too promising!" I try to inject a note of optimism that my long rain-affected drive through Cambridgeshire and Norfolk really doesn't bear out, The forecast is for occasional drizzle" but, instead, depress Buster further, "it says it's gonna be farking fine on my forecast!"

The Norfolk Arena changes almost every time I arrive since the Chapmans are passionate about its ongoing development and continually strive to enhance the facilities and customer experience. Some of the modifications are small, whereas others require considerable investment. Tonight it's instantly noticeable that they've rearranged the entrance area just inside the turnstiles to provide a completely new seating area kitted out with a large number of trestle tables. Fans will now have somewhere to linger with the food they've bought from the on-site catering outlets, though this will appeal more in the summer rather than October. After the fans have eaten, they'll be able to visit the new-look trackshop which, though it looks slightly similar, is now located inside a much more substantial wooden structure than previously was the case. Inside it's a bit more spacious and the majority of the speedway merchandise has already been put out on display. Indoors Johnny Barber is fulminating against the complaint culture that often afflicts the die-hard speedway supporter on the terraces but is worn as a badge of honour on the Internet forums. "Two tactical rides is one of the best ever rules introduced - this season the racing has been worse in the Elite League and that's one of the important factors. Another is the riders - the Elite League is the best league in the world in my opinion - but only if the riders take it seriously! Everyone knows before the season starts that the Elite League is 40 meetings. So you sign if you want to ride those and not if you don't. If I was Bob Brimson I'd have sacked Nicki Pedersen by now as he only rides when he thought he wouldn't get injured for the GPs. The other problem is the Poles. I wouldn't have them - Ippo [Ipswich] have really suffered 'cause of that - when they get told they have to come back for a practice they do, otherwise they'll be sacked from their league team. And in British speedway we just say 'oh, okay!' Another thing, *Sky* is one of the best things ever to happen to the sport. It's got so ridiculous that people complain on the Internet about Nigel Pearson shouting. So what! For 20 years we were begging for any coverage - people amaze me sometimes. I reckon about 200 new people come to speedway each year 'cause of *Sky*. We wouldn't get them without *Sky* and who can tell who they tell? I don't understand people who knock it! We have the most exciting league in the world. Alright some of the racing hasn't been so great this year but when it's good there's nothing better."

During my drive I'd listened to the ever-excellent Laurie Taylor on his BBC Radio 4 programme *Thinking Allowed*. Today the sociological concept of "proximity of sensibility" has been discussed in relation to the so-called unique characteristics of British comedy. As a nation, we always pride ourselves on our advanced and (according to Ken Dodd) superior chuckle muscles - apparently unaware that our ability to relish our own humour and enjoy laughing at our own jokes, while other nationalities remain baffled, is also a subtle way to construct our national identity. Indeed this is, in fact, the primary function of this discourse since it instantly differentiates us as a group from others (who, in this case, don't share our humour) and also immediately fosters group unity since it functions to set us aside as both different and 'unique' from others who, by definition, are then foreign or 'other' to us. Humour aside (and speedway so often is no laughing matter), it immediately struck me how these ideas applied to my experience of speedway round the country. In essence speedway fans pride themselves on our broad-church approach and the supposedly warm welcome they give out towards other fans and casual visitors unaware that, in reality, contrary to our stated beliefs that we'd like to increase the popularity of the sport, we're actually a sub-cultural group that delights in defining itself as insular or away from the mainstream. Indeed, we do this unconsciously without noticing - the understanding we have of complex rules, the way we casually brush aside the injuries and element of danger or our decrepit stadia, the paraphernalia of programme boards and air horns, the difficulty of completing the programme accurately, even the need for garden chairs, sandwiches and flasks - all instantly exclude the casual visitor. Or, until they adapt to our norms, we mark them out as strangers in comparison to ourselves - people who are in the know and who are part of a community. We don't all share the same views but, because we enjoy a "proximity of sensibility", our sense of inclusion and belonging is, bizarrely, something that turns off or turns away others. Thought about in comedy terms if one group shares a certain sense of humour that another finds completely unfunny, then the people who laugh together are signalling they belong with each other and enjoy shared values and outlook. Almost unbeknownst to us all, this both binds and bounds the group while it operates to exclude others. This might explain why so many armchair viewers of speedway stay just that because on the sofa they're part of the speedway television community, whereas at the track (in the unlikely event they should ever venture there) almost everything they experience communicates their difference to the norm and marks them out as outsiders.

A tradition in the trackshop is the weekly sweepstake when Johnny Barber and Mike Moseley have to predict the outcome of the meeting. Johnny explains, "we always try to forecast the exact score before each meeting - blind - he goes first and I go after. Usually we think differently but tonight we both put 45 all. What do you think will happen? It's a challenge meeting between two sides owned by the Chapmans - it's bound to happen! How uncanny that we both don't predict a score correctly all season and then, maybe, get this one correct?" Mike tells me proudly, "I'm one-nil up in the series though last year JB won one-nil. One thing that isn't going to happen is King's Lynn losing their unbeaten home record and I'm usually the optimistic one!" Johnny harrumphs, "No comment."

Ever keen to help my sales efforts Johnny chortles, "I should only give you two plastic bags but, being an optimist, I'll give you a handful! I enjoyed your ELRC blog where you said you set a record low sales number of one copy sold. You've been on quite a run of those since then [laughs]!" Luckily, I know that tonight I have a couple of secret weapons to improve book sales. One of these is the Cambridge University Press book display holders that enable me to display some of my books in an upright position. This marketing gimmick - well, more the Cambridge University Press name and logo - attracts the eye of Jonathan Chapman as he passes my table. "Do they know you've got these?" he enquires and my reply that as I do freelance work for them they have kindly given me some used display holders (on the verge of breaking) gets the response, "Oh, so stealing from your employer then!" However, my main secret weapon is the help and support of Steve Chilton who produces the Leicester Lions Supporters' Club newsletter. Indeed, he has specially produced a full-colour leaflet advertising a special offer for Leicester fans who purchase a copy of *Shale Britannia*. The leaflet looks lovely and he's kindly handed them out to all the fans on the coaches they've brought over to Norfolk to watch tonight's speedway. Like many Leicester fans, Steve switched his speedway allegiance to Coventry when the club closed its doors, though this hasn't made the longing for the Lions re-emergence diminish. This dream now has the best-ever chance of becoming reality since its lamented closure. Steve has kept me up-to-date with developments as they happen: the news of the Chapmans involvement, the launch of the website (www.leicester-speedway.co.uk), the local media coverage, Supporters' Club activity as well as his encounters with his boyhood hero Ray Wilson, along with opinion on Coventry and news of his Pink Floyd tribute band alter-ego. Consequently, as a result of his marketing activities, interest in my books is high.

One of the many charms of speedway is the ready availability of the riders, staff and officials to the fans. Though many fans relish and enjoy the interaction, I'm sure that this isn't always completely a fun experience for those involved. SCB official Tony Steele is stretching his legs prior to his duties and his stroll back from the pits takes him along past my table to the trackshop. While he's en route to his duties in the box, a fan comes up to debate with him the exact thinking behind the abandonment decision at the relatively recent Peterborough versus Belle Vue fixture on August 16th. The bone of his contention appears to hinge on the annoyance felt by some fans (including him) who had paid and entered the stadium to watch a meeting that subsequently didn't happen. These feelings of betrayal and anger had been exacerbated by Tony's choice of footwear, "What were you wearing white plimsolls for?"

Patiently Tony explains, "Because I couldn't stand up in my ordinary shoes - they're not SCB issue by the way."

"Well, it was a scandal to call it off. We just sat there with the tractors going round and round and you walking on the track with those others."

"The team managers."

"Yeh, the bloke next to me said, 'look at them all doing nothing out there - even the ref is poncing about in white plimsolls' - you'll never live it down![1] The worst thing was I took two ex-Belle Vue fans who hadn't been for decades with four children and they were so disgusted at the wait and the attitude that they tore up their re-admission tickets in disgust and said, 'if that's how they treat people, we're never coming back!' I don't care about the adults but the children are our future!" "Well, the track was rideable when I got there but once Trevor [Swales] - without asking anyone - started work things changed and, after consulting with the captains, Hans Andersen and Joe Screen, I had no choice but to postpone it."

[1 Particularly as Tony was pictured in the *Speedway Star* wearing said natty footwear for the track inspection]

Apart from the spectacle of the racing, another delight of any meeting at King's Lynn is the chance to be entertained by speedway presenter Mike Bennett. He has some sensible advice for children, "always be suspicious if a speedway rider comes up to you and says, 'do you want a sweetie?' Thank you, Kevin [Doolan]" Tonight with the arrival of the Leicester Lions, Mike conducts a virtuoso master class in the dark art of speedway presentation mixing his trademark condescension with a potent but beyond pastiche combination of minimal research, gratuitous comment and fatuous opinion. Ex-Leicester rider Norman Hunter is in the stadium as an honoured guest of the promoters and I'm sure that his arrival is a thrill for die-hard Lions fans. However, Mike appears to operate under the impression that the closure of the club and a lack of motor vehicles has trapped everyone within the city limits of Leicester, thereby preventing them for a couple of decades from venturing more widely in search of alternative sources of speedway entertainment.

[MB] "Is this the first speedway meeting you've been to in years?"

[NH] "Nah, I was very kindly invited to Swindon last year."

[MB] "Well, I'm sorry! You'll enjoy your speedway here tonight!"

The brief interview over and the guest of honour dismissed, Mike turns to the task of explaining the team line-ups. The nature of the beast for a challenge meeting against a club that doesn't really exist requires that the team will be comprised of a variety of 'guests'. An attractive Lions team has been hired for the fixture and the line-up includes Lewis Bridger, Chris Holder and Sergey Darkin, though Mike mostly ignores these riders in order to big up the return of ex-Stars riders Kevin Doolan and "the most guested rider, if there is such an expression, we call him 'Lambo-Rambo'[!] - Simon Lambert." On the sidelines, a proud Steve Chilton tells me, "It's a disappointment we've lost David Howe but I think we've got a nicely balanced side."

Mike bangs on all night with his cookie-cutter, one-size-fits-all chosen theme of the return of the Leicester Lions. Mostly his comments are speculative but we do learn the fact that announcer Edwin Overland used to work at Blackbird Road and we're treated to a few heartfelt words from Edwin: "It's a nostalgic night but also exciting for the future to think that speedway might return to Leicester. What happy memories!" That's about as much sincerity as we're allowed before Mike decides to regale the assembled Leicester faithful with news of (I think) a tabard autographed by the riders ("it's all signed written"). Along with a painfully slow outline of the basic rules of speedway, "it's 3 points for first, 2 points for second, 1 point for third and no points for fourth - good grief, I sound like that bloke off *Sky* now!" The idea that the people who've come over on the Supporters' Club coaches wouldn't know the rules of speedway is thoughtless at best, but then blithely criticising Swindon speedway and Nigel Pearson in your opening remarks isn't exactly bright either. Luckily, a moving presentation by "Pete [Brennan] - a big King's Lynn fan" distracts Mike and shortly afterwards the racing starts with a 1-5 heat advantage for the Lions gained by the exciting partnership of Kevin Doolan and Lewis Bridger. "Anyone who thought the riders would just go through the motions has been put right - I imagine a wheelie demonstration could be on the cards here - it doesn't take a genius to work that out!" Lewis often does exuberant wheelies before the race and usually afterwards too, irrespective of his finishing position, so (for once) this isn't an inaccurate or wild surmise.

The Leicester fans or the riders aren't the only ones available for Mike to talk down to here tonight - there's also a large contingent of young people in the crowd who're enthusiastic pupils from the King's Lynn Stars Speedway Study Centre. After he easily goads them into some teenybopper cheers, he retorts, "they've been on the Smarties and the Sunny D!" To Mike's delight (but a muted reaction from the crowd), the Stars reply with a 5-1 in Heat 2 before they fall behind again in the next race. Before the fourth heat, Mike implores the assembled teenagers, "come on you guys from the Study Centre, you're supposed to cheer when our boys come out!" I'm stood by a distressed steward who worries about the possibility of rider injuries, "I don't know why we're having this meeting now with so many important fixtures later this week, never mind in the next few weeks." Chris Mills beats his notionally illustrious rival Sergey Darkin to win Heat 4 and is rewarded with a centre green interview for his troubles. I've noticed on previous visits a marked reluctance among the King's Lynn riders to submit themselves to the interactive cut and thrust of the standard Mike Bennett interview. The usual technique of such almost Brechtian interviews were later described to me as something along the lines of, "I'm not listening to you, you're boring me, I'm not paying any attention other than to listen to the sound of my own voice!" This solipsistic style of interview is sadly on the wane at most tracks, but I always relish the chance to experience first-hand Mike's casual narcissism. This most-gifted practitioner of the speedway presentational craft needs no second invitation to repeatedly interview Chris Mills throughout the season.

[MB] "The reason we call him Chris-Milk-It-Millsy is 'cause he loves to milk the adulation!"

[CM] "Hopefully we'll have three finals in the last month of the season."

[MB] "Oh come on, it's better than a proper job, isn't it?"

[CM] "Huh huh, yeh, I suppose so."

[MB] "How do you feel about the win against Darkin?"

[CM] "He's an Elite League rider and he rides for his country so he's a good rider. He made the start but I made a move on him using my local knowledge, I suppose 'cause I ride here every week and he doesn't!"

The fifth race sees Lewis Bridger relegated to third place by Daniel Nermark, "Lewis has been given something to think about - nice easy meeting, I don't think so!" The competitive nature of the meeting is emphasised in the next race too, when Paul Lee snatches second place on the line from a surprised Darkin. "Let's find some Leicester fans to speak to - to put it politely, they're hardly teenagers. When did you last see a Leicester team race?" Silence is followed by an inaudible mumble before Mike Bennett snaps irritably, "The answer is 1983! To let you know the correct answer." Obviously, Mike's thorough preparations for the meeting have, at least, extended to minimally checking what year Leicester formally closed but, inevitably, this is in fact the wrong answer. Stood a short distance away from me, while sporting a giant red and yellow Doctor Who style home knitted scarf ("I wore it to Birmingham's first meeting"), supremely knowledgeable speedway fan Arnie Gibbons can barely contain himself from heckling at the idiocy of Mike's claim, "1986 was the last time Leicester rode as a team at Long Eaton."[2] Clearly disappointed at the poor quality of the people he has to practise his art on, Mike manfully chunters on regardless, "you've got a big enough petition!" A loud low-flying plane interrupts his monologue-cum-interview and we hear a rare flash of real wit from him, "Hang on - if we've left the landing lights on, we could be in trouble."

Between heats six and eight the scores remain tied, something that leads Johnny Barber to note, "How uncanny that we both don't predict a score correctly all season and then we both seem to get this one right!" An interview with Jonathan Chapman - obviously seeking a look of greater authority tonight since he's resplendent in an SCB anorak - on the centre green is bound to be richer and more fertile ground for any eager listeners since he can be relied on to overcome the paucity of Mike's questioning. Consequently, we learn in quick order that the Leicester fans have seized the chance in numbers to see their team ride again ("there's probably three or four hundred here tonight"), though personally I'd say there's a touch of the BSIs at Cardiff here and so would question the exactitude of the maths. Media interest has got off the ground ("they'll be doing a back page in the local paper [*Leicester Mercury*] tomorrow") and optimism abounds, "hopefully next year we'll get another match somewhere for Leicester to keep the bandwagon rolling!" Interview over, Mike looks ahead to a possible bumper crowd if Lynn win the first leg of the play-off semi-final at Owlerton, "they'll be a lot if we win at Sheffield tomorrow night. If you remember last year's Play-Off Final - we took over the third and fourth bends and they hated it!" If the Leicester fans have enjoyed their night out and wish to relive the experience with the added benefit of further commentary and entertainment from Mike then he's quick to remind them endlessly, "we're making a film of this one tonight - check it out on our website www.mikebennettspeedway.co.uk!"

Though it's difficult to choose, one of the most irksome aspects of Mike Bennett's presentational approach is the way he interrupts each race to start his 'analysis' before the riders have even entered the last corner. A win on the line for the yellow-helmeted Lewis Bridger in Heat 11 has him exclaim, "I tell you that Lewis Bridger has improved!" Sadly as the words boom out over loudspeakers Lewis crashes on the first bend before he's even had the chance to go around on his warm-down celebration lap. "I think we'll need to have a chat with Lewis about that one." In the trackshop, though the scores are still close enough for a draw to be a likely outcome, Johnny instead savours the gifts of the presenter, "for some reason Mike Bennett reminds me of Roland Rat when he used to say 'Hello Rat fans!'"

[2 The next day Arnie emails to say, "the last Leicester meeting was more recent than I thought, it looks like: 9.9.92 Long Eaton 52 (Stekkers 15 max) Leicester 38 (Dave Blackburn top scored with 9 in a team that included 5 of the 1983 Lions line-up - Les, Neil, Courtney, Regeling and Cook). It was a good night last night, not only seeing the Lions - although only Darkin [who lodged in Leicester] can claim any connection with the City! - but also watching Tony in action from the ref's box."]

As if to confirm that the riders really are keen to compete tonight, the re-run of Heat 12 sees Chris Holder (on gate 3) have quite a tussle with Daniel Nermark (on gate 2) almost on the start line. The Australian puts his arm on and across Nermark who buckles but then blasts him aside causing Holder to gesture pleadingly at Tony "referee from Leicester" Steele in the forlorn hope of his intervention. Just in case we haven't noticed or have temporarily forgotten, Mike reminds us, "It's all entertaining stuff here tonight!"

I retreat to the new-look hut that houses the trackshop in the hope that the continuous barrage of faux bonhomie is muffled by the more substantial looking walls it now has. Johnny has been in touch with his brother, "I just texted Nick and said Jeff's sold 14 and he texted back 'you've put in a 4 by mistake' and I said no, no, I'm serious." Mike Moseley jokes, "I know you've got your doubts about our predictions, so shall we name the winning time of the next one to convince you? Let's try 60.74!" In fact Tomas Topinka wins in a time of 60.96 to retain the Lynn advantage on the night at a scoreline that should reputedly bathe everyone in happiness, namely 40-38. Lewis Bridger has been tempted out onto the centre green but his arrival only gets a muted reaction. Mike is outraged, "Come on Leicester fans - cheer - he's racing for you!" before he effortlessly segues with Alan Partridge-like ability into his first 'question', "Lewis - obviously, you always enjoy it when you come here!" I zone out the rest of the 'interview' and listen instead to Mike Moseley talk about a different Scunny to the one I've experienced, "Lots of fans walk to Scunthorpe and on dark nights they have to walk through the druggie area and the red light district - that's what a Scunthorpe fan told me anyway."

The meeting draws to its exciting conclusion - with one heat to go the scores are tied at 42 each - but has gone on too long for the young people from the study centre. "Could the owner of a white Ford [blah blah] move your car 'cause you're stopping 60 schoolchildren going home on their bus. If you don't move it, the boys in blue will!" Suddenly seized by clairvoyancy (but not a thousand tongues) Mike continues, "We know that Chris Holder will be out in the last one and we can guess that Lewis Bridger will be there as well. We could not have predicted this one could we? A last-heat decider! I know it's great for you guys [Leicester fans] just to be here, getting racing again!" Meanwhile Johnny has news of further drink-driving shame for a major Elite League club in Dorset to follow on from the Lindback affair, "Me dad just rang to say that Jason Doyle just lost his licence for a year at Blackpool magistrates court for drink driving - what is it with these Poole assets?" On the track at the Norfolk Arena, Nermark wins the final race in the fastest time of the night (60.3) under the close attentions of Chris Holder. And, with Topinka third, King's Lynn emerge victorious 46-44 ("I've lost all faith in match fixing" smirks Johnny).

There's still time for some post-meeting interviews. Though stone last in the final race, Kevin Doolan has read the script, "Let's hope it sparked some Lions pride! You never take it easy against your mates, do you?" A sizeable horde of Leicester fans listen to the interviews before they contentedly wend their way back out into the car park towards their coaches. A satisfied Steve Chilton stops for a brief word to luxuriate in the racing on the night and look forward to more positive developments with regard to planning permission for a stadium in Leicester. He also proudly mentions how the Leicester fans had bought seven tyres for the Lions team tonight, "They'd got the tyres - when we got here they were already on the bikes!" As I pack away, Jonathan Chapman passes and lets me know "the racing was excellent!" Shortly afterwards I overhear Buster chatting with some stragglers, "It was a really poor crowd for us tonight. Most of the Lynn fans stayed away but you brought a good few - the racing was as good as ever but you missed seeing how many kids we get here!"

3rd October King's Lynn v Leicester (Challenge) 46-44

Chapter 48. Eastbourne v Swindon v Belle Vue: Many hands make light work

6th October

Tony Millard	*"Can David Norris win this one?"* [pitted against William Lawson and Theo Pijper]
Havvy	*"Yeh, I think he can, he's out against two reserves"* [it was three reserves since Doolan was also a reserve for Belle Vue]
Tony Millard	*"The 27-year-old Dutchman really was the flying Dutchman in that one ... the Pijper indeed calling the tune!"*
Jonathan	*"Welcome back to Arlington where the tractor is on the track. What are they going to do about the track?"*
Kelvin	*"Bob Dugard knows this track inside down"*

The triangular tournament that is the Craven Shield nowadays arrives at Arlington for the second leg semi-final to pit the Eagles against Belle Vue and Swindon, who hold a 9-point lead from Blunsdon and remain firm favourites to qualify for the final. It would be safe to say that Eastbourne promoter Bob Brimson's first season hasn't quite gone to plan, in fact he's been unluckily dogged with the unexpected almost from the get go, when he learnt that Jon Cook would leave the club to work at Lakeside. It was the sort of news that could put you on the back foot from the outset and, coupled with a bad run of injuries from March onwards, results haven't been sufficiently good to get the fans rushing through the turnstiles on a regular basis. Though still laudably keen as mustard about the club, increasingly Bob's other work commitments have required him to miss the odd meeting here and there. It's widely understood that he has to continue with his work to staunch the steady but inexorable financial losses racked up at Arlington. Nonetheless, he's remained buoyant and the only visible sign of stress is his obsessive chain-smoking (almost as though he's on a sponsored smoke) though I gather this isn't speedway induced. I fully expect him to smoke up another storm in the pit lane tonight.

Recent weeks have seen the green shoots of recovery appear both in the performance of the team and the comparative lack of injuries, albeit this has happened too late to do anything other than lift the Eagles away from the nightmare possibility of finishing stone last at the basement of the Elite League (though, technically, that position would have fallen to Oxford). Any victory over local rivals Poole is greeted with considerable delight and so hammering them at home 53-37 last weekend regained some vestige of local bragging rights and indicated that the team was finally starting to gel together as the season closed. Because of injuries and other absences, speedway is famous for the use of guest riders but at Eastbourne this season - along with the team - even the columns in the programme use replacements on a regular basis. Tonight's 'Promoters Piece' features a stern looking photograph of Bob but the affable language of the text tells you it's written by Trevor Geer without even a glance at the by-line. Trevor took some pleasure in the performance against Poole - a performance notable for the Eagles having "six fit riders" in attendance as well as, much more significantly, the fact "we did look and ride like a team." Everyone contributed and "it was also good to see our new signings Simon [Gustafsson] and Roman [Povazhny] scoring well." However, it wouldn't be Eastbourne if inevitably there wasn't a jinx just around the corner, "not even 24 hours later I get a phone call from Poland to say our top two riders are both in hospital following separate crashes in the same meeting at Wroclaw. Nicki has damage to his shoulder and is suffering from concussion and Davey has aggravated his neck injury, which he's been riding with since May". That all said, tonight the Eagles track a team that looks less make do and mend than it has on numerous other times during this season. Partly

Many hands make light work

Parade truck congratulats Nicki

No ponytail

this is because there are only six riders required for Craven Shield meetings, while Eagles asset Edward Kennett replaces Davey Watt and, something that has become more noticeable this season, there's no Nicki Pedersen. Though to be fair to him, not only has he performed exceptionally to ram in the points (with 8 full or paid maximums) in the new-look Eagles race tabard but he has often ridden when not fully fit. Martin Dugard tells me Nicki would be absent tonight anyway, "It's in Nicki's contract that he doesn't have to ride any Craven Shield meetings - he's probably still recovering from his crash last Sunday in Poland too!" All this is no consolation to Marlin Dadswell in the trackshop who pointedly asks me rhetorically, "Guess who hasn't ridden in any of the seven Elite League meetings I've been to away this season?"

When I arrive it's more crowded in the pits than on the terraces and some people worry that the attraction of alternative speedway meetings at both Lakeside and Rye House will attract the floating speedway fan to take their custom elsewhere. This might be understandable as not only is there no Nicki on display but also the Swindon team sports a 'rum without Coke' look about its line up as they appear without their talismanic captain, Leigh Adams. With the sole addition of guest Shaun Tacey, only Belle Vue field what looks like a 'full-strength' team and even might mount a strong challenge though, given their travails all season, the formbook indicates otherwise. A glance at the racecard in the programme tells us that the Swindon captain is "TBA" and, bizarrely, that Belle Vue will have Nigel Wagstaff as team manager. If there are (needless) worries that there might not be a large crowd on the terraces to watch the meeting, there are no such fears in the Lewis Bridger section of the pits. Not only has he enlisted the expert mechanical help of "ex-Eagle from about 20 years ago Malcolm Ballard" (wearing the fashion *of white socks with his sandals) but when his throaty-sounding bike ("the technical term is it's running like a sack of poo") is revved up on the pits concourse I count a stunning 14 people helping or standing round looking at it. These include Malcolm, his granddad Tony, Lewis, Bob Brimson, Trevor Geer, Dennis Isaac, Morten Risager, two youths with excess hair gel and a variety of other people - some with spanners. You don't get this much help in the pit lane for a tyre change at a Formula 1 Grand Prix! Dave Fairbrother from the *Speedway Star* tells me confidently, "It's the carburettor."

By the time the riders go on parade, what counts for a sizeable crowd this season has shown up on the terraces. At least something has been won at the club this season, albeit away from East Sussex by Nicki Pedersen. The riders load themselves into the Meridian Marquees pick-up truck driven (as always) by sponsor Dennis Isaac that he's now had decorated with signs on the driver and passenger doors that say 'Nicki Pedersen World Champion 2007'. I think there's some Eagles pride in Nicki's achievement - and I found one of the real pleasures of my Writer in Residence position at the club was the chance to spend many meetings only a few yards away from his section of the pit that Ray and Mark Blackwell effortlessly ran - but this is definitely one consolation during a poor season. Resident presenter Kevin 'KC' Coombes highlights some alternative reasons for celebration "It's Andy Moore's 25th birthday" (and later we learn it's Start Marshal Alan Rolfe's too). He goes on to talk up the perceived glamour of the contest with the claim, "Belle Vue look very strong even" with a solid team that includes the latest star in their midst "PLRC winner James Wright". Ever one to make a virtue of the race format, he continues, "we have 18 top quality heats for the price of 15!" Looked at from behind, it appears that Belle Vue are about to embark on a speedway revolution of their own by tracking a lady rider at number 4 - though I soon realise my error since it's only Adam Skornicki who, tonight, wears his hair loose rather than in his traditional ponytail. Roman Povazhny is billed as "the man from Russia with the touch of attitude" and, reiterating news of a smoking ban that some members of the regular Arlington congregation appear reluctant to embrace, Kevin warns, "if you smoke within an enclosed area you're going to get a bucket of cold water thrown over you!"

The additional help with his equipment appears to have saddled Lewis Bridger with a much meaner machine and Roman feels the full force of this when his team mate powers under him on the first bend and gives him a good thump. He's experienced enough to ride through such inconveniences and the Eagles top scorer in the first leg at Blunsdon had just forced himself back into contention when Lewis repeated the medicine on the third bend of the second lap. After a bit of a struggle with the laws of gravity, Roman eventually falls and is excluded for his troubles by referee Frank 'fast fingers' Ebdon. In the fourth heat ex-Eagle but now a Swindon rider, Andrew Moore, briefly rides determinedly by the rider who replaced him at Arlington (Cameron Jackson Woodward) before he trails off into third place ("not so far away was young Andrew Moore"). The resulting Eagles 5-1 massages the scoreline to 9-10-5, a bizarre-looking formulation brought on by the triangulation effect of the Craven Shield. This still leaves the Robins ahead on the night and on aggregate in what, ignoring the participation of the Aces, Assistant Team Manager Paul Bailey calls "the battle of the bird cages!" Stood next to me as she has been for the majority of the season is the Eagles club physiotherapist Jane Wooller whose team loyalty has caused her to set aside her natural inclination to always help others, "Andrew [Moore] asked me earlier if I could look at his neck as it was stiff after his fall at Swindon and I had to tell him 'Sorry, honey, you don't ride for us any more so I can't look at it till afterwards' - when I'll only be too happy to!"

Heat 6 sees Edward Kennett comprehensively outgate Simon Stead and hold his advantage into the first corner before (on the second bend) Stead zooms aggressively underneath him. Edward bravely keeps the throttle held open to repel the challenge and skip away to victory, thereby meeting with full approval from Eastbourne team manager, Trevor Geer, in the pits, "That's quick! That woke him up, didn't it!" In these triangular fixtures it's essential that you beat your main rivals when you go head-to-head with them in alternate races. This aspect of the script looks likely to go awry for the Eagles in the seventh when the unlikely but dominant Robins pairing of Mark Lemon and Tomasz Chrzanowski look set to win. Well, until they enter the third bend of the third lap when Cameron decides to gatecrash the party by barging past Lemon and flashing his elbow to boot. The need to ride aggressively and show no quarter is something his mechanic Ashley Wooller has tried to gradually inculcate into the armoury of this most affable of young Australian men and, having just seen his advice put into action, he's gleeful as he runs to greet Cameron in the pit lane. The need for steel on the track goes against Cameron's natural outlook off it, where he's a hard-working, conscientious, slightly sensitive but easy-going bloke who's a credit to his family and nation thousands of miles away (though tonight his proud and attractive mum Jenni Woodward is again in the pits - on her month-long visit to see her son and watch him race competitively in England). Indeed, Cameron is so laid back he doesn't even bother with the traditional travelling Australian superiority complex about their national brilliance at sport. My attempt to get a reaction to the Aussie defeat in the Rugby World Cup only elicits a shrug ("I'm not interested in rugby") from Cameron and an explanation from his mum, "It's not a big sport in Australia, definitely not in the Mildura area."

The Andrew Moore who thinks he's actually Leigh Adams has turned up at Arlington this evening, as evidenced by his racing in Heat 8 and the manner in which he winds it up down the home straight and then blasts by a bemused Kevin Doolan in the first corner of lap two. Watching over the bend-two air fence Bob Brimson's plain-speaking brother, Greg asks me, "Who's that?" I tell him it's a rejuvenated Andrew Moore who used to ride here and work during the winter in a Mr Kipling factory, "He looks like he likes cakes!" Greg is much more impressed by how the diffident Morten Risager has responded to the additional responsibility of being named club captain, "I like to see Morten geeing everyone up on the team. I've watched him do it all night. He encourages everyone - like a proper captain should - we've been missing that so far this season!" The decision to name a loanee rider as skipper arguably bucks the trend without setting a precedent! Heat 9 sees Roman take the path of least resistance, so he sensibly opts to let Lewis have his favoured outside line and a maximum heat advantage against the Aces 'power partnership' of Joe Screen and Adam Skornicki looks the likely outcome until the Russian's chain snaps. This season Eastbourne wouldn't have any luck but for bad luck and, typically, this sudden unexpected rub of the green effectively ends any lingering hopes that the Eagles challenge might take them into the final stages of the competition since the aggregate deficit behind the Robins already looks insurmountable. This realisation takes a little longer to sink in with Greg Brimson who appreciatively watches a drawn heat with Swindon (won by Edward Kennett) even though the score still looks ugly at 21-25-14. A keen judge of racing form and team spirit, has Jane Wooller savour another daredevil ride from Andrew Moore for second place. She tells her husband Ashley (who used to be Andrew's mechanic), "He's riding really well - he's not braking in the corner like he did sometimes but just going flat out!" Something else that is also flat out is the Eastbourne 2007 challenge for a trophy to place in the cabinet and, the unusual sight of Billy Forsberg diving under Morten Risager to ensure an Aces 5-1, finally convinces Greg all is now lost, "That was a great move! Fark it - that's us done for!"

During the interval, Kevin Coombes grabs Swindon team manager Alun 'Rosco' Rossiter to pick his brain about "where do we go with British speedway?" Rosco appears to have a giant bee in his bonnet about the stupidity of ever listening to the opinions of the paying public and a lesser gripe about how the iniquitous influence of Reading (in their Bulldogs incarnation) has afflicted the organisation of the sport. "I was pretty disappointed when we changed things from last year. We listened to the supporters and that was a mistake, just 'cause of Reading! We should have stayed where we were [regarding the regulations governing tactical rides] - last season was the best yet in the Elite League. One of seven teams could have made the play-offs. This year we should have spread the riders out evenly, I do realise that - we were strong this year but that was the way it fell! Again, 'cause Reading lost the play-off 'cause of it, we got rid of one of the tacticals which was silly."

I arrive in the gent's toilets just in time to overhear two blokes loudly discuss the latest iteration of the ongoing mechanical sagas of Lewis Bridger. "Not being funny about granddad - he's a lovely bloke - but Ballard has done a few things and Lewis already has 5 points with a longtrack engine round here! Farking typical our new engine blew up before the parade."

"Just back from Neville's, yes?"

"Yeh, I don't farking believe it! A carb most likely."

As luck would have it, Lewis is out in the first race (heat 13) after the interval during which not only does his bike backfire three times with a sound like a pistol shot but he also rides in typically harum-scarum fashion throughout, even though he's at the front. Well, he is until the third bend of the third lap when he nearly gets thrown off his machine but, through sheer riding skill and agility on the bike, somehow stays mounted. Chrzanowski takes this chance to pass and when, on the final lap, Lewis repeats this loss of control within a yard or so of the initial incident, he causes Mark Lemon to fall off.

A race maximum for Kennett and Gustafsson in Heat 15 that featured an enthralling race between two teammates brings the Eagles to within 2 points of Swindon at 30-32-28. A heat advantage from Povazhny ("the end of the season and Roman's coming good") and Bridger over the Robins partnership of Gjedde/King immediately follows to create a score of 34-34-28, a pleasing spectacle at a speedway meeting but strange vital statistics in a woman. Sadly for Eagles followers, this is as good as it gets since the race format structure of the Craven Shield beast then sees the Chrzanowski/Lemon combination race to an easy 5-1 against Stead/Tacey. All that remains is for Cameron to frighten Joe Screen with a temporary loss of control before he somehow stays on his bike in the last heat ("Screenie almost shat himself there and backed off sharpish"). As usual the victorious team rides round the stadium on a celebratory lap-cum-parade to wave to the fans from the back of a pick-up truck emblazoned with Nicki Pedersen's (rather than Leigh Adams') world championship credentials. In the crowd on the fourth bend, loyal Eagles fan John Hazelden sportingly cries out, "Well done Swindon!" as they pass. It's a sentiment that appears to visibly startle Rosco!

6th October Eastbourne v Swindon v Belle Vue (Craven Shield semi final, second leg) 37-39-32

Chapter 49. Eastbourne v Belle Vue: 'Norman the Fox' arrives at Arlington

14th October

The true genius of speedway administration in this country is further confirmed by the staging of a rare Sunday afternoon Elite League meeting at Arlington. The club has repeatedly staged meetings on their regular Saturday race night in direct competition with various stages of the Grand Prix series but strangely, as the season ends, decided not to run against the attraction of the Gelsenkirchen round. This afternoon's meeting pits Eastbourne against Belle Vue a mere 13 days after Coventry have been confirmed as Elite League champions![1] Only in speedway could you engineer a situation where a meaningless end-of-season encounter is scheduled after the climax of the season. In terms of speedway, this does represent a significant improvement on some other years recently when the entire programme of Elite League didn't even get finished, thereby ensuring the final table had a lopsided look and further destroyed the last vestiges of credibility the sport has in print and broadcast media circles. Not that Eagles fans would have welcomed it - though it would have typified the season - but, at one point, it did very much look that this meeting could be a battle for the wooden spoon. Fortunately, at this time, last place in the Elite League doesn't include the outside possibility of relegation to the Premier League (though it will in 2008 via a wonderfully convoluted play-off system). Even if they somehow engineer their second shock away win of the season to go with the one they got at Reading (46-47), the Aces will still definitely finish bottom of the league. To be fair to them, at the outset of the season it looked like they would track a weak team likely to struggle. And so it proved. Whereas the Eagles looked strong on paper but turned out to be frequent visitors to medical practitioners or totally out of luck under the enthusiastic tutelage of new promoter Bob 'Jonah' Brimson.

Exemplifying the peculiar weather that has been in force all year, the day has dawned gloriously sunny and by early afternoon the temperature is positively balmy. Just the sort of conditions that you'd imagine would attract a big crowd to Arlington for the penultimate meeting of the season. It's also the kind of weather to attract the local constabulary to operate a roadblock down the country lanes at the railway level crossing just a few miles from the stadium. Though it's laudable to remove drink drivers from the roads, you have to ask yourself whether it's a tad ambitious to expect to capture that many drink-drivers on early afternoon on a Sunday (though that said, there are likely to be even fewer drivers to breathalyse on other days of the week). Personally I'd suggest the weeks leading up to Christmas or after pub closing at weekends in city centres might be a better use of resources. The uniformed officer leans in my window and says, "Sussex Police Safety Check - have you consumed any alcohol this afternoon?" I haven't, but the way the season has gone it's a surprise that Bob Brimson hasn't been driven to alcoholism.

[1 proving that nothing is new under the speedway sun, there was the famous case of the Coventry v Leicester Midland Cup Final being staged a week before Coventry actually qualified by beating Wolves in the second leg of the semi-final]

Off for introductions

A pensive Bob Brimson

Controlled carnage

Thankfully, he's only stuck to chain-smoking cigarettes but other less strong-minded Eagles fans might understandably have taken to the demon drink. If they had already this afternoon, they wouldn't have made it to the meeting if they'd travelled there on this particular back route. Judged by the number of cars in the car park, the stadium should be packed but the reality of modern travel is that everyone appears to have their own transport and invariably travels without passengers so, consequently, inside it looks incredibly sparsely populated. Except, of course, for the pits area and pit lane which, as usual this season, looks totally packed with riders, track staff, mechanics and guests. In his programme notes, Bob Brimson accentuates the positive, "today's meeting is a battle against time for our captain Nicki to get fit, especially with last night's Grand Prix in Germany to take account of. As World Champion, he was desperate to take his place at that meeting, and we all hope that his efforts over there won't have had a detrimental effect, and that he can take his place in our side today." The great unsaid of this hopeful comment is that although already crowned victorious in the 2007 GP series, like any entrepreneurial rider, Nicki wouldn't want to rule himself out of the chance to race for the so-called "richest prize in speedway" of $100,000 on offer to the winner of the final race at Gelsenkirchen.[2]

In the pits the feedback on the German GP is pretty uniform. Eagles Financial Officer (when did these kind of job titles arrive in the sport?) Phil Orr actually went to the meeting and reports, "It was a great spectacle but the racing was awful - Nicki really didn't look on it." Whereas club physio, Jane Wooller, who watched at home reports that *Sky Sports* continued to take the piss out of the armchair speedway viewer when they started the coverage "over half an hour late 'cause of the rugby - not even the World Cup rugby either". This, thereby, deprived the stay-at-home GP fans of the early action from the "richest minute in motorsport". Luckily, they missed nothing of note as the meeting was subject to the traditional BSI SGP specially prepared indoor track designed to look lovely but inevitably de-skill the riders and reduce the contest to a lottery with the provision of a ropey racing surface. It's all very well boasting about the logistics of delivering the shale, constructing the track or the notional comfort of the stadia at (Cardiff and) Gelsenkirchen but I'd still imagine 99 out of 100 genuine

[2 the ongoing scandal-cum-travesty that is the deleterious impact on British speedway of the BSI (latterly IMG) owned Speedway Grand Prix series - in terms of rider availability and the havoc it plays with the Elite League fixture list - can be experienced most weeks by the fans and reviewed on the FIM website. A glance here shows the rules and regulations that govern all motorcycle activities that fall under its jurisdiction and, most revealingly, the execrable level of the official/approved pay rates that lead the riders to effectively bastardise our enjoyment of top-level speedway in this country. Given the importance the riders clearly attach to individual success in this competition, you'd probably imagine that the rewards on offer would be a king's ransom. After a 2007 campaign, when Nicki has really performed without rival or close comparison, you'd expect him to have really coined it in terms of the prize money he earned. In fact, his total winnings were a comparatively paltry $88,150 (roughly £45,000) and would have been the highest figure earned by any rider during the 2007 GP series but for the boost to Andreas Jonsson's earnings ($143,150) from his last (richest) race victory in Germany. Clearly this level of remuneration doesn't even begin to cover the investment in equipment, staff, accommodation and travel a GP campaign requires from any rider. So, the conclusion must be that the rewards that drive the riders to sacrifice so much to compete for individual glory in the GP series must come from somewhere other than the prize money on offer. This elsewhere is likely to be the attraction the sponsors immediately feel about the regular television appearances of riders emblazoned with their logos guarantee. The financial rewards will also come from the higher rates of guarantee, points money and signing-on fee a rider can negotiate/command from their club sides in Poland, Sweden, England and Russia as a consequence of the success or notoriety by competing in the GP! Clearly this isn't a sustainable situation or one that is good for the long-term future or development of British speedway!]

speedway fans would settle for fewer creature comforts in exchange for competitive racing on a decent surface. [3] While a clearly out-of-sorts Nicki Pedersen applied himself sufficiently to make it to the semi-final stage, his exertions proved too much for anything like a sensible recovery from his injuries and so, for the 16th time this season in 43 fixtures (though three of these in the Craven Shield he wasn't contracted to ride so that really makes 13 missed out of 40 or an absence percentage of 32%), Eastbourne take to the track without him. Luckily this isn't likely to prove fatal against Belle Vue and club asset Edward Kennett has, once again, been drafted into the team. The Aces have drafted in Jordan Frampton at reserve and Kevin Coombes informs us that they'll run rider replacement for "ill victim - Adam Skornicki".

Right from the first race, Bob Brimson lives each race on his nerves and alternates between deep drags on his perpetually lit cigarette or pacing impressively long distances up and down the pit lane parallel to the back straight. Though mid-October, it's sunny enough for it still to be shirtsleeve weather and Bob cuts an absorbed, passionate but lone figure with his closely shaven head. Between races, I catch a moment or two of his time and he confesses that he's not had a chance to glance at my latest magnum opus *Shifting Shale*. "After the ways things have gone, the last thing I want to do before I go to bed is read about speedway!" The second race proves problematic to bring to a conclusion and, in the first attempt to run it, referee Chris Gay manages to anger the usually taciturn Cameron Woodward by waiting until he's nearly reached the third bend before he puts on the red lights to stop the race.[4] Cameron gestures at the box - something that, by his mild-mannered standards, almost counts as rushing up the stairs to the box to head butt him in the face with his crash helmet. Physio Jane is equally mystified, "That was terribly late!" In the re-run, the riders fall like skittles (or, perhaps, dominoes) with Billy Forsberg departing his transport on bend one and Jordan Frampton abandoning his steed on bend two. A re-re-run with all four back is the adjudication and Cameron doesn't need a third invitation to win handsomely. Bob looks on glumly, "I'll be glad when this season is over - it's all ended with a damp squib if you look at the crowd. I had to run otherwise I wouldn't get my *Sky* money. If you don't complete your fixtures you're stuffed! Peterborough can claim *force majeure* for not completing their fixtures and get away with it. Whereas I'm *persona non grata* with the BSPA now - but I can't really go into it." Nearby his brother Greg Brimson surveys the comparatively meagre crowd morosely, "Small gate and a big payday - what a great combination for Bob!"

The early Eagles lead is wiped out in Heat 4 when inexperience from Simon Gustafsson after a promising start out front (with Morten Risager) sees him passed on the inside by both Forsberg and Doolan, thereby enabling the Aces to level the scores with a 1-5. Just like a disgruntled Bob Brimson ("that's 5-1 thrown away"), the softly spoken Ben Orr, son of Financial Officer Phil and the man with probably the smallest, neatest handwriting in speedway, equally can't believe the evidence of his own eyes though he prescribes optimistic medicine as the solution, "they should have team rode!" A 4-2 for the Eagles in the next with a win ahead of the fast-riding Simon Stead from Roman Povazhny on his rider replacement outing in place of the injured Davey Watt, has Phil Orr showing none of the caution you'd traditionally associate with the accounting world and, instead, he's immediately sensing what Thatcher-era Tories used to term the 'green shoots of recovery', "now the tide has turned!" It's a win that has also pleased Sid Shine who delights every week in his campaign to instruct me to move from where I'm stood in the pit lane to somewhere else "so we can put the crash barriers out" or advises me about the hazard I face with club sponsor Dennis Isaac at the wheel of the Meridian Marquees pick-up truck he uses to parade the team ("watch out the car is reversing", "mind yourself - the car is moving"). However, Sid is even happier when he's compiling or checking the statistics he's amassed for his column in the programme ('Sid's Statistics'). The win for Roman has Sid sidle alongside me to gleefully report, "that was Roman's best time of the season by point four of a second - though it helps when you're being chased." There's always something of interest to be gleaned from his page in the programme and this week not only do we learn, "Davey Watt is one of only 11 riders to win heats at every Elite League track so far this year," but also that referee Chris Gay was born in Huddersfield (as stated before but worth repeating - you can always tell a Yorkshireman, but not much) in 1962 and boasts "three Christian names" - Chris, James and Mark. Fortunately, Sid is retired otherwise I'd have to advise him against giving up his day job to further his career as a budding comic based on the evidence of this week's attempted humour featuring one joke I completely don't understand, plus another

[3 All GP tracks are prepared/managed to the orders and specifications of Ole Olsen. Despite much evidence to the contrary, Ole reputedly claims that slick tracks produce 'close' racing. The reality is that these smooth surfaces minimise the disruption caused to the all-so-important live television schedules rather than provide entertainment for the paying public in attendance!]

[4 Chris Gay does this deliberately for safety reasons having adjudicated at a meeting at Eastbourne that saw Mark Loram pile into the fence when the rider in front of him pulled up abruptly. To avoid unnecessary injury, Chris now waits until the riders are strung out and have the length of the straight to properly see the red lights.]

side-splitting one about Chris Gay's work that will probably have the St John Ambulance booth overrun. "His job is a Senior Officer for HM Customs. This means it is inadvisable for riders to attempt to smuggle through the starting gate when nobody's looking!"

A rider in superlative form this afternoon is Cameron Woodward who appears to think that he's an Australian version of Nicki Pedersen, if judged by his aggression in the first corner and his exhilarating speed round the track in heat 7. He celebrates the win ecstatically when he crosses the line and Jane Wooller comes over all maternal, "He's well chuffed with that - I wish his mum were here to watch that." Phil Orr leans over with a quizzical look on his face to tell us, "This is what Elite League speedway would be like without the GP stars and a 38- or 39 point limit!" Having seen the future, I can't in all honesty say that I can see the difference or notice the join. Well, other than to realise that we've had many more close races. Though, equally, It's true that no one has shown the superlative speed and grace that you see when riders like Nicki or Leigh Adams strut their stuff. Kevin Coombes is quick to grab Cameron to investigate the factors behind his impressive display. Cameron underplays his return to full fitness after an early season injury or his recent increased confidence on the bike and instead we quickly learn, "I've borrowed an engine off Davey Watt." Stuck for an illuminating response, Kevin settles for, "Ah, the Wattster - that's interesting," before Cam interrupts to explain his personal philosophy gained through the bitter experience of his sacking at Edinburgh when he fully expected to ride for them again the next season in the Premier League, "You've got to finish strong, otherwise you're out of a job! I set myself a goal of a 5-point average and I think I'm close!"[5]

With little or no drama, the Eagles swoop to victory led by guest number one Edward Kennett who scores 17 points from six rides (strangely dropping his only point of the meeting in Heat 15 to Kevin Doolan). He's ably supported by a fast-gating, hard-riding Cameron who scores 12 points from five rides. For the Aces, only Kevin Doolan (paid 14 for six rides) and Billy Forsberg (paid 12 from seven rides) offered any real resistance. Joe Screen endured a particularly disappointing return to Arlington (no points from three rides) and the newly crowned PLRC champion, James Wright, was plagued by engine problems and inconsistency (3 points from five rides).

The razzamatazz that forms an essential part of all sport nowadays appears to get out of hand when a seemingly 'rogue' Fox mascot invades Arlington around the time of the interval. The reaction of pretty well everyone was to scratch our collective heads to try to figure out what exactly a fox mascot was doing at an encounter between Eagles and Aces? I ask, "What the fark is that?" only to be told "That's Norman - the Fox!" Strangely I could already see it was a fox, though as it appeared to be slightly duck-toed perhaps 'Norman the Duck-Toed Fox' would have a better ring to it? It turned out said mascot was a gimmick to promote the Brighton Bonanza in December though, in the way of the world, this has been re-branded as the "Indoor Speedway" after the departure of Jon Cook from the management team in charge of the event. Arguably, the new nomenclature more succinctly describes the product on offer, though it does lack the flamboyance implied by the word 'bonanza'. Greg Brimson looks at the mascot disdainfully, "Foxes eat eagles - that has to be the biggest farking *faux pas* of the season so far - the mascot eats the club!" Weirdly this comment could also be viewed differently when it was announced that, after one season at the helm, Bob Brimson would relinquish his ownership of the Eastbourne promotional licence to the newly formed and more experienced partnership of Martin Hagon and Bob Dugard. So, in that sense, the (Dugard) Fox had eaten the (Brimson) Eagle. Questions are raised about who is actually inside the mascot. Greg has his own pet theories, "No, it's going too fast for Floppy! Hello, it's stopped for a snack on the way round - it's Deano!"

14th October Eastbourne v Belle Vue (Elite League B) 55-37

[5 Cameron would finish with an average of 5.40 from his 34 meetings for the Eagles. During the close season his mechanic and friend Ashley would tell me an illuminating story. "When I retired after 20 years of international competition, I didn't know what to do with myself - I went abroad 30 times in that last year and then nothing. I couldn't handle it and, to be fair to him, neither can [David] Norris - when I came along here and watched over the fence, I thought I can't do this, do nothing, I have to be involved - and I worry about Lewis 'cause he won't either. Whereas Cameron will 'cause he's carried on with his apprenticeship as a plumber. He's working at this very moment in 40 degrees heat on a corrugated roof - plumbing is different there [in Australia] - it involves roofs too! When he broke his collarbone at Wolverhampton he was in tears in the medical room - floods of them - there was just Jane, me, Bob Brimson and the doctor. I didn't know what to do or what to say, it won't be in the manual. He wasn't crying 'cause of the pain 'cause he was holding his hand up and it wasn't the pain of the broken bone, it was 'cause he thought he'd be sacked - like he was at Edinburgh when he broke his ankle. Bad experiences like that don't leave you. He thought he'd have to become a plumber again not a speedway rider, a top speedway rider, like is his dream. He was inconsolable and, I think it was the best thing he ever did, Bob [Brimson] was so impressed at what it meant to him that he stuck by him and told him he wasn't going to be sacked. He cried all the way home in the back of the van, on the floor with a broken bone 'cause we didn't have a bed in it then. I don't think we got back till quarter to six. We rang his mum so she could talk to him but he just cried 'cause he still didn't really believe he wouldn't get sacked. It [speedway] means that much to him! But he knows there's a life outside too, if that don't sound silly." When I quizzed Bob Brimson about the Cameron Woodward injury situation he replied modestly, "One thing I do know is that with talented people (basically mad people) you try and let them do what they do and make them feel good about it. Then you stand back and enjoy it! After years of searching I have discovered my luck is that I have no talent at anything at all"]

Chapter 50. Oxford v Plymouth: Antepenultimate speedway meeting at Cowley Stadium?

15th October

Though I've planned to visit every single track in the country again this season, the vagaries of the weather and the complexities caused to my travel (and work) schedule by the rearranged fixtures mean that my chance to get to Plymouth to see them ride has come to nought. The best I can manage is to catch their trip to Cowley Stadium for the Conference League Play-Off Semi Final Second Leg following an initial encounter that they'd won handsomely by 17 points 10 days previously at the St Boniface Arena. In his hard-hitting column entitled 'the Cheetahs' Lair', club promoter Allen Trump states, "talking of Plymouth, although I am writing these notes prior to our meeting with them last Friday [!], I have no doubt that on paper we should have got a hiding. With no Lee, Danny, Jordan or Bargee, it was a very weak side that we sent down to the West Country and those of you who read John Gaisford's piece in the *Oxford Mail* will understand how futile the meeting was. Unfortunately the alternative could have been a £5,000 fine for not completing our fixtures!"

Given the club nearly went out of existence, even to be still riding is a huge achievement in itself, let alone mounting a challenge for the Conference League Play-Off Final. Interestingly after the demise of the Elite League incarnation of the club, the BSPA received a couple of alternative offers to run things at Cowley Stadium. Allegedly a higher money offer from the King's Lynn Chapmans was turned down in preference to giving the committed speedway enthusiast and successful businessman Allen Trump the opportunity to prove himself in speedway circles as a promoter. It's been a steep learning curve managing the rich tapestry of demands and requirements that go to make up the day-to-day life of a promoter. One ongoing issue is coordination, "I've lost count of the hours I've spent trying to fit a quart into a pint pot and with the absolute cut-off date of 31st October, by which time all speedway meetings must be run, the pressure piles up." One of the many things that was immediately resolved upon Allen's arrival was the appointment of Peter Oakes to the 'Director of Speedway' position. Peter has forgotten more than many people know and has gained his hard-won experience over the years in practically every way imaginable - from promoter, to team manager and speedway journalist. Quite how he manages to fulfil the various positions he holds in speedway during 2007 - Coventry (co-team manager), Great Britain (Under-21 team manager), journalist (speedway and other sports), Oxford (Director of Speedway) along with his Academy League work - is nothing short of impressive. Obviously, though some of these positions are remunerated, like so many in the sport he works many additional hours and incurs costs at his own expense in order to fulfil his responsibilities professionally and to the standard he requires of himself. When I bump into him in the pits before the meeting, he talks guardedly of a "tough meeting ahead where it'll be difficult to make up the aggregate points deficit" and he gives even less

Plain clothes track walk

GRA infrastructure investments continue

away about the widely held prospect that Coventry will make a clean sweep in all competitions to add to their Elite League championship triumph. "We don't have a full trophy cabinet, it's just a possibility at the moment!"

This injection of Peter's support and experience into the club by Allen Trump has been a vital part of the equation of the recent Oxford Conference League success story but then, also, of greater significance has been the long hours of voluntary work and service given to the club by a loyal band of Oxford enthusiasts in a whole variety of vital but unpaid positions. Without the practical and administrative details getting sorted for every fixture, there would be no speedway or club. Whatever League you compete in you require people to write and produce the programme, work on the turnstiles, track or in the pits never mind elsewhere in the grandstand or within the stadium. Unlike the previous incumbents, Allen Trump makes a point to offer praise where praise is due. Though he praises the "superb track surface we now enjoy" (in contrast to the situation during the "infamous Coventry thrashing [when] the third and fourth bend resembled a ploughed field"), the people who made that possible are the real focus of his congratulations, "take a bow Geoff Barber, Colin Meredith and Nobby Hall, your work is appreciated by everyone."

Another man who, like his parents, works tirelessly behind the scenes on behalf of the club is Robert Peasley. Among other things he's the unofficial club historian, programme editor along with Bryn Williams, trackshop manager and meeting reporter on the website, where his account of the action mixes insight, detail, slightly partisan support and a wide vocabulary, leavened with his characteristic sense of fair play. Tonight he's already set out the trackshop stall in the far left-hand corner of the upstairs bar and restaurant they have in the home-straight grandstand at Cowley Stadium. From this vantagepoint, Rob has a panoramic view of proceedings on the track and apart from laying out the range of merchandise on offer, he has also organised this nest of tables to ensure that his seat is cordoned off from the rogue bottoms of the paying public. He has also kindly placed a table for my display of books adjacent to the corner of his stall. Wherever possible I try to avoid watching speedway indoors and particularly from behind glass as you lose the immediacy of the noise and the smell, ignoring the inevitable distance the barrier of glass creates. Nonetheless, the chance to observe Rob twitch, shout and pirouette while he's totally absorbed as he watches his beloved Cheetahs compete for glory on the track is a unique opportunity and almost enough compensation for the lack of the usual sights, sounds and smells of speedway.

When the outcome of the meeting is hugely important to both teams, you definitely want the services of an experienced speedway referee and, fortunately tonight, we have the services of Tony Steele who's renowned for his shrewd handing of people as well as his knowledge of the rules. On his way to the referee's box located through a door by the cafe, up two flights of green-painted stairs to an eyrie perched close to the grandstand roof, Tony stops for a few words. I quiz him about the recent Grand Prix in Gelsenkirchen. "I thought the ref [Wojciech Grodzki] was terrible! Some of the decisions were awful in the semi-final and the final never mind not excluding Scott in the run-off. Then, it's easier when you're the son of the Vice President of the F.I.M., it tends to make it easier than for anyone who's good at the job!" Given Tony's legendary diplomacy this has to count as a savage excoriation of Wojciech's competence and fitness for the position. "They say the staging costs at any Grand Prix varies between £230,000 and £280,000 - that was £280k excluding prize money. It was never expected to make any money. They say the attendance was 25,000 but they gave away loads of tickets just to boost the numbers because the capacity is 66,000."

Not that we knew it at the time, but this would be one of the last (for the foreseeable future as I write) Oxford speedway meetings at Cowley Stadium because, subsequently after the season closed, promoter Allen Trump was unable to secure agreement on what he viewed to be an acceptable rental valuation for the 2008 season. Sensibly avoiding the naive tactic of lambasting the stadium owners on local radio, attempts at an amicable resolution still eventually came to nought. One of the reasons that was given as a contributory factor behind this decision was the apparent shortfall in revenues earned by the stadium landlords from the bar and restaurant on speedway race night. The question of the profits from catering and refreshments was always going to be a difficult aspect of the relationship to resolve since not only were Conference League crowds never likely to be excessive but the 'older' age demographic of the typical speedway audience ensures that there is no real tradition of excessive alcohol consumption, never mind that many fans invariably bring their own seating, sandwiches and flasks!

However, if every Oxford fan had known it was their patriotic duty to buy some food and drink from the various stadium outlets every other week in order to keep the place open, then a campaign could surely have been organised. As it is, this all sounds rather like a retrospective justification and post-hoc explanation cunningly thought up by the stadium landlords, the Greyhound Racing Association. If the GRA were being fair, they'd take into account the trading environment and business context in which food and drink would find itself competing for the attention of potential customers every race night. Firstly, if you bring a family into the stadium and purchase programmes you're already going to have spent a tidy sum before you've even seen a wheel turn. And, not wishing to be presumptuous about how people organise their family lives and household budgets, but given racing doesn't actually start until 7.30 p.m. many people will have dined before arrival. Or, possibly, brought sandwiches and snacks to tide them over until they get home to eat. Equally, if they've set off from the house (or straight from work) without eating, then the Tesco superstore directly adjacent to the stadium (it's hard to imagine it could get any closer) also has a restaurant offering a good selection of hot and cold food as well as the added lure of Clubcard points. Never mind, that only a short distance further away, there are some national fast-food outlets. Even more importantly, the prices Tesco charge are significantly keener that those of the GRA outlets though, that said, if you dine upstairs at Cowley Stadium you have the additional benefit that you can either stare out over the vacant track or watch the bikes (or tractor) going round. You can't do this from Tesco unless you have X-ray eyes.

Handwritten in marker pen on the white board next to the serving hatch of the Racers Food Stop, the "Speedway Menu" features quite an emphasis upon chips. Indeed, you can have all the following with chips: Cheeseburger (£4.10), Beefburger (£4.00), Hot Dog (£4.50), Sausage (£3.00) or without you can have Cheeseburger (£2.60), Beefburger (£2.50), Hot Dog (£3.00) or chips (£1.50). If this were a Mensa test and you had to spot the odd one out, you'd notice that "Sausage" should also have been offered at £1.50 and, perhaps, it's the absence of this item from the "Speedway Menu" that stifled the exponential demand on race night that would have saved the club? Once you've loaded up with your first course, you still have a few choices for sweet: Chocolate Fudge Brownie (£1.20), Vanilla Ice Cream Tubs (£1.00) and "Ice Cream Sundries" (£2.65) that you can wash down with Tea (£1.00), Coffee (£1.10) or Hot Chocolate (£1.10). Even more compelling than the comestibles on offer within the upstairs area of the Cowley Stadium home-straight grandstand is the excess of signage on display on almost every available wall and door. All the usual favourites are here - Emergency Exit; Fire Escape; Grandstand Restaurant Strictly Diners Only; Litter → - along with my favourite sign of the speedway season, which has been strategically placed above many of the rubbish bins "please do not throw your empty glasses in the bin thank you". Who would have thought you'd need to issue such an instruction, let alone place such a sign above the litterbins? My curiosity was aroused enough to venture to the bar to check whether they did, indeed, use glass glasses to serve alcohol (they did). Given the lack of custom the GRA identified as one of the contributory factors behind the need for a rental increase at the stadium, I can only assume that (given their superiority in numbers and greater frequency of visits to

Important notice

the stadium) the punters who watch the dogs (rather than those fans who watch the speedway) throw the majority of glasses away? On that basis, the lack of profitability of the bar sales at the stadium was, in fact, helped by the lack of speedway drinkers who by not using or throwing the glasses away actually contributed to the profitability of the operation here! Not wishing to help Clive Feltham become a better, more rounded businessman but, perhaps, if he looked at profitability rather than the less helpful (but still important) basic business variable of headline gross revenues, he might have reached a more nuanced conclusion about the use of his catering outlets by his tenants at Cowley Stadium.

An A-board sign close by to the bar (one I imagine that might cause a health and safety hazard) indicates to me that the experts among the Oxford Cheetahs faithful don't really expect to make up the 17-point deficit required in order to qualify for the Conference League Final. I come to this conclusion as the notice on the A-board from the OSSC (Oxford Speedway Supporters' Club) implores me to buy a £5 ticket in order to try to win a £400 prize - "your last chance to sign up - draw to be made tonight". If confidence of victory were really as high as some fans claimed to me, then the draw would surely be made during the Cowley leg of the final against Scunthorpe? Anyway, I settle instead for raffle tickets ("£1 a strip, £2 for three") for the "Raceday 50/50 draw" sold to me by Rob Peasley's mum, Hilary. Over the tannoy the announcer ramps up the pre-meeting anticipation with news of the teams, the sale of my books ("a very worthy purchase") and the claim, "certainly a good crowd is building up!"

Once the racing starts, inside the total exclusion zone he has created for himself with the trackshop tables, Rob only has eyes for his speedway mistress - the Oxford Cheetahs - rather than for guarding the merchandise on display. Not that anyone shows any inclination to avail themselves of this distraction because, almost without exception, they're similarly absorbed. Having lost the intimacy of the crowd along with the essential speedway noise and smell, it has to be admitted that the view is excellent and, even better, you get instant replays on the bank of television screens that line the length of the grandstand viewing area and are also dotted throughout in strategic places, such as by the bar and restaurant serving area. Obviously, these are really provided for the joy and delectation of the greyhound fans as they watch their possible fortunes depend on the dogs they have chosen to favour but, during the meeting itself, we're treated to the benefit of instant video reruns. Earlier the screens had all been showing *Sky* News in ideal viewing conditions - with the sound off - though the shouty red ticker tape headlines at the bottom of the screen still bellowed information at us. Unusually tonight, there was actually some 'breaking news' that could just about qualify for this label, namely the resignation of Liberal Democrat Party leader, the Rt Hon. Sir William Menzies 'Ming' Campbell. Personally I was shocked at the decision but everyone else greeted the news with a sustained campaign of studiously ignoring it, though I have my doubts whether speedway fans are a natural constituency for Lib Dems or, even, ever really that interested in politics. Except, of course, when it comes to the local variety concerning speedway planning applications, noise objections and campaigns to stop immigration or re-introduce capital punishment.

The evening starts well enough for the Cheetahs with a win for Lee Smethills over the experienced Seemond Stephens and third for Sam Martin in the re-run of the first race. In the initial running, Tim Webster's attempt to move past Sam Martin into third place results in his exclusion after a challenge that causes him to fall after he's clipped the back wheel of his rival. Rob allows himself a small hip thrust of delight as the riders cross the line before he attentively completes the necessaries in his programme in between frequent glances at the replay on the screen almost directly above us. Rob then shows little reaction to the outcome of Heat 2 other than a slouch of the shoulders - a 1-5 for the visitors gained through Ben Hopwood and Jaimie Pickard - and, afterwards, barely glances at the screen. He is much keener to study this intently after the next race that sees Andrew Bargh and Jordan Frampton reply in kind. The race also features a fall and remount for Plymouth's Tom Brown "He always has at least one fall here - he's got it out of the way early tonight!" Just before the fourth race, a pesky customer - a teenage girl from Plymouth - demands, "I want one of those horns you press", and thereby interrupts Rob's absorption and concentration just as the race is about to start! Poor timing is an immutable law of trackshop life but, luckily, Rob is able to multitask with the change and simultaneously watch the race. There is a hint of celebration from Rob when Danny Betson wins and with third place being secured by Brendan Johnson, after Ben Hopwood helpfully falls, things look all right on the night (so far) for the Cheetahs.

After he's studied the replay, Rob gives me a brief run down on the history of the club air fence - an item of furniture that you rarely see at this level. "Allen bought Waggy's air fence on eBay when Waggy went into administration - our original one is at King's Lynn not being used - and we have the old one back! So we've changed air fence colour, it's green now and the old one was supposed to be blue and yellow but it was sort of purple and orange - I dunno how Airtek could get the colours so wrong?" Heat 5 sees Tim Webster fall for the second time in two outings and, just after he's remounted, the red lights come on to temporarily exasperate Rob, "What's that? Why's that? He better bloody award it!" The subsequent award of the race as a 5-1 for the Cheetahs satisfies all the home fans and contentment levels increase further with yet more of the same in the next race when Smethills and Martin combine to advance the score on the night to 24-12. Before the next race, over the tannoy we learn, "The sponsors of this heat are the Faulkner Scooter Centre - so if you want a scooter give them a call or go to Botley and see what they've got to offer for yourself!" This would be the ideal opportunity to try to get an answer to the eternal question, 'should mopeds be allowed on motorways?' but the riders are already under orders at the start line. The race gets no further than the first corner before it ends in a tangle of men and machines. Rob is keen to offer Tony Steele some plaintive advice, "Come on Tony - exclude yellow [Rob Smith] it was his fault!" Tony Steele rules it as an unsatisfactory start, so as all four riders begin to return to the start line to attempt the race again, we watch the replay. This clearly shows that Oxford's Danny Betson knocked Rob Smith into Scott Campos. Rob backs down on his initial appeal for an exclusion, "Well, okay, maybe not!" But, instead, goes on to question the tactical naïvety of the visitors, "I'm surprised that they didn't decide to use a black and white as they'd have got 4 points with Scott [Campos] in the race." This prediction proves prescient since Betson wins easily and Campos finishes tailed off at the rear. The 50/50 draw winner gets to go home with £115 and I get to rip up my losing tickets.

One race too late according to Rob, Plymouth bring in Tom Brown to replace the out of form/luck Tom Webster and have him ride as a tactical substitute off 15 metres. Though Sam Martin wins the race, Plymouth riders occupy the minor placings to ensure a 3-5 heat win. Rob shouts encouragement throughout, "Go on Brendan - keep third!" Sheer effort of mind and aggressive racing sees Nicki Glanz intimidate the home pair of Andrew Bargh and Jordan Frampton sufficiently on the first three bends of Heat 9 to win with some comfort. "This is going to the last heat," says Rob knowledgeably. The next heats are drawn including a four-all in Heat 11 when tactical substitute Seemond Stephens finishes second behind Danny Betson in a race that sees Tim Webster fall, remount and then retire with an engine failure. Wearing the number two race tabard, Tim Webster's final three-race haul of nil points doesn't really reflect the effort expended or the entertainment he's provided but equally, during a tight meeting, Plymouth could point to his lack of contribution as possibly a decisive factor on the night. Another fall and remount, this time for Jaimie Pickard, helps the Cheetahs eek out a further heat advantage to advance their lead on the night by a further 2 points to 44-32. Another heat advantage in Heat 13 extends the lead further and has Rob hopping about the carpeted area of the trackshop like an expectant father with severe cramp in his foot. With Oxford in the lead by 14 points and Plymouth ahead on aggregate by 3, the penultimate race requires steady nerves or a flash of inspiration. Though Jordan Frampton wins, the Plymouth pair block out Brendan Johnson who, upstairs in the grandstand bar, has Rob howl his encouragement, "C'mon Brendan! C'mon Brendan!" to no avail. Though nervous, Rob remains phlegmatic, "It was bound to happen - another last heat decider!" (To determine the final aggregate score over two legs).

The responsibility to get the 5-1 that Oxford LCD Publishing Cheetahs require to win and go through to the final and certain defeat against Scunthorpe falls to Danny Betson and Lee Smethills. While to guarantee their appearance and similar subsequent defeat to Scunthorpe, the Plymouth Devils track Tom Brown and Seemond Stephens. With the tension manifesting itself as an expression of studious concern on Rob's face, the tapes fly and Danny Betson makes a lightning fast start to gain the lead. Behind him Stephens has second and Smethills third until the Oxford rider forces his way through on the inside. When the Oxford riders hit the front, Rob leaps into the air as though he's either just scored a goal or been stung by a wasp. For the remainder of the race he combines hopping anxiously from foot to foot with a hip-thrusting motion - as though, reduced fluidity of movement aside, he's Oxford's answer to Elvis - to draw the riders round the circuit to victory. Making a last-gasp dash round the outside that will see his race end in either great glory or brave failure, Tom Brown tries to find his way past through a challenge for a gap that really doesn't exist. Without sufficient speed to pass but enough to tumble into a heap trying on the third bend of the last lap, Tom Brown crashes out of the race to loud cheers of triumph (rather than *Schadenfreude*) from the Oxford faithful. Even as he dances around gleefully in an exalted moment of a 1- point aggregate victory, Rob remains a true speedway fan at heart when asking loudly of the still stricken and prostrate Plymouth rider, "Is Brown alright? Is he alright?" Quite who can answer I don't know since the total exclusion zone of the trackshop tables has ensured we uninterruptedly remained kings of our own particular castle throughout the meeting. With the victory parade just about to take place, Rob is keen to rush into the cold outside air to savour the moment with the majority of the Oxford fans. He packs away the Cheetahs merchandise with such impressive speed and confident familiarity that, for a moment, I suspect we've been told to evacuate the building.

The announcer tees up his interview with the club promoter by saying, "Allen Trump has done it - he has resurrected Oxford speedway!" In a voice filled with emotion and one that genuinely sounds on the verge of tears, Trump says, "I don't know what to say - I'm so emotional! I think they should give us the championship trophy tonight based on that performance! We always knew we would pull it back. We left it a bit late but we knew we would. Plymouth did a lot of shouting about how they would stuff us and get lots of points but it didn't happen! Rob Godfrey was down here watching tonight and we've given him something to think about for the final."

15th October Oxford v Plymouth (CL Play-off Semi Final, 2nd leg) 56-38

Chapter 51. Rye House v Sheffield: Ironing, triumph and humble pie

20th October

Kelvin	*"It's all in the boiling pot tonight"*
Jonathan [before Heat 12] **Kelvin**	*"Heat 14 - unlikely to be the decider!"* *"Well, it could be"*
Jonathan [later] **Kelvin** [with two heats to go still]	*"We said Heat 14 could be vital - and it is!"* *"This meeting has had everything and I don't think it's over yet"*
Jonathan [on Premier League] **Kelvin**	*"It's a massive, massive league"* *"It really is quite a big league!"*
Jonathan [on Tai Woffinden]	*"He comes from a family"*
Nigel [as race finishes]	*"Amazing! One more lap and it might have been different!"*
Jonathan	*"Tai, tell us how old you are and everything?"*

A long hard Premier League season arrives at its conclusion with a finale in Hoddesdon that all Rye House fans, the majority of neutrals and all but the most optimistic of die- hard Sheffield supporters confidently expect will result in victory for the home team. Both clubs ride at tracks that visitors find difficult to master, let alone excel on sufficiently enough to make it a close contest. Though undoubtedly this provides great entertainment for the diehard faithful, there is a school of thought that, as the old T-shirts used to claim, says 'happiness is 40-38' and ideally close contests should really be the order of the day. If you ignore that the number of heats has changed since this message gained popularity, the fact that both of these teams racked up a significant number of meetings where they scored 60 points or more (Sheffield six times and Rye House 11) or won comfortably with scores between 55 to 59 points (Sheffield 15 times and Rye House five) says it all. The prowess of the Rye House Silver Ski Rockets round their own circuit isn't disputed but it was their performance during their visit to Owlerton two nights previously when they held their margin of defeat to 9 points that effectively secured them the Premier League crown. In the media, Rockets team manager John Sampford expressed satisfaction at the way his team "managed to subdue bits of the Sheffield team" but played down talk of automatic triumph, "this is a good result for us and I can understand why so many people now make us favourites, but you won't hear me or any of the boys saying we're favourites."

It's a beautifully sunny afternoon when I arrive at the stadium, the track looks in pristine condition and clear skies ensure that the meeting will definitely go ahead, albeit with the promise of a cold night later. Andy Griggs has already set out the majority of the merchandise on his stall. While he pays obsessive attention to ensuring that all the riders' pens are lined up in rider order symmetrically, Doug Boxall fusses over hanging up a wide variety of clothing. There are bargains galore to be had tonight for Rye House fans - the pens will retail at a bargain £1 (rather than £1.50), there are glow in the dark whistles at 60p and lots of the Rockets-logoed clothing is aggressively marked down for a quick sale - though sensibly, given the likelihood of excessive and exuberant celebrations later, the price of air horns (£4.75) and air horn refills (£3.00) haven't been discounted. The organisational powerhouse behind the continued success of the club off the track, Heather Silver, dashes zealously about the place doing many things in a flurry of activity and last-minute instructions to ensure everything operates seamlessly. One of the ladies on the

The lolly boys

Tireless fundraisers George and Linda Barclay

Famous Rye House catering

entrance gate turnstiles has a bad hangover, while just inside the entrance gates two young boys sit patiently by two giant tubs of fizzy lollies that they'll hand out to every child that comes along tonight. My eyes are continually drawn to them. Though my taste buds have been stimulated by the sight and thought of the lollies, no matter how many times I accidentally pass by to request a lolly from the boys, the youngsters are adamant that I can't have one! The indefatigable George and Linda Barclay, who have worked so tirelessly to raise funds and awareness for the Speedway Museum at the nearby Paradise Park through their regular travel to every (or almost every) speedway track in the country, actually have the Premier League trophy with them. They place it on a blue box-cum-pedestal in the centre of the table they've set up to draw attention to tonight's raffle to raise monies on behalf of the Speedway Riders' Benevolent Fund. The fine details of which are advertised on specially printed plastic cards which George and Linda display prominently on the table and also hang round their necks to further draw the eye.

When I bump into Craig Saul - the Rockets supremely entertaining announcer with the virtuoso language skills that surely someday should take him to the bigger stage of the Cardiff Grand Prix - he can't be bothered with the pretence of false modesty about the likelihood of a Rye House victory. "The only question is which heat will Sheffield use their tactical ride in? Ashworth never rides well here, so it'll be Compton so [looks at programme] I guess Heat 7 or maybe 10. Doesn't really matter who we have riding, it's just not going to happen for them!" Much more guarded about the likely outcome or the stock that he's pre-ordered in for tonight and has hidden under his table is Rye House trackshop owner, Andy Griggs. When I enquire, "Do you have any 'Rye House Silver Ski Rockets 2007 League Champions' badges here?" He tells me "no comment!" in a manner that brooks no dissent. I decide it would be best not to ask about the availability of any other commemorative memorabilia such as fleeces, caps and the like that he may have pre-purchased to specially have in stock for this very night of potential triumph.

In his 'Len's Lines' column in the programme, Len Silver draws attention to the ongoing development of the facilities at the club including upgraded and brighter floodlights as well as a bigger car park on the River Lee side of the stadium on a strip of unused land (owned by the Rye House pub) that has been levelled and cleaned. Even if you ignore the professionalism of pretty well any aspect of the presentation you care to consider or name here on speedway race night, it's clear that Len takes great pride and care to ensure that appearances meet his high standards - even when it comes to the car park! He notes with some pride that not only is there "extra space" but "also the way in which it makes that area much more attractive." However, while the majority of his column ostensibly only really deals with the climax of the Premier League season ("tonight's event is, surely, one of the most important we have staged since our re-opening for speedway in 2000"), it really is a thinly veiled but sustained attack on the practices, ethics and philosophy of King's Lynn speedway, albeit without explicitly naming them. "One of the reasons for my pleasure in the Tigers qualification and visit tonight is that the philosophy of the management at the Steel City is very similar to my own and speedway is presented at Owlerton with the basic idea of fair play to both teams. Neil Machin does not stoop to tricks or bias and if his team wins it is because they are the better team and not because, for example, the track has been made difficult for the visitors. Not that the Rockets find the huge and speedy bowl at Owlerton a happy hunting ground, it couldn't, frankly, be more different from our own strip - but, and this is the point, it is always safe and smooth. Sadly there are other promotions in our league who are not as fair minded and there have been times when our riders' safety has been in jeopardy because of deliberate actions to make the racing surface difficult. Sheffield have themselves had cause for complaint about this very issue, and not very long ago either."

Someone else who has also seen it all before, but still has quite some time before he achieves Len's longevity in the sport is Malcolm Wright, who until this season used to be the co-promoter at Sheffield. Old habits die hard and Malcolm has distanced himself from the grinding day-to-day administration of the sport but has still (despite his intentions to the contrary) been a regular fixture at speedway meetings featuring Sheffield. "It can't be right can it? Birmingham finish second and they're not in the play-offs. King's Lynn win the league and yet they're third. Isle of Wight finish fifth and qualify and we could still finish second or first. Well, actually, the only time we've rode well here in recent years was when it had rained really heavily. Len didn't want to race but the ref said it was fine so he had to. Nature had done its work so there was actually a bit of grip for once. We still lost though - by 6 or 8 points! Some have said that Graham [Drury] didn't try to complete his fixtures by the cut-off 'cause he knew that four Young Shield meetings would be easier and more lucrative for him than the play-offs." Travel is definitely something that excites and occupies Malcolm much more than speedway, "I'm just back from Ecuador. Our guide - a professor, really articulate man - collects banana labels from round the world. He has over 30,000 and travels the world over to get them. Every distributor in every country has their own versions that they change all the time!" This sounds more obsessive than the passionate people who collect speedway programmes and badges. I ask about those people who collect airline sick bags and learn things are no longer what they once were, "I have a friend who collects them but cost cutting means they're all plain standard ones nowadays."

As usual, Len Silver marches out on parade in military fashion ahead of his troop of track staff closely followed by the riders to the sound of the tune of 'Those Magnificent Men in their Flying Machines'. The introductory formalities include a chat with Len apparently in the style of 'What-the-veteran-promoter-saw'. He ranges widely in free associative fashion, "I had a call 15 minutes ago from Buster Chapman wishing us the best of luck! I must admit I was at King's Lynn when Sheffield won [through] and I must admit that what I saw makes me welcome Sheffield here tonight." All that is then left to do is to adhere to the Hoddesdon tradition of the throw of the ceremonial coin after the toss for gate positions, "Sheffield take one and three and Len lobs the £2 coin into the crowd!" The stadium is packed, the children all have their lollies but the meeting is effectively over as a contest almost from the outset. Heat 2 is drawn when a Sheffield rider in the form of James Cockle actually wins a race. Apart from that it is a pretty constant diet of 5-1s until there is another drawn heat when Andre Compton wins race seven, after that no Sheffield rider wins again. With little in the way of competition on the track, Craig Saul ramps up the celebratory feelings among the home fans from the off, "Yes, we've already got a real party atmosphere this evening already!" When Steve Boxall wins Heat 4 to take Rye House into the overall lead on aggregate (let alone the meeting advantage of 12 points), Craig notes, "The fist in the air says it all!" Clutching at descriptive straws for his comments on the Sheffield 'opposition' as early as Heat 5 we learn, "the Tigers edge up to 7 [points]." Joel Parsons appears not to have ridden to the start line on the leaden bikes favoured tonight by his team mates and, instead, shoots from the start gate to lead for nearly a lap before Chris Neath overtakes him on the first bend of the second lap and Stefan Ekberg eventually passes him on the third bend of the last lap. The lovely George Barclay brings the irredeemably positive outlook of his faith-healing work wherever he goes and so consequently delights in the spectacle, "Some of the passing is fantastic!"

At least there is still an air of mystery about who will win the raffle, though Len can't resist some further light-hearted banter at the expense of their Norfolk rivals with a pretend draw of the winner, "what's that - Jonathan Chapman of King's Lynn?"[1] He continues, "I hope you're having fun - I certainly am. We've raised over £500 for the Riders' Benevolent Fund which takes it to over £2,200 this season!"

[1 The raffle prize that night was the chance to present the Championship trophy to the winning team, which was the reason for his aside]

Andy Griggs in action

Victory flag

Champions on parade

The Tigers send out Andre Compton for a tactical ride in Heat 10 as Craig correctly predicted beforehand, but to no real avail though his second place does ensure a rare drawn heat. The Rockets roar to their eighth 5-1 when they win Heat 11, "Once again the heroes max out and are so close to taking that championship." A disgruntled Sheffield fan asks me, "Who's to say whether losing the Play-off Final is better than winning the Young Shield?" Heat 12 sees Compton and Tai Woffinden battle for supremacy all the way to the finish line and, stood on the fourth bend, I award the win to the Tiger and mark my programme accordingly. Controversially to my mind, referee Chris Gay adjudges Woffinden to have won (though this balances up his Heat 2 decision, when Adam Roynon appeared to win a race the scorecard shows James Cockle had won). George Barclay is also surprised to learn that Andre hadn't won but typically remains evenhandedly philosophical, "I thought he had but you can't tell from here." Afterwards, Chris Gay confirms that we were both mistaken and highlights that referee's boxes are most often (though there are exceptions) traditionally sited in the best position to overlook the business sharp end of the finish line. Nonetheless, these 2 points were to prove vital and ensured that the Tigers eventually lost 69-26 and thereby didn't suffer the total humiliation of again being on the end of a 70-point score (they humiliatingly lost 75-15 at King's Lynn earlier in the season).

Off-duty referee Christine Turnbull says, "There was a bit of pride there", though you have to say that throughout the night it was mostly conspicuous by its absence from the Sheffield team. Such nuances are lost in the unalloyed celebrations of the crowd as well as the riders' and pits' crew who rush en masse onto the track surface. Presenter Craig Saul also enthusiastically leads the way in his own inimitable fashion, "Mathematically and every other way, Rye House are confirmed as Premier League champions - I think it could take a while to get these guys off the track!" If this were football, then there would be a pitch invasion by the home fans but, as this is speedway, delight abounds but civility reigns - except for the cacophony of air horns. At the trackshop, Andy Griggs celebrates in his own unique way by doing some ironing! Personally I hadn't previously seen him as a domestic goddess. But, while the crowd are distracted, he works away diligently ironing his previously hidden but cunningly pre-prepared 'Rye House Premier League Champions 2007' iron-on transfers onto every top of the range blue garment he can lay his hands on at his stall in anticipation of imminent demand on the night. I sense now wouldn't be a good time to interrupt him since not only does he have a narrow time window of opportunity to prepare said merchandise, but also his tongue-out look of concentration is a picture (that sadly doesn't come out).

Elsewhere in the stadium, Craig has a couple of important announcements, "Lost and found - it's a large slice of humble pie awaiting a Mr Jonathan Chapman if he'd like to come and collect it![2] And don't forget the championship merchandise will be available at the trackshop this evening."

[2 Craig later elucidated: "The 'humble pie' note actually came up to the announcer's box from a die-hard Rye House supporter and I think I said (in as serious a tone as I could work up) that he had found this item of lost property and that it could be reclaimed by the owner. Credit where it is due: this was not my original. (Honest, Jonathan, honest.)"]

The final Rye House scorecard makes impressive reading with every rider gaining a win or a paid win. There were paid maximums for Stefan Ekberg (10+2), Tai Woffinden (12+3) and Tommy Allen (14+1) as well as an impressive roster of support from Chris Neath (9+1), Steve Boxall (10+1), Luke Bowen (7+3) and Adam Roynon (7+2). For Sheffield, Andre Compton top scored with 11 points from five rides with James Cockle and Joel Parsons joint second highest scorers on a lowly 4 points, while Paul Cooper and Jordan Frampton failed to even trouble the scorer. Len Silver is understandably ebullient, "We are the best team in the League bar none and that includes King's Lynn! You could have stayed at home to watch England in the [Rugby] World Cup Final but you chose to watch the Rockets and that's wonderful - thank you!"

DVD saleswoman, Kirstie Burnett, wonders how the night of celebrations will pan out for some of the riders from the victorious Rye House team: "I have a question - what do they give them to drink? Because Tai Woffinden, Adam Roynon and Luke Bowen are all too young to drink!"

20th October Rye House v Sheffield (Premier League Play-Off Final, Second Leg) 69-26

Chapter 52. Ryton-on-Dunsmore: Rapt atmosphere envelopes

3rd November

With speedway racing over for the 2007 season (outdoors, at least), my continuing education into the ways of the shale takes another interesting turn when I travel to the Sports Connexion Centre at Ryton-on-Dunsmore near Coventry. In the "Nick Barber Sporting Auction" catalogue, the event is billed as the "Collectors' Fayre Speedway beginning at 9-9.30 a.m." with "auction viewing" beginning at 9.30 a.m. and continuing until 12.45 p.m. before the "auction begins prompt 1 p.m.". This keenly anticipated event is the speedway equivalent to attendance at a prestigious art auction at Christie's or Sotheby's. All the big names are in attendance there and the lime-green catalogue lists the "stallholders for the day" as "Martin Dadswell, Alan Boniface [without links with Plymouth], Nick Barber, Alan Hunt, Alan Morgan, Lindsay Gray, Chris Stockwell". For those in the know, this is an exhibitor listing to thrill the imagination and get the heart pounding. The classifications and instructions contained on the inside page of the catalogue hint at the arcane complexity of the collector's world. "Commission bids" can be sent by post but "note final bids are received by Friday 2nd November 2007". I'm not quite sure what this exactly means but I assume you can submit a sealed bid for any particular items for auction that catch your fancy, even if you don't attend the event. Judged by the commission bid form on the back of the catalogue this is an intricate process. "I request Nick Barber Auctions to bid on my behalf as stated below. All lots will be purchased as cheaply as the reserve price and other bids allow. Bidding increments are 2-5-8-0 i.e. 22/25/28/30 or above 50 in 5s, above 100 in 10s. So please bid accordingly. Note a buyer's premium will be added to bids."

Sensibly enough payment is only cash or cheque, though it is possible to pay by credit card via PayPal on the Nick Barber Auctions website with the proviso that "there will be a charge to cover costs" (PayPal usually charge 5.25% of the item value). The rules that govern postage charges are comprehensive and straightforwardly expressed. The catalogue extends to 56 closely typed pages but, since this is a two-day affair, only 29 of these pages relate to speedway memorabilia and the remainder are for the "Collectors' Fayre Football and Speedway" that takes place on the Sunday. Nonetheless, there are 1014 lots of speedway goodies from yesteryear on sale and each has a listing that identifies the item itself, its provenance, age and condition as well as an estimated sale price. There is also a series of helpful identifiers: vgc (very good condition), ph (punch holes), slcr (slightly creased), cr (creased), inc (including), tcm (team changes marked), smf (score marked on front) and nmn (no maker's name). Given speedway as a sport has its own complex rules and rituals, I'd always assumed that understanding the action and the ability to mark the score in your programme represented the best sign of your fitness to join its cloistered world. I now realise that existing alongside this world during the speedway season is a parallel universe where the weight of history and past achievement finds expression in speedway memorabilia and collectables.

Though I'd been dimly aware that some people attached a great deal of importance to collecting, say, programmes, badges and tabards - I'd never really appreciated the scale and significance of the pent-up interest or the sheer volume of merchandise sold. They say one man's rubbish is another man's treasure and this is borne out at car boot sales every weekend and on eBay every day of the week. Inevitably, there is an element of 'dead man's shoes' that contributes to the trickle of rare items onto the market from bygone days. Usually when relatives dispose of the detritus and junk collected over a lifetime by a loved one or close family member, often blissfully unaware of its true value but keen to get rid of the clutter. Given speedway started in this country in 1928 as well as being a sport widely acknowledged as characterised by the older fan/ageing demographic in its base support, I now realise that the flow of items onto the market from the pre and post-war eras will have gathered real pace as the owners die off. These treasured possessions will inevitably change hands in a private sale or end their days recycled into the hands of other adoring owners at an important trade event like this one. Indeed, though the surroundings aren't plush, there's no escaping the fact that this event is the speedway memorabilia market's equivalent of the Chelsea Flower Show or Crufts, possibly even the Oscars. *The Speedway Star* describes the Fayre organiser, Nick Barber, as a "leading souvenir shop boss" with a chain of eight (soon to be nine with the addition of Belle Vue) "tracks under the wing of his Felixstowe-based business" but clearly this is only part of a more complicated story. Though the trackshop sales provide the bread and butter, nuts and bolts of a regular income stream, they are possibly only important as a vehicle to provide constant access to the flows of speedway memorabilia. Something I now (finally) realise is the cornerstone and revenue engine of Nick's business empire.

Outside in the car park of the Sports Connexion Centre, the place buzzes with activity. Some of this is from the various vans of speedway memorabilia being unloaded and the early arrival of keen collectors but, mostly, the place is overrun with Dalmatian dogs for the show that takes place in the sports hall (like a large Nissen hut) that is the adjacent building. Later in the day, when I leave the Fayre the car park is still full of proud dog owners, albeit the breed on display is the altogether flightier Red Setter. Apart from their dogs, everyone carries the paraphernalia you also need to possess if you own a show dog - tartan blankets, cages, leads, cut glass home-counties accents and, today it seems, a large numbered lapel badge. The Collectors' Fayre itself is located upstairs in the Connexion Centre in a large L-shaped room just off the main bar area. It's already filled with tables some already loaded down with speedway merchandise and others in the process of being laid out. Towards the top of the L-shape a veritable mountain of chairs are stacked dangerously high and, judged by the partition walls, the space we occupy can be reconfigured to adapt to whatever sized meeting will take place within. Martin Dadswell informs me, "We'll educate you into the ways of the memorabilia world by the end of the day!" He then dramatically clutches to his chest a soiled looking document from his stall and flourishes it under my nose, "Look at this pre-World War Two programme," before he then waves his arm expansively over towards his table, "and all these pre-war books." Given they sometimes struggle to sell nowadays at a memorabilia Fayre, I ask the question 'will my books sell when they're old?' only to learn, "some of the old books don't sell when they're old!"

Though the Fayre has yet to officially open some of the stalls are already mobbed by eager males of a certain age. They're so keen to get their hands on the latest treasures that a group of twenty or so avid men storm the exhibitors' area before the official opening time of 9 o'clock. Whether the stock is already set out on display or in the process of being unpacked doesn't concern them as they politely search-cum-ransack the merchandise for prized goodies. There isn't much conversation or noise (other than to establish price) since an atmosphere of rapt concentration has descended on the room. It's the kind of expectant frisson that I imagine you find at the introductory drinks stage of an orgy organised and staffed by supermodels - everyone's panting for it but still presently attempting to amiably keep their behaviour just about within the accepted protocols and bounds of polite society. Still, the late twentieth-century Thatcherite version of capitalism has taught us that there is no such thing as society. So, really, if the average speedway collector is to 'succeed', he definitely needs to compete ruthlessly to win what, ultimately, is a zero-sum game. The veneer of civility just about remains intact - this is still speedway, after all - but there is some surprising speed and agility shown by the collectors as they scamper from table to table in search of the missing items they require to enhance or complete their collections. Many people conduct their search in a structured and carefully planned manner. Consequently there is

Donald Walton and Andy Brickell

Memorabilia overflow area

Eager anticipation prevails

much flourishing of ring binders, notebooks and scraps of paper as the merchandise is compared to the authoritative inventory already personally owned by the punter.

I soon realise that the urgency is partially caused by a peep-show type level of interest but is also driven by a desire to have quickly scavenged the stock on display in order to have 'done' the exhibitors' part of the Collectors Fayre before moving on to the real focus of the day - the catalogued auction stock. These particular treasures are located in a large but anonymous room accessed through an incredibly squeaky door that leads from the bar. To the keen collector, this is an Aladdin's Cave of highly desirable collectables mixed in with some dross. Sorting the wheat from the chaff and also ensuring that the cornucopia does what it says on the tin (well in the Auction catalogue) requires that you thoroughly check the merchandise before it goes on sale. Once it has been scrutinised, you can then formulate the appropriate size of what will be your winning (or maximum) bid. This process requires that the collectors sit down at one of a long line of tables and - by item number - request the opportunity to closely peruse the object of their desire.

The sale items are held in individual large brown envelopes stacked inside a row of boxes away from the row of inspection tables and are retrieved for the interested collector after they've been requested from the helpers who administer the viewing process. Only the addition of white gloves to handle the merchandise would add to the mystique and overall veneration of the process. Since there are a limited number of chairs and only three and a quarter hours before the inspection phase ends, the first-come-first-served rule applies and the collectors scrimmage for a seat almost as soon as the doors open. Some items are more in demand for inspection than others. So not only is there an element of waiting in your seat (or worse, waiting for your chance to be in a seat looking at the merchandise) but there's also an element of show and charade, bluff and double bluff as you seek to examine the REAL object of your desire, while simultaneously throwing others off the scent about your particular target. Equally given that different people have different needs and/or collections - though, almost without fail, it appears everyone has brought a list of what they already have at home - the nature of specialisation dictates from a lot list of 1,014 items, some goodies will only attract certain collectors. If the atmosphere was earnest in the exhibitors' area, then inside this room it is positively febrile and collectively verges on a heightened degree of pleasure that they rather elegantly call in modern French (philosophy) *jouissance*. If a fire alarm were to sound, it would be curious to see who would try to save what!

Inevitably, reminiscences flood out at such an event, even more so than at any speedway meeting where memories still abound. One man born in 1925 wistfully recalls, "I've been going since I was four and went to Birmingham. I was black! I went 20 times a season until the War and then in the 50s followed Birmingham and Cradley everywhere, and went all over Europe. I used to collect badges and programmes but I lost all the programmes in a fire and haven't collected them since. The price of badges is ridiculous nowadays, some of those

I have sold for £400 or £500. I think the most I've ever paid for a badge is £45. Then everything is so expensive now! I'm 82 now and can't afford to watch speedway any more but, I have some doubles of badges of riders few people have, so I can swap them for other ones I'm missing."

As part of my ongoing education, I soon realise that not only can you collect physical items of memorabilia but also you can collect and tabulate information. The fans who indulge in this branch of the speedway world are known as 'results collectors'. Based on my observation at this one event, they come armed with larger and even more impressive looking ring binders than other collectors. They're twirled with practised ease and excitement. John Vass confides, "Since 1946, I have 574 results for which I need heat details - first, second and third places but not fourth - this sounds a lot but when you think there are 10,000 results that's not bad. Of these, I have some of them partially from other results collectors - people like Mark [Sawbridge], Tim, Hugh Vass and, of course, the Speedway Researcher website is fantastic - but you have to check to make sure! Because programmes have often been completed incorrectly, either wrongly at the time or from incorrect information afterwards. The worst one is when the *Speedway Star* and the *Speedway News* don't add up! Then you buy a programme of the result you're missing for £5 to check and they've used the *Star* to fill it out wrong. To give you an example [of the importance of results collecting], if you want George Hunter's average in 1965 you can do that easy. If you want it for 1964, it's impossible. The advent of the British League in 1965 was a spur to statisticians and the collation of stats, before that you have to do it yourself." It clearly must be a hobby that is passed down through the generations. When we're joined by Wolverhampton Speedway historian (and results collector), Mark Sawbridge, he excitedly interjects, "I need to sit down with your dad and swap results!" Mark has been allowed out with strict instructions from her indoors, "I've got me money intact now - when I left the house, the wife said 'watch what you spend! [laughs nervously]"[1]

Though, to my untutored eyes, all of the memorabilia has been created equally musty, weathered and (often) tattered - it's noticeable that some stallholders are besieged, whereas others only attract passing attention but no sustained scrabble for real or imagined treasures. The affable Don Walton from Belle Vue (whom I met at Kirkmanshulme Lane during my lively night there at the Swindon meeting) kindly explains, "He's got the biggest crowd 'cause he's got the best selection of gear!" Don has disciplined himself to only buy what he really wants or absolutely needs for his collection. So far today that is only a black-and-white photograph that he slips out of its protective sleeve to proudly show me. He avidly explains what I'm looking at, "that's the solid silver National Trophy - it used to be kept in the vaults of the *Daily Mail* - there's Norman Parker, Barry Briggs and Wimbledon winning it. I reckon mid-50s; that's Norman Greene who was the promoter - he has the look of a film star!" We're joined by a fellow collector Don knows, who has come along today with a set of ten Ivan Mauger badges dated from 1955 to 1985. He's already had a reconnaissance of the exhibits that will be sold at auction later, "have you seen there's a lot of 15 Ivan Mauger badges for sale in the auction? I have 6,000 badges but I still haven't catalogued them to figure out what I'm missing yet. I need to get together with some other collectors to photograph and catalogue our badge collections. It's urgently needed as many of the people who know about the pre-War badges are dying off more frequently nowadays!"

As it's the close season, the talk isn't only of yesteryear but of the season just gone, the season ahead and possible crimes that will be committed to the rules and regulations of the sport at the BSPA Annual Conference later in the month. Someone who made a big impression in a short time at Belle Vue last season was Antonio Lindback, albeit most of the attention was ultimately given to the off-track activities (in Sweden) that forced his premature retirement from the sport. Don Watson has a lot of sympathy for Antonio and tells me his version of the famous drink-driving incident, "he worked on his bikes at his parents' house 'cause they were away and went home and had a few beers as he is wont to do, when he remembered he'd left his parents front door unlocked!

[1 After the event I asked Mark for some more information on the arcane world of the results collectors. "I've got an application form for the 'Get a Life Club' somewhere, I must fill it in! But seriously, I don't think us results collectors have a common noun (my memory tells me that Dave Allen used to do a monologue about this - 'a clutch of drivers', 'a lot of Sodomites' and so on ...). 'Results collectors' makes us sound a bit dull. The guy you were talking to when I approached is John Vass, the son of a fellow results collector - his dad is called Hugh Vass (he called here once and my wife Sally picked up the phone, and said "Mark, it's Hugh Jass for you," but I don't think he heard). Hugh is one of those really nice people that you seem to meet at speedway tracks and we've swapped a lot of information over the years. My ambition is to get averages published for every official meeting from 1946-64 (and perhaps pre-war too). Of the 574 I'm outstanding, about half of those are where I'm missing last places, or have odd queries. Bit by bit, the list goes down each month. There are those of us who are even more dedicated. At Colindale in North London is the National Newspaper Library and groups of results collectors gather there to scrutinise newspapers. Some of the Scottish guys get the overnight coach once a month and spend a day there. Pre-war speedway was quite well reported so this is a prime focus for them. I'd love to join them, but I have this thing called 'work' which does prevent me from this activity. One friend of mine writes to reference libraries around the country to ask if they'd copy bits of information out of the old papers and send it over. Some of them (Motherwell, for example) couldn't be more helpful. Some charge a fortune for the privilege. Have you ever seen the *Speedway Researcher* magazine? It's manna from heaven for people like me. The website, www.speedwayresearcher.org.uk is a wonderful resource."]

Lots of lots

Close, silent study

Brian Oldham and Kenneth Brown

He drove over and locked up and on the way back he saw the blue lights come on and tried to escape. He took the corner too quickly and overturned the van but then ran off. Not a big mystery for the police as his name is all over the van, never mind in Sweden he stands out a bit. Once he'd been home for a few hours and thought he'd sobered up, he remembered the dog was in the back of the van still. When he got there and opened the back, the policeman sitting inside snapped on the cuffs. It could be a custodial sentence, given he has previous but, hopefully, they'll take account of his situation and be lenient."

Later another man stops by my stall to ask, "What have you done to upset Mike Bennett? I've heard him grumble about you a few times now. I thought it was out of order at the ELRC that he rubbished your books to the crowd. If people did that about his DVDs and said they were in the shop but don't buy them, he really wouldn't like it! He was away from the sport for years and now he comes back as the big 'I am'. He's stuck in a time warp, I just don't like the bloke. His ego is massive and when the other year I saw a thread on the forums of 'Mike Bennett for Cardiff' I had to double check it wasn't April 1st or someint!" The lack of activity at my stall elicits a gleeful response from Martin Dadswell while he displays a distinctive and well-practised gesture with his hand, "Reading a paper - that says it all. What - no sales? They're collectors, wha'didya expect?" Later talk turns to the season enjoyed at Peterborough, "They say Danny King was hoping to be paid the eight weeks' money he was owed at the Peterborough Dinner Dance. I heard Hans Andersen asked if he could borrow Colin Horton's Ferrari and then said he could only have it back when he paid him. It's such a great story I like to think it's true but it's probably an urban myth, like the idea the riders haven't been paid in full yet, which I'm sure they have!"

It also sounds like the life of a SCB referee isn't always a bed of roses away from the track if judged by anticipation levels before the annual get-together for the officials. "Chris van Straaten and Peter Toogood will be there, so most people won't say anything. Pete Toogood is the type of bloke who likes to get his retaliation in first with a sharp and/or cutting comment to provoke. Graham Reeves will turn up and we won't have an agenda, he'll just ask, 'What should we talk about?' He does it for the money people say. Something has to change with their rulebook - they set the rules and they're just too complicated! Many phrases have three or four interpretations. This season five or six decisions had to be amended after the meeting. Some of these featured refs like Tony Steele, Jim Lawrence and Jim McGregor. If experienced refs like those can't get it right - what hope is there for ordinary mortals like the rest of us?" With a gathering of like-minded men (and there were very few women in attendance) keen on speedway of yesteryear, much joy was to be had from overheard snatches of conversation premised upon the assumption that the original version of things was always better. In the space of one five-minute conversation, two of the great speedway club names were talked about almost identically, "You know when Belle Vue closed - the real Belle Vue ..." closely followed by, "When it was proper Wimbledon - Plough Lane was Plough Lane with crowds and a decent track - not the recent thing there!"

Dick Jarvis from Sittingbourne Speedway is at the event. Though he might have ventured away from Kent and his usual speedway work in the pits, as ever, he still wears the uniform of his usual somewhat oily eggshell-blue anorak. "I don't care what they do with the Elite League at the BSPA Conference so long as it doesn't mess up the Conference League. [In the CL] They need to bring in averages instead of grades, have a low points limit - say around 35 - and thereby get rid of the 'professional' Conference League riders like Danny Betson to only name one of many. You can never get rid of the money, there's always one or two promoters who overpay - if, for example, Allen Trump wants to pay £40 a point, that's his business - but, at least, this would even it up. It's so sensible [Peter] Morrish [the Conference League co-ordinator] probably won't do it!" Dick loves his speedway and what the Sittingbourne club represents within the sport. Many young riders have passed through on the club on their way to career success, whereas others have lived the dream before reality bites them again. The club in its own way tries to help other clubs that have fallen on harder times, "I said to Nick Taylor at the four-team tournament [at Sittingbourne featuring trackless Wimbledon] 'where's Perkin then?' and he said 'he won't come 'cause it's us [the Independent Supporters Club] but, at least, we're doing something not just talking about it!' I wonder if they'll ever come back with him in charge?"

Suddenly the trade exhibition is deserted by all but the odd remaining stallholder since practically everyone else has departed next door to watch, participate in or administer the auction. Nick Barber is an understated but effective Master of Ceremonies and the early pace of the event is swift as the items on offer are, apparently, not so highly sought after. You have to attend through the standard bread-and-butter items in order to get to the premium and highly sought-after articles. That said, the bidding does occasionally splutter into competitive life though, after a flurry of quick-fire bids Nick soon has the item "Going once, going twice, sold for [blah] to the man on my left." I recognise many faces in the audience from my journeys round the speedway tracks of Great Britain. The squeaking door separates the room used for the auction from the bar where on a giant screen Arsenal versus Manchester United has just started. Peterborough and Arsenal fan Steve Miles sits nursing his hangover and watches the flickering figures flitting hither and thither on the large screen. It's quite a contrast! The eagerly anticipated clash of Arsenal and Manchester United will allegedly draw a worldwide audience of 220 million, whereas the next-door auction of speedway collectibles has attracted an audience of around 120 people. Though there is much less noise in the hushed auction room, arguably the intensity, devotion, thrill and concentration is just as great in Ryton-on-Dunsmore as elsewhere. As a speedway auction virgin, everyone is keen to help me lose my novice status. Some are more forgiving and less cynical than others. When I ask Johnny Barber when does it get exciting, he replies, "Dunno, when they start really bidding - probably around [lot] 120 when we get to the badges!" Someone else (who shall remain nameless) says, "Is this your first time? What do you think? All these blokes who smell of BO and piss, who've lost interest in women - if they ever had it! And spend all their money on old speedway stuff - programmes, badges and other assorted stuff. You'll be amazed what some of the prices get to and then Trump [Allen not Donald] out bids them all at the end and pisses them all off." As if on cue, an item for sale has attracted a flurry of bids and, the totally in his element Master of Ceremonies Nick Barber, then says, "I'm bid £x - Allen?" Everyone sits there completely absorbed - there's almost the rapt devotional silence of a church service - while the lots are sold with thrills to be savoured, whether you're the buyer, the seller or a voyeur.

There is a school of thought within speedway that slyly holds the dedicated fans who continue to remain faithful to the sport in almost complete and utter contempt. This applies across the industry from riders to promoters and includes some track staff, helpers as well as certain *Sky Sports* television employees and even the trackshop stallholders (obviously BSI, through the deleterious impact of its actions, must hold British League speedway in contempt too). Whether you get paid for your participation or give it voluntarily, among some people this feeling of superiority through privileged access (or plain outright contempt) definitely exists - often just as much in the pits as on the terraces - and, sad though this is, that is their prerogative. However, I believe that this not only sells the sport and themselves short (both emotionally and spiritually) but denigrates so many others who relish and hold dear the speedway world with its old-fashioned sense of community and increasingly superseded values. So what if some of the people who come along to events like this might stick out like a sore thumb at a Royal Garden party. Or, heaven forefend, have some behavioural or sartorial idiosyncrasies? I can't say that I have any desire to buy anything myself or even get remotely this obsessed about speedway artefacts from yesteryear. Like pretty well everyone, I have enough of my own other obsessions already, thank you very much. Nonetheless, you can feel the love and sense of belonging, the mutual respect and rubbing along together nature of our community at this gathering. These people, like the fans who pay weekly at the turnstiles, are all part of a complex and variegated speedway community spread throughout Great Britain. Like many other things, it's emblematic of what makes the sport (our sport) as it's lived by the fans - rather than by the participants or the second tier of people involved in servicing these performers - something to be proud of and savoured! Our modern-day involvement in the collective experience of something surprisingly special - an activity that is often romanticised in the hype as something more significant than it really is - still has a tradition that stretches back before us, captures us here and now but also, hopefully, will continue in some form long after we have gone. So, the fans and the stadiums may look a little battered round the edges but nonetheless remains something culturally special that we underestimate at our peril and could still lose thoughtlessly. An intelligent, perceptive and kindly man I've stood with a number of times at Owlerton, Kenneth Brown, leaves early with the auction barely 20 minutes old to make his long way home on public transport. I suspect he lives alone but also gather that his passion for speedway over the decades still really animates him. It also provides a purpose and a passion, while it gives his life a force that so many people of his age and generation lose late in life. Ultimately, I don't know him from Adam, I've just bumped into him occasionally but he's part of the extended family that is speedway. Equally, despite outward appearances, he's got something we can learn from if only we're prepared to listen. "It's alright for those who like it but I've spent enough today and I'm happy with what I've got already! You can't get much on a pension anyway!"

3rd November - Winners: Everyone who left with a bargain or a treasure

Chapter 53. Brighton: "I nearly wet my pants!"
9th December

The traditional speedway season finale takes places at the Brighton Centre as usual, though there have been some significant changes behind the scenes. Following the shock departure of Jon Cook from the Eagles to the Hammers and after ten years working together to organise and run the event, the management partnership of Jon and Martin Dugard have also gone their separate ways. As if to signal the significance of the change, as well as probably for tax reasons, the name of the meeting has changed too from the Brighton Bonanza to something more in tune with the Internet age *IndoorSpeedway.co.uk*. The weird use of the URL is too complicated for everyone to have remembered, so rather than adopt the shortened version 'Indoor Speedway' most people still call it the Bonanza in the same way that vacuum cleaners remain Hoovers or, for older people, photocopies still get called Xeroxes. The mechanics and logistics of staging the event indoors still remains just as impressive as it always has and, as ever, requires the hard work and dedication of a hardy band of volunteers. In the article promoting the event in the *Speedway Star* beforehand, Martin made light of the sheer effort and skill involved in the process to install the track and all its essential accoutrements, "we can usually put it all together in between six and eight hours - we've got it down to quite a fine art. Last year [2006] Ed Kennett, Chris Geer, Jon Cook and I went in and put all the outer fence and white line up and shale in four hours." Strangely this wasn't my recollection since I'd spent nearly eight hours helping only Edward, Martin and Jon (without Chris Geer) on the Friday before the event doing the basic layout of the white line and the fence! I missed the installation of the shale on the Saturday.

If like the song some things remain the same, then the biggest and most visible change in evidence has been the extensive promotion of the event locally in Brighton and throughout the East Sussex area. At one point this involved a giant display board in a field that was visible to drivers on the A23 into Brighton, though a short while after it appeared said sign was removed having fallen foul of council planning regulations. This being speedway a way to work round the exact letter of the law was soon found, so the sign returned but only after it had been placed on a trailer and technically, provided the sign moves (fractionally) every day, planning permission is no longer required for its erection as it is deemed a 'temporary' (rather than permanent) structure. There were also a greater number of distinctive and luminously coloured posters dotted everywhere, a dedicated website appeared months beforehand and, extremely responsively for a promoter, Martin even posted updates of his plans on a regular basis on the British Speedway Forum. At one point, sources 'in the know' claimed that it was a cast-iron certainty that the calibre of the field assembled by Martin for the 2007 event would feature some top quality riders strutting their stuff indoors at Brighton. Clearly to do so would have required significant financial investment but, equally, would have boosted the crowd level as well as address the frequent dilution of quality complaint (from attendees and non-attendees alike) that quick comparisons with the field assembled for yesteryears apparently provided. The past always looks better through rose-tinted spectacles but it is the case that in the early days Grand Prix riders like Greg Hancock, Mark Loram and Peter Karlsson could be persuaded to interrupt their winter

Model rider display

Ready for action

Baby Tai

break to take part and race indoors. After scepticism that such suggestions were far-fetched, this year there was confident talk that Martin was in discussions with key big-name riders and we would see riders such as Nicki Pedersen, Scott Nicholls and Chris Harris take part. Whatever the reasons, this hasn't happened but the assembled field will still provide an entertaining mix of youth and experience as well as indoor experts like Edward Kennett, Martin Dugard or Shawn McConnell along with the flamboyance of Lewis Bridger. Not that this impresses stallholder and Sheffield trackshop man Mick Gregory, "the days of Scott Nicholls and Greg Hancock riding here have long gone - I've never watched it, but I certainly wouldn't watch it nowadays!" As is the way of the modern world, along with the new name for the event there is also a new strapline to emblazon on all the marketing and publicity materials - "anything can happen on the next four laps!"

If the rider line-up has a string element of *déjà vu*, then the same can be said of the stallholders who attend the Collectors' Fayre. There's the odd absence through retirement (John Jones) though his place has been taken by Andy Griggs. This is the last real hurrah before Christmas for both the sellers and buyers of speedway merchandise and memorabilia, though mostly expectations border on the jaundiced side of the equation. Despite deliberate appearances to the contrary, the allegedly richest practising speedway trackshop owner is the Croesus-like Dave Rattenberry who has sent along his able deputies in the form of Bill Gimbet and Steve Davies to person his stall while he spends his hard earned watching football in Cyprus. The Barber family in the form of brothers Nick and Johnny - who along with Dave Fairbrother organise the Fayre - obviously attend as do *Backtrack* (Tony and Susie), *Re-Run Videos* (Steve Girdwood, girlfriend Jo and their really cute baby Tai), Mick Gregory, Martin Dadswell and his sidekick Alan Boniface, Andy Griggs and Doug Boxall along with various other stallholders including the Polish people whose names I don't learn. I'm in my usual prime position by the Gents toilets adjacent to Mick Gregory. Unlike the previous two years, I'm solely selling my books rather than almost invisibly and cack-handedly helping out behind the scenes.

Across the way from Mick Gregory's stall is the mountain of well-chosen and keenly priced merchandise that the Barbers' have attractively set out over a large number of tables. Their stall attracts a lot of interest during the event but, in the many hours before the revolving doors of the Brighton Centre open, the chance to catch up on the close season world of speedway with the extremely knowledgeable and well-informed Johnny is hard to resist. "We stayed in Crawley last night - we've stayed in Brighton before and weren't impressed. [His sister] Bev has been asking to come for years and we told her it was awful, now she's been she don't wanna come back. We're gonna pack up after they go on for the second meeting. Not being funny but it's not worth hanging about for the sake of £30, especially with the torrential rain and 80 mph winds forecast." Johnny suggests that I should attend the first King's Lynn fixture of the 2008 season, which will be a meeting against Ipswich. "Some of their fans hate Mike Bennett with a passion going back years - I know that some Ipswich fans refused to go to the ELRC 'cause he was commentating there. For an Ipswich meeting they have no choice but to attend." At that point we're joined by a fresh-faced, smilingly cheerful Adam Roynon sporting a pristine looking blue Rye House anorak.

[JB] "Are you riding?"

[AR] "Yeh, don't you read the forums?"

[JS] "Gomolski dropped out."

[AR sharply] "Nah, I was always in it!"

[JB] "How you gonna do?"

[AR] "Me and Danny King said we have to ride together and we are. Otherwise we'd get paired with some Pole or someone who can't ride the track. We're gonna win, I think!"

[JB] "When are you gonna sign for King's Lynn?"

[AR] "I'm not! I'm waiting on Coventry sorting out what they're doing, so I can't get anywhere till then." Johnny gives him a theatrical look and raises his eyebrows, "I'll only be a squad member."

[JB] "There's no doubling up this year! They say Scott might get released by Coventry."

Gomolski provided some mystique and much-needed glamour in the original line up but has withdrawn due to injury sustained in the gym. Today he's replaced by Tommy Allen who has been promoted from reserve to earn a place from the start and will later take up his place alongside Shawn McConnell (25 years his senior) in the Pairs. His brother Ollie will also ride in both events and partners Simon Gustafsson.

Having come up for the day from Swindon to help out on the Barbers' stall is the friendly Lucy Aubrey who, like on race nights at Blunsdon, has also come along with her boyfriend Lee Poole.

[LA] "If Davey Watt gets recalled to Poole, you'll have Lee Richardson as your number one!"

[JS] "At least he'll not have the distraction of the GPs and be able to ride every Saturday."

[LA] "Nah, he'll be out all the time with man flu or whatever it is that he gets!"

[JS] "James Wright is a good signing for youse - he looked great at the PLRC."

[LA] "Problem is four nights later he looked awful for Belle Vue but with Leigh in the pits he's bound to improve!"

The Brighton Centre appears to specialise in employing slightly bolshie and overly officious staff in positions of notional management responsibility. When Kath Rolfe passes by to ready the tables that will form the programme stall, a lady staff member from the Centre repeatedly calls to her in haughty fashion, "Excuse me! Excuse me!" Kath eventually twigs that she's the one being spoken to and replies brusquely, "I'm with the thing, the show, I work here!" The lady retreats to the glass swing doors of the entrance and instead guards them officiously until the opening time of 11 a.m. Alan Boniface looks over morosely, "Once upon a time there used to be a bloody queue to get in here but the weather will put them off if nothing else will! It's crap, init? I thought of buying a ticket but came to help Martin instead." I think Alan means the weather forecast for later, as presently bright sunlight streams in through the smoked glass windows of the Brighton Centre. When the synchronised watches of the Centre staff agree that we are 'officially open', there's an initial rush towards my stand from the small gaggle of keen fans who have waited patiently for a few minutes outside. This posse of fans fail to stop at my stall but instead storms straight into the toilets except for one lady who stops, hovers and then asks Nick Barber, "Where are the toilets?" Nick nonchalantly waves at the opposite facing door to the Gents and says confidently, "They're there!" Only they're not, as that door turns out to be an alternative exit from inside the Gents. Once they can concentrate, the early arrivals wander from stall to stall but many have clearly only come to savour the pre-meeting atmosphere, gossip and window shop rather than dig deep in their pockets. Mick Gregory isn't impressed, "I'm supposed to be in Sri Lanka now [watching the cricket] but I'm here. The first half-hour has gone and I haven't taken a penny, same as last year. If you want to get some business, perhaps you should show them my picture? That's the best photo (in *Shale Britannia*) that's ever been taken of me!" With Mick "I support four teams" Gregory conversation invariably turns to football. "I support Rangers, Montrose, Derby and Real Madrid - since 1960 when they beat Eintrach Frankfurt 7-3 (Puskas scored four and di Stefano three). I always supported them except when Derby played them in the European Cup - we beat them 4-1 at home and lost 5-1 away!"

I'm fortunate that I have the lovely and hard-working 'Scary' Sheila Le-Sage - who has come down on the coach organised by the Lakeside supporters club - working the room on my behalf. She hands out leaflets on my latest books to the fans as they arrive in the building and advises them of my presence and her glamorous cover girl status. She's certainly very effective at promotion as many people pass my stall clutching these postcards and one bloke rushes up to say, "I've got this - can you autograph it for me?" Various important people from within the sport pass by and stop for a chat including Dave Fairbrother from the *Speedway Star* whom we also see regularly on our TV screens - dressed in what appears to be a dapper leather jacket - when, live on satellite, he helps administer the draw for gate positions during the final stages of the Grand Prix every fortnight. He recently saw his expensively bought football team, Chelsea, beat mine and wasn't impressed with the spectacle. "Youse were the worst team we've had at Stamford Bridge all season - for years even. That Roy Keene talks a good story but you're useless! Your first shot was after 32 minutes and it just rolled along the ground! We were quiet 'cause it was crap and there was nothing to cheer about. That player - you know whatsisname - came on and kicked Miller in the balls and that's why he pushed his face. Silly mistake [thereby getting himself sent off] but that's modern football init. If you'd have had 12 rather than 10 it would have made no difference."

Notoriously, Edward Kennett prepares for his outings on the indoor track at the Brighton Centre on the small track that they've specially constructed at the quarry owned by his employer, Mick Robins, the genial owner of Robins of Herstmonceux. Edward's long-time mechanic and friend Chris Geer reports that this track is no more, "He destroyed it this week after someone complained to the council. It wasn't hurting anyone, we only rode on it a couple of times a week and, if you didn't know it was there, you wouldn't have found it 'cause it's hidden away on the top. Someone went up there to dump some rubbish, so it's someone they know but we can't figure out who, so far."

Arnie Gibbons, the well-travelled speedway enthusiast, accountant, Liberal Democrat party member and unofficial historian of Reading Speedway drops by to update me on his progress and some of the research behind his forthcoming book on the Racers with the catchily alliterative title, *Tears and Glory: The Winged Wheel Story*. The nature of diligent research is that it can throw up some surprises and, after hours poring over the back issues of many local newspapers held at Colindale Library in North London, Arnie has discovered exciting information on the California track in Berkshire. "I've never seen California in the list of tracks who ran in the War - books edited by Robert Bamford, in his excellent *Homes of Speedway* reports the 20th August 1939 as the last meeting - whereas I've found in the *Wokingham Times* (that didn't usually cover speedway very much) that a further meeting at California was run on the 24th September 1939. He also hinted that he had unearthed details of a previously unknown venue for speedway in Berkshire (I'm sworn to secrecy), where a meeting was held on September 17th - in some fields - and ridden by the usual California crowd [of riders]." Back in the present day, the widely anticipated decision by the new Racers management of Malcolm Holloway and Mark Legg to drop down from Elite League back into the Premier League has generally met with warm approval from the Smallmead faithful. "I went to the Reading Forum and it was amazing how upbeat we all were, even though we were dropping down a league! It sounds like we'll have a solid rather than exciting team next year - we all now know that remaining solvent is the priority above anything else!"

The affable founder of the speedway breaking-news Internet portal www.worldspeedway.com (and Eastbourne Eagles supporter) Nick Ward drops by my stall, "I went to the press and practice day but after the Poole meeting I didn't go again and couldn't wait for the season to end, if I'm honest. I think things are going to be a lot better next year and I'm sure I'll go more often." Martin Dadswell informs me with his customary grace and politeness (though said as if he's talking to a particularly slow-on-the-uptake adult) that he will help me gain access to the auditorium, "Come on numbnuts, let me show you where the VIP pass area is!" I tag along behind Martin who says incredulously to Nick Barber, "The Eastbourne 2007 DVD is five and a half hours long!" Nick shrugs, "Imagine how long it would have been if Nicki had rode more often!"

I arrive and take my seat in the East Balcony of the grandstand reserved for sponsors, guests and the press (behind Dave Pavitt who continues to wear his winter coat indoors), just in time to witness the Lewis Bridger and Marcin Liberski partnership get into a complete tangle with each other on the tight first bend on their third lap together. Generously SCB referee Dan Holt ordered a re-run with all four back only to be jovially mocked by resident Master of Ceremonies, Kevin Coombes, "Ah, I see what you're doing - getting the crowd on your side early!" To my left, the main grandstand is almost completely full and the opposite West Balcony is sparsely populated, though by the time of the Individual Championship in the evening the crowd numbers had swollen appreciably. The next race features Jason Lyons and his entrance onto the track is greeted enthusiastically by a large contingent of Birmingham Brummies fans that have made the journey down to Brighton seafront in order to cheer on their adopted idol. Jason is one of the bigger names that Martin Dugard has persuaded to take part in this year's revamped Indoor Speedway meeting and, since he combines experience, skill on his machine and an excellent rapport with the fans, this is a shrewd decision. His participation in the event lasts no longer than the few seconds it took him to journey from the start line to then crash painfully on the first corner. My vantagepoint gives a superb view of the majority of the track but, sadly, there is a blind spot that covers the apex of the first bend so I'm unable to see the incident that causes Jason's withdrawal. For a few moments there's hope that the Australian will soldier on in later heats ("Jason Lyons is resting himself after that fall and is replaced by Jason King") of the Pairs competition. One Jason is replaced by another - King for Lyons - and though he gates poorly, the younger Jason shows great determination to win a hard-fought race with Adam Roynon. "Coming out of the box last but becoming the winner is Jason King - full throttle action is what it's all about!" Kevin Coombes announces excitedly.

One thing with tracking unknowns rather than star names in the line-up is that the newcomers apply themselves in a wholehearted manner that more experienced and 'professional' riders might not bother to do. The fifth heat certainly confirms Martin Dugard's school of thought that entertainment levels would be higher. In fact, this is the fourth race in five to be re-run, though this time it is because Edward Kennett is so determined to beat his friend and occasional spannerman that he exceeds the bounds of fair play and rides very aggressively into the first corner. Martin Dugard collapses to the floor clutching his ankle and Kevin Coombes euphemistically notes, "Martin's taking a bit of a rest at the moment." Later, it is suspected that when he briefly got his foot caught in the back wheel, Martin chipped his anklebone. Booed for his zealous determination by the crowd ("do you think Edward Kennett was a bit dodgy?"), after they have been consulted and a large number of red cards have been brandished (the yellow and red card system is unique to this indoor event and it allows the crowd to help adjudicate some of the less contentious decisions), Edward has to start the re-run seven metres back, "Ed - you're penalised my man for dodgy gamesmanship!" The arrival of new riders on the scene allows Kevin to delight us with some exotic pronunciations of their names; safe in the knowledge that we have no real idea whether he's doing so accurately or with extreme artistic licence. One of the four Polish riders on show for the first time in this country is 20-year-old Sebastian Brucheiser, which Kevin pronounces as "BRUS-Ketter" as though he's mistaken him for some tomato-covered Italian bread. A short while later he tries out another version for size this time calling him "PREW-chay-SIR". One of the Brighton crowd favourites is also the oldest rider on display, Shawn McConnell. Not only does he ride in a wily but also determined fashion, he appears to want to entertain when on the track and, very noticeably, goes out of his way to mix and mingle with the fans off the track. You can safely bet if any rider is going to wander round the Collectors' Fayre, stay later to sign autographs or chat amiably and at length by his pick-up truck, then it will be Shawn. On the track he is no slouch but prefers to gain his points through trackcraft and shrewd thinking. Heat 6 is a case in point, Shawn doesn't bother to crouch over his handlebars as the riders come under orders at the start but instead sits bolt upright on his machine as though on a straight-backed chair. He rarely leaves the start line with anything approximating speed but instead looks at the configuration of riders ahead of him to plot his best route through them to the front. In most races this involves idling forwards to hug the inside white line of the first corner before a tactical blast aggressively underneath the apparently unsuspecting younger riders as they exit the second bend. He has done this time and again over recent years and the 2007 meeting is no exception, even though you'd have thought the other riders might have twigged his tactics by now? This time his progression through the field takes slightly longer than usual but, by the start of the second lap, he's found second place and comfortably slots in behind his partner Tommy Allen. When I say slots in behind, the reality is that he covers the track in such a manner that any rider behind him finds it impossible to rush past. Partly this is due to the pace of each race round the small circuit (not necessarily fast but each race is over quickly) but also because he deliberately invites a challenge in the open space he's created before then 'shutting the door' once anyone takes the bait to try!

Apart from the fix of racing during the close season and the aromatic smell of the exhaust fumes, the informality of the event along with the thrills and spills is another real appeal. There's always a fair share of spills, primarily caused by first-bend bunching on the narrow confines of the specially laid track, though there are also a good number of other incidents elsewhere. In the seventh heat, Lewis Bridger smashes into the fence on his second lap as he exits the fourth bend but, though quickly back on his feet, he's unable to clear the track because his footrest has got jammed under the wooden safety fence. Though these fences look insubstantial, they can reputedly easily withstand the velocity of a runaway speedway bike (with or without rider) since they're tough enough to cope with five tons of pressure. With Lewis excluded for his troubles and while we await the fifth re-run in seven races, Kevin announces, "News from pit lane isn't great about Jason [Lyons] - after high siding, he's withdrawn from the meeting on medical advice!" The favoured King-Roynon partnership have no problem defeating their lone rival when the race is run and, bizarrely given he's comprehensively third, Kevin claims Marcin Liberski is "really adapting rather quickly to this tight Brighton race bowl." Race eight sees the venerable Ollie Allen line up at the tapes on the outside gate as the elder statesman of the group, "an old man at 25 - gosh!" There's definitely life in the old dog yet since he wins the race only to immediately then crash into the safety fence as he crosses the line, thereby causing the closely following Ricky Wells to slither off his machine after they clatter bikes together. Kevin notes with some understatement, "That fourth bend really seems to be catching a few riders out!"

There's a brief interval while the riders pull themselves and their machines back together and I retreat to my bookstall. A young boy called Kelsey is the only person to show any interest and he absorbedly thumbs through my photograph book. He tells me that he would like to become a speedway rider and practises whenever he can on a smaller engined bike ("I'm on a 140"). I gather his dad [Martin Dugard] rides but injury might hold him back ("my dad's hurt his foot"). He's a polite and curious youngster and leaves pleased to have been given one of my free postcards. Later in the evening, he makes a point to return the favour and gives me a free 'British Speedway' grey wristband ("would you like one of these, Jeff?"). The re-run of the first race after the interval sees Lewis try to batter Brucheiser into submission on the first bend of the second lap only for the Pole to survive but then immediately pull up with an engine failure. Lewis then turns on the style when he smashes into the safety fence by the start line, turns 180 degrees on his bike before he falls to the shale only to promptly remount and finish in third place. During a brief interval spent away from the auditorium, I've clearly missed the major close season Eastbourne news. Luckily, ever the professional, Kevin repeats it, "in case you were out getting a beer or whatever, Eastbourne announced the signings of Lewis Bridger, Edward Kennett, Scott Nicholls! And Lee Richardson."

Dan Giffard tries to win the 'Silly Fall of the Night' award with a virtuoso effort prior to the start of Heat 11 while he lines up at the tapes. Once the tapes rise, Jason King falls to gift Dan a third place point. Away to my left, I notice that not only does the Brighton Centre have 'Executive Boxes' but also they are actually in use at the Bonanza. Quite why is a total mystery to me as sitting behind glass when already indoors (!) means that you lose two of the primary joys of the experience - the sound and smell of the bikes! People never cease to amaze me with the lengths they'll go to appear different, assert status or emphasise their superiority. On the track Marcin Liberski is determined to offer entertainment every time he appears with a varied range of falls. In Heat 14, he tastes shale again ("he's bitten the dust again then!") before he then remounts to chase his long gone rivals, "it's what they do in Poland, they start racing again - NUTTER!" Though only second behind Lewis, Shawn tries without success to snatch the chequered flag off Start Marshal Alan Rolfe as a memento to take back to the United States. The last race before the final between the partnerships of Allen/McConnell and King/Roynon sees US-based New Zealander Ricky Wells win the race. Kevin Coombes is quite keen on him, "16 years of age - riding for the first time at the Brighton Centre, alright Ricky - Ricky Wells!" While we wait for the riders to appear for the six-lap final, Kevin initiates some homemade entertainment for the crowd, "We'll start the Mexican wave in the East with Big Dave [Pavitt] from the Isle of Wight!" When you ride in Pairs, it is essential that you've discussed your tactics before the race. This is clearly the case with Shawn and Tommy Allen since the younger rider shoots away from the start to win (and thereby becomes the holder of the Dick Bellamy Trophy) while Shawn contents himself by diligently blocking the charge of their erstwhile rivals.

I miss the presentations when I rush back to my stall for the half-expected rush of business during the extended interval between the Pairs and the Individual Championships. Though the winds are strong, it's a sunny winter afternoon and many fans leave the Brighton Centre to get some refreshments or join the Christmas shoppers in nearby Churchill Square. As the majority of fans stream down the stairs and head in the opposite direction from the Collectors' Fayre and out of the smoked glass doors, Bill Gimbet exclaims morosely "they're all turning left!" and, quick as a flash, Steve Davies replies "that's what they do in speedway!" They both obviously have the devil in them this afternoon as they decide they'll phone Dave 'the Rat' Rattenberry on his football ground hopping trip in Cyprus to update him on how badly business has gone at the Fair, so far, for them. Even if sales are slow, many people pop by for a chat including a tall man I met at Swindon (Graham Ramsey) who's a recent newcomer to the sport, "I will say this - as you say in your book *Showered in Shale* - speedway is a very blue collar sport. I took my wife to Reading and she almost immediately said, 'I don't like this!' It was interesting in your book that many promoters didn't really want to talk as if there was some fear of talking to strangers. It's not like that with the fans - I find that people help me all the time and say to me now 'see you next week'. I don't think you get that elsewhere so much."

No sooner has the revelation that Eastbourne have signalled their ambitions to challenge for league success in 2008 with the high calibre signing of Scott Nicholls than die-hard Eagles fans start to complain. One such is Sid "I've done a million miles following speedway" Greatley who strangely dismisses Scott, "he's a dirty bastard!" A few minutes later he concedes, "Nicki was no angel" before he goes on to speculate, "it was Nicki not turning up so often that cost Brimson dear last year." Whenever I see Sid, we're only ever a few words away from a trip down memory lane or his recollections of the riders of yesteryear, "I may be old but there's not much I forget!" he calls out as he wanders off doing a good impression of 'young' Mr Grace from *Are You Being Served?* unaware that he's left behind two programmes he'd placed on my table. Many other Eagles fans decide to focus their worries upon the absence of an announcement about who will be the club number seven rider. "Who can we sign on an average of 3.26? Whoever it is will know how much we need them and be able to ask for nearly as much as Nicki as a guarantee!" My reaction is to immediately quiz Johnny 'Crystal Ball' Barber with the question, How did you know Scott Nicholls would sign for Eastbourne?" he laughs, "I didn't! I heard he was available last Tuesday and I thought who needs a rider like him and where does he ride really well? It's a no-brainer really, especially when Poole aren't letting Eastbourne talk to their asset Davey Watt. With the side of Englishmen Eastbourne have next season, I'm really pleased we're back [at the trackshop] there!"

Never frightened to swim against the tide of popular opinion on the Internet forums, Johnny is equally bullish about the prospects for the 2008 after the changes made at the BSPA Annual Conference. "I think the changes made by the promoters should be supported. With the introduction of promotion and relegation, meetings that no one wanted to see last season in a cold October, like Ipswich versus Eastbourne, would get big crowds and could be something *Sky* would really sell. Just as I, not being funny, would watch Sunderland in a relegation battle (though you're having them already!), when I wouldn't otherwise!" Johnny remains phlegmatic about the possible absence of Nicki Pedersen from British Speedway in 2008, "Nicki said last year that there were too many meaningless meetings and that he wanted to ride 20 meetings here not 40 and, the way it has worked out, he's got what he wanted - only less so! I didn't hear Nicki's mechanic Ray [Blackwell] complaining about the poor quality of the third heat leader averages last year - like he is this - when Ipswich had Robert Miskowiak on a 5-point average. I'm sure Nicki will be back when there's an injury or in 2009."

When the racing restarts in the evening, news of the withdrawal of last year's winner Martin Dugard through injury double underlines Edward Kennett's status as favourite to regain his individual indoor crown. His not-so-secret weapon is his use of an upright bike rather than the modern lay-down machines favoured by all his rivals for glory. First time out in Heat 2, this choice of equipment appears inspired, despite the gremlin of bits falling off his machine during the race, "winning Heat 2 without a footrest - and that's impressive - was Super Ted!" Apart from his exclusion for a fall in his fourth race (Heat 15) when he competed against possible rivals Shawn McConnell and Lewis Bridger, 'Super Ted' showed his liking for the circuit he helps construct every year by remaining unbeaten all night! Lewis has been as good as his word, "I'm not gonna go out there and injure myself trying to win it! But I'm gonna use my head to make the final." Changes to the rules of the sport at the BSPA Conference don't bother him either, "I don't really care what happens so long as I've got a good track and a good team!" It's only a few years ago since the BSPA conducted market research among the fans - something they didn't publish - just like the more in-depth look at the sport by the experienced, independent sports consultant Svend Elkjaer that also never saw the light of day. With all the secrecy to allow greater and more uninterrupted violin practice, it falls to Kevin Coombes to conduct the only publicly available speedway market research of the 2007 season when he conducts a show of hands in answer to a series of basic questions he poses. Unsurprisingly a big show of support greets both "How many of you go to speedway regularly?" and "How many of you went to the GP this year?" It's predictable that anyone who attends Brighton will most likely be a die-hard, fanatical speedway fan. Particularly given the peculiarity of the indoor racing experience compared to that served up outdoors. Plus, over recent years, the event has struggled to retain an audience, which in itself must be an indication that the casual punter prepared to forgo the joys of Christmas shopping and just drop in is an elusive quarry. The question "Will you be going again this year [to the Cardiff GP]?" elicits a much smaller show of hands in response, possibly an early indication that the perfect storm of processional racing, extortionate prices and an awful track surface every year has finally had a cumulative impact upon collective enthusiasm. Paid to be there himself as an announcer, Kevin ignores the evidence of his eyes inside the Brighton Centre and proceeds to relentlessly talk the so-called significance of the Chris Harris victory up. "How fantastic was that? When Chris Harris overtook on the last bend - I nearly wet my pants!"

During the interval, the Collectors' Fayre has a much more Spartan look since many of the experienced trackshops have already packed up their gear and have left or are about to leave. This is a sensible decision as by this time, it seems no one is remotely interested in purchasing last-minute gifts. On his way for a cigarette outside, speedway photographer Steve Dixon stops for a few words. Many of his photos used to appear regularly in the *Speedway Star* but the volume has dropped in recent times, "the *Star* used to use a whole variety of photographers but nowadays it's mostly Mike Patrick - it's probably cost cutting!" While we talk we're standing near one of the key people keeping the community ethos alive in modern speedway with his tireless work at Sittingbourne, Graham Arnold. Though (if we asked him) he'd be quick to point out that this is a team effort built on the endless hours of voluntary service given selflessly by many people. "Oh, that's Graham is it? I had a funny experience with Steve Ribbons at Sittingbourne. I went there and took some photos when Scunny went there a couple of years ago and one of their people laid Ashley Johnson's dad spark out when I was photographing. The story goes, Ashley Johnson's dad went to step over a cord held across the pit entrance, the guy holding it lifted it as he did so, pulling the cord up between his legs. Ashley's dad vented his anger in some way (don't know how) and some local yob, known to Ribbons and his merry men, came from nowhere and sparked him! Police were called and Ashley's dad wanted to press charges but it would have meant packing up and leaving the meeting so decided not to. The yob was ejected and life carried on. I put it in a gallery along with my other photos as usual, yet on the forums it was claimed that I was some sort of paparazzi figure! When all I did is photograph what I saw, if they want to punch people at speedway that's up to them! I did say I would remove any photo if requested to do so by anyone pictured. Steve Ribbons got in touch and I removed one photo of him pointing and running on the track."

The business way nowadays is to cut back on headcount in practically every industry and make the workers left behind do even more work for the same money (or less if you can get away with it). While I'm sure that they don't pay a king's ransom, the Brighton Centre staffing policy appears to buck this trend since they seem to have uniformed staff everywhere to supervise the fans, look after security or manage the people doing these tasks. There are more uniformed people on display here than at a regional military tattoo. Guarding the entrance to the East Stand balcony and dispensing occasional advice from the comfort of her chair is Hilary Carrington. I make the assumption that she's not a fan and have no expectation that serendipity and the historic popularity of speedway will once again prove itself. I ask if she's not tempted to move her chair to inside the doorway and watch rather than sit alone outside. "I can't stand to watch 'cause I think it's someone's little boy really - trying so hard and pretending they're not hurt when they really are when they fall off. Is this the same that used to be on cinders? I went on my first ever date to speedway at the Bulawayo Showground and we sat on the bend. It was the first ever speedway meeting they'd held there - I was 16 or 17 at the time, I'm 70 now. Afterwards, I was like a coalminer! The queues to get out were horrendous and when I got home really late, my mum refused to believe me that I hadn't been up to no good!"

9th December Indoor Speedway Brighton

Winners: Pairs - Tommy Allen and Shawn McConnell; Individual - Edward Kennett

Afterword

I hope that you enjoyed the journey.

Phew! What a fantastic year I had and what another brilliant experience. I was genuinely overwhelmed with the kindness of strangers and amazed how people went out of their way to help me.

Obviously all mistakes remain my own and I apologise if I have accidentally upset anyone. If you have any comments, of either persuasion, please get in touch via my website on www.methanolpress.com

Every effort has been made to get in touch with all copyright holders and many people featured in the photos but, again, I would be delighted to hear from you to make the appropriate credits or acknowledgements.

I mentioned earlier that I have been overwhelmed with help and kindness. I hesitate to name everyone as, inevitably, I will make a mistake and miss someone I'm extremely grateful to, so, with sincere apologies to those who I do manage to miss out I would like to thank the following people: Peter Adams, Rachael Adams, Graham Arnold, Stephanie Babb, Mike Bacon, Paul Bailey, Graeme Bailey, Andrew Baker, Robert Bamford, Nick, Johnny, Bev, Molly and Colin Barber, George and Linda Barclay, Derek Barclay, Dick Barrie, Phil Bartlett, Norman Beeney, John Berry, Mike Berry, Alun Biggart, Ray and Mark Blackwell, Joyce and Malcolm Blythe, Richard Bott, Bob and Greg Brimson, Jim and Steven Brykajlo, Brian Burford, John Campbell, Alison Chalmers, Karen Chappell, Karen Chick, Steve Chilton, Jon Cook, Graham Cooke, Kevin Coombes, Dougie Copland, David Crane, Lucy Cross, Dave Croucher, Jonathan Chapman, Keith and Cheryl Chapman, Martin Dadswell, Andrew Dalby, Paddy Davitt, Gordie Day, Nigel Dean, Anita Dennington, Alan Dick, Chris Durno, Tim Durrans, Graham and Denise Drury, Steve and Debbie Dixon, Neil Dyson, Svend Elkjaer, George and Joan English, Dave Fairbrother, Ben Findon, Richard Frost, Cory Gathercole, Chris Gay, Chris Geer, Trevor Geer, Arnie Gibbons, Bill Gimbeth, Darcia Gingell, Rob Godfrey, Mike and Anita Golding, Mick Gregory, George Grant, Rob Griffin, Andy Griggs, Nobby Hall, Keith Hamblin, Tim Hamblin, Steve Hilliard, Liz Hunt, John Hyam, John, Jordan, Karen, Mark and Judy Hazelden, Jim Henry, Andy Higgs, Mike Hinves, Richard Hollingsworth, Dave Hoggart, Charles Howgego, Paul Hunsdon, Lynn Hunt, Mike Hunter, Tony Jackson, Sue Jackson-Scott, Wendy Jedrzejakski, Adam Jennison, Edward Kennett, Elvin King, Tim Lang, Jo Lawson, Mark Lawton, Sheila Le-Sage, Kevin Ling, Gary Lough, John Louis, Roger Love, Joanna Lunde, Michael Max, Tony and Susie MacDonald, Ella MacDonald, Phil Mackie, Ian and Jean Maclean, Neil Machin, Lee Maclaughlin, Julie Martin, Martin Mauger, Iain McBride, Dennis McCleary, Charles McKay, Allan Melville, Steve and Sarah Miles, Howard Milton, Jayne Moss, Martin Neal, Bill Norris, Peter Oakes, Paul Oughton, Brian Owen, Gordon Pairman, Shane and Anji Parker, Dave Pavitt, Michael Payne, Nigel Pearson, Rob Peasley, Di Phillips, Mark Poulton, Andy and Win Povey, Colin Pratt, Dave Rattenberry, Julie Reading, Dave and Margaret Rice, John Rich, Gareth Rogers, Laurence Rogers, Wayne Russell, Craig Saul, Mark Sawbridge, Sid Shine, Len and Hazel Silver, Andrew Skeels, Derek Smith, Phil Spence, the late Tim Stone, Tony Steele, Trevor Swales, Shaun Tacey, Dave Tattum, Caroline Tattum, Peter Toogood, Stuart Towner, Ian Thomas, Tony (Grandad) Thompson, Stefan Usansky, Dave Valentine, Chris Van Stratton, Peter Waite, Barry Wallace, Nick Ward, Paul Watson, Alf Weedon, The Reverend Michael Whawell, Bryn Williams, Scott Wilson, Cameron Woodward, Ashley and Jane Wooller, Dave Wright and Malcolm Wright.

To pick out anyone in particular would be invidious. However, I owe so many 'thank you's'. The book wouldn't look as lovely as it does without Vicky Holtham's design and artistic skills, along with her stubborn persistence. There would be many more errors than there are without the diligent proofreading of Caroline Tidmarsh and Vy Shepherd along with speedway fanatic Billy Jenkins who has kindly encouraged and advised in so many thoughtful ways. Graham Russel has shown tremendous pedantry and knowledge to wrangle with my words to convert them into some sort of sense. My true friend Sue Young has encouraged me often in so many things and really saved me when I needed that most - for which she has my eternal gratitude. Of course, without the love and guidance of my parents - Mary and Alan - none of this book or so many other things would have been possible. Finally, you can never have too many teachers and I was lucky enough to have been inspired to write my speedway books by a truly great teacher, poet, musician and wit - Michael Donaghy. He remains greatly missed.

Finally, if you go to speedway already why not make a point of taking even more friends this year and if you haven't been for a while or have never been, now is as good a time as any to start!

Yours in speedway!

Thank you for getting this far.

Brighton

1 June 2008

Jazz Musicians

www.billyjenkins.com

The one and only Billy J - tho incomparable speedway/bowls loving Bard of Bromley and progenitor of a distinctively British kitchen-sink jazz sound

Accommodation

All the following warmly welcome speedway fans and have special rates for them:

Waverley Hotel, Workington
01900 603246
www.waverley-hotel.com

Lower Farm, Harpley, King's Lynn
01485 520240

Garrison Hotel, Sheffield
0114 249 9555
www.garrisonhotel.co.uk

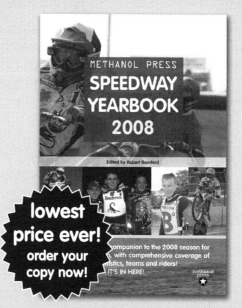